TRANSNATIONAL
FRANCE

TRANSNATIONAL
FRANCE

The Modern History
of a Universal Nation

TYLER STOVALL

University of California, Santa Cruz

WESTVIEW PRESS

A MEMBER OF THE PERSEUS BOOKS GROUP

Westview Press was founded in 1975 in Boulder, Colorado, by notable publisher and intellectual Fred Praeger. Westview Press continues to publish scholarly titles and high-quality undergraduate- and graduate-level textbooks in core social science disciplines. With books developed, written, and edited with the needs of serious nonfiction readers, professors, and students in mind, Westview Press honors its long history of publishing books that matter.

Copyright © 2015 by Westview Press

Published by Westview Press,
A Member of the Perseus Books Group
2465 Central Avenue
Boulder, CO 80301
www.westviewpress.com

Every effort has been made to secure required permissions for all text, images, maps, and other art reprinted in this volume.

Westview Press books are available at special discounts for bulk purchases in the United States by corporations, institutions, and other organizations. For more information, please contact the Special Markets Department at the Perseus Books Group, 2300 Chestnut Street, Suite 200, Philadelphia, PA 19103, or call (800) 810-4145, ext. 5000, or e-mail special.markets@perseusbooks.com.

Cover photo: Brooklyn Museum Archives. Goodyear Archival Collection. Visual materials [6.1.015]: Paris Exposition lantern slides. Paris Exposition: Eiffel Tower and Celestial Globe, Paris, France, 1900.

Designed by Linda Mark

A CIP catalog record for this book is available from the Library of Congress.

ISBN: 978-0-8133-4811-7 (paperback)
ISBN: 978-0-8133-4812-4 (e-book)

10 9 8 7 6 5 4 3 2 1

CONTENTS

CHAPTER 3: IMPERIAL DEMOCRACY? FRANCE UNDER THE SECOND EMPIRE, 1852–1870

CHAPTER 4: PARIS: THE MAKING OF A WORLD CAPITAL

CHAPTER 5: THE UNIVERSAL REPUBLIC

CHAPTER 6: THE REPUBLICAN EMPIRE

PREFACE

THE TURN TOWARD TRANSNATIONAL HISTORY THAT INSPIRED THIS book arises from imperatives not only methodological but personal and political as well. I am a historian who has spent his professional life trying to make sense of another country's history, an endeavor at times illuminating, frustrating, and mystifying. My own professional history has thus shown me both the importance of transnational perspectives and the necessity of dealing with the reality of the nation-state. At the same time the new awareness of the global nature of the human experience in the past as well as the present has inspired many contemporary historians to explore how crossing borders has created the modern era, and how millions of people's lives in the past have both shaped nations and transcended them. In addition, in an era in which "globalization" is often viewed as shorthand for neoliberal hegemony, transnational history must embrace the political task of showing the making of a globalized world in all its complexities and messiness.

This is a tall order, and in undertaking it I depended on the support and expertise of many individuals. I must first thank my two editors, Priscilla McGeehon and Kelli Fillingim. Priscilla suggested this project to me, then guided me through the process of crafting a proposal as well as reading and commenting on my first chapters. Kelli took over the project midstream, encouraging me to finish it even when the schedule she suggested seemed impossible, somehow enabling me to see the process through. My work with both of them has been inspiring and gratifying, while at the same time reminding me to what extent a book in final form transcends the intentions of its author.

I have also benefited from the advice and suggestions of many colleagues. At Berkeley, Alan Karras, Emily Gottreich, and Peter Sahlins listened to and/or read pieces of this project, and I value their input greatly. Several colleagues and friends in Santa Cruz, including Nathaniel Deutsch, Noriko Aso, Gail Hershatter, and Wlad Godzich, were kind enough to consider this project and offer suggestions. I was fortunate to be able to present talks based on the book at two conferences, the California World History Association in Berkeley, and France and its Global Histories at the University of St. Andrews in Scotland. Presenting work based on a textbook is unusual at scholarly conferences, and I am very grateful to the organizers of these two meetings for making it possible for me to do so. Finally, I thank the anonymous reviewers at Westview Press for their enthusiasm and their very helpful suggestions.

I am also indebted to friends and colleagues in France for help with this project and many others as well. Over the years Richard Allen, Elisabeth Altschull, Jim Cohen, and François Gaudu have helped me in numerous ways, from concrete assistance in finding housing to valuable insights about life in France. François passed away as I was beginning this project, and his very French perspectives on universalism and national identity informed our last conversations and helped shape this book. I would also like to thank Sylvain Pattieu, Audrey Celestine, Xavier Vigna, and Emmanuelle Sibeud for inviting me to talk about my work in France, and for making excellent suggestions and observations.

Any textbook must rely on the experience of teaching the field, and I am grateful to my students who have taken this subject seriously and at times have forced me to rethink my approach to it. Like writing a textbook, teaching makes you step away from the narrow confines of your own research to ask the big questions and argue for the broader importance of your subject. Consequently, I'm very grateful to all who have studied French history with me over the years; my experiences in those classes have gone a long way toward creating this book. In particular I would like to thank my graduate students Christopher Church, Felix Germain, Robin Mitchell, and Kim Nalley for their help with this project, as well as their insights and support.

Finally, a big thank you to all those who helped with the technical aspects of producing this book. Lots of appreciation to the staff of Berkeley's Undergraduate Division, especially Paul Schwochow and Frank Naughton, for facilitating my research and writing by helping with computer questions. A very special thank you to Justin Stovall for helping select the images that have made this a much more engaging book.

Thank you all! I hope you enjoy this book and see yourselves reflected in it, at least in its strengths. I of course bear sole responsibility for its weaknesses. Whenever I read or discuss it I will think of you all, in appreciation and gratitude.

Tyler Stovall

Berkeley, California

INTRODUCTION

MISSION IMPOSSIBLE?
A TRANSNATIONAL HISTORY OF THE NATION

In the modern era, history and the nation-state have been close companions. Historical analysis has traditionally regarded the nation as a central unit of analysis and to an important extent has created the very idea of the nation-state. To this day most historians define themselves in national as much as temporal terms, especially in the modern period. Working on sabbaticals often funded by national governments, they use research collections housed in national archives, libraries, and museums. They even tend to embed the history of manifestly global events, such as the world wars, in national discourses.

Much of this is now changing or at least is being questioned. Contemporary intellectual and political themes like globalization, immigration, diaspora, and multiculturalism increasingly call into question the centrality and uniqueness of national institutions and experiences. In recent decades the rise of first social and then cultural history, as well as the new attention to colonialism and postcolonialism, has spurred many historians to look beyond national boundaries in trying to grasp the human experience. At the same time, some have recognized that we cannot simply dispense with national histories in attempting to come to terms with the modern world. To take one example, some

Map I.1. France.

students of the African diaspora recently challenged Paul Gilroy's vision of the black Atlantic, arguing that the international heterogeneity of black populations, and the conflicts among them, often results from their affiliation with national cultures. Even when individuals move from one nation to another, they take with them the marks of the country they left behind. Just as interdisciplinarity is based on the relationship between disciplines, not their absence, transnational history does not so much ignore the nation as interrogate it critically and place it in a comparative and global context. As such, it shares some kinship with other critical analyses of social and cultural dominance, notably the study of masculinity and whiteness.

Transnational history must also recognize and analyze the importance of national citizenship in ideas of human progress. In our contemporary era, when "globalization" is often a shorthand expression for the imposition of neo-capitalist hegemony, it is important to acknowledge that many movements of popular resistance and liberation, ranging from anticolonial and antifascist struggles to the American civil rights movement, have appealed for *national* liberation and the rights of citizenship. A fully transnational history of the nation must illustrate both the potential rewards as well as the limitations of the nation-state and national citizenship.

Transnational France applies these insights to the study of French history from the great Revolution to the present day. Like other historians, students of modern France have been influenced by the intellectual trends in favor of transnational approaches mentioned above. Equally, if not more important, have been the often agonized debates in contemporary France about multi-culturalism, race, and national identity. Recurring controversies about the veil, debates about memories of the nation's colonial heritage, and the social tensions of the troubled suburbs have all underscored the importance of global perspectives on the French past. For example, over the last twenty years or so the field has witnessed a massive shift toward a previously neglected area of concern: colonial history. In large numbers, historians of France are not just writing about the imperial experience but are also traveling to colonial and former colonial archives as well as learning languages other than French. A key tenet of the new colonial history is the idea that "France" is not just limited to the European hexagon but is itself a product of the colonial encounter, both at home and overseas. At the same time the (often conflicted) history of Franco-American relations, politically, socially, and culturally, has received new attention, as historians consider not just the American impact on twentieth-century France but more fundamentally the similarities and differences between the two great republics. For a variety of reasons, therefore, it makes sense to write French history in a transnational context.

This still leaves us, of course, with the fundamental question of how to square the circle: how to write the transnational history of a nation. More particularly, how to write the transnational history of *the* nation, of a country that invented much of the ideological and administrative apparatus of the modern nation-state. In taking a transnational approach to the history of modern France, I have chosen to focus on a key aspect of French political culture:

universalism. The product of the French Revolution, which remains to this day possibly the most studied single event in world history, universalism argues that the core revolutionary values of liberty, citizenship, and Enlightenment principles of reason are at the same time central components of French national identity and the province of humanity as a whole. In short, France is a nation that sees its civilization as both specifically grounded in the nation's history and equally a part of the heritage of all the peoples of the world. In recent times this concept has come in for substantial criticism from intellectuals and activists who decry its limitations and see in it a failure to recognize or accept other cultures, whether of foreigners, immigrants, or colonial subjects. In labeling it "ethnocentrism," Tzvetan Todorov has argued that "ethnocentrism thus has two facets: the claim to universality on the one hand, and a particular content (most often national) on the other."[1] While I share Todorov's concerns, I also contend that the universalist tradition, a central theme in modern France and still powerful there to this day, underscores the validity of a transnational approach to that country's history. It emphasizes national exceptionalism and at the same time places it in the broader context of the culture of humanity as a whole. This book therefore focuses on the ways in which the universalist tradition has shaped both France's interactions with other nations and its internal debates about diversity and national identity. It approaches the study of France as the history of a universal nation.

In exploring the transnational history of France, this book concentrates primarily, although not exclusively, on the nation's relations with three areas of the world. The first, Europe, is the easiest to approach, thanks to a wealth of university courses and textbooks on modern European history and western civilization. The second, France's colonial empire, has, as noted above, benefited from a wealth of recent historical studies. Finally, the third, the United States, has a long history of relations with France, its first national ally, and the two nations share many characteristics and concerns. Considering France's different relations with these three areas, politically, socially, and culturally, will provide new insights into both the nature of French identity and the making of the modern world in general.

ETERNAL FRANCE

Although the borders of the metropole, the nation without its colonies, have changed over time, much of what constitutes contemporary France has been

French for a long time. France lies at the heart of western Europe; along with Spain, it is the only nation with coastlines along the Atlantic Ocean and the Mediterranean Sea. Geographically France is one of the largest nations in Europe, stretching roughly six hundred miles from north to south, and the same from east to west. Starting in the early nineteenth century French geographers referred to the shape of France as a hexagon, and this has since become a popular nickname for metropolitan France.

Within the hexagon lies a land of unusual diversity. At the beginning of its history France was a heavily forested area, inhabited by large animals like bear, deer, and wolves. The spread of human habitation and agriculture led to a gradual clearing of the woodlands, however, so that by the late Middle Ages the country had to import lumber from northern Europe. Much of the land, especially in the northern and eastern parts of the country, consists of flat plains and low rolling hills. This is especially true of the Ile de France, or Paris basin, historically a wealthy agricultural region blessed with rich soil, and an area like Normandy, which for years has been the nation's classic dairy land. In the center and the south of the country, in contrast, the landscape becomes mountainous and rugged. France has a number of mountain ranges, notably the Alps to the east, the Pyrenees to the south, and Vosges to the northeast. All of these lie on the nation's borders, but the Massif Central, a mountainous plateau composed in part of extinct volcanoes, dominates the south-central part of the country.

France is also blessed with several major rivers, which have historically provided ample water for drinking and agriculture and have also facilitated transportation among different regions. The Loire River, the nation's longest, rises in the Alps to run over six hundred miles from east to west across the country into the Atlantic. The Rhone also originates in the Alps, but instead runs south into the Mediterranean. The Saone, another long river, runs into the Rhone at the city of Lyon, so that like the Mississippi and the Missouri rivers in America they form one long internal waterway. The Seine, nearly five hundred miles long, runs through Paris and northern France before reaching the sea in Normandy. Other major rivers include the Garonne and the Dordogne in south-central France. Finally, one of Europe's great rivers, the Rhine, forms part of the nation's eastern border.

The French have ample contact with salt as well as fresh water. The nation has a coastline over two thousand miles long. While not as extensive as those in Britain, Italy, or Norway, it compares favorably with most other European nations. Much of the country's northern border consists of what the British rather arrogantly name the English Channel; the French term for it is La Manche, the sleeve. The northeastern part of France touches on the North Sea, while the Mediterranean forms much of the nation's southern border, and the Atlantic its western edge. More than most European nations, therefore, France is both a continental and a maritime country. Many of its most prominent cities, including Marseilles, Bordeaux, Le Havre, and Nantes, are major seaports, as is Paris itself, thanks to commerce along the Seine. At the same time France has large agricultural plains, and for most of its history it has been a major breadbasket for Europe as a whole. Moreover, the country is blessed with a relatively mild climate, colder and foggier in the north, warmer and sunnier along the Mediterranean. All in all, it is a prosperous country with many natural resources and beautiful landscapes.

A major theme in French history since the Middle Ages has been the attempt to expand to the nation's "natural" or geographical, boundaries. To the north, west, and south, oceans and mountain chains formed major barriers that helped define the hexagon. The northeast was less well defined by geography, and although some ambitious French people would consider the Rhine River in its entirety France's natural eastern border, this was never feasible militarily, politically, or culturally. Nonetheless, there has long been a sense in France that geography has made France a coherent and distinct nation, internally diverse but all the same a unified land.

Finally, it is worth considering the borders and outlying regions of France. Since the seventeenth century, at a time when metropolitan France was expanding to its present size, the nation also began expanding overseas. At the beginning of the 1600s France established a presence in North America, founding Quebec City in 1608 and Montreal in 1611. In the early seventeenth century it also became a power in the Caribbean, creating colonies in Saint-Domingue, Martinique, and Guadeloupe as well as other islands, and the Ile Bourbon, the present-day Ile de la Réunion, in the Indian Ocean. Thus for most of the modern period French geography has not been limited to the metropole but has encompassed a wide variety of climatic zones ranging from northern forests to tropical islands. In Europe, metropolitan France belongs both to the north and the south at the same time. In the north people make roofs with blue slate, for example, whereas in the south they use red tiles; in the north they cook with butter, in the south with olive oil. In many ways a key to French history has been the gradual blending of different peoples, ranging from the Celtic and German tribes of the early historical period to the Poles, Italians, Portuguese, and North Africans of today. France has also bordered throughout its history on other powerful European nations, namely Spain, Italy, Germany, and England, experiencing both conflict and cooperation with all of them. The geography of France has thus both defined the nation and underscored its transnational and global character at the same time.

A LONG AND RICH HISTORY

Archeologists have shown that the presence of modern *Homo sapiens* in France dates back for tens of thousands of years. Early French men and women have left tantalizing clues to their history, including prehistoric monuments of standing stones, or *menhirs*, such as in Carnac in Brittany, and the great cave paintings of animals at Lascaux in southwestern France. The recorded history of the nation begins in the millennium before the Christian era. Celtic peoples gradually populated what is now France, founding settlements that gradually grew into cities like Paris, Bordeaux, and Toulouse. Greeks founded colonies along the Mediterranean, including Marseilles and Nice. But it was the Romans, who conquered what they called Gaul at the beginning of the Christian era, who first gave shape to what would become France. The Romans controlled Gaul until the fifth century AD, making it a province of the Roman Empire. They built roads and arenas, founded cities like Lyon and Narbonne, taught the local population Latin, and integrated the Celtic Gauls into Roman culture.

By the middle of the fifth century the empire was collapsing, gradually withdrawing its legions from provinces like Gaul to protect the Roman heartland from invading Germanic tribesmen. In 486 Clovis, leader of the Franks, defeated the Romans and united much of Gaul under his reign. He thus became the undisputed ruler of the Franks and in many ways the founder of the French nation. Ten years later he accepted the Christian faith and enforced it as the state religion for his kingdom. The first of the major Germanic leaders to do so, Clovis won for France recognition by Rome as "the eldest daughter of the Church." The idea of France as special, as a light to other nations, thus started in the early Christian era as a part of Christian universalism: the belief in universal salvation. This foundational moment in the birth of France also lies at the origins of the idea of the universal nation.

Although the reign of Clovis has traditionally been seen as the beginning of the French nation, the country in no way resembled its modern form. After

Clovis's death France was divided between different Frankish kingdoms and also faced new invasions. In 732 the Franks defeated Muslim invaders from Spain at the Battle of Tours, breaking the momentum of Arab expansion into western Europe. At the end of the century a powerful new ruler, Charlemagne, united the Frankish kingdoms, as well as conquering northern Italy, northern Spain, and western Germany. In 800 Pope Leo III crowned him Emperor of the Romans, and his reign marked the height of Frankish power. After his death Charlemagne's three grandsons divided up his empire in 843; out of that division emerged the west Frankish kingdom, the ancestor of modern France. During the ninth century the country suffered greatly from Viking raids; most notably the Northmen seized control of Normandy, which has borne their name ever since. In 987 the Carolingian dynasty came to an end with the election of Hugh Capet as king. Capet would found the Capetian dynasty, which would rule France until the fourteenth century.

Life in France during the Middle Ages was characterized by weak monarchies and powerful local lords, who ruled over a peasantry tied to the land as serfs. Monarchs representing France as a whole struggled to impose their power on both the powerful lords who ruled the provinces and the international power of the Church. As a result, during these years the outlines of modern France gradually emerged. Over the centuries the language spoken by the Franks turned into French, although many people in the country, especially Brittany and Provence, did not speak it. The Capetians made Paris the permanent capital of France, and under their rule it emerged as the political, economic, and intellectual center of the country. During the twelfth century the French began building both Notre Dame and the Louvre, and during the thirteenth founded the Sorbonne. At the same time the kingdom was torn by international and overseas conflicts. In 1066 William Duke of Normandy invaded and conquered England, closely linking the two countries with dynastic and other ties. In 1095 Pope Urban II launched the First Crusade to conquer Palestine and the Holy Land for Christianity, and thousands of French nobles and commoners took place in successive crusades over the next two centuries. One of France's greatest kings, Louis IX or Saint Louis, died in the Eighth Crusade. In 1337 the Hundred Years War began between France and England, which controlled much of the French mainland. The war, combined with the outbreak of the Black Plague in the fourteenth century, devastated much of the country, but France's ultimate victory in 1453 sharply reduced the English presence on its lands, as well as providing the nation with one of its greatest heroes, Joan of Arc.

During the early modern era, the sixteenth and seventeenth centuries, France grew in prosperity and power, but also witnessed a series of internal conflicts. Although the overwhelming majority of the population remained rural, French cities grew in these years, Paris reaching a population of over 200,000 by 1550. French consolidated its position as the dominant language of the country, and in general France developed a greater sense of national unity. It was also a period of seemingly incessant military conflict, most often directed against the Habsburg dynasty which, controlling both Spain and the Holy Roman Empire, threatened to encircle the nation. For over half a century the French fought the Habsburgs for control of Italy, ultimately annexing the city of Nice. The Reformation triggered a series of religious civil wars in France, which only came to an end in 1598 with the victory of King Henry IV, the founder of the Bourbon dynasty that would last until the early nineteenth century. The presence of a powerful Protestant minority, the Huguenots, remained a problem for the French state for many decades thereafter. In the early seventeenth century the Thirty Years War erupted in central Europe, ending with a major French victory over the Habsburgs. During these years France also began to establish overseas colonies in North America, the Caribbean, and the Indian Ocean.

THE SUN KING AND THE AGE OF FRENCH GLORY

In 1643 Louis XIV became king of France at the age of five but did not actually rule his kingdom until 1661. He reigned for seventy-two years, dying in 1715, so that his regime became the most durable in European history. Under Louis XIV's rule France became the leading power in Europe, besting the Habsburgs and their allies in several major wars and increasing its national territory to its present-day extent. In many respects the reign of Louis XIV, nicknamed "the sun king" for the splendor of his reign, was one of the high points of French history. Under his rule, France not only developed a greater sense of itself as a unified country but also began to conceive of itself as the center of civilization. Louis XIV thus inaugurated the image of France as a universal nation.

One of the great king's two major concerns was to solidify the power of the monarchy and tame the aristocracy, which still clung to feudal ideals of a powerful independent nobility and a weak sovereign. His father King Louis XIII, aided by his brilliant counselor and chief minister Cardinal Richelieu, had already done a lot to promote royal power, including destroying most of the nobility's castles. The resentments such policies caused among the aristocracy led to the revolt known as the Fronde, from 1648 to 1653. Louis XIV, king but still a boy at the time, was forced to flee Paris until order was finally restored. This experience confirmed for him the importance of royal authority, leading him to embrace the doctrine of absolute monarchy. According to this principle kings rule by divine right, owing nothing to their subjects or anyone else. Once Louis XIV began ruling in 1661 he dispensed with the office of chief minister, emphasizing direct control and oversight of state affairs. Among other reforms, he reorganized the military to make it both more efficient and to reduce the power of the nobility. One of his most dramatic reforms was building the sumptuous royal palace of Versailles outside Paris, and relocating the French court there. The magnificence of the chateau was meant to illustrate not just the power of the monarchy but the wealth of France in general. Moreover, by forcing the great aristocratic families to move there and spend their time in the endless rituals and intrigues of the court, Louis XIV weakened their ability to conspire against him. There would be no more revolts like the Fronde against the monarchy; Louis XIV made the power of the centralized state a key aspect of French political life which continues to this day.

Louis XIV also desired to make France supreme in Europe and break the power of the Habsburgs once and for all. During his reign France fought several wars, establishing his nation as the leading European power and expanding the national territory, especially with the annexation of Alsace in the east. French explorers carved out a new colony in North America, naming it Louisiana after the sun king. Increasingly under Louis's reign other European nations, notably England, Prussia, and the Dutch republic, regarded France as the main threat to stability and the balance of power, and at times joined alliances against the French. Louis XIV did not win every battle, and the cost of his wars imposed a heavy burden on the French treasury. But he did succeed in underscoring France's military power and prestige, as well as permanently weakening the Habsburgs, especially Spain. Military prowess was an essential part of the grandeur of Louis XIV's reign.

The glory of the sun king involved more than battlefield victories, however. Louis XIV vigorously supported the arts, making Versailles a showcase of culture as well as royal power. The seventeenth century was a golden age of classical French literature, led by writers like Molière, Racine, Corneille, and La Fontaine. They and others brought a new range of sophistication to French, helping to confirm its position as the leading language in Europe, as well as creating an important repertoire of national culture. Music and architecture also prospered under the reign of the sun king, led by composers like Lully and Couperin, and architects like Le Brun, Le Vau, and Vaux-le-Vicomte. The patronage of the royal court nurtured many artists and intellectuals, making France the cultural as well as military leader of Europe in the seventeenth century.

By the end of Louis XIV's reign France was more prosperous and powerful than ever before in its history. It had a population of 20 million people, making it the second largest country in Europe after Russia, and its capital city had 600,000 inhabitants. It had a vibrant cultural life and a strong economy, based on bountiful agriculture and skilled artisanal manufacture. In addition, France was a power not only in Europe but overseas as well, with a strong network of colonies in the New World. Although the nation would lose both Canada and Louisiana in 1763 as a result of the Seven Years War, the sugar colonies of the Caribbean, above all Saint-Domingue, generated enormous profits that played a key role in the nation's prosperity. It had for the most part expanded to natural and defensible borders with its European neighbors, borders that would remain fixed for most of its modern history. In short, France in the early eighteenth century was an exemplary nation, admired by many beyond its boundaries. The chapters that follow will explore how the French dealt with and expanded this powerful legacy during the modern era, adopting universalism as a key aspect of national identity and building a core sense of themselves as a universal nation.

Suggestions for Further Reading

Celestin, Roger, and Eliane DalMolin. *France from 1851 to the Present: Universalism in Crisis.* New York: Palgrave Macmillan, 2007.

Conklin, Alice L., Sarah Fishman, and Robert Zaretsky. *France and Its Empire Since 1870.* New York: Oxford University Press, 2011.

Haine, Scott W. *The History of France.* Westport, CT: Greenwood, 2000.

Parry, G. L., and Pierre Girard. *France Since 1800.* Oxford: Oxford University Press, 2002.

Popkin, Jeremy D. *A History of Modern France*. Upper Saddle River, NJ: Prentice-Hall, 2001.

Schor, Naomi. "The Crisis of French Universalism." *Yale French Studies* 100 (2001): 43–64.

Wright, Gordon. *France in Modern Times*. Chicago: Rand McNally College Publishing, 1974.

Notes

1. Tzvetan Todorov, *On Human Diversity: Nationalism, Racism, and Exoticism in French Thought*, trans. Catherine Porter (Cambridge: Harvard University Press, 1993), 2.

one

FRENCH REVOLUTION, WORLD REVOLUTION

IN 1798 NAPOLEON BONAPARTE, LEADER OF FRANCE'S REVOLUTIONARY armies, invaded Egypt and attempted to win local hearts and minds by claiming, among other things, that the French people were Muslims. A year later, a group of French expatriates allied themselves with the sultan of the south Indian kingdom of Mysore to set up a Jacobin club in his kingdom and mobilize to fight the British. In 1802, when Emperor Napoleon Bonaparte's forces invaded Guadeloupe to reinstate chattel slavery, his armies faced the former slaves. Both sides brandished tricolor flags, and men of both armies fought and died to shouts of *liberté, égalité, fraternité.*

The French Revolution constituted a foundational event in the rise of globalization. It lay at the heart of what historians have termed the age of revolution, influencing people throughout the Atlantic basin and beyond. Yet even as events in France had an impact far beyond the nation's borders, the global context helped shape the pace and direction of the Revolution at home. The barricades of revolutionary Paris arose from local concerns, but at the same time the conquerors of the Bastille often reacted to events beyond the nation's borders. The French Revolution was one of the great world wars of the modern era, a conflict fostered by continuing interactions between Parisian radical politics and developments abroad.

1.1. *The Storming of the Bastille,* 1789. *Source:* Bibliothèque nationale de France.

The Revolution created the idea of universalism in modern France and welded the identity of the French nation to that idea. The revolutionaries considered themselves motivated by principles applicable to all of humanity, and they fought for a better world as well as a more just France. At the same time they forged the identity of a nation, based on universalist principles. Thus was born the paradox of national universalism, which more than anything else has shaped not just the political culture but the very identity of France since 1789.

In many ways, the French Revolution created the idea of modernity, both for France and for the world in general. It was the first modern revolution, against which all subsequent political upheavals would be measured. It established the norm for the modern nation-state, grounded in both political institutions and the powerful political culture of nationalism. Finally, it created the modern idea of empire, radically reshaping this traditional political form. At the same time, it fundamentally reshaped social and cultural life in France, breaking down old social divisions and fostering new ones. Consequently the great Revolution became the lodestone of French national

Map 1.1. France in 1789.

identity in the modern era, making France a global symbol of progressive change. However, it also tied France as a nation-state to the influences and fortunes of the wider world, inscribing a global dimension at the heart of the modern nation.

FRANCE AND EUROPE IN 1789

"Happy as God in France," runs an old Yiddish saying, and indeed life for the French in the eighteenth century seemed fortunate in comparison to the rest of Europe and the world. France was a nation of unusual prosperity, blessed with abundant and fertile farmland, the greatest city on the European continent, and a lively commercial and intellectual life. When France went to war, for example during the Seven Years War, such conflicts were fought far away from the national homeland. The kind of military anarchy that had devastated central Europe in the Thirty Years War had no place in living memory. Above all, France had a prosperous and independent peasantry, which made up the vast majority of the population. Many owned their land, if only a tiny parcel, and most (but not all) could generally live life free from want and starvation.

The substantial advantages of life in rural France, and to a significant extent in the country as a whole, appear more evident when compared with conditions in the rest of Europe. France occupied an intermediary position between the burgeoning capitalist societies of Britain and the Low Countries, on the one hand, and the more traditional societies east of the Rhine River, on the other. In contemporary England, life in the countryside was being rapidly transformed by changes such as crop rotation and better methods of swamp drainage, collectively known as the agricultural revolution. These new methods sharply raised agricultural productivity, and the increased food supply in turn prompted population growth, urbanization, and ultimately the industrial revolution. However, local peasants often did not benefit from such innovations. The enclosure movement, a key aspect of the agricultural revolution in England, rationalized farming by privatizing the village common land, often essential to the survival of the poorest peasants. New foodstuffs, most notably those miraculous American imports, corn and the potato, helped somewhat, but many of the most vulnerable farmers in Britain and the Netherlands found themselves confronting a choice between flight from the land or starvation.

In central and eastern Europe, by contrast, farming seemed to have improved little since the Middle Ages. Agricultural techniques remained traditional, and consequently productivity remained low. Peasants, the overwhelming majority, ate sparingly, mostly hard bread, and often worried about getting enough. Moreover, the independence of the French peasantry largely eluded them. In contrast to western Europe, the early modern era saw growing serfdom in the east. Far from owning land, many farmers in eastern Europe were still bonded to it. With relatively few cities or towns to offer an escape from the travails of rural life, peasants in east and central Europe often led a precarious existence.

From these perspectives, French peasants, and the nation as a whole, were fortunate. Only a small minority were serfs, and popular ideology identified the country as the land of free men. At the same time, French commercial and landowning interests lacked the power of their British counterparts to force the enclosure of common lands. Consequently the landowning peasant remained a staple figure of the countryside and indeed the nation's image of itself. Traditional enough to offer many of the protections of earlier centuries against the harsh new logic of capitalism, yet modern enough to provide a vibrant urban sector and a high standard of living, eighteenth-century France did in many ways seem to outsiders a blessed land, one of prosperity and contentment.

So how did such a happy nation produce one of the great revolutions of modern times? The poorest of the poor do not usually trigger revolutionary upheavals, but rather those who have some social means and standing but feel unfairly restricted by the political and institutional structure of their society. Eighteenth-century France, having characteristics of a dying feudal order and a nascent capitalist one, illustrated this. In 1789 France had 26 million people, divided into three estates whose origins went back to the Middle Ages. The first estate, the Catholic Church, owned about 10 percent of the land in France and was dominated by officials of noble origin. The second estate, the nobility, constituted roughly 1–2 percent of the population yet owned a quarter of the land. The aristocracy dominated positions in government and administration, constituting the wealthiest sector of society. To an important extent the first two estates enjoyed exemption from major taxes like the *taille*, a tax on land.

The fact that the last of the three, the third estate, included everyone else in France and thus accounted for nearly 99 percent of the population, graphically demonstrated how obsolete this system of social rank and privilege had become. The peasantry, who alone accounted for four-fifths of the nation, owned roughly half of French land. This group varied widely, ranging from the wealthy farmers known as the "cocks of the village" down to the poorest landless peasants. France also had a substantial and growing middle class, concentrated in the cities and towns, as well as large urban working-class communities. The various social classes of the third estate had little in common, except for the fact that they lacked the privileges of the first two estates. The middle class, or bourgeoisie, saw its share of the national wealth increase during the eighteenth century, yet its members lacked the social and political status that a noble title could bring. Many peasants paid substantial dues of feudal origin to aristocratic landowners, and they resented having to pay taxes not imposed on the nobility. The divisions between the estates were not absolute: the wealthiest members of the bourgeoisie not only lived like nobles but often socialized with them. Nonetheless, hatred of the nobility was widespread in France during the late eighteenth century, frequently serving to unite an estate that would soon don the mantle of the nation as a whole.

ENLIGHTENING THE WORLD

Hostility toward the nobility helped bring about the Revolution, but such hatred was nothing new in France. The rise of new ideas and values collectively known as the Enlightenment not only challenged the old feudal order but also provided an alternative to it. The relationship between the Enlightenment and the French Revolution is by no means clear-cut. Its main figures emphasized reform, not insurgency, and the majority of people in France knew little about it. It did, however, help undermine the status quo in French society and politics. Emphasizing progress, change, and the primacy of human reason over superstition and traditional authority, the Enlightenment provided a language revolutionaries could use in their assault against the reigning order of things in 1789.

Even more than the Revolution, the Enlightenment was both French and global at the same time. The flight of French Protestants from their homeland in the late seventeenth century played a key role in the origins of the intellectual movement. Not only did the exile of the Huguenots loom large as an example of irrational religious intolerance, but French Protestants based elsewhere in Europe attacked the established order far more harshly than critics within France. Pierre Bayle's *Dictionary*, which questioned the authority of the Bible, was a case in point. By the middle of the eighteenth century, the high point of the Enlightenment, intellectual circles devoted to its ideas could be found throughout Europe as well as across the Atlantic, in both North and South America. David Hume and Adam Smith in Scotland, Immanuel Kant and Moses Mendelssohn in Germany, and Thomas Jefferson and Benjamin Franklin in British North America all belonged to Denis Diderot's Republic of Letters. Even the works of French Enlightenment writers often took an international perspective, such as the Baron de Montesquieu's *Persian Letters* and Voltaire's *Letters Concerning the English Nation*, and they frequently published their works abroad to avoid censorship laws in France.

At the same time, French thinkers dominated the Enlightenment. The vibrant intellectual and social life of the French capital, the largest city on the European continent, played a major role in this. By the late eighteenth century most Parisians could read, and many took part in the public culture of cafés and newspapers, whose numbers mushroomed during the eighteenth century. On the eve of the Revolution, Paris had one hundred Masonic lodges, drawing men from a wide variety of social backgrounds committed to Enlightenment values of progress. The city's famed salons, social gatherings usually hosted by women of the aristocracy, provided opportunities for Enlightenment thinkers, or *philosophes*, to spread their ideas among the Parisian elite. Also important, however, was the fact that France combined an active public sphere with a repressive monarchy and clergy. This clash between modernity and tradition, similar to that between feudal and capitalist views of society, made France's *philosophes* more focused than elsewhere on fighting the established order and thus championing the new. A key feature of modern French life, the politically engaged intellectual, was born in the Enlightenment.

Key to Enlightenment philosophy was the belief that its ideals applied to all men at all times. Universalism defined the movement, both in France and on a global scale, for several reasons. Inspired by the scientific revolution, Enlightenment thinkers saw themselves as taking the general principles governing the physical world and applying similar insights to the study of humanity and society. Just as nature was shaped by universal laws and standards, so too was the human experience. The central clash between the Enlightenment and the Church also shaped the universalist expectations of the former, a negative mirror of the Christian universalism long espoused by Rome. The emphasis of the *philosophes* on the centrality of the French language underscored the fact that the universalism of the Enlightenment was very much a *French* universalism; in 1780 King Frederick II of Prussia wrote an essay on German literature praising the clarity of French. As the Enlightenment gained power and influence in eighteenth-century France, so too did the assumption that French culture would play a central role in realizing its universalist aims. The French Revolution would go a long way toward putting that assumption into practice.

During the forty years before the Revolution broke out, French Enlightenment thinkers successfully challenged the authority of the Church and the monarchy. They demanded freedom of speech and of the press, and insisted that human reason, not religion or tradition, should be the supreme arbiter of human affairs. In 1751 Denis Diderot started publishing the massive

Encyclopedia, a collective work featuring the work of leading *philosophes* that aimed at nothing less than the application of reason to all fields of human knowledge. Officially banned by the royal censors, the *Encyclopedia* was simply too massive and prominent to suppress entirely, so it soon reached a wide reading public. Editions of Enlightenment works published outside France, especially in Switzerland and the Netherlands, also undermined the efforts of French censors to restrict the new ideas. During the 1760s the *philosophes* established their dominance over Parisian intellectual life, infiltrating institutions of official royal culture like the Académie-française. By the time Voltaire and fellow *philosophe* Jean-Jacques Rousseau died in 1778, influential members of both the Church and the royal court had embraced their ideas, and France as a whole seemed to be moving along the path of reform laid out by the Enlightenment.

For this reason, although the ideas of the Enlightenment certainly influenced the upheaval of 1789, we must look elsewhere for its causes. Ultimately the Enlightenment preached reform, not revolution. The national universalism of the movement was one of its greatest legacies, but a different aspect of international concerns had a more immediate impact in triggering the birth pangs of modern France.

FROM CRISIS TO REVOLUTION

A combination of international concerns and domestic problems brought about the collapse of the ancien régime in France. The French monarchy had viewed France as the leading nation in Europe, devoting great energy and treasure to realizing French continental hegemony. The foreign policy ambition of Louis XIV had established a model of French greatness on an international scale. Yet it was an expensive model, and even though France was a wealthy nation the governments of the ancien régime were unable to mobilize its resources efficiently. As 1789 would demonstrate, absolute monarchy could no longer realize the dreams of French universalism; the Revolution would provide a new model for modern France.

The first major upheaval in what would come to be called the age of revolution took place not in France but in Britain's North American colonies. Although fundamentally different from France's great revolution in many important respects, the American war of independence foreshadowed it in at least two ways. First, it drew strongly on Enlightenment principles, thus demonstrating that that movement's vision of a progressive republic was indeed feasible. Second, it helped bring to a head the fiscal crisis of the French monarchy, thus directly precipitating the events of 1789.

The American revolution had an enormous attraction for the progressive intellectuals of France. Widely interpreted as an uprising for liberty and human rights against a despotic king, the cause of the American colonists seemed to draw directly from French Enlightenment philosophy. The American declaration of independence sounded major Enlightenment themes of liberty and human rights. The central roles played by *philosophes* like Benjamin Franklin and Thomas Jefferson only added to its allure, as did the opportunity it offered France to take revenge on Britain for the latter's seizure of Canada during the Seven Years War. As a result, the French monarchy found itself supporting a revolution for liberty and republicanism. The triumph of the Americans made their cause extremely popular in France. Benjamin Franklin, who lived in Paris between 1776 and 1785, was lionized by Parisians, and French soldiers who had fought in America returned full of admiration for the new republic.

French support for the American revolution also illustrated the less positive side of Enlightenment universalism. The new American state was not only a republic but a republic of slaveholders, and a major impetus for separation from Britain had been London's attempts to restrict the colonists' dispossession of America's native peoples. Moreover, the new republic enfranchised men only, suggesting that the Enlightenment offered relatively little to women. While in theory Enlightenment universalism applied to all people, the new American republic clearly demonstrated that ideas of liberty and human rights did not in fact apply to all. This would become a major issue during France's revolution and ultimately loomed large in the modern history of French universalism.

More concretely, the French crown's substantial expenditures in favor of American independence stretched its own finances to the breaking point. For the past century the monarchy's pursuit of power and *gloire*, both at home and abroad, had strained the nation's resources; for example, the cost of building Versailles was so high that Louis XIV destroyed the receipts. Two major wars in the mid-eighteenth century, the War of Austrian Succession (1740–1748) and the Seven Years War (1756–1763), revealed the financial weaknesses of France's government for all to see. The fact that the Church and the nobility, accounting for much of the nation's wealth, enjoyed immunity from many taxes was the central problem but not the only one. The tax farming system, in which the crown sold the right to collect taxes to private individuals, also limited its ability to raise needed revenue. As a result, the government turned time and time again to borrowing, becoming hopelessly mired in debt. By the middle of the eighteenth century the monarchy was desperately looking for ways to modernize its tax structure and gain control over its bureaucracy.

This was easier said than done, for the nobility and other vested interests fought hard to retain their privileges. Absolutist France had no functioning legislature; the closest equivalent, the Estates General, had last met in 1614. However, regional estates continued to meet in some provinces, usually resisting attempts at centralization and reform. More important were the thirteen *parlements*, aristocratic law courts that had the power to suspend the enforcement of new laws. Wealthy nobles dominated these courts and used their power to resist what they considered royal despotism, often inspired by Enlightenment thinkers. The *parlements* forestalled efforts by Louis XV to reform the national economy in the 1760s, leading to a political clash and their suspension in 1770 by Chancellor René Maupeou. This act did tame resistance to royal authority somewhat, but it also underscored the problems facing attempts at reform.

When Louis XVI was crowned king in 1774, he assumed power over an increasingly restive nation. Although French agriculture increased in productivity during the eighteenth century, it was outstripped by the country's dramatic population growth which crested in the 1770s. High levels of production during much of the century ensured that the additional mouths could be fed, but unfortunately starting in the late 1760s France experienced a series of poor harvests that drove up the price of bread, by far the most important food for most people in city and countryside alike. Food shortages led to a general economic crisis for the next two decades. The new king, well-intentioned but inexperienced, sought to restore public faith in the monarchy by restoring the *parlements* and liberalizing the economy. Comptroller-general Jacques Turgot introduced a series of reforms, notably the abolition of the guilds and of restrictions on the grain trade, accompanied by sharp limits to government spending. These measures proved effective in dealing with the government deficit but provoked widespread discontent. As a result, backing down in the face of resistance by the *parlements* as well as popular riots over the price of grain, in 1777 the king appointed the Swiss banker Jacques Necker to replace Turgot. Whereas Turgot had acted boldly, Necker pursued a more hesitant policy of economic reform. Yet his proposals to collect taxes more efficiently and reduce government expenditures also encountered powerful opposition, leading to his dismissal in 1781.

By the 1780s France was clearly in a state of crisis, desperately needing economic reforms but lacking the political structures necessary to realize them. Interest payments on the national debt alone consumed over half of the crown's annual income. Matters came to a head in 1786. In August the latest comptroller-general, Charles-Alexandre de Calonne, informed the king that France needed to repay the loans it took out to support America's war of independence but lacked the funds to do so. Like his predecessors he realized that the monarchy had to find a way to tax the Church and nobility, but he also understood the political resistance such measures would elicit. He therefore proposed that the king lay his case before the nation by convoking an Assembly of Notables to discuss the situation. The assembly met in January 1787 but proved unwilling to support Calonne's reforms. Louis XVI then replaced Calonne with the archbishop of Toulouse, Lomenie de Brienne, who dealt with the burgeoning opposition to the monarchy by abolishing the *parlements* altogether.

This was a fateful step. The government's prestige had already been weakened by the failures of earlier reform efforts and continuing economic stagnation. Abolishing the *parlements* caused a firestorm of protest, including major riots throughout the country. For many this was an act of despotism pure and simple, and opponents of the king began to call for convening the Estates General to counteract royal power and to address the problems confronting France. Faced with a tidal wave of opposition, Louis XVI and his ministers saw no alternative but to reinstate the *parlements* and, more significantly, to accept the call for a new Estates General. With this action the king appeased popular opinion for the moment. But in seeking to resolve the political crisis, he laid the basis for a revolution instead.

THE LIBERAL REVOLUTION

In 1789, therefore, France set about the process of convening the Estates General, scheduled to meet in May. Reviving an institution that last met 175 years earlier is easier said than done. One important question concerned the way the people of France would elect the new body. Traditionally, voting for the Estates General had followed its division into three estates: each would have the same number of representatives, and people would only vote for representatives of their own estate. Such a proceeding would have ensured that the first two estates, with less than 3 percent of the nation's population, would control the Estates General.

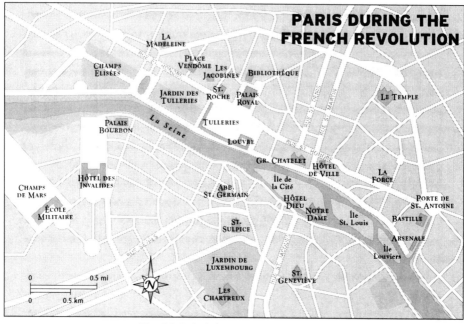

Map 1.2. Paris during the French Revolution.

This was not at all to the liking of many members of the third estate, however. In the fall of 1788 a radical cleric, Abbé Sieyès, published *What Is the Third Estate?* a pamphlet claiming that the third estate represented the nation as a whole and should rule the Estates General. Sieyès's pamphlet was one example of a vast outpouring of writings prompted by the summoning of the Estates General. In organizing the elections, royal officials called on people throughout France to submit lists of grievances (*cahiers de doléances*), and thousands did so. French writers also published over 3,000 pamphlets in 1789 and founded 184 new newspapers. This formidable mobilization of public opinion forced the king to agree to "doubling the third," giving the third estate as many representatives as the first and second combined. Far from resolving the issue, however, this move only increased the determination of many members of the third to fight for full legislative control. The alliance between aristocrats in the *parlements* and bourgeois activists that had forced the king to bow before the challenge to absolutist rule was already breaking down.

The question of representation would dominate the new legislative body. The Estates General that opened on May 3, 1789, in Versailles represented a wide range of opinion among its twelve hundred deputies. A strong majority supported the king, whereas others pushed for more radical steps, including a written constitution and freedom of the press. Immediately deputies wrestled with the issue of how to vote: by estate, as most of the clergy and nobility wished, or by head, the solution desired by members of the third estate. As it became clear that Louis XVI would side with the first two estates, thus handing them effective control of the Estates General, members of the third decided to recast themselves as a unified legislature, which the deputies of the other estates were free to join. On June 17 they, along with a few clerical deputies, unilaterally proclaimed the creation of the National Assembly. The king rejected this challenge to his authority and on June 20 locked the third estate deputies out of their meeting halls. They responded by adjourning in emergency session to a nearby tennis court, the only location large enough to house them, and swearing not to leave until they had written a constitution for France.

The Tennis Court Oath showed that France would not go back to 1614. After denouncing the move by the third estate, on June 27 Louis XVI capitulated, ordering the deputies of the other two estates to join the third in the new National Assembly. The delegates of the third greeted their victory with an outpouring of joy and emotion; one deputy literally died of happiness. The deputies then set about the task of establishing a constitutional monarchy that would balance the legitimate powers of the king with a strong, popularly based legislature. A complex task, to be sure, but in the afterglow of the creation of the National Assembly many considered it eminently feasible. As events would soon show, however, such a view failed to reckon with national popular opinion and activism. The interactions between legislators and militant citizens would become a key theme of the French Revolution, giving the movement its fundamentally transformative character.

The elections to the Estates General and the crafting of the *cahiers des doléances* had mobilized, indeed created, public opinion on a scale unprecedented in France. Millions throughout the country followed the deliberations of the newly elected deputies, and were incensed by noble and clerical resistance to the idea of a National Assembly. Popular anger was fueled by the continued economic downturn and the harsh winter of 1788–1789, which sharply increased unemployment and sent the price of bread climbing to new heights.

Louis XVI's initial support of the first two estates, and his decision to assemble troops around Paris, further stoked popular suspicion of a royalist plot to starve the people of France into political submission. The breaking point came when the king dismissed Jacques Necker, whom he had recalled to replace Lomenie de Brienne as comptroller-general in the fall of 1788. Many viewed Necker as the one pro-reform moderate among the king's counselors (doubling the Third was his idea, for example), and they saw his dismissal as proof that the king intended to suppress the revolution by force.

The people of Paris responded immediately and powerfully. Officials announced Necker's dismissal on Sunday, July 12, and Parisians taking their Sunday strolls began debating the news, then crowding into theaters and museums to demand action. At the Palais Royal, a popular gathering spot, the young Camille Desmoulins harangued listeners to arm themselves and resist despotism. Soon a crowd of several thousand had formed and began searching for firearms to challenge the king's soldiers. By the next day armed mobs of Parisians were attacking granaries and customs houses, even a monastery, to obtain stores of grain. On Tuesday, July 14, the insurgency culminated with the armed seizure of the Bastille, a royal fortress and prison that, to many, symbolized royal despotism and tyranny. The Bastille was only lightly held and counted only a few prisoners in 1789, but the prison governor's rash decision to fire on the mob unleashed its anger, prompting attackers to smash their way into the fortress with cannon taken from the Invalides, a military museum and hospital in Paris. The victors cut off the poor governor's head and paraded through the city with it suspended on a pike, a grisly demonstration of the power and anger of the Parisian crowd.

The capture of the Bastille not only furnished modern France with its major national holiday but permanently inscribed the French Revolution in the history and geography of Paris. Parisians were not the only ones to react to the debates in the National Assembly, however. Provincial cities also witnessed conflict as supporters of the assembly seized power from royal officials. At the same time rumors of marauding brigands in the pay of the nobility swept throughout the countryside, prompting peasants to rise up in arms and attack the chateaux of the aristocracy across France, often burning records of seigneurial dues and reclaiming common lands. If the attack on the Bastille made the Revolution in Paris, this so-called Great Fear gave it a national scale and impact. The violent acts taken by hordes of French men and women made the Revolution a reality far beyond the debates in Versailles.

Again, in the face of such turmoil Louis XVI saw no alternative to conceding. He had consistently failed to grasp the significance of the movement or to anticipate effective means of controlling it. When the Duke of Liancourt informed him that the Bastille had been taken, the king asked, "Is it a revolt?" The duke replied, "No sire, it is a revolution."[1] The king soon accepted the demands of the crowd, recalling Necker and sending the royal troops back home to the provinces. Deciding not to flee the country, he instead traveled to Paris and formally accepted the new tricolor cockade, uniting the red and blue of the city of Paris with the white of the monarchy. Clearly the king had lost control of events, and it was now up to the National Assembly to chart out the future of France.

The members of that body thus had to confront a radically changed political landscape. While many rejoiced that the king no longer threatened the Revolution, they were often aghast at the turmoil in Paris and the countryside. France had known peasant revolts before, but this threatened to turn into a national insurgency against property rights in general. The deputies thus felt they had to act to prevent the nation from descending into anarchy. Accordingly, on August 4 they passed the first major legislation of the Revolution, a decree abolishing feudalism. It targeted all feudal obligations and distinctions. In one sense the assembly was simply enacting in theory what the nation's peasants had already effected in practice. Nonetheless, this was a radical measure: it essentially abolished the nobility and the entire notion of a society based on castes in favor of a nation of citizens. The assembly followed this up on August 27 with the famous Declaration of the Rights of Man and Citizen. Inspired by Enlightenment thinking and America's declaration of independence, the seventeen-article declaration established that men were citizens, not subjects, and that sovereignty resided in the nation, not the king. Like much Enlightenment writing, the declaration used the language of universalism, suggesting from the outset that the French Revolution should and could apply to all of humanity. The declaration and the abolition of feudalism were impressive achievements that would transform France, remaining bedrocks of the nation's political culture to the present day.

While the National Assembly debated, the new citizens of France went about organizing political life in earnest. What often started as spontaneous meetings in cafés gradually turned into organized political clubs, the ancestors of modern political parties. Most of these clubs supported the cause of the Revolution, in part because popular agitators sometimes attacked conservative groups. The most prominent was known as the Jacobin Club, from the name of the monastery in Paris where it met. By 1791 it could claim over four hundred provincial affiliates. One of its early leading members was a young lawyer from Arras, Maximilian Robespierre, destined to become the leader of the radical Revolution. Clubs generally charged dues, which meant they were limited to the middle classes, and usually excluded women, who sometimes responded by forming their own political clubs. Nonetheless, the clubs played a vital role in spreading awareness of the Revolution throughout the population. French municipal governments were also reorganized in ways that facilitated popular activism. The city (*commune*) of Paris was divided into forty-eight sections, which would become centers of revolutionary militancy. Finally, the National Guard, a citizens' militia first established in Paris in July to defend the National Assembly, offered ordinary Frenchmen the ability to fight for the Revolution.

Events in October 1789 made it clear that an aroused citizenry was not prepared to give the king or National Assembly a blank check. Continued high bread prices, as well as Louis XVI's failure to endorse the new declaration publicly, stoked popular anger. Rumors of a lavish army banquet in Versailles where soldiers trampled on the tricolor cockade produced an explosion. On October 5, thousands of women gathered in Paris in protest, carrying arms and dragging cannon. They marched the twelve miles to the royal palace at Versailles, demanding an audience with the king. When the crowd broke into the royal apartments the next morning and massacred two palace bodyguards, the king accepted their demands that he and his family move back to Paris. They soon set out, "the baker, the baker's wife, and the baker's son," accompanied by the mob and followed by the members of the National Assembly. Henceforth the king and government would work in Paris under the watchful eyes of the city's militant citizenry.

The October 1789 march highlighted the central role of women in the revolutionary process. Most of the leading revolutionaries were male, and the political work of the National Assembly detailed the rights of men as citizens, while largely excluding women. Many of the new political clubs admitted men only. Yet women insisted on their right to a political voice, and time and time again used the platform of the streets to make that voice heard. As October demonstrated, they often led the revolutionary crowds. Thus the distinction between legislative and popular politics that did so much to shape the Revolution was also a gendered distinction. The Revolution thus created a space to allow for the expression of female political agency. In 1791 Olympe de Gouges would take the Declaration of the Rights of Man as a model for her Declaration of the Rights of Women.

The move to Paris in October 1789 calmed the situation, and the National Assembly, installed in its new quarters, got to work drawing up a constitution for France. For the next two years the political situation was relatively calm, allowing the nation's representatives to draft a number of foundational laws that transformed France from an absolute to a constitutional monarchy. According to the terms of the constitution of September 1791, the king would remain in power and have the right to delay (but not fully veto) legislation. Real power would rest in a Legislative Assembly, to be elected by all adult males who paid the equivalent of three days wages in taxes annually. The National Assembly formally abolished the nobility, the guilds, and the *parlements*. It got rid of the traditional provinces, dividing France up instead into eighty-three *départements*. It also created a new system of law courts to administer justice from the village to the national level.

The National Assembly devoted particular attention to the question of religion. It separated religion from citizenship, confirming the civil equality of Protestants and then granting the same rights to Jews. These moves provoked some controversy, especially in areas with a history of competition between Protestants and Catholics, but most accepted them. Dealing with the Catholic Church was more difficult. In November 1789 the assembly voted to expropriate the Church's landed property and sell it to private concerns, enabling France to avoid bankruptcy and winning the loyalty of those (mostly wealthy bourgeois) who acquired the new lands. The next year the assembly took further moves to restructure the Church, including popular election of priests. But the move that provoked the most controversy, and ultimately massive counterrevolution, was the Civil Constitution of the Clergy, passed by the assembly in July 1790. The constitution made all Catholic priests civil servants and required them to swear allegiance to the nation. This new law split the Church, and France, in two: nearly half of all French priests refused to accept it, especially in the west and south of the country, and within a year the pope had formally denounced it and the Revolution in general. This clash of universalisms, between the Church and the revolutionaries, would play a key role in the history of the Revolution and modern France as a whole.

Taken collectively, the actions of the National Assembly created the institutional structures of modern France, making the country a model for people throughout the world. It constituted a liberal revolution, implementing the values of freedom of speech, religion, and the press, as well the accountability of government to its citizenry. It was equally a bourgeois revolution, limiting the franchise to people of means (though the breadth of the franchise, enabling nearly half of all French men to vote, was radical in Europe at the time) and in general defending property rights. The 1791 Le Chapelier law, for example, outlawed trade unions in France. Moreover, by excluding women and the slaves of the Caribbean from politics, it demonstrated the limits of Enlightenment universalism.

Nonetheless, the achievements of the National Assembly represented real progress for France, and many at the time considered the Revolution essentially over. It had, after all, accomplished the main goals of Enlightenment reformism, affirming freedom of expression, the equality of all citizens before the law, and constitutional monarchy. Yet the Revolution did not end. Starting in 1791, it took a new, radical turn that plunged France and all of Europe into unprecedented turmoil. The reasoned moderation of the National Assembly ultimately satisfied neither the right-wing opposition, concentrated among the conservative nobility and the Church, nor the *menu peuple*, the working people and others of modest means in Paris and throughout France. The clash between those forces prevented any quick or easy stabilization.

Another central factor was the increasing internationalization of the revolutionary movement. The liberal Revolution of 1789–1791 had been essentially a domestic affair, taking place in a France consumed with its own problems. This would change after 1791, making the Revolution increasingly a European and even global event. Those outside France regarded the nation's transformation with horror or admiration but rarely indifference, and many saw it as key to their own condition. At the same time, many French revolutionaries felt inspired by a mission to spread the achievements of the Revolution beyond the nation's borders. In consequence, the idea of universalism à la française achieved a new urgency and concrete level of expression that would permanently mark the new French nation.

RISE AND FALL OF THE RADICAL REVOLUTION

The French Revolution broke upon Europe like a thunderclap. With a few exceptions, notably Britain, Europe in 1789 was governed by absolutist monarchs who viewed their power and legitimacy as a matter of divine right. Royal power varied widely across the Continent, and Enlightenment ideas had influenced some notable rulers like Frederick the Great of Prussia and Joseph II of Austria, who styled themselves "enlightened despots." Nonetheless, the prospect of a legislature, not to mention armed masses of commoners, forcing its political will on a sovereign and proclaiming that political power derived from the people, not from God, filled Louis XVI's colleagues with horror. If such things could happen in France, in its day the most powerful monarchy in Europe, who knew what the future held for their own lands?

Refugees from the turmoil in France stoked aristocratic fears, both by their words and by their sorry plight. Starting with Bastille Day, conservative opponents of the new order began fleeing the country to save their fortunes and, ultimately, their lives. This flight was led by the aristocracy, including the king's brothers, the Comte de Provence and the Comte d'Artois, who fled to Germany and England, respectively. The increasing violence and radicalism of the Revolution swelled the ranks of the emigration, so that many commoners also fled France. The Rhine River city of Coblentz became a center of the French emigration, and consequently of counterrevolutionary activism. Emigrés could be found throughout Europe, and many traveled to America, forming settlements not only on the East Coast but also in the Ohio River Valley and Texas. Like the Huguenots a century before them, the émigrés from the French Revolution spread throughout Europe and beyond, preaching to any who would listen their tale of woe and pleading for armed intervention to overthrow the evildoers in Paris.

Yet if Europe's monarchs and nobility feared and condemned the momentous events in France after 1789, many commoners, from wealthy bourgeois to poor peasants, drew inspiration from them. The abolition of feudalism and the establishment of a constitutional monarchy won praise from educated urban elites in much of Europe. In Germany students met in the ancient university cities of Heidelberg and Tübingen to discuss the exciting news from France, while peasant uprisings broke out in Baden, Saxony, and Silesia. Revolts also took place in Italy, a country with a large progressive middle class and masses of discontented peasants. In the southern Netherlands (now Belgium) a popular uprising in 1789 expelled the Austrians and created a republic, only to be overthrown by Austrian troops the following year. Such activism further hardened royal and aristocratic distrust of the Revolution, reinforced by its moves against the Church.

More than anywhere else, the French Revolution had a major impact in Britain. Public opinion there had largely favored the early stages of the movement, seen as making France a more progressive constitutional monarchy along British lines. Yet as the Revolution grew more radical, many came to condemn it. In November 1790 Edmund Burke published his classic *Reflections on the Revolution in France*, which attacked the Revolution for violating historical traditions and property rights. The next year Thomas Paine, already famous for his defense of the American revolution, published *The Rights of Man*, which energetically defended the movement. Paine's pamphlet was tremendously popular, selling almost 1 million copies (in contrast to Burke's sales of 30,000), and was read by small craftsmen, workers, Protestant dissenters, and other members of Britain's middle and lower classes. It inspired many to form political clubs to support the ideas of the French Revolution, notably the London Corresponding Society of 1791, one of the first working-class organizations in modern Europe. Such radical mobilization was more than the British government was willing to tolerate, and it responded by suppressing the local Jacobin movements in 1792–1793 and transporting many of their activists to penal servitude in Australia.

Interest in the French Revolution was not just a European phenomenon. The shock waves of the explosive events in France traveled across the Atlantic to trouble the azure waters and green islands of the Caribbean. In the late eighteenth century the Caribbean basin was dominated by European mercantile capitalism, which used African slave labor to produce sugar and other valuable crops for export. As such it played a central role in European imperial rivalries, so that during the Seven Years War the British navy had laid siege to France's Caribbean possessions. More than any other colony, the French possession of Saint-Domingue, on the island of Hispaniola, felt the impact of revolutionary events in France. In 1789 Saint-Domingue was the most valuable colony in the world, with eight thousand plantations employing the largest slave population in the Caribbean. It alone accounted for 40 percent of France's overseas trade and produced nearly 50 percent of all the sugar and coffee consumed in Europe and the Americas. The colony's population in the late eighteenth century was divided into three groups: whites, free people of color, and black slaves. Whereas the first two communities each had roughly 30,000 people, the slaves (many of whom had recently arrived from Africa) numbered 500,000. The specter of slave revolts hung heavily over the white colonists, and the growth of antislavery and abolitionist sentiment in France itself only increased their fears.

When Louis XVI agreed to call the Estates General in 1788, the whites of Saint-Domingue sent delegates to Paris to demand representation in it, a demand that was granted. They excluded not only the slaves but also the free people of color, who responded by sending their own delegation, led by the lawyer (and slave owner) Vincent Ogé. His appeals to whites to join forces against the slaves fell on deaf ears. In Paris, those representing whites defended the right to own slaves and maintain white supremacy in the colonial Caribbean against proposals by antislavery delegates. As the debate over slavery intensified, many white planters reacted by suggesting that Saint-Domingue secede from France and declare independence. In Saint-Domingue itself tensions increased between whites and people of mixed race, who now demanded full equality. In October 1790 Vincent Ogé, who had returned home from Paris, led other free blacks in an armed attack against the capital city of Cap Français. Soon suppressed by both white planters and government forces, Ogé's revolt illustrated the complexity of local reactions to the Revolution in France and hinted at the massive violence to come.

Like the Revolution in France, the struggle in Saint-Domingue began as a fight between elites, in this case white planters and free people of color. As would soon happen in Paris, however, revolutionary ideology and activism spread to the rest of the population, fundamentally transforming the Revolution. While the whites and free people of color debated, the black slaves in Saint-Domingue listened and made their own plans. On August 22, 1791, they rose up in revolt, launching one of the biggest slave insurrections in world history. Within a few weeks 100,000 slaves had joined the revolt, burning hundreds of plantations to the ground and frequently massacring their owners. For whites the revolt was a vision of the Apocalypse, as all the cruelty they had visited upon their slaves came back to them in brutal vengeance.

News of the uprising quickly spread around the Caribbean basin, so that within a month slaves in Jamaica were singing songs praising it. Refugees fled the island and settled in Philadelphia, New Orleans, and other American cities, inspiring fears (or hopes) of slave revolts in the United States. Over the next decade and beyond the struggle of the Saint-Domingue slaves for freedom, and the reaction of various Parisian governments to it, placed the question of slavery and emancipation on the front burner throughout the Caribbean, creating a revolutionary crisis in the area as a whole.

No part of the world outside Europe was more affected by the French Revolution, and nowhere did its logic of liberation go so far. Historians have generally portrayed the insurrection in Saint-Domingue as a reaction to events in France, yet it is worth considering what impact the slave revolt may have had on the French Revolution. Enlightenment political theorists had at times compared their struggle against despotism to a revolt against slavery, yet what happened in Saint-Domingue was no metaphor. If a central trope of the Revolution was the entry of the armed people into elite politics, the 1791 uprising in the Caribbean prefigured the creation of a sustained *sans-culotte* movement in Paris. Social and racial elites fled from both and tended to portray members of both groups as murderous savages, not freedom fighters. Did the news of slaves battling for liberty in the distant Caribbean, which reached France just as the new Legislative Assembly opened in October 1791, inspire people in France to do the same?

If Europe, the Caribbean, and elsewhere watched the Revolution unfold with bated breath, in 1791 and 1792 the leaders of the movement in France became increasingly aware of their revolutionary nation's place in a conservative world. After the relative calm of the past year and a half, during which the National Assembly had outlined the governing structures of a new French nation, the direction of the Revolution once again became a matter of political conflict in the summer of 1791. Louis XVI precipitated this new crisis. The king had long resented the Revolution but felt powerless to do anything about it. In particular, he refused to take effective action against the émigrés, including his own brothers. On June 20, he decided to join them. Wearing a disguise, he fled Paris in a coach headed for the German border and left behind a manifesto denouncing the Revolution. But authorities in the small town of Varennes recognized him and the queen, and forced them to return under guard to Paris. The flight to Varennes caused an uproar in the National Assembly, with radicals condemning the king as a traitor and calling for the abolition of the monarchy. It also underscored the link between counterrevolution and foreign interests, making the unity of national patriotism and progressive ideology a central theme of the Revolution, a theme that would shape the history of modern France.

The new Legislative Assembly, which opened in October 1791, was dominated by moderates but included substantial numbers of radical republicans, who wished to push the movement further, as well as royalists, who openly hoped for foreign intervention to end the Revolution. The attitude of Europe's monarchs seemed ever more threatening. In August 1791 the kings of Austria and Prussia issued the Declaration of Pilnitz, calling for the restoration of order in France. This, plus continuing agitation by the émigrés in European royal courts, intensified the anger of the French, confirming their fear that the main danger to the Revolution lay abroad. In April 1792 the Legislative Assembly decided to push for war, in spite of the objections of Robespierre, who feared the consequences of a military defeat. Hostility focused on Austria, whose emperor, Leopold II, was the brother of the reviled French queen Marie Antoinette. When Austria refused a French ultimatum

to expel the French émigrés, France declared war on April 20, 1792, precipitating a conflict that would last for over twenty years and establish a key
dynamic in modern history: the link between war and revolution.

At first the war went badly, in part because most of the French army's
officers were aristocrats whose loyalty to the new regime was shaky at best. A
combination of military defeats and continuing economic troubles provoked
an upsurge of patriotic activism in Paris. The year 1792 saw the return of the
Parisian crowd to active political participation. The *sans-culottes*, representatives of the city's artisans and lower classes who supported the radical left,
began mobilizing in the Paris sections and making alliances with progressive
members of the Legislative Assembly. They used the celebration of July 14 to
mobilize supporters from all over the country to come to the capital and begin plotting to overthrow the monarchy. Parisians were particularly struck by
the ardor of the volunteer soldiers from Marseilles, whose marching song, the
"Marseillaise," would become the country's national anthem.

A proclamation by the leader of the military alliance against France, the
Duke of Brunswick, threatening the French people if any harm should come
to Louis XVI, outraged popular opinion to Paris and led the plotters to take
action. On August 10, 1792, thousands of *sans-culottes* invaded the royal resi-
dence at the Tuileries Palace, massacring some six hundred Swiss guards who
defended it. Fearing for their own lives, the deputies voted to abrogate the
constitution and hold new elections (based on universal manhood suffrage)
for a National Convention. This *journée*, or revolutionary day of action, was
followed by another upsurge of violence a few weeks later. During the first
week of September, in response to Prussia's capture of the strategic fortress
of Verdun, panicked Parisians invaded the city's prisons. Believing that traitors
at home were aiding the enemy abroad, they massacred over a thousand prisoners, roughly half of the city's prison population, on frequently trumped-up
charges of counterrevolution and treason. The September massacres made it
clear that ordinary Parisians were prepared to take not only justice but also
politics into their own hands.

The violent actions of the Parisian *sans-culottes* transformed French politics, initiating what many historians have called the Second Revolution. For
these militants, the fight against counterrevolution and the war against foreign
enemies were one. Volunteers also flooded into the revolutionary armies and
on September 20 handed the Prussian and Austrian armies a signal defeat at
Valmy, stopping the advance on Paris. The German poet Goethe, who witnessed the fanatical ardor of the French troops, observed that "from here and

today begins a new epoch of world history."[2] A day later the new National Convention met in Paris and immediately voted to abolish the monarchy, establishing the first republic in French history. In a period of political anxiety and threatened invasion, the French people created the political form that would dominate the history of the modern nation.

They did so in a transformed political landscape. Many conservatives and moderates had left the country because of the violence in August and September. The Marquis de Lafayette, leader of French forces in the war for American independence and a strong supporter of the liberal revolution, fled to the Austrian Netherlands. The Jacobins had won the parliamentary elections and consequently dominated the new convention, but they now split into two factions, both mostly composed of middle-class lawyers and professionals. The Girondins, many of whom came from the Gironde department around Bordeaux, supported the republican idea but tended to represent the interests of the bourgeois elites and oppose the radical activism of the *sans-culottes*. In contrast, the Montagnards (so named because its members generally took the highest seats in the convention) frequently supported and worked with Parisian militants. Led by Maximilian Robespierre and the fiery young orator Saint-Just, the Montagnards called for a radical vision of the republic, and their alliance with the *sans-culottes* would make this vision possible.

The fate of Louis XVI also divided the two Jacobin factions. Whereas the Girondins saw no benefit to prosecuting the king further, the Montagnards, bowing to popular anger, insisted on trying him for treason. At his trial in December 1792, Louis XVI denied all charges, but the discovery of letters he had written to sovereigns elsewhere in Europe denouncing the Revolution weakened his defense and hardened the views of many deputies. As a result, the convention voted, by a majority of 380 to 310, to condemn him to death, and he was formally executed by guillotine, "the national razor," in the Place de la Concorde on January 21, 1793. Like the execution of King Charles I in 1649 during the English revolution, putting Louis XVI to death sent a clear message to France and the world that there would be no turning back, that the Revolution, led by the people in arms, would determine the future of the nation.

The execution of Louis XVI horrified the rest of Europe, turning the struggle against revolutionary France into a holy crusade to save civilization. By the spring of 1793 Spain and Britain entered the anti-French coalition, and the Austrians made headway in the Netherlands and along the Rhine. Moreover, a massive internal revolt confronted the convention. In March, peasants in the deeply Catholic region of the Vendée, in the west, rose up in revolt against the national government, spurred on by hatred of the attacks against the Church and attempts to draft local men into the army. At the same time continued poor harvests and inflation sapped working-class living standards, stoking popular anger in Paris and across the country. At the end of May units of the Parisian National Guard, controlled by the *sans-culottes*, invaded the convention and forced the ouster of the Girondins, leaving the Montagnards in control of the government. Two-thirds of French departments protested their expulsion, and the Girondin leaders fled to their strongholds in the provinces, instigating revolts against Paris in Caen, Bordeaux, Marseilles, and Lyon. The Revolution had entered its darkest hour.

Far from compromising its ideals and policies, the convention responded to the crisis with a *fuite en avant*, a series of new laws and policies that increased the radicalism of the movement. In April it appointed a Committee of Public Safety to lead the war effort, a small group that in July would come under the control of Robespierre and form an effective dictatorship. In August, the convention responded to the threat of foreign invasion and domestic counterrevolution with the *levée en masse*, a modern system of conscription that created new revolutionary armies of unprecedented size. In September, abandoning economic liberalism in order to retain the loyalty of the *sans-culottes*, the convention passed the Maximum, fixing the price of wheat and other food staples; speculation in the price of grain became a capital crime. These and other measures centralized government control over France, anticipating the welfare and military policies of twentieth-century nation-states.

These new radical policies became collectively known as the Terror, symbolizing the wrath of the Revolution militant. In particular, the Terror referred to the trials and executions of those suspected of counterrevolutionary activities. In September the convention passed the Law on Suspects, giving the government broad new powers to arrest suspects and defining as traitors those who emigrated or failed to prove their patriotism sufficiently. Under this law a revolutionary tribunal guillotined several thousand French women and men in Paris and the provinces. Many more were imprisoned, and over 100,000 fled France. In October 1793 the government guillotined Queen Marie Antoinette for treason. Although the Terror focused at first on nobles and refractory priests, it mostly took the lives of members of the lower classes whose patriotism was in question. In November, for example, the government executed Olympe de Gouges, a self-educated butcher's daughter who came under suspicion because of her ties to the Girondins.

The Terror was not just a policy of political repression, however; it looked to the radical remaking of France as a nation and as a culture. Cultural change had been a key part of the Revolution ever since 1789. In the aftermath of the seizure of the Bastille revolutionaries planted "liberty trees," ceremonial poles, throughout France and founded ceremonies to celebrate the movement. On July 14, 1790, a national Festival of Federation inaugurated the tradition of celebrating Bastille Day. Under Montagnard rule, however, government attempts to eradicate all aspects of the ancien régime took cultural change to an unprecedented level. The heart of this effort was a massive program of de-Christianization. For example, the convention replaced the traditional Christian calendar with a new revolutionary one, divided into twelve months with names like Floréal and Brumaire (based on the seasons), and divided the month into three ten-day weeks. The revolutionary leaders even created a Cult of Reason to replace Christianity, and in November 1793 turned Notre Dame Cathedral into a temple of reason, consecrated with a ceremony in honor of the goddess of liberty. Activists also pressured priests to renounce their vows and to marry. Across France revolutionaries destroyed religious statues, books, and churches.

De-Christianization was just one aspect of the politicization of everyday life under the Revolution. Public names referring to the Church or the monarchy were changed, so that in far-off Martinique the city of Fort Royal became Fort-de-France. In daily discourse people dropped the formal *vous* for the more comradely *tu*, or "Citizen." Wearing the revolutionary cockade, colored red, white, and blue, became a prudent means of demonstrating personal patriotism. Ostentatious displays of wealth frequently gave rise to suspicion of aristocratic leanings, so dressing down became the order of the day. In regions like Provence or Alsace, where people spoke languages other than Parisian French, learning French became a symbol of patriotism, and the refusal (or inability) to speak it a possible sign of counterrevolutionary tendencies. During the Terror, therefore, revolutionary commitment went beyond politics to become a way of life.

These changes were important to many, but the ultimate task of the Terror was to defeat the Revolution's enemies. The *levée en masse* created a huge new French military force, some 700,000 strong. This plus the application of ruthless discipline and the promotion of skilled younger officers enabled the French to turn the tide by the end of 1793, even though they were at war with most of the major European powers. By the summer of 1794 French forces mounted an offensive in the Austrian Netherlands, the Rhine valley, and

Savoy. The convention portrayed its conquest of these areas as a revolutionary war of liberation against despotism. Some local inhabitants concurred and worked with the French, but others saw the French presence as an occupation rather than an emancipation. The convention also succeeded in defeating insurgencies at home, largely thanks to the disorganization of its opponents. Revolutionary armies, sometimes with guillotines mounted on wheels, rampaged across France, burning towns and fields and imprisoning thousands of suspects. The war against the Vendée revolt was particularly brutal: at one point government troops threw several thousand insurgents into the Loire River to drown.

The Terror has gone down in history as an evil, bloody dictatorship, yet for many French men and women at the time it represented the most just regime they had ever lived under. The Terror treated opponents or suspected opponents with brutality, but it won the loyalty of the *sans-culottes* and many others by its measures to support the poor, and by its embrace of patriotism. The Maximum kept the price of bread down, making life far easier for the poor who depended on it. The convention also tended to favor the interests of peasants over landlords, and went so far as to suggest that land confiscated from those convicted of treason should be given free to the poor. Above all, the convention's successful prosecution of the war showed its ability and determination to defend the Revolution against all enemies. For the *sans-culottes* and their allies, the bread of freedom had to be watered with the blood of the oppressors, and the Terror's willingness to do just that ensured their support.

The image of the Terror as a symbol of liberty becomes clearer if we look to the Caribbean. While tentatively offering equal status to the free people of color in Saint-Domingue, the Legislative Assembly did nothing to address the raging slave revolt or the conditions that had created it. In February 1794, however, in defiance of orthodox opinion in much of Europe as well as the young United States, the convention formally abolished slavery in the French empire and offered citizenship to (male) former slaves. More than that, the convention sent a fleet to the Caribbean to retake Martinique and Guadeloupe from the British and free the slaves there as well. In alliance with the rebel slaves of Saint-Domingue, led by the remarkable general Toussaint L'Ouverture, the French freed their islands from British control and briefly invaded the island of Saint-Vincent in support of a slave revolt there. Although Napoleon would later reverse French support of the Saint-Domingue slaves, the actions of the convention left a powerful legacy, convincing the people of the French Caribbean that the republic equaled liberty.

The Revolution's impact in the Caribbean and the Americas as a whole spread far beyond France's own territories. In an area dominated and shaped by the Atlantic slave trade, the question of African slavery and the resistance to it dominated public life, and no event in history mobilized people around it like the French Revolution. The combination of the Revolution's high-flown rhetoric about liberty and the massive war for freedom in Saint-Domingue threw the entire region into turmoil. Slave revolts had erupted throughout the Caribbean basin ever since the beginnings of African slavery, and in many ways the uprising in Saint-Domingue was merely the latest and most powerful example.

The Revolution in the Caribbean also drew inspiration from another local tradition: piracy. Pirates ranged far and wide across the Caribbean during the seventeenth and early eighteenth centuries, terrorizing the established order and holding forth an alternate vision of liberty. Pirate ships, whose crews frequently included escaped slaves, were generally run along democratic lines, emphasizing the equal rights of all. Long before the taking of the Bastille, a libertarian model of equality flourished on the high seas of the Americas. In building on the (often brutal) heritage of both slave insurgencies and pirate ships, the revolutionary Caribbean illustrated how people far from Paris interpreted the French Revolution according to their own ideas and desires.

In short, the Terror brutalized many, but to many more it held out the prospect of a brilliant future of liberty, equality, and fraternity. In spite of this support, however, the Terror did not last much more than a year. The Committee of Public Safety increasingly lost the ability to distinguish between political opponents and traitors, so that even after the dangers of invasion and counterrevolution had been tamed it continued to arrest suspects and guillotine people from all walks of French society. Repression reached its height in June and July of 1794, a period known as the Great Terror, after the revolutionary armies had scored signal victories on all fronts. In April 1794 the Committee tried and executed the so-called Indulgents, those who wanted to rein in the Terror, including famous and committed revolutionaries like Georges Danton and Camille Desmoulins.

Perhaps more importantly, the Terror also began attacking the leadership of the *sans-culottes*, bringing them more firmly under the control of the convention. At the end of 1793 it began banning popular clubs, especially those organized by women. In March 1794 the committee executed the journalist Hébert, leader of the Ultras, and his followers. This step effectively demobilized the *sans-culottes*, which meant they could no longer threaten the

Jacobins' control of the convention, but also meant that they could no longer support them against their enemies on the right. It broke the unity between radical politicians and popular activists, with fateful consequences.

The end came swiftly. On July 27, 1794 (the ninth day of Thermidor according to the revolutionary calendar), convention deputies arrested Robespierre, Saint-Just, and their associates, fearing yet another round of executions. The demobilization of the *sans-culottes* movement prevented them from mounting any effective resistance, and the leaders of the Committee of Public Safety met their fate on the guillotine. The fall of Robespierre unleashed a massive counterreaction, as the victors moved to dismantle the edifice of terror. They released large numbers of political prisoners from jail, abolished the Revolutionary Tribunal, and banned the Jacobin Club in Paris. They also terminated the Maximum, setting off the runaway inflation of grain prices. The Thermidorians soon found they had unleashed a powerful movement beyond their control, as some of those victimized by the Terror now sought revenge. Upper-class youth known as the *jeunesse dorée* went on the rampage, beating and even killing Jacobin militants throughout France. The violent political repression and the tremendous economic distress of the poor prompted one more Parisian *journée*, when *sans-culottes* invaded the convention, but soldiers and vigilantes easily suppressed the movement. Clearly the radical Revolution was over.

What would follow was less clear. Those who overthrew Robespierre and the Jacobin dictatorship wanted to continue the Revolution, but they disagreed about the form it should take. Moreover, the swing of the political pendulum back to the center allowed those who rejected the Revolution altogether to press their ideas in public debate. To guard against a return to authoritarian radicalism, after Thermidor the convention drafted a new constitution that sharply restricted the democratic character of French politics. It abolished universal manhood suffrage, restricting the franchise to the wealthy. The new constitution also created a bicameral legislature, a Council of 500 and a Council of Elders, whose structure promoted conservative stability over revolutionary innovation. It vested executive authority in a committee of five directors whose title, the Directory, gave the new regime its name. This was a regime created to safeguard bourgeois interests and fortunes, and to exclude most French people from the kind of political activism that had shaped the radical Republic.

During its four years in power, 1795–1799, the Directory sought a middle way between the excesses of Jacobinism and royalism. As is often the case in such situations, the regime succeeded in pleasing neither side, and consequently has been judged wanting. Yet as some historians have noted, the new regime did score solid successes. It was able to curb the runaway inflation of the previous years by returning to a metal currency and writing off much of the public debt. It also succeeded in rationalizing tax collection, the issue that had touched off the Revolution in the first place. Moreover, it created a network of leading educational institutions, such as new medical schools and the Ecole polytechnique, that made Paris a world center of scientific scholarship.

Another success of the Directory, yet one that ultimately proved its Achilles' heel, was the prosecution of the war. The last years of the Jacobin regime had seen the revolutionary armies take the offense on a number of fronts. France's armies, the largest in Europe thanks to the *levée en masse*, had become well trained and professional as the old aristocratic leadership gave way to the new citizen's military. This progress continued under the Directory, so that in 1795 France conquered the Netherlands and in following years scored important victories in Germany and Italy.

Yet in spite of a strong economy at home and military victories abroad, the Directory remained vulnerable to attacks from both left and right. Royalists attempted two insurrections in 1795: a landing of émigré nobles in Brittany in June and an armed uprising in Paris in October. In May 1796 the Directory arrested Gracchus Babeuf, leader of the Conspiracy of Equals, who plotted to overthrow the regime and return to the social egalitarianism of *sans-culotte* ideology. In 1797 royalists won big in the elections to the Council of 500, prompting the directors to annul the results. They did the same thing in 1798 when neo-Jacobins in their turn won several seats. Even in good times, therefore, the Directory failed to create the solid center that would support it, and the good times did not last. By 1798 the economy had once again turned sour, increasing discontent throughout French society. Moreover, a powerful new European coalition against France, involving Britain, Austria, and Russia, dealt a series of major defeats to French forces, leading to the prospect of a military collapse. By 1799 the Directory was clearly falling apart, and the only question was what would replace it.

The answer came soon enough. One effect of the revolutionary wars was to produce a new crop of capable young officers who had risen through the ranks thanks to their own talents. Among these the Revolution would find its man of destiny. Napoleon Bonaparte, the product of the minor nobility from the backwater island of Corsica, was physically unimpressive but gifted with a powerful personality that made him a natural leader. Born in 1768, he attended military school in Paris and joined the army as an artillery officer; unlike many aristocrats, he remained in the army after the Revolution broke out. He first attracted the attention of the army leadership with his brilliant conquest of Toulon, which had fallen to opposition forces, in 1793. Napoleon continued his rise to power under the Directory, winning renown for suppressing the royalist revolt of October 1795. The Directory sent him to command the revolutionary army in Italy, where against all expectations he crushed the Austrians and made France the dominant military power. Next the Directory sent Napoleon to invade Egypt, hoping both to cut Britain's links with India and to send the increasingly popular general as far away from Paris as possible. In July 1798 Bonaparte arrived in Egypt, quickly conquering Alexandria and Cairo. However, the British navy under Admiral Nelson moved into position, trapping Bonaparte's forces. Faced with this, Napoleon deserted his forces in Egypt and secretly returned to France alone.

Napoleon came back to Paris in October 1799, where he was hailed as a hero, the conqueror of Italy and Egypt. Just thirty years old, he symbolized dynamism and the future. He arrived at a time when the Directory was largely discredited and many were looking for alternatives. One of these was the Abbé Sieyès, who after pursuing a complicated trajectory during the Revolution (he later said his main accomplishment was that he survived) had become a director in June. He had decided that the Revolution needed a strongman to put things right, and he thought Napoleon would be the perfect candidate, vastly popular but also young and inexperienced enough to be controlled. He approached Napoleon, who agreed to support Sieyès and his co-conspirators. They appointed Bonaparte commander in chief of the army in Paris. On November 9, 1799 (or, on the revolutionary calendar, Brumaire 18) Napoleon's troops surrounded the convention and forced it to vote full power to a new government of three consuls: Napoleon, Sieyès, and fellow director Roger Ducos. Much to Sieyès's surprise, Bonaparte soon made it clear that he was no one's puppet, and his control of the army ensured his control of the nation. Once again, following a key trope of the Revolution, warfare abroad determined the political situation at home. No riots or insurrections greeted Napoleon's seizure of power, as the Directory passed into history largely unlamented. In December a plebiscite approved the new regime, the Consulate, by nearly 100 percent of all votes cast. A new era had begun, and for the next fifteen years Napoleon Bonaparte would reign unchallenged as the master of France.

1.2. *Napoleon Crosses the St. Bernard*, Jacques-Louis David.
Source: Bibliothèque nationale de France.

THE FIRST EMPIRE

Bonaparte's long reign, during which he created many of the institutions of modern France, was much more than just a coda attached to the end of the Revolution. The ultimate symbol of the great man in history, and of the self-made man, Napoleon inspired controversy and admiration among both his contemporaries and later historians. Much of the controversy swirls around his relationship to the Revolution. Did Napoleon reinforce and sustain the principles and achievements of the ten revolutionary years, or did he bring them to an end? Proponents of the first perspective emphasize his support for religious tolerance, his codification of French law, and his abolition of serfdom throughout Europe. Advocates of the second perspective focus on his abandonment of the republic for an empire, his reconciliation with the Church, and his restoration of slavery in the French Caribbean. Good arguments exist on either side, but perhaps Napoleon's most important legacy was the myth of individual achievement he created, a myth that would inspire millions in the decades to come and would become a core belief of bourgeois society in modern France.

Napoleon Bonaparte is especially important for transnational approaches to French history. He reaffirmed the significance of the Revolution for Europe as a whole, destroying medieval institutions across the Continent. However, the way in which this imperial mission reshaped France is also important, and intriguing. Out of the ashes of royalty and republicanism Napoleon created an empire, a political formation whose significance for modern France has not always been acknowledged. This is paradoxical on a number of levels. In general, the history of modern government has been away from multinational empires and toward more unified nation-states, yet the French case is much more complicated. What is the historian to make of Bonaparte's empire, containing so many features of the French nation-state yet at the same time claiming to apply its principles to all imperial subjects? The Napoleonic empire represented the most powerful example of French national universalism up to that time, one that would constitute a leitmotif for both French society and its relationship to the wider world ever since.

It is also important that this universalism would take the shape of empire. Students of French colonialism have often been perplexed to discover that, in doing library searches on the term "French empire," they come up with references to Napoleon's regime as much as to colonial Africa or Indochina. This is no mere semantic coincidence, for the first empire did in fact lay out the basic outlines of French overseas imperialism in the modern era. Bonaparte failed to make France a global power, thanks largely to the power of the British navy. He abandoned Egypt, sold the vast Louisiana territory to the Americans, and failed to reconquer Saint-Domingue. Yet his expansion of French dominance throughout Europe anticipated in many respects the themes of empire in Africa and Asia. It would eventually inspire another European leader, Adolf Hitler, to attempt his own version of empire in Europe. Moreover, his complex blend of revolutionary and imperial themes would make empire an enduring part of the heritage of 1789; the Third Republic, which made permanent many of the achievements of the Revolution, would also take the paradoxical form of a republican empire.

Napoleon's imperial vision rested on the revolutionaries' belief that they were engaged in a war for liberty against the tyrants of Europe, a war of liberation rather than conquest. As we will see, while this vision inspired one of the greatest series of military triumphs in modern world history, it failed to convince many Europeans that French arms had come to free them. Instead, the French occupation often inspired the birth of local nationalist movements, modeled on France's revolutionary patriotism and ranged in opposition against it. Both the outlines of modern empire and of wars of national liberation in response have come down to us from the Napoleonic empire, a model for France and the world as a whole.

Within a few years of the Directory's overthrow, Napoleon Bonaparte had secured his power at home and abroad. The new constitution of 1799 made him first consul with complete executive authority and an essentially powerless legislature. It was the first French constitution since 1789 that made no mention of the rights of man. He also increased government censorship of the media and of free expression, sharply reducing the number of newspapers in Paris and submitting all artistic performances to government approval. In 1802 Napoleon signed a concordat with Rome; while affirming state control over the Catholic Church, it restored religious holidays and the religious calendar, recognized Catholicism as the faith of most French people, and ended the religious conflict that had traumatized the nation for a decade. This step, plus his overtures to the nobility, healed some of the wounds caused by the Revolution and helped secure the new leader's authority.

Bonaparte's continued success on the fields of war and diplomacy also facilitated his claims to absolute rule. In 1800 he renewed the war against Austria, defeating that nation handily at the battle of Marengo in June. He then made the Austrians sign a peace treaty accepting French control of Belgium and parts of Italy. With Austria out of the war, and Russia distracted by conflict with the Ottoman Empire, Napoleon forced the British to sign the Peace of Amiens in 1802, in which London recognized French conquests in Europe and also returned the Caribbean colonies it had seized from France. With this new treaty France was finally at peace for the first time in a decade. Napoleon took the opportunity to proclaim himself consul for life in 1802, a decision that was duly ratified by a plebiscite. However, this did not satisfy the great general, who worried about his legacy for France. Several assassination attempts convinced him he needed to found a dynasty, so on December 2, 1804, in an elaborate coronation ceremony in Notre Dame Cathedral, he took the title "emperor of the French," becoming France's first emperor since Charlemagne a thousand years earlier. Ever the self-made man, rather than wait for Pope Pius VII to crown him he seized the crown from the pontiff and crowned himself. It was a fitting gesture, perhaps, for a new type of monarch.

By 1804 Napoleon Bonaparte had realized the dream of both Louis XIV and the Revolution, centralizing state power to an unprecedented degree. Showing a talent for administration as well as warfare, he transformed the French state. He reinforced the departments by creating the office of prefect to administer them; the prefects resembled governors of American states, except for the fact that they were appointed by the central government (namely, Napoleon himself), not locally elected. Prefects in turn had the power to appoint mayors, while at the same time Paris appointed all judges. More than ever before, the capital became the center of France.

One of the emperor's greatest achievements was the creation of a unified legal system. The Civil Code, or Napoleonic Code, ensured the equality of all French men before the law. It also confirmed the end of feudal laws as well as the transfers of land under the Revolution, a move that won Napoleon the support of those who had acquired new property. It reaffirmed rights to religious liberty, while sharply limiting the rights of employees. Most strikingly, it inscribed a strongly patriarchal vision of French society into national law. Reversing the gains that women had made under the Revolution, the Civil Code made wives legally dependent on their husbands and restricted their right to divorce. It also strengthened the authority of fathers over their children, for example, allowing the former summarily to imprison the latter for up to six months. The Napoleonic Code created the legal basis for bourgeois patriarchal society, and not just in France. One of the modern world's most influential documents, it was widely adapted and imitated throughout Europe and Latin America.

In other ways Napoleon reshaped France according to his desires. Building on the work of the Directory, he invested heavily in education, creating the *lycées*, schools, which dominate French secondary education to this day. He also founded the Bank of France to ensure efficient management of the economy. He engaged in a massive construction program, especially in Paris, building the Arc de Triomphe to commemorate his many victories, as well as other neoclassical monuments. In addition, Napoleon wooed both the aristocracy and the wealthy bourgeoisie by reestablishing a system of noble privilege, but one based on wealth and achievement rather than historical lineage. To deal with those not seduced by these accomplishments, Napoleon also improved and increased the police force, including secret police constantly on the lookout for seditious comments. Thanks to all these measures and more, Bonaparte not only modernized France but also forestalled any serious domestic challenges to his reign.

For all these important achievements, however, Napoleon's primary interest, and his ultimate reputation, lay with military conquest. Perhaps no other world leader in modern times has been so closely identified with triumphs on the battlefield. Time and again Bonaparte overwhelmed opposing forces with a combination of brilliant military strategy and the patriotic ardor of a huge citizen army, something the largely mercenary forces of the rest of Europe could rarely resist. Britain and France went to war again, and Britain eventually paid both Austria and Russia to join a new coalition against Napoleon, one soon joined by Prussia as well. Yet British subsidies went for naught, as French armies crushed all three nations in a series of brilliant victories in 1806 and 1807. Napoleon's armies occupied Berlin in 1806, then took Vienna in 1809. By 1810 France controlled the largest European empire since the Romans, directly ruling or in close alliance with countries from Spain and Portugal through the Low Countries, Italy, Germany, Austria, and Poland. The little man from Corsica had in short order become not only the emperor of France but the ruler of Europe.

Napoleon's one great military failure during the first decade of his rule came in the Caribbean. In 1801 Toussaint L'Ouverture proclaimed the independence of Saint-Domingue, taking the name of Haiti for the new nation. A year later Napoleon sent a fleet to invade the young nation and restore slavery. His forces successfully overthrew the revolutionary regime in Guadeloupe and reestablished slavery on that island. Haiti proved a harder nut to crack. Bonaparte captured Toussaint and imprisoned him in an alpine fortress, where he died in 1803. However, the Haitians fought back fiercely, this time aided by the British, and much of the French occupying force perished from yellow fever and other tropical diseases. What was left of the French force finally surrendered in 1804, making Haiti once again an independent nation and France's first former colony.

For the millions who lived under French rule, the Napoleonic occupation of Europe brought unprecedented changes, some desirable, some not. In less than a decade Bonaparte implemented the innovations of the Revolution on a Continental scale. He abolished feudalism and serfdom, prompting the sale of millions of acres of land, often to wealthy commoners. He imposed the legal standardizations of the Napoleonic Code as well as religious toleration. Napoleonic troops liberated Jews from ghettos throughout Europe, and in 1807 he convened an international body of Jewish theologians to debate the future of its people in the Great Sanhedrin, an ancient rabbinical body that had not met for eighteen centuries. Bonaparte also built bridges and canals, unified customs areas, and promoted a uniform system of weights and measures. Most dramatically, he redrew the map of Europe. He created a new Polish state, replacing the one gobbled up by Prussia, Russia, and Austria in 1795. He reduced the number of Italian states and reorganized the peninsula into two kingdoms. In 1806 Napoleon abolished the centuries-old Holy Roman Empire, reducing the number of German states from over three hundred to roughly thirty, organized in the new Confederation of the Rhine. In effect, Napoleon ruled Europe as the ultimate enlightened despot, imposing progress and reason through the power of the sword.

Napoleon's policies and the ideology they represented benefited, especially at first, from considerable support among Europeans. Urban elites and members of the middle class often applauded (and benefited from) his abolition of the feudal order. Religious toleration offered Jews and other religious minorities opportunities undreamed of by earlier generations. These reforms succeeded best in the Low Countries, Switzerland, the Rhineland, and other relatively prosperous areas. In Mediterranean and eastern Europe, in contrast, they encountered resistance. The French takeover of Spain in 1808 triggered a massive insurgency that gave the world the term *guerrilla*. But even in the areas that had greeted French troops as liberators, the occupation frequently provoked significant resistance. In large part this arose from the nature of the occupation. As was traditional with European armies, the French imposed heavy duties and reparations on the countries they occupied, but theirs were unusually large, in part because of the sheer size of the revolutionary armies. Whereas many French people saw this as legitimate, believing the people of Europe should help foot the bill for their own liberation, those who had to pay often viewed it as a conqueror's tax. Moreover, the siphoning off of considerable European wealth to France (a major reason for the strength of the French economy under Napoleon) turned many against the occupation, as did the damage to trade caused by the economic boycott of Britain, which devastated the economy of the Netherlands and other areas. As in France, attacks on the Church often prompted resistance, especially in southern Europe. Finally, the increasingly repressive nature of the occupation and its promotion of a new nobility rather than the forces of democracy cost Napoleon the support of many. What had begun as a revolutionary liberation now seemed to be the imposition of foreign rule by force.

As a result, the Napoleonic occupation of Europe helped create the very nationalism it exemplified, but this nationalism was now directed against the French. Germany became a prime example of this. Many German intellectuals had welcomed the French Revolution and hailed Napoleon's rise to power. As Bonaparte became increasingly authoritarian, some reconsidered their earlier support of him. The great composer Ludwig van Beethoven had initially dedicated his *Eroica* symphony to Napoleon, only to tear off the dedication page in disgust upon learning of his intention to proclaim himself emperor. At the same time, writers and thinkers began to consider a German patriotism that could inspire resistance to Napoleon. Lacking a single nation-state, they focused instead on language, history, and culture, inspiring a cultural movement that would blossom as romanticism. It challenged the rationalism of the Enlightenment, so that German resistance to France was not just political but cultural as well. Bonaparte himself had contributed to this new idea of German unity by sharply reducing the number of German states. The new German nationalism thus owed much to France even as it excoriated the French invader.

French rule did not produce a nationalist resistance everywhere in occupied Europe: Italy and Poland were two noteworthy exceptions. Nonetheless, the rise of anti-French movements in Napoleonic Europe testified to the failure of national universalism. Napoleonic rule, and the revolutionary precedents on which it rested, could not be both French and the property of all men at the same time. The fact that German intellectuals turned from enthusiastic membership in an international Republic of Letters to an embrace of their own cultural and national traditions illustrated the depths of this failure. For the variety of reasons outlined above, even though Napoleon carried out many reforms long desired by Europeans, he could not convince them that this was a liberation rather than an occupation. Without their support, Napoleon's dominance of Europe had to rest on France's strength and his own formidable military genius. Ultimately this was not enough.

Napoleon's France was at the height of its power by 1810, completely dominating the Continent. Only Britain and Russia actively opposed Bonaparte. The emperor's fortunes soon turned, however. In 1812 the army that had defeated all other opponents invaded Russia. Napoleon scored several major victories but could never trap and destroy the Russian armies, which retreated across eastern Europe destroying everything in their path that the French might use. Moreover, hundreds of thousands of French troops were tied up fighting the insurgency in Spain, thus weakening the emperor's forces. In October, after occupying Moscow, Napoleon ordered a general retreat, too late to escape the brutal Russian winter. Cold and hunger decimated the French armies: less than one in ten of those who had set out from France returned. The clear weakening of French strength inspired the Prussians and

Austrians to rejoin the war against Napoleon. In 1813 this new coalition took the field, defeating France at the Battle of Nations near Leipzig in October. At the same time, Britain's Duke of Wellington invaded southern France with an army of British, Spanish, and Portuguese soldiers.

By 1814 Napoleon's situation was desperate: the allied armies were closing in and the French people did not respond to his pleas for more men and treasure to fight the invaders. Like Robespierre in 1794, Napoleon discovered that repression only weakened his power base. At the end of March the allies reached Paris, prompting Bonaparte to abdicate the throne on April 6, 1814, after his generals told him that they would no longer fight. The victors treated Napoleon generously, exiling him to the Italian island of Elba, which they turned into his own personal kingdom. This proved to be a mistake; on March 1, 1815, Bonaparte escaped and made his way back to France. During the extraordinary episode known as the Hundred Days, Napoleon quickly regained control of the country, forcing the new king, Louis XVIII, into flight, and raised an army to liberate France from the allies. Yet this dream sequence would not have a happy ending. Bonaparte met the British and Prussian armies in battle at the small Belgian town of Waterloo, only to suffer a crushing defeat. Once again the allies exiled him, this time farther afield to the island of Saint Helena off the African coast, where he died in 1821 at the age of fifty-two. The extraordinary saga of one of world history's greatest figures had finally come to an end.

Waterloo conclusively ended the French Revolution, over a quarter of a century after the storming of the Bastille. During those years some 8 million Europeans died in warfare, and the struggles unleashed in Paris transformed the Continent. What did these tumultuous decades mean, for France and for the world as a whole? What changed as a result of the Revolution, and what legacy did it leave to future generations? Historians, political activists, and many others have debated such questions from 1789 down to the present day, and the debate is far from over.

The French Revolution launched the idea of modern political universalism, writing the script for future movements that aimed to change the human condition. The very notion of ideology, a comprehensive view of the world, was born in the Revolution and testifies to its universalist character. Modern liberalism, conservatism, nationalism, and socialism originated in the cauldron of revolutionary Paris, as did the very concepts of political left and right, which began with the seating choices of deputies in the National Assembly. Such ideologies, and the concept of ideology in general, have been adopted by peoples and political movements throughout the world, constituting perhaps the greatest global legacy of 1789.

For France itself, the Revolution brought momentous changes. While scholars have challenged the notion of a bourgeois revolution, noting that the aristocracy survived and that landed property remained the dominant form of wealth, in 1815 France was a much more liberal society and economy than in 1789. The rise of Napoleon, and his emphasis on achievement over pedigree, conformed to bourgeois ideology and constituted a powerful bequest to the people of modern France. At the same time, the Revolution vastly increased the powers of the centralized French state, realizing to a much greater extent the dream of Louis XIV. The Revolution transformed French men from royal subjects to citizens equal before the law. It introduced new rights for women, even if in large part it reaffirmed patriarchal double standards. Finally, it abolished slavery in the colonies, a process of abolition that only a second revolution in 1848 would render permanent.

Above all, the Revolution pioneered the concept of France as a universal nation, a central theme of modern French history. Core values of liberty and citizenship took shape in the context of struggles not just in France but also throughout Europe and the Caribbean, so that the idea of France as a light to all the people of the world became inseparable from French identity. Millions of French men fought for the Revolution abroad, bringing home with them a core belief in both the superiority and the universality of French ideas of freedom and justice. France's national universalism may have failed to win over many Europeans, but for the French themselves it provided a new way of defining their country in an era that challenged previously dominant monarchical and ecclesiastical paradigms. The enduring influence of the Revolution throughout the world would only underscore this vision of universality. The Revolution also created the two primary forms of universal nationalism, the nation-state and the empire, and the interaction of these two would shape the history of modern France.

Suggestions for Further Reading

Bell, David A. *The First Total War: Napoleon's Europe and the Birth of Warfare as We Know It*. Boston: Houghton Mifflin, 2007.

Blackburn, Robin. *The Overthrow of Colonial Slavery*. London: Verso, 1988.

Censer, Jack R., and Lynn Hunt. 2001. *Liberty, Equality, Fraternity: Exploring the French Revolution*. University Park: Pennsylvania State University Press, 2001.

Chartier, Roger. *The Cultural Origins of the French Revolution*. Durham, NC: Duke University Press, 1991.

Cole, Juan. *Napoleon's Egypt: Invading the Middle East*. New York: Palgrave Macmillan, 2007.

Dubois, Laurent. *Avengers of the New World: The Story of the Haitian Revolution*. Cambridge: Harvard University Press, 2004.

Furet, François. *Revolutionary France, 1770–1880*. Cambridge: Harvard University Press, 1992.

Goodman, Dena. *The Republic of Letters: A Cultural History of the French Enlightenment*. Ithaca, NY: Cornell University Press, 1994.

Hunt, Lynn. *Politics, Culture, and Class in the French Revolution*. Berkeley: University of California Press, 1984.

Israel, Jonathan. *Radical Enlightenment: Philosophy and the Making of Modernity, 1650–1750*. Oxford: Oxford University Press, 2001.

Lefebvre, Georges. *The Coming of the French Revolution*. Princeton, NJ: Princeton University Press, 1947.

Moreau-Zanelli, Jocelyne. *Gallipolis: Histoire d'un mirage américain au XVIIIe siècle*. Paris: Harmattan, 2000.

Palmer, R. R. *The Age of the Democratic Revolution: A Political History of Europe and America, 1760–1800*. Princeton, NJ: Princeton University Press, 1964.

Schama, Simon. *Citizens: A Chronicle of the French Revolution*. New York: Knopf, 1989.

Scott, Joan. *Only Paradoxes to Offer: French Feminists and the Rights of Man*. Cambridge: Harvard University Press, 1997.

Soboul, Albert. *The Sans-Culottes: The Popular Movement and Revolutionary Government, 1793–1794*. Princeton, NJ: Princeton University Press, 1980.

Notes

1. Jack R. Censer and Lynn Hunt, *Liberty, Equality, Fraternity: Exploring the French Revolution* (University Park: Pennsylvania State University Press, 2001), 53.

2. Lesley Sharpe, ed., *The Cambridge Companion to Goethe* (Cambridge: Cambridge University Press, 2002), 154.

[two]

Restoration, Revolution, and Empire: France, 1815–1852

After the turbulence of the French Revolution, many in France, Europe, and beyond looked with hopeful anticipation toward quiet, peace, and stability. Yet such was not to be. The first half of France's nineteenth century witnessed an impressive level of turmoil both at home and abroad, so that the period seemed dominated by a series of aftershocks following the great earthquake of 1789. In less than two generations France experienced four different political regimes: two royal dynasties, a republic, and an empire. As with the Revolution itself, instability and innovation spread far beyond politics. A number of modern cultural movements, including social Catholicism, feminism, and artistic and literary modernism, took shape in these years. The rise of modern industry fundamentally transformed France's economy and society. Finally, the first half of the nineteenth century brought about the transition from old forms of overseas empire, centered around plantation slavery in the Caribbean, to new types of colonial expansion in North Africa.

The magnitude of these changes shows that for France the years between 1815 and 1852 were far more than a replay of the Revolution of 1789. The ideas and institutions generated on an experimental basis during the revolutionary whirlwind began to achieve concrete and enduring shape during the

2.1. *Liberty Leading the People*, Eugène Delacroix. *Source:* Bibliothèque nationale de France.

decades that followed. Even the restoration of monarchical rule made it clear that many of the Revolution's achievements were permanent, that France would never return to the days of royalist absolutism. The spread of both liberal philosophy and radical democratic activism would shape the political turmoil of the era, ultimately producing the political and ideological synthesis of liberal democracy under the Third Republic in the late nineteenth century. In a similar vein, the period from 1815 to 1852 witnessed another political conflict, that between republic and empire. Both forms had their day in this period, again resulting in a synthesis of the two after 1870.

Finally, the theme of national universalism so evident during the Revolution retained considerable force after 1815. The French occupied a smaller place on the world's stage than during the height of Napoleon's empire, and modern France would not dominate European affairs as it had during the reign of Louis XIV. Yet the nation would continue to play an important role as a trendsetter, politically, socially, and culturally, in the nineteenth century. Its pioneering interactions of liberalism and democracy, of republicanism and imperialism, of industrialism and social tradition, would help set the tone for the evolution of the modern world. At the same time the French would see their lives transformed by foreign and global influences, from British industrialism to German romanticism and the siren song of gold rush California. Out of these diverse strands the French wove their own distinct culture, which in the nineteenth century became the symbol of modernity.

LIFE IN EARLY-NINETEENTH-CENTURY FRANCE

Whatever the political changes in Paris, the essence of French life in the decades after Napoleon continued to be rural; like their ancestors, most French women and men worked the land for a living. In 1814, 75 percent of France's citizens were peasants. Nonetheless, the turmoil of the Revolution had changed peasant life in France, mostly for the better. Although the land experienced bad harvests from time to time, crises that still had the power to shake national politics, French peasants lived relatively well in the early nineteenth century. More efficient farming techniques raised productivity, enabling peasants to live off their small plots of land. Much of this new productivity was caused by the bourgeois landowners who had purchased farmland during the Revolution; the decision of the Restoration to respect revolutionary property transfers after 1814 was the single most important impact of national politics on local life. The Revolution had transformed traditional inheritance laws, mandating that property should be divided equally between heirs rather than going to the eldest. This ensured that peasant plots would continue to be modest in size; France would remain a land of smallholders rather than witnessing the rise of large estates that transformed rural life in Britain and Germany.

A major reason for the prosperity of French peasants was the gradual integration of agriculture into national and even international markets. This was a slow process, so that local farm goods, such as wine and cheese, were not readily available nationwide until the late nineteenth century. Yet the transportation improvements of the 1830s and 1840s, canals and above all railroads, enabled farmers to send their goods farther and farther afield. The growth of towns and cities increased the market for food, pushing peasants to shift from self-sufficiency to market specialization. Another reason for rural prosperity was, paradoxically, the development of industry. Many who lived in the countryside and considered themselves peasants took side jobs in the new workplaces that sprang up as France industrialized in the early nineteenth century, at times deriving the bulk of their income from these employments rather than from agriculture. Such moonlighting acted as a hedge against bad times, helping to preserve small family farms that otherwise might not have survived.

Nonetheless, the conditions of life on the farm in the early nineteenth century remained harsh. If there was any improvement, it was all too often, in the words of Gordon Wright, a shift from misery to poverty. While starvation no longer represented an omnipresent possibility, peasant diets continued to be meager, relying mostly on the coarsest of black bread. Visitors from towns and cities continued to be shocked by the rudimentary living conditions of rural denizens, as well as by their low levels of culture (many adult peasants were still illiterate), and frequently compared them to African and Asian savages. Nonetheless, for the peasants themselves life was better than it had been. Perhaps the most important proof of that was the relatively high birth rate in the countryside. France's peasant population reached its largest size in history during the 1840s. After midcentury, the number of French men and women who worked the land would decline, both absolutely and relatively.

In this respect France's rural population was exceptional, for one of the most striking and ultimately important characteristics of national life was the low and declining birthrate. This phenomenon had begun under Napoleon, perhaps resulting from the new inheritance laws which led peasants to fear that having several children would make farms too small to be viable. Another factor may have been the decline in death rates, especially rates of infant mortality, so that it was no longer necessary to have lots of children in order to ensure the survival of a few. For whatever reasons, the tendency to have fewer and fewer offspring gained momentum during the early nineteenth century. This was not noticeable at the time. Thanks largely to the countryside, France's population grew from 30 million to 36 million between 1815 and 1851. But after 1830 the national birth rate declined more sharply than the death rate, and the general rate of population growth slowed, setting the stage for a smaller and older France in the late nineteenth and early twentieth centuries. During the seventeenth and eighteenth centuries French international power had rested to an important degree on the fact that the nation was the largest in Europe. By the late nineteenth century this would cease to be true, with important, perhaps troubling, implications for France's relationship to the rest of the world.

Paradoxically, the implications of population decline were clearest in the place where the number of people was increasing most dramatically, Paris. With a population of roughly 600,000 in 1815, the French capital mushroomed to a metropolis of over a million people by 1851. Between 1830 and 1840 it added roughly 20,000 people every year.[1] At the same time, it had some of the highest death rates in the country. For most of the period deaths far exceeded births, and some one-third of infants born did not live to see their first birthday. As a result, Paris soon gained the image of a murderous city, a killer or corrupter of youth, and a den of crime and violence. Balzac's famous character Vautrin, the brilliant master criminal and intriguer, symbolized the physical and moral danger of the capital.

The city's growth, whose rate matched that of London and other major European cities, came almost entirely from immigration, both domestic and foreign. Most new Parisians came from northern France, especially Normandy and Brittany. Crowding into festering slums, they sought opportunity and a better life but instead found hardship and exploitation. Often disdained as savages by native Parisians, especially members of the upper classes, these rustic newcomers would nonetheless transform and overwhelm the city by their sheer numbers. This vast new population would make Paris a symbol of the problems of poverty and social justice in the new industrial society. As both 1830 and especially 1848 would demonstrate, France's greatest city had become a world capital of revolution.

The Revolutionary and Napoleonic eras had thus brought widespread and permanent changes to French society. The majority of French people alive in 1814 had either a dim memory or no personal knowledge at all of the years before 1789. Consequently, any attempt to restore the monarchical past would have to contend with the delicate task of trying to force old wine into new bottles. Yet that is exactly what the post-Napoleonic leadership of France considered in the years after 1814. Their debates about how, or even if, to accomplish this task, and the resistance they encountered, would shape the life of the nation in the decades after Waterloo, in large part explaining the tumultuous nature of character of politics in early-nineteenth-century France.

THE RESTORATION

In September 1814 the victorious allies gathered to celebrate the defeat of revolutionary France and to chart out the future of Europe in the sumptuous aristocratic environs of Habsburg Vienna. Ably led by Austria's chancellor, Klemens Wenzel von Metternich, the sovereigns and statesmen who took part in the Congress of Vienna had one overriding preoccupation: to prevent France, and the social revolution it represented, from ever again threatening the established order in Europe. Napoleon's dramatic, brief return to power in March 1815, while the congress was still in session, underscored the danger of political instability and the importance of containing it. Against the threat of revolution the congress upheld the ideal of absolutist monarchy and authority, an ultimately futile attempt to force the genie of liberty back into the bottle.

The restoration of royal authority in France was central to the goals of the Congress of Vienna. In 1814, seeing the imminent demise of Napoleon's empire, a group of his supporters led by his foreign minister, Talleyrand, negotiated with Louis XVI's closest male relative to take the throne. The prince agreed, returning from exile to be crowned as Louis XVIII. Generally an unimpressive figure, the new king understood that he lacked a solid power base in his kingdom, a point dramatically underscored by Napoleon's triumphant return from Elba and Louis's own ignominious flight to Belgium in March 1815. He also understood, as many of the leaders at Vienna did not, that France could not simply erase the last twenty-five years of its history: there would be no return to royal absolutism. The new regime established by Louis XVIII was a limited monarchy featuring a written constitution, the Charter, as well as a popularly elected legislature. As under the Directory, only a small minority of the population was entitled to vote for the lower house, the Chamber of Deputies; the upper House of Peers consisted of nobles appointed by the king. Yet many of these had gained their titles from Napoleon, and the king did not restore the prerevolutionary aristocracy. Many other legacies of the Revolution, such as the administrative reorganization of France into departments, the revolutionary land settlements, and civil and religious liberty and tolerance, also endured.

Nonetheless, the renewal of the French monarchy did satisfy the Congress of Vienna that France now belonged to the forces of order in Europe. In May 1814 France signed the Treaty of Paris with the allies formally ending the wars of the French Revolution. The allies initially treated France generously, permitting the French to retain some of their military conquests. After the Hundred Days, however, they imposed more draconian terms, including a large indemnity. Nonetheless, France kept its independence and essential territorial integrity. Thanks largely to Talleyrand's adroit diplomacy, the Congress of Vienna accepted the France of Louis XVIII as an ally and fellow great power rather than a defeated enemy. Restoration France became a member of the Concert of Europe, entrusted with the task of safeguarding the reestablished conservative order, by force if necessary.

If the allies approved of France's new royal government, many French men and women were less accepting. Members of the nobility, in particular those who had returned from exile, rejected *any* compromise with the Revolution and argued strenuously that only a society based in hierarchy and tradition could endure and prosper. For the so-called Ultras, the very idea of a constitutional monarchy was anathema. It soon became clear that they were a force to be reckoned with. After the collapse of the Hundred Days and Napoleon's final deportation, the king and many royalists took punitive measures, sometimes violent, against the former Bonapartists. The legislative elections of October 1815 took place in this climate of retribution against the left, and the Ultras won most of the seats in the new Chamber of Deputies. For the next few years, therefore, France presented the curious spectacle of a country with a sovereign who wished to reign as a constitutional monarch but was frequently opposed by a conservative faction that advocated absolutism while using the structure of constitutional rule—its control of the legislature—to do so. Ironically, the Ultras' opposition to Louis XVIII ensured the survival of one of the Revolution's key victories, an independent legislature.

Louis XVIII's years in exile had taught him, unlike many of his fellow émigrés, the virtues of compromise, so he resisted the Ultras' demands for a complete return to the past. While bowing to their insistence on removing some leading followers of Bonaparte from the government, the king stood by the idea of a constitutional monarchy, supported by a group of moderates known as the Doctrinaires. In September 1816 he dissolved the chamber and held new elections that substantially reduced the power of the Ultras. Four years later, however, the Ultras roared back as new electoral laws intended to reduce the power of the left gave them renewed success. In 1821 they persuaded Louis XVIII to appoint one of their own members, Joseph Villèle, as prime minister. Their power increased further when Louis XVIII died in 1824 and was succeeded by his very conservative brother, who took the throne as King Charles X. For most of the Restoration, therefore, the monarchist right was firmly in the saddle.

A key factor in their success, and centerpiece of their worldview, was the religious revival that swept through France and Europe in the aftermath of the Revolution. Anticlericalism had been one of the great principles of the Revolution, as well as one of the key factors in opposition to it. Napoleon's concordat with the Church in 1801 had opened the door to a renewal of religious life, but this took off in earnest after 1815. The new emphasis on religion represented a reversal of the international flow of ideas during the Enlightenment and Revolution, when new thoughts seemed to radiate from Paris outward. During the eighteenth century the western world had experienced not only an emphasis on reason but also an outpouring of religious conviction, marked by the rise of Methodism in Britain, Pietism in Germany, and the first Great Awakening in what would become the United States. This tidal wave of spiritual fervor had largely passed the French by, but during the Restoration religion took on a new importance in politics and national life in general.

Much of the new Catholic philosophy in France harshly criticized the legacy of the Revolution, pointing to the Terror as the ultimate consequence of Enlightenment godlessness. Joseph de Maistre, in works like *On the Pope* (1819), argued that sovereignty came from God, not man, and any deviation from this principle could only bring disaster. Chateaubriand's massive *Genius of Christianity*, first published in 1802, emphasized religious faith as the center of personal and political well-being. The new spirituality touched many who never read such scholarly works. These ideas directly inspired the creation of a major new missionary revival movement in France. Consciously imitating the mass revivalist strategies of Anglo-American preachers, the missionaries in France organized meetings throughout the country, emphasizing emotion rather than liturgical reasoning to bring the masses to God. Like Maistre and Chateaubriand, they emphasized the unity of throne and altar, of "the Bourbons and the Faith."[2] Under the reign of Charles X, whose coronation at Reims was a religious and traditional ceremony, the power of the Church increased, especially over the nation's education system.

As is often the case with religious movements, however, the new Christianity had more than one political face. Some of its advocates, such as Henri de Saint-Simon and especially Felicité de Lamennais, saw spirituality as a force for social progress, not conservatism. More generally, it shared much with the dominant intellectual current of the early nineteenth century, romanticism. Like the new Christianity, romanticism rejected the classicism of the Enlightenment, emphasizing emotion over reason, the heart over the mind. It also emphasized the importance of natural beauty and historical tradition. *The Genius of Christianity*, in which Chateaubriand declared, "My conviction came from within my heart," had a major influence on the movement.[3]

Also like the Catholic revival, romanticism in France drew on foreign sources, notably German. As noted in the previous chapter, German romanticism constituted in part an intellectual resistance to the Napoleonic occupation at the beginning of the century, and its ideas soon spread to France. In 1810 Madame de Stael, a leading figure in the romantic movement in France, published *Germany*, an account of her travels in that country and a manifesto for the new cultural movement. French romanticism also drew on British influences, notably the poetry of Byron, Shelley, and Keats, and the medieval fantasy novels of Sir Walter Scott, in particular *Ivanhoe*. Romanticism never loomed as large in French culture as it did elsewhere; Cartesian rationalism remained the bedrock of the nation's intellectual identity. Its importance during the Restoration nonetheless underscored the fact that France was shaped by its neighbors even as it influenced them.

Given the movement's emphasis on emotion rather than intellect, it is no surprise that its main achievements came in fields like poetry, painting, and music, rather than philosophy or scholarship. Alphonse de Lamartine and the young Victor Hugo were among the most prominent French writers to embrace the new aesthetic. In music, Hector Berlioz's *Symphonie Fantastique* (1830) flaunted a fascination with the macabre, the beauty of nature, and the allure and tragedy of frustrated love. Perhaps the most widely recognized romantic artist was the painter Eugène Delacroix. His dramatic canvases, bursting with life and vibrant color, frequently took as their subject exotic and historical scenes. Paintings like *The Massacre at Chios* (1824) and *The Death of Sardanapalus* (1828) conveyed a sense of passion alien to the classical tradition. Delacroix's most famous work, *Liberty Leading the People* (1830), portrayed less the specific events of 1789 (or the revolution of 1830, for that matter) and more the drama of the people fighting for freedom.

The work of Delacroix highlights two other important themes of the romantic movement. One was orientalism, the interest in and attraction to the cultures of the east. Napoleon's 1798 expedition to Egypt brought about the discovery of the Rosetta stone and major advances in knowledge about the ancient Egyptians. The French conquest of Algeria arose out of this fascination with the orient and reinforced it. In 1832, for example, Delacroix traveled to North Africa, eventually producing scores of paintings depicting his impressions of those lands. For many romantics the "primitive" cultures of the east strongly resembled those of ancient and medieval Europe, thus increasing their appeal. At the same time, orientalism developed a vision of nonwestern cultures as fundamentally different from European, characterized by sensuality and emotion rather than reason or progress. Such stereotypes ultimately confirmed images of these people as inferior, in ways that could justify the need to civilize them through colonial rule.

The second theme was the struggle for liberty. Romanticism inspired not just conservatives but also liberalism, both perpetuating and redefining the intellectual legacy of the French Revolution. If conservatives emphasized the beauties of religion and order, liberals and radicals focused on the popular desire for liberty and for national identity. During the Restoration the government of France, along with the other regimes that upheld the Concert of Europe, faced nearly constant challenges from those inspired by romantic visions of the revolutionary heritage. Ultimately these movements for liberty would triumph, proving that neither in France nor elsewhere could one hope to turn back the clock to 1789.

THE STRUGGLE FOR LIBERTY

While the royal governments of Restoration France embraced the reactionary values of the Concert of Europe, many other French men and women drew inspiration from the Revolution's legacy and reaffirmed their commitment to the values of liberty and progress. Under the reign of Louis XVIII, liberals regrouped in a series of moderate political factions, notably the Constitutional and Independent parties. They pressed the monarchy to respect the Charter as a genuine constitution, and to safeguard civil liberties and freedom of expression. However, the parliamentary liberals represented a small, elite segment of society. Others took a more radical view of the political situation, prompting a series of revolts that culminated in the revolution of 1830.

Radical movements in Restoration France took place in the context of revolts across Europe against the conservatism of the Congress of Vienna. While Paris remained an important symbol of revolution, Europe was no longer simply reacting to popular insurgencies in France but instead leading the struggle for liberty. North, south, east, and west, the combination of a desire for freedom and a new emphasis on national identity and liberation, both fueled by the romantic movement, inspired conspiracies and revolts targeting the established order. Moreover, the turmoil was not limited to Europe but had an important dimension in the Americas. The transnational character of liberal and revolutionary movements in the early nineteenth century illustrated the continuing influence of France's revolutionary heritage as well as demonstrating how it was shaped by forces beyond the nation's borders.

The history of the Charbonnerie provides an important example of these interactions. During the summer of 1820 a number of secret societies in France laid plans for a general insurrection in August to overthrow the monarchy. The government discovered the plot, however, forcing its leaders to flee the country. Two of them, Joubert and Dugied, went into exile in Italy where they contacted members of the Carbonari, a revolutionary secret society in the kingdom of Naples dedicated to the struggle against Austrian overlordship. In July 1820 the Carbonari staged a revolution in Naples that achieved some important successes before collapsing in 1821. Inspired by this example, Joubert and Dugied returned to France in 1821 and founded the Charbonnerie. Some thirty to forty thousand people joined the secret society, including the Marquis de Lafayette and several other notables; most members came from the upper echelons of society. Over the next few years it attempted a number of uprisings. None succeeded, but they testified to continuing discontent with the Restoration political order.

The creation of the Charbonnerie in France reflected a wave of liberal agitation across Europe in the early 1820s. German university students demonstrated for press freedom and national unification, opposing the monarchs of Prussia and Austria. In 1821 the Greeks rose up in revolt against Ottoman Turkish rule. Their war for independence captured the imagination of European intellectuals, notably Britain's Lord Byron, who traveled to Greece to fight alongside the rebels. Thanks to divisions among the major powers, the Greeks won their freedom. In 1825 dissident army officers in Russia staged the Decembrist revolt, a failed attempt to overthrow Czar Nicholas I.

The Iberian Peninsula witnessed a series of popular revolts against the Restoration order. Like Louis XVIII in France, Ferdinand VII was restored to the monarchy of Spain in 1814, and soon showed himself even more intransigent and hostile to the winds of change than his northern neighbor. His refusal to convoke the national parliament, the Cortes, and his reestablishment of the Inquisition stoked the fires of revolt. The revolutions against Spanish rule in the Americas, which had begun during the Napoleonic occupation of Spain, returned with a vengeance after Argentina declared its independence in 1816. Within a decade the country lost one of the greatest empires in world history. The struggle to retain the colonies, combined with an economic downturn, exacerbated discontent at home and led to the outbreak of revolution in Spain in 1820. A similar uprising took place the same year in Portugal. The government of Louis XVIII sharply opposed both revolutions and in 1823 invaded Spain, occupying Madrid and returning Ferdinand VII to power.

The invasion of Spain underscored the central role played by France in the struggle between restoration and revolution in Europe after 1815. As long as the French monarchy firmly embraced the reactionary outlook of the Concert of Europe it was hard to foresee the success of the liberal opposition either at home or abroad. Those who hoped for such success were bitterly disappointed when Louis XVIII died in 1824 and was succeeded by his brother, Charles X. The new king soon proved more resistant to change than the old, rejecting the idea of constitutionalism and embracing the most conservative interpretation of Catholicism. His 1825 coronation in the ancient royal city of Reims, complete with courtiers in sixteenth-century costumes and flights of white doves, was an orgy of religious and traditional royalist symbolism. As king, Charles X allied himself firmly with the Ultras in parliament, agreeing to laws that increased the power of the Church and government censorship. As far as he was concerned, under his reign France would embrace the power and unity of throne and altar; the future of France would be modeled on the prerevolutionary past.

It soon became clear that many French people were not willing to accept this. In response to the politics of the Catholic revival a wave of popular anticlericalism swept the nation. Liberals produced songs, poems, plays, and other works that satirized the Church and the king's allegiance to it. Anticlericals disrupted church services, sometimes leading to popular riots. They also revived Molière's seventeenth-century play *Tartuffe*, a pointed critique of religion and hypocrisy, staging performances throughout France between 1825 and 1830. Attempts to prevent its performance in Rouen in April 1825 prompted a month of popular disturbances in the city.

Liberal opposition, combined with a crop failure in 1826 and a resulting economic downturn the following year, led to a major defeat for the monarchy and the Ultras in the parliamentary elections of 1827. A chastened Charles X responded by appointing a more moderate government headed by the Vicomte de Martignac in 1828. Distrusted by king, Ultras, and opposition alike, Martignac's government achieved a few small successes but ultimately could not overcome the increasing polarization of French politics. In August 1829 Charles X dismissed Martignac and appointed a new government headed by Prince Jules de Polignac, a leader of the Ultra faction and one of the most uncompromisingly reactionary figures in French politics. This only increased the determination of the liberal opposition, convincing many that no significant change or progress would occur as long as Charles X was king. When 221 liberal parliamentary deputies signed a petition against the government, the king responded by dissolving the assembly in March 1830. In the new elections that followed in July, not only were 202 of the 221 deputies reelected, but the liberals went on to win a majority of seats in the new parliament. Clearly the stage was set for a confrontation.

The year 1830 would witness the return of revolution to France, underscoring the permanence of the heritage of 1789. It was also a turning point in the history of French overseas expansion, as France conquered a new colony, Algeria, that would become a centerpiece of the nation's modern empire. The desire to restore the old order and the determination to continue the fight for liberty shaped France's colonies as well as the French metropole in the early nineteenth century. In 1830 the relation between revolution and empire, a key legacy of Napoleon for modern France, took an important new turn.

THE RESTORATION AND FRANCE OVERSEAS

Just as revolution in the French Caribbean had meant the overthrow of slavery, so did the Restoration mean its return. Little distinguished the Bonapartist regime, which had reinstituted bondage in Guadeloupe and Martinique, from the monarchist regime after 1814. For the white inhabitants of the French West Indies, the restoration of monarchical rule in France signaled a return to the moral order violently torn apart by the revolution in Saint-Domingue. Pierre Dessalles, a planter in Martinique, commemorated the execution of Louis XVI every January 21 in his diary, characterizing the anniversary in 1837 with the words "What a crime! Consequently, France has not known tranquility since that atrocity was perpetrated."[4] Slavery, the classic opponent of liberty, dominated the French Caribbean in the years after Napoleon's fall.

Opposition to slavery constituted the main form of resistance to the Restoration and took two principal forms. First and foremost was the slaves' resistance to their masters and the institution of bondage in general. As during the eighteenth century, numerous slave revolts and conspiracies erupted in Martinique and Guadeloupe during the early nineteenth century. The existence of a free Haitian republic as a model helped inspire such movements there and throughout the Americas. At the same time, the future of the slave economy was cast into doubt by the rise of sugar beet cultivation in Europe and the international ban on the slave trade imposed in 1807. Growing economic pressure on slave owners often translated into greater oppression of their slaves, at times sparking revolts. In 1822 a major slave uprising erupted in Martinique, the same year Denmark Vesey staged his conspiracy against American slavery in Charleston, South Carolina. Other forms of resistance also appeared; many whites in Martinique were convinced that their slaves were trying to poison them, sparking a series of trials in the 1820s.

The other form of resistance to slavery took the form of political abolition movements, located primarily in the metropole. The crusade against slavery and the slave trade during the early nineteenth century, notably in Britain and America, attracted mass followings and became a key tenet of liberal philosophy. The movement in France was smaller and less successful, both because liberalism was weaker and because the country lacked a mass-based movement like Methodism to attract middle-class and working-class activists. During the 1820s the leading abolitionist group, the Société de morale chrétienne, rarely counted more than four hundred members at a time. However, these members came from the leading ranks of the Protestant and Catholic nobility, including names like the Duc de Broglie, the Marquis de LaFayette, and even the Duc d'Orléans himself, the future King Louis Philippe. Under the Restoration French abolitionism achieved little beyond keeping the issue of Caribbean slavery in the public eye and affirming the liberal belief that French civilization could bring progress and liberty, not oppression, to the peoples of the world.

If the belief in what Napoleon had already dubbed "the civilizing mission" could lead some to oppose old forms of empire, it also marshaled support for new types of imperial expansion. Indeed, the campaign to suppress the slave trade played an important role in French colonization of Africa; intervention against the slave traders led Europeans farther into the African interior to stamp out the trade at its source. At the same time, new "scientific" theories of western racial superiority and orientalist philosophy promoted a paternalist view of non-Europeans waiting to be civilized. During the Restoration the French tried to expand their already existing trading posts along the African coast into full-fledged colonies, driven by both moral imperatives and the hope of founding new agricultural colonies. Such efforts bore little fruit but did lay the groundwork for future colonial expansion and the creation of a new French empire.

The conquest of Algeria in 1830 was the most significant example of Restoration colonialism, and colonial Algeria would become the centerpiece of the new French empire. The roots of the conflict went back to the gradual decline of Ottoman authority in North Africa and the problem of Algerian piracy in the Mediterranean. Attacks on shipping had bothered western powers for years, and the first military campaign of the young United States was the war against the Barbary pirates in 1801. Piracy and unpaid debts led to French protests against the Dey of Algiers, the ruler of the province of Algeria under the authority of the Ottoman sultan. Things came to a head in April

1827 when, during a heated discussion, the Dey slapped the French consul in the face with a fly swatter. Stung by this insult, the French government sent a naval squadron to blockade Algiers. The blockade proved ineffective, so in January 1830 the Polignac ministry decided to invade Algeria. Domestic political considerations factored heavily into this decision. Faced with increasing discontent at home, Charles X hoped that a successful military adventure abroad would (as it had for Napoleon) win him the goodwill of his subjects. Precisely for this reason the liberal opposition condemned the expedition, although under a new monarch more to their liking they would strongly rally to the cause of French colonialism in Algeria.

The French flotilla landed in Algeria on June 14 and quickly overwhelmed the Dey's forces. Within three weeks France proclaimed victory and the tricolor flag was hoisted over the Casbah of Algiers. This was a signal triumph for the French king, all the more so in that it had cost few French lives. Yet it did not bring the political rewards he had hoped for. The easy victory over the Algerians gave Charles X an inflated sense of power without significantly mollifying the opposition. A few weeks later a revolution broke out in Paris that would cost Charles X his throne. It was perhaps the ultimate irony of the Algerian expedition that, by removing a large part of the French army to the other side of the Mediterranean, it hindered the ability of the king's forces to suppress the revolt. Not for the last time, war in Algeria and political change in France would go hand in hand.

THE REVOLUTION OF 1830

By the summer of 1830 Charles X confronted widespread unrest in his kingdom. The economic downturn that began in 1827 showed no signs of abating, and the failure of the Martignac ministry clearly demonstrated the king's determination to pursue his own course in spite of widespread opposition to it. This opposition spread far beyond the ranks of the liberal elite in Paris. In the department of the Ariège, for example, bands of men dressed as women staged widespread attacks against royal forest guards in defense of traditional rights to pasture and lumber. Throughout the countryside peasants staged violent revolts against royal tax collectors, prompted by hard times and the increasing pressures of a national capitalist economy. Artisans and skilled workers in Paris and other cities demanded not only higher pay and shorter workdays but also liberty and national glory. Economic depression and political discontent thus combined to produce a revolutionary crisis of the regime.

The king's stubborn actions brought this crisis to a head. Rather than respond to his electoral defeat with compromise and conciliation, he decided on a frontal challenge to his opponents. On July 26 the Polignac ministry published the four July Ordinances, which drastically increased press censorship and changed election laws to favor the Ultra party. The liberal opposition viewed this as direct attack against the Charter and responded forcefully. Led by the young journalist Adophe Thiers, they drew up a manifesto denouncing the ordinances and distributed it throughout Paris. That evening many merchants and manufacturers decided to close their businesses the following day, freeing their employees to take to the streets.

That day, July 27, saw the beginnings of mass protests. Polignac mobilized the army and had it occupy key points throughout the capital. At the same time students and workers began to gather in the streets of Paris, and the first barricades appeared. After a relatively calm night the revolution began in earnest on Wednesday, July 28 as crowds rampaged throughout the city, frequently aided by soldiers called out to suppress them but who decided to join the revolt instead. The rebels occupied key points in the capital, including the city hall and Notre Dame Cathedral, crying "Down with the Bourbons! Long live the republic! Long live the emperor!"[5] The next day saw the triumph of the revolution. By noon some six thousand barricades had appeared throughout the city, and insurgents stormed the Louvre palace, routing the army detachments stationed there to defend it. By sunset most of Paris was in the hands of the revolutionaries and the army abandoned the capital.

That afternoon Charles X decided to retract the ordinances, but his action was too little, too late. The next day a self-appointed provisional government in Paris proclaimed the end of his reign and demanded the proclamation of a republic. On August 2 the king formally abdicated in favor of his grandson, eventually fleeing the country to spend the rest of his days in England. The insurgency, promptly baptized the "three glorious days," had triumphed.

The spirit of revolution had returned to France with a vengeance and, as in 1789, its repercussions were soon felt elsewhere in Europe; the desire for liberty and national independence proved a volatile combination. The 1830 crisis in France spread north to Belgium, at the time ruled by the Netherlands. In August a popular revolt erupted in Brussels against Dutch rule, forcing the Dutch king to send troops to the rebellious provinces. The rebels forced the soldiers to withdraw and secured recognition of Belgian independence from the great powers. Renewed efforts by the Dutch to subdue the country were forestalled by French military intervention in 1831. Poland experienced a very different outcome, having ceased to exist as an independent nation after being carved up by Russia, Prussia, and Austria in the 1790s. Russian Poland was governed by the czar's brother Constantine, who during the 1820s increasingly encroached on the prerogatives of the Polish parliament and civil liberties. Inspired by events in Paris, in November young army officers led a popular armed revolt that overthrew Constantine. The czar intervened the next year, however, capturing Warsaw and imposing military rule on Poland.

In short, France retained its ability to inspire and lead those who fought for liberty. Where it would lead them, however, was not entirely clear during the heady days of July. Many of those who manned the Parisian barricades hoped for a republic along the lines of 1793, but they were disappointed. Instead, France's parliamentary and political leaders chose to appoint a different kind of king, a true constitutional monarch. In August the Duke of Orleans took the crown as Louis Philippe, king of the French (*not* king of France). The choice horrified Europe's aristocratic establishment, but many French looked to Louis Philippe to become a citizen king, a ruler who would represent continuity with the royal past but also lead France into the new world of rapid economic and social change. Under his reign France became an industrial nation, and within a generation the stresses and strains of that transformation would help produce yet another revolution.

INDUSTRIAL REVOLUTION

The first half of the nineteenth century transformed the French economy and society, making France one of the world's leading industrial powers. While industrialization in France lacked the drama and scope of Britain's industrial revolution, it nonetheless created vast new sources of wealth, tied the nation together to an unprecedented degree, and established a new series of social and political cleavages that would in many ways set the tone for the modern era. During the July Monarchy, France invested heavily in advanced technologies, most notably railroads, and industrialists increasingly assumed leadership of the nation as a whole. A new bourgeois society and culture, which would come in many ways to symbolize French life as a whole, took center stage during these years. Paris grew massively, doubling in size from roughly 500,000 in 1801 to over 1 million inhabitants by 1851, becoming more than ever the heart of the French nation.

Yet overemphasizing the magnitude of these changes would be a mistake. In recent years historians have challenged the idea of the industrial revolution as a sharp break with the agrarian past, emphasizing instead continuities with earlier forms of manufacture. France is an excellent example of this. The overwhelming majority of French people at midcentury still lived on the land or in small towns; in 1851 only a quarter of the nation's population lived in cities, defined as settlements of two thousand people or more. For all the attention devoted to factories as the symbol of the industrial age, most workers were employed in small workshops. In small towns and cities many people worked in both industry and agriculture, according to the opportunities and the needs of the season. Rural industry, performed by women and men who essentially saw themselves as peasants, still accounted for much of French manufacturing.

This was true of industrializing Europe in general, so France was not exceptionally backward, even though the French lagged significantly behind their neighbors across the Channel. Britain in the early nineteenth century became the symbol and standard bearer of the new industrial economy, and its head start made it the leading nation in Europe during the nineteenth century as well as the greatest global power of the age. It underscored the end of an era of French dominance of European affairs that stretched from Louis XIV to Napoleon. Population statistics reveal that whereas in 1800 France had roughly two and a half times the population of Britain, a century later the two nations were essentially equal in size.

Historians have pointed to several reasons for this relative delay, including a lack of entrepreneurial spirit and drive in the French, at least compared to the British. French industrialists on the whole proved more conservative in their choices, less likely to take the risk of investing heavily in new technologies or building large factories. The survival of the small family farm in France, in part due to the Revolution, made French agriculture relatively unproductive, not able to feed a large urban and industrial population. At the same time it enabled French peasants to resist proletarianization to a much greater extent than their British peers. Low levels of urbanization meant reduced markets for industrial products. Finally, the fact that in France (unlike Britain) iron and coal deposits were often located far from each other increased the cost and difficulty of establishing modern manufactures.

Yet these were only *relative* disadvantages. France remained a strong and prosperous nation with a vital citizenry that adapted to the new economy. While the turmoil of the revolutionary era had in some respects hindered industrial progress, it had also established a national economy and tax structure; destroying guilds and banning unions favored the efforts of French manufacturers. The end of war in 1815 and the peace of the next few decades allowed the fruits of such innovations to ripen. French agriculture became more productive in these years, especially as farmers shifted to a three-field crop rotation system that boosted yields. In 1830 the advent of a new political regime dedicated to economic growth helped provide the dynamism needed for an industrial takeoff. Under the July Monarchy France took its first major steps into the industrial age.

As in Britain, industrialization in France started in the textiles industry. Entrepreneurs began building cotton factories during the 1820s and sharply increased their efforts over the next two decades. Northern and eastern cities like Lille and especially Mulhouse in Alsace became the centers of French textiles production, a smaller version of England's Lancashire. They focused on producing cotton cloth, drawing their raw material from Egypt and the slave plantations of the American South. While most cloth in France still came from handlooms and traditional workshops, this new industrial sector held forth the promise of the future.

The new textiles factories needed machines, so as in Britain this industry stimulated iron and steel production; a mechanical loom of even modest size required over a ton of iron. During the 1830s and 1840s entrepreneurs started creating new companies, such as the Schneider ironworks in 1836. The coal deposits of the Nord were especially attractive to fledgling industrialists, who created sixty-eight new companies there between 1836 and 1838. Modern industry also needed power, and in the early nineteenth century that meant above all steam engines. The number of steam engines used by French industry nearly doubled between 1835 and 1840, as did the number employed in the iron industry. Certain regions of France, notably the Nord, Alsace, and the Loire valley, saw their landscape and their way of life transformed by the new industrial economy.[6]

Structural changes facilitated the growth of industry during the July Monarchy. The government of Louis Philippe created a more investment-friendly climate by easing bankruptcy laws, making it easier to form corporations, keeping business taxes low, and maintaining tariffs to protect key industries, notably textiles, from foreign competition. Starting in the late 1830s French banks began to take a more active role in investing in industry. The founding of the Caisse generale du Commerce et de l'Industrie in 1837 created a new model for industrial finance, one soon followed by other banks. As industry became more extensive, requiring more capital for start-up expenses, the role of bankers became more important. The Rothschild bank, headed by James Rothschild, became a symbol of the new financial wealth during the 1840s.

These changes came together to produce the signal event of industrialization in France under the July Monarchy: the development of the railroads. Creating efficient transportation systems was key to building a national economy, enabling industrialists to market their goods as widely as possible. Although French engineers and industrialists followed the expansion of this dramatic new technology in Britain during the early nineteenth century, France did not at first move to adopt it. During the Restoration and early years of the July Monarchy governments devoted more attention to expanding and upgrading the country's canals and river transportation networks, an effort encouraged by the invention of steamships and their increasing use on the nation's waterways. Not until the beginning of the 1840s did political and business leaders decide that the railroad had come to stay and begin to plan for a French network. Whereas in Britain, private interests had created the railways, in France the government took the lead. In 1842 the Chamber of Deputies approved the Legrand Plan, which created France's first national railroads. The plan, which combined public and private financing, created several main lines radiating out from Paris to major provincial cities. Completed in the 1850s, it reinforced Parisian dominance in France while failing to link provincial regions to each other.

In many ways, political, administrative, and military considerations trumped the needs of industry in guiding railroad construction. Nonetheless, railroad construction provided a major boost to the French economy: from 1842 to 1845 France experienced its first industrial boom. Not only did railways sharply cut the time it took to travel (or send goods) across the country, but the scope of the new industry stimulated other businesses. They were a major reason for the expansion of the iron industry during the 1840s, and their needs for capital (and the profits they generated) encouraged the expansion of France's banking sector. More generally, the impact of the railroad went beyond economics to symbolize the dynamism of the new era. Wherever France was going, it would get there by train.

A new France was thus born during the July Monarchy. The fact that much of the old France remained intact, especially in the countryside, does not detract from the momentous changes the nation experienced in the 1830s and 1840s. When social commentators considered contemporary affairs, they tended to focus on the emergence of new social strata and ways of life. The self-confident bourgeoisie and the troubled working class, both seen as products of industrial society, fascinated the public imagination, itself a product of the new society. A world of (often closely juxtaposed) privilege and poverty, of glittering success and abject misery, France in the 1830s and 1840s embodied some of the central conflicts that have shaped the modern world.

WINNERS AND LOSERS: THE NEW INDUSTRIAL SOCIETY

The July Monarchy continued and reinforced a trend that had begun during the Napoleonic era: the displacement of the traditional aristocracy by new elites whose social position was based on achievement and, increasingly, wealth rather than inherited privilege. The aristocracy remained but no longer set the tone for society as a whole. Instead, a new elite of wealthy bankers, industrialists, lawyers, and businessmen occupied center stage. Their dynamism not only propelled them to positions of leadership but established a view of France as a quintessentially bourgeois nation for many years to come.

This new orientation started at the top. Louis Philippe, the last king in French history, heartily embraced the values of the new bourgeois society. Eschewing the traditional finery of the aristocracy, he dressed in the somber black clothing favored by businessmen and sent his sons to the *lycée* for their education. Styling himself "the citizen king," he prided himself on working long hours to master statecraft. He was scorned by the old aristocracy, which had supported the Bourbon Restoration, as an *arriviste*. Many Legitimists withdrew from public affairs, thus leaving a social and political vacuum that members of the new bourgeoisie rushed to fill.

Broadly speaking, the bourgeoisie that loomed so prominently during the July Monarchy consisted of people who owned property, were well educated, and had a standard of living much higher than that of the population as a whole. It was primarily an urban population, located not just in Paris but in provincial cities and towns. It was also a diverse group. At the top was the *haute bourgeoisie*, the great industrialists, merchants, and Parisian bankers. Below them was a wide stratum of professionals, business owners, and state bureaucrats, as well as a much larger *petite bourgeoisie* of small shopkeepers and skilled artisans. In the early nineteenth century many bourgeois were self-made men and ran family businesses. Those who prospered (and not all did) frequently invested their money in land, still perhaps the greatest source of social prestige, but also industry and government bonds. In later years some would become *rentiers*, people who lived off inherited wealth and the proceeds of family investments.

Yet the bourgeoisie was a culture and a lifestyle every bit as much as an economic class. To be bourgeois meant above all to look to the future rather than the past (the classic characteristic of the aristocracy). Among other things, this entailed a heavy investment in childhood, so that bourgeois families increasingly focused on nurturing the next generation. The middle classes also had a strong faith in the importance and power of education. Sons were supposed to attend a *lycée* and perhaps even one of the *grandes écoles*, such as the Ecole Polytechnique. The bourgeoisie also cultivated the value of hearth and home. Houses, and in Paris apartments, were the centers of family life and became larger and more elaborate. Many featured comforts like carpets, works of art, and musical instruments, notably the piano. The home became the province of the wife and mother, who increasingly abandoned the paid labor force and was expected to devote her time to raising the children and supervising the servants that a proper bourgeois home was expected to have. Finally, the middle classes expected a certain level of culture, of acquaintance with literature, history, and the fine arts— in short, good taste.

The lives of the working poor seemed light years removed from this world. Like the bourgeoisie, many viewed working-class France as essentially a creation of the industrial revolution, an oversimplification in both cases. Just as most workplaces remained small and relatively unaffected by the new production methods during the July Monarchy, most French workers labored not in large factories but in small, traditional workshops. Also like the bourgeoisie, the working class was so varied that it is difficult to speak of it as a single entity. Levels of skill played a key role in differentiating among those who worked with their hands. Artisans usually possessed the greatest skills and often worked for themselves as independent craftsmen. This was especially true in Paris, where they had dominated the insurgent crowds of the Revolution while they continued to turn out the luxury goods that earned the French capital fame around the world. Although the guilds that had governed such professions since the Middle Ages no longer existed, artisans still had important traditions of training and association, such as the Tour de France ritual: journeymen artisans were expected to travel around the country for years before being accepted as master craftsmen.

In contrast, unskilled laborers led a precarious existence. Most came from rural areas to cities and towns during the early industrial era, fleeing rural overcrowding in search of a better life. This produced a major wave of urban expansion in the early nineteenth century: Paris alone doubled in size to over 1 million inhabitants. The newcomers usually found lodgings in boardinghouses, often frequented by others from their hometowns or regions. These generally existed in the worst slums, areas that were horribly overcrowded, lacking even basic sanitation and prey to disease and crime. Settled working-class families rented apartments, often no larger than one room. An entire family slept on a thin straw mattress, and their rooms were sparsely furnished, usually lacking indoor plumbing or even heat. Entire urban neighborhoods packed with such miserable lodgings horrified bourgeois observers, feeding the image of working people as debased savages.

French workers labored in a variety of industries and occupations during the July Monarchy. A few worked in large factories, especially in the north and east of the country. Male workers in cities found employment in a variety of trades, notably carpentry and construction as well as more skilled crafts like silk weaving in Lyon. Women worked overwhelmingly in the textile industry, often as seamstresses, or in domestic service, employed as maids and governesses by bourgeois families. Some women, often servants who had become pregnant, ended up as prostitutes, an all too common and tragic fate of young girls from the countryside. Victor Hugo's portrait in *Les Misérables* of Fantine, the unemployed seamstress reduced to selling herself in order to care for her two-year-old daughter, depicted a classic dilemma in dramatic terms. Finally, many French children worked in industry, often in the new textile factories. French peasant children had often worked on the farm and continued to do so, but the prospect of the very young in factories horrified commentators and spurred official action. In 1841 the French government passed a law restricting child labor, the state's first workplace regulation.

The contrast between bourgeois and worker, between rich and poor, characterized for many the new industrial society in France. It bears repeating that the majority of French men and women belonged to neither group, but instead lived in small towns and the countryside, tilling the soil in the manner of their ancestors. Nonetheless, the new social cleavages captivated the public imagination. They were most marked in the cities, above all in Paris; the influx of rural and small-town migrants into slums like the Ile de la Cité and the Faubourgs Saint-Marcel and Saint-Victor fundamentally transformed life in the French capital. This contrast also set the tone for the July Monarchy, a regime dedicated to the interests of the *haute bourgeoisie* and challenged by working-class unrest. France's last monarchy struggled to reconcile these diverse interests and manage the affairs of a new era. All too soon, like the Restoration earlier, it proved unable to do so.

THE JULY MONARCHY

France's last royal regime began and ended in revolution. Like nineteenth-century liberalism in general, the July Monarchy sought a middle ground between the forces of reaction and revolution.

The decision of the Chamber of Deputies to grant the crown to Louis-Philippe, a member of the Orleans branch of the royal family, came as an unwelcome surprise to many at home and abroad. Many European sovereigns looked askance at the new king's embrace of constitutionalism and his acceptance of the crown from the hands of the revolutionary mob. France's Ultras were appalled at this turn of events, a defeat for everything they believed in. Styling themselves the Legitimists, they continued to believe that only a Bourbon monarch could be France's true king.

Members of the left also expressed discontent. The crowds who had built the barricades in July had called for a republic, not a new king. Whereas the liberal elite might desire a constitutional monarchy and a revolution along the lines of England's 1688 Glorious Revolution, many working people had hoped for a fundamental change of regime. As a result, popular unrest resurfaced with a vengeance. In 1831 the artisan silk workers of Lyon staged an uprising against the regime, followed by a larger one three years later. In Paris, rioters sacked the palace of the city's archbishop in 1831, and the following year attempted an uprising. The colonies were also restive. As is often true in colonial wars, the initial French conquest of Algeria soon gave way to wars of "pacification," lasting for the better part of twenty years. In 1842 Abd-el-Kadir launched a major revolt against French rule. In the French West Indies revolts against slavery continued, notably a major slave insurrection in Martinique in 1831. Further revolts, as well as assassination attempts against the king, erupted in both Paris and the provinces throughout the July Monarchy.

Both at home and in the colonies the government of Louis-Philippe met resistance with brutal repression. On April 15, 1834, in response to an uprising of Parisian workers, national troops pursued rioters into the small Rue Transnonain, on the right bank. They invaded a building and went from floor to floor, shooting all the inhabitants. Nineteen people, men, women, and children, died in what became the famous massacre of the Rue Transnonain, a symbol of government repression and a cherished memory of the French left. In large part this incident owed its fame to a lithograph drawn by Honoré Daumier, the greatest cartoonist in French history and a determined opponent of the regime. His drawings mercilessly satirized the king and the bourgeois elite of the July Monarchy as corpulent, corrupt, and arrogant. In *The Massacre of the Rue Transnonain* (1834), he showed the other side of the regime: its bloody violence. An abortive attempt on the king's life in 1835 led the regime to pass the September laws, enacting new restrictions on press freedom and political activism. Founded in the name of liberty, the July Monarchy did not hesitate to embrace the authoritarianism of other royal regimes.

This paradox, far from daunting the government's progressive opponents, motivated them anew to fight for change and reform. The 1840s witnessed a flowering of new forms of French left-wing ideology that had global impact. These new forms both reinforced the legacy of the French Revolution and adapted it to new social and cultural conditions. They reaffirmed France's position as a world center of new ideas and political movements.

BEYOND LIBERTY? NEW PATHS
TO REFORM AND REVOLUTION

The widening social divisions caused by industrialization and the growing unpopularity of the July Monarchy lay at the base of the new social and political movements in early-nineteenth-century France. Socialism, feminism, and bohemianism all loomed large, not just as challenges to the regime but also as new visions of society. All had begun before 1830, yet under the regime of Louis-Philippe they assumed a new prominence, or notoriety. At the same time, all embraced an internationalist vision, seeing their struggles in France as part of a broader effort to remake the world. Thanks in part to them, Paris retained and renewed its significance as a world capital.

As elsewhere in Europe, the traumas of industrialization inspired many in France to protest the misery of working-class life. Working people themselves challenged the new capitalist order. Although strikes and unions were illegal, skilled workers adopted both as means of struggle. The July Monarchy saw a proliferation of working-class mutual aid societies, which collected funds to help members in time of need. Ostensibly devoted to caring for the sick and unemployed, mutual aid societies also served as rudimentary labor unions, their members often figuring prominently in strikes. Skilled workers also started both producer and consumer cooperatives, inspired by the belief that such mutualist economic endeavors would benefit working people concretely with better wages and cheaper goods, as well as ultimately rendering capitalists obsolete. France's first consumer cooperative opened in 1834, in the same

Lyon neighborhood, La Croix-Rousse, that had been a center of working-class insurrections in 1832 and 1834.

Working-class poverty and exploitation also inspired broader efforts to re-think the nature of French capitalist society in general. France in the early nineteenth century witnessed the birth of modern socialist ideology, a new po-litical form that drew on the revolutionary legacy of 1789 and concerns about the impacts of industrialization. Historians have used the terms "utopian" or "romantic" socialism to characterize the early years of this movement, under-scoring the tendency of many leading thinkers to develop idealistic schemes for the wholesale remaking of society. At the same time, like the romantics, early socialists emphasized not just economic exploitation but equally the im-portance of changes to personal and emotional life as part of the process of building a new, more just world.

During the Restoration Charles Fourier and Henri de Saint-Simon led this new wave of thinking about society. Fourier grew up in a bourgeois family in Besançon but as a young man rejected commerce and invented grandiose schemes for improving the human condition. A sharp critic of bourgeois do-mesticity, Fourier argued that men and women should live as equals in com-munal societies he termed "phalansteries." In these ideal societies all would be free to express their own desires, and bourgeois individualism would give way to a spirit of cooperation. Fourier's socialist ideal combined a desire to end poverty with a mystical cosmology that viewed human happiness as the ultimate social goal. Count Henri de Saint-Simon also embraced a spirit of mystical cooperation as a way to reform humanity. Unlike Fourier, however, he felt that the new society should be hierarchical, but based on productivity and technology rather than inherited wealth or social position. His emphasis on science and technology attracted many wealthy young people dissatisfied with contemporary society and less concerned with social justice than with the creation of an educated elite.

After 1830 socialism evolved along more practical lines, moving away from the fantasies of middle-class thinkers and toward working-class activism and politics. Etienne Cabet was a kind of transitional figure in this shift. Cabet also advocated a communally organized utopian society, one he popularized in his novel *Voyage to Icaria* (1840). His doctrines appealed to thousands of artisans, creating a new model for a mass-based socialist movement. Other socialists during the 1840s shifted their focus from creating an ideal future society to overthrowing the one that currently existed. Louis Auguste Blanqui agreed with the ideals of a communal society but argued that it could only come by violent revolution. From an elite social background (his brother Je-rome Adolphe Blanqui was a leading liberal economist), he contended that the working class could not liberate itself but had to be freed by a small core of professional revolutionaries. Blanqui practiced what he preached and was imprisoned in 1840 for an attempt to overthrow the regime.

Like Blanqui, Louis Blanc emphasized the importance of politics and rev-olution. Unlike Blanqui, however, he looked to the state to achieve the great socialist transformation. Through political action workers could take control of government and use it to improve working-class living conditions and ul-timately socialize the means of production. For Blanc, therefore, political ac-tivism was key, and he ardently advocated universal suffrage as a means of seizing control of the state through democratic and peaceful means. In sharp contrast, Pierre-Joseph Proudhon saw the state as the problem, not the solu-tion. He felt that by defending the rights of private property the state ensured the exploitation of the poor by the weak. (In 1840 he answered the rhetorical question "What is Property?" with "Theft!") Proudhon rejected politics and political movements in favor of small-scale organizations of producers, advo-cating the abolition of the state.

Socialism in its various guises drew on and in turn inspired other protest movements and ideologies. During the Restoration the Breton priest Félicité de Lammenais had moved from Ultra politics to a new vision of Catholicism attacking ecclesiastical and political corruption and embracing a liberal view of society. During the early years of the July Monarchy he developed these be-liefs further, arguing that religion must oppose economic liberalism and bour-geois individualism. The hostile reaction of France's clerical establishment did not stop Lammenais from publishing *The Words of a Believer* (1834), in which he called for nothing less than a religious version of revolutionary democracy. This brought a formal condemnation from the pope, but at the same time in-spired a potent strand of social Catholicism that would remain a force within the modern French left.

Early-nineteenth-century France was also a landmark era in the rise of modern feminism. During this period socialism and feminism overlapped in a number of respects. The romantic socialists, with their emphasis on mo-rality, the family, and sexuality, often foregrounded the role to be played by women and gender in the new socialist society. Some even portrayed gender inequality and oppression as the ultimate symbol of capitalist society. Prosper Enfantin, the leader of the Saint-Simonians after the death of Saint-Simon in 1825, made the question of women's emancipation the central question of the movement in the 1830s. When Enfantin changed his ideas about gender equality, several prominent women in the movement broke away to found the journal *La Tribune des Femmes* (The Free Woman), the first feminist journal in French history.

Other socialists were drawn to feminism by observing the plight of working-class women. A prime example of the nexus between feminism and socialism was the writer and activist Flora Tristan. Tristan experienced both poverty and gender discrimination personally when the French state confiscated her Peruvian father's fortune upon his death and declared her illegitimate, plunging her and her mother from opulence to misery. She spent her life campaigning for equal rights for women and for socialism, arguing that all workers, men and women alike, must be liberated. Tristan was an early advocate of unions, whose advantages she spelled out in her 1843 book *The Workers' Union*. French feminists also played leading roles in consumer cooperatives.

Feminism was not just a variant of socialism under the July Monarchy. Women wrestled with questions of gender equality in personal relationships, in families, in careers, and before the law. A few intellectuals from affluent backgrounds, notably George Sand (born the Baroness Aurore Dupin), were able to establish independent careers and choose partners and lovers on a basis of equality, yet this remained a dream for most. Some questioned marriage as an oppressive institution but had to contend with the difficulty of supporting a family on their own. While middle-class and aristocratic women tended to dominate feminist movements, working-class women also got involved in socialist feminism, especially during times of political upheaval. In these years French feminists articulated some core demands, including equal wages, the right to divorce, and legal equality within marriage, that would set the tone for women's political activism well into the future.

Rejection of the July Monarchy and of bourgeois society also took cultural forms, largely inspired by the romantic movement. The 1830s witnessed the birth of bohemianism, a movement of disaffected young people from bourgeois backgrounds. Rather than going into business like their elders and peers, bohemians typically adopted a low-budget lifestyle devoted to the pursuit of art, beauty, and Truth. They rejected the materialism of the age, living in slum conditions (the classic Parisian garret or attic room) and wearing defiantly unfashionable clothes. They gravitated to Paris, above all the Latin Quarter, where they whiled away endless hours in conversation at cafés with other aspiring artists, day and night. Eschewing bourgeois morality, they embraced free love, alcohol, and drugs. Their lives were consciously constructed both as works of art and as a protest against the prevailing values of the age.

The bohemians became famous in part because of their novelty, but especially because they produced so many leading young artists and writers. In this case, the revolt against the bourgeois order came from within the heart of the bourgeoisie itself. Middle-class young people also played prominent roles in socialist and feminist movements, showing that the critique of the new establishment was less sociological than ideological.

The poet Charles Baudelaire fled his wealthy family at the age of eighteen to live the bohemian life in the Latin Quarter, where he produced much of his greatest work. George Sand left her husband and bourgeois domesticity behind to move to Paris, wear men's clothes, and live as a novelist and intellectual. Yet the bohemians also played into the broader rethinking of the politics of protest and liberty in early-nineteenth-century France. They made Paris the center of a new type of revolution that would inspire urban avant-garde and youth movements around the world during the modern era. The global hippie movement of the 1960s owed more than a little to the drug-smoking sexual radicals of the July Monarchy.

The ultimate global impact of Parisian bohemianism underscored the transnational character of the new social movements during the 1830s and 1840s in France. Like the republican conspiracies of the Restoration, the social movements of the July Monarchy resonated far beyond the nation's borders. The very term "bohemian" came from the traditional French word for the gypsies of eastern Europe; like them, the bohemians of Paris wished to lead a free, vagabond life. Romantic socialism frequently looked abroad for inspiration and opportunity. Followers of both Fourier and Cabet ended up creating utopian settlements in the United States, like the English Owenites who founded New Harmony, Indiana, and the German Pietists who created Iowa's Amana colonies. French socialists, especially in Paris, interacted with socialist exiles from other nations, in particular Germany. From the outset, socialism defined itself as an international movement that proclaimed the global solidarity of the working class. It represented a new type of universalism that rejected the nationalism of the French Revolution while owing much to it. When reformers and revolutionaries spoke during the July Monarchy of changing the world they meant that literally; as during the great revolution the process might start in Paris, but it certainly wouldn't end there.

By 1848 the concept of liberty in France had become both dominant and increasingly fractured. Whereas the bourgeois establishment might speak of economic and civil freedoms, the socialist left increasingly defined freedom in social terms, while feminists and bohemians focused on freedom from cultural constraints. In 1848 the clash of these contrasting interpretations would produce an explosion that started in Paris but, as in 1789, made princes and potentates tremble throughout Europe and beyond.

THE REVOLUTIONS OF 1848

For France, 1848 was an exceptional year, in terms of the nation itself as well as its relationships to the rest of Europe and the empire. To a greater extent than during the Revolution, political upheaval in Paris led directly to turmoil and revolution elsewhere. The 1848 revolutions in France also shook the colonies, at long last bringing an end to colonial slavery. At the same time, the differences between political life in France and in the rest of Europe, already in evidence during the Napoleonic era, loomed ever larger. In 1848 the peoples of Europe took inspiration from the French to demand what France already had: national integrity and independence. In Italy, Germany, and elsewhere insurgent peoples challenged the old imperial structures with the clarion call of democratic nationalism. The defeat of these movements everywhere restored, at least for a few more decades, the tradition of absolutism. France both conformed to and deviated from this model, in the process revealing its challenges and its limits. As during the Revolution itself, in 1848 France embodied the challenge and the limits of the new. The tumultuous year thus gave a new lease to the idea of France as a universal nation.

The collapse of the July Monarchy was by no means a foregone conclusion in 1848. After a difficult and tempestuous beginning, the regime had achieved a certain stability by the 1840s. In October 1840 François Guizot became prime minister, a position he would keep for over seven years. A staunch economic liberal, Guizot would become famous for telling those who protested the restriction of voting rights to the wealthy to "Enrichissez-vous!" (Get rich!) He also helped develop a sophisticated system of patronage politics (by 1846, for example, 40 percent of parliamentary deputies were employed by the state) that kept the political establishment firmly in control, at least as long as the money held out.[7] Political corruption and repression worked together for a time to silence much of the opposition to the regime.

Things took a turn for the worse with the massive economic crisis of the mid-1840s. Known as "the hungry forties" in Britain, hard times ravaged Europe. The harvest was poor in 1845 and worse in 1846, when a major disease struck potatoes—a traditional staple of the poor. The potato shortage brought hunger across France and throughout Europe, most notably causing the great famine in Ireland. These hard times in agriculture were followed by an industrial crisis in 1847, as overinvestment and speculation in the railways produced a short-term economic collapse.

The lackluster response of Guizot's government to the crisis, conforming to the tenets of liberal ideology, did not help. However, the key threat to the regime came not from impoverished workers or peasants but from the dissatisfied and increasingly alienated republican middle classes. The key issue remained restrictions on voting. Paradoxically, under a bourgeois monarchy most members of the middle classes could not vote. As a result, the most potent opposition to the regime materialized as an electoral reform movement, which emphasized its respectability and moderation.

In 1846 the republican opposition launched a new tactic to win electoral reform. Organizers began holding reform banquets (to get around the law against political meetings) throughout the country. At these banquets speakers would address the burning issues of the day, notably the need for voting reform. The banquet sponsors charged an attendance fee, hoping to restrict the movement to the relatively affluent. As the movement gathered steam in 1847, however, members of the lower classes gathered in support of the banquets, cheering on the attendants and increasingly voicing their own demands. Thus the official bourgeois protest movement had its own doppelganger, a popular mobilization of anger against the regime. As in 1789, the combination of the two would produce an explosion.

The campaign was scheduled to culminate with a gigantic banquet in Paris on February 22, 1848. The king, who had attacked the movement the previous December, responded by banning the banquet. While this intimidated the banquet organizers, it also provoked a popular explosion of anger. Large crowds demonstrated in Paris, demanding the ouster of Guizot. Louis Philippe immediately capitulated and dismissed the unpopular minister, but it was too little, too late. That night troops fired on the crowd, killing forty people. This prompted street fighting the next day, as barricades sprang up all across working-class Paris. The turning point came when the Paris National Guard, mostly composed of middle-class volunteers, took the side of the insurgents. On February 24 crowds invaded the National Assembly and Paris city hall, where they proclaimed the end of the monarchy and the creation of the Second Republic. The revolution soon spread to the provinces, welcomed by republicans throughout the country. Louis Philippe, who was in his seventies, decided not to fight. After an abortive attempt to have his grandson crowned king, he fled to England and exile. His ignominious departure ended the French monarchy.

Although in some ways the new revolt seemed similar to the *trois glorieuses* of 1830, the refusal to accept a new king marked a major difference. Others would soon surface. Instead of a new king, the Chamber of Deputies chose a provisional government headed by the romantic poet Alphonse de Lamartine. The members of the new regime included both bourgeois republicans and radical democrats and socialists, notably Louis Blanc. Unlike 1830, the new government immediately adopted universal manhood suffrage, appealing at one stroke to the principle of republican ideology that had motivated bourgeois opposition to the regime and the desires of the working class and poor masses for true democracy, or *la république sociale*. This was a momentous step: henceforth France would allow all men to vote, ultimately extending the franchise to women in 1946. More immediately, it underscored the entry of the majority of the French population into political life, in a way that had not happened since the Jacobin dictatorship. The "social question," the division between rich and poor that had loomed so large during the July Monarchy, now assumed a central role in French politics.

Once again Paris had become the insurgent capital of Europe, and the fires of revolution soon spread far beyond France's borders. But in 1848 the French led by example rather than by force. Lamartine, the new government's minister of foreign affairs, assured nervous leaders across the Continent that France would not actively export revolution as it had in the 1790s. Yet many Europeans took matters into their own hands and in March initiated revolutionary movements throughout Europe. The news of the February revolution reinforced antigovernment protests in Bavaria, prompting demonstrators to build barricades in the streets of Munich and forcing King Ludwig I to abdicate. Throughout Germany, aristocratic regimes made concessions to liberal and republican forces. In Berlin protestors also took to the streets, prompting a counterattack by the army that massacred 250 demonstrators; as in Paris, military overreaction produced a political crisis, forcing Prussia's King Frederick William IV to grant civil liberties and convene a constituent assembly. Later that spring German liberals organized elections to an all-German assembly, the Frankfurt parliament, which would plan national unification along liberal and republican lines.

The news from Paris also prompted insurrections in Italy, directed primarily against conservative regimes like the Papal States and against Austrian rule in Lombardy and Venetia. In the south, insurgents forced King Ferdinand II of Naples to accept a constitution. In Milan on March 18, the people of the city staged massive demonstrations followed by five days of street fighting (named "the Five Glorious Days" following the French example). They succeeded in driving out the Austrian army and establishing a republic. Venetians followed suit a few days later, expelling the Austrians and restoring the Republic of Saint Mark. Perhaps the most dramatic event of Europe's revolutionary spring took place in Vienna. A clash between demonstrators and royal troops forced the emperor to sack Prince von Metternich, the architect of the Concert of Europe and symbol of aristocratic reaction. Crowds demonstrated for joy as Metternich fled the Austrian capital for London, his departure symbolizing the triumph of republicanism and a new day in Europe. Even in Britain, supposedly immune to the contagion of revolution, the news from the Continent radicalized the Chartist movement, prompting leaders to organize a mass demonstration in London for working-class political rights.

The 1848 revolution also had a major impact on the French empire. As soon as it came to power, the provisional government made clear its intention to abolish slavery. In early March the republican abolitionist leader Victor Schoelcher persuaded the government to form a Commission for the Abolition of Slavery to explore the issue. After a month of deliberations the commission recommended immediate and complete abolition, crafting a decree that was signed into law by the provisional government on April 13, 1848. The decree established a waiting period of two months before the slaves would actually be freed, a concession to colonial interests. However, this concession failed to take into account the desires of the slaves themselves. Slaves in Martinique soon learned of the February revolution from visiting British sailors, who told them the new provisional government had announced its intentions to abolish slavery. They began organizing demonstrations, which escalated to an insurrection in the capital city of Saint-Pierre on May 23. Fears of a Saint-Domingue style general slave revolt prompted the governor of Martinique to decree immediate emancipation the same day, with the governor of Guadeloupe following suit four days later. Thus by the time the official decree of emancipation reached the Caribbean from Paris, the slaves of Martinique and Guadeloupe had already seized their own freedom. Once again the republic had brought liberty to the French Caribbean by empowering the slaves to free themselves.

France thus served as a global model of liberty in 1848, but those who followed the French example had their own ideas of what liberty meant. Insurgents in Germany and Italy crafted a model of national liberation, linking social and political reform to the struggle for national independence. Hungarians fought for freedom from the control of the Austrian empire, while at the same time resisting demands for liberation by the Serbs, Croats, Czechs, and Romanians within Hungary. The Frankfurt parliament wished above all to unify Germany as a constitutional monarchy, offering the imperial throne to Prussia's king in 1849. The idea of national liberation derived in large part from the European resistance movements against Napoleon, but this time the enemies were the reactionary empires of central and eastern Europe. Revolutionary France, in contrast, represented the kind of liberal, powerful nation all others aspired to be. The events of 1848 thus reinforced for the French the idea of national universalism, the idea that France could lead the world to a new era of human liberty. More even than 1789, these events affirmed a powerful connection between national and global liberation.

If Europeans differed about the nature of liberty, so did the French. Republicanism was now the dominant belief in France, but the ideology had changed and evolved since the Restoration. A wide gap now yawned between classic liberal versus radical democratic and socialist visions of the republic, a gap reflected in the contrast between rich and poor. The overthrow of the July Monarchy led to a flowering of radical politics and activism in France. Paris alone had over two hundred clubs representing a variety of progressive perspectives, often meeting several times a week. At one point George Sand tried to find a locksmith to let her into her building, only to be told that they were all at a political meeting. The revolution brought a revival of feminist activity, as women demanding that the provisional government grant them the vote as well. Women's clubs appeared throughout Paris and the countryside, along with a renaissance of feminist newspapers. Socialists and Christian progressives also organized to press their causes. Whereas for bourgeois republicans the fall of the monarchy marked the end of their struggle, for many others it was only the beginning.

The provisional government's efforts to address the "social question" highlighted the tensions between the revolutionary right and left. In an attempt to relieve the unemployment crisis, which the revolution had only worsened, the regime established national workshops, hiring jobless laborers in Paris and paying them minimal wages to perform public works like repairing train stations and paving roads. A concrete manifestation of the provisional government's affirmation of the right to work, the national workshops mushroomed in size: the number of Parisians employed there skyrocketed from 6,000 in March to over 100,000 in June. The workshops did succeed in easing mass employment, but conservatives charged that this was simply make-work at public expense. Worse, it seemed that because there was not enough actual work to go around, workers spent much of their time relaxing or discussing socialist ideas. The provisional government also empowered Louis Blanc to investigate working-class conditions. His Luxembourg Commission likewise attracted conservative criticism as a forum for socialist propaganda.

Concrete proof of this hostility to the republican left soon surfaced. Immediately upon taking power, the provisional government decided to hold elections for a new constituent assembly in April. Ideologically consistent with the belief of the republican and socialist left in universal manhood suffrage and popular sovereignty, this decision gave Parisian revolutionaries little time to bring their message to the provinces and the countryside. Instead, rural voters tended to listen to the local *notables*, who raged against the Parisian radicals for spending their money on workshops for people who weren't working. This was a powerful argument because the provisional government had enacted a 45 percent tax to pay for social measures that mostly benefited city dwellers. When they looked at the new republic, therefore, many peasants and villagers saw mostly costs, not benefits.

The result was a triumph for the right. Held on April 23, 1848, the first mass-based elections in French history produced a conservative majority. Monarchists of various factions dominated the new National Assembly, joining together in common opposition to the Second Republic. Moderate and conservative republicans formed a sizable minority, while radical republicans and socialists got barely 10 percent of the vote, mostly from Paris and other large cities. Workers in Limoges and Rouen staged uprisings to protest the electoral results, uprisings soon snuffed out by government troops. A few weeks later, inspired by the wave of democratic revolutions across Europe, Parisians took to the streets to demand aid for Polish nationalists. Members of the city's radical clubs invaded the National Assembly and tried to overthrow the government, but unlike in February the National Guard sided with the regime, suppressing the movement and arresting many of its leaders. The forces that had together overthrown Louis Philippe now opposed each other, espousing increasingly divergent views of the republic and the revolution.

Matters came to a head in June. Right after the elections the new conservative majority had expelled Louis Blanc from his leadership position but had hesitated to close the workshops for fear of the political consequences. The failure of the May 15 uprising convinced the majority it no longer need fear the Paris crowd. Consequently, on June 21 the assembly voted to disband the workshops in the capital and send their members either to the provinces or to the army. Not surprisingly, many Parisian workers saw this as a frontal attack on the city's working class and reacted with a fury. The insurrection that would come to be known as the June Days began on June 23, and by the next day barricades had arisen throughout the poorer neighborhoods of the city. Some 50,000 Parisians took part in the revolt, both women and men, mostly artisans and working poor or unemployed. However, unlike in February the insurgents failed to capture city hall or to win soldiers to their cause. The government brought in National Guard units from the provinces and on June 25 engaged in a systematic, bloody reconquest of the capital. Led by Gen. Eugene Cavaignac, government soldiers demolished barricades and pursued insurgents through narrow streets and up the stairways of apartment buildings, at times summarily executing those they caught. Up to 3,000 rebels died during the June Days, and some 15,000 were arrested. After the repression had triumphed the government moved swiftly to suppress the left. It banned many revolutionary clubs, reinstituted press censorship, and dissolved the Luxembourg Commission. France was still a republic, but a conservative one that, like the Directory before it, had for the time being turned its back on the radical vision of *la république sociale*. If the three revolutionary days of July 1830 had been glorious, those of June 1848 were tragic.

Just as the overthrow of the July Monarchy in February had sparked revolutions throughout Europe, the defeat of the June insurrection likewise signaled a new period of counterrevolution. As in France, the transition from broad antimonarchist alliances to conflicts between bourgeois and workers proved fatal for the insurgencies of 1848. On June 16 the Austrian army crushed a nationalist uprising in Prague, putting an end to the hopes of the Pan-Slav Congress gathered there. Vienna's turn came a few months later, when, as in Paris, workers revolted after the closure of national workshops. Emperor Ferdinand responded by shelling the city with cannon fire and killing some three thousand insurgents. The winds of change in central Europe suffered a mortal blow in April 1849, as Austrian troops invaded Hungary to stamp out the nationalist regime of Lajos Kossuth and Prussia's King Frederick William dissolved the Frankfurt parliament. By the end of the year the revolutions in Italy had also come to an end, defeated by invading French and Austrian forces. Europe's springtime of peoples had given way to a bitter winter.

The rise and fall of the 1848 revolutions resounded not only in Europe but also in France's overseas empire. As noted above, the overthrow of the July Monarchy brought about the final abolition of French slavery. However, the end of formal bondage did not necessarily translate into freedom, at least in the sense that the former slaves conceived of it. Like most postemancipation societies in the Americas, formal liberation did not bring about the wholesale transformation of the former slave societies. The men of Martinique, Guadeloupe, and Guyana might now be French citizens in theory, but in reality the *bekés*, the former slave owners and their descendants, still controlled the land and the reins of political power. As in the metropole, the winds of change that swept the French Caribbean soon brought disenchantment in their train.

As in 1830, Algeria figured significantly in the revolutions of 1848. By that year the French had finally quelled indigenous resistance in their new colony: Abd-el-Kadr formally surrendered to General Bugeaud in December 1847. February 1848 brought new possibilities, however, as the people of Algeria, like those of Martinique and Guadeloupe, saw in France's revolution an opportunity for change. As one French officer noted, the Arabs observed that France had kicked out its sultan, and if the French could not rule themselves they had no right to give orders to the peoples of Africa.[8] As a result revolts erupted throughout the colony, leading to a declaration of Islamic holy war against the French.

French troops quickly put down this new insurgency and on March 2, 1848, the provisional government changed the status of Algeria from a colony to three formal departments of France (Algiers, Oran, and Constantine), complete with representation in the National Assembly. Native Algerians, however, did not become French citizens, so the vote was restricted to the few French residents. One of the first delegates to be elected to the National Assembly under this new system was General Cavaignac, who had served with distinction in the Algerian wars since 1832. Arriving in Paris in May, he took the lead in the new government's repression of working class discontent, directing the savage repression of the June Days. Cavaignac and other officers from the Armée d'Afrique applied anti-insurgent techniques that they had developed in Algeria, using the same methods in Paris they had deployed to clean out the *medinas* of Algiers and Oran. As Friedrich Engels noted, "Until then, people had no idea that this brand of Algerian warfare could be used right in the center of Paris."[9] The June Days therefore illustrated the interplay between metropolitan and imperial politics.

Algeria also served as a depository for the losers of the June insurrection. The European tradition of deporting criminals and revolutionaries to the colonies went back to the seventeenth century; in 1848 Britain transported hundreds of Chartist activists to Australia. French authorities had long debated how to encourage French settlement in North Africa, and sending Parisian revolutionaries there seemed a natural solution on several levels. Not only would it get them out of the capital, but hopefully the experience of living on the frontier in a healthy rural setting would change them for the better, both politically and morally. Consequently authorities deported some four thousand people arrested for political crimes in June to new lives in Algeria. However, they did not just stop at insurgents. Government officials considered the broader problem of the thousands of unemployed in the capital, people whose despair had led to revolution in June, and decided to launch an ambitious new program of French settlement in Algeria. All told, the government sent nearly 5,000 families, over 13,000 men, women, and children, to North Africa in the aftermath of the June Days, spending some 55 million francs to buy them land, livestock, and agricultural materials. For a variety of reasons the program was less than successful; many of the settlers died or eventually returned to France. Nonetheless, the program did establish the idea of Algeria as a French settler colony and pave the way for others in the future.

America likewise beckoned those looking for safe harbor from the revolutionary upheavals of 1848. Again, this was a European rather than specifically French phenomenon. After the Frankfurt parliament collapsed, thousands of German "red '48ers" fled the turmoil in their homeland for new lives across the Atlantic, founding vibrant new communities throughout the United States and Mexico. For French men and women looking to escape economic and political difficulties at home, the main lure was the California gold rush. French settlers had a long history in California, including the French sailors and French Canadian trappers who traveled to the area when it was under Mexican rule. But the discovery of gold there in January 1848 made California a household name throughout France: bars named Café de la Californie sprang up in cities and small towns alike. Frenchmen (and a few Frenchwomen) left by the thousands bound for the legendary Eldorado in the west, aided by some ninety companies bearing names like La Californienne. By 1851 some 20,000 French citizens had come to California, where locals called them "the Keskydees" (a corruption of qu'est-ce qu'il dit, or "what is he saying"). Many went immediately to the gold fields, leaving for posterity place-names like Frenchman's Creek and Matelot (sailor) Gulch. Others settled in San Francisco, which by the early 1850s had a sizable French community supporting cafés, shops, offices, theaters, and even its own firefighting brigade, the Lafayette Hook and Ladder. While none matched the success of Levi Strauss, the Bavarian immigrant who invented blue jeans, French immigrants founded one of San Francisco's leading department stores, the City of Paris.

FROM REPUBLIC TO EMPIRE

Events of 1848 thus inspired, or required, many French men and women to leave their native land in search of new lives elsewhere. In France itself, after the June Days politics focused on the impending elections for president. Fearing the dangers of "excessive democracy," the conservative government had written a new constitution for the republic that featured a strong executive branch to balance the actions of the National Assembly. General Cavaignac, who after June had ruled as provisional leader of the republic, was widely expected to win the election. However, a number of candidates stood for election, including the socialist Ledru-Rollin and Alphonse Lamartine, leader of the February revolution.

The most unusual candidate was Louis-Napoleon Bonaparte, nephew and heir of the great emperor. Forty years old in 1848, Louis-Napoleon had spent most of his life in exile, growing up in Switzerland and Germany. Arrested when he entered France, he escaped prison in 1846 and fled to England. The fall of the royal regime in February 1848 cleared the way for Louis-Napoleon to return to France; he did so promptly and won election to the National Assembly in April. Many in France did not take him seriously, arguing that he knew little of his country and even spoke French with a German accent, but Bonaparte's nephew had three great advantages he used to maximum political effect. The first was his lack of any clear, consistent ideological position, which enabled people to see in him what they wanted to see. While some of his ideas seemed vaguely socialistic, he also represented order and tradition. Second, Louis-Napoleon had not taken part in either the February or June revolutions, so both sides could claim him for their own. By far the most important advantage, however, was simple name recognition. Everyone knew the name Bonaparte, and those who understood little of contemporary politics but nonetheless romanticized the past glories of imperial France were naturally drawn to him.

In spite of this, many leading figures of French politics dismissed Louis-Napoleon as a nonentity or a buffoon. The presidential elections of December 10, 1848 were a tremendous shock for such people, and a huge surprise for the nation as a whole. Louis-Napoleon won in a landslide, receiving over 5 million votes. His closest competitor, General Cavaignac, got less than 3 million and Lamartine, the hero of February, only earned eight thousand. In a nation just getting used to mass politics, Louis-Napoleon won support as a man who stood above the partisan fray, who represented not sectarian interests but France as a whole. His stunning victory suggested to many commentators that 1848 would unfold along the same lines, from radical to conservative republic and perhaps to empire, that had characterized the great Revolution. It inspired the young Karl Marx to declare famously that history does indeed repeat itself, first as tragedy, second as farce.

Although he was not their first choice, Louis-Napoleon's crushing defeat of the left reassured the monarchists and bourgeois elites who had constituted the bedrock of the July Monarchy, and thus won the allegiance of the Party of Order, which dominated the assembly. The new president moved swiftly to cultivate their support. In May 1849 his government dispatched troops to Italy, intervening against the revolutionaries of the Roman republic. After an initial setback, the French defeated the republicans, occupying Rome and restoring the Church to power. This intervention placed Louis-Napoleon's France squarely on the side of the counterrevolution in Europe. At home as well, the president attacked the left, suppressing radical and socialist organizations. Assured of Louis-Napoleon's support, the assembly moved to overturn the legacies of the revolution. In March 1850 it passed the Falloux Law, which empowered the Church to run its own school system and mandated Catholic instruction in the public schools. In May it dispensed with universal manhood suffrage, introducing a three-year residency requirement for voting that disenfranchised over 2 million French men. Since many of these were workers who traveled frequently in search of employment, the new law sharply reduced the electoral power of the left.

Louis-Napoleon's relations with radicals and socialists were more complicated. Many workers had voted for him, and he at times expressed his concerns with the plight of the poor. He distanced himself from the assembly's vote to restrict the franchise, if not actively opposing it. However, in power Louis-Napoleon pursued a systematic policy of repressing the left. Such measures included arresting radical republican and socialist leaders, banning unions and other working-class organizations, and dismissing leftist teachers and mayors. The government even attacked the symbols of the Revolution itself, banning the Marseillaise as well as red caps (the color red had become identified with revolution by the early nineteenth century) and uprooting liberty trees throughout the country.

Faced with this assault, and handicapped by restrictions on the franchise, radical republicans and socialists went underground. Secret societies flourished, as they had under the Restoration. More significantly, progressive activists began to spread their beliefs into the countryside. The prosperity of rural France in the early nineteenth century had brought peasants into contact with town dwellers as they were integrated into regional and national markets. The artisans (many of whom lived in small towns or the countryside) who dominated radical politics were thus able to reach out more effectively than in the past to their agrarian brethren. This happened especially in the south, an area that would eventually become known as the *rouge Midi*, or red South. Quietly, therefore, the left began to establish itself among French peasants, going beyond its urban roots and creating a national vision of French politics.

Louis-Napoleon's complex relations with both right and left underscored the basic contradiction of his position: he had been elected president of a republic in which he did not believe. The constitution of the Second Republic limited the president to one four-year term; he could not stand for reelection. Therefore, Louis-Napoleon would have to leave power in 1852. But he had no intention of doing so. The growing power of radical republican and socialist forces, who won a number of by-elections in 1850 and 1851 and seemed poised to take power during the national legislative elections of 1852, represented a threat to both the president and the Party of Order in the assembly. Conservative legislators had rejected Louis-Napoleon's pleas to amend the constitution to permit him to remain in power. Louis-Napoleon gambled, correctly, that they would acquiesce to his desires rather than risk another revolution, by electoral means or otherwise. To underscore the gravity of the situation, the government declared martial law in several regions during the fall of 1851. Meanwhile, Louis-Napoleon made sure to station his supporters in key military and government positions.

The president made his move on December 2, 1851, the forty-sixth anniversary of his uncle's great victory at Austerlitz. He dissolved the National Assembly, arrested much of its membership, and declared his intention to replace parliamentary incompetence with the decisiveness and glory of the Napoleonic tradition. A few deputies who escaped called for armed resistance, and barricades appeared in some Parisian neighborhoods. Yet compared with 1848 relatively few people took part, and Louis-Napoleon's forces easily smashed the barricades and defeated the insurgents. The same scenario played out in other major French cities. Few desired to risk life and limb to defend a National Assembly that had not supported them.

The real action took place in the countryside, above all in Provence. The steady activist work of the radical republicans and socialists bore fruit as 100,000 artisans and peasants took up arms against the coup d'état, forming spontaneous armies and marching on local towns. It was the largest insurrection in France during the nineteenth century, and it reversed the traditional pattern of radical cities confronting a conservative countryside. At first taken unawares, Louis-Napoleon's forces quickly rallied and soon defeated the insurgents, but the movement revealed the extent to which the left had permanently transformed the landscape of French politics.

Once in firm control, Louis-Napoleon announced that he would draw up a new constitution and submit it to the voters for approval. He also, as an olive branch to the left, announced his intention to restore universal manhood suffrage. On December 20 he held a plebiscite which (not surprisingly, given that much of the nation was under martial law and the leaders of the opposition mostly in prison) overwhelmingly approved the new constitution. The National Assembly remained in existence, but the tightly controlled elections in early 1852 mostly brought Louis-Napoleon's supporters to power. However, even the constitution's provisions for a ten-year presidency and the title "Prince-President" were not enough. The new president had always dreamed of restoring the empire, out of personal and familial vanity as well as out of the conviction that France had never been more powerful or glorious than under imperial rule. At the end of November 1852 in a second plebiscite 97 percent of the electorate voted to abolish the Second Republic in favor of the Second Empire. Exactly a year after his coup d'etat, on December 2, 1852, Louis-Napoleon took the title Emperor Napoleon III (Napoleon I's son having died young), and Bonapartism once again ruled France.

The 1848 revolution, like that of 1789, thus came to an end at the hands of an emperor named Napoleon. Napoleon III, like his namesake and predecessor, stood above the fray of everyday politics, symbolizing a rejection of republic and monarchy alike. France once again had moved toward democracy then lurched back from it, still hesitating between the rule of tradition and government by the people. Yet 1852 was not 1800: France, Europe, and the world had changed greatly during the previous half century. The Second Empire would adopt new policies and approaches to governing the nation, establishing a fundamentally different relationship to Europe and the world than the first. Napoleon might reign again, but it was a new Napoleon, and more importantly a new France.

In contrast to the revolutionary era, France during the early nineteenth century had a more complicated, two-way relationship with the world beyond its borders. Paris remained the great center and symbol of progressive politics and avant-garde culture, and the nation as a whole was still one of the most powerful and prosperous in Europe. Yet the French also borrowed heavily from other national experiences, whether it be British industrialism, German romanticism, or Italian conspiratorial politics. The nation never regained the military dominance of Europe it had enjoyed under Napoleon, nor did it find a colony as lucrative to replace the lost Saint-Domingue. By the July Monarchy London had replaced Paris as the largest city in Europe, a position it would keep during the modern era.

Local and global interactions nonetheless continued to shape not only French life but also the very idea of France in this period. France remained the world's greatest incubator of new ideologies, all of which espoused a universal vision that owed not a little to their French heritage. The new industrial economy increasingly integrated the nation's peoples, in both cities and towns, into national and global networks of production, labor, and trade. As the world moved into the modern era, Paris became a leading symbol of cultural modernity. Perhaps most of all, the French of different political and cultural persuasions still tended to view the nation's major concerns as intimately connected with global problems and events. In short, the turmoil of the Restoration and July Monarchy reinforced the emphasis on universal nationalism at the heart of French identity. Both the republic and the empire, by 1850 the two dominant political forms in France, drew heavily upon a universalist vision. The next fifty years would illustrate the conflicts and confluence between these two forms of French universalism.

Suggestions for Further Reading

Agulhon, Maurice. *The Republican Experiment, 1848–1852.* Cambridge: Cambridge University Press, 1983.

Andrews, Naomi. *Socialism's Muse: Gender in the Intellectual Landscape of French Romantic Socialism.* Lanham, MD: Lexington, 2006.

Beecher, Jonathan. *Charles Fourier: The Visionary and His World.* Berkeley: University of California Press, 1987.

Horn, Jeff. 2006. *The Path Not Taken: French Industrialization in the Age of Revolution, 1750–1830.* Cambridge: MIT Press, 2006.

Landes, David. *The Unbound Prometheus: Technological Change and Industrial Development in Western Europe from 1750 to the Present.* London: Cambridge University Press, 1969.

Margadant, Ted W. *French Peasants in Revolt: The Insurrection of 1851.* Princeton, NJ: Princeton University Press, 1979.

Merriman, John M. *The Agony of the Republic: The Repression of the Left in Revolutionary France, 1848–1851*. New Haven, CT: Yale University Press, 1978.

Pinkney, David. *The French Revolution of 1830*. Princeton, NJ: Princeton University Press, 1972.

Pomeranz, Ken. *The Great Divergence: China, Europe, and the Making of the Modern World Economy*. Princeton, NJ: Princeton University Press, 2000.

Sewell, William. *Work and Revolution in France: The Language of Labor from the Old Regime to 1848*. Cambridge: Cambridge University Press, 1980.

Sperber, Jonathan. *Karl Marx: A Nineteenth-Century Life*. New York: Liveright, 2013.

Tilly, Louise, and Joan Scott. *Women, Work, and the Family*. New York: Holt, Rinehart & Winston, 1978.

Notes

1. Patrice Higonnet, *Paris: Capital of the World* (Cambridge: Harvard University Press, 2002), 77.
2. Guillaume de Bertier de Sauvigny, *The Bourbon Restoration* (Philadelphia: University of Pennsylvania Press, 1966), 321.
3. Sauvigny, *Bourbon Restoration*, 301–302.
4. Pierre Dessalles and Robert Forster, eds., *Sugar and Slavery, Family and Race: The Letters and Diary of Pierre Dessalles, Planter in Martinique, 1808–1856* (Baltimore: Johns Hopkins University Press, 1996), 95.
5. Savigny, *Bourbon Restoration*, 447.
6. David Pinkney, *Decisive Years in France 1840–1847* (Princeton, NJ: Princeton University Press, 1986), 28–29.
7. Jeremy Popkin, *A History of Modern France* (New Jersey: Prentice Hall, 2001), 94.
8. E. Perret, *Les Francais en Afrique: Récits Algériens, 1848–1886* (Paris: Bloud et Barral, 1886), 2–11.
9. Osama W. Abi-Mershed, *Apostles of Modernity: Saint-Simonians and the Civilizing Mission in Algeria* (Stanford, CA: Stanford University Press, 2010), 120.

[three]

Imperial Democracy? France Under the Second Empire, 1852–1870

"First time as tragedy, second time as farce." Karl Marx's famous satire of Louis Napoleon has haunted the memory of Louis (Napoleon III) and his regime ever since. Generations of French historians, especially those of republican or leftist persuasion, have dismissed the Second Empire as a comic opera regime of no real consequence or, worse, as a repressive, authoritarian government that futilely resisted France's march toward democracy and social justice. Few figures in the history of modern France have been as wickedly lampooned as Napoleon III, often portrayed as the lesser spawn of a great political and military hero. The empire's sordid origins in a military *coup* and its ignoble end in military disaster have obscured the accomplishments of the years in between. For the political leaders of the Third Republic, the Second Empire offered little more than a long tale of mistakes it was determined not to replicate.

In recent years more nuanced, even positive, perspectives on the regime of Napoleon III have predominated. Some historians have noted the exceptional growth of the French economy during the Second Empire, arguing that this progress not only brought unprecedented prosperity but also helped create a

3.1. *Napoleon III Frees Abd-el-Kadir,* 1852.
Source: copyright © RMN-Grand Palais/Art Resource, New York.

national market and a national culture. Others have noted the democratic aspect of the regime's politics, how the empire combined authoritarianism with universal manhood suffrage, thus leaving an important legacy for French political life in the twentieth century. Still others have pointed to the empire's transformation of Paris into a glamorous world capital, controversial at the time but almost universally regarded as an impressive achievement ever since. While Napoleon III failed to equal the military success of his more illustrious uncle, his regime nonetheless laid the economic and political groundwork for the emergence of modern France.

Love him or hate him, Napoleon III and the empire he led for eighteen years had a major impact, both at home and abroad. Viewed from a transnational perspective, the Second Empire is important for a number of reasons. It provides a fascinating example of a key theme of the mid-nineteenth century in Europe and America: the struggle to create liberal democracy. Both liberalism and democratic republicanism had emerged out of the convulsions of the French revolutionary era as major political movements, but as June 1848 demonstrated their proponents were not necessarily allies. Both in France and abroad, the third quarter of the nineteenth century would gradually outline a synthesis between the two that would henceforth dominate the politics of the modern era. The history of the Second Empire highlighted the other major theme of the mid-nineteenth century: nationalism and the rise of the mass-based nation-state. While Bonapartism at home struggled to weave various ideological strands into a common French political culture and identity, abroad it intervened to aid, and sometimes oppose, the forces of popular nationalism. The deeply contradictory regime of Napoleon III, caught between democracy and authoritarianism, dynasty and nation, cosmopolitanism and reaction, city and country, exemplified all the tensions of the modern age.

France's relationship to the wider world preoccupied the Second Empire, as it did the first, but with significant differences. Bonapartism retained its paradoxical heritage of support for liberty abroad and commitments to preserve the status quo, and the contradictions between the two positions loomed even larger than they had half a century earlier. Increasingly, France under Napoleon III loomed as an obstacle to the new forces of national unification shaking central and southern Europe. At the same time, the Second Empire, much more so than the first, extended the search for imperial glory well beyond the borders of Europe. Both with his successful ventures in Africa, Southeast Asia, and the Pacific, and with his disastrous Mexican campaign, Napoleon III redefined the meaning of empire to focus on overseas expansion. Finally, France's long rivalry with Germany essentially began under the Second Empire, as the French emperor faced the brilliant Prussian chancellor Otto von Bismarck, bent on making a united Germany dominant in Europe. Unlike the Restoration and July monarchies, the Second Empire collapsed as a result of military defeat, a theme that would resurface more than once during the twentieth century.

During the reign of Napoleon III the French became more conscious of their identity as a nation, a process that would continue and accelerate under the Third Republic to follow. This process owed much to the economic advances of the era, notably the rise of a national market facilitated by transportation and communications improvements. The growth of mass-based nationalism abroad also contributed to this new sense of identity; increasingly surrounded by other unified nations, France could not but become more conscious of its own national character. The regime's end with the signing of German unification at Versailles, on French territory, dramatically underscored the links between French and foreign nationalisms. The idea of French republicanism as a universal value did not disappear, but was instead complemented by a growing sense of French distinction. Both the decline of provincial economic and cultural economy, and increased national awareness elsewhere in Europe, fostered a new sense of the singularity of France. Yet, paradoxically, this awareness rested more than ever before on the heritage of the French Revolution, so that modern views of French identity both challenged and reinforced the idea of France as a universal nation.

EUROPE AND THE WORLD IN THE MID-NINETEENTH CENTURY

Two essential political, social, and cultural movements, the rise of the nation-state and the emergence of liberal democracy, dominated the affairs of much of Europe and the world during the Second Empire. In Europe, popular nationalism and social equality had mounted a frontal challenge to the established order in the first half of the nineteenth century, only to be beaten back in the aftermath of the 1848 revolutions. Yet it was clear that the forces of reaction could not triumph permanently, that the powerful political movements unleashed by the French and industrial revolutions would have to be accommodated, if not entirely accepted. Both liberal democracy and the nation-state represented such accommodations, the former a way of conceding popular rule while protecting the sanctity of property rights, the latter a means of enfolding demands for popular national sovereignty within conservative social hierarchies. Beyond Europe, people struggled to reframe traditional regimes and policies to fit new models of liberal nationalism, in part as a way of imitating Europe's power and success, in part to resist ever more aggressive European imperialism. The paradoxes that typified France's Second Empire thus resonated in many different parts of the world.

The creation of the new nation-states of Italy and Germany out of a hodge-podge of independent cities and states was perhaps the most dramatic instance in Europe of the new nationalism. As we will see, Napoleon III played an important role in both struggles. In both cases, national unification came from above, from the aristocracy so bitterly opposed by the revolutionaries of 1848. In Italy foreign intervention and papal hostility had defeated the populist nationalism of 1848, led by Giuseppe Mazzini and Giuseppe Garibaldi. Although revolutionary nationalism remained a potent force, the leadership of the unification movement passed to the conservative kingdom of Piedmont-Sardinia, the most powerful independent Italian state. Led by the royal minister Count Camillo di Cavour, the kingdom negotiated alliances with France to defeat the Austrians, as well as securing the loyalty of Garibaldi after the veteran guerrilla fighter seized power in southern Italy and marched on Rome.

In similar fashion, the Prussian monarchy engineered the unification of Germany. In the aftermath of the Napoleonic wars Prussia had emerged as the most powerful state in Germany, rivaling the Austrian empire for the dominance of central Europe. Here too the forces of liberal and popular nationalism had failed to bring about unification in 1848. In 1862 the Prussian king appointed minister-president Otto von Bismarck, one of the greatest diplomats of the modern era. Provoking wars with Denmark, Austria, and ultimately France, Bismarck used his control of the Prussian state, and Prussia's powerful army, to push through the unification of Germany on conservative terms, so that the Prussian king became the new German emperor. For both Germany and Italy, conflict with France played a decisive role in national unification; both became unified nations in 1871, in the aftermath of the Franco-Prussian War.

For other nations, the era of the Second Empire brought new definitions of national identity and popular sovereignty. The mid-nineteenth century was the height of Britain's imperial power and unquestioned leadership of the world economy. The Crystal Palace Exhibition of 1851, which attracted over 6 million spectators, convincingly demonstrated the nation's industrial prowess. For Victorian Britain, a key question was how to extend the benefits of progress to the people of the nation as whole: how to incorporate the working classes into the liberal consensus. In 1867, after years of debate, Parliament passed the Reform Bill, effectively enfranchising millions of male workers. It was not universal manhood suffrage, and it certainly did not address the political role of women, but it did represent a major step toward liberal democracy that would prove irrevocable.

Extending freedom to new sectors of the population also took place in the two countries that would dominate the history of the twentieth century, Russia and the United States. The American Civil War (1861–1865) not only ended slavery in that country but also unified the nation to an unprecedented extent. Henceforth the United States would no longer be half slave and half free, but federal authority would prevail throughout the country over the desires and prerogatives of the individual states. By unifying the nation economically, it also laid the basis for the unprecedented economic growth of the late nineteenth century. In 1861 Russia liberated the serfs, bringing a final end to this relic of medieval society. The emancipation measure granted legal rights to the former serfs, making them members of the national community to a much greater extent. In both cases liberation had its limits, often seeming more theoretical than real. Both ex-slaves and ex-serfs often remained tied to the land of their forebears. Nonetheless, these acts of emancipation created new visions of national unity, visions accompanied in both cases by major waves of territorial expansion and conquest, westward in America and eastward in Russia.

The era of the Second Empire also brought new visions of nationalism and national unity to Asia. There, people were forced to confront Europe's new power and aggressive expansionism, to adapt traditional regimes and societies to new times. Japan proved most successful in this regard. After American warships forced the country's Tokugawa rulers to accept diplomatic and commercial relations with the west in 1853, the threat of foreign domination sparked a revolution. Misleadingly labeled the Meiji Restoration because the rebels used the Meiji emperor as a figurehead to advance their own designs, the revolution overthrew the Tokugawa regime and launched Japan on a crash course of modernization and national unification. As a result, Japan became one of few nonwestern countries to resist colonial domination successfully.

India and China were not so fortunate. In these nations colonialism also sparked revolutions, but in both cases the political upheavals failed to bring about national transformation. British expansion in India, and especially its transformation of village economy and society, triggered the massive 1857 revolt. British forces prevailed, transferring control of India from the East India Company to the crown and imposing direct colonial rule. The era of the British Raj made rule over India increasingly central to ideas of British nationality, while at the same time the memory of the great 1857 revolt became a legacy for the Indian nationalist and independence movements that began to develop later in the century. Imperialist expansion and local resistance produced an even greater revolt in China. After the Opium War with Britain had demonstrated the weakness of the Qing dynasty and subjected the proud Chinese empire to humiliating concessions to the west, a huge uprising broke out in southern China in 1850. Taking the name Taiping, the rebels combined mysticism, nationalist anti-imperialism, and appeals for social justice in a movement that mobilized millions against the Qing regime. As in India, the opposition of both the west and of local elites doomed the Taipings, enabling the Qing dynasty to survive for another half century. Also as in India, however, the Taiping Rebellion helped inspire future, more successful nationalist and anti-imperialist movements in China.

During the middle of the nineteenth century societies around the world struggled with the political implications of the rise of political liberalism, nationalism, and democracy, as well as the increasing power of capitalism as a global system. While elite states imposed national unity from the top down in Europe, nationalism remained a potent force for democratization, especially in regions where it meshed with anti-imperial struggles. At the same time, national identity became increasingly entangled with imperial might in nations like Britain and France. The regime of Napoleon III combined nationalism, empire, and democracy in an often confusing and unstable mix that reflected all the uncertainties of the global era. In making Bonapartism the ruling political system for the last time in French history, the people of France embraced a government that had contradictory affinities with many major ideologies, including authoritarianism, empire, nationalism, and representative democracy, of the modern age. The Second Empire therefore represented a key turning point in the history of both France and the world as a whole.

THE AUTHORITARIAN EMPIRE

Historians have traditionally divided the Second Empire into two phases, the authoritarian empire of the 1850s and the liberal empire of the 1860s. During the first period Napoleon III set up a ruling system that promoted obedience and suppressed dissent, while during the second he experimented with more inclusive forms of governance. The distinction between these two phases is useful, but it must not be allowed to hide some essential continuities in the life of the Second Empire. Both authoritarian and liberal political measures were adopted by the regime as means to an end: strengthening imperial power in France and maximizing French power and influence in Europe and the world.

The most important and unusual characteristic of the Second Empire was its paradoxical interpretation of political sovereignty and legitimacy. When Louis Napoleon took power as emperor Napoleon III, he based the political structure of the Second Empire on that of the first. Like Napoleon I, Napoleon III blended representative and democratic forms with authoritarian content. The Second Empire had both a bicameral legislature and a ministry to lead the day-to-day affairs of the state. However, the minister was chosen by and answerable to the emperor alone, not to the legislature, as in true parliamentary democracies. The legislature also lacked any real power: its sessions were closed to the public, and elections occurred only every six years.

Voting and elections stood out as paradoxical. Whereas the ministers and members of the Senate, the legislative upper house, were appointed by the emperor, members of the lower house, or Legislature (the *Corps legislative*), were elected according to universal manhood suffrage. The Second Empire thus restored the practice of mass voting briefly established by both the first and second republics, and made it a permanent part of French political culture. France thus became the first major nation in Europe to institutionalize mass democracy, and it did so under an authoritarian imperial regime. The powers of the electorate, and of the lower house, were circumscribed by restrictions on legislative autonomy and by a general climate of press censorship and police repression. Nonetheless, for many throughout the nation, especially the rural majority, the Second Empire gave them their first enduring lessons in electoralism, and made voting a regular part of daily life.

The regime reinforced its electoralism by the use of plebiscites: national referendums based on universal manhood suffrage. Three times during his imperial reign, in 1851, 1852, and in 1870, Napoleon III turned directly to the people of France, asking them to vote yes or no on a given political question. The plebiscite of December 1851 ratified the coup d'état of that year, the plebiscite of December 1852 approved the creation of the Second Empire, and the plebiscite of 1870 supported the new liberal constitution proposed by the regime. In all three cases the yes votes carried the day overwhelmingly. Not surprisingly, given the military repression that accompanied the birth of the empire, the cowed electorate ratified the first two plebiscites, but the government also won handily during the more liberal environment of 1870. The emperor argued that, whereas parliamentary politics and representative democracy were divisive, the plebiscites showed that the people of France as a whole supported him; he alone represented the nation. In a perspective that looked back to Rousseau and forward to twentieth-century fascism, Napoleon III viewed himself as the embodiment of the general will of the French people.

The regime's success with the plebiscites owed a lot to political repression; nonetheless, the Second Empire enjoyed considerable popular support. This came primarily, if not exclusively, from two major social groups. Not surprisingly, the wealthy bourgeoisie strongly backed the emperor and his regime. They viewed him as both a supporter of the *nouveaux riches* and a bulwark against republicanism and revolution. Many wealthy French men and women opposed the Second Empire, especially members of the traditional aristocracy who continued to hope for a Legitimist revival. But for those focused on future profits rather than past glories, Napoleon III, like his famous uncle, represented the capitalist entrepreneurialism and the social stability they craved. The regime's other major source of support was the French peasantry, still the overwhelming majority of the national population. For many peasants, the Second Empire recalled the glories of the first, and many others agreed with the emperor's repression of the urban left. Moreover, the regime won rural loyalty by its institutionalization of the forms (if not necessarily the content) of democracy, giving peasants their first real taste of electoral participation. For many, a vote for the emperor represented a stand against the traditional *notables* of aristocracy and Church who had dominated village life for so long. The existence of such mass support, clearly reflected in the outcomes of the plebiscites, underscored the regime's claims to be a democratic empire.

To a great extent, popular support for Napoleon III during the 1850s rested on the dramatic economic expansion of that decade, and during the regime as a whole. As some historians have noted, the Second Empire in part simply inherited a dynamic economy from the July Monarchy, frequently taking credit for a situation it had not itself created. It is nonetheless true that the empire brought a major period of economic growth for France. From 1852 to 1870 France's industrial production doubled, and its foreign trade tripled. One key to, and symbol of, this industrial dynamism was the railroad, whose importance we have already noted under the July Monarchy. By 1870 France had five times the amount of railway track, some 10,000 miles, than it had in 1852. Railroad expansion contributed to the development of a national unified economic market, which was becoming a reality by the 1860s. Farmers increasingly produced specialized goods for the national market rather than growing or making most of what they needed for themselves. This encouraged the rise of regional specialties, such as Camembert and other types of cheese, that would become the signature glories of French agriculture and cuisine. At the same time, the increase in French wealth made the nation a major international exporter of capital. French investors helped finance one of the great engineering projects of the age, Ferdinand de Lesseps's Suez Canal, which opened in 1869.

More than any other French government during the nineteenth century, the Second Empire took a direct and extensive role in promoting economic growth. The regime acted decisively to expand the nation's credit supply, enabling investors to find the capital necessary for new business ventures. New banks sprang up to invest the capital generated by industrial expansion. In 1852 the Pereire brothers founded the Crédit Mobilier, a major new

investment bank that loaned money to a wide variety of French businesses until it went bankrupt in 1867. Napoleon III also loosened government restrictions on joint-stock companies (*sociétés anonymes*), encouraging their growth.
The Second Empire embraced the idea of free trade to a much greater extent
than any previous French government. Finally, the regime invested heavily in
public works projects, most notably Haussmann's renovations of Paris, which
we will consider in the next chapter.

One result of sustained good times was a regime that seemed to glorify
wealth, ostentation, and material excess. Like the July Monarchy, but to an
even greater extent, the society of the Second Empire was dominated by the
haute bourgeoisie, elites who had made their money in finance and industry
during the boom times. As during the First Empire, social status depended
almost entirely on wealth rather than aristocratic pedigree. Emperor Napoleon III himself set the tone for this emphasis on the accumulation and
display of riches. He surrounded himself with wealthy individuals who used
their positions to enrich themselves further. He also established a public persona emphasizing unashamed opulence. In 1853 he wed Eugénie de Mon-
tijo, a Spanish princess and the new Empress Eugénie. The wedding was a
lavish affair, condemned by many as being in bad taste; seamstresses made
fifty-four dresses for the wedding party, and gifts to the bride, including a diamond necklace worth 600,000 francs from the Paris city council, poured in
from throughout the country.[1] The conservative, firmly Catholic empress took
the lead in setting a tone of extravagant fashion and display. Paris became a
symbol of affluence, a city where the wealthy occupied luxurious apartments
along the new boulevards, where rich women could spend tens of thousands
of francs on fashionable clothing and rich men could lavish similar sums on
the city's elite courtesans. A pronounced tendency toward the *nouveau riche*
materialism, manifesting itself in everything from flamboyant architecture to
the splashy operettas of Jacques Offenbach, typified imperial Paris and the
Second Empire in general.

This emphasis on wealth at the heart of the authoritarian empire underscored the vast gulf between French elites and the nation's working people.
The regime had some working-class support, especially during the boom
years of the 1850s. Working people also benefited from the prosperity of the
decade, if to a lesser extent than the bourgeoisie. Workers ate more food, and
more varied kinds of food, than their parents who had depended overwhelmingly on coarse bread. Not only food but also jobs were plentiful during the
early Second Empire. The regime's major public work projects, above all the

rebuilding of Paris, provided employment for both skilled artisans and un-skilled manual laborers. Full employment meant rising wages for many working families, translating into the beginnings of working-class consumerism. Moreover, like many peasants, some working people admired the nationalist appeal of Bonapartism.

The Second Empire was born in the repression of the working-class left, however, and in spite of Bonapartism's populist aura it never won over the mass of urban workers. Even with the rising standard of living, working-class life was still very difficult. As during the July Monarchy many urban laborers were rural migrants who had to adjust quickly to a harsh and radically different environment. Manual laborers generally worked thirteen to sixteen hours a day, six days a week. Affordable housing was scarce and of poor quality, especially in Paris and other large cities, where families lived in one unheated room. Skilled workers and artisans, still a major proportion of the French working class, feared that the unskilled rural migrants would lower wages and worsen working conditions, a prospect made all too real by the rise of large factories. For all its populist rhetoric, the regime made its loyalty to the interests of the *haute bourgeoisie* clear by banning strikes and unions. In 1854 it created a mandatory worker's passport (*livret ouvrier*) to control the ability of workers to change jobs and in general submit them to police surveillance.[2] In the face of such repression, paternalist initiatives like plans for model workers' housing did little to win working class support.

The combination of economic prosperity and political repression forced the republican and socialist left underground during the authoritarian empire. These forces did not disappear, however, and when conditions changed during the 1860s they reemerged as the heart of opposition to the imperial regime. Obscured by the glitter and opulence of bourgeois society during the boom years of the 1850s, Napoleon III's failure to win working-class support would ultimately prove fatal for the Second Empire.

FRANCE CONFRONTS A CHANGING WORLD

For the emperor, the prosperity of the 1850s was a major achievement, but it did not alone assure the greatness of France and the regime. Imperial expansion and glory had always lain at the heart of the Bonapartist vision, and for Napoleon III foreign policy and conquest were at least as important as domestic politics. Like his illustrious uncle, the emperor considered foreign victories a key means of securing popular support for the regime from the

French people, as well as contributing to the glory of the nation in general. The Second Empire's record in foreign policy compares poorly with that of the first, however. Whereas Napoleon I subdued all of Europe to his will, at least briefly, Napoleon III's successes were less impressive. France remained a great power, but not *the* dominant nation on the Continent it had been half a century earlier. While the regime made solid international achievements during the 1850s, it ended with a military and diplomatic disaster that weakened the nation for decades to come.

The middle of the nineteenth century witnessed important shifts in the meaning of empire for the regime and for France as a whole. At the beginning of the century imperial expansion focused strongly on Europe. Napoleon I had so little interest in overseas colonies that he sold the vast Louisiana Territory to the infant United States for a song. In contrast, the Second Empire emphasized colonial expansion beyond Europe. Building on initiatives taken during the July Monarchy, notably the acquisition of Tahiti in 1842, the Second Empire gradually redefined the word "empire" to mean overseas colonialism. The Third Republic would make this new view of empire dominant in the modern era. Napoleon III's regime thus played an important traditional role in redefining not just democracy but also imperialism in the history of modern France.

The Second Empire's foreign policy, like its domestic, was often contradictory. Above all, the emperor wanted to maintain and restore the power and prestige of France in a rapidly changing Europe. During the reign of Napoleon III France would see its population surpassed by that of Germany, a demographic inferiority underscored by the defeat of 1870 and the creation of a unified German state. Britain, the traditional enemy, by midcentury counted almost as many people as France, and London was by far the largest city in Europe, almost twice the size of Paris. Consequently, unlike his uncle, who could dominate Europe through military brilliance and brute force, Napoleon III had to use diplomacy and alliances to ensure France's influence in European affairs.

Particularly during the 1850s this strategy scored some important successes. Paradoxically, in contrast to his largely conservative orientation at home, Napoleon III's foreign policy challenged the power of other European empires. This liberal orientation abroad brought about one of the most striking aspects of Second Empire foreign policy, the tacit alliance with Britain. In 1854, alarmed by Russia's increasingly aggressive stance vis-à-vis the fading Ottoman Empire, both France and Britain declared war on the czarist regime. Although the French forces performed better than their British allies, they failed to achieve the kind of lightning victory so characteristic of Napoleon I, instead laying siege to Russia's Black Sea fortress of Sebastopol for over a year. Nonetheless, France and Britain eventually triumphed, negotiating a peace treaty with Russia that protected Ottoman sovereignty and the European balance of power, at least for a while.

Toward the end of the decade the Second Empire also became involved in the struggle for Italian unification, renewing the Bonapartist concern with peninsular affairs. In 1858 Napoleon III made an alliance with Piedmont, the Italian state whose prime minister, Camillo di Cavour, led the movement to unify the peninsula. In exchange for French help against the Austrians Cavour agreed to cede Nice and Savoy to France. The next year France and Piedmont went to war against Austria, winning the battle of Solferino and capturing Milan. The Austrians negotiated a treaty that surrendered Lombardy to Piedmont, although they retained control of Venice, much to Cavour's displeasure.

In both the Crimean and Italian wars the Second Empire demonstrated that France was still a dominant power in European affairs, and one committed to the struggle for liberty. At the same time these campaigns fell far short of achieving the military glory of the First Empire. French forces performed solidly, but not brilliantly, on the battlefield, and both wars depended on alliances and diplomacy rather than overwhelming military prowess. Nonetheless, Napoleon III's foreign policy, like his reign in general, worked well during the 1850s, something that would change dramatically during the following decade.

NEW VISIONS OF EMPIRE

To a greater extent than the First Empire, the second undertook imperial expansion beyond Europe. Unlike the Third Republic that followed it, the regime of Napoleon III had no defined colonial policy but often supported the initiatives of French adventurers and others in Asia and Africa, sometimes gaining new French colonies. This divergence between Parisian and local perspectives on empire was especially pronounced in the case of Algeria. By the beginnings of the Second Empire the French army had largely pacified Algeria, with the exception of Kabylia, which was finally subdued in 1871. The emperor visited Algeria twice in the early 1860s, coming away with very favorable impressions of indigenous leaders while looking down with disdain on the burgeoning community of European settlers as venal and self-centered. In consequence he identified himself a friend of the Arab people, proclaiming in a speech that "Algeria is not a colony . . . but an Arab kingdom . . . I am as much the emperor of the

Arabs as of the French!"[3] Napoleon III restored military rule over Algeria, much to the displeasure of the civilian *colons*, or settlers. Yet the latter population continued to grow, taking advantage of new laws on property rights to strip the Muslim population of more and more of its land. Ultimately the emperor's fantasies of an Arab kingdom in Algeria came to naught, and after the collapse of the Second Empire the French *colons* asserted full control over Algeria.

The autonomy of imperialist forces was greater in sub-Saharan Africa and Asia, places farther away from France and less familiar to the emperor. For black Africa the Second Empire represented a transitional period, from the previous era of small trading posts left over from the days of the slave trade to the full-fledged territorial expansion and occupation of the late nineteenth century. A key imperative during these years was free trade and opening African markets to French commerce. Business interests in Bordeaux, for example, pushed for greater trading opportunities in Africa. Whereas commercial relations during the era of the slave trade had been largely controlled by Africans who jealously guarded access to the interior of the continent, now French traders and soldiers pushed to establish both business and military dominance. In 1854 Paris appointed Gen. Louis Faidherbe governor of the French colony of Saint-Louis at the mouth of the Senegal River. Over the next few years Faidherbe expanded the French presence in the interior and successfully waged war against African kingdoms. In 1857 his forces seized the African city of Ndakarou, rechristening it the French colonial city of Dakar. While the Second Empire approved of these conquests, they occurred largely without its direction, resulting instead from clashes between ambitious French soldiers and local rulers.

France's most dramatic colonial expansion during the Second Empire took place in southeast Asia. During the mid-nineteenth century French forces intervened extensively in Asia and the Pacific, driven by a global vision of the French empire that required naval bases and trading posts around the world, as well as the activities of French missionaries. In 1853, for example, France annexed the large Pacific island of New Caledonia, drawn to its physical and strategic value as well as acting to avenge the mistreatment of French missionaries there. Missionaries also led the way to the creation of French colonies on the Asian mainland. Men and women of the cloth from France had a long history in Asia, dating back to the voyages of Francis Xavier to Japan and Alexandre de Rhodes to Annam in the sixteenth century. Competition between French Catholic and British Protestant missionaries led France to declare a protectorate over Tahiti in the 1840s.

France had traditionally protected Catholic interests in Vietnam, and the increasing persecution of missionaries there by the Vietnamese emperor, including the execution of French priests, led Paris to take action. In 1858 Napoleon III, egged on by the intensely Catholic Empress Eugénie, sent a naval flotilla to Cochin China. In 1859 the French conquered Saigon, giving France a major Asian port many hoped would rival Hong Kong. By the end of the 1860s French forces, not always with the direct approval of Paris, had conquered most of southern Vietnam and established a protectorate over Cambodia. Napoleon III could thus justly claim to have created a new French empire of global proportions.

While expanding in Asia and Africa, France retained its foothold in the Caribbean. Now considered the "old colonies." Martinique, Guadeloupe, and French Guiana bridged the transition from one imperial era to another. No part of France more underscored the contradictory character of the Second Empire than the French Caribbean in the postemancipation era. The revolution of 1848 had not only abolished slavery but also made all residents of the French Antilles citizens of France equal to those of the metropole. They voted in local and national elections, choosing their own representatives to serve in the National Assembly in Paris.

At the same time, however, they remained colonies, subject to the dictates of the colonial and naval ministries. Moreover, emancipation had done little to promote true equality in the French Caribbean. Control of most of the land and wealth remained in the hands of the *bekés*, the white former slave owners and their descendants. As elsewhere in the Americas after emancipation, many ex-slaves continued to work for their former masters as sharecroppers. In order to ensure the survival of the plantations and to prevent labor shortages that would give the freedmen greater bargaining power, white Caribbean elites sponsored massive labor immigration from India, China, and even Africa, often from the same areas that had provided slaves in the past. In Martinique, Guadeloupe, and Guiana the legacy of the slave past coexisted uneasily with formal political equality. As was so often the case in the modern Caribbean, class and racial conflicts intersected, so that the struggle between the dominant conservative aristocracy and the republican bourgeoisie was equally a struggle between white *bekés* and the largely mixed-race descendants of the free people of color. In the French Caribbean, therefore, electoralism did not necessarily mean freedom. Here the imperial vision combined authoritarianism and democracy in an extreme version of the Second Empire's politics in general.

Most dramatic, and notorious, of all Napoleon III's foreign initiatives was France's ill-starred intervention in Mexico. In 1862 the liberal Mexican government of Benito Juarez, the nation's first leader of Indian origin, announced it was suspending payments on its foreign debts, prompting military intervention by Britain, Spain, and France. Although London and Madrid soon withdrew, Napoleon III decided to seize this opportunity to create a new French empire in the Americas. The French launched a major invasion in early 1862 and over the next two years succeeded in subduing most of the country. They then created a new regime, Mexico's Second Empire, headed by the Austrian Hapsburg Archduke Maximilian. Maximilian's regime, like that of Napoleon III's in France, blended liberal reformism and imperial authoritarianism in a way that pleased neither Mexico's conservatives nor liberals. When the US Civil War ended in 1865 the Americans began pressuring France to withdraw, leading Napoleon III to recall French forces the next year. As a result the liberal nationalist forces of Juarez quickly overwhelmed Maximilian's regime, capturing and executing the emperor in June 1867. Napoleon III's attempt to export liberal imperialism thus ended in defeat, a disaster that would foreshadow the demise of his own regime a few years later.

Both the foreign and colonial policies of Napoleon III thus blended authoritarianism practices with a certain liberal, even emancipatory vision. French diplomats and soldiers did not hesitate to use force to achieve the nation's ends, sometimes allying themselves with conservative forces to do so. The defense of the Ottoman Empire hardly spoke to the imperatives of national liberation. At the same time, however, both in Europe and overseas the Second Empire often articulated a progressive message, such as in its support of Italian unification, or the emperor's ideas about an Arab kingdom in North Africa. It is worth noting that Napoleon III, unlike his famous uncle, made no attempt to restore slavery in the French Caribbean after the fall of the republic that had abolished it. In some ways, France's actions in the wider world foreshadowed the turn toward liberal empire in the 1860s. Ultimately, however, they underscored the contradictory nature of the regime that would soon bring about its downfall.

THE LIBERAL EMPIRE

In 1859 Napoleon III proclaimed that it was time to "crown the [imperial] edifice with liberty."[4] Over the next few years he implemented a series of reforms promoting greater freedom of expression and increasing the power of the legislature. By the end of the 1860s France seemed to be moving toward a full-fledged imperial democracy. Had the regime not collapsed after the French military defeat in 1870, it might have gradually matured into a constitutional empire, much as Britain managed to combine monarchy and democracy. As it was, the combination of a strong executive and an active legislature was a powerful political legacy for France, one ultimately realized under the Fifth Republic a century later.

Why did Napoleon III undertake such a striking about-face? The simplest answer is that it wasn't a reversal at all. As we have seen, even at its most authoritarian the Second Empire contained aspects of democratic practice, and the emperor often preached liberal and progressive political values. For Napoleon III, and to an important extent for Bonapartism in general, imperial democracy represented a real proposition, an alternative to the parliamentary democracy embraced by the republican left. Far more than self-interested legislators, the national leader represented the desires of the people as a whole. Authoritarian rule might have been necessary to forestall the danger of revolution, but once that threat had passed liberty could flourish. Having achieved an important measure of stability, by the 1860s the emperor felt it was time to emphasize the more progressive aspects of his regime.

More concretely, the growing power of the French left, as well as the failure of the emperor's earlier efforts to win working-class support, made this imperative. Combined with the decline of the Legitimist right, it paved the way for a new liberal interpretation of the Second Empire. In the elections of 1852 the greatest opposition came from the right, whereas by 1857 the left constituted the primary threat to the government. The shift to liberalism, like so much of Napoleon III's regime, reflected a combination of principle and opportunism.

Imperial liberalization during the 1860s meant above all granting more rights to the legislature and relaxing censorship. The imperial decree of November 24, 1860, the formal beginning of the liberal empire, gave the legislature greater power over the government ministry as well as the right to review the emperor's annual speech. The following year Napoleon III authorized the legislature to review and approve the imperial budget. In 1864 the regime relaxed its control over the press, a move that prompted the rise of a new era of mass journalism, notably in Paris. In 1868 Napoleon III passed a new law permitting freedom of assembly in France.

In trying to win support for a kinder, gentler empire, Napoleon III paid particular attention to winning over urban workers. The working people of

Paris and other French cities had generally shown little enthusiasm for his policies or his reign, and to a large extent constituted the mass base of his republican and socialist opponents. The emperor therefore courted them more aggressively, believing that winning their approval was crucial to ensuring the future of his regime. By the middle of the 1860s the Second Empire had granted workers the right to form unions and go on strike, a major shift from the pro-business policies of a decade earlier. Most dramatically, in 1862 the regime not only allowed but also paid for worker representatives from France to attend the International Exposition in London, the successor to the Crystal Palace Exhibition of 1851. There delegates met with British socialists, as well as being welcomed by Karl Marx himself. Two years later these meetings and conversations bore fruit with the founding of the First International, a global organization of socialist parties whose creation was a landmark event in the history of socialism.

The Second Empire's foreign policy also expressed this liberal turn. As we have seen, support for liberty had been a strong theme of Napoleon III's relations with the outside world since the beginning of his reign. His de facto alliance with that ultimate symbol of nineteenth-century liberalism, Great Britain, epitomized his progressive view of the world. On January 23, 1860, the two nations signed the Cobden-Chevalier treaty, establishing the principle of free trade between the two nations. This was a major shift for the French. Until this point the nation's industries had been protected by large tariffs to secure them from British competition. Yet Napoleon III believed in free trade, seeing it as a major source of British prosperity, and pushed to adopt it in France. To the political alliance with Britain symbolized by the Crimean War the emperor now added an economic alliance. France, like its great neighbor across the Channel, would now combine economic and political liberty.

The 1860s thus brought a new vision for the Second Empire, one that seemed to be evolving toward full-fledged imperial democracy by the end of the decade. The various liberalization measures undertaken by the emperor did not, however, produce increased popular support for the regime. The economic downturn of the 1860s was one important reason for this. The 1850s had been a boom decade, fueled primarily by railroad expansion and modern banking and credit structures. After 1862, however, the French economy stalled and remained relatively weak for the rest of the decade. The textile industry, still the most important in France, suffered as a result of the American Civil War and the shortage of cotton resulting from the North's blockade of the South. In 1867 the Credit Mobilier, a creation of the Second Empire and one of the leading banks in France, declared bankruptcy, casting the regime's economic policy in doubt.

Economic hard times did not by themselves explain the mounting opposition to the imperial regime, however. The end of the prosperity of the 1850s certainly did not please the bourgeois elites who had constituted the bedrock of the Second Empire, but specific government policies transformed their discontent into anger and even opposition. Most opposed the Cobden-Chevalier treaty, believing that French industry was still too weak to compete with the British on equal terms. Napoleon III's embrace of free trade was unpopular and constituted one of the few periods in the history of modern France that the government abandoned its traditional protectionism. Business elites also looked askance at the emperor's overtures to labor, especially its legalization of unions and strikes, which had been banned since the French Revolution. Those who had supported and benefited from the authoritarian empire found little to admire in its new liberal incarnation.

More surprising, perhaps, was the regime's inability to win the support of the republican and socialist left. For many, Napoleon III's reforms seemed a classic case of too little, too late. Instead of winning over his opponents, the weakening of authoritarian rule seemed only to empower them. Newspapers, such as the *Siècle* and the *Opinion nationale*, took advantage of the new press freedom to publish fierce attacks against the emperor, attacks that would have landed their authors in jail a decade earlier. The relaxation of restrictions on freedom of assembly facilitated the political organization of republican factions throughout France, while the emperor's sponsorship of the worker's delegation in London only nurtured the growth of French socialism. Moreover, the rise of an organized opposition during the liberal empire coincided with and contributed to a decline of imperial patronage politics at the local level, practices that had always undergirded the regime's mass base. The republican inroads into small town and rural life that had begun during the Second Republic had been forced underground during the authoritarian empire but could now resurface. Provincial mayors, a bedrock of imperial rule, found themselves increasingly challenged and often defeated by opposition candidates. Wealthy republicans used their money to mount extravagant campaigns for office, in the process creating a republican political culture throughout France.

The 1863 parliamentary elections graphically demonstrated the failure of liberal reform to mollify the opposition and win the support of the French people. In spite of the best efforts of the Duc de Persigny, the emperor's minister of the interior and right-hand man, the opposition more than doubled its vote total from the last election, winning over 2 million votes. The vote against the empire was particularly strong in Paris and other urban areas, but also notable in those areas of the center and southeast that had opposed Louis Napoleon's coup d'état in 1851. Only in the west did the empire maintain and improve its support. The elections underscored a geographical dividing line, between the liberal northeast and the conservative southwest, that would dominate French politics for generations to come.

Persigny and others viewed the election results as proof that liberalization had failed and sought to persuade the emperor to return to authoritarianism. Instead, Napoleon III chose to continue and intensify the shift to liberal empire. From 1864 to 1868 the emperor gave more freedom to the press, to political and workers' organizations, and to the legislature. These measures only increased the strength of the opposition, which won over 3 million votes in the elections of 1869, some 45 percent of the total vote. The fact that Napoleon III did not renounce the liberal experiment at this point underscores its importance to him on principle rather than grounds of expediency. In January 1870 he responded to the election results by approaching a leader of the moderate republican opposition, Emile Ollivier, to form a government and draft a new constitution. This move appealed to many liberal republicans, both as a sign of conciliation from the emperor and as a means of preventing the further growth of the republican and socialist extreme left. Napoleon III charged Ollivier's government with drafting a new, more liberal constitution. In a few months it produced a draft that outlined a full-fledged constitutional empire. To strengthen his position vis-à-vis the opposition, he staged the last plebiscite of his regime in May 1870, calling on the people of France to declare whether or not they approved the proposed constitution. Over 80 percent of the electorate voted yes, a result the emperor interpreted as a validation of his policies and the idea of liberal empire. It seemed that the gamble on liberalization had paid off after all.

This proved to be an illusion; a few months later the Second Empire lay in shambles. Whatever its domestic successes, like the First Empire the fate of the regime was determined by events abroad. Setting a pattern that would also characterize the Third Republic and Fourth Republic that followed, the Second Empire collapsed as a result of military defeat. As Napoleon III would discover to his sorrow, an emperor who could not win battles would not long remain an emperor.

THE FRANCO-PRUSSIAN WAR
AND THE FALL OF THE EMPIRE

As we have seen, the liberal face of the Second Empire dated from the beginning of the regime. Liberalization after 1860 produced some echoes overseas, especially in the colonies. The emperor's call for an "Arab empire" in Algeria certainly reflected this liberal tone. In the French Caribbean, wealthy men of color used the new political climate to press their demands for political inclusion against the hegemony of the *békés*. Yet for the most part attempts to liberalize colonial rule came to naught, frustrated by local white populations as well as the designs of the empire itself. In 1865 the emperor granted all Algerians French nationality but not citizenship, which they could only acquire by renouncing Muslim law and thus effectively abandoning Islam. This underscored the idea of French law, and French nature in general, as universal, something that other peoples must embrace to be civilized. In the Caribbean, political opportunity remained largely closed to the nonwhite elite, not to mention the black majority. In the last analysis, liberalization meant little to the residents of the French colonies in the 1860s.

France's foreign policy, its relations with other nations in Europe and overseas, took a decided turn for the worse in the 1860s, one that ultimately proved fatal. During the 1850s the Second Empire had scored two major successes, in the Crimean War and in Italy. A decade later, by way of contrast, it seemed to go from one disaster to another. French colonial adventurism, such as the conquests in Southeast Asia and an 1860 expedition to Syria, raised the suspicions of the British and helped cool relations with London in spite of the Cobden-Chevalier treaty. The disastrous misadventure in Mexico made the regime look authoritarian, opportunistic, and incompetent to both its domestic critics and its European neighbors. By the latter half of the decade Napoleon III had squandered much of the respect his regime once enjoyed in foreign capitals.

The last years of the Second Empire were dominated by its increasingly tense relations with Prussia. Faced with Bismarck's iron determination to unify Germany under the leadership of the Prussian monarchy, French diplomacy proved hesitant and inept. Far from realizing the threat posed to French interests by an increasingly powerful Prussia, Napoleon III helped arrange a treaty between Berlin and the new Italian state in 1866. When Prussia went to war with Austria that same year, this alliance helped defeat the Austrians (winning for the Italians the prize of Venetia). France, like much of the rest of Europe, had underestimated Prussia's military strength, expecting a long war that it could ultimately help resolve through diplomatic mediation. Instead, the Prussians defeated Austria and their south German allies in seven short weeks during June and July, leaving the French emperor powerless to influence events. The French did demand Prussian support for their plans to annex Belgium and Luxembourg, a request that would later come back to haunt them. But they had no power to enforce such a demand, and Bismarck refused.

All in all, the Austro-Prussian war was a humiliation for the Second Empire, and the desire to overcome this embarrassment as well as attacks by the opposition partly explains the emperor's decision to further liberalize his empire. Some in France, notably the prominent opposition leader Adolphe Thiers, warned that the Prussian threat needed to be taken seriously. Yet the regime seemed incapable of contending with the new political and military situation in central Europe. Napoleon III suffered from poor health during the last few years of his reign, accentuating his tendency toward lassitude and indecision. Hopes for alliances with Italy and Austria-Hungary went nowhere, so that by the end of the 1860s France could scarcely claim a leading role in European diplomacy, becoming more isolated than ever.

Such was the state of affairs when a new diplomatic crisis erupted in July 1870. Two years earlier the queen of Spain had been overthrown, leaving the Spanish throne vacant. One of the candidates considered for the position was Prince Leopold of the Prussian royal family, the Hohenzollerns. The French reacted with fury to the prospect of Leopold becoming king of Spain, fearing that France would then be surrounded by Prussian rulers. Egged on by the Spanish-born empress, Napoleon III's government demanded the retraction of Leopold's candidacy, threatening to declare war if it did not receive satisfaction. The Prussians soon complied, persuaded by the opposition of the other major European powers. This was not enough for the emperor, however. He sent his foreign minister, the Duc de Gramont, to negotiate with the Prussian king, William I. During their meeting in the Rhineland town of Ems, Gramont demanded that the Prussians renounce all designs on the Spanish throne. The king then sent Bismarck a telegram describing the encounter. Bismarck, however, changed the wording of what became known as the Ems dispatch, making the tone of the meeting seem much harsher than it was and strongly implying that each side had insulted the other. Predictably, this caused outrage in both France and Prussia. Reluctantly, because he felt he had no choice if he wanted to preserve French national honor, on July 19, 1870 Napoleon III declared war. The Franco-Prussian War was on.

As both the emperor and Prime Minister Ollivier were painfully aware, France was in no shape for such a contest. The nation did have some advantages. The standard army rifle, the *chassepot*, was superior to Prussian firearms, and the French had begun introducing a weapon that would play a great role in the twentieth century: the machine gun. Yet the Prussians had better artillery. More importantly, along with their south German allies they were able to field a much larger army, 500,000 against barely 250,000 for the French side. Moreover, Prussian army officers were generally better trained and more competent, in contrast to French officers who often received promotions thanks to their wealth and family connections. In addition, France found itself diplomatically isolated in 1870. Bismarck had cleverly negotiated agreements with Austria, Russia, and Italy to ensure that they did not intervene in a war with France. He also conveyed to the British the emperor's 1866 note about annexing Belgium and Luxembourg; given that Britain had always insisted on preserving the neutrality of the Low Countries, this was enough to ensure France would receive no aid from London. The Second Empire thus entered the war against Prussia unprepared and alone.

The result was an unmitigated disaster. Cursed with an antiquated, chaotic mobilization system, the French were still pulling their armies together when the first German troops crossed the frontier into France. The French scored some initial successes, managing to occupy the Rhenish city of Saarbrücken on August 2. This proved their only victory of the war, pinning them down in a relatively unimportant military sector while General Von Moltke's massive armies moved rapidly to the front. In quick succession the French lost the battles of Wissembourg, Spicheren, and Froeschwiller in the first week of August, forcing them to abandon the province of Alsace to the enemy. By August 16 the Prussians had surrounded one of the two main French armies, led by General Bazaine, in the old fortress town of Metz, in Lorraine. This prompted the fall of Ollivier's government, abetted by the empress. French commanders then sent their remaining army, led by General MacMahon, to rescue Bazaine's forces, hoping to break the Prussian siege of Metz.

This was the final error, not just for the empire but for the emperor personally. Hoping to invoke the inspirational leadership of his famous uncle, Napoleon III had elected to accompany his forces into battle, the last French national leader to do so. Leaving Paris on July 28, the emperor was in such pain he could barely ride his horse, a pathetic postscript to the glory of the Napoleonic legend.

He accompanied (rather than "led") MacMahon's forces on their ill-fated show-down with the Prussians. Unfortunately, the faster Prussian armies soon caught up with the French and forced them into a confrontation in the city of Sedan on August 31. The next day, the Prussians crushed the French armies in the battle of Sedan, taking over 100,000 prisoners. Among these was Napoleon III himself, who was deprived of his hopes for a glorious death in battle. So fell the last emperor of the French, not with a bang but a whimper.

The news of this military disaster caused a political earthquake in France. Public opinion had been divided over the war. In contrast to the general political pattern—the empire being strongest in the countryside and weakest in the cities—Parisians and other urbanites generally cheered the onset of war, whereas peasants were less enthusiastic. Paris in particular displayed a flamboyant level of war fever: crowds marched along the boulevards singing the (until recently banned) "Marseillaise" and cheering on soldiers in uniform. In the countryside, by contrast, peasants (who were more likely to be drafted because they were in better health) feared the impact of war. As Capt. Claude Lombard noted on the eve of battle:

> What a calamity war is! What end will it serve? May God protect us! How my poor wife will suffer! How many cruel moments will she have to endure! Who knows if I'll return? What then will be her destiny? May God give her the strength to stand this absence which, alas, may be very long, and may He protect her, as well as our child, my father, my godparents, all those who are dear to me and will suffer more than me from this war.[5]

This split between city and country would soon play out in a dramatic fashion. The news of the defeat at Sedan and the emperor's imprisonment reached Paris on the evening of September 3. Lyon and Marseilles had already risen up in insurrection the day before, proclaiming the overthrow of the regime. The new hard-line prime minister, Comte de Palikao, summoned the legislature to a midnight meeting, where he tried to win support for an interim government. Many members, even republicans, were willing to cooperate, but it was too late to save the empire. The next morning ordinary Parisians heard the news and immediately took to the streets. Huge crowds marched to the Palais Bourbon, the seat of the legislature, invading the session and boisterously demanding the deposition of the emperor and the proclamation of a republic. Led by radical republican leaders, notably the lawyer and political activist Léon Gambetta, the crowd then marched to the Hôtel de Ville and proclaimed the republic, like their forebears in 1830 and 1848. No one lifted a finger to save regime, which simply disappeared into history. Empress Eugénie fled to Britain, soon to be joined there in exile by her husband. France's Third Republic was born on September 4, 1870, but no one had a clear idea of what this political change would bring. Facing the prospect of a Prussian invasion, its future seemed far from certain.

The regime of Napoleon III ended badly, yet the emperor's eighteen-year reign transformed France in many important ways. Both the economic expansion and the political mobilization of the era knit the nation more closely together than ever before. Thanks to the railways in particular, France became a unified economic and consumer market, and both the political organization of the empire and the mobilization of those who opposed it made women and men throughout the country more conscious of being one nation and one people. The very idea of France as a nation-state, as a nation united by law, politics, and culture, became a concrete reality under the Second Empire.

This is of course deeply ironic, and fully in keeping with the paradoxical character of the regime. Historians of modern Europe have generally viewed empires and nation-states as mutually opposed to each other, the former generally giving way to the latter. The French case, in which the nation's last empire gave way to a series of republics, would at first glance seem to support this. The Second Empire, however, contained many traits, notably universal manhood suffrage, inherited by the Third Republic. More notably, France's last formal empire gave way to a republic that undertook the greatest imperial expansion in the nation's history. Although Napoleon III was France's last emperor, the theme of empire would remain central to modern French history.

It is also ironic, and very much in keeping with a central theme of this book, that French national identity owed so much to a man who lived much of life abroad, spoke French with an accent, and saw a global vision as key to the success of his regime. Napoleon III seemed a hybrid between the traditional antinational cosmopolitanism of the monarchy and the nationalism of the republican leaders who would succeed him. As such, he exemplified the idea of universal nationalism that had become part of the French character. Under his leadership, France could and should continue to be a light to all nations. In large part, his regime ultimately failed because it could no longer lead by example and found itself outstripped by other European nations.

At the same time, however, the Second Empire was instrumental in fostering the growth of another aspect of French universal nationalism: the rise of French culture. During the reign of Napoleon III France became a symbol of avant-garde art and thought, of modernity in general. Paris became a world capital during those years, the symbol of all that was new and daring in the world. In many ways the invention of modern Paris was the Second Empire's greatest legacy, a story to which we now turn.

Suggestions for Further Reading

Bierman, John. *Napoleon the Third and His Carnival Empire*. New York: St Martin's, 1988.

Cunningham, Michele. *Mexico and the Foreign Policy of Napoleon III*. New York: Palgrave, 2001.

Dehan, Thierry, and Sandrine Sénéchal. *Les français sous le Second Empire*. Paris: Éditions Privat, 2006.

Hazareesingh, Sudhir. *From Subject to Citizen: The Second Empire and the Emergence of Modern French Democracy*. Princeton, NJ: Princeton University Press, 1998.

Howard, Michael. *The Franco-Prussian War: The German Invasion of France, 1870–1871*. New York: Routledge, 2001.

Lecaillon, Jean-François. *Été 1870: La guerre racontée par les soldats*. Paris: Bernard Giovanangeli, 2002.

McMillan, James F. *Napoleon III*. New York: Longman, 1991.

Plessis, Alain. *The Rise and Fall of the Second Empire, 1852–1871*. Cambridge: Cambridge University Press, 1985.

Zeldin, Theodore. *The Political System of Napoleon III*. New York: Norton, 1971.

Notes

1. John Bierman, *Napoleon the Third and His Carnival Empire* (New York: St Martin's, 1988), p. 134.
2. Thierry Dehan and Sandrine Sénéchal, *Les français sous le Second Empire* (Paris: Éditions Privat, 2006), p. 140.
3. Benjamin Stora, *Algeria, 1830–2000: A Short History* (Ithaca, NY: Cornell University Press, 2001), 5.
4. John Merriman, *A History of Modern Europe: Volume 2, From the French Revolution to the Present* (New York: Norton, 1996), 834.
5. Jean-François Lecaillon, *Été 1870: La guerre racontée par les soldats* (Paris: Bernard Giovanangeli, 2002), 15.

four

PARIS: THE MAKING
OF A WORLD CAPITAL

DURING THE SECOND HALF OF THE NINETEENTH CENTURY PARIS became no longer just the capital of France and one of Europe's greatest cities but a global symbol of the modern age. In some ways this heightened international presence seems ironic. Other major cities like New York, Berlin, and Tokyo had or would soon surpass it in population size, while at the same time French politics depended less on events in the capital than during the era of the Revolution, as the suppression of the Paris commune by national troops based in Versailles would make graphically clear. Nineteenth-century Paris was no longer the biggest city in Europe, just as France was no longer the biggest country.

But Paris more than made up for its relative loss of population with increased cultural prominence, even brilliance. More than ever before, people throughout the world looked to the French capital as the ultimate arbiter of all that was new and daring. Paris became the world's city of fashion, not just in clothing but also architecture, ideas, and the arts. At the same time, the most powerful imagery associated with the city, ranging from the broad new boulevards to impressionism and the Eiffel tower, originated during these years. Thanks to its artists, writers, intellectuals, and architects, Paris the modern city became familiar to millions of people

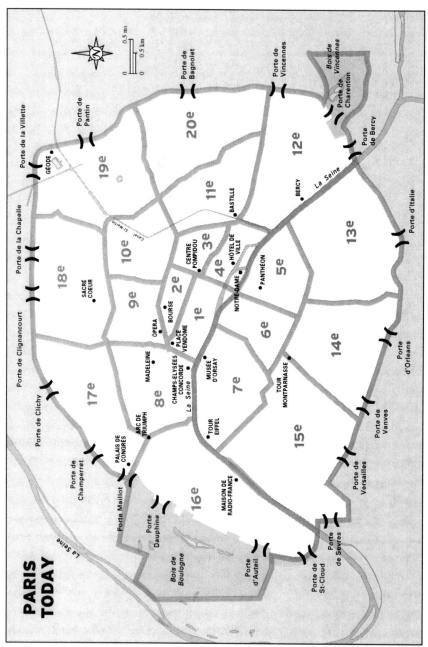

Map 4.1. Paris today.

throughout the world who had never set foot there; as an Italian noted in the 1870s, "one never sees Paris for the first time; one alwa, s sees it again."[1]

The fifty years that spanned the Second Empire and the first half of the Third Republic thus witnessed the emergence of modern Paris as one of the world's great capital cities, a symbol of both French greatness and global modernity. Combining these two roles, it became a powerful symbol and vector of universal nationalism in modern France, a city that welcomed outsiders from near and far, drawing on their talents while at the same time integrating them into local communities and cultures. Paris displayed French culture as both rooted in the national experience and shaped by influences and individuals from many different lands. At the same time, the city's powerful cultural impact gave global modernism a distinctly French cast. In the late nineteenth century to be a Parisian, especially a Parisian artist or intellectual, was to be a citizen of both the nation and the world.

THE RISE OF WORLD CITIES

During the second half of the nineteenth century levels and rates of urbanization increased on a global scale. A few of the largest urban areas, such as London, New York, and Tokyo, became so large and influential that they functioned as world cities. Peter Hall has defined world cities as those that play a leading role, at both national and international levels, in a wide variety of fields, including politics and government, trade and finance, media and information, education and the arts, and conspicuous consumption. While sheer size is important, world cities are above all global centers of power and influence.

World cities can only exist in a united world, which came into being between 1850 and 1900. Technological achievements, like the advent of transatlantic steamship travel in the 1830s, the invention of the telegraph in the 1840s, and the beginning of telephone service in the 1870s, all helped make the world a smaller place. The tremendous expansion of capital during the early nineteenth century created global markets for trade and investment, so that British stockholders helped finance railroad construction in Argentina and French capital bankrolled economic growth in Russia and the Middle East. The so-called Long Depression, which began in 1873 and lasted on and off until 1896, affected people around the world, confirming the rise of a united global economy. The rise of powerful nation-states, as well as the increasing role of central governments in the daily lives of inhabitants, broke down regional particularism, exposing people throughout the world to broader horizons. The late nineteenth century also witnessed Europe's scramble for empire, bringing most of Asia and Africa under European control and formally binding much of the world together. Finally, the era saw millions of people migrate between regions and continents, especially but not only from Europe to the Americas. As a result of these changes, by 1900 no people on earth lived in isolation from global affairs.

The increasing interconnectedness of the world played a major role in the rise of the great cities. As the functions, such as finance, industry, politics, and communications, that leading urban centers traditionally fulfilled became more and more important on a global scale, so did great cities assume a larger place in modern life. Between 1850 and 1900 the number of European cities with more than 250,000 inhabitants mushroomed from ten to forty-eight. By 1900 London had over 7 million residents, Paris nearly 3 million, and Berlin, Vienna, and Glasgow over 1 million. The rise of megacities was not limited to Europe. Between 1850 and 1900 Calcutta and Cairo more than doubled in size, the former counting over 1 million residents, and newer colonial cities like Sydney and Hong Kong grew even more dramatically. The United States also witnessed rapid urban growth. By 1900 New York had 3.4 million people, while Chicago grew from 100,000 in 1860 to 1.7 million by the turn of the century.

Big cities offered both advantages and disadvantages to those who lived there. Residents of cities like London, Paris, and New York could rightly feel themselves at the heart of things, with privileged access to power and information. The latest fashions, consumer goods, and ideas came to them first. Most great cities were also political capitals (with the signal exception of those in America), and often defined their culture as the culture of the nation. Their sheer size and access to political power also often made them key sites for political movements, most notably the rise of labor movements and the left in the late nineteenth century, but also causes like feminism. At the same time, life was more expensive and frequently more difficult than in smaller cities or the countryside. Public health conditions, notably for the poor, were often terrible, and big cities usually had high mortality rates. The late nineteenth century saw increases in residential class segregation in urban areas, as the affluent sought to distance themselves from the working class and poor. A major reason for this was the fear of crime, a key social concern in big cities in particular. Increasingly, social analysts viewed crime as rooted in poverty, which seemed more extreme in cities not so much because urbanites had less money than peasants (they usually had more) but because the contrast between wealth and poverty was so much more immediate and obvious there. In short, those who lived in the world's great cities experienced the extremes of modern life, either for good or for ill.

Finally, great cities, and above all capital cities, provided the crucial nexus between the nation and the world as a whole. Not only were national capitals full of foreign embassies and diplomats, but they also tended to have exceptionally diverse populations, including immigrants from other countries. At the same time foreign images of a given nation frequently focused on its largest and most prominent city as the prime example. Capital cities often showcased the culture and achievements of the nation as a whole with impressive government buildings, national museums, and monuments. These were meant to impress not only the nation's citizenry but also visitors from other countries.

Paris had become a great city as the capital and largest urban center of France. During the late nineteenth century, however, it developed a new profile as a symbol of urban modernity. In its role as the prototypical world capital, Paris blended characteristics of modern great cities with the specific character of French culture, and a key aspect of that culture was its universalist vision. The fact that people looked to the French capital for all that was new and fashionable arose from the idea of France as a universal nation and reinforced it.

THE HAUSSMANNIZATION OF PARIS

Athough in 1850 Paris was one of Europe's greatest cities, and the capital of one of the world's leading nations, its inhabitants lived in conditions often little improved from those of the Middle Ages. Whereas the city had doubled in population since the French Revolution, physically it hadn't grown for centuries. The central neighborhoods of the Right Bank had some of the highest urban densities in the world, as newcomers crammed into ever-smaller spaces. For all its monuments, the legacy of previous regimes, dreary tenements dominated the cityscape of the French capital, buildings five or more stories high on narrow streets often delineated by gutters instead of sidewalks. The Ile de la Cité, the island heart of the city and the site of Notre Dame, had degenerated into a dismal slum with 14,000 people living in squalor. Paris lacked adequate sewage and drinking water systems, so the Seine often served as both, with terrible consequences for public health. France's biggest city and in many ways a symbol of national glory, Paris also had the nation's highest mortality rate. In the 1830s and 1840s two major cholera epidemics killed tens of thousands of Parisians, focusing public attention on the city's toxic health conditions and dilapidated state in general.

Renovating the French capital became a major concern of Napoleon III, and ultimately his most successful and enduring endeavor. Inspired by the Roman emperor Caesar Augustus, who boasted of having found Rome a city of wood and left it one of marble, Napoleon III undertook the biggest urban renewal project in Parisian history. Paris would become the symbol of French grandeur, an example of beauty and majesty to dazzle the world. To implement these visions of urban greatness the emperor chose Baron Georges Haussmann, an Alsatian Protestant trained as a civil engineer. In 1853 Napoleon III appointed Haussmann the prefect of the Department of the Seine, making him in effect master of the French capital. Haussmann used his authority to remake Paris massively, transforming it into the modern urban jewel we know to this day.

Haussmann modernized the city by addressing both seen and unseen dimensions of urban life. The process we know as Haussmannization is famous above all for its boulevards, broad avenues that not only improved traffic circulation but also gave the French capital striking views and a sense of monumentality. Haussmann did not invent the Parisian boulevard. The most famous of them all, the Champs-Elysées, had achieved prominence by the end of the eighteenth century. But the prefect did make them much more common, widening and lengthening streets like the Rue de Rivoli, the Boulevard de Sébastopol, and the Rue Lafayette on the Right Bank, and the Boulevard Saint-Germain and the Boulevard Arago on the Left Bank. The modernization of the city's streets was so extensive that according to Haussmann the average width of city streets in central Paris in 1869 was twice what it had been in 1852.[2]

This helped ease traffic flow in the city, but the modernization of the street network, like much of Haussman's work, also had an important aesthetic and social dimension. Many of the boulevards were designed or redesigned to end at major monuments, offering Parisians and visitors a series of impressive visual displays. Haussmann began the work (completed under the Third Republic) of opening up the Avenue de l'Opéra to lead to one of the Second Empire's most impressive new buildings, architect Charles Garnier's Paris Opera house. The brand new boulevards de Sébastopol and Strasbourg ran straight from the Seine at the Place du Chatelet to the Gare de l'Est, one of the city's main railway stations, providing a striking urban vista. Haussmann had the new boulevards lined with apartment buildings of six to eight stories.

Generally designed for bourgeois residents, they conformed to height and size regulations, thus giving the city's streetscapes a uniform appearance that characterizes Paris to this day.

If Haussmann's street renovations provided new housing for the affluent, they often proved disastrous for working-class and poor Parisians. The new and renovated boulevards often cut through crowded popular areas, wiping out ancient streets and displacing their inhabitants. The prefect destroyed most of the slum housing on the Ile de la Cité, replacing it with sterile government buildings. All told some 350,000 Parisians, mostly lower income, were displaced by Haussmannization, which destroyed entire neighborhoods and the rich local cultures that had shaped them.[3] The renovations of Paris under the Second Empire permanently reclaimed the city center for the affluent, forcing those of modest means into peripheral areas and ultimately out of the city.

This massive displacement had an important political dimension. Haussmannization destroyed or reduced many neighborhoods that had been the centers of working-class insurrection from 1789 to 1848. Many of the new streets were designed to encircle and thus control revolutionary areas, like the Faubourg Saint-Antoine now surrounded by the boulevards Voltaire and Diderot. Moreover, the width of the new streets made it difficult for insurgents to block them with barricades. Haussmann hoped that the new streetscape would not only facilitate circulation in the city but also render it riot proof. As we will see, these hopes were not realistic in the short term, but they did provide another rationale for the beautiful new boulevards of the French capital.

In addition to building impressive new streets, Haussmann modernized unseen Paris. The prefect built a massive new sewer system to dispose of the city's waste and make it a healthier place to live. By the end of the Second Empire almost all streets in Paris had their own drains, which channeled waste water well away from the city. As Edwin Chadwick, British public health crusader, commented to Napoleon III, "May it be said of you that you found Paris stinking and left it sweet."[4] By dumping the city's waste several miles downstream, a curse for residents of those suburban communities, Haussmann made the Seine in Paris once again an attractive natural resource. He also constructed several new aqueducts to bring fresh water from the surrounding countryside to the capital, and the new buildings on the boulevards usually had their own plumbing systems. By the beginning of the 1870s the majority of Parisian apartments had running water, bad news for the porters who once carried fresh water up several flights of stairs to private domiciles.

Haussmann's vast expansion of the city's park system combined beauty and salubrity. In 1850 Paris had few public green spaces, and as the city's population grew, this also posed problems for public health. Napoleon III had been very impressed with London's Hyde Park during his British exile, and he and Haussmann decided that Paris needed more parks along the lines of English romantic gardens, in contrast to the formal French style typified by Versailles. Haussmann created what remain the two biggest parks in the French capital, the Bois de Boulogne in the west and the Bois de Vincennes in the east. In addition he took an abandoned tract of land, formerly the site of public executions, in northeastern Paris and transformed it into the Buttes-Chaumont Park, one of the most beautiful green spaces in the city. The change was dramatic: in 1850 Paris had less than 50 acres of public parkland; by 1870 it had over 4,500.

The city that Haussmann transformed grew dramatically under the Second Empire. Provincial migrants had a long tradition of coming to Paris in search of work, especially during the summer construction season. Haussmann's public works projects, employing thousands of laborers, vastly increased the city's allure. The provincial *départements* near the capital experienced a major exodus of workers; as one administrator in the Seine-et-Marne noted, "The extraordinary stimulus given to buildings by the creation of immense projects in the center of Paris has depopulated the countryside."[5] The dynamism of modernizing Paris made it more attractive than ever to provincial migrants and confirmed its status as the leading city of France.

Paris also grew by expanding its municipal boundaries and annexing neighboring suburban communities. As Haussmannization depopulated the central slums of the city, new migrants tended to settle in the areas between the city limits and the Paris fortifications. Innovations in public transport, notably the creation of a unified city bus network in 1854 and the beginnings of a streetcar, or tramway, system the same year, began to break down the classic localism of Parisians and facilitate commuting between peripheral neighborhoods and the city center. As a result, communities like Belleville, Vaugirard, and most famously Montmartre saw their populations expand by leaps and bounds during the 1850s, so that by the end of the decade many had populations larger than most provincial capitals.[6] Consequently, in 1859 Napoleon III's government decided to annex these areas, expanding the boundaries of the French capital to their present-day limits. Since taxes were lower in the suburbs than in the city some commercial interests objected, but in general the move proved very popular, officially going into effect on January 1, 1860. The annexations doubled the surface area of Paris and increased its population to over 1.6 million inhabitants. Napoleon III also divided the city administration into its current twenty *arrondissements*, or districts. Integrating the new areas, many of which retained the character of provincial villages, took time and money, but the annexations ensured that Paris would remain one of the biggest and greatest cities in Europe, if not the world.

To achieve his ends Haussmann often ran roughshod over local and political opposition, and his methods of financing this massive project seemed questionable to many. As a result, political opponents forced the emperor to call for his resignation, and he left office in January 1870, only a few months before the collapse of the regime he had served so well. Yet Haussmann's work outlived the Second Empire, becoming not only its greatest legacy to the future of France but also the defining moment for the emergence of Paris as a world city. The influence of Haussmannization spread far and wide beyond the nation's borders. The prefect's great boulevards inspired imitators from Mexico City, where Emperor Maximilian designed the Paseo de la Reforma in clear imitation of the Champs-Elysées, to Chicago's great boulevard, Michigan Avenue. Belgian leaders redesigned Brussels in the 1860s and 1870s along similar lines, and the City Beautiful movement in the United States drew inspiration from Haussmann's attention to urban parks. In short, the classic themes of Haussmannization, including broad, majestic boulevards, modern sewer and water systems, and abundant green space, became the signature of progressive urbanism throughout the world, and Paris the ultimate example of the modern world city.

The French capital's global prominence after the middle of the nineteenth century rested on more than beautiful boulevards and parks, however. Cultures of modernity, reflected not only in Haussmann-style architecture but also philosophy, literature, and the visual arts, made Paris the world's center of modernity during the second half of the century. Many of the images that continue to shape contemporary views of the City of Light, such as impressionist painting, date from these years. Haussmann may have made Paris beautiful, but its artists and intellectuals made it modern. Together they transformed the French capital into a place that many from near and far regarded as the greatest city in the world.

PARIS AND THE CULTURES OF MODERNITY

The link between cultural modernity and entertainment that distinguished Paris during the modern era had first become noticeable under the July Monarchy. As noted in Chapter 2, the rise of bohemian subcultures in the French capital and the cultural sway of romanticism during the 1840s had given the city a reputation for fashion and good times that reached far beyond the nation's borders. This trend continued during the late nineteenth century, but with some important differences. Not only had Haussmannization and the annexation of the suburbs made Paris bigger and more modern than it was during the July Monarchy, but the increased globalization of French society, evident in transportation, finance, and imperial expansion, gave the modernist cultures of Paris a much greater impact. Artistic and intellectual innovations in the French capital influenced writers, painters, and thinkers in many different lands, making Paris the world capital of modernity during the late nineteenth century.

A crucial dimension of this new modernist culture was a shift toward realism in the arts and social sciences. By the 1850s the romanticism of the July Monarchy had become passé, and many now looked to the sciences for intellectual inspiration. French scientific research scored major triumphs during these years, although French scientists began to lag behind their German colleagues, who had access to better universities and laboratories. Still, the French could point to the achievements of men like Louis Pasteur, whose innovations in germ theory revolutionized biology. The achievements of modern science, both in France and abroad, inspired the philosophy of positivism, which would have a major impact on French intellectuals. Developed by the philosopher August Comte during the July Monarchy, positivism argued that scientific rationalism should be applied to the study of humanity as well. A frontal attack on religion and metaphysics, positivism not only played a key role in the development of modern social science but also attracted writers and artists searching for new ways to understand the human experience.

In literature, the romanticism of writers like Victor Hugo had been challenged as early as the 1830s by the realism of Honoré de Balzac. By the 1850s realism had come to dominate French creative writing. In 1857 Gustave Flaubert published *Madame Bovary*, a study of a bored provincial housewife who dreamed of Paris and rebelled against the strictures of her narrow life by having adulterous affairs before eventually committing suicide. The novel's realism and amorality won it the condemnation of much of Parisian society and an attempt to ban it by the French courts. The same year poet Charles Baudelaire published *Les Fleurs du mal* (*The Flowers of Evil*), a dark meditation on the superficiality of modern urban society. Baudelaire, who coined the term "modernity," viewed urban life as sexually degraded and evil, and his graphic descriptions also provoked the outrage of polite society.

During the 1860s a new, scientifically oriented version of literary realism arose in France. Known as naturalism, it emphasized the objective portrayal of social conditions. Its champion was Emile Zola, who based his massive novels in the Rougon-Macquart series tracing the history of one large extended family based on extensive research into social conditions. Zola spent months in coal mining communities researching his great novel of a mining disaster in northern France, *Germinal*. Scientific theory also played an important role in naturalist literature. Naturalist writers viewed life as shaped by factors like heredity and social conditions far beyond the individual's control, a generally bleak assessment of the human condition.

Realism also had a major impact on the visual arts in mid-nineteenth-century France. French inventors Joseph Niépce and Louis Daguerre had invented photography in the 1820s and 1830s. Its popularization by the advent of the Second Empire inspired many artists to strive for exact representation of human subjects, rejecting the idealism of romanticism. In the 1850s, the Barbizon painters, who were based in a village of the same name near Paris, created realistic portrayals of rural life. The leader of the realist school of painting, Gustave Courbet, emphasized painting people as they were, not as they were supposed to be. In paintings like *Burial at Ornans* (1850) and *The Stone Breakers* (1849) he depicted the daily lives of ordinary people, not religious figures, eminent individuals, or historical subjects.

Important as the realist school of painting was, it paled in importance to the revolutionary impact of the artistic movement that followed it. The birth of impressionism in 1860s Paris signaled the advent of modern painting, as well as the modern era in general. Although the term "impressionism" did not come into existence until the 1870s (and even then many leaders of the movement rejected it) as an artistic school it began to coalesce in the last decade of the Second Empire, led by a few seminal artists. Like their realist predecessors, the impressionists rejected an emphasis on classical and romantic themes, preferring instead to represent modern life with all its warts and imperfections. They differed sharply, however, in their opinion of what constituted reality. Abjuring a positivist, objective approach to daily life, they insisted instead on the importance of momentary impressions and feelings in structuring how the artist, and people in general, perceived the world. Moreover, in contrast to the dark tones and traditional representational styles of an artist like Courbet, the impressionists gloried in bright colors and a more abstract approach. Their emphasis on inner feeling and subjectivity in particular heralded the birth of modern art.

The world first learned of the impressionist movement in 1863, at the annual Paris Salon. The salon, originally created in the seventeenth century, was the nation's most prestigious art exhibition. To be chosen to exhibit there was to win recognition as a leading French artist. By the mid-nineteenth century the salon had become known for aesthetic conservatism, its judges and juries favoring conventional, academic works. A scandal erupted in 1863 when the judges rejected paintings by several artists, including Edouard Manet, Paul Cezanne, and Camille Pissarro, who would come to be identified with the new movement. Many in the art world reacted furiously, and to appease the critics Napoleon III allowed those who had been turned down to organize their own exhibit, the Salon des Refusés, so that the public could judge for itself.

￩ This Salon of Rejects became in effect the first modern art exhibit, and with it impressionism was born. During the 1860s the major artists of the school, including Manet, Pierre Auguste Renoir, Claude Monet, Berthe Morisot, Paul Cezanne, Camille Pissarro, and Edgar Degas, came to know each other, to work and paint together, and to develop a common (if not identical) aesthetic. They did not hold their first formal exhibit until 1874, but impressionism had already become a coherent, revolutionary aesthetic movement in the waning years of the Second Empire.

The writers and artists of midcentury Paris produced works that helped shape the idea of modernity as a global phenomenon, and their ideas attracted fans and imitators around the world. But global influence flowed two ways, and Parisian avant-garde art and literature drew on influences from abroad. For example, the painting of Dutch artists Rembrandt and Frans Hals had a major impact on Edouard Manet. Foreign artists, like James McNeil Whistler and Vincent van Gogh, made important contributions to the impressionist movement. One of the key influences on impressionism was *japonisme*, the vogue for Japanese art and culture that swept midcentury France. Many impressionist painters admired and found inspiration in the *ukiyo-e*, or woodblock prints of Japanese artists. In 1887, for example, Vincent van Gogh painted *The Blooming Plum Tree*, which drew heavily on the style of Hiroshige. Intellectual and literary realism also developed in dialogue with foreign influences. Comte's positivism attracted a number of followers in England, notably George Eliot, and literary realism was heavily influenced by the great Russian novelists of the nineteenth century, in particular Dostoevsky.

While they had an important global dimension, the new art and literature were also intensely Parisian. Emile Zola wrote several novels about

Paris, notably *L'Assommoir* (1877), which graphically portray
of the city's periphery. The impressionists became famous f
ings of the French capital, including Gustave Caillebotte's *Paris, Rainy Day*
(1877) and Camille Pissarro's *Boulevard Montmartre* (1897). In their work
they portrayed Paris in all its diversity, from Caillebotte's self-assured bourgeois strolling down Haussmannized boulevards to Edgar Degas's ballet
dancers and barflies, to Manet's suburban rag pickers. Parisian artists and
writers not only viewed but also made their city the world's great symbol of
the modern age.

The modernist art of Second Empire Paris illustrated and exemplified the
tensions that would soon explode in revolution. While many artists and writers
sympathized with the republican left and criticized the new bourgeois paradise that Napoleon III and Haussmann had wrought, they also depended
on a bourgeois and aristocratic clientele to support their work. During the
Second Empire Napoleon III had built on the image of Paris as the capital of
gaiety, fashion, and pleasure inherited from the July Monarchy. Exemplified by
the operettas of Jacques Offenbach, life in Paris was lighthearted, amorous,
and luxurious, and Haussmann's elegant new boulevards and townhouses only
added to its glamour. But there was another side of Paris, one shut out from
the sparkling brilliance of Second Empire society. In 1870–1871 this Paris
would once again brutally seize center stage, shattering the imperial regime
and showing up the emperor's dream of permanently banning insurrection
from the capital for the illusion it was.

THE FRANCO-PRUSSIAN WAR AND THE SIEGE OF PARIS

As we saw in the preceding chapter, the military disaster at Sedan led Parisians to rise up in revolt, overthrowing the Second Empire and proclaiming a
new republican government. Following the pattern of 1848 rather than 1830,
the initial seizure of power represented the beginning of the revolution, not its
culmination. Neither did the *journée* of September 4, 1870, end the war with
Prussia. With the downfall of the emperor republican politicians in Paris had
hastily organized a government of national defense. Although in effect lead by
Léon Gambetta, deputy from Paris and a leader of the republican left, most
of its members sympathized with the perspective of Adolphe Thiers, a conservative who would famously argue that "the republic must be conservative or it
will not be." On September 6 the government rejected Prussian proposals for
an armistice, vowing to continue the fight. Faced with this intransigence, the

Prussian forces and their German allies continued their invasion of France, unhindered by any effective resistance.

On September 18 they reached Paris, surrounding the fortifications built by Louis Philippe and placing the city under siege. Members of the provisional government fled for the provinces, hoping to organize resistance against the Germans. On October 8 Gambetta dramatically escaped from the capital in a hot air balloon, floating over the German lines and making his way to Tours, where he worked feverishly to reorganize France's army and fight the Prussians. At first the French had some successes, but at the end of October Bazaine's besieged armies in Metz surrendered to the Prussians, enabling Bismarck to redeploy his forces against the capital. This doomed the provisional government's attempts to relieve Paris, as well as the war effort itself.

The siege effectively cut Paris off from the rest of France. As a result, Parisians had to endure the increasing privations that came with German encirclement. Although many wealthy members of the city had fled in advance of the Prussian armies, their places were taken by the suburbanites who left their homes to take shelter behind the city's fortifications. The city soon filled up with soldiers, members of both the national armies and the city's National Guard. As a result, the city's population swelled to over 2 million during the siege, a fact Parisian authorities did not realize for months. This was crucial, because estimates of necessary food supplies proved woefully inadequate. Prussian authorities opted not to bombard the capital on humanitarian grounds, deciding instead to starve it into submission. Parisian authorities had not prepared for this possibility, most believing that the siege would be very brief. Their lack of preparation would have real consequences, military and political.

For the next four months the people of the capital had to tighten their belts dramatically. Meat, a central part of Parisians' diets, became scarce. In mid-October Parisian authorities began rationing. Once most traditional animals, like cows and pigs, had been consumed, people turned to other sources of protein. The Horse Eating Society having proclaimed the benefits of equine flesh, Parisians gobbled up everything from thoroughbred horses to mules. Dogs, cats, and even rats went from being pets and pests to comestibles. Restaurants catering to the wealthy even prepared special dishes using rat meat. When these proved insufficient Parisians set their sights on the last remaining source of meat in the city: the Paris Zoo. Castor and Pollux, two popular elephants, were butchered and eaten, along with antelopes, zebras, and camels. The big cats escaped this fate because they were too dangerous, and zoo officials also spared the monkeys because, thanks to Charles Darwin, they were considered too close to human beings. The meat was sold to butchers and soon appeared in restaurant menus as exotic dishes with names like kangaroo stew and terrine of antelope with truffles.

Food was not the only thing in short supply. The blockade also kept fuel out of the city, and the winter of 1870–1871 was exceptionally cold in Paris. Crowds stole wood from timber yards and then chopped down most of the city's trees for fuel. Trying to keep as much coal gas as possible for heating, city authorities stopped illuminating public lamps, so that the City of Light was no more. Decent clothing, especially for the winter months, was also hard to come by, so that people began making shirts out of newspapers. These privations had a terrible impact on public health, and disease rates skyrocketed under the siege. The *gamins de Paris*, the children of the poor, suffered and died most of all.[7]

The siege placed a particular burden on Parisian women. They did most of the food shopping and had to learn how to make a thin soup feed an entire family. The siege also caused unemployment, and many women lost their jobs, particularly in the garment industry. Men also lost their jobs, but many found paid employment in the National Guard, whose ranks swelled to some 300,000 during the siege. Unemployed unmarried women did not have this option, so they had to get by as best they could. Their experience of desperate poverty, at times approaching starvation, radicalized many Parisian women during the siege, helping prepare the ground for the uprising to follow.

In spite of their increasingly untenable situation, however, the majority of Parisians adamantly refused to yield to the enemy. If anything, the siege heightened the patriotism and war fever of the capital's people, who saw themselves bravely fighting for the entire nation. Many viewed negotiations for anything less than total victory as a betrayal of the people. Working-class Parisians especially felt this way, pointing to the bourgeois who had fled the city in its hour of need. As during the French Revolution, patriotism and social radicalism marched to the same tune. Many members of the government wanted to negotiate a surrender but feared that Parisian workers would respond with insurrection as they had in September. When news of Bazaine's surrender had reached the capital at the end of October, thousands of Parisians had taken to the streets and briefly laid siege to the Hotel de Ville. People remembered the miraculous victories of the *sans-culottes* armies against the Prussians during the Revolution, hoping against hope that the revolutionary patriotism of Paris could once again bring about a miracle.

This hope proved vain. By January 1871 food was running out; in the middle of the month the government decreed a daily portion of 300 grams of bread per adult, and half for children.[8] On January 4 the Prussians began shelling the city several hours each night. While the bombardment failed to break the morale of most Parisians, it did convince their leaders that the end was only a matter of time. Adolphe Thiers and other government leaders had been pursuing secret negotiations with the Prussians for some time, all the while assuring Parisians they would resist to the bitter end. After a final sortie against the Germans failed miserably, with over four thousand French casualties, the French government capitulated at the end of January, agreeing to Bismarck's terms for an armistice. On January 28, after four bitter months, the great siege of Paris ended in defeat.

Parisians reacted with fury to the news of the armistice. The failure of the January 18 sortie had triggered an uprising in Belleville four days later, and the announcement of the armistice confirmed for many working people that their leaders had betrayed them. The publication of the terms of the peace only intensified these feelings. Not only would France have to pay a large wartime indemnity to Germany, but the new German empire would annex the (largely German-speaking) provinces of Alsace and Lorraine. To add insult to injury, Bismarck insisted on the right of German troops to stage a victory march in Paris. If Parisians were indignant at the surrender, the rest of the country, especially the rural districts, rejoiced that the bloodletting had ended. In February the nation held parliamentary elections, marked by low voter turnout, that decisively rejected the republican position and elected a chamber dominated by monarchists. For many Parisians this underscored the ungrateful attitude of the provinces. The new National Assembly chose to meet in Versailles rather than Paris, further convincing many Parisians that even though the siege was over the capital still stood alone.

Further outrages followed in short order. During the siege the government had imposed a moratorium on eviction for nonpayment of rent. Now landlords, many having fled the city during the siege, began demanding back rent, even though the city's economy was in shambles and thousands were unemployed. The National Assembly backed them up, passing a law that required tenants to pay all wartime debts, including rent, in forty-eight hours. Small shopkeepers were ordered to pay outstanding bills immediately. On March 1, the same day the French government ratified the final terms of the peace treaty, the triumphant German armies staged a ceremonial parade through, and symbolic occupation of, the French capital. Thirty thousand soldiers marched under the Arch of Triumph and down the Champs-Elysées under the proud gaze of William II, king of Prussia and newly crowned emperor of Germany. Parisians bitterly watched the humiliating display, hanging black flags from windows and beating up spectators who seemed too friendly toward the enemy troops. For many working-class Parisians, the idea that a national government would allow foreigners to defile its capital called into question its legitimacy.

If anger propelled the people of Paris toward revolution, the weakness of the national government made it possible. The city was still full of hundreds of thousands of National Guard troops, over whom the government in Versailles had no effective control. Most of them came from working-class districts of the city, and precisely for that reason the government had never really trusted them. Accordingly, it provided them with only minimal training and arms, doubtful of their military value but hoping they would keep order in the city. During the siege the National Guardsmen did little beyond serve sentry duty, and during the January sortie only the units from bourgeois districts saw actual combat. Like many other Parisians, the members of the National Guard were outraged by France's surrender to Prussia, reinforced by the decision of the national government to stop paying them after the war had ended. They nonetheless constituted the only armed force in the city, and they reacted to the election of a conservative National Assembly in February by organizing at the *arrondissement* level and forming their own citywide Central Committee. The committee represented a spectrum of political positions, including different socialist organizations, rather than a unified program. Its members shared a sense of outraged patriotism, a hostility to the government now sitting in Versailles, and an increasing sense that Paris might have to go it alone if need be.

This presented the National Assembly with a problem. Its army only had 12,000 soldiers versus a National Guard of hundreds of thousands. Yet unless it could disarm the Parisians, it could not assert its authority over the capital. Attempts to negotiate differences proved fruitless; as one monarchist delegate noted, "We provincials were unable to come to an understanding with the Parisians . . . it seemed as though we did not even speak the same language, and that they were prey to a kind of sickness."[9] Therefore the prime minister, Adolphe Thiers, decided he must take action. A conservative republican who had helped suppress working-class revolts under the July Monarchy, Thiers was adamantly hostile to the Parisian left and concluded that its insubordination could only be met with force. In particular, he worried about the National Guard seizing cannons left behind by the army during the siege and positioning them in working-class districts of the city. Thiers decided to seize the cannons, and his attempt sparked a revolution.

4.1. *Two Members of the Paris Commune at a Barricade atop Montmartre. Source:* copyright ©
BHVP/Boyer/Roger-Viollet/The Image Works. Bibliothèque Historique de la Ville de Paris.

THE PARIS COMMUNE

On March 18, 1871, Adolphe Thiers directed national troops in Paris to com-
mandeer the cannons held by the National Assembly. They immediately ran
into trouble in Montmartre, a solidly leftist working-class neighborhood and
the highest point in the city. Local women intervened to prevent the removal
of the guns, challenging the soldiers to join them instead of fighting them.
Louise Michel, one of the most prominent communard leaders later nicknamed "the Red Virgin," described the scene:

> Montmartre was waking up; the drum was beating. I went with others to
> launch what amounted to an assault on the hilltop. The sun was rising and we
> heard the alarm bell. Our ascent was at the speed of a charge, and we knew
> that at the top was an army poised for battle. We expected to die for liberty.[10]

The troops refused to fire on the women, instead arresting their general
and shooting him a few hours later, thus joining the revolt. Similar actions

took place throughout the city, as National Guardsmen mobilized to support the Paris crowds. By the end of the day Thiers, who had come to Paris to oversee the operation, realized the game was lost and fled with his ministers to the safety of Versailles. That night the National Guard Central Committee occupied the Hotel de Ville, hoisting the red flag from the belfry and proclaiming the triumph of the revolution.

So began the Paris commune, the last of the French capital's great nineteenth-century revolutions. It would go down in history as the first communist uprising, but in reality it was anything but. The name itself referred not to communism but to the municipality of Paris (*commune de Paris*), and the leaders of the movement ranged from moderate republicans to democratic socialists to Marxists and anarchists. Nor did the communards, or *fédérés*, intend to secede from the rest of France. Rather, they hoped their appeals to patriotism and social justice would spark similar risings throughout the country. Insurrections did take place in Marseilles, Lyon, Toulouse, and elsewhere, but they soon collapsed, leaving the capital isolated and alone. The flame of revolution might still burn bright in Paris, but unlike what happened in 1789, 1830, or 1848, it no longer lit a path for the nation to follow.

Undaunted, the communard leaders set out building a revolutionary society in Paris, hoping that the nation and eventually the world would follow its example. The National Assembly decided to withdraw its troops from the capital for the time being, massing its forces at Versailles, and then invading the city and crushing the commune once it had achieved military superiority. This gave revolutionaries breathing space to organize the defense of Paris and create a new society. In order to reorganize society, however, the commune first had to organize itself. This was no easy task in a city whose every neighborhood had a local committee that jealously guarded its own autonomy, not to mention the hundreds of thousands of armed National Guardsmen who refused to follow orders from politicians. A week after seizing power the commune held elections, won overwhelmingly by radical republicans and socialists (in large part because most bourgeois did not vote). The elected delegates composed a Communal Council, the commune's central parliament. To administer public affairs it created a series of commissions, dealing with issues like education, labor, foreign affairs, and justice, headed by an executive commission of seven members. Workers composed the majority of delegates, a first in France if not the world.

From the start the commune saw itself, and was viewed by many in France and abroad, as not just a French movement but a symbol of world revolution.

The Franco-Prussian War had attracted broad international attention. At first, most commentators supported Prussia, thanks to Napoleon III's poor reputation, but then the collapse of the empire and the creation of the Third Republic, as well as Bismarck's harsh peace terms, won the French widespread sympathy abroad.

The commune itself polarized opinion in Europe, as it had in France. Many on the left interpreted "commune" to mean "communist," hailing it as the world's first proletarian seizure of power. Trade unions and socialist parties abroad, notably in Germany, sent fraternal messages of support. The commune was especially important for the socialist First International, founded in London in 1864. Many abroad viewed the commune as a creation of the exiled Karl Marx, although in fact the anarchist followers of Proudhon had greater impact. Both Marxism and anarchism claimed the commune, with Marx writing a key theoretical work about it, *On the Civil War in France*. The Paris commune contributed to the growing split between Marxists and the anarchist followers of Mikhail Bakunin that would destroy the organization by 1876.

If the left embraced the communards, establishment forces viewed them with a horror not matched since the days of the Jacobin republic and the Terror. Political and social elites all over Europe railed against the sinister doings of the communards, widely characterized as murderous anarchists. Many blamed the commune on foreign agitators and the French capital's traditional hospitality toward them. Not only did conservatives push Thiers to invade Paris as quickly as possible, many also called on Bismarck not to do anything to hinder the effort. There was no possibility of that; not only did the Prussian leader say that if the French couldn't suppress the commune Germany would do it for them, he also accelerated the release of French POWs so they could join in the struggle against it. Overseas, American journalists hastened to condemn the commune in the most lurid tones: as the New York *Herald* put it, "Murderers let loose on society could not be worse than the Paris Commune."[11]

The commune embraced a universal vision of its significance. Rejecting the traditional xenophobia of the French left, the commune welcomed foreigners, many of whom took part in its leadership. Gustave Cluseret, a naturalized American, headed the Military Commission, and Leo Frankel, a Hungarian Jew who had headed up the International's German-language section in France, lead the Labor Commission. In debating whether or not it was appropriate to appoint Frankel to such an important position, the communal council enthusiastically decided in the affirmative, noting "We consider that the flag of the Commune is that of the universal republic."[12] The commune's use of the red flag, rather than the tricolor emblem of France, underscored its revolutionary internationalism. Even more than the French Revolution, the Paris commune embraced a vision of revolutionary universalist nationalism, emphasizing that the struggle for social justice had roots in both the nation and the world.

Exercising power for an embattled seventy-three days, the commune had little time to implement its vision of a new society. Yet it did pass several laws that were models of progressive social legislation. In its first day of operation, addressing the issues that provoked the uprising, the council abolished the standing army, "an agent of repression and imperialism," canceled all back rent, and banned eviction for nonpayment of rent. Other important reforms included abolishing night work for bakers, supporting free and mandatory elementary education, and decreeing the separation of church and state. The commune also supported more radical measures, such as sponsoring workers' cooperatives to challenge the capitalist mode of production, and expropriating the factories of those who had fled Paris and allowing their workers to run them.

Women's welfare was a key concern of the communards, and they enacted several measures in favor of gender equality. Thousands of Parisian women participated actively in the work of the commune, and they did not hesitate to voice their demands in the neighborhood meetings that seemed to go on constantly. Not only did the commune legalize divorce, banned in France since 1816, and advocate for girls' education, but it also took measures to employ women, creating workshops to sew uniforms for the National Guard. It also sought to aid working women by organizing day care facilities. Many communard women went further, demanding equal pay for equal work, for example. Drawing on the socialist feminism of the romantic era, the communard leadership viewed gender equality as a key aspect of human liberation, and did more than any previous French government to make it a reality.

These were hard days for Parisians: food was still in short supply, the city had endured a ruinous siege and a hard winter, and the future was by no means certain. It is therefore striking that many accounts of the commune emphasize the festive air that seemed to pervade the capital, the sense of joy at the prospect of building a new world. As Gustave Courbet, an enthusiastic communard and member of the Arts Commission, commented, "I get up, have breakfast and preside over meetings for 12 hours each day. My head has begun to spin, but despite this mental torment which I am not used to, I am enchanted. Paris is a true paradise!"[13] Louis Barron, a young army veteran who came to Paris to join the commune, described the atmosphere in these terms:

Even in these fearful times I enjoy public festivities, where the real people, moved by lofty ideals or generous sentiments, reveal their naïve and playful curiosity, their enthusiasm, their spontaneous kindness. One cannot be bored in their company. Never having been dulled by a surfeit of pleasure, they are entertained by anything . . . This is how viable revolutions begin and develop. One returns from such exalted experiences as one would awake from a dream, but the memory remains of a brief moment of ecstasy, an illusion of fraternity.[14]

Public ceremonies reinforced this feeling of festival. The communards destroyed the Vendome column, erected by Napoleon I and a hated symbol of empire, to the wild cheers of the crowd. During the commune working-class Parisians celebrated their reconquest of the city center from which Haussmann had expelled them, their right to stand at the heart of national life.

The commune's other major task, and its critical failure, was organizing the defense of the city against the national government. While the communards debated matters of social justice, Adolphe Thiers was mobilizing his forces to crush the revolution. He had abandoned Paris for strategic reasons, believing it better to leave the city and return in strength rather than try to fight the revolution at its inception, and now he prepared to do just that. In contrast, although the Paris National Guard numbered hundreds of thousands of troops, it was poorly organized and its members often had little to no military training. Its units generally refused to follow the orders of the commune's military leadership, instead making their own decisions about when and where to fight. Ultimately, the commune was unable to resist a professionally organized and led army.

Thiers had another important advantage: the increasingly hostile attitude of the nation toward the Parisian rebels. Many people in France viewed the commune with horror as the uprising of a savage mob driven by envy and immorality. The fact that the revolt occurred while parts of northern France were still under German occupation convinced many in the provinces that, far from representing patriotism, the communards were a disgrace to the nation. Many of the soldiers called up from rural areas knew nothing of the commune's progressive ideology, seeing it instead as an anarchistic urban mob that had betrayed France and must be dealt with summarily. Even a writer as sympathetic to the working class and the left as Emile Zola portrayed the communards harshly in his novel Le Debâcle. Although some sympathized with the progressive social vision of the commune, in general French public opinion strongly supported the government's war against it.

By the end of April Thiers had managed to mold a stream of provincial recruits into a formidable fighting force. French troops began shelling the city, ironically doing the most damage to the bourgeois neighborhoods in the west. After threatening to do so for weeks, the French army invaded Paris on May 21, entering the city through the Point du Jour gate that government sympathizers had left unguarded. The week that followed, soon known as *la semaine sanglante,* or Bloody Week, marked one of the saddest episodes in the history of modern Paris. Rather than mounting an effective resistance to the invaders, the commune's troops fell back, trying to defend their neighborhoods by building barricades and rallying their supporters for the last defense of the regime. Thiers's heavily armed forces advanced inexorably, smashing through the barricades and conquering the city section by section. The communards responded by executing hostages, notably the archbishop of Paris, and by setting fires throughout the city. Wild rumors circulated of savage women arsonists, the famous *petroleuses*, using bottles filled with gas to ignite buildings, hoping to burn Paris to the ground. By the end of the week the Hotel de Ville, the Tuileries Palace, and the Palais Royal had gone up in flames; the City of Light had become a city of fiery destruction, its world-famous boulevards a vision of the Apocalypse.

The national troops reacted with unprecedented fury. They took tens of thousands of prisoners and summarily executed many of them: men, women, even children. These included many innocent bystanders, working people who had nothing to do with the fighting but happened to be in the wrong place at the wrong time. Soldiers shot women carrying milk bottles, suspecting them of being *petroleuses*. As the Versailles troops pushed the communards toward their eastern strongholds of Menilmontant and Belleville, the fighting intensified, both sides resorting to atrocities as it became clear that no quarter would be asked or given.

The end came on May 28 in the Père Lachaise cemetery, at the heart of working-class Paris. After overwhelming the city's last barricade, in the Rue Ramponneau, the national soldiers lined up 147 captured communards against a wall, henceforth known as the *mur des fédérés* ("wall of the communards"), in the cemetery and shot them dead. The bullet holes remain to this day. At least 25,000 Parisians were massacred during Bloody Week, with some journalists estimating as many as 50,000. Many others were convicted and transported to the colonies, thousands, including Louise Michel, being

,ed to New Caledonia in the Pacific. Entire working-class professions, including house painters, shoemakers, and plumbers, lost much of their membership. Amid flames and unprecedented slaughter, the revolutionary dreams of the Paris commune came to a horrifying, bitter end.

The fall of the Paris commune marked an important turning point in French history. It was the last hurrah of the insurgent Parisian crowd that had surfaced so dramatically in 1789 and had been a major factor in French politics ever since. France would experience no more revolutions that began with the seizure of the Hotel de Ville. It confirmed the expulsion of the working class to the city's outskirts and the suburbs beyond, making the city ever more bourgeois and conservative. Finally, it underscored the fact that revolutionary politics was increasingly a national and international affair. A city might lead by example, but it could not impose its will on the whole nation. At the same time, the commune created a powerful legacy for the future, and to an important extent this legacy was international. Many communard leaders escaped the repression by fleeing abroad, carrying the message of the commune well beyond France's borders. A month after Bloody Week, former communard Eugène Pottier wrote the words to what would become famous as "The Internationale," the anthem of world communism and one of the greatest revolutionary songs in history. Communism would also adopt the red flag from the commune as its symbol. During the twentieth century the Soviet Union would embrace the memory of the commune; when the Soviets shot the satellite Sputnik into space in 1957, among other items it carried a piece of a communard flag.

PARIS: WORLD CAPITAL OF CONSUMER CULTURE

The defeat of the Paris commune brought the effective end of a long contest between two fundamentally different visions of the French capital: the city of popular politics and revolution represented by the *sans-culottes* of 1789, and the bourgeois consumer paradise developed by the July Monarchy and the Second Empire. Haussmann's renovation of Paris did not prevent the commune, and insurgents managed to build barricades in spite of the destruction of many old streets and the building of wide boulevards. But even after 1871 the old revolutionary Paris did not simply fade into history; radical movements and even barricades would reappear in the French capital during the twentieth century. In addition, this opposition was by no means absolute; as we will see, there were many points of contact between the boulevard and the barricade. Nonetheless, the conservative idea of the city did prevail in general terms, reconfirming the

4.2. Poster for the Paris Universal Exposition of 1889.
Source: Bibliothèque nationale de France.

image of Paris as a glittering world capital. During the late nineteenth century Paris became more than ever a symbol of the modern age.

Recovery from the ravages of the terrible year did not happen overnight. Paris remained under martial law for five years after the commune was destroyed, and the national government did not move back there from Versailles until 1879. The loss of so many skilled workers depressed Parisian industry for years. The new Third Republic moved swiftly to rebuild the city, however, so that Paris regained its glamour and allure sooner than many expected. Not only did the national government repair and rebuild many of the buildings and streets damaged by the fires of the commune (with the exception of the Tuileries Palace, which it razed to the ground), but it also completed many of the projects Haussmann left unfinished, notably the construction of the Paris Opera. More generally, builders and government officials continued to favor the bourgeois apartment blocks so typical of Haussmann's Paris, increasingly furnished with modern conveniences like elevators (introduced in the 1880s), gas lighting, central heating, and running water. The Third Republic thus continued the urban design pioneered by Haussmann, making his vision of Paris permanent.

In November 1878 the French government sponsored a massive world's fair in Paris to celebrate the nation's recovery from the Franco-Prussian War and the commune. The Second Empire, inspired by Britain's 1851 Crystal Palace Exhibition, had sponsored major fairs in 1855 and 1867, but the 1878 exposition was on an entirely different scale, the biggest ever held in not only France but the world as a whole. It covered sixty-six acres in the Champs de Mars and attracted 13 million visitors. Organizers consciously conceived of the exposition as a world's fair, with exhibits from countries around the globe organized along a central Avenue des Nations. Half of the exhibits came from France, and a third from Britain and the British Empire, but other nations also sent displays. The exhibits focused predominantly on modern technology, so Alexander Graham Bell demonstrated the new telephone, and Thomas Edison displayed a phonograph. One of the most impressive French displays was the recently completed head of the Statue of Liberty; eight years later, the statue would take its place in New York harbor. The 1878 exposition also marked the first appearance of electric street lighting in Paris, dramatically illuminating the Avenue de l'Opéra. The 1878 exposition thus marked the recovery of Paris from the commune, and underscored its importance as a world capital.

If continuity typified the urban planning of Paris in the late nineteenth century, it also characterized the city's culture of modernity more generally. The idea of the French capital as a world leader in modern ideas, entertainment, and consumerism had first arisen under the July Monarchy, strongly reinforced by the Second Empire. After 1871 the city remained world famous as an urban center and the ultimate example of urbanity and style. Paris continued to grow in the last third of the century, increasing in size from 2 million in the 1870s to 2.7 million by 1901, with another million people living in the suburbs. Its ever-larger crowds and the very public nature of Parisian life, centered on boulevards and in cafés, underscored the city's dynamism and perpetual novelty.

Consumer culture played a key role in the reputation and allure of modern Paris, in at least two important respects. First, the French capital became increasingly famous as a place that offered wonderful things for sale. It married a tradition of fine artisanal craftsmanship with an innovative spirit of marketing to render the very name of Paris an important trademark and symbol of commercial prestige. This emphasis on commerce was closely tied to the increasingly bourgeois character of the city. Dominated by a class that defined its identity in large part by what it bought and displayed, the French capital seemed a place where everything was for sale. Second, many viewed the city as a place to be enjoyed and consumed. In Paris one could purchase top-notch entertainment, food, and clothing, one could enjoy the city's matchless beauty, one could admire and purchase its works of literature and art. Strolling along the boulevards, marveling at the spectacles on display, or enjoying the city's impressive architecture meant engaging in acts of urban consumption. During the 1860s Charles Baudelaire had described the *flâneur* as a disinterested observer of the crowd and of modern life in general, and the idea of *flânerie* remained a key characteristic of Parisian life in the late nineteenth century. Ironically, given that Paris remained one of Europe's great centers of industrial production even after 1871, its fame, notoriety, and world significance rested increasingly on its reputation as a center of consumer culture, both French and global at the same time.

The culture of the boulevard was one of the greatest symbols of Parisian modernity, and no area represented this better than the Grands Boulevards. A series of broad avenues stretching continuously from the Place de la Bastille in the east to the Place de la Madeleine in the west, the Grands Boulevards had emerged as an important site of urban leisure and consumer culture under the July Monarchy. During the Second Empire they became the leading space for public life in the capital, and this reputation only increased after 1871. Both men and women enjoyed strolling down the boulevards in the afternoon and evening, not just members of the city's elites but also working people.

The Grands Boulevards also became a place for news. Many Parisian newspapers had their offices on or near the boulevards, and the latest newspapers were available. Street kiosks covered with posters advertising events, products, and stores provided another type of information. The widespread use of posters, pioneered in the 1870s by Parisian artist Jules Cheret, transformed the streetscape of the Grands Boulevards, filling it with vibrant but ephemeral splashes of color and bits of information emphasizing the new and dramatic. Numerous cafés lined the boulevards, where individuals could rest and observe the passing throngs. The Café de la Paix, opened in 1862, soon became one of the city's prime gathering spots.

The culture of the Grands Boulevards became a quintessential symbol of Parisian life by the end of the nineteenth century. It represented key themes of modernity, notably constant change, the importance of form and display, the shock of the new, and increasing amounts of information. The diversity of people and products on display underscored the idea of the boulevards and Paris as a city at the center of the world. As one commentator noted, "It's a kaleidoscope where objects and people, diversely, but always picturesquely colored, change each step and each instant."[15]

Department stores, the *grands magasins*, constituted another great example of Parisian modernity in the late nineteenth century. The first major department store in Paris, the Bon Marché, began as a small store in 1838 before moving in 1852 to a sumptuous new building designed by Gustave Eiffel, who would go on to create the Eiffel Tower. Over the next few decades several similar stores opened, such as Printemps (1862), the Belle Jardinière (1867), La Samaritaine (1870), and the Galeries Lafayette (1895). The department stores were huge buildings, often several stories high, which offered all the goods of the world to their customers. Their size enabled them to offer consumers lower prices as well, and they pioneered marketing techniques like frequent sales to attract shoppers away from more traditional retail establishments.

But their appeal went well beyond providing a wide array of goods at reasonable prices. In older stores clients generally entered in search of specific objects and negotiated the price with the store clerks; reaching an agreement obligated the customer to purchase the object. In contrast, the department stores fixed prices on goods, dispensing with traditional haggling, but also invited customers to enter the store and look around without an expectation to buy. Instead, they used techniques of display and advertising to convince people to buy goods, whether or not they initially desired them. Stores specialized in creating elaborate displays to tempt and dazzle the customer. The buildings not only were constructed on a monumental scale, frequently adorned with statues and other lavish decorations, but also had huge windows to attract passersby and illuminate the goods within. The stores created a fantasy of opulence, luxury, and refinement, emphasizing the fashionable modernity of the dream world they invited the customer to enter. Functioning as interiorized versions of the boulevard, they cast the shopper as a *flaneur*, someone there to stroll among luxurious displays, dazzled by the allure of the new.

The department stores catered to all who could afford them, but they became the province of bourgeois women. They offered a somewhat more refined space for those not quite at ease with the rough-and-tumble spectacle of the boulevard. Women could stroll the department stores in perfect respectability and comfort. Moreover, they featured goods, especially clothing and home décor, increasingly defined as a feminine province. What historian Colin Jones has called "cathedrals of consumption" symbolized the allure of Paris for women, and indeed the idea of Paris as a city of women. In his novel *The La-dies Paradise (Au Bonheur des Dames)*, Emile Zola gave a classic fictionalized portrait of the Bon Marché, one so real that the actual department store copied some of the displays described in his book. The novel portrays bourgeois Parisi-ennes as carried away by the fantasy world of goods, at their extreme subject to hysteria eerily reminiscent of the fury of the *petroleuses*.

Both the Grands Boulevards and the *grands magasins* heavily emphasized exotica, the romance of the new and unfamiliar. Like the world's fairs of the era, which usually included displays of colonial objects (and sometimes sub-jects as well), department stores and boulevards offered a glimpse into the cultures of a world far removed from Paris. On the boulevards newspapers trumpeted the events of the world, and the cosmopolitan crowds numbered people from every corner of the globe. As Paris became a prime tourist desti-nation, visitors in search of the unusual and picturesque flocked to the bou-levards, their very presence adding to the area's diversity. Department stores gloried in their role as emporiums of the world, and frequently organized dis-plays around exotic themes. In one scene of *The Ladies' Paradise*, Zola de-scribes an exhibit used to sell oriental carpets:

> Then they disappeared in the vestibule, which was transformed into an oriental salon.
>
> From the very threshold it was a marvel, a surprise, which enchanted all of them . . . This sumptuous pasha's tent was furnished with divans and arm-chairs, made with camel sacks, some ornamented with many-coloured lozenges, others with primitive roses. Turkey, Arabia, and the Indies were all there. They had emptied palaces, plundered the mosques and bazaars. A barbarous gold tone prevailed in the weft of the old carpets, the faded tints of which still preserved a somber warmth, as on an extin-guished furnace, a beautiful burnt hue suggestive of the old masters. Vi-sions of the East floated beneath the luxury of this barbarous art, amid the strong odour which the old wools had retained of the country of vermin and of the rising sun.[16]

Consumerism and colonialism came together in the Parisian department store.

The consumer culture of late-nineteenth-century Paris, attracting visitors, shoppers, and goods from near and far, defined the French capital as a world capital. It underscored the idea of modernity as a world of instability, political ultural, of ever-changing ideas and institutions, always open to the new and daring. At a time when French national prestige had seen better days, the star of France's capital paradoxically had never shone brighter. By the 1880s electric lighting became commonplace on the city's boulevards, making Paris more than ever before the City of Light. It became the object of fantasy for people throughout the world, the ultimate consumer good for the modern generation. The late nineteenth century created the class image of modern Paris, an image that continues to dazzle and inspire to this day.

MONTMARTRE AND THE RISE OF A NEW BOHEMIA

The commercial consumerism of late-nineteenth-century Paris had a strong impact on the world of the arts. Impressionist artists like Renoir (*Les grands boulevards*, 1875) and Pissarro (*Le Boulevard Montmartre*, 1879) painted the dazzling public life of the capital, creating canvases that would become world famous. Yet many also criticized the new opulence of the city, retaining an interest in the world of the working class and the barricade. By the 1880s the Parisian avant-garde had created its own alternative to the consumer society of the boulevard in the picturesque neighborhood of Montmartre, transforming it into the art capital of the nation, and perhaps the world.

At first glance, Montmartre seemed an unlikely spot to gain such renown. Far from the city center, it had been an independent village for many centuries, only becoming a part of Paris with the annexations of 1860. Yet Montmartre had a physical and cultural presence that made it a place apart in the French capital, a distinctiveness that attracted the best of Parisian artists in the late nineteenth century and made it the birthplace of impressionism. For millennia the neighborhood had displayed two faces, sacred and profane. Its hilltop location made it a religious center going back to the Roman Empire, and its name (Martyr's Mount) came from the martyrdom of Saint-Denis, one of ancient Gaul's first Christian missionaries, on its slopes. Ignatius of Loyola founded the Jesuit Order there in 1534. By the eighteenth century, however, Montmartre had also developed a reputation for gaiety and good times. The area had a number of vineyards, thanks in part to the efforts of the local Benedictine abbey, and wine was readily available. Moreover, because Montmartre lay just outside the city limits, wine consumed there was not taxed as heavily and therefore was cheaper. The village consequently developed a number of cabarets and wine shops where visitors could enjoy country air and a good vintage. As Paris grew in the early nineteenth century, Montmartre retained its village-like aspect, increasingly appealing to those who wanted to escape the city yet remain close to it.

Even after being annexed to Paris in the 1860s, Montmartre seemed a place apart. Its hilly topography and peripheral location prevented Haussmann from renovating the area, so that except for the boulevards at the base of the hill Montmartre remained a warren of narrow winding streets and small houses. It thus constituted an alternative to the bourgeois boulevards and tall apartment blocks of Second Empire Paris, populated largely by working people displaced from the center city. Both its popular character and picturesque scenery made it popular with Parisian artists, who began moving there in large numbers during the 1860s. Montmartre offered cheap rents, scenic vistas, and clean country air, as well as distance from the establishment Ecole des Beaux Arts across the river. It also became a place where those disdainful of bourgeois culture could interact with working people in cafés and dancehalls. Many painters took young working women from the neighborhood as both models and lovers. A notable example was Suzanne Valadon, illegitimate daughter of a local laundress who modeled for Renoir, eventually becoming a noted painter in her own right. In addition, Montmartre had a thriving vice trade, prostitutes working the boulevards, that also contributed to its raffish air.

By the 1870s Montmartre had become the center of artistic and bohemian life in the capital. Its central role in the commune underscored its rejection of the establishment, both political and aesthetic. Manet, Renoir, Degas, Pissarro, Cezanne, and other leading artists had studios there and socialized together. They gravitated toward the top of the hill, or *butte*, where the rents were cheapest. Cafes, cabarets, and dance halls fostered the combination of avant-garde art and entertainment that became the signature of Montmartre. Artists, writers, and intellectuals routinely gathered at the Café Guerbois in the Rue des Batignolles. There in December 1873 Monet proposed that young painters stage a special group exhibition.[17] Held in 1874, the exhibition gave birth to the term "impressionism," after an art critic dismissed Monet's *Impression: Sunrise* (1873). Other cafés, like the Nouvelles Athènes, depicted in Degas's *L'Absinthe* (1876), also promoted the social and intellectual life of the avant-garde. For the impressionist painters, Montmartre underscored the importance of painting the daily lives of ordinary people.

The neighborhood became most famous, if not notorious, for its dance halls. For the most part these clustered at the base of the hill, on the Boulevard

Rochechouart. The most famous was the Elysées-Montmartre, a huge space with a dance hall, restaurant, and gambling rooms. In 1874 Emile Zola held a party there to celebrate the success of *L'Assommoir*, his famous novel of working-class Parisian life set nearby. Another was the Moulin de la Galette, originally a windmill dating back to the thirteenth century. A very ordinary dance hall with a working-class clientele, the Moulin de la Galette became famous after the Montmartre intelligentsia "discovered" it. In the 1870s Renoir became a fixture there, memorializing it in his 1876 masterpiece *Le bal du Moulin de la Galette*. Cabarets featuring poetry, music, and theater performances also sprang up in Montmartre by the 1880s. In 1881 the poet Rodolphe Salis opened the *Chat Noir* (Black Cat). Salis, a larger-than-life figure who delighted in ridiculing his customers, attracted a wide clientele of artists, writers, and those who wanted a glimpse of bohemia. He helped create a mythical image of his beloved neighborhood, at one point proclaiming "Montmartre the free city, Montmartre the sacred hill, Montmartre the germ of the earth, navel and brain of the world."[18]

Although the avant-garde culture of Montmartre stood against the commercialism of establishment Paris, by the 1890s it also was becoming commercialized to an important degree. One reason was the increasing acceptance and success of the impressionists, who made bohemia central to the art world. Another had to do with the growing commercialization of vice, from the casual sexuality of the young bohemians to organized prostitution and drug rackets. Nothing better represented this shift than Montmartre's greatest dance hall, the Moulin Rouge, opened in 1889. Built to acknowledge the tradition of windmills in the neighborhood, it was a successful attempt to cash in on the notoriety of Montmartre as the pleasure capital of Paris. A cavernous space featuring a huge stage, the Moulin Rouge featured professional dancers performing while customers danced and drank. Here performers like Jane Avril and La Goulue titillated clients by dancing the can-can, lifting their skirts and flashing their *derrières*. Henri de Toulouse-Lautrec, the impressionist artist most closely associated with the Moulin Rouge, became a fixture there, having affairs with various dancers and drinking "the green fairy," absinthe. As one visitor noted, "When the hours grow late the scene becomes almost indescribable. The slumbering passions of dancers are roused by their frequent visits to the refreshment tables, and in this place no passions need be curbed."[19]

The Moulin Rouge symbolized both the bohemian gaiety of Montmartre and its transformation into a site for commercialized pleasure. By the turn of the century the dance hall had become one of the largest prostitution markets in Europe. It also hosted a thriving commerce in illegal drugs, notably morphine and cocaine. In part thanks to the availability of such pleasures Montmartre also became a major tourist attraction, the very embodiment of what Americans called "gay Paree." As the neighborhood became more popular, it also became more cosmopolitan. Not only did tourists visit from throughout the world, but it also attracted many foreign performers, including the African American dancers who popularized the cakewalk there in the 1890s. Increasingly Montmartre became a global symbol of the shock of the new, a place only imaginable in Paris.

Not surprisingly, conservative elites looked on bohemian Montmartre with horror, regarding it as a symbol of political, cultural, and moral degeneration. In the aftermath of the terrible year and the commune, Catholic leaders decided to build a new church in Paris to symbolize the expiation of the sins they felt had caused such misfortunes. Given the popularity of the Order of the Sacred Heart among French Catholics, they decided to name the new church Sacre Coeur (Sacred Heart); moreover, they chose to place it at the top of the Montmartre hill. The National Assembly voted in 1873 to allocate the land for the new church, which would be funded by donations from the Catholic faithful. As the archbishop of Paris observed, "It is here that the Sacred Heart should be enthroned, to draw all to itself, on the summit of the hill upon which Christendom was born in the blood of the first apostles, the monument to our religious rebirth should be raised."[20]

Bohemian Montmartre reacted with horror to the prospect of its neighborhood being dominated by a monument that represented everything it opposed. Not a single local artist contributed to it. Moreover, local politicians made their displeasure manifest by naming streets up to the basilica after noted anticlerical figures and people persecuted by the Church; for example, the Rue du Chevalier de la Barre commemorated a man executed by Louis XV for insulting a religious procession. Throughout the late nineteenth century, during the glory years of the Montmartre avant-garde, the massive basilica slowly rose above the area, a white church frowning disapprovingly on a red city.

Sacre Coeur was not completed until 1914, and not formally consecrated until 1919. Although the political and artistic left continued to despise it, by then it had become a symbol of Montmartre, giving shape to the hill's skyline and appearing in multiple faux impressionist posters and postcards. It has remained so ever since. The building of Sacré Coeur underscored once again Montmartre's long history as a religious site, a sacred hill overlooking

Paris. For both the Catholic right and the avant-garde left it was indeed sacred ground. The construction of Sacré Coeur in Montmartre, like the increasing commercialization of its avant-garde culture, thus illustrated both the contradictions that shaped modern Paris and commonalities that existed among the extremes of urban life.

PARIS ON DISPLAY TO THE WORLD

In 1889 and again in 1900 the French capital hosted major world fairs, which enabled Parisians to marvel at the latest technological achievements from across the globe and showcased the beauty of the City of Light. For the millions who visited the fairs Paris itself was on display, the ultimate consumer product and symbol of modernity. Moreover, the fairs left a permanent mark on the city, contributing some of its most notable landmarks. They completed the transformation of Paris into a world capital, decisively shaping popular images of the city that still exist today.

The second half of the nineteenth century up to World War I was the classic era of the world's fair. The rise of industrial capitalism as a global system, knitting together the people and commerce of the world to an unprecedented degree, encouraged nations to display their technological prowess and modernity in world fairs, hosted by leading world cities. Starting with London's Crystal Palace Exhibition in 1851, every few years nations would organize a world fair both to show off their own accomplishments and display the work of inventors and scientists from near and far. In 1876, for example, Philadelphia hosted the International Centennial Exhibition in honor of the one hundredth anniversary of American independence. Chicago hosted the Columbian Exhibition in 1893 to mark the four hundredth anniversary of Columbus's discovery of the Americas. In general the fairs had two main themes. The celebration of new technology as a symbol of human progress was perhaps most important. Ethnography, a fascination with the exotic and far away also occupied an important place; fairs often featured exhibits of "primitive" cultures and peoples. The late nineteenth century was an age of empire, and the opportunity to see the fruits of empire drew many to the fairs. The presence, and opposition, of the scientist and the savage shaped not just the world fairs but, in the minds of many, the condition of the world as a whole.

Such fairs had enjoyed great popularity in France for decades. Napoleon III had welcomed them as opportunities to display French genius. He hosted two in Paris, one in 1855 and one in 1867, using the latter to show off

Haussmann's renovations of the French capital. As we have seen, the Third Republic staged the third Parisian world fair in 1878 to showcase the city's recovery from the siege and the commune of 1871. In 1889 the French government mounted a new world fair in Paris, the Exposition Universelle, to celebrate the centennial of the French Revolution. Like its predecessor in 1878 it took place on the Champs de Mars and featured impressive examples of science and engineering. A centerpiece of the fair was the vast Machinery Hall, the largest interior space in the world, constructed of iron and glass. The fair featured popular and exotic exhibits from around the world, including several buildings devoted to France's burgeoning colonial empire, and from the United States Buffalo Bill's Wild West Show, starring sharpshooter Annie Oakley.

But the clear star of the show, and a building that more than any other has symbolized Paris ever since, was the Eiffel Tower. Designed by architect Gustave Eiffel, the tower soared almost a thousand feet into the Parisian sky, at the time the tallest building in the world. The ultimate symbol of modernity, it broke with traditional architecture, composed of steel beams and bolts rather than wood, stone, or plaster. It also symbolized the triumph of form over function, for the tower had no purpose other than to represent human ambition and progress. Eiffel compared it to the pyramids of Egypt and proclaimed that France now had a thousand-foot flagpole. The Eiffel Tower shocked and dismayed many Parisians, however. A committee of three hundred artists and intellectuals, led by Charles Garnier, designer of the Paris Opera, denounced it in no uncertain terms:

> We, writers, painters, sculptors, architects and passionate devotees of the hitherto untouched beauty of Paris, protest with all our strength, with all our indignation in the name of slighted French taste, against the erection . . . of this useless and monstrous Eiffel Tower . . . To bring our arguments home, imagine for a moment a giddy, ridiculous tower dominating Paris like a gigantic black smokestack, crushing under its barbaric bulk Notre Dame, the Tour Saint-Jacques, the Louvre, the Dome of les Invalides, the Arc de Triomphe, all of our humiliated monuments will disappear in this ghastly dream.[21]

Others, however, admired a building that broke so boldly with tradition, embodying the dynamism and shock of the modern age. Like Sacré Coeur, another new Parisian monument that seemed to stick out like a sore thumb, the Eiffel Tower provoked controversy and opposition but went on to become a beloved Parisian landmark and icon. For many into the present day, its marriage of grace and modernity made it the perfect symbol of Paris as a world city.

Eleven years later another world fair took place in Paris, the Exposition Universelle of 1900. Although France had recently hosted an international exposition, it decided to stage another one after learning that Germany planned a similar event; Berlin might have won the war of 1870, but Paris would remain the capital of world fairs! Entitled *Paris: Capital of the Civilized World*, the exposition was the largest yet, ultimately attracting over 50 million visitors. Forty-seven nations took part and twenty-two built pavilions along the Champs de Mars. The African American scholar W. E .B. Du Bois organized an American Negro exhibit to illustrate black contributions to the United States. Technological achievements remained important: new inventions like the automobile, the bicycle, and cinema attracted lots of attention from fairgoers. Electrical engineering proudly displayed its progress, illuminating the Eiffel Tower and the Champs de Mars with a dazzling display of nighttime lights.

At the same time, the arts and consumer culture came into their own in the 1900 exposition. The fair represented a triumph of the art nouveau movement, a new aesthetic symbol of modernity. Its most dramatic example was the Alexandre III Bridge, the most ornate span in Paris, named after the Russian czar. The French government also built the Grand Palais and Petit Palais, two enormous buildings used for art displays. More generally, the exposition showcased French style, drawing on and contributing to the image of Paris as a city for the modern woman. At its entrance stood a five-meter statue of a fashionably dressed woman, entitled *La Parisienne*, welcoming people to the fair. The Pavilion of Decorative Arts, the Palace of Woman, and the Palace of Fashion proved highly popular, exhibiting all manner of consumer goods. In general the exposition overwhelmed fairgoers with things to see, buy, and do, underscoring the idea of the French capital as a place of unparalleled stimulation and excitement.

Yet for all the attractions of the 1900 exposition, its most important and enduring legacy was largely invisible. For years public officials had debated the possibility of building a subway system in the French capital. London had opened the world's first in 1863, followed by Glasgow in 1891, Budapest in 1896, and Boston in 1897. Parisians had long enjoyed the benefits of public transit. Buses had been operating since the 1820s, and a street tramway system started in 1855. The subway, however, was not only more practical for a city that began to see increasing vehicular street traffic, but also symbolized urban progress and the life of great cities. Simply put, in order to be a world-class metropolis Paris had to have a subway.

With the looming 1900 international exposition as incentive, engineers led by Fulgence Bienvenu, "Father Metro," began planning the new system. Construction started in 1898 on what would be the first subway line in Paris, running across the Right Bank from the Porte Maillot in the west to the Porte de Vincennes in the east. On July 19, 1900, the Paris Métropolitain, or Metro, opened its doors to Parisians for the first time. It immediately proved immensely popular, counting 500,000 voyages in its first two weeks, and 17 million by the end of the year. The station entrances, designed by Hector Guimard in a dramatic art nouveau style, became major examples of public art in Paris. The Eiffel Tower might be more dramatic, but ultimately the Metro was far more useful and present in the daily lives of Parisians. In many ways it defined the city, especially as locals began to define where they lived by which Metro stop they used. As Paris entered the new century, its brand-new subway provided the most dramatic distinction between its past and its future.

In the second half of the nineteenth century Paris hosted no less than five world fairs, more than any other city before or since. Gigantic events that celebrated new achievements in science, technology, and art, the joys of strolling through spaces chock-full of marvels, and the exoticism of faraway lands, the world fairs provided the ultimate experience for the *flâneur*, the consumer of urban life. They drew on and contributed to the French capital's reputation as the world's capital of modernity. As we will see in the next chapter, the French would continue to confront political, social, and economic challenges. But as long as the lights of its brilliant, beautiful capital continued to sparkle, attracting visitors from near and far, France could convincingly claim to be a universal nation.

Suggestions for Further Reading

Becker, George J., ed. and trans. *Paris Under Siege, 1870–1871: From the Goncourt Journal*. Ithaca, NY: Cornell University Press, 1969.

Cate, Phillip Dennis, and Mary Shaw, eds. *The Spirit of Montmartre: Cabarets, Humor, and Avant-Garde, 1875–1905*. New Brunswick, NJ: Rutgers University Press, 1996.

Coffin, Judith G. *The Politics of Women's Work: the Paris Garment Trades, 1750–1791*. Princeton, NJ: Princeton University Press, 1996.

Crane, Diane. *Fashion and Its Social Agendas: Class, Gender, and Identity in Clothing*. Chicago: University of Chicago Press, 2000.

De Marly, Diana. *The History of Haute Couture, 1850–1950*. New York: Holmes & Meier, 1980.

Edwards, Stewart, ed. *The Communards of Paris, 1871*. Ithaca, NY: Cornell University Press, 1973.

Eichner, Carolyn J. *Surmounting the Barricades: Women in the Paris Commune*. Bloomington: Indiana University Press, 2004.

Gluckstein, Donny. *The Paris Commune: A Revolution in Democracy*. Chicago: Haymarket, 2011.

Green, Nancy L. *Ready-to-Wear Ready-to-Work: A Century of Industry and Immigrants in Paris and New York*. Durham, NC: Duke University Press, 1997.

Gullickson, Gay L. *Unruly Women of Paris: Images of the Commune*. Ithaca, NY: Cornell University Press, 1996.

Hahn, Hazel H. *Scenes of Parisian Modernity: Culture and Consumption in the Nineteenth Century*. New York: Palgrave Macmillan, 2009.

Horne, Alistair. *The Terrible Year: The Paris Commune 1871*. London: Macmillan, 1971.

King, Ross. *The Judgment of Paris: The Revolutionary Decade That Gave the World Impressionism*. New York: Walker, 2006.

Jones, Colin. *Paris: The Biography of a City*. New York: Viking, 2004.

Jullian, Philippe. *Montmartre*. Oxford: Phaidon, 1977.

Lees, Andrew, and Lynn Hollen Lees. *Cities and the Making of Modern Europe, 1750–1850*. Cambridge: Cambridge University Press, 2007.

Nord, Philip. *Impressionists and Politics: Art and Democracy in the Nineteenth Century*. London: Routledge, 2000.

Rose, June. *Suzanne Valadon, Mistress of Montmartre*. New York: St Martin's, 1999.

Schwartz, Vanessa R. *Spectacular Realities: Early Mass Culture in Fin-de-Siècle Paris*. Berkeley: University of California Press, 1998.

Steele, Valerie. *Paris Fashion: A Cultural History*. Oxford: Berg, 1998.

Troy, Nancy J. *Couture Culture: A Study in Modern Art and Fashion*. Cambridge: MIT Press, 2003.

Williams, Rosalind H. *Dream Worlds: Mass Consumption in Late Nineteenth-Century France*. Berkeley: University of California Press, 1982.

Zola, Emile. *The Ladies' Paradise*. Introduction by Kristin Ross. Berkeley: University of California Press, 1992.

--------- **Notes** ---------

1. Colin Jones, *Paris: The Biography of a City* (New York: Viking, 2004), 337.
2. David Pinkney, *Napoleon III and the Rebuilding of Paris* (Princeton, NJ: Princeton University Press, 1972), 70.
3. Jones, *Paris*, 318.
4. Pinkney, *Napoleon III*, 127.
5. Ibid., 162
6. Ibid., 170.
7. Alistair Horne, *The Terrible Year: The Paris Commune 1871* (London: Macmillan, 1971), 77–78.
8. Roberto Naranjo, "The Siege of Paris during the Franco-Prussian War," eHistory.
9. Stewart Edwards, ed., 1973. *The Communards of Paris, 1871* (Ithaca, NY: Cornell University Press, 1973), 23.
10. Donny Gluckstein, *The Paris Commune: A Revolution in Democracy* (Chicago: Haymarket, 2011), 3.
11. Philip Katz, "'Lessons from Paris': The American Clergy Responds to the Paris Commune," *Church History*, September 1994, 395.
12. Gluckstein, *Paris Commune*, 30.
13. Ibid., 9.
14. Edwards, *Communards*, 142–143.
15. H. Hazel Hahn, *Scenes of Parisian Modernity: Culture and Consumption in the Nineteenth Century* (New York: Palgrave Macmillan, 2009), 130.
16. Emile Zola, *The Ladies Paradise* (Berkeley: University of California Press, 1992), 79.
17. June Rose, *Suzanne Valadon: Mistress of Montmartre* (New York: St. Martin's, 1999), 28.
18. Philippe Jullian, *Montmartre* (Oxford: Phaidon, 1977), 82.
19. Ibid., 97.
20. Ibid., 51.
21. Henri Loyrette, *Gustave Eiffel* (New York: Rizzoli, 1985), 174.

[five]

THE UNIVERSAL REPUBLIC

UNTIL THE LATE NINETEENTH CENTURY, REPUBLICANISM HAD BEEN
an exceptional phenomenon in French political life. The first two republics
were short-lived and violent, and republicanism as a movement mostly existed
in opposition to the established order, both political and social. Moreover, nowhere in Europe had it fared any better; the United States stood alone among
the world's great nations in embracing a republican form of government. Monarchy in its various forms, ranging from the constitutional monarchy of Britain
to the imperial despotism of Russia, still dominated European politics in the
late nineteenth century, and even after the collapse of the Second Empire it
was hard to argue that France would be any different.

The Third Republic gave the lie to this perspective. Surprising many contemporaries, the new regime not only survived its shaky beginnings in war and
defeat but went on to become the longest regime in modern French history,
outlasting even the reign of Louis XIV. From 1870 to 1940 France assumed its
modern form as a nation, and key to this form was the establishment of the
republic as the country's dominant type of government. By the time the long
regime came to an end with another German defeat, republican political culture had become an integral part of France; for many, to be French meant to
embrace the values of the republic.

Key to this political culture was the idea of universalism and of France
as a universal nation. For the builders and supporters of the Third Republic,

modern French identity had its origins in the Revolution and subsequent struggles to realize its liberal and democratic ideals. The regime's great challenge, inherited from the insurgents of 1789, was to reconcile these two (often contradictory) ideals. Ultimately it achieved this task, making liberal democracy the political standard for twentieth-century France, by elaborating a vision of national identity centered around core political values rather than geography, language, or race. These values, including progress, reason, and liberty, could be (and in the opinion of republicans should be) embraced by anyone and everyone. Propagation of these universal values, therefore, was central to building the republic and the nation it represented.

The next two chapters will consider the history of the Third Republic in the seminal years from its founding in 1870 to the beginnings of the twentieth century. This chapter will examine how the republic survived its challengers to dominate French politics, and how it spread republican institutions and values throughout France. The next chapter will consider the unprecedented expansion of the nation's overseas empire during this period. During this period, perhaps more than at any other time of French history since the Revolution, a desire to spread and ultimately universalize republican values brought together domestic and imperial history. This had some odd effects, producing, for example, that strangest of political phenomena, the republican empire. Nonetheless, these two dimensions of republican expansionism underscored the centrality of the universalist vision during the Third Republic to the making of modern France.

GLOBAL CHANGE: THE SECOND INDUSTRIAL REVOLUTION AND THE RISE OF MASS SOCIETY

France in the last decades of the nineteenth century found itself part of a wider world increasingly interconnected and driven by major technological innovation. During these years the planet achieved unprecedented integration. The world economy functioned more and more as a unified system, not only generating exceptional profits and wealth but also giving rise to the first global depression. The rise of powerful nation-states in Europe and America broke down local cultures and created a new awareness of belonging to a unified people. Imperialism, both informal and increasingly formal, tied Europe, Africa, Asia, and the Americas together, changing not only the lives of the "natives" but also those of the Europeans who colonized their lands. All sorts of factors, from the search for ever-more profitable investments to the romantic lure of far horizons, conspired to unify the globe. Such an era of seemingly limitless possibilities fully justified a universalist view of France's heritage and its place in the world.

Central to this era of progress was what has come to be known as the second industrial revolution. From the 1870s until the outbreak of World War I, a series of spectacular technological breakthroughs fundamentally reshaped life in Europe, America, and to an increasing extent the world as a whole. If iron and coal dominated the first industrial revolution, steel ruled the second. After the 1850s the Bessemer process, named after British inventor Henry Bessemer, made the production of steel more efficient and dramatically lowered its cost. The increased use of steel, stronger and more flexible than iron, made it possible to build much larger and more powerful machinery. At the same time, new sources of power freed industry from its traditional dependence on coal. After Thomas Edison's path-breaking experiments with electric lighting, electricity emerged as a major source of industrial power in the 1880s. By the end of the century internal combustion engines powered by petroleum rather than coal had begun to transform transportation, especially maritime travel. The burgeoning chemical industry provided another major source of innovation for consumer products like soap as well as industrial materials. The growth of steel and chemicals, as well as new sources of power, encouraged the dramatic expansion of heavy industry at the end of the nineteenth century.

The second industrial revolution was also an era of spectacular technical inventions, many of which would shape life in the new century to come. In 1885 German engineer Karl Benz invented the world's first automobile, launching one of the modern era's most important industries. The revolution in transportation it sparked went along with major innovations in urban mass transit, especially the development of subway systems. Both means of transport dramatically shortened the time it took to get from one place to another, creating a new emphasis on mobility and speed. The Wright brothers' invention of the airplane in 1903 would provide the ultimate example of technology's conquest of time and space, of its ability to bring the world together.

New technologies made it possible to build factories with hundreds, even thousands, of workers, but heavy industry could only survive by selling its products to mass markets. A key aspect of the second industrial revolution, therefore, was the rise of mass consumer society. As noted in the previous chapter, the late nineteenth century witnessed tremendous urban growth, so that factories drew on cities as both sources of labor and consumer markets. Both urbanization and industrialization brought a new focus on consumer life, exemplified by the new prominence of commercial advertisements on urban boulevards and in metropolitan daily newspapers. Innovations like department stores and installment purchase plans enabled even those of modest means to enjoy the fruits of consumer society. At the same time, the ever-increasing size of major cities provided a market for heavy industry, especially in construction and transportation. As the invention of the cinema in 1895 demonstrated, technological progress went hand in hand with the rise of mass society and culture, creating a world that was ever more closely tied together.

This was not a period of uninterrupted prosperity, however. The Long Depression that lasted roughly from 1873 to 1896 demonstrated some of the perils of early globalization. The depression began with a series of financial panics, especially in Vienna and New York, in 1873. Many factors, notably speculation in a variety of economic sectors, caused the collapse. For example, the completion of the transcontinental railway network across the United States in 1869 enabled Americans to ship grain cheaply to Europe, lowering grain prices in general. The economic crisis evolved in different ways in different places, oscillating between periods of depression and prosperity. In general, production slowed significantly during these years and prices fell on most commodities. The global downturn encouraged a number of reactions, including a turn from economic liberalism to protectionism, a scramble for overseas markets and ultimately colonies, and massive waves of population migration.

This combination of industrial and technological dynamism with economic uncertainty in the late nineteenth century lay at the heart of the rise of mass society and mass politics. To an important degree, the breakdown of localized life by global forces took place in the context of the nation-state, more and more the dominant form of political organization in Europe and America. Nations organized educational facilities and policies, regulated and often subsidized business and economic life, and mounted ever-larger standing armies and navies. The growth of government bureaucracies in these years symbolized the rise of mass society in general. Above all, modern nation-states increasingly owed their legitimacy to popular consent, measured in terms of popular opinion and, more and more, elections. Nationalism, the political culture of the nation-state, played an increasingly central role in the lives of millions of people. Forces opposed to nationalism, from Catholicism on the right to socialism on the left, also organized themselves as mass-based popular movements. To a significant extent, therefore, national institutions and cultures paradoxically arose from and fostered the mass society that was key to an increasingly globalized age.

Like many other nations, France elaborated the essential outlines of its national political culture during these years, the first half of the Third Republic. Above all, this culture centered on the values of universalism inherited from the French Revolution and developed by progressive forces ever since. The triumph of the republic was thus the triumph of France as a universal nation, one whose core identity focused on ideas considered to be the property of all right-thinking men and women. In a world made increasingly of self-conscious nation-states and peoples, the idea of the universal nation expressed France's own historical heritage as well as the tenor of the contemporary world.

UNIVERSALISM AND THE THIRD REPUBLIC

On March 11, 1882, Professor Ernest Renan presented a landmark lecture at the Sorbonne: "What Is a Nation?" Renan, holder of the chair in Hebrew at the Collège de France, was a scholar of formidable if controversial reputation. His 1863 study *The Life of Jesus* had scandalized many Catholics by treating Christ as a historical figure, subject to the same rigorous standards of historical analysis as any other man. In his 1882 lecture Renan argued against the idea that national identity was based in race or language. Instead, two things made a nation: a sense of a common history and the consent of the nation's citizens. As Renan put it:

> A nation is a soul, a spiritual principle. Two things, which in truth are but one, constitute this soul or spiritual principle. One lies in the past, one in the present. One is the possession in common of a rich legacy of memories, the other is present-day consent, the desire to live together, the will to perpetuate the value of the heritage that one has received in an undivided form.[1]

In making this argument about national identity, Renan laid out the principles, and to an important extent the culture, of republican universal nationalism. His vision of the nation clearly derived from French experience, emphasizing the importance of both history and popular sovereignty. For the republicans of late-nineteenth-century France had a heritage, that of the Revolution, which had molded the nation and given the people the right and ability to choose its own national identity. But that heritage was precisely a universalist one, based in a global understanding of the rights of man and applicable to all people. Moreover, the very structure of Renan's lecture, its emphasis on rational argument and its tendency to derive broad principles from specific historical cases, resonated strongly with republican political and intellectual culture under the Third Republic. For Renan, therefore, the answer to the question What is a nation? was at the same time historically specific and universal.

The values embodied in Renan's great address dominated the political and intellectual culture of late-nineteenth-century France, becoming as much symbols of French national identity as the Eiffel Tower. As one scholar has noted, the Third Republic was the golden age of French universalism.[2] What were these values? First, a strong faith in progress: the idea that today was better than yesterday and tomorrow would be better than today. Progress was not automatic but occurred when and because men strove to make a better world. Key to this was human liberty, both the cause and consequence of human progress. Freedom *from* a variety of evils, not only tyranny and injustice but also ignorance, superstition, and poverty, was a central and cherished value. Knowledge and enlightenment were fundamental tools in freeing man and enabling him to reach his greatest potential. In particular republicans embraced reason and positivism, the rigorous application of the scientific method to all fields of knowledge, as keys to progress. Finally, republicans emphasized the importance of human rights, safeguarded by the nation but fittingly the property of all people. From the perspective of the late nineteenth century, the Revolution had first introduced these principles, and the Third Republic had finally succeeded in making them dominant in France.

Much of the history of the Third Republic centers around the republican struggle for mastery in politics as well as in society and culture. Republican principles may have claimed universality, but not everyone accepted them. Not until the end of the century was the triumph of the republic assured in France. At the same time, republican universalism did not apply to everyone equally. Republicans cherished the ideal of universal adult male suffrage, but this of course marginalized the half of the population that was female. The Third Republic was also an era of extensive foreign immigration, as well as colonial expansion, and neither foreigners nor colonial subjects enjoyed the rights of French citizens. In the end, it seemed, republicanism defined itself as universal as much by those it excluded as by those it included. Nonetheless, by sometimes holding out the prospect that those who embraced republican values could become French no matter what their origins, republican universalism proved attractive to many beyond the nation's borders.

Third Republic France embraced, finally and permanently, the heritage and values of the great Revolution in the name of mankind as a whole. The strength and widespread acceptance of these values to a large extent explains why the republic lasted for so long, in spite of numerous challenges and difficulties. Ultimately it would take not one but two world wars to bring it to an end, and even then the political culture it championed survived. In elaborating this vibrant political culture, the Third Republic not only represented the culmination of the nineteenth century but equally set forth some major themes for the twentieth. As such, no other French regime more fully represents the history of modern France as a whole.

THE "REPUBLICANIZATION" OF THE REPUBLIC

The Third Republic was only expected be a brief prelude to a restoration of the monarchy. The provisional government appointed in September 1870 needed above all to defend the nation against the Prussians; when it became clear that continued resistance was useless, the government sued for an armistice so it could conduct elections for a regular government that would negotiate the final peace from a position of authority. These elections took place in early February after an electoral campaign of barely a week, at a time when a large part of the country lay under enemy occupation and communications were hopelessly disrupted. The results were paradoxical, to say the least. A nation that only a few months earlier had overthrown an emperor and proclaimed a revolutionary republic now elected a solid majority of antirepublican monarchists. By a two to one margin, the people of France voted for aristocratic representatives pledged to make a king once again the ruler of the land.

The monarchists owed their stunning victory primarily to two factors. First, during a time of great disruption many peasants voted for the most familiar leader, and that was often the local *seigneur*. More important, the central issue in the election was support for war or peace, and many in the countryside saw the republicans as the war party. In contrast to the Parisian radicals loudly calling for a struggle to the bitter end, the monarchist right posed as advocates of peace as soon as possible. Given the widespread hostility to the (now essentially lost) war in much of the country, this proved the right's trump card. The election results did not mean, however, that the majority of the country hoped for a restoration of the monarchy; as soon became clear, the republican ideal had deep roots and broad support in France. Nonetheless, for the time being the right dominated the National Assembly and could claim a mandate for royalist rule.

One of the new assembly's first acts was to elect the conservative Republican Adolphe Thiers head of the provisional government. Thiers immediately pursued peace negotiations with the Prussians, leading France to accept the draconian treaty imposed by Berlin on March 1, 1871. As we saw in Chapter 4, Thiers then moved to suppress the Paris commune, eliminating the last resistance in the capital by the end of May. Thiers's actions in both cases reassured many in France that the republic could be bourgeois rather than revolutionary, serving both to reinforce his own power in the assembly and to increase the strength of republicanism in general. For the next two years Thiers concentrated on floating government bonds to pay off the indemnity imposed by the Germans, something he did with remarkable success. By 1873 Paris had paid the indemnity and German troops evacuated the nation eighteen months ahead of schedule. Thiers also rebuilt the shattered French army and helped restore the nation's sense of self-confidence so badly damaged by the events of the terrible year.

While Thiers worked to restore France, the monarchist majority in the assembly remained committed to the return of the king. This initiative soon ran into considerable difficulties, however, on a variety of fronts. First, by-elections soon demonstrated that the February 1871 vote had been a fluke. The ink was barely dry on the peace treaty when the republicans scored a significant victory in local elections during April. They followed this with an even more impressive success in July, winning ninety-nine seats in by-elections, as opposed to twelve for the monarchists. As they watched their parliamentary majority dwindle, monarchists strove to come up with a restoration plan, but this also proved difficult. They were divided into two factions, the Legitimists who looked to the Bourbon monarchy and supported the Comte de Chambord, and the Orléanist faction who supported the Comte de Paris; in other words, the Restoration versus the July Monarchy, 1814 versus 1830.

In spite of the long-standing hostility between these two royalist factions, it seemed at first that they could resolve this issue very easily. The fifty-year-old Comte de Chambord had no children, whereas the Comte de Paris was in his early thirties and had already sired a male heir. Therefore, the two sides agreed to appoint Chambord as the next king, with the title Henry V, and Paris as his successor. Ultimately, however, Chambord's personality derailed royalist dreams of a new monarchy. The grandson of Charles X, the last reigning Bourbon king, Chambord had fled into exile in 1830 and remained there ever since, eventually settling at a castle in Frohsdorf, near Vienna. When the monarchists approached him about taking the crown, he returned to the chateau of Chambord and proclaimed his intention of becoming king on July 5, 1871. Unfortunately he showed he knew little about contemporary France and had learned nothing from history. Not only did he reject any notions of constitutional monarchy, he also made clear that he would accept the crown only if France abandoned the tricolor flag in favor of the traditional fleur-de-lis standard. Many monarchists, who had hoped for a modern constitutional monarch along British lines, were shocked and bitterly disappointed, but Chambord refused to be swayed by their pleas. For him, everything since the Revolution had been a gigantic mistake, and he would reign by divine right or not at all. Subsequent attempts to advance his cause proving fruitless, he returned to Austria, dying there in 1883.

It is easy to ridicule the stubbornness and shortsightedness of the Comte de Chambord, but his defiant posture underscored the extent to which the heritage of the Revolution had permanently marked France. Generations of French women and men had sworn allegiance to the tricolor flag, in some cases shedding their blood and dying for the nation it represented. The 1789 Revolution and its aftermath had become an indelible part of the history of modern France, and no one could simply pretend that the last eighty years had not happened. Most monarchists recognized this, but without a viable pretender who agreed, a latter-day Louis Philippe, royalism had no future in France. Henceforth, the nation's destiny would be ruled by the republican form of government first born of the Revolution.

Stymied by the obstinacy of the Comte de Chambord, the monarchists decided to play for time. In May 1873 they maneuvered Thiers into resigning, replacing him with Patrice de MacMahon, a marshal of France whose credentials included amassing a losing record in the Franco-Prussian War and helping to suppress the Paris commune. Appointing him as president for a seven-year term, the monarchists hoped during that time Chambord would either come to his senses or else die and leave the field to a more reasonable pretender (he did neither). MacMahon's royalist government of "moral order" condemned republicanism as dangerous to France and increased censorship laws to hinder the opposition. This proved vain: the by-elections of July 1873 were a triumph for the republicans, who won ninety-nine seats out of one hundred and fourteen up for grabs. Subsequent elections confirmed this trend, further reducing the monarchist majority. The royalist dream of a restoration was fast ebbing with the political tide.

The major task of the new assembly was to write a constitution for the Third Republic. This was no easy task since, as would become typical, the assembly was split into several factions. On the right, the monarchists were divided into Legitimists, Orléanists, and a few Bonapartists, while on the left republican forces ranged from the radicals led by Léon Gambetta to conservatives like Adolphe Thiers. The resulting constitution, passed in 1875, owed much to a strategic alliance between moderates from both sides. Those on the right accepted the principle of universal manhood suffrage, whereas a solid faction of the left agreed to the creation of a bicameral legislature, composed of a lower house, the Chamber of Deputies, and an upper house, the Senate. The new Senate, whose members would be elected by the nation's mayors and not by popular vote, represented a conservative, rural-dominated force in the new regime, something anathema to left republicans who dreamed of a revolutionary unicameral legislature. Léon Gambetta led many to accept it, winning for himself and his followers the title of "Opportunists." Yet like Thiers before him, Gambetta believed one must make concessions to the right in order to ensure the viability of the new regime. As in that other great republic, the United States, a semidemocratic Senate served in Third Republic France to reassure elites and forestall the possibility of abrupt and potentially dangerous political change that might threaten property rights. Finally, the new constitution made provisions for a president elected by the members of the legislature, but left vague how much actual power that individual would have.

At the end of 1875 the assembly disbanded to make way for elections to the new legislative body. Republicans won a solid majority in the new chamber, with 340 seats to 155 for the monarchists. However, as expected, the right controlled the Senate and President MacMahon remained firmly in the royalist camp. While the nation as a whole clearly supported republicanism, the monarchists continued to hope for the triumph of their cause. Instead of appointing Léon Gambetta, the clear republican leader, as head of the new government, MacMahon instead chose the more moderate Jules Simon, hoping to anger Gambetta and split the republicans. This failed: Gambetta loyally supported Simon's government, which had to confront the hopeless task of trying to balance republican and monarchist aspirations, represented by the chamber and the president.

After months of tension and frustration MacMahon took action. On May 16, 1877, he sent Simon a letter demanding his resignation, which he received the next day. The republican majority in the chamber reacted with shock and fury, speaking of a coup d'état, and refused to approve the monarchist

MacMahon nominated to replace Simon. MacMahon responded by dissolving the chamber and scheduling new elections for October. In spite of the strident campaigning undertaken by the president along with his royalist and Church supporters, the republicans once again won a solid majority of the vote. Thus reinforced, the chamber again refused to accept MacMahon's choice of premier until he named a republican, Jules Dufaure. In spite of urging from his most impassioned allies to call out the army, MacMahon accepted the popular will and let the new government do its work without interference. In 1879 further legislative victories gave the republicans control of the Senate. MacMahon concluded there was little he could do as president and resigned, leaving the field free for republican control.

The crisis of May 16, 1877, was an important turning point in the history of modern France. For perhaps the first time, a major political turning point took place peacefully, without barricades, revolutionary crowds in the streets, or seizures of government buildings. Over the preceding decades Frenchmen from Paris down to the smallest villages had learned to vote and use elections as the ultimate arbiter of political power and legitimacy. At the same time, the crisis spelled the final end of monarchism in France. The resignation of MacMahon, followed by the death of the Comte de Chambord four years later, left the royalist party with no standard bearer, and the consistent drumbeat of republican electoral victories left no doubt as to the sentiments of the French people, and indeed the prevailing winds of history. The aristocracy would retain a great deal of wealth and influence in France, but it would no longer constitute a political force of any significance.

Above all, the crisis of May 1877 made the Third Republic a real republic. Republicanism now became, and would remain, the dominant (if not unchallenged) political culture in France. The Third Republic would retain an important conservative dimension, highlighted above all by the semidemocratic Senate. It would also be a parliamentary rather than a presidential regime. When MacMahon resigned, the legislative republicans promptly replaced him with the colorless Jules Grévy, and the presidency soon became essentially a ceremonial position (the republican equivalent of a constitutional monarchy). In years to come many would criticize the absence of a strong executive, leaving the government of the country at the mercy of fleeting parliamentary majorities. But this arrangement seemed to guarantee the integrity of the democratic system, ensuring that no new Napoleon would arise.

As of 1879, therefore, the republicans had taken firm and permanent control of the French government. A bigger task now confronted them: making

France a thoroughly republican nation. During the last decades of the nineteenth century they undertook a variety of initiatives to make republicanism not just an ideology or system of government but a national political culture. Republicans must spread their values throughout the country, down to the smallest, most isolated villages. Their success in doing so would not only give the Third Republic its unusual longevity but more importantly remake the character and identity of France.

THE REPUBLICANIZATION OF FRANCE

Once the republicans had reduced MacMahon and the monarchists to political impotence, they moved swiftly to remake France along liberal democratic lines. Starting with symbolic changes, they soon implemented more substantive policies that both transformed the nation and underscored how much it had already changed. The new nation that came into being during the last decades of the nineteenth century was created in the image of republican universalism, and the policies implemented by the republicans would indelibly mark the face of modern France.

A key characteristic of the opportunist republic was a weak executive and control by the Legislative Assembly. In part this reflected the personalities that dominated the new government. Léon Gambetta, by far the most prominent republican leader, was the natural choice to lead the regime after 1877. Yet his enemies combined to prevent him from becoming prime minister until 1881, and then managed to overthrow his government a few months later. Gambetta was succeeded by Jules Ferry who, more than any other man, would come to symbolize the opportunist republic. A quiet manager rather than a charismatic leader, Ferry and his followers would push through major reforms while retaining the image of moderation and judicious government. This combination would characterize the Third Republic in general, helping to account for both its triumphs and its challenges.

During the first few years after their victory in 1877 the republicans inscribed the legacy of the Revolution in the nation's political culture. Starting in 1879, they reversed a series of laws restricting freedom of expression and assembly. In 1881 the government abolished censorship of the press and political cartoons. In 1884, a banner year for republican reform, the regime legalized trade unions, allowed most municipalities (with the signal exception of Paris) to elect their own mayors and city councils, and restored the right to divorce banned since the Restoration. Symbolic measures also demonstrated the new hegemony of republicanism. In 1879 the "Marseillaise" was restored to its position as the French national anthem. In 1880 the government made Bastille Day a national holiday and legitimized the image of Marianne, seen as subversive under the Second Empire. In 1882 it legalized secular public funerals, which at times became republican festivals. Events like the burial procession of Léon Gambetta through Paris on January 6, 1883, attempted (not always successfully) to mobilize public opinion in favor of the regime. In 1885, 2 million Parisians took part in demonstrations marking the funeral of Victor Hugo and celebrating his progressive ideas.

The opportunist republic went beyond symbols, enacting measures that would reshape the nation. In economic affairs it pursued a relatively conservative path designed to favor property owners rather than promote rapid economic growth. The adoption of the Méline tariff in 1892 rejected the free trade orientation of the Second Empire in favor of widespread protectionism and heavy duties on imports. Perhaps the most important innovation was the Freycinet plan of 1879, which built over five thousand miles of new railroads throughout the country. The plan's goal was to ensure that everyone in France had easy access to a train, and therefore to demonstrate the modernity and vitality of the republic at the local level. At the same time it would provide jobs and stimulate commerce, thus providing both economic and political benefits.

By far the most significant reforms undertaken during the opportunist republic concerned education. Before the 1880s most children attended primary school, but it was neither required nor free. Secondary education, especially for girls, was a luxury. Moreover, the Church dominated the educational system, especially in rural areas whose local governments could barely afford to maintain public schools. For the republicans, education reform assumed pride of place for several reasons. The increasing importance of technology demanded a more highly skilled workforce in the late nineteenth century, and the growth of print culture gave significant advantages to those with at least a modicum of education. But perhaps the most important consideration was political. Jules Ferry and other republican leaders viewed education as their best tool for winning over France's population by instilling the values of the republic. Schoolteachers would instruct the nation's youth, both boys and girls, in the glorious heritage of the Revolution and their duty to defend it against enemies at home and abroad.

Jules Ferry was minister of education from 1879 to 1885, and during his tenure he pushed through a series of school reforms known as the Ferry laws. First and foremost, Ferry made primary education free and compulsory for all children in France. The nation's youth would henceforth learn standardized forms of French language and history as well as math and science, in schoolrooms adorned with maps of France and the tricolor flag. The reform created a new large cohort of public elementary school teachers, both men and women, who became the de facto representatives of republican ideology in villages and towns throughout the country. They faced many difficulties, especially single young women teachers in the countryside, and yet they embodied the France of the future. For many peasants in particular the prospect of people who could earn a living without hard physical labor came as a revelation, offering new opportunities for small town youth. Both by their ideas and their presence public schoolteachers represented the growing power of the French state, the *fonctionnaires* or public employees who would become an ever-greater part of the national population in the century to come. Not for nothing did many contemporaries term them the "black hussars" of the republic.

The republicans' determination to control French education, and ultimately the nation's future, brought them into direct conflict with one of the most powerful institutions in France: the Catholic Church. As a result, bitter battles pitting religion against secularism became a leading theme of the early Third Republic, suffusing both public and private life. It is no accident that the establishment of the republic as a universal political culture would lead to a fundamental clash with a long-standing champion of a very different universalist vision. The republic's confrontation with the Church reinforced its own sometimes fanatical universalism, so that in their intense struggle these two opponents increasingly resembled each other. To Catholicism's belief in spirituality and the divine, the republic opposed its own conviction in reason, science, and the civic virtues inherited from the Revolution. In the sphere of education above all, republican universalism would tolerate no rival.

In challenging Catholic control of the schoolhouse, the Ferry laws struck at the heart of the Church's power in France. Before the 1870s Catholic primary schools were at least as widespread as their secular rivals, and the Falloux Law of 1850 had created a flourishing system of parochial secondary schools. In particular, the Church dominated the education of girls, whose parents frequently viewed public schools as low in prestige if not morally suspect. Moreover, the Falloux Law required religious instruction in all public schools, and many public school teachers were priests and nuns. Ferry's reforms changed all that. While rejecting demands from radical republicans to close the religious schools, they did ban religious instruction in public schools, replacing it with "civic" (i.e., republican) instruction. They also banned members of Catholic orders from teaching in the public schools after five years (a law that was never completely enforced). In addition, the reforms created lay secondary schools for girls, seeing young women as key to religious political culture.

The conflict over education set the republic and the Church on a collision course for decades to come. Religious leaders denied the political legitimacy of the regime, at times referring to the republic as *la gueuse* (the slut). Many villages, such as Plozévet in Brittany, so memorably described by Pierre-Jakez Hélias, found themselves split between the republican schoolmaster and the Catholic priest. More generally, the Church fought to retain its central role in French life. The Assumptionist Fathers, founded in 1845, launched a massive campaign against the republic during the 1870s. The order sponsored the national subscription to build Sacré Coeur in Montmartre, and its newspaper *La Croix* had a circulation of several hundred thousand. As historians have pointed out recently, church/state conflict was at times less extreme than it appeared. For example, in small towns the priest and the teacher, often the most educated individuals in their communities, sometimes worked together. Nonetheless, during the late nineteenth century the Church remained a resolute opponent of the republican regime, and the new right-wing movements that emerged in the 1880s found ready support in the nation's pulpits.

Jules Ferry's educational reforms achieved their objectives. First, they made literacy nearly universal in France by the end of the nineteenth century. Second, they knit the nation together to an unprecedented degree on the basis of republican political culture. The new elementary curriculum was extremely centralized, prompting the joke that at any moment every French child in a given class was turning the exact same page of the exact same book. Even young people in the colonies of Africa and Asia repeated lessons about "our ancestors the Gauls," according to popular legend. Perhaps more than any other single measure, the Ferry laws united France, making it a nation governed by a universal republican vision.

In large part, Ferry's educational reforms succeeded because they conformed to the new shape of French society at the end of the late nineteenth century. Above all, they expressed the worldview of the burgeoning middle class that increasingly shaped the self-image of Third Republic France. The July Monarchy and the Second Empire had witnessed the triumph of the *haute bourgeoisie* in French politics and society, usually in alliance with the more progressive members of the aristocracy. Both groups retained substantial economic influence after 1870, although the legend of France as a country controlled by two hundred prominent families was more mythical than real during these years.

Increasingly, however, political and cultural leadership passed into the hands of the less wealthy but much larger *moyenne* and *petite bourgeoisie*, the middle and lower middle classes. These groups grew substantially during the late nineteenth century. The rise of large industry and commerce created a need for more clerks and managers, white-collar workers with more education and social status than the workers below them, even if they also depended on wage labor. The expansion of education produced more trained professionals, teachers, doctors, and lawyers, who were often the most notable individuals in small towns throughout the country. In addition, the growth of government increased the number of middle-class jobs. The number of people working for the public sector in France doubled from roughly 250,000 to 500,000 between 1848 and 1914, and many of these individuals considered themselves middle class.[3]

These were the people Léon Gambetta termed "the new social strata," and they constituted the bedrock of the Third Republic. Republican political culture identified itself with the "little man," and it held up the small town lawyer, businessman, and civil servant as the heart and soul of France. To be middle class was more than just a matter of occupation, however, it was also a way of life. It meant having enough money to dress properly (conservatively rather than fashionably) and to live in a house or an apartment with a well-furnished living room as well as sleeping quarters. It meant not engaging in manual labor, and providing an education (at least at the secondary level) so one's children wouldn't have to work with their hands either. In addition, it meant having a high level of culture, a knowledge of literature, music, and the arts. Middle-class French men and women were people of respectability, social standing, financial solidity, and good taste.

Finally, the broad middle class of the Third Republic held core ideas that amounted at times to a secular faith. Strongly influenced by mid-nineteenth-century positivism, they believed in science and reason, and the progress that such ideals would inevitably bring about. Education was of paramount importance, not only as a way of teaching rational thought but also because it was key to social mobility and middle-class status. The middle class believed strongly in the tradition of the French Revolution as the heritage of both France and mankind in general, and in particular in its attack on inherited privilege. The desire for social justice only went so far, however, and never questioned property rights. In the tradition of nineteenth-century liberalism it upheld equality of opportunity but not of condition, and consequently often turned a deaf ear to the sufferings of the working poor. To a great extent, therefore, to be middle class in the Third Republic meant embracing the ideals of the universal republic. No other social group believed so strongly in the republican mission, or lived so completely according to its principles.

One important yet paradoxical aspect of bourgeois life under the Third Republic was the rise of modern feminism. As we have seen, demands for female empowerment and gender equality have a long history in France, going back at least as far as the Revolution. Middle-class life in the late nineteenth century hardly seemed devoted to women's rights. The bourgeois family ideal included a wife who did not seek paid labor but instead devoted herself to home and children while her husband made all the key decisions about their life. As many historians have argued, republican doctrine, with its emphasis on fraternity and the rights of man, was heavily gendered male. Moreover, stereotypes of women as emotional and spiritual rather than rational led many men to justify denying them the vote, arguing that they would look to the priests for political guidance and therefore reinforce the power of the Church. Republicans did believe in educating girls in order to liberate them from superstition and republicanize the family. Nonetheless, aside from the legalization of divorce in 1884 the Third Republic did little to promote gender equality and the rights of women. Husbands controlled the property of married women, and a Frenchwoman who wed a foreigner automatically lost her nationality on the presumption that a woman should belong to the same country as her spouse.

Nonetheless, it was precisely the contradiction between egalitarian rhetoric and patriarchal realities that inspired the rebirth of feminism under the Third Republic. A Frenchwoman, the radical feminist Hubertine Auclert, who had founded the Society for the Rights of Women in 1876, invented the term "feminism" in 1882. Also in 1882 veteran activists Maria Deraismes and Léon Richer founded the French League for the Rights of Women. The rebirth of French feminism took place in the global context of first-wave feminism, which sought above all to win women the right to vote.

In comparison to their militant sisters and brothers in Britain and America, women's rights activists in France took a more moderate approach, emphasizing legal equality and property rights rather than enfranchisement. Whereas in the early nineteenth century feminism had developed in close conjunction with socialism, as demonstrated by women like Flora Tristan and Louise Michel, after 1870 the movement for women's rights had a strongly bourgeois character. The marked feminist orientation of the commune, as well as the tendency of male workers to see women in factories as contributing to lower wages and deskilling, certainly contributed to this more conservative orientation. At the same time, Third Republic feminism was strongly influenced by the dominant middle-class culture of that era. Many feminist activists, for example, shared the anticlericalism of the republicans and saw themselves as demanding for women the rights guaranteed by the republic to men. Like bourgeois men, they also displayed little sympathy for working people, refusing, for example, to support shorter hours for (mostly female) servants.

The refusal to focus on suffrage clearly illustrated the moderate character of French feminism during the late nineteenth century. Feminists shared the fear of republican men that the enfranchisement of women might benefit the Church and conservative forces in general. Many also feared that such demands were unrealistic, and focusing on them could distract the movement from more attainable goals. This reluctance to press for women's suffrage split the feminist movement in France; at an 1889 conference in Paris Deraisme and Richer agreed to suppress discussion of the issue, much to the anger of Hubertine Auclert, who argued that political rights for women should be a top priority. Feminists did score some victories during this period. They won full legal rights for single women, and women began to enter the elite professions, like medicine, in small numbers. But political enfranchisement remained a distant dream for French feminists, and would not be realized for another half century.

As influential as the middle classes were, they constituted no more than 20 percent of the French population. The success of the new republic also rested on demographic shifts among the nation's two large popular classes: peasants and workers. Life in the countryside changed substantially in these years. During the first half of the Third Republic peasants ceased to constitute a majority of the French population, dropping from over 50 percent in 1870 to roughly 40 percent by 1914. The nation experienced a substantial rural exodus, marked not only by the growth of cities and towns but also by the declining number of farms. Those who continued to work the land had to learn to grow food more efficiently for increasingly faraway markets, as subsistence agriculture could no longer adequately provide for a family. Spurred by foreign competition and the impact of the Long Depression, the price of grain dropped substantially during the late nineteenth century. The most dramatic example of new agricultural realities was the phylloxera epidemic that ravaged the French wine industry in the 1870s. A disease native to American vines, phylloxera arrived in Europe during the 1850s with the introduction of rootstock from the new world. The disease largely destroyed the wine industry, especially in Languedoc and the south, and only the introduction of new vines from the United States, naturally resistant to the disease, to French vineyards saved the nation's viniculture. This was an expensive process, so the disease forced many small vineyards out of business and made the industry as a whole more market oriented. In general, farms became fewer, larger, and more modern during this period, and those who worked them less peasants in the traditional mode and more farmers and agriculture workers.

The changing demography of rural France facilitated the implantation of the new republican culture to an important degree. Certainly, many saw the increased presence of the national institutions in their local lives as an imposition. Teachers emphasized that one must learn the national culture, and helped stamp out dialects like Breton in Brittany or Occitan in Languedoc. The imposition of national military service after 1870 took young men (whose labor was needed on the farm) far away from their homes and families, sometimes never to return. The world portrayed in Parisian newspapers often seemed foreign even to those who could read them easily. Yet many others found these new ideas attractive and valued the opportunities that broader horizons could bring. Gradually the world of the village *notable*, the local politician, the teacher, and the journalist, became the world of the French peasant, and especially of the peasant's sons and daughters.

In 1904 Emile Guillaumin, a peasant turned writer, published *The Life of a Simple Man*, a fictionalized autobiography of a man much like himself born in the 1820s. Guillaumin's novel describes in captivating detail traditional rural life in France and how it changed over the course of the century. At the end of the novel Guillaumin relates a conversation between "Tiennon" and his young grandson Francis, a conversation about memory and history that illustrates just how much peasant life has changed by the dawn of the twentieth century:

> Francis would often beg me to tell him stories . . . I knew some of the old stories which we hand down on the farms from generation to generation. I knew "The Green Mountain," "The White Dog," "Tom Thumb," "The Devil's Bag of Gold," and "The Beast with Seven Heads."
>
> But it was not long before Francis knew my collection of stories and riddles and funny tales as well as I did, and I was no longer able to amuse him. He then began to tell me the things he was learning at school. He talked of kings and queens, of Joan of Arc, Bayard, Richelieu, Robespierre, of crusades and wars and massacres. He seemed to know all that

had happened down the centuries. Of course I listened with only half an ear and was too old to remember all those things when he asked me afterwards in what year such and such a battle took place, at what time such and such a king had reigned, and what had been the exploits of such and such a famous man, I would make stupid mistakes, even to the extent of being a thousand years out. With geography it was the same thing. I confused the names of countries, seas, *départements* and towns—which made him laugh a good deal.[4]

Life of a Simple Man portrays not only classic peasant life but also the republican culture that was replacing it at the end of the nineteenth century.

By 1900 the working class had become almost as large as the peasantry, nearly 40 percent of the French population. Yet in contrast to farmers, widely courted by the politicians of the Third Republic and frequently lionized as the soul of the nation, working people existed at the margins of society. French workers were a diverse class, including rural laborers and urban craftsmen in a variety of different industries and occupations. The second industrial revolution and the growth of French heavy industry reshaped working-class life. By the 1880s and 1890s the skilled craftsmen who had dominated working-class politics earlier in the century were gradually being replaced by skilled factory workers as large factories became more common in France. A few crafts, notably glassmaking, disappeared entirely, but more commonly the sons of artisans took up factory work rather than following the trades of their fathers. Semiskilled workers, those with only a modicum of training and little formal education, became more common as mechanization reduced the need for sophisticated technical knowledge. The gradual flattening out of working-class skill levels made life on the job less rewarding for many, but by reducing differences between workers it also made it easier to organize unions and political parties.

French labor did not become completely homogeneous, however. The late nineteenth century witnessed a massive wave of foreign immigration into France, and the majority of immigrants took up working-class employment. Immigrants usually came from neighboring countries, such as Belgium, Germany, and Italy, but in the 1880s large numbers of Jews from central and eastern Europe also settled in France. For the most part, these newcomers moved to Paris and other large cities or to industrial regions like Lorraine and the Nord. Immigrant workers tended to concentrate in specific occupations like construction or clothing, often living and working in isolation from French laborers.

Their native colleagues often reacted to them with suspicion and anger, accusing them of stealing jobs and undercutting wages. In 1893 French workers in the southern city of Aigues-Mortes rioted against Italian immigrants, killing as many as 150. Hostility to Asian immigrants, almost nonexistent in France, led French unions to salute Chinese exclusion laws in California. Ideas of working-class solidarity in France clearly had their limits.

The living conditions of French workers showed some improvement during the late nineteenth century but in general remained poor. While the Long Depression may have hurt salaries, it lowered prices on many basic goods, so that real wages tended to rise during this period. Workers ate better than their parents or grandparents had, enjoying richer and more diverse diets, and they began to have enough disposable income to take part in the burgeoning consumer culture, especially in Paris. However, lodgings remained small and dismal, with French workers experiencing some of the worst housing conditions in western Europe. Moreover, health standards remained poor, so that young working men were rejected from military service on grounds of poor health at higher rates than any others in France. Public authorities took few measures to improve the working-class condition, in sharp contrast to imperial Germany, which offered health and disability insurance. The standard workweek remained twelve hours per day, Monday through Saturday. Finally, and perhaps most important, if working-class living standards were rising slowly, the middle classes seemed to be finding prosperity more rapidly. Wealth and poverty are always relative concepts, and compared to others in society many French workers felt relatively poorer by the turn of the century.

Increasing ideas of class solidarity and class immiseration, combined with a liberal regime that tolerated unions and unfettered freedom of expression, fostered the rapid growth of the labor movement during the early Third Republic. In France workers organized along two main lines: trade unions and socialist political parties. Both had been effectively smashed by the repression of the Paris commune, and since many leading activists had been killed or forced into exile it took some time for labor to start organizing again. After years of debate, the republican-dominated assembly voted a full amnesty for all communards in July 1880, prompting many to return from prison or exile. The amnesty not only benefited these individuals but also reflected a new tolerance for the left. That and the legalization of unions which followed in 1884 marked a new beginning for organized labor in France.

Unions in the Third Republic first took the form of the *bourses du travail*, or labor exchanges. Originally conceived as centers where workers could socialize, read, and get news about employment, the *bourses* gradually began to defend labor interests collectively. The first was founded in Paris in 1885 with the aid of Gambetta's government, which hoped to use them to win workers over to republicanism. Some businessmen also supported them, seeing the *bourses* as a more wholesome alternative to working class cafés. The guiding spirit of the *bourses du travail* was Fernand Pelloutier, a revolutionary journalist who believed in worker self-management and independence from capitalism. In 1891 outrage over the repression of a strike at Fourmies, where soldiers massacred nine demonstrating workers, pushed the movement in a more radical direction. The next year Pelloutier helped found the Federation of the Bourses du Travail. Three years later the federation merged with another union group to create the Confédération Générale du Travail (General Confederation of Labor), or CGT, which to this day remains France's largest labor union organization.

Led by Pelloutier and others, the activists of the CGT embraced the idea of revolutionary anarcho-syndicalism (*syndicalisme* being the French word for unionism). Anarcho-syndicalism consisted of a few essential principles. First, it was resolutely anticapitalist, believing that only the overthrow of capitalism and its replacement by worker self-management would liberate the working class. Second, it emphasized the necessity of direct action to attack and ultimately destroy the capitalist system. Anarcho-syndicalists revered the strike as not just a movement for higher wages or better hours but even more as a body blow against the economic ruling class. Ultimately, they foresaw and hoped for the merging of separate industrial actions into an apocalyptic general strike that would prompt the revolutionary overthrow of capitalism. Third, anarcho-syndicalism rejected political struggle, in particular, participation in electoral campaigns, in favor of direct action. They thus refused to cooperate with any political parties, even those on the left, arguing the workers must liberate themselves. Anarcho-syndicalism drew on earlier strands of French socialism and anarchism, notably the philosophy of Proudhon as well as the cooperative movement, adapting them to the new realities of industrial labor.

An important socialist movement, or movements, also developed in France during the late nineteenth century. More than before 1870, Marxism featured prominently in the French far left. Before the ideas of Marx and Engels had been only one belief, and not the most important, held by socialist militants, and few Marxists had figured among the leadership of the Paris commune. Both the decimation of that leadership, and Marxism's orientation toward mass political parties and electoral participation, gave it new standing among

French socialists. Modern socialism had always been an international movement, of course, and the greater prominence of Marxism in France reflected the situation in Europe as a whole. Marx died in London in 1883 but his tradition of "scientific socialism" continued to win adherents and inspire new socialist parties as European society became increasingly industrial. In 1889, on the centennial of the French Revolution, a socialist congress in Paris formally created the Second International, the umbrella organization for socialist parties throughout Europe and the world. By the end of the century Marxist parties had enrolled millions of supporters across the Continent in a movement they claimed would overthrow capitalism and bring the working class to power.

In France the main representative of Marxist socialism was the French Workers Party led by indefatigable militant Jules Guesde. A hard-line Marxist also known as the Red Pope, Guesde worked together with another French socialist (and Marx's son-in-law) Paul LaFargue to organize the first major socialist congress in France in 1879. Guesde believed that the problems of the working class could only be resolved by socialist revolution, and that all else must be subordinated to that goal. The Guesdists believed in supporting labor actions and in participating in elections; Guesde himself was elected to the National Assembly from Lille. However, such actions should only be a means to the revolutionary end, not ends in themselves. Not all socialists in France agreed with this uncompromising posture, and in 1883 the party split into two factions, Guesde's French Workers Party and the French Socialist Workers Federation, led by Paul Brousse and Jean Allemane. Nicknamed "the Possibilists," this party emphasized reform over revolution, and encouraged participation in elections and cooperation with progressive republicans. French socialism would remain divided until 1905, after that enjoying a brief period of unity until World War I.

The conflict over reform versus revolution would become the central socialist concern in the new century. Its emergence during the early Third Republic illustrated the rise of republican political culture, the fact that reform was a real option in contrast to the early nineteenth century. But at times this dichotomy was more rigid than it seemed. Guesde, Brousse, and Allemane, all veterans of the commune, might differ in rhetoric but all agreed on the need for radical political change and engagement in the electoral process. Moreover, some republicans also identified as socialists, or "republican-socialists," holding to the old principal of "no enemies on the left," and saw the socialists as potential allies rather than enemies. Revolutionary convictions aside, it seemed quite possible that socialism could be integrated into a broader republican consensus.

Political developments in the last two decades of the nineteenth century made this manifestly clear. The real challenges to the republic arose not on the left but on the right, and were so powerful at times as to call into question the survival of the republican experiment. The hostility of powerful institutions, notably the Church and the army, to the republic blended with the rise of a new right-wing movement, one adapted to the politics of mass society. Once again France confronted conflicts born of the Revolution, and once again it became a nation bitterly divided.

THE REPUBLIC IN DANGER

By the mid-1880s the Third Republic could point to some solid achievements, notably in the field of education. Not all were happy with republican rule, however, and the legislative elections of 1885 brought a sharp setback for the Opportunists. Not only did right-wing parties double their vote from the previous election, but the radical republicans, or simply Radicals, emerged as a powerful bloc in their own right. The economic downturn perhaps best explained this electoral reverse, as well as the generally colorless character of the regime, and the fact that it seemed to have run out of ideas. The fact that no party or coalition had a clear majority led to a series of weak, unstable governments over the next few years. The regime's reputation was further tarnished by scandal in 1887 when it came out that President Grévy's son-in-law, Daniel Wilson, had been selling government decorations for cash. To many, the time seemed right for radical change.

The agent of that change arrived on horseback. Georges Boulanger was a career military officer who had risen through the ranks to become a general, serving in Italy, Indochina, and Algeria. He was decorated for bravery in the Franco-Prussian War and participated in the army's attack on the commune. As it happened, an injury prevented him from taking part in the final bloody massacre of the communards, a fact that would prove politically useful later. Boulanger also had strong ties to radical republicans, and had been a high school classmate of the radical leader Georges Clemenceau. In January 1886 he became war minister and proceeded to implement a series of popular reforms, such as improving soldiers' mattresses and allowing them to wear beards. When miners staged a bitter strike in Decazeville that same month, he won the approval of the right by leading army troops against it, and the support of the left by refusing to allow soldiers to fire on the strikers, instead directing them to share their rations with the miners. Moreover, the handsome general cut a dashing and charismatic figure, electrifying the Parisian crowd astride his black horse during a military parade in the Longchamps racecourse. Compared with the lackluster and scandal-ridden regime, he attracted many on all sides of the political spectrum. Monarchists at a loss for new strategies viewed him as a potential ally, and Bonapartists saw in him a potential new version of the famous general.

A key factor in Boulanger's appeal was the rise of a new nationalist spirit in France. Until the Third Republic, patriotism had been the province of the French left; even the commune had seen itself in large part as a patriotic uprising against a defeatist government. By the 1880s, however, many on the right had adopted national pride as a central value, spurred principally by resentment against Germany and its seizure of Alsace-Lorraine. In 1882 Paul Déroulède, a veteran of the Franco-Prussian War, founded the Patriots League. This organization, devoted above all to the cause of *revanche* (revenge) against Berlin, quickly attracted tens of thousands of members. The new nationalists attracted support in diverse quarters well beyond those of the traditional right. The economic crisis had hurt many shopkeepers and artisans, facing competition from large industries and department stores. Moreover, the relative economic decline of France, which had now slipped well behind Germany and the United States as an industrial power, seemed to parallel both the plight of the small producer and the nation's humiliation in 1870–1871. Some workers, and others, also saw themselves threatened by rising immigration from abroad. In particular, a disturbing new strain of anti-Semitism accompanied the rise of the new nationalism, although France's Jewish population remained quite small.

The political movement that coalesced in support of General Boulanger not only drew from both left and right but reshaped them and the French political landscape in general. By the end of 1886 Boulanger had become one of the most popular men in France. As war minister he took steps designed to provoke Germany, fanning the flames of revanchist sentiment at home. A new government dismissed him from his ministerial post in May 1887 and tried to bury him in a provincial command, but he remained the darling of the Parisian crowd, which assaulted the train station attempting to prevent his departure. The Wilson scandal convinced Boulanger to throw his hat into the political ring, and in 1887 supporters began submitting his name in a variety of legislative by-elections, all of which he won handily. Afraid of his growing popularity, the government forced him to retire from the army, unwisely as it turned out, since now he could devote his efforts full-time to political activism. By 1888 Boulanger had won the support of many Radicals and socialists, as well as funding from key monarchists and Bonapartists. To many it seemed inevitable that he would triumph in the legislative elections the following year and soon seize the reins of power one way or another.

Unfortunately for his supporters, however, Boulanger the man did not measure up to the movement that bore his name. In January 1889 the general scored his most spectacular victory yet, handily winning a by-election in Paris despite energetic republican opposition. His ecstatic Parisian followers thronged the streets of the capital, while political organizers planned to nominate him for election in every district in France. Many hoped he would use the momentum generated by his triumph to seize power in a coup d'état. Yet Boulanger let the moment pass him by, and when the interior minister tricked him into believing the government had proof of treasonous actions on his part, the general fled across the border to Belgium in April. As a result the movement quickly collapsed, the Boulangist faction winning only a few seats in the legislative elections of July. Boulanger's saga ended ignominiously two years later when he committed suicide in Brussels, shooting himself in the head at the grave of his mistress.

For all its melodramatic qualities, the Boulanger episode signaled some important changes in French life. It heralded the first appearance of the new nationalist right on the political stage, making it clear that the era of mass politics did not favor just the left. If the idea of the populist general and strongman looked back to Napoleon, it also anticipated twentieth-century French leaders like Philippe Pétain and Charles de Gaulle. Boulangism's authoritarian tendencies and its balancing act between left and right have been seen by many historians as foreshadowing fascism, and not just in Europe: the future leader who most resembled him was Argentina's Juan Perón. Finally, the movement's fundamental impact on Parisian politics is worth noting. Until the 1880s the national capital had always been a left-wing stronghold in the modern era, as the commune made clear. Its support for Boulanger marked a sea change, however, so that ever since Paris has voted for the right in local and national politics. The gradual movement of Parisian workers out of the city and into the suburbs played a key role, but this shift would first become clear in the Boulanger era. Thanks largely to the general's own political ineptitude the republic had survived, but not all believed it would continue to do so.

The turbulence of the Boulanger episode ushered in the 1890s and what the French call the *fin de siècle*: the turn of the century. It would be an era of continued turmoil not only politically but also culturally, and bring challenges to the dominant republican political culture from both left and right. Immediately after the general's demise a new scandal erupted in public life. In 1880 Ferdinand de Lesseps, the builder of the Suez Canal, organized a new company to build a canal across Panama to link the Atlantic and Pacific. Thanks to poor management the company rapidly lost money and in 1888 it bribed several legislators to win approval of a public loan. In 1892 the scandal broke. Edouard Drumont, an anti-Semitic journalist and author of *Jewish France*, a notorious and influential racist tract, began an investigation. He focused on two Jewish company representatives, but his research uncovered the depth of the corruption involved. The public outcry forced the government to stage a formal inquiry and put the accused legislators on trial, but little came of this and public authorities soon swept the entire matter under the rug.

For many, the weakness revealed by the Panama scandal seemed emblematic of a broader French malaise. For all the positivist belief in progress, ideas of national decadence also became popular in the *fin de siècle*. Above all, this was linked to France's anemic birthrate, which had been declining for decades and by the 1890s was the lowest in Europe. From 1891 to 1895 it veered into the territory of negative population growth, as deaths outnumbered births. Contrasted with the robust fecundity of other nations, especially the national rival and enemy Germany, this worried many. Moreover, France led Europe in rates of both alcoholism and suicide by the turn of the century. In addition, the nation's relative economic decline, even after the end of the Long Depression, underscored this sense of decay.

Many social and cultural commentators linked French decadence to urbanization and modernity: the culture of the new. Psychiatrists testified to an epidemic of female hysteria, which some linked to lack of exercise and sexual frustration. Jean-Martin Charcot, a pioneering French neurologist, developed his theories on hysteria (which he claimed was not limited to women) while working at Salpetrière hospital in Paris. He had a strong influence on the young Sigmund Freud, who studied with him in the mid-1880s. Men too had their own trendy nervous disease, neurasthenia, considered the result of stress, overwork, and overstimulation. For many, both the military defeat of 1870 and the nation's low birthrate indicated a major crisis of French masculinity, underscored by urban decadence.

Paradoxically but not surprisingly, the era also witnessed a major expansion of organized sports, primarily among the middle classes and social elites. Cycling became popular among both men and women. In 1896 Pierre de Coubertin, a scion of the Parisian aristocracy, succeeded in reviving ancient Greece's Olympic Games, becoming the father of the modern world's premier sporting event. Inspired in large part by British educator Thomas Arnold's use of sport in the Rugby School, as immortalized in *Tom Brown's School Days*, Coubertin believed that an emphasis on peaceful athletic competition would both strengthen French manhood and promote world peace. The revival of the Olympics demonstrated the extent to which French social concerns had an important universal dimension.

Many social commentators saw urban life as the source of French decay in the *fin de siècle*. In 1895 the writer Gustave Le Bon published *The Psychology of Crowds*, a psychosocial study that viewed urbanization as a destroyer of social cohesion and traditional values. Having witnessed both the Paris commune and the Boulanger affair, he decried the descent into irrationality and lack of individuality that the "crowd mentality" could bring. The writer Maurice Barrès, a pioneer of extreme nationalism at the turn of the century, also saw urbanization as a cancer on the national body. He developed a mystical belief in *la patrie*, calling for a return to the soil and rural life that were the sources of French genius.

Other intellectuals attacked the positivism that dominated French culture and was the heart and soul of the republican worldview. In 1886 the poet Jean Moreas published "The Symbolist Manifesto," and went on to found a literary journal, *Le Symboliste*, later that year. Symbolism, which had a major impact on French literature and music, was a reaction against the realist and naturalist schools. It argued that true meaning and understanding was intuitive rather than rational, that art must go beyond the superficialities of reason. In its emphasis on emotion, on the heart over the head, symbolism strongly recalled the romanticism of the early nineteenth century. In the visual arts as well, impressionism gave way to postimpressionism, a movement led by artists like Vincent van Gogh and Paul Cezanne. These artists emphasized intense psychological struggles in their work rather than trying to portray society. Perhaps no French intellectual did more to undermine positivism than the philosopher Henri Bergson, who emphasized subconscious inner drives, the so-called *élan vital*, over rational thought. Bergson's ideas were highly popular at the turn of the century, and his lectures at the College de France became a social and intellectual sensation.

Republican political culture thus experienced a variety of challenges during the 1890s. Yet the Opportunist republic could also point to some solid achievements in the early years of the decade. One came from an unexpected source. In 1890, with the support of the Vatican, France's Cardinal Lavigerie launched a policy called *ralliement*, advocating ecclesiastical acceptance of the Third Republic. In 1892 Pope Leo XIII officially reinforced this with a formal papal encyclical. While much of the Church hierarchy continued to oppose the regime, *ralliement* legitimated Catholics who had reconciled themselves to the republic.

Economic changes also helped bolster the Opportunist republic. The Long Depression came to an end by the middle of the decade, and although the return of prosperity did not benefit all, it did benefit peasants and small producers, the republic's main constituents. To ensure this support continued, the regime abandoned the tradition of free trade capitalism practiced since the Second Empire in favor of economic protectionism. In 1892 the government adopted the Meline tariff, which placed heavy import duties on a wide variety of foreign goods. Perhaps more than any other measure, the Meline tariff underscored the republic's identification with "the little guy," small landowners, shopkeepers, and other members of the *petite bourgeoisie*. The tariff helped them enormously, enabling France to remain largely self-sufficient in food and protecting small industry. It was widely criticized, at the time and ever since, for protecting inefficient economic sectors and retarding the growth of the French economy, especially in comparison with those of Germany and the United States. It also led many wealthy French men and women to invest their money abroad, notably in Russia, rather than at home, thus depriving the national economy of needed capital. Defenders of the Meline tariff countered that it spared France from the kind of massive social dislocation experienced by other industrial societies. The nation might not claim the dynamism of its powerful rivals, but at least for the average French man and woman life remained sweet.

Perhaps most importantly, the republic could point to a major breakthrough in foreign policy during the 1890s. Thanks in part to his defeat of France, one man, German Chancellor Otto von Bismarck, had completely dominated European diplomacy after 1870. Apprehensive about French anti-German hostility thanks to Berlin's annexation of Alsace-Lorraine (a step he had never favored personally), Bismarck devoted much of his formidable intelligence and diplomatic skill to keeping France isolated among the great powers of Europe. In many ways this did not seem a difficult task: Britain and France had been at odds for centuries, a rivalry reinforced by colonial expansion, and Russia and Austria-Hungary were autocratic empires that had much more in common with imperial Germany than republican France. This strategy had its weaknesses, notably rivalry between St. Petersburg and Vienna over control of eastern Europe, a rivalry accentuated by the rise of anti-Austrian pan-Slavism at the end of the century. Nonetheless, Bismarck was able to juggle these conflicts adroitly, preventing France from gaining any important allies.

All this changed by the early 1890s. French investors began devoting increasing attention to the lucrative Russian market, especially the railroads, supplanting the Germans as Bismarck suspended loans to Russia to pressure the czar against attacking Austrian interests in the Balkans. In 1888 Emperor Wilhelm I of Germany died, leaving the throne to his son, Wilhelm II. The elderly chancellor and the young emperor clashed almost immediately, resulting ultimately in Bismarck's forced resignation in 1890. Lacking the venerable chancellor's diplomatic acumen, the new government stood by as France and Russia, each fearing isolation, signed a series of accords, from a friendship treaty in 1891 to a full-fledged military pact in 1894. The idea of an alliance between the nineteenth century's great symbols of reaction and revolution did not come easy to either side, and many on the French left opposed the treaties. Nonetheless, the chance to win a powerful ally that might make dreams of *revanche* a realistic possibility carried the day in France. Parisians honored Czar Alexander III by building the city's most beautiful bridge, the Pont Alexandre III, to commemorate the treaty.

All in all, in spite of the many challenges the republic faced, things seemed to be looking up in the *fin de siècle*. It had overcome the threat of a would-be Napoleon. The economy was prospering, in both foreign and colonial affairs the regime seemed stronger than it had in a while, and by the early 1890s it had already lasted longer than any French regime in a century. By the middle of the decade, however, the Third Republic would face its greatest trial to date.

THE DREYFUS AFFAIR

France entered the twentieth century in the throes of one of the greatest peacetime controversies in the nation's history. The intense public and private battles over the putative guilt or innocence of army captain Alfred Dreyfus split families, caused riots in courtrooms and in the streets, and in general resembled a bloodless civil war. The convulsive nature of what became known as the Dreyfus affair both revealed and produced profound fault lines in the Third

Republic. Unlike earlier periods of political strife in France, however, the conflict did not pit past versus future. Both the republican left and the nationalist right were creations of modern French society, and in spite of the eventual victory of the former both would play major roles in the France to come.

The case of Captain Dreyfus at first showed no signs of becoming a major national issue. In September 1894 a cleaning lady (actually a French spy) working in the German embassy in Paris discovered a discarded scrap of paper, the famous *bordereau*, listing French military secrets for sale to the Germans. Nothing of course identified the writer of the note, but a secret investigation soon decided that the most likely culprit was Captain Alfred Dreyfus, from an affluent Alsatian family and the only Jewish member of the army general staff. The clearly weak case against Dreyfus might have gone nowhere except for the fact that Edouard Drumont, the nation's leading anti-Semite, got wind of the matter and accused the army of pardoning a rich Jewish traitor. As a result, Dreyfus was promptly court-martialed and, despite the fact that aside from questionable handwriting analysis no evidence linked him to the crime, convicted. In December, in a heartbreaking public ceremony, a symbolic execution, at the Ecole Militaire, the army stripped Dreyfus of his epaulets and broke his sword, while a crowd shouted "Death to Judas, death to the Jew."[5] Upon hearing the judgment, Dreyfus cried out to the soldiers present, "Soldiers, they are degrading an honest man. Soldiers, they are dishonoring an honest man. Long live France! Long live the Army!"[6] He was then shipped off to the notorious colonial prison Devil's Island in French Guiana.

That, it seemed, was that. Or was it? Evidence soon surfaced that in spite of Dreyfus's arrest the German government continued to receive French military secrets. In early 1896 the new head of army intelligence, Georges Picquart, launched his own investigation. His suspicions fell on Commandant Ferdinand Esterhazy, an officer of Hungarian origin whose handwriting much more closely resembled that on the *bordereau*, and who was known to have significant gambling debts. When he supported his findings to his superiors, however, they refused to reopen the case, concerned about damaging the prestige of the army. Another army officer, Col. Joseph Henry, forged documents purportedly confirming Dreyfus's guilt. The army then tried to hush up the entire matter, transferring Picquart to a remote outpost in Tunisia. As in 1848 and 1871, defeat meant exile to the colonies.

The army's efforts might have succeeded but for two factors. First, before his transfer Picquart had shared his suspicions with Auguste Scheurer-Kestner, the vice president of the Senate, who pressured the army to investigate

Esterhazy further. Second, Dreyfus's family, almost the only ones in France to defend the unfortunate captain, began to win allies. In 1895 the captain's brother, Mathieu Dreyfus, met with Bernard Lazare, a Jewish literary critic. Lazare, like many on the French left, had initially agreed with the verdict, feeling little sympathy for a man he condemned as a wealthy bourgeois. Mathieu Dreyfus went over the lack of evidence against his brother with Lazare, and was able to convince the writer not only that Dreyfus was innocent, but that anti-Semitism had largely sparked his conviction. Lazare then took action, publishing *A Judicial Error: The Truth About the Dreyfus Affair* in November 1896. This and other initiatives made the Dreyfus case a matter of great public interest, forcing the army to court-martial Esterhazy in January 1898.

By the time the court-martial opened the trial had become a *cause célèbre*, with people throughout France following it and choosing up sides. The law restoring freedom of the press had caused a proliferation of newspapers by the end of the century, and the rise of mass politics meant many of them appealed to specific ideological points of view. The anti-Semitic press had a field day with the case, which seemed to confirm all their suspicions of French Jews. On the other side, left-wing intellectuals and journalists, persuaded by the arguments of Lazare and others, swung increasingly to the view that Dreyfus was innocent. Esterhazy's court-martial only added fuel to the controversy. The army quickly acquitted Esterhazy, hoping to bury the matter once and for all. But two days later the great novelist Emile Zola published a landmark editorial in Clemenceau's newspaper *L'Aurore*. Entitled "J'Accuse," Zola's essay attacked the army in no uncertain terms for wrongly convicting Dreyfus, covering it up, and in general betraying the cause of justice and the principles of the republic. The editorial broke on French public opinion like a thunderclap, polarizing both sides of the debate and making the case of Captain Dreyfus *the* burning political question of the day. Authorities quickly arrested, tried, and convicted Zola for slandering the army. Nationalist mobs waited outside the courtroom, hoping to lynch the great writer, who fortunately succeeded in escaping to Britain.

Emile Zola's trial highlighted the deep national divisions over the Dreyfus case. Family members argued bitterly, newspapers thundered in editorials, and men fought duels on a daily basis. Particularly in Paris and other cities, the case dominated public life. A famous cartoon of the period showed two scenes: In the first, people sit down to an elegant dinner, with a caption saying "Above all, let's not talk about the Dreyfus affair!" The second shows the same scene in utter chaos, with all the guests at each other's throats. The caption reads simply "They talked about it."

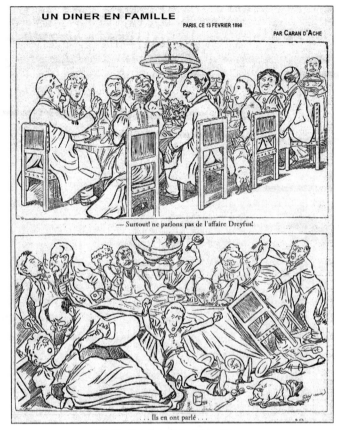

5.1. The Dreyfus affair divides France.
Source: Bibliothèque nationale de France.

Why did the guilt or innocence of one army captain so convulse the nation at the end of the century? For both Dreyfusards and anti-Dreyfusards, the affair touched on issues that went to the heart of their beliefs. The nationalist right, which had first surfaced during the Boulanger episode, led the anti-Dreyfusard party. This group, dominated by the military and the Church, saw Dreyfus as a threat to the nation, even if he was technically innocent. Allowing concern for an individual to trump the security and stability of France as a whole could not be permitted. This new conservative movement embraced nationalism, unlike the traditional right, but saw the nation as an organic, even racial unit, very different from Ernest Renan's idea of an entity bound by the consent of the governed.

This idea of the nation gave pride of place to anti-Semitism, a rejection of Jews as permanent outsiders. The late nineteenth century saw anti-Semitism shift from primarily religious to increasingly racial, and not just in France. Once a component of traditional bigoted beliefs, it became more and more a symbol of modernity, or rather antimodernity. For many in France, Jews symbolized alienation from the land, the problems of urban life, capitalism, and socialism all at once. They represented both plutocratic financiers like the Rothschilds who oppressed small shopkeepers and the eastern European immigrants who took French jobs. Finally, many saw Jewish men as effeminate, a symbol of the nation's crisis of masculinity. Humiliating Dreyfus by breaking his sword, a symbolic castration, spoke directly to these fears.

From this perspective Dreyfus was guilty, no matter the facts of the case, because he was born guilty. As a result, anti-Semitic agitation and activism flourished. *La Croix*, the conservative Catholic journal, called for stripping all Jews of citizenship. Anti-Jewish riots broke out throughout the country, horrifying the nation's small Jewish communities. The fact that they could happen in a nation that symbolized religious tolerance and Jewish enfranchisement was particularly shocking. One man who observed the affair closely was Theodor Herzl, the Jewish Viennese journalist who lived in Paris and reported on the controversy. His despair at the outbreak of anti-Semitic outrages in a country as civilized as France helped lead him to the conclusion that Jews had no future in Europe and could only be safe in a country of their own. He went on to found modern Zionism, becoming the spiritual godfather of the state of Israel.

For their part, the Dreyfusards were also less concerned about Dreyfus the man than what he represented. To them the increasingly transparent persecution of Dreyfus symbolized the intolerance and narrow-mindedness of the right, and its hostility to the values of the republic and the Revolution. The central role of monarchists and the Church, the inveterate enemies of the Third Republic, in the anti-Dreyfusard party was enough to damn it in their eyes. While not necessarily motivated by opposition to anti-Semitism (Picquart, to take one example, hated Jews), the Dreyfusards strongly rejected the idea of religious persecution, and even more fundamentally opposed condemning a man for crimes he did not commit. They believed in the universalist idea according to which anyone who embraced French values was French, and should be treated as such. Moreover, if the affair underscored the new nationalism of the right, it also created a new spirit of antimilitarism on the left. In a sense it represented the final death of Bonapartism, a permanent parting of the ways between ideals of military glory and social justice.

In short, the Dreyfusards viewed the persecution of Captain Dreyfus as an attack on the republic and responded accordingly. The position of French socialists during the case was particularly interesting. Like Bernard Lazare, many initially saw Albert Dreyfus as an affluent bourgeois whose fate held little interest for the working class. A certain strain of working-class anti-Semitism, as revealed by the Boulanger episode, also prevented some socialists from getting involved in the case. None of significance joined the anti-Dreyfusard camp, however, and as the broader implications of the case became clear most swung around to support the defense of a republic they paradoxically hoped would be overthrown one day by a socialist revolution. A case in point was the great socialist leader, Jean Jaurès. Widely regarded as the greatest socialist in France, Jaurès combined intellectual brilliance and spellbinding oratory. A southerner like Léon Gambetta, Jaurès seemed at ease with people ranging from small town coal miners to Parisian writers and professors. Unlike the Marxist Jules Guesde, Jaurès thoroughly embraced the values of the French Revolution, seeing socialism as essentially the next step in that tradition. One of his most prominent books was *A Socialist History of the French Revolution*. For Jaurès it made sense to support Dreyfus as a way of opposing those antirepublican forces who were also enemies of the working class. He participated energetically in the Dreyfusard coalition, swinging many workers and socialists around to its support.

Matters came to a head in the summer of 1898. In August Colonel Henry confessed to forging the evidence against Dreyfus and committed suicide shortly thereafter. Meanwhile, Colonel Esterhazy fled to England where, safe from prosecution, he admitted to being the author of the *bordereau*. Given the complete disappearance of any credible evidence against Dreyfus, it seemed only natural that he be released. In June 1899 the appeals court dismissed his conviction and scheduled a new trial for September, to take place in the Breton capital of Rennes. Dreyfus was allowed to return from Devil's Island after five years of horrible punishment, and the army undertook a new court-martial. Amid an atmosphere of huge demonstrations by groups like the Anti-Semitic League, the army once again convicted Dreyfus in spite of all the evidence. This unbelievable action prompted a worldwide firestorm of protest, prompting the public burning of French flags as far away as Minneapolis. Ten days later the French president, Paul Loubet, officially pardoned Dreyfus and allowed him to return to his family. He was not fully exonerated until 1906, but with his pardon the Dreyfus affair came to an end. The left had vanquished the right, and the republic was safe.

THE RADICAL REPUBLIC

The Dreyfus affair reshaped French politics and society in a number of ways. It powerfully reaffirmed the universalist tradition of the republic, underscoring its centrality to French political culture. The victory of the left furthered the global reputation of France as a land (perhaps *the* land) of liberty. At the same time, it made the new nationalist and populist right the dominant force among French conservatism. Even monarchists had to abandon their traditional elitism and cultivate a mass base. One of its most important legacies was a new role for intellectuals in French society. Not since the Enlightenment had the ideas of learned men and women weighed so heavily in political debate. Intellectuals like Lazare, Zola, and Jaurès could justly claim to have made history during the Dreyfus affair. This was not just true of leftists. Conservatives like Edouard Drumont and Maurice Barrès mobilized millions in support of their ideas. In 1899, for example, dissidents from the League for the French Fatherland founded the Action Française. Led by the monarchist literary critic Charles Maurras, the Action Francaise combined integralist Catholicism, anti-Semitism, and antirepublicanism into a powerful movement that many historians have considered a key precursor of French fascism.

Most notably, however, the Dreyfus affair brought the Radicals to power. Before 1890 they had been a loose gathering of progressive republicans, but the affair forged them into a united and distinct organization. Unlike the Opportunists, who waffled over whether or not to support Dreyfus, Radicals like Georges Clemenceau had stood at the heart of the Dreyfusard movement. In large part because of their alliance with the socialists during the affair, the Radicals tended to look to their left rather than their right for support. In 1889 they in effect took control of the government formed by moderate Pierre Waldeck-Rousseau. It became the first French ministry to include a socialist, Alexandre Millerand, a move harshly attacked as collaborationism by the followers of Jules Guesde. In 1901 the Radicals constituted themselves as a formal political party, the Radical and Radical Socialist Party. Under various guises, the Radicals would dominate French politics for most of the early twentieth century.

More than anything else, what united the Radicals was a visceral hatred of the Church, one greatly intensified by the Dreyfus affair. They wasted little time in acting on this hatred. In 1902 the Radicals and their socialist allies won a majority in the assembly, and they used it to replace the moderate

Waldeck-Rousseau with the extremist Emile Combes, who made restricting ecclesiastical power the key concern of his government. In 1904, for example, the radical regime broke relations with Rome and closed thousands of religious schools. These efforts culminated with the 1905 law formally separating Church and state. The greatest assault on the power of French Catholicism since the Revolution, the 1905 law renounced the concordat between Church and state established by Napoleon in 1804. It abolished all state financial support for religious officials, whose salaries had been paid by the government, and transferred Church property to the government. The end of state subsidies hit Catholic education particularly hard, causing a sharp drop in the number of parochial schools and students.

The Church reacted with a fury. Although some liberal Catholic voices still hoped for an accommodation with the regime, they were overruled by the majority and the Vatican. The pope ordered all good Catholics to resist and, to underscore the point, excommunicated all assembly members who voted for the law. Resistance, sometimes violent, occurred, especially in conservative and rural regions whose people saw the law as an attack on their communities. Public authorities trying to enter village churches to inventory their property at times encountered peasants with shotguns, and in one famous case a wild bear chained to the church door.

Eventually, however, both sides adjusted to the new reality. Religious life went on, and Church officials found that the quality of recruits to the priesthood went up, since they were now motivated more by religious conviction than hopes for easy jobs. Locally, public and religious authorities worked together to soften the impact of the law, especially in small towns. At the same time, the 1905 law probably intensified the pace of de-Christianization, especially in the countryside. Finally, the law brought to an end the wars between religious and secular France that had so consumed the Third Republic. The bitter divorce of 1905 gradually gave way to humdrum coexistence.

To an important extent, the separation of Church and state represented payback for the Dreyfus affair. The Radicals also took measures to purge the army of those disloyal to the republic, going so far as to spy on officers who attended mass. It was the culmination of the broader conflict between two visions of universalism: one religious, one political. The Third Republic did not just defeat the Church but also strove to take its place. Republican political culture became a kind of secular religion; like Catholicism, it assumed that all men and women could and should adopt its principles, and that its essential truths were eternal. After 1905 there would be room for only one type of universalism in France: the universal republic.

The year 1905 represented a watershed in the history of modern France, both the end of the nineteenth century and the dawn of the twentieth. Not only did it bring the permanent resolution of conflicts between Church and state, but more generally it underscored the dominance of republican political culture. After 1905 the monarchist and Bonapartist right faded into political irrelevance. New conflicts, notably between capital and labor, would assume pride of place during the twentieth century. By 1905 republicanism had become firmly grounded in the French countryside, making both the local lord and the Parisian revolutionary mob increasingly obsolete. France thus entered the new century as a nation united to an unprecedented degree, and at the same time a leading representative of the cultural dynamism of the modern age.

France's relationship to the wider world also underwent fundamental change during these years. In some ways this was a period of relative decline, especially economic, vis-à-vis more aggressive powers like Germany and the United States. At the same time the late nineteenth century represented an unprecedented era of imperial expansion, so that the French flag flew over more lands and peoples than ever before in the nation's history. The interaction between nation and empire, between colony and metropole, not only became increasingly central to French life but also fundamentally reshaped ideas of France as a universal nation. It is to that interaction that we now turn.

Suggestions for Further Reading

Dreyfus, Alfred. *Cinq années de ma vie, 1894–1899*. Paris: Fasquelle, 1962.

Forth, Christopher E. *The Dreyfus Affair and the Crisis of French Manhood*. Baltimore: Johns Hopkins University Press, 2004.

Gildea, Robert. *France, 1870–1914*. London: Longman, 1996.

Graetz, Michael. *The Jews in Nineteenth-Century France: From the French Revolution to the Alliance Israélite Universelle*. Stanford, CA: Stanford University Press, 1996.

Guillaumin, Emile. *The Life of a Simple Man*. Hanover, NH: University Press of New England, 1982.

Harris, Ruth. *Dreyfus: Politics, Emotion, and the Scandal of the Century*. New York: Holt, 2010.

Helias, Pierre-Jakez. *Horse of Pride: Life in a Breton Village.* New Haven, CT: Yale University Press, 1980.

Laskier, Michael M. *The Alliance Israélite Universelle and the Jewish Communities of Morocco: 1862–1962.* Albany: State University of New York Press, 1983.

Leff, Lisa Moses. *Sacred Bonds of Solidarity: The Rise of Jewish Internationalism in Nineteenth-Century France.* Stanford, CA: Stanford University Press, 2006.

Lehning, James R. *To Be a Citizen: The Political Culture of the Early French Third Republic.* Ithaca, NY: Cornell University Press, 2001.

Malino, Frances, and Bernard Wasserstein. *The Jews in Modern France.* Hanover, NH: University Press of New England, 1985.

Mayeur, Jean-Marie, and Madeleine Reberioux. *The Third Republic from Its Origins to the Great War, 1871–1914.* Cambridge: Cambridge University Press, 1984.

Nord, Philip. *Paris Shopkeepers and the Politics of Resentment.* Princeton, NJ: Princeton University Press, 1986.

Rodrigue, Aron. *French Jews, Turkish Jews: The Alliance Israélite Universelle and the Politics of Jewish Schooling in Turkey, 1860–1925.* Bloomington: Indiana University Press, 1990.

Smith, Bonnie. *Ladies of the Leisure Class: The Bourgeoises of Northern France in the Nineteenth Century.* Princeton, NJ: Princeton University Press, 1981.

Watson, D. R. *Georges Clemenceau: A Political Biography.* London: Eyre Methuen, 1974.

Weber, Eugen. *Peasants into Frenchmen.* Stanford, CA: Stanford University Press, 1975.

———. *France Fin de Siècle.* Cambridge, MA: Belknap, 1988.

Notes

1. Ernest Renan, "What Is a Nation?" in Homi K. Bhabha, ed., *Nation and Narration* (London: Routledge, 1990), 19.
2. Naomi Schor, "The Crisis of French Universalism," *Yale French Studies* 100 (2001): 43–64.
3. Theodore Zeldin, *France, 1848–1945: Ambition and Love* (Oxford: Oxford University Press, 1980), 114.

4. Emile Guillamin, *The Life of a Simple Man* (Hanover, NH: University Press of New England, 1982), 173, 176.

5. Ruth Harris, *Dreyfus: Politics, Emotion, and the Scandal of the Century* (New York: Holt, 2010), 1.

6. Alfred Dreyfus, *Cinq années de ma vie, 1894–1899* (Paris: Fasquelle, 1962), 54.

[six]

THE REPUBLICAN EMPIRE

DURING THE LAST THIRD OF THE NINETEENTH CENTURY FRANCE expanded its overseas empire to the greatest extent in the nation's history. Only Britain, master of fully 25 percent of the globe, possessed more colonies. Even before 1870 France had an important imperial presence, controlling not only the "old colonies" of the Caribbean and Indian Ocean, but also Algeria, Tahiti, and southern Indochina. The Third Republic would build on and expand this legacy, bringing new colonies into the national fold and reinforcing the French presence in old ones. By the start of the twentieth century the French flag flew over every major continent and many islands in the world's seas. France might no longer dominate the affairs of the European continent, and Paris no longer reigned as Europe's biggest city, but the French empire ensured the nation's continued role as a great world power.

It was no accident that the triumph of the republic and of overseas empire occurred at the same time. The vision of the universal republic transformed France, but it also fundamentally altered the nation's relationship to the wider world. As we have seen, republicanism and imperialism both played significant roles in the construction of the French nation during the nineteenth century, and while they opposed each other in many ways they also had important points in common. In particular, the first empire under Napoleon had combined authoritarian rule with a populist vision and a commitment to extending the values of the Revolution beyond France's borders. The Third

6.1. Poster for the 1906 Colonial Exposition in Marseilles.
Source: Leemage/UIG via Getty Images.

Republic inherited much from the second empire, notably building on this legacy by expanding the nation's colonial empire to an undreamed-of size. At the same time, the new regime based itself on the principle of universal manhood suffrage and popular sovereignty, making the citizen the undisputed ruler of France.

The combination of these two imperatives produced that strangest of political formations: the republican empire. By traditional definition a republic cannot have a monarch because only its citizens are sovereign, whereas an empire must be ruled by an emperor or empress. Yet after 1870 France was a republic ruled by citizens in control of colonies populated by subjects, an empire without an imperial sovereign other than the French people. This rather bizarre structure both embodied the interactions between republic and empire in France during the nineteenth century, and also underscored key themes in modern French life whose implications went well beyond questions of colonial rule.

Above all, it illustrated the complex relations between universalism and democracy in a regime firmly committed to both. France in the late nineteenth century was a democratic nation with an authoritarian empire, where citizens in the metropole could enjoy the benefits of sovereignty but subjects in the colonies could not. This essential paradox lay at the heart of modern French life and rested on two fundamental characteristics of republican thought. One was the belief that people must be made ready for citizenship, that only a sufficient intellectual and moral level would render the republic viable. One must teach the people to be free, as the regime's heavy investment in education illustrated. The other was the growth of scientific racism toward the end of the century. The idea that humanity was divided into separate and unequal races, and that such racial differences were essentially fixed, increasingly permeated republican thought in the late 1800s. It made the prospect of a republican empire largely divided between white citizens and nonwhite subjects understandable, if not desirable. In general, then, the growth of the empire under the Third Republic underscored both the power of the universal ideal and its limitations.

THE NEW IMPERIALISM

Nothing more dramatically illustrated the rise of the west to world domination than the heyday of European imperialism in the late nineteenth century. Whereas in 1800 Europe controlled 35 percent of the world's surface, by 1914 it controlled 84 percent.[1] The change was most striking in Africa. Until 1880 European nations possessed about 10 percent of the continent's land, mostly coastal settlements. A generation later virtually the entire continent had come under their control, with only Liberia and Abyssinia retaining formal independence. The British loved to proclaim that the sun never set on their empire, and the new imperialism assured Europeans of their place at the center of world affairs.

Several factors explain the striking expansion of European colonial power. Economics played an important role. A major concern of the leading powers was securing profitable markets to nurture their growing industries. During the early nineteenth century Britain was the world's leading industrial power. But because it was so much more advanced than any other nation it could undersell their products, so it had no need for formal colonies. By the end of the century, however, the British faced other competitors,

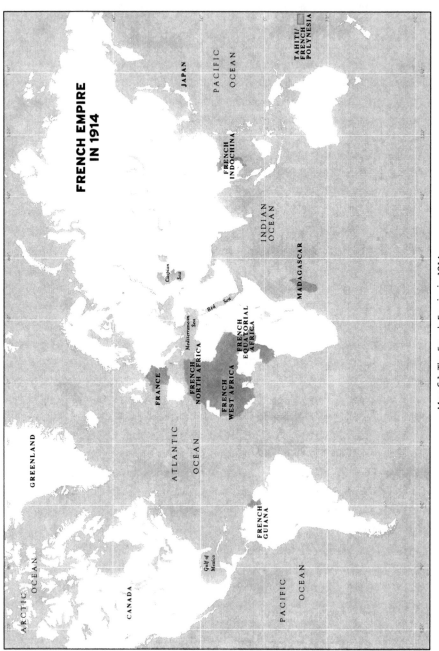

Map 6.1. The French Empire in 1914.

all striving for lucrative overseas markets. The constriction of world trade caused by the Long Depression led many nations, as we have seen, to pass new tariffs in order to protect their own industries at the expense of others. Many statesmen and business leaders thus argued their nations needed formal colonies in order to prevent other countries from taking control of them and using tariffs to restrict the entry of foreign goods. The race for colonies was thus to an important extent a race for secure markets. In many ways it was based on speculation: most industrial nations traded much more with each other than with their colonies, and overseas investment followed similar patterns. Colonial markets might not be especially profitable in the short term, but in an era of economic anxiety many saw them as a hedge against an uncertain future.

Colonies were useful not just to increase wealth but also to maintain social peace. If industries could not find markets for their goods, they could not hire workers, so that unemployment would increase, perhaps leading to social discord or even revolution. Chancellor Bismarck, initially no fan of overseas empire, eventually came round to the belief that Germany should have colonies to appease the masses at home. Given that the German industrial model emphasized heavy industry and low wages, domestic consumption did not suffice to absorb the profits of its factories, so overseas markets were all the more important. Perhaps the most important advocate of what came to be known as social imperialism was Cecil Rhodes, the British/South African businessman who more than anyone else symbolized the age of high empire. In 1898 Rhodes described watching socialist leaders harangue a working-class crowd in the East End of London. He concluded that imperialism was crucial to providing the kind of prosperity that would guard against the temptation of socialist revolution. "The Empire, as I have always said, is a bread-and-butter question. If you want to avoid civil war, you must become imperialists."[2]

The new imperialism did not respond solely to economic needs, however. It also suited an age of heightened nationalism and increased attention to national glory. Stories about the heroic exploits of colonial regiments became a staple of mass journalism, what the British called the penny press. More and more, colonial possessions became a symbol of power and greatness; a leading nation must have an empire. In 1898, for example, naval forces from Britain, Germany, and the United States converged on the Pacific nation of Samoa, each determined to acquire it as an imperial possession. The fact that a remote territory with a small population and few natural resources could provoke such interest underscored the importance of national prestige in the spread of the new imperialism. Another factor was European technological superiority. Before the late nineteenth century African and Asian peoples had often successfully resisted outside aggression, but the development of sophisticated arms like the machine gun gave imperial forces overwhelming military superiority. At the battle of Omdurman, Sudan, in 1898, the British forces of Lord Kitchener overwhelmed their indigenous opponents, killing over ten thousand while losing less than one hundred of their own. As a popular jingle went, "Whatever happens we have got/The Maxim gun, and they have not."[3]

Finally, and in many ways paradoxically, humanitarianism often motivated the new imperialism. A key reason for attempts to push into the African interior was the movement to stamp out the slave trade. Missionaries, who often constituted the avant-garde of imperialism, sought not only to save the souls of the heathen but also to bring them modern education and health care. Many European feminists supported imperial ventures, seeing them as a way of enlightening native women and freeing them from the patriarchal oppression of native men. At the base of these humanitarian motivations lay the conviction that European civilization was superior, and that the rest of the world would benefit by exposure to and integration into it, by force if need be. What Rudyard Kipling called "the white man's burden" was not just a rationalization for conquest but equally a sincere belief in the power of Europe to improve and remake the world in its own image.

European incursions overseas had been under way for centuries, and by 1850 foreigners controlled substantial parts of India, the East Indies, and Vietnam. During the two decades from 1880 to 1900 the new imperialism gathered steam, however, turning into a race to annex any part of the globe not already seized by another colonial power. At the heart of this massive expansion lay the so-called scramble for Africa. During this period the British occupied Egypt and then moved into the Sudan, the French took over large portions of western and central Africa, and Germany moved to establish colonies in what are now Cameroon and Namibia. The most bizarre example of the new imperialism in Africa was the Congo; there King Leopold II of Belgium moved to create his own personal empire at the heart of the continent. In an attempt to bring some order to this frantic rush for empire France and Germany organized the Berlin conference of 1884–1885. The conference recognized Leopold's holdings, set down basic rules for imperial expansion in Africa, and pledged to continue action against slavery and the slave trade. By 1900 only Liberia and Abyssinia, where local forces had inflicted a humiliating defeat on the Italians in 1896, remained free of European rule.

For both the elites and the masses of Asians and Africans, the new imperialism was often a disorienting, traumatic experience. Overwhelmed by western military superiority and forced to adapt to new structures of governance, people struggled to make sense of the new era and adapt to it. Many reacted with sustained resistance, so that brief wars of colonial conquest often gave way to extended periods of "pacification." Others sought to learn from their imperial rulers, to master the technology and science that would hopefully one day set them free. For a few imperial rule opened up new possibilities, especially in education and careers. A particular shock for many was the imposition of European racism, of being forced to acknowledge the superiority of whites and their own inferiority. Finally, harsh oppression became a reality for many under imperial rule. To take the most extreme example, the brutal use of forced labor in King Leopold's Congo Free State caused an international scandal and cost the lives of literally millions, forcing the Belgian government to take over direct rule of the colony. In general, Africans and Asians had to confront a radically new world; as the Nigerian writer Chinua Achebe observed in his great novel *Things Fall Apart*:

> The white man is very clever. He came quietly and peacefully with his religion. We were amused at his foolishness and allowed him to stay. Now he has won our brothers, and our clan can no longer act like one. He has put a knife on the things that held us together and we have fallen apart.[4]

The new imperialism brought unprecedented political unity to the world, reinforcing and building on the rise of a global economy. It graphically demonstrated European technological superiority and that continent's position at the center of world affairs. France's imperial adventures and conquests responded to this general pattern and had deep roots in the nature of French society and politics. The rise of a new French empire, and its conjunction with the triumph of republicanism, would write a new page in the history of France as a universal nation.

JULES FERRY *LE TONKINOIS* AND THE NEW FRENCH EMPIRE

Already possessing an important colonial empire, France during the 1880s significantly increased its overseas holdings, so that it remained second only to Britain as an imperial power. To an important extent this major effort was led by one man, Jules Ferry, the Opportunist prime minister during the early 1880s. Colonial and educational expansion were the two signature undertakings of his political career, and indeed they had much in common; Ferry regarded both as promoting the economic well-being of the nation by integrating masses of people into the values of republican France. So great was his commitment to imperialism that many, both supporters and detractors, referred to him as Jules Ferry "the Tonkinese" (le tonkinois).

Not an avowed imperialist at first, Ferry soon became a convinced advocate of the benefits of overseas expansion. In March 1881, during his first administration, a series of Tunisian raids across the Algerian border led to a major French invasion, forcing the Bey of Tunis to turn his country into a protectorate of France, a colony in all but name. The occupation of Tunisia was not Ferry's idea initially, but the experience won him over to the importance of colonial expansion. For Ferry imperialism had two main justifications. First, it was important to the French economy; colonies provided both important raw materials and markets for industrial products. As he noted in a speech to the National Assembly, "Colonial policy is the daughter of industrial policy . . . The field of action for capital, like the demand for labour, is measured by the size of the foreign market."[5] But Ferry also argued that colonialism was good for the colonized, that France had a right to civilize its subjects: "Gentlemen, we must speak more loudly and more honestly! We must say openly that indeed the higher races have a right over the lower races. . . . I repeat, that the superior races have a right because they have a duty. They have the duty to civilize the inferior races."[6] Jules Ferry and other proponents of imperial expansion thus adapted the civilizing mission, initially developed under the first empire, to justify the conquest and control of overseas colonies. Here imperial ideas of forcible rule and republican ideas of education and uplift met in a colonialist synthesis.

During his second administration, from 1883 to 1885, Ferry moved forcefully to implement his imperial vision. His major target was southeast Asia, where France had already established control of southern Vietnam, or Cochin-China, under the second empire. During the 1860s the French had consolidated their hold over the south, formally annexing much of Cochin-China in 1867 and taking advantage of dynastic turmoil in Cambodia to establish a protectorate over that country in 1863. Ten years later the French, led by the officer Francis Garnier, invaded Tonkin, using as a pretext a dispute between the local authorities and the French businessman Jean Dupuis over trading rights. In November 1873 Garnier captured the capital city of Hanoi, forcing the Vietnamese to agree to French protectorates over Annam and Tonkin. Tonkinese officials, lacking the strength to withstand the French, appealed to a Chinese bandit army known as the Black Flags to intervene on their behalf. The Black Flags, led by Liu Yongfu, arrived at Hanoi in force in December, forcing the French to withdraw and killing Garnier.

In 1883 Ferry led the French to attempt the conquest of Tonkin once again. This time France seized upon the activities of pirates on the Red River in northern Vietnam who were seizing European ships and disrupting trade in general. Paris sent a new army to seize Tonkin, capturing Hanoi, only to face a determined counterattack from the pirates who succeeded in capturing and beheading the leader of the expedition, Henri Rivière. At this point, stung by the second such military disaster in ten years, Ferry ordered an all-out invasion of Tonkin. This prompted intervention by China, leading to the Sino-French war of 1883–1885. In March 1885 Chinese forces defeated the French in a battle, prompting an outcry in Paris and the fall of Ferry's second government. French troops in Tonkin rallied nonetheless, going on to win the war against China and reaffirm their control of Tonkin and Annam. In 1887 the French formally organized the Government-General of Indochina, consisting of the Vietnamese provinces of Cochin-China, Annam, and Tonkin, as well as Cambodia. A decade later France took control of Laos, integrating it into French Indochina as well. Ferry might no longer be prime minister, but his vision of imperial expansion had yielded France a major new colony.

Under Jules Ferry and his successors France also expanded its holdings in Africa. As in earlier years, French adventurers on the ground often led the way, with the government supporting and taking over their initiatives post facto. The pursuit of the war in Indochina necessitated a refueling station in East Africa for French ships. Since the British refused to let France use its facilities in Aden, the French took over the port city of Djibouti on the Red Sea. The small colony flourished, becoming France's foothold in east Africa. In west Africa the French continued their expansion into the interior of Senegal, controlling most of the area known as the Casamance by the 1880s. In 1881 they established a protectorate over the key Muslim state of Fouta-Djalon, between Senegal and Guinea. In central Africa Pierre Savorgnan de Brazza, one of the most remarkable of France's imperial conquerors, staked French claims over a vast territory. Born in Rome and naturalized French at the age of twenty-two, Brazza made several voyages upriver into the heart of the Congo between 1875 and 1885. Undertaken on behalf of the French navy, Brazza's trips became the stuff of legend; heavily covered in the French press,

Brazza gave detailed observations of local customs, flora and fauna, emphasizing the wealth of the land and its potential benefits for France. He managed to convince Africans to accept treaties granting French rule without using force, although he made it clear that force was an option; as he commented to one African chieftain, "The white . . . has two hands: one full of presents for his friends, the other that death itself arms against his enemies–there is no alternative."[7] Brazza secured for France its major colonies of French Equatorial Africa, giving his name to its capital, Brazzaville.

In addition, Ferry helped lay claim to a major new colony in the Indian Ocean. Madagascar is larger than metropolitan France, and its strategic location on sailing routes from South Africa to India and east Asia had long attracted the attention of French and other European explorers. The French presence in the Indian Ocean dated back to the conquest of the island of Réunion in the mid-seventeenth century, and its growing interest in both Africa and southeast Asia two hundred years later increased the region's importance to Paris. Divided between several ethnic groups, Madagascar had been ruled with an iron fist by the Merina dynasty since the early nineteenth century. This period also witnessed growing contact with Europeans, especially missionaries, who by the middle of the century had converted a substantial proportion of the island's population to Christianity. In 1869 they succeeded in winning Queen Ranavalona II over to Christ, leading her to make Christianity the official creed of the nation and to ban indigenous religious practices, including polygamy.

France's interest in Madagascar, stoked by the presence of French businessmen, adventurers, and priests, came to a head in the 1880s. In 1855 a Malagasy prince had signed a vague agreement with a French slave trader, Jean-François Lambert, granting France economic concessions in the island. The Lambert Charter was of dubious legality, but it did provide Paris some grounds for claiming rights in Madagascar. In 1883, after years of increasing tensions with the Malagasy monarchy, the French claimed Madagascar had violated the Lambert Charter and took military action, bombarding cities on the island's coast. Queen Ranavalona III rallied her troops and resisted the French invasion, but after two years was forced to grant France's demands for a partial protectorate and a large indemnity. French colonization of Madagascar had begun in earnest.

During the two regimes of Jules Ferry in the early 1880s France thus embarked on an unprecedented expansion of its colonial empire. Ferry was enthusiastic about imperial policy, yet as we have seen he did not build the new empire by himself. The late nineteenth century also saw the development of a powerful *parti colonial*, or colonial lobby, in France. The members of this lobby were a diverse group of writers, politicians, businessmen, and journalists who came together to advocate for the importance of overseas empire and push the French government to support imperial ventures. Initially they met at formal dinners, such as in Paris's Petite Vache restaurant, to discuss colonial issues, but over time they organized more systematically. In 1874 the economist Paul Leroy-Beaulieu published *De la colonisation chez les peuples modernes* (*On Colonization among Modern Peoples*), one of the first of a number of theoretical studies of empire. Scientific and scholarly organizations like the Paris Geographical Society, founded in 1821, helped promote interest in overseas expansion. By the early 1890s French men and women had created a number of institutions to promote imperial interests. In 1892 members of the National Assembly founded a colonial group to coordinate political efforts. A year later businessmen created the French Colonial Union to lobby for commercial interests overseas. Political and business interests in port cities, notably Marseilles and Bordeaux, often took the lead in advocating colonial policies. In addition, religious organizations like the Jesuits who engaged in missionary work exhorted their congregants to support the French presence overseas.

Not everyone in France approved of the new imperialism, however. Some criticized it on humanitarian grounds, attacking human rights abuses in the colonies and even questioning the right of France to impose its civilization by force on other peoples. Such critiques came mostly from the socialist left, which in general tended to regard colonialism as a way of propping up capitalism and a diversion from the class struggle. In 1905 the socialist Paul Louis published *Le Colonialisme*, a pamphlet that coined the modern term "colonialism," portraying it as the result of capitalist competition and decay. More commonly, however, French critics attacked imperial policy as an expensive and unwarranted use of resources. As Georges Clemenceau put it in 1885, "My patriotism lies in France . . . While you are lost in your colonial dreams, there are at your feet men, Frenchmen, who call for useful and beneficial efforts to develop French genius."[8] Some of the harshest opposition to the new colonialism came from the ranks of the nationalist right. Many of those who thirsted for revenge against Germany saw Ferry's new emphasis on imperial expansion, not without reason, as a distraction from the holy quest to recover Alsace-Lorraine, a suspicion reinforced by Ferry's cooperation with Bismarck to arrange the Berlin Conference. At one point nationalist leader Paul Déroulède accused Ferry of offering France twenty Negroes in exchange for her two lost daughters.

Hostility to imperial ventures played an important role in Ferry's final fall from power in 1885. Nonetheless, in important respects the greatest challenge confronted by Jules Ferry and the colonial lobby was not organized opposition but general indifference. With some important exceptions, such as the nation's ports and maritime regions like Brittany, most French paid little attention to questions of empire. The nation's primary school textbooks only gave cursory coverage of the colonies, and France lacked a tradition like Britain's Empire Day to increase popular awareness and support of imperialism. As a result, in France colonialism lacked the enthusiastic mass base found elsewhere in Europe, remaining instead the concern of a minority of politicians and businessmen. This was a powerful minority, however, and even after the fall of Jules Ferry they were able to win government support for further imperial expansion at the end of the nineteenth century.

FRANCE AND THE SCRAMBLE FOR AFRICA

In November 1884 representatives of the major European powers met in Berlin at the invitation of Chancellor Bismarck to consider the future of Africa. Both concerned by the danger to the international order represented by imperial adventurism, most notably that of Leopold in the Congo, and also mindful of their own colonial interests, the diplomats at the Berlin Conference took the next several months to map out a systematic approach to European exploitation of the African continent. The meeting concluded at the end of February, having mapped out zones of influence for each major colonial power and established principles by which each could secure its holdings. The scramble for Africa was on.

The Berlin Conference recognized French predominance in west Africa, and Paris moved quickly to make this a reality. During the late 1880s and 1890s French troops moved inland from coastal settlements, often encountering fierce African resistance. They had already established a formal protectorate over the Muslim state of Fouta-Djalon, and by the mid-1890s took effective control of the country. In 1882 French forces came into conflict with Samory Touré, one of the great rulers of west Africa. Touré had created a disciplined military force and, using firearms purchased from the British, managed to repel a series of French invasions during the 1880s. The following decade brought increasing pressure from France, and in spite of bitter resistance and a scorched-earth policy to hinder the invading troops, Touré was forced to surrender in 1898.

During the same years the French established control over the Ivory Coast and launched a military campaign against the kingdom of Dahomey. That country's king, Béhanzin, fought ferociously against the invaders, in 1892 boldly proclaiming his defiance: "I am the king of the blacks, and the whites have nothing to say about what I do. The villages of which you speak are indeed mine, they belong to me . . . I would like to know how many independent French villages have been attacked by me, King of Dahomey . . . if you want war, I am ready."[9] In spite of his courageous words, however, French forces overwhelmed Dahomey in three successive military campaigns, taking the brave king prisoner and exiling him to Martinique.

These conquests brought the French solid control of coastal west Africa, areas with valuable resources in both raw materials, especially groundnuts, and labor. Guinea, Dahomey, the Ivory Coast, and Upper Volta joined Senegal as French colonies. The adventures that really fired the French imagination, however, were those that lay claim to the west African interior and the Sahara desert, linking the nation's colonies on the gulf of Guinea with its possessions in North Africa. By the early 1890s French fantasies of African conquest focused on the legendary city of Timbuktu, in Mali. Situated where the great Niger River meets the Sahara desert, Timbuktu had emerged during the twelfth century as a major urban settlement thanks to its position astride trans-Saharan trading routes, where merchants bought and sold valuable commodities like gold, ivory, and slaves, sending them in caravans as far as Morocco, Egypt, and Ethiopia. It was a leading city in first the Mali then the Songhai empire, and by the sixteenth century had become a center of Islamic scholarship.

By the late nineteenth century Timbuktu had become legendary in Europe both as a place of great wealth and learning, and as a very remote location, a mysterious hidden city. During the 1880s the French sent several expeditions up the Niger River hoping to reach Timbuktu, but all failed, defeated both by the rigors of navigation and by the resistance of the area's Tuareg inhabitants. These failures only increased the city's attraction and the determination of the French to find it. In 1893 two French officers, Eugène Bonnier and Gaston Boiteux, staged in effect a race for the fabled city, Bonnier marching overland and Boiteux sailing up the Niger. Boiteux won, reaching Timbuktu on December 16, 1893, taking possession of the city peacefully and raising the French flag over it. The capture of Timbuktu represented a triumph of imperial expansion, winning it control of the colony of Mali. What the French found in Timbuktu, however, was a poor, somnolent small town in the desert, far removed from the legend that had lured them so powerfully.

During the 1890s France also secured control over the colony it named Niger, expanding eastward from Mali. Paris and London had agreed to divide up region in 1890, but the British ended up with by far the most valuable colony, Nigeria, whereas France's share was mostly desert, with few resources and little value. Moreover, for over a decade the Tuaregs resisted French rule energetically, so that the colony was not "pacified" until shortly before World War I. The 1890s also saw France expand its presence in neighboring Chad, as several military expeditions explored that vast territory. These initiatives led some French strategists to think of expanding all the way across the continent to link up with the outpost of Djibouti on the Red Sea as well as controlling the territory between the Niger and Nile rivers. This brought France directly into conflict with Britain, however, busily developing its own control over the Sudan in order to connect Egypt and British East Africa.

These conflicting imperial imperatives produced what became known as the Fashoda incident. In July 1898 a large French force led by Major Jean-Baptiste Marchand arrived at the town of Fashoda, on the tributary of the Nile River called the White Nile. In September Britain sent its own smaller but more heavily armed detachment, led by Sir Herbert Kitchener, to Fashoda. The British, fresh from their great victory over the Mahdi's indigenous forces at Omdurman, insisted that the French withdraw, but Marchand refused. Both armies raised their flags over the city and then sat, awaiting instructions from Paris and London. While diplomats negotiated over the next two months crowds in both Britain and France called on their governments to stand firm for imperial glory, and for a while it seemed the two countries might go to war for empire. Ultimately cooler heads prevailed and the French backed down, so that Fashoda became a symbol of Britain's dominant role in the scramble for Africa.

By the beginning of the twentieth century France had by no means done badly, however, in terms of imperial conquest. In 1894 the French launched a major invasion of Madagascar, one resisted by the Malagasy government for several years until it was overwhelmed and France annexed the island as a colony in 1899. After years of complex negotiations and rivalry with Germany, in 1912 Paris took full control of Morocco as a protectorate, completing its dominance of the Maghreb, or northwest Africa. By this point France controlled fully one-third of the African continent, organized primarily in two great colonial federations: French West Africa, established in 1895 with its capital at Dakar, and French Equatorial Africa, established in 1910 with its capital at Brazzaville. Combined with French control of the Maghreb and Madagascar, these new African colonies gave France the largest empire in the nation's history, larger even than that of Napoleon, and made it the world's second imperial power. The nation's greatest republic had become the nation's greatest empire. In the colonies republican ideology would drive imperial policy, yet at the same time be changed by the colonial experience. At the same time, overseas empire would have its own impact on life in the French metropole, making the country an imperial republic.

THE OLD COLONIES AND THE NEW EMPIRE

By the end of the nineteenth century France had created a vast empire, and the tricolor flag flew over territories scattered across the globe. Although the Third Republic had greatly expanded it, the French empire was not entirely new, however. The nation's colonies in North Africa, the Indian Ocean, and the Caribbean had been French for decades, in some cases centuries. Like metropolitan France itself, they had to adjust to the new regime, and to the new idea of republican empire. The Third Republic's imperial vision thus developed not only on virgin soil, but also in areas much more intimately associated with the nation's history.

No place had been part of the French empire longer than the Caribbean colonies of Martinique, Guadeloupe, and French Guiana. As in the metropole, the Third Republic in the Caribbean began in insurrection. In September 1870 a major uprising broke out in the southern part of Martinique, prompted both by the news from France and particularly by the unjust treatment of a black man, Léopold Lubin, by white planters. The revolutionaries, mostly black small farmers and agricultural laborers, called for the overthrow of the white plantocracy and the establishment of a Haitian-style regime. "Long live the Republic, death to the whites!" cried the insurgents.[10] Opposed not only by the white elite but also much of the mulatto bourgeoisie, the movement nonetheless lasted nearly a month and threatened to overwhelm the island entirely before it was finally suppressed. As for the communards of Paris, for many in the French Caribbean the republic equaled revolution.

The establishment of the Third Republic in the Caribbean in some ways replicated metropolitan patterns, but at the same time demonstrated local particularities. In particular, the political divisions between monarchists, moderate and radical republicans, and socialists took on a strong racial dimension, as the quotation in the previous paragraph suggests. The white elites and former slave owners had the same disdain for the republic as did monarchists in the metropole, and often boycotted the elections. The black former slaves also largely abstained from voting, partly due to the influence of their former masters and current employers, and also (especially in Martinique) due to disillusionment with the republic after its suppression of the 1870 insurrection. The Third Republic thus brought the third major group in French Caribbean society, the mulatto middle class, to power. This group embraced the republic, seeing it as its pathway to equality and progress; it was a parliamentary deputy newly arrived from Martinique, François Marc Godissart, who cast the deciding vote in favor of ratifying the 1875 constitution. In contrast, not until the rise of socialist and union organizations in the 1890s did the majority black population begin to achieve significant political representation.

In some ways the French Caribbean after 1870 thus represented the paradox of imperial republicanism at its most extreme. Its residents had the same voting and citizenship rights as did those of the metropole, yet Guadeloupe, Martinique, and Guiana remained colonies, subject in important ways to the minister of colonies in Paris. Republican politics there took on a crucial racial dimension that contradicted the republican ideal of equality before the law. The economic conditions of the French Caribbean strongly reinforced this republican political paradox. The white elite could abstain from politics because it kept a firm control over sugar production, by far the dominant economic sector. The great sugar refineries were all owned by the *bekés*, and much of the population had to work for them in order to survive. This control, and the well-being of the French Caribbean in general, however, was increasingly challenged by the decline of the sugar economy after the mid-1880s. The rise of other sites of sugar production, such as Cuba and Hawaii, as well as the increasing use of beet sugar, spelled disaster for what had been known as the "isles of white gold." The Méline tariff of 1892 also hurt the Caribbean by sharply increasing the prices of imports. The crisis of the sugar economy plunged many of the people of the islands into poverty, prompting major strikes and insurrections in both Guadeloupe and Martinique at the turn of the century. These challenges paled in comparison, however, with the eruption of Martinique's Mount Pelée on May 8, 1902. The greatest volcanic cataclysm of the twentieth century, it emitted a vast cloud of poison gas that wiped out Saint-Pierre, the island's greatest city. Some thirty thousand people, 15 percent of Martinique's population, died within minutes. This freakish natural disaster, which shocked the world in 1902, underscored the idea that France's Caribbean colonies could hardly be seen as a triumph of the imperial republic.

The "old colonies" of Martinique, Guadeloupe, Guiana, and Réunion were not the only parts of the empire to have colonial citizenship under the Third Republic. The oldest French settlements in west Africa, like those in the Caribbean, date back to the seventeenth century, and some two hundred years later their residents also received recognition of their rights by the French. In 1848 the Second Republic extended the right of representation in the National Assembly to the four *communes*, or towns, of Senegal: Saint-Louis, Gorée, Rufisque, and Dakar. The Third Republic followed this up by granting citizen rights to the residents of Saint-Louis and Gorée in 1872, Rufisque in 1880, and Dakar (by then the capital of the colony of Senegal) in 1887. In 1879 Paris confirmed the right of the four communes to elect a representative to the National Assembly, making their inhabitants, known as *originaires*, the only people in colonial Africa to have representation in a European legislature. Whether this all added up to formal citizenship, however, remained an open question until World War I, and in any case few in France considered the *originaires* the equals of metropolitan Frenchmen.

Tahiti became the other colony to grant its inhabitants something approaching French citizenship. The country had been a protectorate of France for decades when the venerable Queen Pomare IV died in 1877, ending a reign of fifty years. Her son succeeded her as king but evidently had little taste for the responsibilities of governance, so in 1880 he resigned and ceded control of the government to France, making the country a full-fledged French colony. A condition of this transfer of power, however, was that all of the king's subjects would be citizens of France. Few Tahitians knew French or had any idea of what it meant to be a French citizen, however, and the agreement did not apply to residents of other island groups in the Etablissements Francais de l'Océanie, such as the Marquesas or the Tuamotus.

The question of citizenship was much more complex in Algeria. The birth of the Third Republic brought important changes to France's stronghold in North Africa. Shortly after news of the disaster at Sedan reached Algeria the local *colons* rallied and overthrew the military in the colony. The new provisional government in Paris supported them, and Adolphe Crémieux moved to reestablish the structures of civilian rule originally set up in 1848. At the same time Crémieux, a strong advocate for Jewish causes and a founding member of the Alliance Israelite Universelle, issued the Crémieux decree granting

French citizenship to the Jews of Algeria. This decree represented a major achievement for the local Jewish population, but at the same time had important consequences for intercommunal relations in Algeria. Many Muslims resented the fact that Jews had received a privilege denied them, while many settlers looked down on the Jews as natives who had no right to legal equality with Europeans. The hostility of the *colons* to Jewish enfranchisement made colonial Algeria a hotbed of anti-Semitism, producing some of the worst anti-Jewish riots in France during the Dreyfus Affair.

The restoration of civilian rule under the Third Republic markedly increased the power of the French settlers in Algeria. In 1871 a major insurrection broke out in Kabylia, prompted by the extreme deprivation inflicted upon the Muslim population due to the destruction of the traditional rural economy. After suppressing the revolt French authorities took measures to control the Muslim population, including expropriating large amounts of tribal land. Much of this land passed into the hands of the settlers, whose numbers doubled during the 1870s to over 300,000. These included several thousand French expatriates from what was now German Alsace-Lorraine. In 1881 the French government recognized the settlers, who had demonstrated their loyalty to the republic in 1870, as full-fledged French citizens, and gave each of the three Algerian departments the right to elect two representatives to the National Assembly. It also moved oversight of Algeria from the Ministry of Foreign Affairs (which administered the colonies until 1894) to the Ministry of the Interior. At the same time, Paris reaffirmed the 1865 ruling that granted Muslims French citizenship only if they agreed to renounce Islam, something very few were willing to do. Like the French Caribbean, therefore, but to a much greater extent, Algeria under the Third Republic combined colonial citizenship with systematic disenfranchisement of particular communities.

After 1870 the old colonies and Algeria represented the limits of republican universalism. Residents of the empire could in some cases be French citizens, yet rarely did colonial citizenship translate into true democracy or bring equality with French men and women in the metropole. Instead, it often resulted in the political dominance of a minority, generally one strongly supportive of republican ideals. In the old colonies, therefore, the republican empire brought important political changes, but universal democracy was not one of them. In the vast new imperial territories, as we will see, imperial republicanism illustrated to an even greater extent the gap between universalist theories and colonial practices.

IDEAS AND REALITIES OF EMPIRE

By the mid-1890s the Third Republic had largely completed its imperial conquests, and it began to turn its attention from military adventure to administration. By the turn of the century France had organized its new colonies into major federations, or governments general: Indochina, French West Africa, French Equatorial Africa, and Madagascar. A governor general ruled each, answering to the minister of colonies in Paris. Below them labored a few thousand French administrators, aided by both members of traditional local elites and, increasingly, young French-trained natives. The overwhelming mass of the colonial population had little to no input in colonial administration. They were subjects, not citizens, of a France struggling to integrate vast new territories and populations into its vision of the universal nation.

In presenting his program for imperial expansion in the early 1880s, Jules Ferry outlined three primary motivations for empire: economic gain, the civilizing mission, and national prestige. While global strategic imperatives and rivalries with other great powers played a significant role in some cases, notably Morocco, the desire for profit and the urge to spread progress and enlightenment dominated the imperialism of the Third Republic. These goals and the policies they inspired often had unexpected consequences, however. As we have seen, France's colonial gold rush did not just emanate from Paris, which often simply responded to local initiatives taken by soldiers and adventurers. Similarly, even after the establishment of colonial rule French administrators had to adapt their ideas to the realities of local life. Republicanism in the empire, to an even greater extent than in the French provinces, thus blended metropolitan republican theories with a variety of colonial interests and pressures.

The economic promise of empire in the late nineteenth century rested on three basic opportunities: raw materials, markets, and investments. The desire for exotic commodities and raw materials had long played a key role in European imperial expansion, and during the ancien régime sugar from the Caribbean lay at the heart of French colonialism. No single colonial commodity achieved anywhere near this importance during the Third Republic, but the French nonetheless imported large quantities of agricultural produce and other raw materials from their colonies during the late nineteenth century. Tropical fruits like the banana became common in French marketplaces, and the coconut had a variety of uses, including the production of margarine and soap. Less exotic commodities like olive oil and rice also came from the colonies. Shortly after the French conquest settlers had developed a major wine industry in Algeria, most of whose people were forbidden by Islamic law from consuming alcohol. Minerals such as nickel from New Caledonia, phosphate from North Africa, and tin from Indochina supplied metropolitan industries. By the eve of World War I Indochina was developing a large sector of rubber plantations, supplying the demand for bicycle and automobile tires, machine parts, and even condoms.

If France imported raw commodities from the empire, it exported manufactured goods to it. This was of course the classic imperial pattern, and the Long Depression made colonial markets more important than ever. As the historian Jacques Marseille has noted, the colonies imported goods from some French industries more than others, so that their impact on the metropolitan economy was uneven. Colonial markets were more important to traditional industries in France, like textiles and candles, than they were to the more advanced industrial sectors. The empire thus contributed to the relative backwardness of the French economy in the late nineteenth century, supporting manufacturers who could not compete successfully in global markets.

Colonial investments followed a similarly uneven pattern. By and large most French investors preferred to send their money elsewhere, predominantly to Russia and Latin America, where rates of return were high and risks generally lower than in the nation's colonies. At the same time, however, the French created several important colonial banks, which mobilized capital to invest in the nation's imperial possessions. The largest of these, the Banque de l'Indochine, proved extremely profitable, establishing branches throughout Indochina as well as New Caledonia, Hong Kong, Shanghai, and Bangkok by the turn of the century. The French began some investment projects in the late nineteenth century, notably railways in its African colonies, but significant infrastructural development would have to wait until the interwar years.

Did the French empire pay? While no colonies in the late nineteenth century produced spectacular profits on the scale of ancien régime Saint-Domingue, nonetheless the empire did make a solid contribution to the French economy. If the primary motivation for the imperial scramble of the 1880s and 1890s was fear of economic crisis and the desire to create protected markets as a safety valve, there are grounds for believing the empire did achieve that end. While the economic realities of French colonialism may have paled next to the glittering fantasies of imperial wealth, many in France derived concrete benefit from the profits of empire.

Financial concerns alone did not prompt the expansion of the republican empire, however. Many French progressives viewed colonialism as a way of bringing Africans and Asians the benefits of modern culture and science, whether they wanted them or not. The idea of the *mission civilisatrice* did not just rationalize imperial conquest for profit, but for many constituted an end in and of itself. The clearest expression of this belief was the doctrine of assimilation, which dominated thinking about empire in early Third Republic France. First developed in the 1830s, assimilation held that the goal of empire should be to make colonial subjects into French citizens by enabling them to master modern civilization. For the leaders of the Third Republic, who had devoted so much effort to integrating provincials into national republican culture, it seemed natural to assume that one could also make colonial natives French. Assimilation was national universalism in its purest form, viewing the values of French civilization as the property of all men.

Yet ultimately the natives did not become Frenchmen, unlike their provincial brethren. This was not completely true: many considered both the old colonies and the four *communes* of Senegal successful examples of assimilation. In contrast, relatively few residents of the new empire in Africa and Asia ever succeeded in obtaining French citizenship. One key reason for this was education. As we have seen, public schoolteachers had served as the shock troops of the republic in the French provinces, spreading literacy, basic skills like writing and mathematical reasoning, and republican values throughout the countryside. French colonial administrators took pride in their efforts to build native schools in the empire, often in competition with the religious schools run by missionaries. In line with assimilationist ideology and the republican tradition of educational centralization, these schools taught roughly the same material as those in the metropole, so that students in Africa, Asia, and the Caribbean learned about French history, literature, and geography but very little about their own countries. However, relatively few colonial children experienced French education, in part because many families could not afford to send their children to school full-time, in part because France invested far less money in colonial than in provincial schools.

This educational gap was important for a number of reasons, not least because schooling could provide a path to French citizenship. Those who demonstrated a mastery of French knowledge and culture could attain the coveted status of *evolué*, or evolved one. While not fully citizens of France, the *evolués* constituted an elite in colonial society. The absence of an adequate educational infrastructure meant that only a tiny percentage of colonial subjects

could rise to this level. In large part this was by design, since colonial authorities felt most natives would work at manual labor and therefore needed little
formal education. Indeed, many French feared the rise of a large educated
colonial population, which might demand full equality that colonial society
was unprepared to give. Most évolués worked in lower level administrative
positions, blocked by their non-European origins and their skin color from
advancing further.

The limits placed on native elites in French colonial society underscore
the central factor of race in the empire. Whatever else rural French men and
women might be, society viewed them as white, in contrast to the nation's
imperial subjects. At first glance a belief in racial difference and inequality
seemed a fundamental contradiction with republican ideology. Ernest Renan
explicitly rejected racial identity in his famous speech "What Is a Nation?"
Yet as some historians have argued, the late nineteenth century saw a rise in
racial thinking in both France and the western world in general. Carole Reynaud-Paligot has described the emergence of a transnational network of institutions devoted to the pursuit of racial science after 1850. Anthropological
societies, the first of which was founded in Paris in 1859, sought to classify
humankind increasingly along racial lines. In contrast to the early nineteenth
century, students and scholars of race after 1850 tended to view racial differences as fixed and immutable, while at the same time adopting earlier ideas
of racial hierarchy which inevitably placed whites at the top and blacks at the
bottom.

The new racial thinking in France arose not just from colonial contacts
but also from life in the metropole. The increase in foreign immigration
during the 1880s and 1890s fed racial attitudes, as we have seen in the case
of the Dreyfus Affair. More generally, questions of race and class often overlapped and reinforced each other. The decline of upward mobility in the late
nineteenth century, as well as the growth of the industrial working class, fostered the idea that working people were separate from the rest of the nation,
a race apart. France's classic study of racial science, Gobineau's *Essay on the
Origins of Inequality*, portrayed the revolutionary workers of Paris as an example of racial degeneracy. In addition, the rise of the modern nation-state,
based on the idea that not just political allegiance but also language, culture,
and tradition united citizens of a nation, contributed to a racial view of the
world. Even Renan proclaimed that "the fact of race is a decisive factor in
human history,"[11] and characterized the war of 1870 as "a great racial struggle."[12] Many French men and women viewed their nation's history through

a racial lens, seeing France as the product of the intermingling between the Gallic and Roman races. The idea of nations as races became widespread by the turn of the century.

Racial thinking had its greatest impact in the empire, however, becoming a central aspect of colonial life. As we have seen, only a minority of colonial subjects achieved citizenship, and even this did not bring them full equality with French administrators or settlers. For the rest, racial difference shaped and underscored their subordinate status, a status enshrined in French colonial law. The *code de l'indigénat*, or native code, was a series of special regulations that applied only to colonial subjects. First developed in Algeria, the Indigenat enabled imperial authorities to fine and jail residents without appeal for a host of infractions, including nonpayment of taxes, insufficient deference to French authority, and failure to adhere to French standards of dress and hygiene. Many administrators viewed it as a means of disciplining lazy natives and often applied it in an arbitrary manner. In effect enabling whites to do whatever they wanted to colonized peoples, the Indigenat became one of the great symbols of French colonial racism.

France's desire to civilize its native population, combined with a belief in its subjects' racial inferiority, shaped other aspects of colonial life. Generally colonial administrators implemented measures combining moral lessons and financial benefits. They imposed a number of taxes on colonial subjects in the belief that colonies should pay for themselves and the natives assume financial responsibility for the benefits of French civilization. The *capitation*, or head tax, levied on most adult males, was the most notorious. In addition to raising funds for colonial administration, these taxes acted to force colonial subjects into the monetary economy by requiring them to have cash to pay their public obligations. The most common way of doing so was working for wages, so colonial rule transformed independent peasants into unskilled workers. Like antebellum American slave owners, French colonial administrators viewed colonial natives as lazy and shiftless, people who needed to be taught the value of hard work. Making them pay taxes helped force them into paid labor. In addition, the French instituted the practice of *corvée*, or forced labor, to save the natives from idleness.

The French also used colonial rule to expropriate vast expanses of land from their indigenous owners. This happened most commonly in settler colonies, above all Algeria, but it occurred throughout the empire. France assumed that as the new governing authority it held title to all public lands. Whereas colonial administrators said they would protect the rights of native landowners, those who could not furnish clear proof of title (and even some who could) often lost their property. Moreover, French colonizers frequently argued that those who could exploit the land more effectively had the right to own it. In contrast to the metropole, where public authorities extolled the value of rural life and the family farm, in the colonies they pursued policies that consciously stripped millions of peoples of their land and forced them into the ranks of the laboring poor.

As France approached the new century, it strove to impose centralized administration and order on its colonies, moving beyond the chaos of the conquest years and applying republican principles systematically. The intricacies of local life often made this more complicated than the new colonial rulers had believed, however, so that imperial republicanism came to look very different on the ground than it did in Paris. As we have seen, a key theme of the Third Republic's political culture was anticlericalism. While Léon Gambetta had led the charge against the Church with his famous words "Clericalism: there is the enemy!" he also proclaimed that anticlericalism was not for export. The colonial administrators of the Third Republic had to confront the fact that the missionaries had arrived before them, and in much larger numbers. In spite of their vaunted anticlericalism, republican administrators often had to rely on the missionaries to help run colonial institutions like hospitals and even schools. At the same time, the missionaries and the Church came to identify more with French nationalism, especially in areas like Tahiti where they competed with British Protestants. Many tensions between colonial Church and state remained, and the rise of the radical republic tended to aggravate them after 1900. Nonetheless, in the republican empire the two universalist ideologies interacted to foster a vision of France as a universal nation.

The struggle against slavery also showed how the republican ideal of empire had to adapt to facts on the ground. Antislavery had been a major reason for France's colonization of west Africa, a concrete expression of the republic's commitment to universal freedom. Yet as Martin Klein has shown, in French West Africa colonial administrators often tolerated slavery. Dependent on slave-owning local elites, they mediated between their interests and directives from Paris. The central role of slavery to agricultural production and the colonial economy frequently led French officials to turn a blind eye to, or even officially accept, the rights of owners over their slaves. In Guinea, for example, colonial authorities routinely returned slaves to masters, only emancipating them when the masters opposed French governance. After 1900 France took a firm stand against west African slavery, prompting a massive flight of slaves to freedom.

The imperial rule of the Third Republic thus represented a complex blend of republican ideas in Paris and colonial realities in the empire. If the colonizers had to adapt to a new world, so did the colonized. As we have seen, the establishment of colonial rule under the Third Republic was in many ways a disaster for the new subjects of France. Indigenous people had to cope with a bewildering transformation of their societies and their daily lives. Many lost their land, and many more were forced into physically demanding, even brutal, labor. The French pointed to their investments in education and health care as concrete examples of its civilizing mission, yet few local residents derived much benefit from these institutions, especially in the years before World War I. To take one example, the population of Tahiti during the late nineteenth century declined sharply as a result of diseases brought by the French. Moreover, the colonized found themselves ruled by foreign elites and subjected to discrimination and humiliation on the basis of their skin color alone.

Colonial rule also opened up new opportunities for some, however. A few, lucky enough to obtain a French education, found posts in the lower levels of the colonial administration as white collar workers. Although never accepted as equals by the French, they did become a kind of Europeanized elite and frequently mediated between the colonizers and the colonized. Many more colonial men joined the ranks of the military, especially in Africa. In 1857 Louis Faidherbe, governor of French West Africa, created the *tirailleurs séné-galais,* or Senegalese rifles. Africans who volunteered for military service received low pay but exemption from some colonial taxes. The Senegalese rifles served widely throughout the empire, taking part in the conquest of Tonkin in the 1880s, and would play an important role in World War I. Other colonial subjects, both men and women, found employment as domestic servants for French settlers. French colonial rule increased the range of employment alternatives for local residents, even if they involved hard work, low pay, and subordination to French employers.

This was especially true for indigenous women. Both missionaries and colonial administrators frequently saw women as the key to successful inroads into native society. They viewed the backwardness and oppression of women as central to the primitive nature of the colonies, arguing that if women could be brought into modernity the whole society would follow. In particular, French colonial authorities advocated educating girls, in societies where schooling for women was rare to nonexistent, as a way of freeing them from traditional patriarchal authority. Colonial administrators also sought to improve health conditions and practices for women and their children. In addition they tried to impose western standards of dress and modesty, whether it be covering up women in the South Pacific or campaigning against the veil in Islamic North Africa. Like men, many indigenous women found employment in the colonial economy. Some performed manual labor on farms and plantations, while others worked as domestics: cleaning, cooking, and taking care of children. Finally, some were forced into prostitution or became the mistresses of French men. Only a few ever obtained the education necessary to qualify for skilled positions like teachers or nurses.

Given the harsh conditions experienced by most French colonial subjects, it is not surprising that anticolonial resistance and rebellion were endemic in the empire. Most colonial wars of conquest involved long periods of "pacification," so that it was often decades before French rule was firmly in place. Even after France had solidified its control revolts broke out at times in the colonies. In June 1878 a series of incidents in New Caledonia sparked a massive armed uprising against the French, led by a chief named Atai. The insurrection lasted for several months before the colonial administration overcame it, costing the lives of two hundred whites and over one thousand indigenous Kanaks. More typically, colonial subjects resorted to subtle, everyday forms of resistance: working slowly, pretending not to understand French, in general cooperating as little as possible with the colonial administration. Indigenous resistance did not seriously threaten French colonialism in the late nineteenth century, but it did demonstrate the failure of Paris to win hearts and minds overseas; its gift of French civilization was only grudgingly received.

FRANCE IN THE COLONIES

For most French people during the late nineteenth century, the empire was a distant phenomenon with little relevance to their daily lives. Some, however, answered the call of faraway horizons, visiting or settling in overseas France. Like America's Wild West or Russian Siberia, the French colonies were both intimidating and alluring. Fears of hostile natives, tropical disease, and isolation competed with fantasies of exotic landscapes, sultry sensuality, and enormous profits. Above all, the empire offered a vision of freedom: the chance to remake oneself anew far away from the strictures of home. The lure of new worlds to conquer was all the more enticing as France became ever more unified and bourgeois. If colonialism offered the possibility of imposing French republican universalism on a global scale, for some it also suggested escape from an ever more interconnected world.

Settler colonialism played a much smaller role in the imperialism of the Third Republic than it had during the early modern era. Only two French colonies, Algeria and New Caledonia, had substantial French populations, and none had a majority of settlers from France. There would be no Quebec or Louisiana in the republican empire. Nonetheless, the empire did attract a variety of people from France. Missionaries, convicts, soldiers and sailors, businesspeople, and others settled in the colonies, in the process transforming at least parts of them into versions of the country they had left behind. As much as the attempts to turn natives into French men and women, their presence in the empire underscored the idea of France as a universal nation.

The initial period of exploration and conquest brought adventurers to the colonies, people who lived lives far removed from traditions of domesticity in Europe. During the Third Republic their time had largely passed, but a few intrepid individuals still set off to the colonies in search of adventure. In 1886 the young Camille Douls set off to explore Mauritania, one of the most remote places in west Africa, after training himself for years by studying Islam and Arabic. Douls lived with the local Moorish population for several months before making his way back to Paris. Two years later he disappeared during an expedition to Timbuktu.

By the late nineteenth century those searching for colonial adventure joined the military rather than setting out on their own. Soldiers and sailors not only conquered the empire for their nation but also featured prominently in French colonial communities. The imperial experience played a key role in shaping the French military during the Third Republic and beyond; many leading generals and admirals cut their teeth on colonial service. At the same time overseas military needs brought many young sailors and soldiers to the colonies who otherwise might never have left France. In Pierre Jakez Hélias's classic memoir of Breton life at the beginning of the twentieth century, *The Horse of Pride*, he mentions in passing a relative who served in Indochina. The ultimate example of imperial military service was the French Foreign Legion. Based in Algeria by the mid-nineteenth century, the legion fought widely in the republican empire, taking part in campaigns in Indochina and Madagascar as well as North Africa. Legends of its deeds became a staple of French colonial adventure and romance.

God as well as guns and glory brought French women and men to the empire. Roughly 50,000 religious workers labored in the French empire, supported morally and financially by more than a million of the faithful back home. Missionaries not only preached the gospel but also ran schools and medical facilities.

Indeed, the Church's mission work in the colonies was one of its strongest selling points in France. The largest group was the Society of Missionaries, founded in 1868 by Father Charles Lavigerie, the archbishop of Algiers; its priests were known as the White Fathers and the associated order of nuns the White Sisters. More than other French people in the empire the missionaries worked directly with the indigenous population, using charitable works as a means of bringing those they considered heathen savages to God. In this their success was mixed: they won lots of converts in Indochina and the Pacific, fewer in sub-Saharan Africa, and hardly any in the Muslim regions of Africa.

Missionaries and members of the military had a lot in common. Members of both groups came to the colonies in service of a collective calling rather than an individual goal, and both gave over personal authority to a powerful organization. Moreover, both lived highly regimented and often extremely rigorous lives in the colonies. Most important, both stood on the margins of civilian society, offering little prospect of creating French communities away from home. As colonial rule stabilized, the rise of such communities became more typical of life in the empire, underscoring the permanence of French control and facilitating the republican idea of turning the colonies into overseas reflections of France.

The largest French populations lived in the settler colonies of Algeria and New Caledonia; Algeria alone, with over 600,000 French settlers by the turn of the century, accounted for a large majority of imperial *colons*. New Caledonia had far fewer residents from France, some 20,000, but since the Kanak population had declined to 27,000 by 1900 it was the most "French" of all the nation's colonies. In both cases the promise of cheap and abundant land attracted the settlers, land that was expropriated from the indigenous population. In New Caledonia locals lost 90 percent of their property holdings, the colonial government frequently removing them to reservations. Also, both colonies drew their "French" populations in part from places outside France. This was especially true of Algeria: many of the *pieds noirs* came from elsewhere in the Mediterranean, especially Spain, Italy, and Malta. New Caledonia's role as a penal colony accounted for many of its first French settlers, notably four thousand deported communards after 1871. By the turn of the century, however, it also attracted immigrants from Australia and New Zealand as well as a substantial Pacific Islander and Asian population. In its settler colonies France thus demonstrated its ability to bring in people from around the world and make them French. They became places where France could reinvent itself in a transnational and universalist approach to empire.

The integration of foreign settlers into French colonial life also under-scored the racial dimension of French universalism. In 1889 the French government decreed that all Algerians of European heritage would become French citizens. It thus made citizenship dependent on race, so that to be white meant to be French and vice versa. Reflecting this, French and other whites in the colonies were commonly referred to collectively as Europeans, emphasizing less their national or even regional origins and more their racial heritage. As we will see, to an important extent French life in the colonies was built around whiteness and white racial privilege. In the empire national and racial universalism blended into each other, crafting a vision of France as a universal white nation.

The racialized character of French colonial life was especially apparent in the empire's cities. Throughout the colonies France created or expanded major urban settlements, which constituted one of the empire's most dramatic impacts and enduring legacies. In the mid-nineteenth century the French founded Dakar, which would eventually become the capital of Senegal and one of the largest cities in Africa. Under the Third Republic French urban planners worked throughout the empire to renovate old cities or, more often, develop new ones along European lines. They endowed them with symbols of urban modernity like broad Parisian-style boulevards, cafés, and modern plumbing and sewage systems. They also erected monumental new buildings to remind them of home and stamp the print of modernity on the urban land-scape. Hanoi's opera house replicated the Paris Opera in Asia, for example, and buildings like train stations, government buildings, and hospitals often had a distinctly European appearance. At times the colonies appeared to be a laboratory for French architectural modernity.

Many French in the empire chose to live in urban areas, while those who had moved to the settler colonies to obtain land often lived on their farms and plantations. Even in New Caledonia, however, the majority of *colons* lived in the capital city of Nouméa, and in Algeria the French developed the new city of Bône next to the Arab town of Annaba, while also creating an extensive new French city outside the old center, or medina, of Algiers. Elsewhere in the empire the French population lived overwhelmingly in the cities. For colonial administrators and businessmen, their work lay in the colonial city, so it made no sense to live elsewhere. The colonial city offered culture, amusements, and most importantly other French people, the possibility of creating expatriate communities overseas. By the end of the nineteenth century French life in the colonies was to a very great extent urban life.

And yet the creation of French expatriate communities did not tell the entire story of colonial urbanization under the Third Republic. The expropriation of indigenous lands and the destruction of rural economies throughout the empire forced many colonial subjects into the cities as well. Traditional native quarters saw their populations grow, and new suburban shantytowns sprang up to house newcomers from the countryside. In most cities poor natives comprised the majority of the population, and the French a privileged minority. The result was what historian Janet Abu-Lughod has called a system of urban apartheid. French colonial cities were rigidly segregated, modern and clean European neighborhoods separated from impoverished native quarters. Ultimately, however, French attempts to create pristine European cities in the colonies uncontaminated by native dirt and disease were only partially successful, and sometimes had unintended consequences. In 1902, for example, Hanoi built a new sewer system, complete with indoor plumbing, for the French section of town. Unfortunately the new sewers facilitated a major rat infestation of the area, leading to an outbreak of bubonic plague the following year.[13] More generally, French settlers depended on servants from the native quarters to clean their homes, cook their meals, and watch their children. Natives and settlers thus interacted constantly, but on a basis of privilege and inferiority. French colonial cities thus became prime symbols of the racism that lay at the heart of republican imperialism.

For French people living in the empire colonial cities offered a welcome range of diversions, including cafés, concerts, plays, and French cuisine. Especially in comparison to their indigenous neighbors, French residents lived well indeed. Colonial French households could afford numerous servants, or "boys" (using the English term imported from British India), and luxurious houses. Both in terms of opulent lifestyle and racialized caste privilege at least a few settlers from France were able to mimic the life of the European aristocracy increasingly unattainable at home. Big game hunting, a traditionally aristocratic privilege in Europe, became an exotic entertainment in the colonies. At the same time, however, life was by no means easy. Setting up a new farm or plantation required backbreaking labor, and natural calamities like droughts and fires could bring all that hard work to naught. Tropical diseases like malaria and dengue fever killed many *colons*. Even in the cities the opportunities for entertainment paled compared to what was available back home. Moreover, the sense of isolation and disorientation resulting from life far from home created a palpable burden for many. Voyages back to France were costly, lengthy (up to six weeks from Asia), and infrequent, and as time went on many settlers felt they no longer belonged there. Yet did not really feel at home in the colonies either. *Le cafard*, or the colonial blues, afflicted many, and drug and alcohol abuse was a common way of coping. If the conquest of empire had produced an image of the virile colonial adventurer, the rise of expatriate French communities generated a counter-image of the white man prey to disease and alcoholism, gone to seed in the tropics.

The lives of French residents in the colonies were fundamentally shaped not only by race but by gender as well. With the exception of female missionaries, most French settlers in the empire were men, especially during the era of exploration and conquest. For many French men the colonies represented an escape from the strictures of bourgeois sexual morality. This plus the absence of French or European women led many to engage in *mariages à la mode de pays*, or common-law relationships with indigenous women. Others resorted to prostitutes or concubines to satisfy their needs for female companionship. Colonial miscegenation both challenged and reinforced hierarchies of race and power in the empire: it emphasized white male dominance while at the same time providing for intimate contacts across the color line. It also produced a significant population of *métis*, or mixed-race offspring, whose presence in the colonies graphically demonstrated France's imperial presence. Those formally recognized by their French fathers became citizens and often obtained French education and good white-collar jobs. Many, however, suffered what American writers have called the "tragic mulatto" syndrome: adrift between two cultures, viewed with suspicion by both and fully at home in neither.

For French women, life in the colonies offered scant possibilities. A few intrepid women saw empire as a chance to escape bourgeois patriarchy at home. For example, Madame de la Souchère founded her own rubber plantation in Indochina in 1909 and became one of the colony's leading planters. By far the most famous example of such adventurous women was Isabelle Eberhardt, a woman of German and Russian heritage who had grown up in Geneva. In 1897 at the age of twenty Eberhardt and her mother moved to Bône, Algeria, to be near her brother who had joined the Foreign Legion. There she embraced Arab culture, studying Arabic and converting to Islam. She also scandalized the local French population by walking around in men's clothing, smoking hashish, and publicly criticizing the racism of the *colons*. She eventually married an Algerian sergeant and consequently gained French citizenship. After more adventures in Algeria and Morocco, she died in a flood at the age of twenty-seven. For Eberhardt, the French empire offered a woman the freedom to live life as she wished, outside the bounds of settled society.

Exceptional cases like Eberhardt's were deeply disturbing to the emerging colonial order. It was one thing for French men to be intimate with colonial women, quite another for French women to enjoy the same privilege. If the colonies could offer some women new opportunities, in general racial boundaries and hierarchies reinforced patriarchy. French women were supposed to represent, not challenge, bourgeois propriety, and their relations with natives should be correct and even caring, but distant. The empire attracted relatively few French women during the late nineteenth century, and most came as either missionaries or wives of colonial administrators. Fears of tropical disease, especially for those who had or wanted to have children, kept all but a few from venturing to the colonies. Those who did often spent their lives caring for their households and learning to manage colonial servants. Others worked in a variety of venues, especially helping professions like teachers and nurse, but also shopkeepers and seamstresses.

Many female settlers from France focused on improving the condition of native women, and some French feminists developed an interest in empire as a way of promoting gender equality. For feminism the issue of empire posed important questions about the comparative and universal nature of women's oppression. In her newspaper *La citoyenne* the noted French feminist Hubertine Auclert wrote extensively about native women in the empire, especially after she moved to Algiers for four years in 1888. Auclert, a socialist feminist, noted that French women often had fewer rights than their Arab sisters, who could keep their own names after marriage, for example. At the same time she generally viewed the Algerians as uncivilized and in need of the benefits French republicanism could provide, especially when it addressed issues of particular importance to women like the abolition of polygamy. At one point Auclert wrote that "the dream of Arab women is to be assimilated and to become French."[14] For Auclert and other French feminists, women's uplift was one of the benefits enlightened republican imperialism could provide.

For a few French people, the empire thus provided a chance for a new life and a vision of freedom. Especially in Algeria, by far the largest *colon* community, it underscored the idea of the transnational nation by offering European foreigners a chance to become French citizens. At the same time, this universal vision rested on a base of racial discrimination and white privilege, making French colonial life an experience in whiteness. This racialized universalism would be an important legacy for the colonies, and France as a whole, in the new century.

THE COLONIES IN FRANCE

While France had a tremendous impact on life in its colonies, the impact of the colonies on life in France was less obvious. Most French women and men regarded the empire (to the extent that they regarded it at all) as interesting and exotic, but distant and of no relevance to their daily lives. Nonetheless, the Third Republic was an imperial republic, and colonialism did shape the lives of its citizens as well as its subjects. Colonial products, images, and stereotypes all circulated widely in the metropole during the late nineteenth century. Moreover, those who had lived in the empire frequently came home to tell their family and friends about their experiences, and colonial subjects at times made their way to France, especially to great cities like Paris and Marseilles. The impact of the colonies on life in the metropole reinforced the idea of France as a universal nation at the center of the world.

The impact of the colonies was most noticeable in contemporary French culture, especially literature and art. Many people liked to read romantic tales about life in exotic, faraway lands, and in the late nineteenth century a small number of writers catered to this thirst for colonialist fiction. The most prominent of these was Pierre Loti, author of some forty novels and collections of stories during the late nineteenth and early twentieth centuries. Born Julien Viaud in the Atlantic port city of Rochefort in 1850, Loti developed a fascination for the exotic at an early age thanks to his older brother's tales of military service in Tahiti. As an adult he joined the navy, traveling in his own turn to Tahiti, and eventually visiting not only most of the French empire but much of the world in general. In 1881 he published what would become his most famous and influential novel, *Le roman d'un spahi* (The Novel of a Colonial Cavalry Man). The novel, which follows the exciting and ultimately tragic adventures of a young French soldier named Péyral in Senegal, gives a lushly detailed and exotic description of colonial life in Africa. This novel and the others Loti wrote with colonial themes proved highly popular in France, enabling the author to beat out Emile Zola for appointment to the French Academy in 1891.

Painting and sculpture in France also frequently took up colonial themes. We have already seen the influential role of non-European styles and subjects in both romanticism and impressionism, and this continued in the new artistic styles of the turn of the century. Paul Gauguin's love of Tahiti and his depictions of those islands in his art are well known. Henri Matisse painted several studies of Morocco after his visits there in 1912 and 1913. Whereas the 1870s and 1880s had witnessed French fascination with Japanese art, during the first decade of the twentieth century the cubist avant-garde discovered the attractions of African sculpture. Artists like Matisse, Pablo Picasso, and Georges Braque saw in African art a primitivist mind-set that challenged western rationalism, using it to inspire their own experiments with abstraction. After World War I this interest in African culture would blossom into full-blown negrophilia, further increasing fascination with the empire.

Visual interest in the French colonies did not stop with great artists and works of art. The invention of photography in the nineteenth century had made the creation and circulation of images a mass art form. Many photographers, both professionals and tourists, took pictures of colonial scenes, monuments, and people, and such images appeared in books and newspapers. One popular form of disseminating these images was the picture postcard, which first appeared in the 1870s and had become popular a generation later. Postcards sent by travelers to friends and family back home often featured colonial scenes and monuments, such as Angkor Wat in Cambodia. Native women frequently appeared in them, sometimes in risqué representations, and French postcards often featured veiled North African women, tempting the viewer to wonder what lay behind the veil.

Commercial product trademarks and advertisements constituted another popular source of colonial imagery in France. A number of companies, especially those selling products of colonial or tropical origin, featured images of natives. In 1909, for example, a Marseilles company introduced a brand of flour named Pousse-Pousse (rickshaw), featuring an Asian man transporting a European woman. Soap and bleach companies frequently contained images of black people being whitened to show how effective their products were. These images, often very demeaning, circulated widely in France, featured not only on the products but also on advertisements displayed in newspapers and on the boulevards of great cities.

The great Parisian world fairs also offered French people an important opportunity to experience colonial life. The universal expositions of 1878, 1889, and 1900 all featured important colonial and exotic sections. The 1889 exposition, for example, included a series of colonial pavilions arranged along the Esplanade des Invalides, designed in the style of native architecture (or French interpretations of native architecture). Perhaps the most popular colonial exhibits were the so-called *tableaux vivants*, live ethnographic exhibits where visitors could watch natives from throughout the empire engage in daily pursuits, all staged for their benefit. The idea of creating zoos featuring people rather than animals both underscored and promoted the view of colonial subjects as racial others. Few bothered to inquire what the natives on display thought, but one newspaper interviewed a jeweler from Senegal who noted, "We are very humiliated to be exhibited this way, in huts like savages; these straw and mud huts do not give an idea of Senegal. In Senegal . . . we have large buildings, railroad stations, railroads; we light them with electricity."[15] The exposition also attracted spectators with performers from the colonies singing and dancing to what was usually billed as traditional native music. This prompted the visiting Jules Ferry to exclaim: "There's all *they* know about the empire—the belly dance."[16]

Not all the colonial subjects in France lived on stage, however. The imperial Third Republic brought a few people from the colonies to the metropole, a phenomenon that would grow into a trickle after World War I and a flood after World War II. This was not the first time that overseas expansion had introduced colonial residents to France. During the eighteenth century the nation had a tiny black population, consisting primarily of ex-slaves from the Caribbean, and in the aftermath of Napoleon I's invasion of Egypt a small number of Egyptians settled in Paris and Marseilles. Under the early Third Republic colonial migration to metropolitan France remained limited, so that most French people, especially outside the great cities, probably never met a native of the empire. It did nonetheless underscore the idea of France as a universal nation, providing a foretaste of changes that would transform what it meant to be French during the twentieth century.

People left the colonies for France for a variety of reasons. Some, especially citizens from the old colonies, came in search of education or opportunity. The future author René Maran left Martinique with his family when his father took a position as a colonial administrator in Gabon. Rather than raise his son in Africa, the father chose to enroll him in a boarding school in Bordeaux. Maran spent most of his childhood there, graduating from a local *lycée*. Felix Éboué, from French Guiana and a future leading colonial administrator, also attended a *lycée* in Bordeaux before moving on to Paris to study at the Ecole Coloniale. Colonial students in France often led a lonely existence, isolated from friends and family, but their stays in the metropole generally paid off professionally.

Others, probably the majority, came in search of work. Although most immigrant workers in France under the Third Republic were Europeans, some colonial migrants also found opportunities there. By the end of the century there were thousands of Algerian workers in France, primarily Marseilles and other parts of the south, working on the docks, in industry, and in agriculture.

Others, especially from Kabylia, crowded into the Paris suburbs in search of low-wage employment. In the 1880s one particularly progressive industrialist built an entire model community for Kabyle immigrant workers in the eastern suburb of Noisiel. For the most part, however, Algerian and other colonial immigrant workers (overwhelmingly single men) had to contend with some of the worst housing and labor conditions in France.

Colonialism and empire were thus a two-way street, changing not only the colonies but France as well. Colonial images and immigrants in the metropole gave French life a bit of exotic spice, as well as confirming the idea that France lay at the center of the world. Napoleon III had made Paris an imperial metropolis, but the republican empire paradoxically reinforced, and to an important extent globalized, the city's role as a world capital. At the same time, the beginnings of colonial immigration in France would begin to introduce paradoxes of republican universalism that would emerge forcefully in the century to come.

The colonial expansion of the Third Republic not only brought France a vast new empire, it also made French republicanism a global phenomenon. French universalism achieved its modern form in the decades after 1870, and its spread beyond the borders of the hexagon was a key aspect of that form. Attempts to integrate the provinces and the colonies into a grand republican ideal occurred at roughly the same time, and as the historian Eugen Weber classically observed, the two phenomena had much in common. Moreover, in a century that saw the rise and fall of both republics and empires, France ended up with a government that combined the two, so that the Third Republic was also in a sense the third empire.

France thus entered the twentieth century as a republican empire, a paradoxical political form that not only encapsulated the conflicts of the past but also foreshadowed important ones to come. The republican empire rested on the conviction that the universalist values born of the French Revolution could be applied to all, and French colonialism represented the most important attempt to date to make this principle a reality. At the same time the experiment in colonial republicanism revealed the limits of French universalism, the extent to which it not only failed to overcome but in some ways reinforced differences between whites and nonwhites, citizens and subjects, men and women. During the new century the French would struggle with these contradictions in their efforts to build a truly democratic republic. The great war that began in 1914 would bring France its greatest trial since the terrible year of 1870. It would reveal both the strengths and weaknesses of the universal nation.

Suggestions for Further Reading

Aldrich, Robert. *Greater France: A History of French Overseas Expansion.* Houndmills, UK: Macmillan, 1996.

————. *Vestiges of the Colonial Empire in France: Monuments, Museums, and Colonial Memories.* New York: Palgrave Macmillan, 2005.

Clancy-Smith, Julia, and Frances Gouda, eds. *Domesticating the Empire: Race, Gender, and Family Life in French and Dutch Colonialism.* Charlottesville: University Press of Virginia, 1998.

Cohen, William. *The French Encounter with Africans: White Response to Blacks, 1530–1880.* Bloomington: Indiana University Press, 1980.

Conklin, Alice L. *A Mission to Civilize: The Republican Idea of Empire in France and West Africa, 1895–1930.* Stanford, CA: Stanford University Press, 1997.

Eichner, Carolyn J. "*La Citoyenne* in the World: Hubertine Auclert and Feminist Imperialism." *French Historical Studies*, Winter 2009, 63–84.

Evans, Martin, ed. *Empire and Culture: The French Experience, 1830–1940.* New York: Palgrave Macmillan, 2004.

Gaugin, Paul. *Letters to His Wife and Friends.* Edited by Maurice Malingue. Boston: MFA Publications, 2003.

Giradet, Raoul. *L'Idée coloniale en France: De 1871 à 1962.* Paris: La Table Ronde, 1972.

Klein, Martin. *Slavery and Colonial Rule in French West Africa.* Cambridge: Cambridge University Press, 1998.

Lorcin, Patricia M. E. *Imperial Identities: Stereotyping, Prejudice, and Race in Colonial Algeria.* London: Tauris, 1999.

Manning, Patrick. *Francophone Sub-Saharan Africa, 1880–1995.* Cambridge: Cambridge University Press, 1998.

Nicolas, Armand. *Histoire de la Martinique: De 1848 à 1939.* Vol. 2. Paris: L'Harmattan, 1996.

Palermo, Lynn E. "Identity Under Construction: Representing the Colonies at the Paris *Exposition Universelle* of 1889." In Sue Peabody and Tyler Stovall, eds., *The Color of Liberty: Histories of Race in France.* Durham, NC: Duke University Press, 2003.

Reynaud-Paligot, Carole. *De l'Identité Nationale: Science, race et politique en Europe et aux États-Unis XIXe–Xxe siècle.* Paris: Presses Universitaires de France, 2011.

Sweetman, David. *Paul Gauguin: A Life.* New York: Simon & Schuster, 1995.

Vann, Michael G. "Of Rats, Rice, and Race: The Great Hanoi Rat Massacre, an Episode in French Colonial History." *French Colonial History* 4, no. 1 (2003): 191–203.

──────── **Notes** ────────────────────────────────

1. John Merriman, *A History of Modern Europe,* vol. 2, *From the French Revolution to the Present* (New York: Norton, 1996), 988.
2. V. I. Lenin, *Imperialism: The Highest Stage of Capitalism* (New York: International Publishers, 1969), 80.
3. Merriman, *History of Modern Europe,* 988.
4. Chinua Achebe, *Things Fall Apart* (New York: Anchor, 1994), 162.
5. Robert Aldrich, *Greater France: A History of French Overseas Expansion* (Houndmill, UK: Macmillan, 1996), 162.
6. Paul Robiquet, ed., *Discours et opinions de Jules Ferry* (Paris: Armand Colin, 1897).
7. Aldrich, *Greater France,* 53.
8. Ibid., 113.
9. Ibid., 40.
10. Armand Nicolas, *Histoire de la Martinique: De 1848 à 1939* (Paris: L'Harmattan, 1996), 2:82.
11. Carole Reynaud-Paligot, *De l'Identité Nationale: Science, race et politique en Europe et aux États-Unis XIXe–Xxe siècle* (Paris: Presses Universitaires de France, 2011), 129.
12. Ibid., 130.
13. Michael G. Vann, "Of Rats, Rice, and Race: The Great Hanoi Rat Massacre, an Episode in French Colonial History," *French Colonial History* 4, no. 1 (2002): 191–203.
14. Carolyn J. Eichner, "*La Citoyenne* in the World: Hubertine Auclert and Feminist Imperialism," *French Historical Studies,* Winter 2009, 63–84.
15. Lynn E. Palermo, "Identity Under Construction: Representing the Colonies at the Paris Exposition Universelle of 1889," in Sue Peabody and Tyler Stovall, eds., *The Color of Liberty: Histories of Race in France* (Durham, NC: Duke University Press, 2003), 291.
16. Wright, op. cit., 301.

seven

THE UNIVERSAL NATION
IN A WORLD AT WAR

NO SUBJECT LENDS ITSELF BETTER TO A TRANSNATIONAL APPROACH than the history of the world wars. The Great War of 1914–1918, known to posterity as World War I, was not only the foundational event of the twentieth century but also created the modern idea of a unified globe. No conflict before it qualified as a "world war," and the diplomats who met in Paris to restore peace after the guns of August had fallen silent gathered to create a universal political settlement, based on diplomatic principles applicable to all people on earth. The development of modern commerce and industry during the eighteenth and nineteenth centuries had created a global economy, and the new imperialism had drawn people everywhere into Europe's orbit. World War I built on these processes of globalization, demonstrating the interactions between technology, strategy, politics, and culture on a worldwide scale. Out of the unprecedented destruction of this conflict arose the idea of one world united in the suffering of the past and hopes for the future.

World War I was a seminal event for France, and the universal nation played a central role in the war. The conflict came at a time when the

Third Republic had overcome domestic challenges to make moderate secular republicanism the dominant political culture in France. The challenge of total war tested the nation to an unprecedented degree but also unified it in ways scarcely imaginable decades earlier. The competing universal visions of republicanism and Catholicism both ardently embraced the defense of the nation, working together to bring about ultimate victory. During the war France also mobilized the resources of its overseas empire more than ever before, making the vision of a globalized nation a concrete reality and establishing important patterns for national life in the new century. Finally, for many French people the war was a national trial of arms that pitted a universal vision of civilization against barbarism and tyranny. As during the wars of the French Revolution, the cause of France was the cause of humanity.

At the same time, the nation occupied a central role in the world conflict. Although World War I was a global affair, convulsing much of Europe, as well as Africa, Asia, and the world's sea lanes, most observers and historians have focused on the appalling trench warfare in eastern France, and the conflict between the French and the Germans. Millions of soldiers and civilians from Europe, America, and the colonial world served in France between 1914 and 1919. Paris offered an exceptionally cosmopolitan array of visitors a window seat on the great conflict of the age. The 1919 peace conference in Paris, which laid out the key outlines of the world as a whole during the twentieth century, only confirmed the main position of France in global affairs. Perhaps never before or since in the modern era have the French played such a central role in world politics. The twentieth century thus began with a dramatic confirmation of France as a universal nation.

Yet this was not the France of Louis XIV or Napoleon. France achieved prominence in World War I as a battlefield, not as the dominant military power of the age. The new global order that arose out of the conflict would highlight the nation's relative weakness vis-à-vis other nations, something World War II would confirm. Domestically as well, France's victory in the Great War would prove bittersweet. The Third Republic survived an unprecedented challenge, military as well as social and economic. Victory gave the universal republican political culture it represented a dominant position in twentieth-century French life. At the same time the tremendous cost of the victory, symbolized above all by the 1.3 million young Frenchmen who never returned from battle, would burden the nation for decades to come. France's wartime mobilization of its colonies demonstrated the value of empire to many, leading to an unprecedented level of interest in *la France outre-mer* during the interwar years, but it also helped foster anticolonialist movements that would burst into full flower after 1945. The nation's triumph in the Great War was hard-won and deeply felt, but as the coming decades would show, it did not bring about the rosy future that so many took for granted as the twentieth century opened.

FRANCE, EUROPE, AND THE WORLD FACE A NEW CENTURY

In the early 1940s, writing in exile amid a world again shattered by war, Viennese Jewish writer Stefan Zweig described the Europe of his youth at the beginning of the twentieth century:

> It may perhaps be difficult to describe to the generation of today, which has grown up amidst catastrophes, collapses, and crises, to which war has been a constant possibility and even a daily expectation, that optimism, that trustfulness in the world which had animated us young people since the turn of the century. Forty years of peace had strengthened the economic organism of the nations, technical science had given wings to the rhythm of life, and scientific discoveries had made the spirit of that generation proud; there was sudden upsurge which could be felt in almost identical measure in all the countries of Europe. The cities grew more beautiful and more populous from year to year. The Berlin of 1905 no longer resembled the city I had known in 1901; the capital had grown into a metropolis and, in turn, had been magnificently overtaken by the Berlin of 1910. Vienna, Milan, Paris, London, and Amsterdam on each fresh visit evoked new astonishment and pleasure. The streets became broader and more showy, the public buildings more impressive, the shops more luxurious and tasteful. Everything manifested the increase and spread of wealth . . . There was progress everywhere. Whoever ventured, won . . . Never had Europe been stronger, richer, more beautiful, or more confident of an even better future. None but a few shriveled graybeards bemoaned, in the ancient manner, the good old days.[1]

Zweig romanticizes a vanished world viewed from the desperation of World War II: the idealization of youth by a man in his sixties shortly before he committed suicide. Nonetheless, in many respects Europe seemed to be at the zenith of its power and prosperity in the years between the turn of the century and the outbreak of World War I, a period the French would call the belle epoque. Along with the undeniably material achievements of the era went, as Zweig observed, a faith in progress and the future, an assurance that life would continue to be sweet and that European civilization would remain the center of all things. World War I would destroy this self-confidence forever. Europe would again know good times, but the assuredness of the belle epoque would never return.

Perhaps the most dramatic manifestation of European power, although not necessarily obvious to its inhabitants, was the global reach of empire. By 1900 virtually the entire world consisted of either former European colonies in the Americas or current European colonies in Africa and Asia. Aside from China, nominally independent but in fact under the collective thrall of the western powers, and Japan, soon to establish itself as a great power on the European model, only a few states like Abyssinia and Thailand survived with their independence intact. As we have seen, imperial domination had an important racial component, so that to be European, or white, became increasingly a marker of superiority. For the average European, even the vast majority who never traveled overseas, imperial expansion brought a sense of dynamism and mastery.

The belle epoque was a prosperous era that brought rising living standards for most people in Europe. During the late nineteenth century working people had lived better than ever before, reflected by sharp increases in the amount of meat and dairy products they ate, as well as the declining percentage of their income they spent on food. The end of the Long Depression in 1896 had ushered in a new period of economic expansion and prosperity. The rapid dissemination of new technologies like the automobile, cinema, airplane, and radio gave Europeans a sense of inhabiting a world of change and progress. Finally, the beginning of the twentieth century was a time of peace in which armed conflicts had been relegated to the margins of Europe or overseas. Relatively few remembered the Franco-Prussian War or the wars of German unification, and the younger generation had known nothing but peace. It was easy to believe that modern science and rational politics had resolved mankind's traditional demons, creating an unlimited era of peace and prosperity.

For all this sense of good times, however, there were also strong indications that all was not well in Europe at the dawn of the twentieth century. Even at its height, European global domination was not complete, and there were significant portents of challenges to come with the new century. By 1898 the United States had matured and reached its contemporary borders, symbolized by its annexation of Hawaii in 1898. The same year it would emerge as an imperial power in its own right, handily winning the Spanish American war and bringing a final end to the greatest European empire of the early modern era. A few years later another rising non-European nation, Japan, would inflict a humiliating defeat on Russia in the Russo-Japanese War of 1904–1905. Challenges to European hegemony also arose in Africa and China. In 1896 Abyssinia defeated Italy's attempt to colonize that nation at the battle of Adowa. In 1899 the Boer War erupted between Britain and the Afrikaner settlers of South Africa, resulting in the creation of the new Union of South Africa. China's Boxer Rebellion mounted a massive, if unsuccessful, revolt against western hegemony, and the turmoil it created helped bring about the collapse of the country's last imperial dynasty in 1911. Imperial Europe might be dominant at the start of the new century, but it also faced increasing challenges.

At home as well, peace and prosperity did not bring about the end of social and political conflict in Europe. After a long period of price stability during the late nineteenth century, the belle epoque saw moderate inflation, triggered in part by the new prosperity and consumerism. As wages failed to keep pace with rising prices, a new spirit of labor militancy was triggered in Europe, at times taking revolutionary form. The years after 1900 saw a major increase in socialist and labor organizing. Activists founded the British Labour Party in 1901, and in the elections of 1912 the German Socialist Party (SPD) became the largest political party in the country. The year 1905 witnessed an unsuccessful revolution in Russia, providing a baptism of fire for the new Bolshevik party. Although much of the socialist movement saw social reform and electoralism as the key to working-class progress, those on the left held up the banner of violent revolution. For many Europeans, apocalyptic visions of class warfare were a reality in the years before World War I.

The rise of militant nationalism in Europe also called into question feelings of political complacency. In large part what the British called "jingoism" represented the domestic results of overseas imperial expansion, as the competition for colonies fed the rivalries between nations. Moreover, imperialism's emphasis on racial superiority found affinities with national competition, leading many to conceive of their own people as distinct races locked in conflict with their neighbors. Near universal literacy in western Europe after 1900 provided a readership for mass-circulation daily newspapers like the *Daily Mail* in Britain and *Le Petit Parisien* in France, which made money by offering a steady diet of military and political triumphs. The new nationalism emphasized not just pride in country but frequently hatred of rival peoples, leading at times to popular fantasies like the hysteria about a possible German invasion that gripped Britain at the beginning of the century.

New directions in art and culture reflected and reinforced the challenge to the liberal order. From the *fin de siècle* on, leading artists and thinkers attacked the emphasis on rationalism, seeking instead to understand and portray the world of emotion and feeling. The popularization of Freudian psychoanalysis, with its view of man as driven by irrational violent and sexual urges, inspired many artists and writers. New artistic movements like the secessionists in Munich and Vienna, and the fauves and cubists in Paris, experimented with both color and form in a departure from classical styles. Some also took inspiration from modern technology, seeing in it a different kind of beauty. None took this farther than Italy's futurists who, reacting against the tendency to view their homeland as a collection of antiquities, embraced speed, daring, and even war.

Therefore, for all its vaunted emphasis on peace, prosperity, and liberal rationality, Europe at the dawn of the twentieth century wrestled with inner demons, forces that would soon erupt in a tremendous military conflict. France exemplified both the successes and challenges of this era. The Third Republic had survived major trials during the late nineteenth century, yet the future was by no means certain. Few French men or women in 1900, however, would have predicted the massive struggle that would confront the nation in less than a generation.

FRANCE IN THE BELLE EPOQUE

For France the years from 1905 seemed golden ones, not just in retrospect but at the time as well. The titanic struggles over the republic and republicanism had finally ended with the complete triumph of the regime. Henceforth, throughout the new century, with the signal exception of the Vichy state, republican ideology would not only dominate national politics but define what it meant to be French. New conflicts and controversies would soon arise, but the people of France could pride themselves on having created a viable and stable liberal democracy in a Europe still dominated by monarchies and empires.

Economic prosperity played a key role in this sense of well-being. Building on the foundations laid by the second industrial revolution, the end of the Long Depression in the 1890s ushered in a period of economic growth unequaled in France since the salad days of the second empire. During the last decade before the war the nation's economy grew by 4.5 percent annually, faster than Britain's. Although French industry remained dominated by small workshops producing for a luxury market, new industries like steel and automobile manufacture gained prominence. France also saw its foreign trade increase sharply, growing by 75 percent between 1896 and 1913. French bankers invested heavily in railroad construction and other new industries in Europe, above all in Russia, which received 25 percent of all of France's overseas capital investment. French economic analysts, at the time and ever since, debated whether the nation's turn to protectionism with the Méline tariff (1892) had promoted or retarded the economic boom. What was undeniable was that, while the French economy grew in absolute terms before the war, it declined relative to other great powers. Whereas France had been the world's second industrial power in the mid-nineteenth century, by 1900 it was fourth, falling behind the dynamism of Germany and the United States. Clearly the nation's relationship to world markets and trends played a central role in its economic life at the dawn of the twentieth century.

Finally, the nation's low birthrate continued to challenge the national economy. By the decade before the war the French birthrate dipped below 20 births per 1,000 people, and in a couple of years the nation achieved negative population growth: fewer births than deaths. By the outbreak of the war it had slipped behind Britain to become the fourth most populous country in Europe, after Germany and Russia. Low natality was a source of great cultural anxiety, as demonstrated by Emile Zola's 1899 novel *Fecondité*. But it also had important implications for the nation's economic productivity, limiting both its labor supply and its national consumer market. It made both immigrant workers and exports crucial to French prosperity.

The growing economy meant broader prosperity for most people in France. Life in the countryside changed markedly, shaped by both the increased presence of national and global economic forces and by the rural exodus which removed the most marginal producers. French peasants became farmers in these years, producing for the market and consuming a wider variety of food and other products than ever before. Urban working people as well continued to enjoy living standards much better than those of their parents or grandparents. The French did not share equally in the benefits of economic growth, however. Many regions of the country, especially in the west and south, saw only slight improvements. Moreover, the expanding economy triggered inflation after the beginning of the century; prices in France rose some 40 percent between 1905 and 1914. For many urban workers in particular, this resulted in declining living standards in the decade before the war.

Rising prices and the resulting decline in real wages not only fostered a sharp increase in labor militancy during the belle epoque, but more generally led to a sense that the national conflict over religion and republicanism had given way to a new social challenge based in class struggle. In April 1905 the various factions of France's political left at last buried the hatchet to create a single socialist party, or SFIO (French Section of the Workers International). Unification was not easy, since not only were there important doctrinal differences between socialists in France, but the two powerful personalities of Jean Jaurès and Jules Guesde struggled for leadership of the movement. A major disagreement concerned the issue of socialist participation in "bourgeois" political coalitions and governments: Jaurès saw socialism as part of the broader progressive coalition that had triumphed during the Dreyfus affair, whereas Guesde believed revolutionaries should have nothing to do with any defenders of the capitalist system. The issue came to a head in 1904, when each side pleaded its case before the congress of the Second International in Amsterdam. The international leadership, strongly influenced by the powerful German Social Democratic Party, ruled in Guesde's favor. Jaurès acquiesced to this decision, paving the way for unification of the SFIO the next year. Not for the last time would the fate of France's far left depend on decisions taken abroad.

The steady growth of the new SFIO, a party at least technically pledged to socialist revolution, during the belle epoque contributed to a sense of imminent social crisis. Even more dramatic, however, was the tremendous strike wave France experienced in the years before the war. The same month that the SFIO was born, a lockout by Limoges's famed porcelain employers prompted workers to stage violent protests, building barricades and singing revolutionary songs. Miners in the Nord went on strike in 1906 after the explosion of the coal mine in Courrières, the worst mining accident in French history that killed over a thousand men. The CGT, or General Confederation of Labor, had been founded in 1895 as the national organization of French unions, and it embraced the revolutionary philosophy of anarcho-syndicalism. Anarcho-syndicalists believed in overthrowing capitalism with a violent, apocalyptic strike of all workers that would usher in the new socialist order, and they saw all strikes as means to this insurrectionary end. In 1906 the CGT announced a general strike on May 1 in favor of the eight-hour day, and over 150,000 workers across France responded. This was followed by an attempted general strike in 1909, and a national railway strike in 1910. In 1908 the philosopher and revolutionary syndicalist Georges Sorel published *Reflections on Violence*, which praised the general strike as a glorious event in the struggle to overthrow capitalism. For the rest of the decade before the war, different groups of French laborers staged a wave of strikes that threatened the social peace of the nation.

Inflation helped stoke the flames of labor discontent, but it was not the only cause. The decision of the Socialists to abandon bourgeois politics had forced the Republican party, dominated by the Radical Socialists who usually went by the name of Radicals, to cooperate with moderate politicians, thus shifting the political landscape's center of gravity to the right. From a valued ally in the struggle against the Church and the army, labor now seemed more of an enemy, and nothing underscored this shift more than the arrival of Georges Clemenceau to power in 1906. Perhaps the dominant figure of the republican left whose progressive credentials went back to his support of the commune and his friendship with Louise Michel, Clemenceau nonetheless believed in protecting the republic at all costs, from enemies on the left as well as the right. Both as minister of the interior and as prime minister he energetically suppressed striking workers, using the police and even the army to do so. In 1908 he even arrested the national leadership of the CGT. Styling himself "France's top cop," he was vilified by his enemies as "Clemenceau strikebreaker."

The muscular opposition of the radical state to organized labor contributed to a sense of inexorable class struggle and reinforced a powerful current of antimilitarism among the French left. Working-class resentment of the army's role both in the Dreyfus affair and in suppressing strikes, combined with peasants' traditional distrust of the military as the arm of the central state that stole their sons, led many to attack not just the armed forces but the idea of patriotism in general. In a sharp departure from the traditional patriotic fervor of the French left, Marxists and anarcho-syndicalists both argued that the worker had no homeland, no *patrie*, but only international class solidarity. The *lycée* professor Gustave Hervé wrote scathing articles denouncing French patriotism. In 1911 Jean Jaurès published *The New Army*, which advocated replacing the national armed forces with decentralized populist militias. Anticapitalism and antimilitarism together suggested a French proletariat bent on nothing less than revolution.

Not all the turmoil came from the working class, however. The biggest protest movement in belle epoque France took place among the peasants and agricultural laborers in the vineyards of southern France, especially the region of Languedoc. The 1890s phylloxera epidemic had devastated the local wine industry, and the restructuring of the industry generally brought lower prices and increased foreign competition. Struggling to maintain not only the quality of their wine but their very way of life, farmers staged protests involving hundreds of thousands in the spring of 1907, overwhelming towns like Montpellier and Narbonne. On the right the Action Française, born in the cauldron of the Dreyfus affair, began organizing a new reactionary movement in French politics. In 1908 it launched its daily newspaper, *Action Française*, and organized a paramilitary youth organization, the Camelots du Roi, which began intimidating left-wing opponents and Jews. Even French feminists, traditionally less militant than their sisters in Britain and the United States, were beginning to demand suffrage for women.

There was, therefore, a lot about the belle epoque that was less rosy than the portrait painted by posterity. And yet for all the turmoil, the political consensus formed around the republic held, and the idea of France as a nation unified by territory, history, and culture took solid root. In 1903 the owners of the daily sports newspaper *L'Auto* decided to profit from the new cycling craze by sponsoring a national bicycle race. On July 1 the Tour de France began, as over sixty avid cyclists raced around the nation's borders. It was a tremendous success for *L'Auto*, enabling it to put rival newspaper *Le Velo* out of business, but it also underscored the idea of French unity at a time when its viability seemed doubtful. For four years the race organizers even received permission from German authorities to go through Alsace-Lorraine, emphasizing the place of the lost provinces in the national imagination. This was revoked in 1911, however, in response to rising international tension. The new threats to peace would put the national unity symbolized by the Tour de France to its greatest test yet.

THE ROAD TO WAR

The outbreak of World War I is one of the great historiographical questions of the twentieth century. Why would a continent enjoying peace, prosperity, and global supremacy throw it all away in a bloodbath of unprecedented scope? In seeking to answer this question, historians have usually differentiated between the immediate causes of the rush to war in August 1914 and the long-term conditions leading to the conflict. Only in the very last moments did the Great War become inevitable, but a variety of factors help explain why it happened.

To an important extent, especially from the French perspective, World War I grew out of the Franco-Prussian War, in particular Germany's annexation of Alsace-Lorraine. That decision, opposed by Chancellor Bismarck at the time, made France and Germany permanent enemies, forcing each to seek allies to defend itself from the other. Germany crafted a close alliance with Austria-Hungary and then in 1882 brought Italy into what became known as the Triple Alliance. At first Bismarck's adroit diplomacy, whose main goal was to isolate France, left the French with few options. The only republic in Europe, France had little in common with the Continent's other major power, Russia. An alliance with Britain also seemed a remote possibility, given not only the enmity between the two countries dating back to the time of Joan of Arc but also the colonial rivalries of the 1880s and 1890s.

This changed at the turn of the century. In 1892, after extended negotiations, France and Russia signed a formal friendship treaty, ending German hopes of isolating Paris diplomatically and presenting Germany with the dangerous prospect of a two-front war. During the next decade France also improved relations with Britain. After nearly going to war over the Fashoda crisis of 1898, the two nations began exploring ways to work together. In 1903 King Edward VII visited Paris to general acclaim, and the next year France and Britain signed a general agreement, or *entente cordiale*, to settle their overseas disputes. In 1907 Britain and Russia signed a treaty leading to the formation of the Triple Entente between those two countries and France. Europe was now divided into two alliance systems, all but ensuring that any dispute between two or more major powers would unleash a general war.

At the same time, imperial rivalry played a key role in the origins of World War I. At a time when Europe was largely at peace, the struggle for colonies in Africa and Asia not only served as a testing ground for European armies but also mobilized European popular opinion in support of national prestige and power. The years just before the outbreak of war witnessed a major nationalist revival across Europe, and much of this arose out of colonial competition. In France, the two crises over the nation's attempts to take over Morocco and German resistance to those plans gave rise to bellicose patriotism. During the first, from 1905 to 1907, Germany pressured the sultan of Morocco to resist French demands for a protectorate, holding an international conference at Algeciras, Spain, to resolve the matter. The conference ultimately approved most of France's demands, but Germany's aggressive stance led many French observers to conclude that war was possible, indeed likely, and the country needed to prepare for it. Such feelings were reinforced by the second Moroccan crisis in 1911, when Germany once again challenged France's increasing hegemony over that nation.

Germany ultimately accepted French control over Morocco in exchange for concessions in central Africa, but the crises over North Africa helped stoke a major nationalist revival in France in the years just before the war. In 1913 Raymond Poincaré, whose family had fled Lorraine after its annexation by Germany, became prime minister, emphasizing a new policy of toughness vis-à-vis Berlin. When Germany increased the size of its army that year, France increased the length of military service from two to three years in response. Inspired by General Mangin's influential 1910 book *La force noire* (*The Black Force*), France also decided to recruit soldiers from Africa and other colonies in defense of the *patrie*. Public opinion shifted sharply away from the antimilitarism of the Dreyfus era to an acceptance, if not a thirst, for military preparedness and national defense.

Ultimately overseas empire and the rise of the nation-state in Europe combined to bring about a military cataclysm. By 1914 France was a centralized nation with a unified national culture based in popular sovereignty, and at the same time a far-flung empire with a republican mission grounded in racial difference and hierarchy. This combination of nation-state and empire, in relation to other imperial nation-states, produced international rivalries that were not only global but European as well. Moreover, the link between popular sovereignty and empire helped produce a racialized vision of the nation frequently expressed in terms of hostility to other nations. A key aspect of the prewar nationalist revival in France and other nations was popular hatred of enemy nations, often expressed in racial terms. Colonial expansion in the late nineteenth century had often centered around race war; now this same phenomenon would come back home to Europe.

When war broke out in the summer of 1914, it happened not in the colonies overseas but rather in the Continent's semicolonial periphery. By the dawn of the twentieth century the peoples of the Balkans had waged a series of successful struggles against the overlordship of the failing Ottoman Empire, but as Constantinople's strength waned other powers, notably Austria-Hungary and Russia, moved in to fill the vacuum. Austria-Hungary's annexation of Bosnia in 1908 provoked a major European crisis, and wars erupted between the Ottomans and the Balkan states in 1912 and 1913. Serbia, with the backing of Russia, opposed both Ottoman and Austrian designs and resented Vienna's annexation of Bosnia.

Matters came to a head on June 28, 1914, when a Serb nationalist named Gavrilo Princip assassinated the Austrian archduke Francis Ferdinand during a state visit to the Bosnian capital of Sarajevo. Vienna blamed the assassination on Serbia and, after some deliberation, in late July delivered an ultimatum to the Serbian government that would have reduced the country to an Austrian protectorate. This brought the Austrians directly into conflict with Russia, which refused to accept the bullying of a fellow Slavic state. Two days after the delivery of the Austrian ultimatum the Russians began mobilizing their army, a lengthy process which all but ensured the vast empire would go to war.

At this point the European alliance system kicked into high gear. Germany had strongly supported Austria-Hungary's ultimatum to Serbia, but it realized that in case Russia attacked the Austrians it would have to fight a war on two fronts: against the Russians and the French. Berlin had long anticipated such an eventuality; General Alfred von Schlieffen had developed a plan to win such a war, based on a rapid deployment of German forces to defeat Russia at the beginning of the conflict, followed by a massive attack against France. It was a complicated plan that depended on both invading Russia before it mobilized and invading France through undefended and neutral Belgium. On July 28 Austria-Hungary declared war on Serbia, initiating the final crisis. As it became clear that neither Russia nor Austria-Hungary was going to back down, Germany and the other major powers began putting their plans for the long-anticipated European war into motion.

The last week of the peace saw Europe plunged into diplomatic chaos. For France, the sudden hostilities came as a great shock. The Balkans were far away, after all, and at first little suggested that diplomacy would not resolve this crisis as it had so many others. Most people in France were less interested in the assassination of the Austrian archduke than another murder closer to home: Madame Henriette Caillaux's murder of *Le Figaro* editor Gaston Calmette in March. Her trial obsessed the French during much of July and up to her acquittal on the same day Austria declared war against Serbia. On July 16 the president and prime minister, Raymond Poincaré and René Viviani, left the country for a lengthy state visit to Russia and Sweden, not returning until July 29. The Austrian declaration of war, and Russia's military mobilization, made it clear, however, that this was a crisis without precedent. French socialists tried to hold back the mounting military tide, vainly attempting to coordinate pacifist action with the German SPD. On July 31 Germany formally demanded France remain neutral in case it went to war with Russia, something no French government could do. That evening socialist leader Jean Jaurès was dining with friends in a Parisian café when a young rightist, Raoul Vilain, shot him to death, fearing he and other socialists would betray France during the coming war. This third assassination seemed to make war inevitable, bringing the reality of it home to the French people. On August 1 Germany declared war on Russia; on August 3 Germany declared war on France and sent troops marching into neutral Belgium. The next day, motivated by the threat to Belgium and its alliances with France and Russia, Britain declared war on Germany. The great world war had begun.

FRANCE GOES TO WAR

On August 1, 1914, church bells rang out across France, in cities, towns, and villages, announcing the beginning of the conflict and the peril of invasion. The French people reacted to the news in different ways. Some, especially in large cities, greeted the war with enthusiasm. After over forty years of hoping for revenge for 1871, now at last the chance had arrived to recapture Alsace-Lorraine and humble the national enemy. As in other European capitals, crowds gathered in Paris to cheer on the troops and support the war effort. For the most part, however, the French marked the beginning of hostilities with an air of determination and resignation rather than celebration. Especially in the countryside, they anguished about the fate of their young men; given that it was late summer, peasants worried about bringing in the harvest without them. As millions of soldiers donned uniforms and gathered with their loved ones in train stations to say good-bye, the often repeated conviction that the war would end by Christmas reflected hope as much as optimism.

In spite of their concerns, however, the overwhelming majority of French people backed the war effort, feeling that Germany had invaded France and they had to defend themselves. This was true even of the socialists and syndicalists, whose previous disdain for a capitalist war had been turned upside down both by the assassination of Jaurès and by the failure of international socialist unity. Instead of protesting, they rallied to the cause of *la patrie en danger*. Almost overnight, Gustave Hervé went from a fanatical antimilitarist to a firm supporter of the war effort. Over the next few days a spirit of unprecedented national unity seized the country. President Poincaré appealed to all French men and women to come together in the spirit of a *union sacrée*, or sacred union. In the Chamber of Deputies lifelong enemies, like the former communard Edouard Vaillant and Albert de Mun, who had helped suppress the commune and massacre its defenders, shook hands or even embraced. Catholics and anticlericals alike turned their backs on the bitter religious conflicts of yesterday, swearing to fight together until victory was achieved. Mourners at Jaurès's funeral on August 4 included not only men and women of the left but also Maurice Barrès, right-wing activist and anti-Dreyfusard. Jules Guesde himself, determined opponent of bourgeois politics, agreed to join the national government. The *union sacrée* represented the triumph of the Third Republic: its ability to mobilize all the people of France in defense of the nation.

This spirit of national unity and determination would be sorely tested during the first few weeks of the war. Like other European nations, France had foreseen the possibility of a general war and had prepared accordingly. The creation of the Triple Entente had given France valuable allies, and considering its greater population and size compared to the Triple Alliance (which was weakened by Italy's decision not to go to war in 1914), France had a very good shot at eventual victory. In the short term, however, it had to face Germany, a nation with a larger population and more powerful industry, and here it was less secure. First, the French were significantly outgunned in 1914, possessing 2,500 machine guns to Germany's 4,500. France's armies were equipped with excellent light artillery, the 75 mm field gun, but they only had 3,800 compared to Germany's 6,000. Most important, the German army's decision to use its reserve troops to invade the west gave it a three-to-one numerical advantage (750,000 to 250,000) over the French.

There were problems with French military strategy as well. To an important extent, Napoleon still represented the ultimate standard of military science. French generals embraced the doctrine of the offensive, using huge numbers of foot soldiers fired up with nationalist zeal, just as the mass armies of the Revolution had overwhelmed their opponents at Valmy in 1792, when this doctrine, the so-called *furia francese*, carried the day. The doctrine of the offensive failed to take into account the great strides in military defense, notably the invention of the machine gun in the late nineteenth century and the development of new types of massive artillery. In general, the superiority of defensive military technology would play a major role in shaping the war. Additionally, French plans for a war with Germany centered around an immediate offensive sally into Alsace-Lorraine, where it was hoped military superiority plus a possible patriotic uprising of the local population would bring victory. Plan XVII, as it was known, arose as much from political as strategic considerations; it did not take into account either the difficulty of mounting an attack in the rugged terrain of eastern France or the possibility that the Germans would invade through Belgium.

For these and other reasons, therefore, the first month of the war went very badly for the French. Plan XVII was a complete nonstarter; within weeks Germany's superiority in machine guns and heavy artillery forced the French armies into retreat, pushing them back across the borders of Alsace-Lorraine. Meanwhile the main German armies, under General Von Moltke, quickly overran Belgium and then moved deep into northern France, encircling the bulk of France's forces. By the end of the month German troops were nearing Paris, much to the consternation of that city's population, which had been led to believe by the censored press that the battle was going well. On August 29 the French government fled to Bordeaux, and hundreds of thousands of ordinary Parisians, especially from the wealthier districts, also evacuated the city. By the first week of September it looked as though the war would be over by Christmas: 1870 all over again.

Several factors intervened to save France, and ultimately to turn what was supposed to be a tidy nineteenth-century war into the grueling conflict of the twentieth. The French defeat and retreat in Alsace-Lorraine actually turned out to be a boon, because instead of being lured farther into German territory the French troops and their British allies escaped to fight the main armies invading from Belgium. After a month of continuous marching in the August heat German armies were suffering from exhaustion, and as they advanced into France their lines became extended and thus vulnerable to counterattack. Moreover, the Germans deviated in important respects from the Schlieffen plan. The core idea of that strategy was to concentrate German forces in the west and knock France out of the war before Russia had time to mobilize. The Russian armies mobilized more quickly than expected, however, and by mid-August they had launched a massive invasion of East Prussia. Faced with this unexpected threat to the homeland, even potentially Berlin, Germany transferred some of its forces to the eastern front. As a result Germany won the battle of Tannenberg, forcing the Russians onto the defensive until they collapsed in 1917. This fateful decision nonetheless helped give the French the breathing room they needed. To an important extent, the controversial alliance with czarist Russia saved France.

In the first week of December French and British forces rallied and stopped the German advance with a series of counterattacks on the Marne River northeast of Paris. As Moltke turned to follow the retreating allied troops, he exposed the right flank of his forces to the French army stationed to defend the capital, commanded by generals Gallieni and Joffre. The French formed a plan of attack and rushed as many soldiers as quickly as possible to the front. On September 6 they famously recruited six hundred of the city's taxis to convey six thousand soldiers to the front (the drivers graciously only charged 27 percent of the meter fare). The next day France launched a surprise attack against the exhausted and overextended German troops. They successfully halted the enemy advance in what became known as "the miracle of the Marne."

Over the next several weeks French, British, and German troops jockeyed for position, each trying to outflank the other in what became known as "the race to the sea." By the end of November the two sides had established a front line that ran from the Swiss border through eastern France and a small part of Belgium to the North Sea. These lines soon hardened as the opposing sides dug themselves in, becoming the infamous western front. The front lines would see some of the bloodiest fighting of the war, indeed of the twentieth century, but they would not shift appreciably until 1918. This small part of occupied and contested France would become for people around the world the ultimate symbol of the Great War.

FRANCE ADJUSTS TO WAR

Published in the newspaper *L'Opinion* in January 1915, one of the most famous French cartoons of World War I showed two *poilus* ("hairy ones," slang for French soldiers) in their trench discussing the war. "We'll be okay as long as they hold out," says one. "Who?" says the other, whereas the first responds, "The civilians." Had this cartoon appeared two years later, perhaps the idea of comparing the travails of the home front to the agony of the trenches might have seemed offensive, but at the time it underscored the fact that the war effort demanded sacrifices from all parts of French society. The sufferings of the soldiers in the trenches were incomparable and unique, but those they left behind faced their own struggles. The mobilization of civilians in support of their troops and the war effort transformed France. Between 1914 and 1918 the French people rose up in defense of the nation, making World War I the first great example of total war in the twentieth century.

It took some time for the French to adjust to the idea of total war. Most believed that the war would be short, so that soldiers departing for the front in the heat of August were not supplied with cold weather clothing. With the battle of the Marne France had prevented a repetition of its 1870 defeat, but there was no recipe for a rapid victory. As trench warfare took hold on the western front by the end of 1914, it became ever more difficult to predict how many months or years the conflict would last, so gradually the French dug themselves in for the long haul.

Even after the miracle of the Marne, Germany occupied some 10 percent of the nation's territory, and would continue to do so almost until the end of the war. Refugees from northern France and Belgium flooded into Paris and other cities, increasing the demand for housing and food. Conditions in occupied France were often desperate. The Germans behaved with brutality, establishing what some historians have termed a reign of terror. Soldiers requisitioned large amounts of food and industrial materials to transport to Germany, engaged in collective reprisals, and established civilian internment camps for those who broke the rules. By 1916 they began deporting large numbers of Frenchmen to Germany to work in the country's war plants. The result of this treatment was hunger, misery, and deep resentment of the Germans, as the refugees' tales elicited anger among people throughout France.

Unfortunately for the French, Germany occupied the most prosperous and economically developed part of France. The northeastern territories under German control accounted for 50 percent of France's coal, 58 percent of its steel, and 64 percent of its iron, commodities indispensable to the war effort. Consequently, a major priority for the French was retooling the national economy for total war. In facing the crisis of wartime production, France scrapped its prewar belief in free market economics with government-lead industrial production. Both ironically and appropriately, the socialists spearheaded this move toward what the British termed "war socialism." The war minister, former socialist Alexandre Millerand, brought together industrialists to encourage armaments production. In 1915 socialist Albert Thomas became undersecretary of armaments, and throughout the war the government closely controlled and supported industry. The occupation of the north and the increased state role in the economy helped make Paris, or more accurately the Paris suburbs, a leading center of heavy industry. The government also had to ensure that war plants had an adequate labor supply, given the crying need for soldiers. In June 1915 it enacted the Dalbiez Law, exempting workers in key war industries from military service.

Ultimately, however, government and industry had to find ways to increase the labor supply. One of the most dramatic results of total war in France was the mass entry of women into the labor market, particularly heavy industry. Many Frenchwomen had toiled outside the home before 1914, but with the departure of millions of men for the front in 1914, France often fell back on female workers to keep essential industries and services going. One French newspaper published a fictional account of a man who fell asleep in September 1914 and awoke in 1916, recording how amazed he was to see women, and only women, working in the Metro, the post office, and many other places. Most important, armaments factories were compelled by the need for labor to admit large numbers of women into heavy industry for the first time, often to the discomfort of male workers who felt the presence of women would lower skill levels and consequently wages. The *munitionnettes* (women workers in war factories) became a fixture of French life during the war, especially in Paris and other industrial areas.

The conversion to a wartime economy involved not just production but also consumption, so that French civilians had to adjust to major shifts in their standard of living. Inflation, which had already become significant during the belle epoque, took off markedly during the war. By 1917 the prices of many basic commodities had tripled since the beginning of the conflict. A major reason for this was the government's decision to finance the war by borrowing and even printing more money, rather than increasing the tax burden on its citizens. The amount of cash in France multiplied by five times during the conflict, and by the war's end the government had borrowed nearly 40 billion francs. At the same time, the shortage of basic commodities caused by the shift to war production also helped increase prices.

At the beginning of the war the government had frozen the price of bread, mindful of the link between expensive bread and social discontent that went back to the Revolution. Yet other foodstuffs, notably meat, dairy products, and sugar, became increasingly scarce and expensive. By the end of the war public authorities introduced rationing of various foods and resorted to other methods, like importing frozen beef, to secure the food supply. Housing became another key concern. At the beginning of the war the French government effectively froze rents and banned evictions, fearing the impact on families whose men had been mobilized of rising housing costs. This policy, which lasted throughout the war, not only infuriated landlords but also created a massive housing shortage, especially in the Paris area as both refugees and migrants attracted to the new war plants flooded into the region. For many French civilians, the war meant shortages of food and housing, long lines in search of the basic necessities of life.

France mobilized to wage war in other ways as well. Public authorities understood the capital importance of maintaining the morale of both soldiers and civilians and took steps to reassure the nation about the military situation. Press censorship, which liberal republicans had fought during the nineteenth century, returned with a vengeance. French women and men got used to reading newspapers with entire sections blacked out by the censors. The manipulation of the press became glaringly obvious at the outset of the war when, after a constant stream of articles lauding the successes of French troops, Parisians realized that the Germans were almost at their doorstep. World War I also saw the birth of modern propaganda. Virtually all French men and women could read and had attended primary school where they learned patriotic historical and cultural narratives. Most had access not only to daily newspapers but to a new media technology: films and newsreels. Finally, the active support of most leading French intellectuals mobilized the nation's cultural leadership squarely behind the war effort. The poet Charles Péguy, who in 1913 had written "Blessed Are Those Who Died in a Just War," volunteered for military service in his forties and died at the front in September 1914. Mobilizing all aspects of French life in pursuit of national salvation and victory was the essence of the *union sacreé*, and the nation's political, social, and cultural leaders embraced the defense of the *patrie* as their highest goal.

More than anything else, adjusting to war meant getting used to the ubiquitous presence of death. Over 300,000 French soldiers died in battle by the end of September 1914, making the first months of the war the bloodiest of all. This came as a shock to families of the fallen and to the nation as a whole, who had become accustomed to nearly half a century of peace. It could take weeks for family members to learn of a soldier's death, so one never really knew if a father, brother, husband, or son were alive until he came home. The sharp decline in infant mortality during the nineteenth century had meant that parents rarely had to bury their children, yet the war reversed that in spectacular, brutal fashion. Within a year after the start of the war there wa. hardly a family in France who had not received official notice that a loved one was dead or missing in action, so that the nation as a whole lived with constant grief. Some historians have noted an increase in deaths during the war among the middle-aged and elderly due not to physical causes but to despair after losing a son in combat. In 1917 Emile Durkheim, the famed scholar and founder of French sociology, died of a stroke near the first anniversary of the death of his only son in battle. Beyond ideology and patriotism, beyond victory and defeat, war meant death above all, and World War I brought this lesson home to the French like no other event in national memory.

In thousands of ways, therefore, France struggled to defend itself in a war without precedent. The hopes of the nation rested on the efforts of its soldiers on the western front, fighting day after day for the breakthrough that would repel the invader from national soil and bring victory and peace. Yet victory remained elusive. For years, French fighting men endured trials without parallel in the annals of twentieth-century military conflict. The trench warfare that ripped apart northern France during the Great War was a national trial that would horrify the world's imagination for decades to come.

BATTLE AND SURVIVAL IN THE TRENCHES

On Christmas Eve 1914, German and British soldiers stationed in the trenches near Armentières, France, spontaneously stopped fighting to celebrate the holiday together. On that first wartime Christmas mortal enemies sang carols together, notably "Oh Come, All Ye Faithful," exchanged greetings and presents, commemorated their dead together, and even played soccer matches. Similar instances of fraternization, some involving French soldiers, also took place during the holiday season. The famous Christmas truces of 1914 have been discussed by historians ever since, most often presented as an outbreak of brotherhood and human kindness amid the insanity of World War I. They also represented, however, an example of what united men across the boundaries erected by nations at war, a vision of the universal as opposed to the nation-state. The Great War, ultimately like all wars, represented not only the violent collision of peoples but also their coming together in strange and unexpected ways.

The truces were held at the beginning of trench warfare; although there were similar incidents later, they were not as frequent nor as widespread as in 1914. In part, this was because military and national authorities on both sides

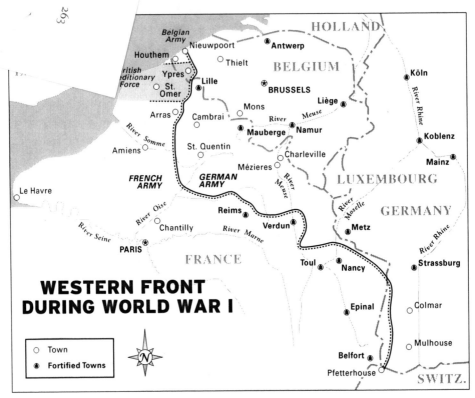

Map 7.1. The western front during World War I.

took steps to prevent them from happening again. More important, however, was the sheer impact of months and years of life in the trenches. The horrors of trench warfare made it almost impossible to see one's opponent as a human being like oneself rather than an anonymous vector of death. For the French, fighting in trenches built on their devastated homeland, the vision of universal brotherhood held little appeal.

To a much greater extent, the French took refuge in a universalist vision of nationalism that portrayed France as the global symbol of civilization and liberty under attack from the forces of barbarism. The idea that Germany had launched an unprovoked attack on France, the brutal occupation of the north, and the horrors of trench warfare combined to create a deadly hatred for all things German. The image of the Germans as barbarians became omnipresent during the war, as exemplified by the term "Boche," the unbiquitous term of insult for the enemy. From this perspective the Germans were not just enemies but savages, and their military assault represented an attack on not just France but on world civilization itself. The experience of trench warfare represented a kind of national martyrdom that united the universalist visions of both Church and republican state in France during World War I. As at other times in modern French history, nationalism and universalism reinforced each other.

The use of the term "Boche" also underscored the racialized character of the Great War in France. As noted earlier, the rise of overseas empire in the late nineteenth century had gradually bled into the ways in which the French and other Europeans defined themselves as nations. The war only intensified this process, so that the conflict between nations became in effect a struggle between races. It created a new idea of the global fight between civilizations, one now within Europe rather than between Europe and its colonies. At a time when French racial thinking was increasingly rejecting the civilizing mission and assimilation in favor of immutable national and racial characteristics, the war with Germany presented a vision of barbarism as something that could only be defeated, not civilized. The Germans were the new savages, and the war against them was a crusade for universal civilization and the salvation of the French race.

The trenches thus separated not just two armies but two worlds. By the beginning of 1915 the trenches of the western front stretched nearly five hundred miles, from Switzerland to the North Sea. Within this strange world men fought, lived, and died in appalling conditions. Each side dug trenches ranging from six to eight feet in depth, deep enough to provide some protection from enemy artillery fire but shallow enough to permit rapid sorties when the order to attack came. There were different types of trenches: those at the front lines, those at the rear for military support and recuperation, and communications trenches linking them together. The trenches were protected by barbed wire and sandbags, but because France's generals continued to believe for years in the prospect of a victorious offensive, they were designed to be temporary and conditions in them were rudimentary. Only toward the end of the war, for example, did some begin to have electricity. Between the opposing trenches stretched the infamous no-man's-land, a zone stretching a few hundred feet filled with mud, artillery shells, pits, and corpses.

Life in the trenches was a mixture of boredom, anxiety, and horror. Soldiers cowered in their shelters hoping to survive the devastating artillery fire launched by the enemy. Generals on both sides adopted the practice of launching massive artillery barrages before major offensives. Although the idea was to soften up the enemy, these volleys also warned the other side of impending attacks. After the barrage usually came the charge of the enemy infantry, masses of soldiers wielding rifles and bayonets. As terrifying as it was to face such an attack, even more frightening was launching one, scrambling across no-man's-land in the face of tremendous artillery fire and deadly machine gun fusillades. The lucky ones lived to return to their trench and face battle another day.

Even when the guns were silent, life in the trenches of the western front was a tale of unending misery. The rainy climate of northern France often turned them into gigantic mud puddles, especially during the cold winters. Lice and vermin infested the trenches, drawn by the soldiers' food and the appetizing lure of death. Enormous trench rats were everywhere, feasting on the dead in no-man's-land and burrowing throughout the trenches. The noise of battle, the smell of dead bodies, the fear of the next offensive, and finally the boredom of waiting for combat and death made the trenches of World War I literally a hell on earth. The worst part, however, was that all this misery and destruction brought virtually no strategic gains. Between the end of 1914 and the beginning of 1918 the front lines in France barely budged. For a nation, and a continent, that had prided itself on progress through technology, science now only brought an agonizing stalemate. In spite of the best efforts of the French army, France remained an invaded, occupied country. Symbolically the trenches resembled nothing more than a gigantic mass grave stretching across northern France.

The great battles of 1915 and 1916 only underscored this. During these years the French general staff, led by Marshal Joseph Joffre, the "savior of the Marne," consistently advocated a major offensive that would break the German trenches and expel the invader. During 1915 the French and the British armies mounted several large attacks against the German lines, hoping for a breakthrough, or *percée*, as the French called it. Joffre hoped these attacks would either produce a major advance or wear down Germany's forces in a war of attrition. At the beginning of May French and British troops began an offensive in Artois that would last until mid-June. The results were bloody but inconclusive, costing the French over 100,000 casualties but not appreciably changing the front lines. In September France launched another offensive, in the Champagne region, which dragged on into October. Again, the French paid a heavy price for no significant military gain. During 1915 France suffered over 1 million men dead or wounded, more than the losses they inflicted on Germany. If this was victory, as many French generals insisted it was, how many more could France survive?

The year 1916 brought the epitome of the tragedy and futility of trench warfare, which could be summed up in one word: Verdun. Situated in the small part of Lorraine retained by France after 1871, the ancient fortress held great symbolic meaning for the French. During the Revolution, France's victory at Valmy had forced the Prussians to abandon the city, and in 1870 Verdun had been the last fort surrendered to the invading Germans. If any city stood for French resistance to Germany this was it, or so calculated German general Erich von Falkenhayn. During 1915 German forces had made major advances in the east but failed to knock Russia out of the war. Falkenhayn therefore concluded that victory must be won in the west first, and he hoped by attacking a spot sacred to the French to lure his enemy into a no-win situation. This battle would bleed France out of the war.

The battle began with a massive German artillery barrage and attack on February 21, 1916. For the offensive Germany had assembled an unprecedented level of firepower, some 1,200 heavy guns and other pieces of artillery equipped with over 2 million shells. The initial bombardment, which lasted for nine hours, was so ferocious that many of the French defenders were literally buried alive in their trenches. For the first few days the Germans seemed to sweep all before them and captured of one of the world's mightiest fortress cities, Douaumont. But the French soldiers, led by Gen. Philippe Pétain, held out against all expectations, and the battle of Verdun degenerated into a killing field of unimaginable brutality. In April and June the Germans launched new offenses, leading French general Robert Nivelle to proclaim on June 23 one of the war's most famous orders of the day: "They shall not pass." On July 1 British and French forces launched a new offensive, the battle of the Somme, which helped relieve the pressure on the defenders of Verdun. Germany staged its last offensive in late July, and then the French gradually assumed the offensive. By the end of October they had retaken Douaumont, and when the battle finally petered out a week before Christmas France could claim victory, having expelled the Germans from at least some of the territory they had overrun in February. But if this was victory it came at a terrible cost: over a quarter of a million French soldiers dead and many more wounded. As Paul Pireaud, stationed with an artillery regiment in Verdun, wrote to his wife:

> Verdun is impossible to describe. It is about 7 or 8 kilometers from here to Douaumont. Not a trench, not a communications trench, nothing but shell holes one inside another. There is not one piece of ground that is not

turned up . . . There are no more woods. Shattered trees resemble tele-graph poles. Not one square of land has been spared. One would have to come here to understand it. One cannot imagine such a thing.[2]

Again, there was no military breakthrough or significant advance by either side.

Ever since Verdun those who have studied the Great War have wondered how soldiers could endure such terrible conditions without breaking, without concluding that the war was insane and not worth the cost. It is easy to blame France's military leaders for pursuing strategies that brought so little gain at such horrendous cost, but at the same time difficult to imagine what else they could have done. If one thing united French men and women during World War I, it was a belief in driving out the invader. In mounting offensive after useless offensive France's military leaders were clearly obeying the national will. But what did this mean to the ordinary *poilu* trapped in the hell of Verdun? The classic view of World War I portrays soldiers as innocents sacrificed to the arrogance and stupidity of leaders on both sides of the conflict. Such a perspective tends to deprive the *poilus* of any sense of agency or ability to determine their own fate. Many embraced the national cause, and like their leaders imagined no other way of pursuing it. Many also took refuge in an intense sense of camaraderie, of loyalty to their fellow soldiers for whom they would, and frequently did, sacrifice their own lives. Rather than underscore the futility of war, for many soldiers the horrible battles of 1915 and 1916 reinforced the desire for victory, for if one did not achieve victory how could one possibly rationalize all this suffering and slaughter? And finally, many fought just to survive: the ultimate goal of the French at Verdun came down to the verb *tenir*: to hold on.

THE EMPIRE GOES TO WAR

World War I tested the resolve of the Third Republic both as a nation and as an empire. For the first time in modern history, conflict mobilized the peoples of the French colonies on a massive scale in defense of the *mère-patrie*, the Motherland. Imperial subjects worked for a French victory both at home and in the metropole itself; hundreds of thousands journeyed to France as soldiers and workers, giving the colonies an unprecedented presence in the French homeland. The view of the postcolonial era as a time when the rigid boundaries between metropole and empire broke down can be traced to the Great

War. The wartime mobilization of imperial France underscored its character as a universal nation whose civilization could claim a global presence. Yet by bringing France's colonies and metropole closer together, World War I also underscored their crucial differences, and the contradictory character of the imperial nation-state. Most fundamentally, it raised a question: Why should colonial subjects fight in France for democratic rights denied them at home? The Great War would in the short term tie *patrie* and empire closer together, while at the same time sowing the seeds of forces that would ultimately break them apart.

After 1914 the empire also struggled against the Germans militarily, especially in sub-Saharan Africa. When the war broke out, the Entente forces laid siege to Germany's colonies. Togo, East Africa, was largely unprotected and surrendered to British and French forces within a few weeks. Cameroon, located between French Equatorial Africa, the British in Nigeria, and the Belgian Congo, proved a harder nut to crack, but combined French and British forces had largely overrun the German colony by the end of 1915. The fighting in Africa was carried on overwhelmingly by black African subjects, to a certain extent resembling an African civil war.

France's most significant military engagement in Africa during World War I had less to do with the global conflict and more to do with traditional colonial warfare. The move to a war footing had important and often negative impacts on life in the colonies, especially when the French began to conscript native men for the war effort. In November 1915 representatives of several villages gathered outside the town of Bona in French West Africa to proclaim a war against French rule, and began mobilizing troops to assert their independence. The next month France sent a large army of 800 soldiers to subdue the uprising, only to be repelled by more than 10,000 African rebels. In the winter of 1916 the French mobilized a new army, the largest it had ever deployed in Africa, to crush the revolt. What had become known as the Volta-Bani war continued throughout 1916, the French waging a total war against the African population and massacring tens of thousands before they finally defeated the insurgency in early 1917.

Little news of this sordid colonial war reached the French homeland, preoccupied with the western front and the war of survival against Germany. In contrast, the arrival of massive numbers of colonial subjects on French soil during the war had an inescapable impact on the life of the nation. Colonial armies had fought under the French flag for generations. During the nineteenth century the Armée d'Afrique had played a major role in the nation's rule over North Africa. World War I, however, by bringing colonial soldiers and other subjects to the French homeland, constituted a major departure in national life. It was this prospect of introducing colonial natives to Europe that had prompted the bitter debates around General Mangin's proposal for a *force noire*, and during the war France was the only country to bring African soldiers to fight on the Continent's battlefields. Shortly after the start of the war the nation began mobilizing units of colonial soldiers to serve on the western front. The most famous were the *tirailleurs sénégalais*, the African troops who saw combat in a number of major battles, notably Verdun, the Somme, and the Chemin des Dames. Stereotypes of Africans as brutal savages paradoxically made them welcome as soldiers in France, where many regarded them as warriors of unparalleled ferocity. One newly arrived detachment of Africans was greeted with the words "Bravo riflemen! Cut off the heads of the Germans!" Colonial subjects from the Caribbean, North Africa, Madagascar, and Indochina also fought for France during the war. All told, over 500,000 men from the French empire served on the battlefields of France during the Great War.

France drew on its colonies to provide workers as well as soldiers. The need for labor in the nation's war industry was so great that by 1915 French authorities were looking literally around the world to find new employees for France's factories and farms. At the end of 1915 the French government sent an official mission, headed by retired army officer Georges Truptil, to China to recruit Chinese workers to come to France. In addition the nation drew heavily on its colonies in North Africa, Madagascar, and Indochina for labor, bringing over 300,000 "exotic" workers to the metropole during the course of the war. Although most worked in the big armaments factories located in the Paris area, the Loire valley, and Toulouse, others were deployed in smaller factories and on farms. Combined with the massive increase of women employed in heavy industry, the war temporarily transformed the face of working-class France.

The use of colonial soldiers and workers in wartime France introduced a large multiracial population onto French soil for the first time in the nation's history, and many authorities worried about its impact on national life. Both soldiers and workers were separated into their own units, ostensibly to provide for language translation but also to keep them isolated from French civilian life. The one exception was soldiers from the Caribbean, who as citizens successfully fought for the right to be integrated into mainstream French units. Colonial soldiers faced extremely difficult conditions, like other soldiers, with the additional problem that many had never before experienced winter. Many nonetheless viewed their experience in France as generally positive. Discipline was harsh, but often less so than in the colonies, and some got to know French soldiers and civilians. They had come to France to fight the national enemy, after all, a fact that often brought them a warm welcome from their hosts.

In contrast, colonial workers frequently encountered hostility and suspicion. Although their labor was vital for the war effort, many French resented their presence in industry not only for potentially lowering wages and worsening working conditions, but also for freeing up young French men to be sent to the trenches. The biggest concerns, however, usually revolved around gender and sexuality. For many colonial subjects, both soldiers and workers, the gendered nature of wartime France came as a great shock: it seemed to be a land without men, where women (in sharp contrast to Frenchwomen in the colonies) worked with their hands alongside men. Paradoxically, in spite of pervasive fears of miscegenation inherited from the colonial encounter, the industrial needs of wartime led French authorities to place large numbers of colonial men and white women in close proximity to one another. As one Madagascan worker noted, "I have noted my great desire to continue to serve the *Patrie*, but in reality I find French women too beautiful and genteel, and I would be crushed if I had to leave them."[3] French fears of such sentiments not only led to outbursts of hostility from French men, including race riots, but also prompted public authorities to keep colonial workers as isolated as possible from the mainstream of national life.

The empire proved its worth to France during World War I, furnishing both its armies and factories with much needed manpower. The war familiarized the average French woman and man with the colonies to an unprecedented degree, setting the stage for the heightened interest in (and romanticization of) empire during the interwar years. At the same time, the wartime presence of colonial subjects in France revealed the porous, artificial nature of the carefully constructed boundaries between metropole and colony, both in the homeland and in the empire. It underscored the paradoxes of French universalism and would bequeath a powerful legacy for the history of imperial France during the twentieth century.

THE CRISES OF 1917

In 1917 the Great War truly became a world war. The entry of the United States into the conflict in April and the Russian revolutions of March and

November broadened the scope of the conflict and began to sketch out some of the main fault lines of the twentieth century. At the same time, the war in the trenches remained stalemated, without any real prospect of victory or defeat, and a harsh winter stretched civilian resources and patience to the breaking point. The year 1917 in France brought a series of crises of wartime morale, both on the front lines and among civilians and it called into question the nation's ability to continue.

By the beginning of 1917 Europe was exhausted. The tremendous battles of 1916, none of which did anything to break the stalemate let alone bring the war closer to an end, made it harder than ever for soldiers and civilians to continue. The bitter cold of the winter of 1916/1917 worsened conditions in the trenches and made food and fuel scarce and therefore expensive for the civilians back home. The "turnip winter," as Germans called it, drove European society to the breaking point. On March 8, International Women's Day, a women's food riot in Petrograd escalated into a major political crisis, forcing the overthrow of the czarist government. The Russian Revolution had begun.

France had suffered heavily, perhaps more than any other nation, from the bloody war of attrition. A large section of the country remained under occupation, the war continued to be fought on French soil, devastating the countryside, and France had the highest casualty rate of any belligerent nation. The national mood remained dominated by grim determination to see things through, but war weariness was starting to take its toll. As one colonel wrote on January 2, "The year is opening in a grim atmosphere. Promises and hopes have been followed by too many disappointments."[4] Could the nation conceivably survive another 1916?

The harsh conditions and enduring stalemate put the French general staff under more pressure than ever before to break the deadlock of trench warfare and defeat the Germans. At the end of 1916 French parliamentary deputies, horrified by the carnage and futility of Verdun and the Somme, had forced Prime Minister Aristide Briand to remove Joseph Joffre from command of the French armies, replacing him with Gen. Robert Nivelle, whose innovative use of successive artillery barrages had helped the French retake Douaumont in October. Nivelle announced that he would prepare yet another offensive for the spring. In spite of considerable skepticism from both military and government leaders, Nivelle won agreement for this new attack on the center of German lines, at the Chemin des Dames. The attack, which began on April 16, achieved some small tactical successes but failed to score the breakthrough that Nivelle hoped for. Almost 150,000 French soldiers died in a few weeks, notably large numbers of the African troops who led the attack. The French gained a few kilometers of ground, and the German lines remained intact.

At this point the French army cracked. The average French soldier continued to believe fervently in the war effort, but many could no longer tolerate being sacrificed in massive numbers for nothing. Starting at the end of April mutinies spread throughout the army, as soldiers refused to obey orders to go "over the top." Unlike those in revolutionary Russia, they did not shoot their officers or make political demands. Rather, over and over again they demanded better treatment and an end to the slaughter. Some units turned into soldiers' democratic assemblies, where individuals debated their grievances and proposed solutions. These were not always consistent; for example, most supported both a peace "without annexations or indemnities" but also the return of Alsace-Lorraine to France. Only a small fraction of the French forces, perhaps no more than 30,000 soldiers, took part in the mutiny, but this was enough to shock the general staff and the government in Paris. General Nivelle was sacked and replaced by Philippe Henri Pétain, who moved swiftly to appease the rebellious troops by improving material conditions in the trenches, granting more leave time, and, crucially, making it clear he would undertake no more offensives like the Chemin des Dames. "We will wait for the tanks and the Americans," he proclaimed. Although several thousand mutineers were court-martialed, less than fifty were actually executed. By midsummer order had largely been restored in the French army.

For the nation's military and political authorities, the mutinies raised the specter of the defeatism that seemed to be sweeping east from insurgent Russia in the spring of 1917 reaching France. In fact, one unit of the Russian expeditionary forces stationed in France mutinied in September, bringing the spirit of revolutionary Petrograd to French soil. Weariness with a seemingly endless war, combined with the harsh winter of 1916–1917, prompted manifestations of pacifism across Europe. At the beginning of April Vladimir Lenin arrived from his Swiss exile at Petrograd's Finland station, proclaiming the need to answer war with revolution. A few days later antiwar dissidents from Germany's powerful Social Democrats founded their own political party, the Independent Social Democratic Party, pledged to ending the war as quickly as possible. In Italy widespread rioting and antiwar activism broke out among both peasants and urban workers.

The spring of 1917 also saw the emergence of opposition to the war, and the collapse of the *union sacrée*, among French civilians. Not everyone in

France had supported the war effort. In 1914 the pacifist writer Romain Rolland protested the war by moving to neutral Switzerland, where in 1916 he published a denunciation of the conflict entitled *Above the Storm*. Members of the socialist and labor left also gradually moved away from their embrace of the *union sacrée* in August 1914, voicing more strident opposition to the war effort. French union delegates attended international antiwar conferences in Switzerland during 1915 and 1916, meeting with German and Austrian activists in defiance of patriotic norms. The most popular French novel of the war, Henri Barbusse's *Le Feu (Under Fire)*, published in 1916, praised socialist internationalism as the road to peace. As the conditions for workers became worsened in France, the antiwar left became more and more prominent in working-class political circles. In 1914 French unions had pledged not to go on strike as part of their contribution to the *union sacrée*, but as inflation first doubled and then tripled the prices of basic commodities they found it increasingly difficult to justify this to their rank and file.

The strike wave that broke out in the spring of 1917 began in an unexpected sector. In spite of wartime production the garment industry remained the largest in Paris, and its overwhelmingly female workforce suffered from not only low wages but the high cost of living. In mid-May thousands of women dressmakers walked off the job in Parisian dressmaking firms, demanding a shorter workweek and a cost of living allowance. Not only were women more likely to do the food shopping, and therefore be intimately affected by inflation, but as women they could not be drafted into the army, a favorite government technique for breaking strikes during the war. By summer strikes had spread to the major metalworking factories in the Paris area, the heart of the armaments industry. Many of these strikers were also women, and the demand for equal pay for equal work figured prominently among their complaints. The strikes were not necessarily revolutionary or even antiwar, although some strikers did brandish red flags as they marched. Nonetheless they did revitalize the socialist and labor left, so that by the end of the year both the Socialist Party and the CGT had substantial and growing minorities clamoring for a rapid end to the war.

Although there was no direct link between the army mutinies and the resumption of strike wave, together they suggested a profound war weariness among the people of France. The war seemed to stretch on and on, miserable and hopeless as ever. As antiwar sentiment mounted it became increasingly clear that without a conclusive victory soon the very fate of the Third Republic was in doubt. As one Parisian wrote in July 1917,

> Life here is becoming impossible, everything is disgustingly bad, even bread, as well as the vegetables we still have. What will happen this winter? There will certainly be a revolution in Paris, and I advise you . . . to close up everything and come to the countryside. It's no joke to find oneself in the middle of riots, all the more because, since this will be a revolution provoked by famine, they will pillage your house.[5]

The most hopeful moment of 1917 was America's long-awaited entry into the war. During the early years of the conflict most Americans were content to observe matters from the sidelines. Moreover, many were hostile to the Entente: Irish Americans opposed doing anything to aid Britain, and many Jews and others from eastern Europe loathed czarist Russia. Germany's pursuit of unrestricted submarine warfare, which targeted ships carrying American passengers, not to mention its maladroit attempts to lure Mexico into an anti-American alliance, turned the tide of public opinion in the US. Accordingly on April 2, 1917, the United States declared war on Germany. On June 13 the first detachment of the American Expeditionary Force, led by General Pershing, arrived in Paris. Accompanied by General Joffre and war minister Painlevé, the two hundred Americans marched in triumph through the French capital, acclaimed by huge throngs of cheering and weeping Parisians. A similarly rapturous welcome greeted the Americans when on July 4, 1917 the next AEF detachments marched through Paris in celebration of America's Independence Day, ending up at the tomb of the Marquis de Lafayette. There Lieutenant Colonel Stanton proclaimed to the listening crowds, "Nous voilà, Lafayette!" Millions of American soldiers would serve in France during the war, creating new ties between the two great republics.

THE FINAL YEAR OF THE WAR

The Americans did not arrive in substantial numbers until 1918, however. Until then, many worried that France might not prevail, that war weariness might overwhelm the Third Republic. That this was no idle fear became abundantly clear in November when the Bolsheviks seized power in Russia. They

immediately announced their intention to pull out of the war by seeking a
separate peace with Germany, a promise they made good on in February 1918
when they signed the treaty of Brest-Litovsk. The Bolshevik Revolution inaugurated the last year of World War I by in effect reducing it to a race. On
the one hand, the Germans redeploying masses of experienced soldiers to the
western front, on the other the seemingly inexhaustible supply of American
manpower slowly but surely making its way across the Atlantic. Whoever won
this race would win the war.

The end of 1917 brought a major political change in France. By this point
the spirit of the *union sacrée* was largely in tatters, and the government seemed
to be floundering in a search for effective policies to win the war. The Radical party remained in control of the government, and in November after the
collapse of the scandal-ridden regime of Paul Painlevé, President Raymond
Poincaré appointed Georges Clemenceau the nation's new prime minister.
Clemenceau had left politics in 1909, and during the war had reemerged as a
virulent critic of the government's failure to defeat the Germans. His tendency
to treat his enemies harshly during his last stint as prime minister had made
him unpopular with many, and his rival Joseph Caillaux had a lot of support.
The choice of Clemenceau over Caillaux, who sympathized with pacifists and
sought to negotiate an end to the war, represented a clear decision to go for
victory no matter what. His inaugural address on November 20 moved and
inspired all who heard it, including the young Winston Churchill, who would
remember his words in 1940.

Clemenceau helped restore the flagging spirits of the nation by visiting
the trenches to praise France's soldiers. Unexpectedly, he also tried to concil-
iate French labor, granting wage increases while also repressing some strikes.
However, when it came to antiwar sentiment the Tiger did not hesitate to
show his teeth. He supported the trial and execution of several high-profile
defeatists like Bolo Pasha, a French adventurer convicted of receiving funds
from the Germans. Most notably, he arrested his own political rival, Joseph
Caillaux, in January 1918, on the charge of treason and held him in prison for
two years without trial. In effect, Clemenceau established a de facto dictatorship in France during 1918, an intolerant regime with some similarities to the
military dictatorship of Generals Ludendorff and Hindenburg in Germany, or
even that of the Bolsheviks in Russia, during the same year. After several years
of war, by 1918 only those regimes tough enough to focus on victory at all
costs hoped to survive. When asked about his policies in March 1918, Clemenceau responded with the same answer to everything: "I wage war!"

In early 1918 it was by no means clear that this would be enough. Antiwar sentiment was not only growing in France but taking on a revolutionary cast, furiously egged on by the new masters of Russia. In the spring and summer of the year massive strikes broke out in the Paris area and the Loire valley, both bigger than those of 1917 and often more antiwar and politically radical as well. Ironically, by signing a separate peace with Germany the Bolsheviks made themselves deeply unpopular with most people in France; even on the left; they were often referred to as "Boche-viks." Nonetheless, both German militarism and socialist revolution threatened the Third Republic during the last year of the war.

On March 21, 1918, less than three weeks after the Brest-Litovsk treaty, Germany launched its final offensive of the war in the west. Starting with the greatest artillery bombardment the world had ever seen, a massive army of a million soldiers attacked British positions, forcing them to retreat with heavy losses and threatening to drive a wedge between them and French forces. In this way Germany hoped to replicate its near success of 1914 and seize Paris. In response, for the first time in the war the Entente powers created a unified transnational military command, under the leadership of French general Ferdinand Foch. Coordinating forces enabled the French and their allies to move reserves rapidly into areas threatened by the German advance and respond more effectively to the enemy threat.

Initially the German offensive seemed to carry everything before it. The reality of the attack came home to Parisians on March 29, Good Friday, when enemy siege guns scored a direct hit on the Church of Saint-Gervais in the capital, killing 156 people. By midsummer German troops had advanced to the Marne River and, as in 1914, threatened to lay siege to Paris. Yet this was Germany's last throw: its forces were able to advance so rapidly because they carried little food or supplies, and they quickly outran their supply lines. Moreover, they took heavy casualties, just as hundreds of thousands of fresh American troops were joining the battle. On July 18 Foch mounted a massive counterattack, forcing the Germans back across the Marne and effectively ending the offensive. By August the German armies were falling apart, their troops often surrendering to smaller Entente units or simply deserting. France and its allies launched a major counteroffensive, pushing the Germans back toward their own border. At last, at last, France seemed poised to liberate its territory and achieve the victory that had eluded it for so long.

At this point diplomats took the upper hand. The German leadership was painfully aware that with the failure of the offensive it had to sue for peace.

After a complicated series of negotiations German and Entente delegates met on the morning of November 11, 1918, in a railway car in Compiègne forest to sign an armistice, with a formal peace treaty to follow. As in August 1914, church bells throughout France pealed to announce the news, and French people in villages, towns, and cities poured into the streets to celebrate—laughing, crying, and embracing each other. Fifty thousand Parisians flooded into the Place de l'Opéra in a massive outpouring of joy and emotion, hugging and kissing friends, family members, and complete strangers, and singing the "Marseillaise." That afternoon Clemenceau made a formal announcement to the National Assembly, stating, "At this terrible hour, great and magnificent, my duty is done."[6] Thus, on the eleventh hour of the eleventh day of the eleventh month of 1918, after nearly 1,600 days of combat, France was saved and the Great War was finally over.

For France, World War I was at the same time a triumph and a horror of unprecedented proportions. Mourning for the more than 1 million soldiers would not stop with the war, of course, and the devastation wrought by World War I would shape the nation for decades to come. Nonetheless the nation, and in particular the Third Republic, had survived at a time when regimes all over Europe were collapsing under the strain. Victory underscored the strength of France as a nation, or a nation-state, and an imperial nation that could call on the resources of all its peoples in the hour of national peril.

The French victory thus underscored the success of national integration under the Third Republic, but it also demonstrated the character of France as a universal nation. The French people saw themselves as inspired both by a defense of the *patrie* but also by universalist principles of liberty and justice, underscored by a racialized perspective on the enemy as the foe of universal civilization. France was a leading theater during the war, so that millions of people from throughout the world got a glimpse of the country during their military service, including all those who died on, and would remain buried in, French soil. Finally, for the first time in its modern history France fought a major war on its own territory in alliance with other countries; its victory belonged not just to itself, but to an important sense to humanity in general.

In November 1918 the French celebrated both victory and peace. Yet November 11, 1918, brought an armistice, a cessation of hostilities, not the final conclusion of the war. It was still unclear what the formal agreement would look like, let alone the postwar world. The peoples of France could justifiably claim to have won the war after four years of national and global travail. Whether or not they would win the peace remained to be seen.

Suggestions for Further Reading

Becker, Jean-Jacques. *The Great War and the French People.* New York: St. Martin's, 1986.

———. *1914: Comment les français sont entrés dans la guerre.* Paris: Presses de la fondation nationale des sciences politiques, 1977.

Darrow, Margaret H. *French Women and the First World War.* Oxford: Berg, 2000.

Downs, Laura Lee. *Manufacturing Inequality: Gender Division in the French and British Metalworking Industries, 1914–1939.* Ithaca. NY: Cornell University Press, 1995.

Fogarty, Richard. *Race and War in France: Colonial Subjects in the French Army, 1914–1918.* Baltimore: Johns Hopkins University Press, 2008.

Hanna, Martha. *Your Death Would Be Mine: Paul and Marie Pireaud in the Great War.* Cambridge: Harvard University Press, 2006.

Hardach, Gerd. *The First World War.* Berkeley: University of California Press, 1981.

Kaspi, Andre. *Le temps des américains: Le concours américain à la France en 1917–1918.* Paris: Publications de la Sorbonne, 1976.

Morrow, John H. Jr. *The Great War: An Imperial History.* New York: Routledge, 2005.

Smith, Leonard V. *Between Mutiny and Obedience: The Case of the French Fifth Infantry Division During World War I.* Princeton, NJ: Princeton University Press, 1994.

Smith, Leonard V., Stéphane Audoin-Rouzeau, and Annette Becker. *France and the Great War, 1914–1918.* Cambridge: Cambridge University Press, 2003.

Stovall, Tyler. "The Color Line Behind the Lines: Racial Violence in France During the Great War." *American Historical Review* 103, no. 3 (1998): 737–769.

Taylor, A. J. P., ed. *History of World War I.* London: Octopus, 1974.

Winter, Jay, and Jean-Louis Robert. *Capital Cities at War: London, Paris, Berlin, 1914–1919.* Cambridge: Cambridge University Press, 1997.

Zweig, Stefan. *The World of Yesterday.* Lincoln: University of Nebraska Press, 1964.

Notes

1. Stefan Zweig, *The World of Yesterday* (Lincoln: University of Nebraska Press, 1964), 192–193.

2. Martha Hanna, *Your Death Would Be Mine: Paul and Marie Pireaud in the Great War* (Cambridge: Harvard University Press, 2006), 78.

3. Tyler Stovall, *Paris and the Spirit of 1919: Consumer Struggles, Transnationalism, and Revolution* (Cambridge: Cambridge University Press, 2012), 125.

4. John Williams, "The French Army Cracks," in A. J. P. Taylor, ed., *History of World War I* (London: Octopus, 1974), 197.

5. Stovall, *Paris*, 77.

6. Leonard V. Smith, Stéphane Audoin-Rouzeau, and Annette Becker, *France and the Great War, 1914–1918* (Cambridge: Cambridge University Press, 2003), 158.

eight

FROM ONE WAR TO ANOTHER: THE UNIVERSAL NATION IN CRISIS

FROM THE VANTAGE POINT OF THE EARLY 1920S FRANCE HAD MUCH to celebrate. The nation had won the war, and the Third Republic had survived its test of arms, unlike most other major nations on the European continent. Moreover, the democratic nation-state symbolized by France had gone from being exceptional to dominating Europe. The French had regained Alsace-Lorraine and were once again the strongest military power in Europe. France had also increased its colonial holdings, thanks to the League of Nations mandate system and the dismemberment of the German colonial empire, and its people appreciated their colonies more than ever before. The economy was recovering from the devastation of the war, and Paris remained in many ways the intellectual and creative center of the world, the global city par excellence. As the burgeoning tourist trade clearly demonstrated, France retained a special place among the nations of the world.

As the nation's most astute leaders realized, however, such a rosy perspective rested on a shaky foundation. By the 1920s France was only the fourth-largest nation in Europe, and its population continued to decline faster than that of any other major country. Germany might be humbled and the infant Soviet Union chaotic, but both nations were potentially much stronger than France economically and militarily. The sharp social divisions that

8.1. André Citroën lights up the Eiffel Tower, 1925.
Source: Boyer/Roger-Viollet/Getty Images.

produced a near-revolutionary situation at the end of the war had been at least papered over, but working-class discontent and political radicalism would continue to threaten the stability of the republic in the decades after the war. Finally, the empire had grown in size and become stronger, but so had the voices of those who challenged colonial rule in the name of anti-imperialist and anti-French nationalism.

The crisis of interwar France was a crisis of the universal nation. World War I revealed and underscored the stability of French national identity, definitively resolving the conflict between Church and state that had absorbed so much of the Third Republic's energy. At the same time, however, it brought to global prominence other universalist visions that challenged those of France. The emphasis on global human rights and democracy during the peace negotiations of 1919 came from Woodrow Wilson, not Georges Clemenceau. The other major global narrative—world revolution—was increasingly centered in Moscow during the 1920s, and French activists who embraced it as a vision of human liberation often found themselves subject to the interests of another universal nation. The rise of fascism and Nazism created an additional narrative, hypernationalist, profoundly anti-universal, and fundamentally opposed to the ideals of the French Revolution. These combined challenges, together with the demographic and political stagnation of the nation, led many to see France as a nation in decline.

Yet France continued to symbolize resistance to other universalisms during the years between the wars. Not for nothing did it become a leading world center for immigrants, refugees, and intellectuals. Paris experienced one of the most brilliant periods of its history during these years, much of it due to the interaction of French and foreign creative spirits. In the end this did not save the French from the horrors of a new war, but it underscored the fact that the decline and fall of France was in many ways a universal tragedy.

THE PEACE OF PARIS AND THE VERSAILLES TREATY

On July 14, 1919, a massive parade took to the streets of Paris to celebrate the Allied victory in World War I. Marking both Bastille Day and the signing of the Versailles peace treaty on June 28, the French government staged a memorable display of military might and universalist nationalism. Led by a contingent of disabled veterans and then Marshal Foch and Marshal Joffre, the march proceeded from the Bois de Boulogne through the Arc de Triomphe, down the Champs Elysées and the Grands Boulevards before concluding at the Place de la République. Delegations from Allied armies joined the procession, bracketed by French military units. In this dramatic piece of street theater, the Allies were integrated into a French procession on a French national holiday proceeding in stately fashion through the French capital. On Bastille Day 1919 the universal nation thus celebrated a universal victory.

In 1919 France had won the war but had to reckon with the tremendous cost of victory. Out of a population of 40 million the French army had mobilized over 8 million soldiers; 1.3 million died in combat, and another 1.1 million came home with permanent disabilities, plus 3 million classified as semi-invalids. Those who never returned left behind them 600,000 widows and 760,000 orphans. The number of French dead and wounded was thus heavier, proportional to its population, than that of any other combatant nation in World War I. In addition to its grievous human losses, France had to contend with the devastation of the regions occupied by the Germans during the war and areas, like Verdun, that had been blasted to smithereens by battle. The occupation had ruined some of the wealthiest areas of the country, so that in 1919 industrial production for France as a whole was less than half what it had been in 1913.

The terrible cost of the war left the French people scarred physically and emotionally. Every village and town of any size erected its own memorial to the dead in the years after the armistice and held memorial ceremonies every November 11. The Paris Metro began its practice of marking seats at the front of the train as reserved for *les mutilés de guerre* (the war wounded), signs that exist to this day. The greatest of all war commemorations took place on the second anniversary of Armistice Day in 1920, when the French government officially buried the Unknown Soldier (using a body recovered from Verdun) under the Arc de Triomphe in Paris. Such public recognition of the sacrifices made by millions became a regular feature of the national landscape in France. The private anguish suffered by those who had lost loved ones endured in a myriad of different ways, but the tremendous extent of the losses made mourning a major part of national life for years to come. For the French, therefore, the search for peace must above all compensate their sufferings, both individual and national, and ensure that such horrors never happen again.

The fact that those goals proved incompatible was ultimately the tragedy of the Versailles treaty. On January 18, 1919, the peace conference opened in Paris. Ostensibly called to write a treaty formally ending World War I, the conference actually had a broader agenda: to create the structures that would shape the world as a whole during the new century. Like the Congress of Vienna a century earlier, it brought together victors and vanquished but on a broader scale. The Paris peace conference represented the first time in history diplomats and politicians conceived of the entire world as a single entity, trying to consult people from around the planet. The fact that it took place in Paris recognized the central role played by France in the Great War, as well its character as a universal nation. Perhaps at no time in its history has France been more central to global affairs than during the first few months of 1919.

For the world as a whole, the 1919 peace conference outlined the major fault lines that would shape the global history of the twentieth century. Not all voices received equal attention from the dominant powers, and the exclusion of many would have important consequences in the long term. The Soviet Union was not invited, and in return it harshly condemned the conference as an attempt to impose capitalist and imperialist hegemony on the world. The military engagement of the Entente powers in the Russian civil war against the Bolsheviks only underscored this opposition, which would continue to resonate globally long after the peace was signed. Delegates from the colonial world who came to Paris to plead for independence or at least greater autonomy received short shrift, learning that Wilson's call for popular self-determination did not apply to them. The peace conference applauded the collapse of empires in Europe but reinforced them for the colonized, setting up the massive struggles for decolonization that would shake the world by midcentury.

Led by Georges Clemenceau as one of the Big Four at the conference (the United States, Britain, and Italy being the other three), France wanted to achieve specific goals from the peace. First and foremost, of course, was the restoration of Alsace-Lorraine. Beyond that, the French government wanted Germany to pay for all the damage caused by the war. This was important for political as well as moral reasons. It was much easier for French politicians to say the Germans would pay for everything than to take measures like increasing taxes or limiting expenses. In addition, France was vitally concerned to keep Germany as weak as possible. Many advocated breaking up the nation or at least establishing buffer states in the Rhineland to be dominated by France. Clemenceau is reported to have said, "The more Germany is split up, the better I'll like it." The French also wanted to establish strong democratic states as allies in eastern Europe, and new colonies from the breakup of the German and Ottoman empires. Finally, France wanted assurances that in the future both Britain and the United States would stand firmly at its side to preserve the peace.

The French were only one of the victorious powers, however, and as such had to contend with the desires and visions of other nations. The United States challenged not only French goals but the idea of France as the dominant power in the peace negotiations. President Wilson arrived in Paris in December 1918 to a tumultuous welcome; hundreds of thousands of Parisians cheered the American president as his motorcade rode up the Champs-Elysées. Wilson's idealism and his belief in the importance of peace over victory, which translated into a relatively benign attitude toward a defeated Germany now ruled by a fledgling republican government, clashed with the desire of Clemenceau and many of his fellow citizens to punish the Germans. The British, represented by Prime Minister David Lloyd George, wanted to restore Germany as an important trading partner and also feared French predominance on the Continent. They therefore tended to resist French attempts to impose harsh conditions on the Germans.

In spite of these differences the French succeeded in wringing a number of concessions from their Allies. The peace treaty that was signed in the

Versailles Hall of Mirrors (the same room where German unification had been ratified in 1871) on June 28, 1919, reflected French desires to an important degree. In addition to ordering Germany to pay massive reparations for war damages, it included the notorious war guilt clause, which stated that the Germans bore full responsibility for starting the conflict. The treaty used the principle of self-determination to support the new democratic regimes of eastern Europe, notably Poland, Czechoslovakia, and Yugoslavia, while at the same time violating that principle to ensure that the new Austrian state would not unite with Germany. Finally, it not only restored Alsace-Lorraine to France but also demilitarized the Rhineland, between the Rhine River and the French border, as well as granting France control for fifteen years over Germany's coal-rich Saar basin.

These were important gains, yet France would go on to suffer as a result of both its victories and defeats at the 1919 peace conference. One of the nation's greatest triumphs, the spread of democracy throughout Europe, would in some ways also prove its undoing. France committed itself to supporting the new democratic states in eastern Europe, notably Czechoslovakia, Romania, and Yugoslavia, seeing them as effective counterweights to Germany and the Soviet Union. In addition, they embodied French democratic ideals. This alliance, however, eventually underscored the fact that the Versailles treaty had been carried out against the two potentially most powerful nations on the European continent; both Germany and Russia had conflicts with the postwar settlement in eastern Europe; ultimately, allying with weak states against strong ones placed France in a no-win situation. Similarly, the collapse of the German second empire and its replacement by the shaky Weimar republic could be seen, as many French socialists argued, as a triumph for democratic republicanism. Yet for Clemenceau and most French, Germany remained Germany, no matter the regime. By insisting on harsh treatment of its defeated rival, far from supporting the extension of republicanism abroad France may well have contributed to its undoing.

Despite its flaws, the Versailles settlement could have prevailed had the victorious powers supported it. But soon it became clear that this was not to be. The US Senate refused to ratify the Versailles treaty, and the American people slipped back into a mood of strict isolationism for a decade. The British made it clear they were more concerned with their empire than the affairs of the Continent. The flaws and contradictions in the treaty contributed to disengagement by Washington and London, but from their perspective intervention in European affairs generally only happened in exceptional circumstances that hopefully would not recur. The absence of their support left France in an untenable position as the sole real guarantor of the peace. The land of Louis XIV and of Napoleon had the military might to sustain such a situation, but not that of Georges Clemenceau. During the interwar years France would maintain a great empire, participate in European alliances, and sustain the largest army on the Continent. Nonetheless, the universal nation would find that when push came to shove, it essentially stood alone.

The tensions between east and west, north and south so evident during the peace negotiations also shaped domestic life in France itself. In 1919 most of Europe east of the Rhine was aflame with insurrection and anti-capitalist and anti-imperialist movements stretching around the world from Seattle to Glasgow, Egypt, India, and China. The Soviet Union might be persona non grata in the diplomatic salons of the peace conference in Paris, but it had important support in the working-class French left. During 1917 and especially 1918 French unions had become increasingly restive due to inflation and war, and both the CGT and the SFIO contained growing antiwar and even revolutionary minorities. The end of conflict removed the key reason for national unity and sharpened these militant tendencies. Lifting wartime price and rent controls sparked a number of popular struggles, especially in Paris. Perhaps most important, with the end of the war the Bolsheviks no longer appeared primarily as defeatists and disloyal allies, so their stock rose sharply in France. Many on the left spoke of a "fresh wind from the east" that would spark the world revolution and sweep capitalism into the dustbin of history. May Day 1919 saw barricades and street fighting between militant workers and the forces of order on Parisian boulevards. The next month hundreds of thousands of metalworkers went on strike for weeks in the capital and its suburbs, demanding higher wages but also shouting revolutionary slogans; in one suburb, Saint-Denis, the socialist municipal government announced it was reconstituting itself as a soviet regime.

Global debates about empire also played a role in French life during 1919. Authorities repressed nationalist revolts in several French colonies after the armistice, reaffirming imperial control. France and its allies prevented a young Vietnamese nationalist, the future Ho Chi Minh, from submitting a petition for human rights in the French colonies to the peace conference. Colonial issues surfaced in the metropole as well. At the end of the war hundreds of thousands of French colonial subjects, both soldiers and workers, remained in France. While the redeployment of the soldiers back home after the end of the fighting seemed to go without saying, the future of colonial workers was less clear.

Postwar reconstruction and the millions of Frenchmen dead and disabled in 1918 meant that France needed to import labor from beyond its borders. In spite of that, French authorities decided to expel colonial laborers from France back to the empire, arguing that the wartime experiment in creating a multicultural labor force had failed. At a time when the colonies had shown their value to France like never before, this decision underscored the boundaries between metropole and colony, separate and unequal. Building on the racialization of national identity fostered by the colonial heritage and World War I, it effectively defined France as a white nation, off-limits to people of color. While diplomats in Paris debated (and mostly ignored) the postwar fate of the colonies, the expulsion of colonial workers in 1919 illustrated the geographical and racial fault lines that lay at the heart of the universal nation.

With the signing of the Versailles peace treaty on June 28 the war was effectively over, although the Allies did not sign an accord with the Ottoman Empire until the Treaty of Sèvres in 1920. France could now turn its attention to rebuilding the nation and preparing for the years to come. Many hoped to put the trauma of war behind them and return to a future that would hopefully look very much like the vanished belle epoque. However, they would discover that the impact of more than four years of total war would not soon disappear.

PROSPERITY AND ANXIETY IN THE INTERWAR YEARS

France between the wars presented two faces to its citizens and the outside world. On the one hand it continued to represent sophistication and modernity. Paris in the 1920s seemed more glamorous and cosmopolitan than ever, thanks in large part to the contributions of foreign artists and intellectuals. The economic revival after the armistice created a dynamic new sector of modern industries. In 1925 one of France's most flamboyant industrialists, car manufacturer Andre Citroën, had his name spelled out in electric lights on the Eiffel Tower. The 1931 census noted that for the first time in history the majority of the French population lived in urban areas. On the other hand, however, much of France remained firmly wedded to tradition. Since according to the French census towns needed only two thousand people to count as "urban," small town and rural life continued to dominate much of France.

The French economy experienced fundamental changes during the 1920s. By 1923 economic production had returned to prewar levels, and by the end of the decade it had gone far beyond them. The leaders of industry demonstrated a new taste for technological innovation and modernization, often borrowed from the United States. Andre Citroën spent time working in Detroit and studying the manufacturing techniques of Henry Ford. The new emphasis on mass production and industrial innovation had begun in the munitions plants during the war and was accelerated in the 1920s. The increased use of assembly lines, unskilled labor, and large factories characterized this new approach to manufacturing. At the same time, traditional industries tended to dominate the national economy. The average French workplace was still small, especially when compared to those of Britain, Germany, or the United States, and many French businesses continued to take conservative approaches to production and marketing.

The prosperity of the 1920s brought few benefits to French workers. The interwar years began with a major victory: the passing of the eight-hour day law in 1919. Many workplaces ignored the law, however, especially the small ones that still employed the majority of French labor, and even where the eight-hour day was enforced, often workers simply took on overtime to compensate for low wages. The collapse of the union movement in 1920 left most defenseless against the demands of their employers, and those who tried to organize on the job often found themselves on the street. The nation avoided a labor shortage, which could have raised working-class wages, by importing large numbers of immigrant workers during the interwar years. Thanks in part to America's closing of its borders to foreigners at the beginning of the decade, by the end of the 1920s France had the largest immigrant population in the world. Immigrant workers in the interwar years came overwhelmingly from Europe, especially neighboring countries like Italy, Spain, and Belgium, but also Poland and other parts of eastern Europe. Smaller numbers came from the empire, especially Algeria, and France also attracted Jewish immigrants from both eastern Europe and North Africa. Most immigrants were unskilled and tended to work in heavy industry.

The large number of immigrants tended to reinforce workers' isolation from the mainstream of French life during the interwar years. Not only relatively low wages but also the scarcity of decent housing meant a poor standard of living for most working people. Particularly in the Paris area, workers increasingly moved to the suburbs during the interwar years. The biggest factories, such as the giant Renault auto plant in Boulogne-Billancourt, were located here. The greatest suburban growth, however, appeared not in the factory towns but in more isolated bedroom communities, where unscrupulous developers sold plots of land to workers from Paris willing to build their own housing. This was usually of very poor quality, in areas without decent sewage, water, or utilities. Nonetheless, these new suburban slums attracted hundreds of thousands of workers between the wars; the town of Drancy, for example, grew from 1,000 to 50,000 inhabitants in thirty years. The one major part of France that significantly increased its population during the interwar years, what became known as the "red belt" around Paris, would form the electoral base of the newest political party in France, the French Communists.

In spite of the dismal working-class standard of living, French workers did achieve some gains. Authorities did not reverse all the benefits of wartime mobilization; for example, rent remained tightly controlled during the interwar years. More generally, the era saw important achievements in welfare benefits, both public and private. Many large factory owners organized employee savings and retirement plans. Concerns with boosting France's population, especially compared to Germany and other rivals, motivated much of the planning for social welfare. In 1923 the government passed a law creating special benefits for large families, and many employers paid special wages to heads of households with lots of children. Since heads of households were universally defined as men, this had the effect of increasing gender inequality at the workplace. In 1928 France passed comprehensive social insurance legislation, including maternity, disability, and retirement benefits, and enacted it in 1930.

Others in French society saw more gains during the boom years of the 1920s. Farmers had benefited from the shortage of food and other agricultural products during the war, and some had amassed significant savings. Few used this money to invest in new machinery or farming methods, so French agriculture continued to be dominated by family farms. There were some exceptions, such as the wheat-growing areas of the north, where mechanized farming techniques were becoming common, but they did not reflect the experience of most French peasants. The new prosperity enabled peasants to improve their standard of living and acquire a taste for urban goods, such as clothing. At the same time, whereas French farmers lived better than their forebears, they were increasingly worse off than their urban countrymen. Agriculture was in many ways the weakest part of the national economy, and in consequence the exodus from the countryside continued, so that by the early 1930s only a third of French families made a living off the land.

For the middle classes as well, the prosperity of the interwar years was mixed. Those associated with the dynamic new economy, not only factory owners and managers but urban professionals in general, did well during the 1920s, and were able to enjoy new luxuries like electrified homes and private automobiles. At the same time many small *rentiers*, those who lived off the interest from investments and annuities, faced hard times or even ruin during the 1920s. The Soviet decision not to honor imperial Russian bonds, a favorite investment before the war, as well as postwar inflation and the weakness of the franc, forced many affluent individuals to make do with less during the 1920s. The increasing popularity in bourgeois homes of the *bonne à tout faire*, the all-purpose maid, reflected both the much ballyhooed servant crisis of the interwar years and the fact that many families could no longer afford a large household staff.

In spite of economic prosperity, therefore, for many there was a palpable sense of decline in the interwar years. The failures of the peace contributed to this pessimism, as did the feeling that the losses and destruction caused by the war could never be fully replaced. At the heart of the nation's malaise, however, lay its poor demographic performance. As we have seen, France's low birthrate was already a matter of grave concern during the belle epoque. The loss of 1.3 million men during the war, plus the deficit of births (often calculated at over 1 million) due to those losses made poor natality nothing less than a national crisis. Birthrates remained low during the interwar years, so that by the early 1930s France slipped from fourth to fifth largest nation in Europe, passed by Italy. The city of Paris recorded the largest population in its history, nearly 3 million, in 1921, then began a decline virtually uninterrupted throughout the entire twentieth century. In contrast, Germany grew robustly during these years, reaching nearly 70 million by 1939. The inability to achieve true reconciliation with Germany made France's low birthrate even more ominous. The baby shortage led to the aging of the French population, which for many translated into conservatism, an unwillingness to take risks, and pessimism about the nation's future.

This "crisis of reproduction" prompted many anguished debates about how to boost the birthrate, and they tended to place concerns about gender at the fore. The war had brought Frenchwomen unprecedented visibility and representation in the public sphere, as workers in previously heavily masculine sectors like metalworking. Even during the war many conservative commentators had argued that working in unhealthy factories harmed women's ability to bear children. Once the war ended industrialists quickly fired women from war plants and replaced them with male workers. In 1920 the French government underscored traditional views of women's roles by enacting a law imposing strict penalties for disseminating information about birth control.

This concern about the blurring of gender roles after the war led to a key political decision in France after the armistice: the failure to grant women the vote. Throughout the western world feminists successfully argued that, because of their service to their countries during the war, women had earned the right to full citizenship and equality with men. As a result, by 1920 most leading nations, including Britain, the United States, the Soviet Union, and Germany, had enacted women's suffrage. The French National Assembly passed a women's suffrage bill in 1919, but it was blocked by the Senate. Not only conservatives opposed women's suffrage however; many on the left were ambivalent about the issue, concerned about the strong influence of the Church on women and thus fearing that female suffrage would just mean more votes for the priests. Ultimately it would take another world war to win Frenchwomen the right to vote. In matters of gender, the idea of France as a leader of universal progress took a backseat to fears for the future of the nation.

This effort to put women back into the home failed in many ways, however. By the mid-1920s rates of female participation in the economy were higher than ever. The decimation of the young male population by the war meant many women would remain unmarried and would have to support themselves. Certain professions, notably the *steno-dactylo*, or secretary-typist, became overwhelmingly female during the interwar years. At times concern for reproduction helped improve the status of women. The interwar years brought increased attention to the health concerns of women in the country-side, so that it became normal for pregnant peasants to consult with doctors in addition to midwives. In 1927 France passed a law liberalizing citizenship requirements, which enabled Frenchwomen who married foreigners to keep their own nationality. Many conservatives supported this out of fear that otherwise the children born to such marriages would be lost to the French nation. Nonetheless, women remained for the most part subordinate to men in French public life. Only a small number succeeded in entering the liberal professions, and working women usually found themselves concentrated in entry-level jobs at low pay.

During the 1920s public opinion (and frequently hostility) tended to focus on those women who embraced the new. The idea of the New Woman was not in fact new at all, having surfaced during the belle epoque, but in the 1920s it was much more prominent, part of a global phenomenon encouraged by the new popularity of radio and cinema. Known as the *garçonne*, or female boy, the French new woman closely resembled the flapper wreaking havoc on traditional gender roles in America at the same time. To a certain extent the *garçonne* was a fashion statement: a young woman with short hair, short skirt, and slim-fitting clothing, "this beast without breasts or hips" in the words of one commentator. The noted designer Coco Chanel became associated with this new look. But the image also reflected a broader social attitude. The new woman smoked and drank, went out in public without a chaperone, engaged in extramarital affairs, and, most important of all, delayed or rejected marriage and children. In 1922 Victor Margueritte published the novel *La Garçonne*, portraying the life of his heroine, Monique Lerbier. Addicted to jazz, drink, drugs, and sex, Lerbier ended up sterile, a cautionary tale for young women tempted by this lifestyle.

Hostility toward young women who rejected motherhood and thereby neglected their primary duty to the nation became a major theme of conservative discourse during the interwar years. In 1933 a young working-class Parisian, Violette Nozière, scandalized France by poisoning her parents, ostensibly to finance a dissolute lifestyle. At her blockbuster trial, the most sensational in France since the Dreyfus affair, Nozière spat defiance, cursing her parents and insisting on her need to live her own life. The right-wing press ignored her sexual abuse at the hands of her father, focusing instead on her numerous lovers and her taste for the cafés of the Latin Quarter. The judge duly condemned her to death while crowds inside and outside the court howled for her destruction. Violette Nozière represented French fears not just of the new woman but of a world that seemed to have lost its moorings since the war.

INTERWAR POLITICS AND DIPLOMACY

This split between forward- and backward-looking France became evident immediately after the war's end. On the left the fascination with the Russian Revolution, and the failure of the revolutionary moment at home in 1919, brought new directions in progressive politics. During 1919 and 1920 both the SFIO and the CGT continued to grow, while at the same time experiencing increasingly bitter splits between reformist and revolutionary factions. In the municipal elections of November 1919 the SFIO took control of several city halls in the industrial suburbs of the capital, laying the base for the future red belt. In the early months of 1920 a number of strikes shook the country, culminating in general strike staged by the CGT in May. After a few weeks the strike collapsed in the face of determined resistance by the government, dealing French unions a blow they would not recover from until the 1930s.

The defeat of the general strike represented the ultimate failure of the anarcho-syndicalist tradition, leading the French left to look to the east for other revolutionary models. In 1919 the Soviets had created the Third International to organize the world revolution, and they invited socialist parties from around Europe and the world to join. During 1920 French socialists journeyed to Moscow to witness the revolution and receive the blessings of its leaders, who encouraged them to create a new socialist party in France. The Soviets also demanded adherence to a list of principles, the Twenty-one Conditions, to ensure that members of the Third International would remain revolutionary and avoid the kind of collapse that destroyed the Second International in August 1914. In December 1920 the SFIO held its annual congress at Tours, and large majority voted to accept the conditions, join the Third International, and rename itself the French Communist Party (PCF). The minority left the new party, staying with the SFIO. This separation also carried over to the labor movement, with the left leaving the CGT to create its own union organization, the CGTU. France's socialist left thus split permanently, and a major French political party increasingly pledged its loyalty to internationalism as defined by a foreign power.

This thunder on the left was matched by thunder on the right. In 1919 conservative parties wrapped themselves in the French flag, championing a hard-line stance against Germany. At the same time, they represented the radical left as a new danger to the nation; posters depicted the Bolshevik agitator as "the man with the knife between his teeth." The dedication of the basilica of Sacre Coeur in October, now viewed as a memorial not just to the victims of the Commune but also those of the war, underscored both the Church's embrace of the conservative republic and the link between patriotism and antibolshevism. In the November 1919 legislative elections the moderate and conservative parties, mobilized in the National Bloc coalition, won an impressive victory. The coalition controlled over two-thirds of the seats in the new National Assembly, the most right-wing since the election of 1871.

The National Bloc would dominate French politics for most of the 1920s. Yet, as in 1871, the right's victory was exceptional rather than symptomatic. The left actually increased its vote totals in 1919, but a new voting system that favored coalitions allowed the National Bloc to win the election. Moreover, its very existence showed important changes in the nation's political life since the turn of the century. Monarchism no longer played a significant role in French politics, and the Church now supported republicanism. The Third Republic's triumph in World War I had driven antirepublicanism to the fringes of French politics. As subsequent elections would make clear, the real political center of gravity belonged to the moderates and the radicals, and during the interwar years power would generally move from one group to the other without really changing anything. It was a system that worked moderately well in good times but would prove incapable of facing the crises of the 1930s.

The new National Bloc coalition quickly replaced the great wartime leader, Clemenceau, with Alexandre Millerand, the onetime socialist turned conservative. The new government emphasized promoting security for France against its enemies, both foreign and domestic. It was, ironically enough, Millerand who led the government's repression of the 1920 general strike, widely if incorrectly viewed as a prelude to revolution. It also advocated a hard-line interpretation of the Versailles treaty, emphasizing that Germany must meet all of its obligations in order to be accepted back into the family of nations. During the early 1920s the National Bloc insisted on prompt payment of reparations, both to punish the Germans and to respond to domestic economic and political pressure. Thanks to its policy of borrowing heavily to pay for the war, when peace finally came France was 26 billion francs in debt, largely to the United States. Large public indebtedness, abetted by the refusal of most French politicians to consider any significant tax increases, inflated prices and put more and more pressure on the stability of the franc. The National Bloc's answer to any reconsideration of economic policy was invariably the same: "Germany will pay."

As a result, after the German government had resisted paying reparations for years, Prime Minister Raymond Poincaré decided to take the offensive. In January 1923 French and Belgian forces invaded and occupied Germany's coal-rich Ruhr basin in order to force Berlin to honor its commitments. The Ruhr invasion was not quite the unmitigated disaster most historians have considered it to be. Even though the French withdrew within a year, it prompted an international commission led by US banker Charles Dawes to develop a new payment plan, and Germany started delivering reparations money in 1925.

The invasion revealed the weaknesses of French policy and of the Versailles settlement, however, and also had ominous consequences for the future. Not only did France's wartime allies oppose it, but so did most of the French left. The young PCF waged an energetic campaign against the invasion, even trying to persuade French soldiers in Germany to mutiny or desert. At least in the short term, the Ruhr invasion cost more than it yielded, and had to be supported by a sizable tax increase. Moreover, it had a profound impact on Germany, leading directly to the incredible hyperinflation of 1923 that so destabilized the Weimar Republic. In November Adolf Hitler and the

young Nazi party would stage the famous beer hall putsch, an attempted seizure of power in Munich that went nowhere but left a powerful legacy for the
future. In addition, the Ruhr invasion made it clear that France stood essentially alone when it came to enforcing the Versailles treaty, and its inability
to do so would have fateful consequences for its hopes of keeping the peace
during the interwar years.

In short, by invading the Ruhr France opted to emphasize financial stability over military security, and ultimately the invasion brought neither.
Instead, it further weakened the franc on international exchange markets.
By withdrawing from Germany and raising taxes, Poincaré stabilized the nation's currency, at least temporarily, but these moves neither addressed the
fundamental problem of high government deficits and low revenue nor reassured French citizens about the soundness of the economy. In 1924 the
National Bloc lost the legislative elections to an alliance of the center left,
the Cartel des Gauches, and Edouard Herriot replaced Poincaré as prime
minister. The Herriot government, dominated by radicals with the support
(but not participation) of the SFIO, negotiated the Dawes plan and, under
the dynamic leadership of foreign minister Aristide Briand, began a series
of initiatives designed to end Franco-German enmity and thus ensure the
peace. Briand managed to forge a working relationship with moderate prime
minister Gustave Stresemann of Germany, resulting in several important
treaties, such as the Locarno agreement of 1925, which promised to open a
new spirit of cooperation in European affairs.

The new government had less success, however, in restoring financial
stability. By 1926 the franc had sunk to less than 10 percent of its prewar
value, paving the way for Raymond Poincaré's return to power as the head
of a new conservative government. Poincaré, whose previous work in stabilizing the franc played a major role in restoring investor confidence, adopted
a program of spending cuts and tax increases. This action helped but was
not enough. In 1928 he took the previously unthinkable step of devaluing
the franc, setting it at roughly 20 percent of its prewar value. This was a
bitter pill for many to swallow, since it wiped out much of their savings, but
they could console themselves with the thought that they did not lose everything, unlike many middle-class investors and savers in Germany. The new
"Poincaré franc" did stabilize the economy, as well as making French exports
cheaper on international markets.

The resolution of France's monetary crisis also brought political stability.
The late 1920s brought an era of growth and prosperity, and while it lasted

the center left and the center right continued to alternate power, together dominating French politics. Raymond Poincaré served as prime minister until 1929, when he was replaced by Aristide Briand and then a succession of radical leaders. Flush from Poincaré's success in stabilizing the franc, the conservatives won control of the National Assembly in 1928, retaining it until the left came back into power in 1932. Governments might come and go in Paris, but as long as the good times held little actually changed in France.

Some of the most interesting developments in French politics between the wars occurred on the margins. Founded at the end of 1920, the French Communist Party (PCF) struggled to find its footing in the postwar decade. Although the overwhelming majority of the SFIO voted to join the new PCF in 1920, ensuring that the new party would take over the newspaper Jaurès founded, *Humanité*, during the next few years most dropped out, in many cases returning to the Socialist party. Many of these were expelled by the Soviets, who made clear their intention of creating a new leftist party along Leninist lines, emphasizing strict limits on internal party democracy and complete subservience to Moscow. This process of "bolshevization," as it was known at the time, came at great cost: by 1925 the PCF had lost most of its initial members and was smaller than the SFIO. At the same time, however, the reorganization of the communists created a more rigorously organized party with a strong working-class orientation. Unlike most political parties in France, the PCF was built for hard times (as its Soviet model, the Bolsheviks, had been). The years of depression and occupation would ultimately reveal the advantages of this new political structure.

If the far left in France developed in line with international communism, the far right also had important international affinities. The Action Française, which had emerged during the Dreyfus affair, continued to fulminate against democracy and the republic during the interwar years, although many conservative Catholics shied away after it was condemned by the Vatican in 1926. The Action Française also faced competition from new right-wing groups, often inspired by Italian fascism, who regarded it as insufficiently militant. Like fascism in Italy these fascist leagues, as they came to be called, stridently, often violently opposed the left, taking to the streets to beat up liberals and socialists. Conservative businessmen often created and bankrolled them as a hedge against the threat of bolshevism. In 1924 champagne magnate Pierre Taittinger founded the Patriotic Youth (*Jeunesses patriotes*), and a year later perfume manufacturer René Coty helped organize and fund the Faisceau. Coty also supported the Cross of

Fire (Croix-de-Feu), founded in 1927. The French fascist leagues trumpeted their hatred of socialists, liberals, Protestants, and Jews, staging noisy street demonstrations and at times physically attacking their political opponents. Yet their hatred of the republic attracted little support in France, at least as long as the prosperity of the 1920s lasted.

THE CRAZY YEARS: NEW DIMENSIONS
IN AVANT-GARDE AND POPULAR CULTURE

The controversy over the new woman noted above highlighted the confluence of fashion, politics, and culture in France between the wars. Modernism had played a key role in France since the *fin de siècle*, but the tremendous, dreadful impact of World War I gave it much greater influence in both elite and popular culture than ever before. The centrality of Paris to both war and peace helped the French capital maintain its global prominence in cultural modernism during the interwar years. At the same time, a brilliant array of foreign artists and intellectuals based in Paris made path-breaking contributions to the culture of modernity on a global scale. The interaction between French culture and global modernism underscored France's position as a universal nation after the armistice.

The interwar avant-garde continued and amplified the prewar attack on traditional rationalism. In 1916 a group of radical young intellectuals in Zurich, led by the Romanian poet Tristan Tzara, came together to launch a new aesthetic revolutionary movement. They christened it Dada, claiming sources for the word including the language of the west African Kru people and the name of Tzara's son's hobbyhorse. The Dada manifesto, which they published in 1918, was a revolutionary statement of intellectual nihilism:

> Dada; abolition of logic, dance of the impotents of creation . . . Dada; of all hierarchy and social equation set up for the values by our valets: Dada; every object, all the objects, the sentiments, and the obscurities, the phantoms and the precise clash of parallel lines, are means in our struggle: Dada; abolition of memory: Dada; abolition of archaeology: Dada; abolition of prophets: Dada; abolition of the future: Dada; absolute indisputable belief in every god that is the immediate product of spontaneity . . . Liberty: DADA DADA DADA, shriek of the shriveled colors, blending of the contraries and of all the contradictions, the grotesques, the inconsistencies: LIFE.[1]

In a world shattered by the insanity of war, Dada represented a frontal attack on the aesthetic and political attitudes that made the slaughter of millions possible.

A global intellectual movement, dadaism established important centers in many western cities, notably Berlin and New York. Paris became a major Dada hub in 1920, when Tzara and other activists moved there from Zurich. For the next few years Parisian dadaists staged art exhibits and plays to a mixed reaction. In 1924 a new group of young intellectuals, led by the writers André Breton, Philippe Soupault, and Louis Aragon, split off from Dada to form their own aesthetic movement, surrealism. The surrealist manifesto of that year emphasized both aesthetic and political revolution, heralding the importance of emotion over rationality and firmly identifying with the Soviet Union and the Communist party. Surrealism embraced artistic techniques like automatic writing, in hopes of bypassing the intellect to express directly one's soul, as well as new cultural media like jazz and cinema. Throughout the 1920s the surrealists railed against the status quo in all forms until the increasing cultural conservatism of the PCF forced a bitter split between political and aesthetic revolutionaries.

Paris remained the capital of French and global avant-garde culture, but the literary and artistic geography of the city had shifted by the 1920s. Whereas artists regarded Montmartre as increasingly passé, dominated by tourists and nightlife, Montparnasse emerged as the new center of bohemian culture. Artists and intellectuals had begun congregating there in the years before the war, renting cheap studio space in buildings like La Ruche and drinking and socializing together in the cafés of the Boulevard Montparnasse. By the 1920s the area had become the most cosmopolitan creative urban neighborhood in the world, home to artists like Pablo Picasso, Tsuguharu Foujita, Jean Cocteau, Diego Rivera, and Marcel Duchamp. More than any other part of the city, Montparnasse came to symbolize the dynamism of the *années folles*, the crazy years, in interwar Paris.

Many different creative spirits came together in Montparnasse between the wars, but none became more famous than the American writers of the Lost Generation. The French capital had an American presence dating back to the days of Thomas Jefferson, and Gertrude Stein, in many ways the spiritual godmother of American expatriates, had lived in the city since 1903. But the 1920s brought an influx of young American intellectuals, many having served in France during the war. F. Scott Fitzgerald, Ernest Hemingway, Ezra Pound, and Henry Miller, to name a few of the most prominent writers, settled into

Montparnasse and the Latin Quarter during the 1920s, frequenting cafés like the Coupole and the Closerie des Lilas. They came to Paris attracted by the city's beauty, fame, and towering intellectual and artistic achievements, as well as the strength of the dollar and the specter of Prohibition back home\ In 1919 Baltimore bookseller Sylvia Beach opened Shakespeare and Company, a bookstore that would serve as a community center for the American expatriate community. In 1922 she published one of the great modernist literary classics, James Joyce's *Ulysses*. Interwar Paris thus became a center of modern American literature, enabling young writers to develop a sense of what it meant to be American in the contemporary world.

Few ordinary French people spent time at the cafés and literary hangouts of Montparnasse, yet mass culture and entertainment between the wars also embraced the new. By the end of the war cinema had emerged as a major cultural force in France, and during the 1920s and 1930s French viewers flocked to movie houses throughout the country. Although the French cinema industry produced important films, like Abel Gance's epic *Napoleon* in 1927, most moviegoers preferred Hollywood productions, making actors like Charlie Chaplin leading stars in France. The most famous American in interwar France was Charles Lindbergh, whose groundbreaking flight from New York to Paris inspired millions in France and throughout the world. Throughout the interwar years, aviation was a major source of popular fascination with its narratives of technological achievement and individual daring. Another new technology, radio, also reshaped interwar French culture. The first radio broadcast in France took place from the top of the Eiffel Tower in 1921, and by the end of the decade the nation had several radio stations and half a million radio receivers. Listeners could also tune in to foreign stations from Britain, Germany, Italy, and Spain, for example, so that radio helped promote a transnational mass culture. At the same time it gave new opportunities to traditional art forms like the Paris music hall, making Maurice Chevalier, Mistinguett, and others national stars.

One cultural trend in interwar France that bridged the worlds of high and mass culture was exoticism and primitivism. Interest in nonwestern cultures, such as the vogue for African sculpture, had begun before 1914. But renewed pessimism about European civilization and the presence of millions of nonwhites on French soil had sharply increased fascination with the other. Both dadaists and surrealists championed so-called primitive art as being more in touch with human emotion than European painting and sculpture. In 1921 the Goncourt Prize, France's top literary honor, went to a novel by a black writer, René Maran's *Batouala*, which harshly criticized French imperialism. During the 1920s jazz also became extremely popular in France, taking dance halls and nightclubs by storm. The triumph of jazz coincided with a kind of dance mania that swept through France after the war. People danced in night-clubs, restaurants, and even city streets during public celebrations. Jazz symbolized a desire to enjoy life and embrace the new during the interwar years.

The popularity of jazz demonstrated how interest in primitivism and hypermodernity went together in interwar France, for the new music represented both the traditional beat of Africa and the machine-age modernism of the United States. This paradoxical combination helped explain the warm reception given to African American expatriates during the 1920s. To cater to desires for this new music a small community of African American jazz musicians took root in Paris, settling in Montmartre, which was more famous than ever for nightlife. For many, Paris represented a kind of paradise, full of easy money and free from the discrimination so prevalent back home. In 1925 a nineteen-year-old black American dancer, Josephine Baker, made her debut in Paris, prompting a level of controversy not seen since the performances of Diaghilev's Ballet Russe in 1912.

> She made her entry entirely nude except for a pink flamingo feather between her limbs; she was being carried upside down and doing the split on the shoulder of a black giant . . . The two specific elements had been established and were unforgettable—her magnificent dark body, a new model that to the French proved for the first time that black was beautiful, and the acute response of the white masculine public in the capital of hedonism of all Europe—Paris . . . She was the established new American star for Europe.[2]

In Baker's appearances on stage and screen, both in 1925 and after, fascination with America and with the colonies came together. Interwar French culture was shaped by both influences, and its responses to both underscored the universalism of the nation.

ONE HUNDRED MILLION FRENCHMEN: IMPERIAL FRANCE BETWEEN THE WARS

The popularity of exoticism arose in part out of heightened interest in the colonies during the interwar years. During the war hundreds of thousands of imperial subjects had journeyed to the metropole, and even though most had departed shortly after the armistice their memory remained. France had mobilized the empire during World War I as never before, and many believed its aid had been crucial to the nation's victory. In the years after the armistice France faced a vengeful and much larger Germany as well as declining support from its wartime allies. Consequently many French people looked to the colonies for military support and national security. Germany might have 70 million people, so the argument went, but 40 million in the metropole plus 60 million in the colonies added up to a nation of 100 million Frenchmen.

Between the wars France's colonies also loomed larger in the national economy, so that the ideal of empire as a source of wealth seemed to be coming true. Whereas in 1913 the empire was only France's third most important trading partner, by 1928 it was first. During the 1920s exports to the colonies grew faster than did those to foreign countries, accounting for one-sixth of all exports by the end of the decade. The nation's declining traditional industries, notably textiles, found ready markets in the colonies. At the same time some parts of the empire developed important agricultural export sectors. These were boom years for the rubber plantations of Indochina, fueled by the growing global popularity of the automobile. North Africa, particularly Algeria, witnessed the growth of its important wine industry; the prospect of a largely Muslim region specializing in alcohol production spoke volumes about the economic and cultural agenda of French colonialism.

Economic development became a priority for French colonial policy. In 1921 Albert Sarraut, colonial minister and former governor general of Indochina, submitted a bill to the National Assembly proposing an extensive program of public works in the colonies, including the development of railroads, port facilities, highways, and other improvements to promote economic activity and prosperity. Two years later Sarraut published his landmark study, *La mise en valeur des colonies françaises* (*The Economic Development of the Colonies*), which laid out his ideas for making the empire pay. Sarraut's plans proceeded in fits and starts, but over the course of the interwar years did succeed in creating an important economic infrastructure that helped make the colonies more prosperous, at least for France, and tie them more closely to the economy of the metropole.

This emphasis on economic development coincided with changing views of the colonies in general. Even before 1914 the doctrine of assimilation was losing ground. For a variety of reasons, including French failure to invest in education and the racial barriers central to colonial life, the prospect of turning large numbers of natives into Frenchmen seemed increasingly remote. Instead a new doctrine, association, achieved prominence. Association argued that different peoples had different cultures and not all could rise to the same levels of civilization. Instead, the duty of empire was to allow each people to pursue its own path. Economic modernization would help by providing greater prosperity. In some ways the doctrine of association served to validate traditional cultures in the French empire. At the same time, it argued that the natives would always remain inferior, largely based on race. The shift from assimilation to association was another face of the interwar crisis of French universalism.

This new view of empire played a key role in the increased prominence of colonial themes and images in France itself. Much more than before 1914, during the interwar years ordinary French men and women learned about France's position as a great imperial power. French advertising often featured colonial themes, notably the famous Banania milk flavoring ads featuring the grinning face of an African soldier. In her numerous stage and screen roles Josephine Baker almost always played a colonial subject instead of an African American, usually a young native woman hopelessly in love with a dashing French officer. In 1930 the government staged a major public celebration of the centennial of the Algerian conquest, and the next year an even more dramatic colonial world fair. The 1931 Colonial Exposition attracted 33 million visitors by recreating colonial architecture, including a full-scale model of Angkor Wat, in the bois de Vincennes on the edge of Paris. Visitors could marvel at real-live native communities, human zoos brought to France and put on display. Rather than portraying the colonies as France in the making, the exposition presented them as exotic and permanently different, in line with the associationist vision of empire. Imperial France might be a nation of 100 million Frenchmen, but clearly not all Frenchmen were equal.

For the colonized, the years between the wars brought new challenges and new opportunities. In the years immediately after the armistice many colonial administrators remarked on the new assertiveness of the indigenous population, especially those who had served in France. Like the African American soldiers who returned after the war demanding better treatment, many former soldiers and workers expected greater respect and rights such as citizenship. Yet this was rarely forthcoming; few of the *tirailleurs sénégalais* won French citizenship, for example. Instead, especially in sub-Saharan Africa, economic development produced a greater monetarization of the local economies, forcing subsistence farmers off the land. At the same time, especially in Africa, the emphasis on economic development often translated into forced labor for the indigenous population. Whereas many of those who worked in France during the war had done so implicitly under duress, now this became increasingly explicit, organized by colonial administrators and conservative local chieftains. This often took place under conditions of extreme brutality; for example, Governor General Raphael Antonetti of French Equatorial Africa built the Congo-Ocean railway during the mid-1920s at the cost of thousands of lives. The system of contract labor that powered the great rubber plantations and mines of Indochina was not much better, using consumer debt and ignorance of contractual rights to force Vietnamese peasants into more or less permanent servitude. An empire founded ostensibly with the goal of combating slavery now developed its own form of bondage.

Forced labor was not the only challenge confronting colonial subjects in France between the wars. Especially in North Africa many peasants were forced off the land, leading to the growth of colonial urbanization in a process similar to that experienced by Paris and other metropolitan cities in the early nineteenth century. Urban slums proliferated in cities like Algiers, Saigon, and Dakar as landless immigrants flocked there in search of a better life, or at least an alternative to traditional communities destroyed by colonial modernization. During these years a small French-educated elite began to develop in the colonies, at times reaching the status of *evolués*. Many looked to France as the homeland of civilization and modernity, while at the same time finding their own upward social mobility blocked by colonial racism.

The combination of an impoverished and destabilized peasantry, a growing poor urban population, and disaffected colonial elites produced new challenges to French imperial rule. Resistance, ranging from everyday acts and gestures of insubordination to mass political and armed uprisings, was a constant of life in imperial France. During the interwar years, however, anti-French activity shifted from attempts to restore the precolonial order to confrontations with the paradoxes of French universalism, demanding either full rights as citizens or autonomy, even independence from France. Much of the new anticolonial activity developed in close collaboration with labor unions and the Communist party, both in the empire and at home in France. The PCF strongly supported the Rif uprising in Morocco in 1925, as well as a major strike wave by Tunisian unions the same year. In 1926 Messali Hadj, an Algerian worker living in the Paris area, founded the North African Star (Etoile nord-africaine) to organize for Algerian independence. Anticolonialism was perhaps the most developed in Indochina, which saw

repeated strikes and agitation by both nationalist and Marxist
February 1930 a mutiny by Vietnamese soldiers at the Yen Bai garrison in
Tonkin sparked a series of uprisings that were brutally suppressed by the
colonial administration, leading to the founding of the Indochina Communist party. To a significant degree, the new anticolonialism of the interwar
years brought together both republican and communist universalism in a
challenge to the republican empire.

During the interwar years small communities of colonial migrants established themselves in the metropole. Algerians constituted the largest single
group of colonial subjects in France. Almost entirely men, they crossed the
Mediterranean to settle in Marseilles, Paris, and other urban and industrial
areas where they generally worked in the worst jobs at the lowest pay. Blacks
from Africa and the Caribbean also migrated to France; during the interwar
years the port area of Marseilles had a small community of black sailors and
longshoremen. Heavily working-class, colonial migrants in France often lived
on the margins of urban life, with Algerians in particular encountering racist attitudes and practices. At the same time, however, their living conditions
in France were an improvement over the colonies. They also brought a new
exoticism to French life, whether it be the Algerian cafés of Marseilles, the
Caribbean dance halls of Montparnasse, or the Vietnamese restaurants of the
Latin Quarter. Some found the metropole an opportunity to engage in anticolonial political activism. In 1931 colonial subjects in France joined with the
surrealists to demonstrate against the Colonial Exposition, claiming it ignored
imperialist oppression in greater France.

Small numbers of colonial students also came to France to pursue an education. In 1931 several black students in Paris, including Aimé Césaire of
Martinique, Léopold Senghor of Senegal, and Léon Damas of Guiana, began
discussions of literature, politics, and black culture that would blossom into
the literary movement *négritude*. Two sisters from Martinique, Paulette and
Jane Nardal, would host regular gatherings of black students and intellectuals at their salon in suburban Clamart, bringing them together with African
American intellectuals like Langston Hughes and Claude McKay who had pioneered the Harlem renaissance in New York. In 1931 the group launched the
journal *Revue du monde noir*, published in a bilingual French/English edition.
Negritude championed black culture and critiqued French colonial racism; its
philosophy embraced a universalist vision of blackness that was French and
global at the same time.

FRANCE AND THE WORLD DEPRESSION

The 1920s and 1930s often appear as opposites in the study of French and world history: the one representing prosperity, modernity, and inebriated gaiety, the other hard times, hard-edged politics, and a descent into the abyss. During the 1930s France saw itself challenged by both global depression and international fascism, so that its attempts to preserve republican democracy seemed more like a retreat into itself rather than an assertion of universalist values. Economic and political crises came together in an unprecedented threat to the universal nation.

Even more than the Long Depression of the late nineteenth century, the Great Depression of the 1930s confirmed the economic integration of the planet. More specifically, it underscored the shift of global economic and financial dominance from Britain to the United States. The collapse of New York's Wall Street stock market in 1929 triggered the worldwide crisis, but the fundamental causes of the Depression lay in the contraction of world trade and increased national debts after World War I. Unlike Britain, America had pursued protectionist policies, so its economic hegemony did little to promote the growth of the world economy. When New York's bankers began to call in their loans, they prompted bank failures throughout Europe and beyond. By 1932 much of the developed world's economy had simply fallen apart; in both the United States and Germany, for example, industrial output was cut in half and unemployment rates rose to 25 percent and above. In Britain unemployed workers staged hunger marches across the country, and everywhere despair and hopelessness seemed to replace the optimism of the late 1920s.

The Depression came late to France, in large part due to the country's relative insulation from global markets. The collapse of Wall Street had little impact because few French firms relied on foreign investment. Not until the end of 1931 did the nation begin to experience the crisis significantly. The economic downturn proved particularly long-lasting in France, however, especially because of the overvaluation of the franc. In 1928 Poincaré had sold his devaluation of the national currency to the French people as a onetime solution to the financial ills caused by the war; asking citizens to accept another financial sacrifice was simply unthinkable. Yet as prices dropped globally, the franc and consequently French exports became overvalued. In the spring of 1931 the British devalued the pound, abandoning the gold standard which had been the bedrock of the international economy for generations. The United States followed suit in 1933. France nonetheless clung to the sanctity of the Poincaré franc, hoping the nation could endure as an island of stability amid a troubled world.

It gradually became clear this was a delusion, as the economic crisis spread throughout the country. Those most advanced parts of the industrial economy, such as the Citroën auto factory in Paris, were the first to suffer, but soon factory closures and unemployment became endemic. Many urban workers dealt with the jobs crisis by returning home to the farm, but agriculture also suffered due to the inefficiency of small family farms and the overpricing of French foodstuffs on global markets. Employers initially reacted to the crisis by laying off immigrant workers, aided by a 1932 law that required hiring French workers first, and also by cutting back on female labor. Industrialists like Louis Renault also fired skilled workers in favor of cheaper unskilled employees. Even more harshly impacted by the crisis were independent small businessmen, farmers, and artisans, the classic "little men" of France and the heart and soul of the Third Republic. Small grocers and food sellers found their businesses increasingly threatened by chain stores like Monoprix and Prisunic. Bankruptcy rates soared among these groups, threatening not just them but the very fabric of republican France.

The economic crisis also had important implications for France's relations with its colonies. In an era of shrinking world trade, the Depression made the empire more central to the national economy than ever, since like Britain, France could restrict foreign commerce with its colonies. Colonial France thus became a kind of protected zone for French industries that could not compete effectively on the world market. By the end of the 1930s the empire accounted for nearly half the world market for French exports. The empire welcomed not only surplus goods but also surplus people. The 1930s saw a small but noticeable increase in the numbers of French men and women settling in the colonies. The lack of jobs at home helped motivate migration to the colonies, as well as improving health conditions. Colonial authorities sought to bring Frenchwomen to the colonies to recreate domestic and family life overseas and to stamp out interracial relations with native women. Cities like Dalat, in the highlands of Annam, developed into miniature versions of France in the tropics, complete with sumptuous villas and social activities including organized tiger hunts, for the French settler population. French women and men could enjoy the middle-class lifestyle increasingly unattainable at home by moving to the empire.

Government attempts to cope with the crisis generally proved ineffective if not actually counterproductive. In 1932 the radicals swept back into power on a wave of disenchantment with conservative failure to stabilize the economy. The government of Edouard Herriot refused to countenance devaluation, however, instead adopting a policy of deflation. This meant cutting state expenditures, especially the wages of state employees, further hurting the middle class and reducing the amount of consumer spending, making things worse. Several ministries rose and fell over the next two years, underscoring the systemic inability of the Third Republic to act forcefully during times of crisis. Increasingly, many in France began to doubt the viability of the political system and looked to alternatives.

Like World War I, the great Depression tested, stretched, and in some cases destroyed regimes throughout Europe. Democracy had already proved a fragile reed in the postwar successor states of eastern Europe, with Josef Pilsudski establishing a dictatorship over Poland in 1926. By the end of the 1930s Hungary, Romania, Bulgaria, and Yugoslavia had followed suit. But all this paled in comparison with the 1933 Nazi seizure of power in Germany. Few nations had been harder hit by the Depression, and for the Germans this was the second major economic crisis in less than a decade, following the hyperinflation of 1923. These combined disasters and the widespread resentment of the Versailles treaty contributed to the meteoric rise of the Nazi and Communist parties after 1929. Following years of parliamentary maneuvering in a vain search for a stable government, Adolf Hitler was appointed chancellor in January 1933. Within six months the Nazis successfully stamped out the communists and all other political opposition, turning Germany into an authoritarian fascist state. Combined with Mussolini's dictatorship in Italy and the collapse of democracy in eastern Europe, fascism seemed to many to be the wave of the future.

In such a world the republican universalism of France appeared increasingly ineffective and outmoded, especially because the Nazis turned around the German economy and the nation was booming again by 1935. Stalin's Soviet Union, whose closed economy and brutal industrialization had largely spared Russia from the Depression, provided another example of authoritarian economic efficiency. Compared to the successes of the two countries that had been outsiders at Versailles, the inability of the Third Republic to remedy the lingering economic crisis in France encouraged domestic opponents of the regime.

The Depression and the dynamism of fascism abroad gave a new boost to fascism at home during the early 1930s. Historians have debated whether far-right leagues like the Croix de Feu and the Camelots du Roi were fascist in a strict sense of the term. Most were stridently religious and some also embraced monarchism, unlike German Nazism or Italian fascism. Yet they also were violently anti-Marxist, militaristic, authoritarian, and often anti-Semitic. By 1934 they had grown significantly: the Croix de Feu had close to half a million members. Their paramilitary bands staged noisy and at times violent demonstrations in the Latin Quarter of Paris, attacking leftists and Jews. For most people in France the fascist leagues held little appeal, but the growth of authoritarianism abroad made it seem to be a threat to the Third Republic.

This was especially true for the French left, above all socialists and communists. The two parties had been bitterly divided since the split at the Congress of Tours in 1920. The smaller of the two at first, the SFIO had grown during the 1920s thanks both to the ex-communists fleeing the ultra-leftism of the PCF and to the rise of a talented new leadership. Léon Blum, a middle-class intellectual and protégé of Jean Jaurès, led the rebuilding of the Socialist party, retaining its theoretical commitment to socialist revolution but in practice turning it into a leftist variant of the Radical party. In 1932 the SFIO supported the radical Herriot government but refused to join it, criticizing its deflationist policies. Meanwhile, in the late 1920s, the PCF, on orders from Moscow, adopted the radical "class against class" doctrine, targeting the socialists as the main enemy of the working class, even calling them "social fascists." This was especially disastrous in Germany, where a divided left played a key role in enabling Hitler's rise to power. The Nazi regime's destruction of German communism forced Stalin to reappraise this policy, searching for new ways to counteract the growing fascist menace.

Matters came to a head in France during the winter of 1934. In January Serge Stavisky, a swindler of Russian Jewish origin, used connections with radical politicians to sell a series of fake municipal bonds. Shortly after the scandal erupted, Stavisky was found dead under mysterious circumstances. The right-wing press quickly claimed that Stavisky had been murdered by radicals to keep him from revealing the depth of corruption in the party, and that the Stavisky affair demonstrated both the corrosive power of Jews in France and the decadence of the republican regime. The fascist leagues and others, including some communists, staged a protest demonstration on February 6 in the Place de la Concorde, across the Seine from the National Assembly. Thousands showed up, and violent confrontations with the police erupted, especially as demonstrators were seen trying to cross the bridge to storm the National Assembly. The police opened fire, killing fourteen and wounding over a thousand. The next day the government of Eduard Daladier resigned.

,ct that fascist violence had overthrown a republican government the French people, confirming for many their fears that international las... on the march could succeed even in Paris. Less than a week later civil war would break out in Austria, with the authoritarian government suppressing the socialists by using cannons to shell the Viennese housing projects that formed the party's stronghold. On February 12 the PCF and SFIO announced a general strike and separate demonstrations against the fascist menace. Often in spite of their leaders' wishes, socialist and communist workers marched together that day in defiance of the far right, the first time since the war that the left had exhibited such unity. In Paris, answering the call of the SFIO, which the PCF decided to support at the last minute, nearly 100,000 people packed into the Place de la Nation.

The great demonstrations of February 12, 1934, were the real beginning of the Popular, or People's, Front. The idea of a broad left-wing political coalition against fascism soon became a global phenomenon, and the French deserve some credit for inventing it. The February riots helped convince Stalin that France, like Germany, could fall to fascism unless the parties of the left found a way of working together. By the summer the Third International had proclaimed the new strategy, and soon communists all over the world were rebranding themselves as willing partners with socialist and other progressive parties. In France the PCF leader, Maurice Thorez, began making overtures to Leon Blum and the SFIO for an electoral alliance. Socialist leaders had their doubts, but most workers pressed for unity, convinced that the division of the left not only contributed to the fascist threat but also had empowered employers at their expense during the Depression years. Accordingly, on July 27, 1934, the two parties signed an agreement to work together. On Bastille Day 1935 throngs of socialists, communists, and others came together to celebrate the national holiday and clamor for change. Thorez then began courting the leaders of the Radical party, downplaying the PCF's revolutionary verbiage and for the first time embracing French patriotism. This was a major departure for the communists, and the radicals required a good deal of persuading, but by October they too were ready to join the Popular Front coalition.

In January 1936 the three parties came together to hammer out an official program for the new coalition, emphasizing moderate goals such as higher wages, a shorter work week, programs of public works to stimulate the economy, and protection of trade union rights. This was not a revolutionary or socialist agenda: it did not advocate nationalizing industry or even devaluing the franc. Instead, it belonged to global programs of reform capitalism that emerged in the 1930s to combat the impact of the Depression. Like Roosevelt's New Deal in the United States, or the reforms undertaken by the Social Democrats in Sweden, the French Popular Front proposed a Keynesian solution to the Depression, improving working-class living standards and purchasing power to increase production and lift France out of the economic crisis. The moderation of the Popular Front did nothing to mollify the right, which viewed it as a thinly disguised revolutionary program dictated by Moscow. In February members of the Camelots du Roi, the paramilitary organization of the Action Française, physically attacked Léon Blum in the streets of Paris, forcing him and his companions to flee for their lives. The idea of a Jewish socialist leading France horrified conservatives, some of whom responded by muttering "better Hitler than Blum." The anti-Semitism of the French right became more pronounced as the electoral campaign began in the spring of 1936.

The Popular Front nonetheless sparked the imagination of many French men and women, who saw in it an antidote to politics as usual and a potential solution to problems, both foreign and domestic. Thousands of people came out across the country to campaign for the coalition. The elections in May resulted in a triumph for the Popular Front and the united left. For the first time in history, the socialists emerged as the largest political party in France, outpolling the radicals. The communists scored the most impressive gains of all, going from ten seats to seventy-two in the National Assembly. When the balloting was finished, the Popular Front controlled nearly two-thirds of the seats in the assembly, and in defiance of the fascist wave so powerful in Europe had elected the nation's first socialist and first Jewish prime minister. Scenes of jubilation broke out across the country, with large crowds acclaiming the victory and shouting *Au boulot!* (Let's get to work!)

It was a personal triumph for Léon Blum, who had rebuilt the SFIO from near extinction in 1920 to the most powerful party in France. Nevertheless, he was no revolutionary; he understood the difference between winning an election and seizing power. This distinction was lost on many of his followers, however, who considered the victory of the socialist- and communist-led coalition as nothing less than the revolution come true. Within a week after the electoral victory a massive strike wave swept across France. Many job actions took the form of sit-down strikes, as workers staged symbolic occupations of their factories. They were almost entirely spontaneous, most union leaders only finding out about them after the fact. The communists vainly tried to persuade workers to return to work, Thorez declaring "one must know how to end a strike." Workers turned the occupied factories into spaces for debate, solidarity, and song, nonstop celebrations of the people's victory. The sit-down strikes graphically demonstrated the power of the Popular Front, and served as a warning to capitalists that the French people would defend it.

Prime Minister Blum certainly did not want revolution and feared the situation would get out of hand. He realized he had to take dramatic action to end the strike wave, so he convened representatives of capital and labor to negotiate a series of far-reaching reforms. These included the forty-hour workweek, sizable pay increases, affirmation of union bargaining rights, and, a first in France, two weeks of paid vacation for all workers. Conservatives in the National Assembly, cowed by what they saw as the prospect of imminent revolution, quickly passed these concessions, known as the Matignon Accords, into law. During the summer of 1936 the Popular Front passed other landmark legislation, including public control of the Bank of France and the aircraft industry, and the abolition of the fascist leagues. Few governments in the history of modern France got off to such a dynamic start.

The Popular Front government emphasized not just solving the nation's economic problems but also creating a new people's culture. For example, it was not enough to give workers more free time by passing the forty-hour workweek; the government also should show them how to benefit from that time. Accordingly, Blum created a new Ministry of Leisure, headed by Léo Lagrange. The very idea of a ministry of leisure prompted great scorn and derision from the right (many referred to it as the ministry of laziness), but Lagrange used his office to support amateur sports programs, youth hostels, and discount rail tickets to resort areas. The minister of education, Jean Zay, increased funding for educational and cultural programs, notably in film and radio. Other government cultural initiatives included the creation of the National Center for Scientific Research (CNRS) and the Cannes film festival. Such programs had a tremendous impact in France, ranking among the most popular and enduring achievements of the Popular Front. During the summer of 1936, for the first time, working people flocked to the country's beaches and mountain resorts in massive numbers, creating the tradition of the annual August holiday in France and democratizing the idea of vacation. The Popular Front represented the people as a whole laying claim to all the riches of France; as the title of the 1936 communist documentary directed by Jean Renoir put it, *Life Belongs to Us*.

The Popular Front also represented a wind of change in the colonies. The socialists had long been ambivalent about colonialism; once in power they focused on reforming its abuses rather than challenging the system as a whole. Blum's government took steps to end or at least reduce the use of forced labor in the empire, and also increased rights for colonial labor unions. The Popular Front amnestied many of the victims of colonial repressions, notably the Vietnamese imprisoned during the Yen Bai uprising. In addition, Blum endorsed a plan by socialist leader Maurice Violette, which would have expanded citizenship in Algeria to a small percentage of the indigenous population. The Popular Front did not achieve much in reforming colonial life, as local officials and the French settler population strenuously resisted many of its initiatives. As in the metropole, however, it did for a brief period foster hope in the possibility of a better day for imperial France.

If the Popular Front represented hope for the working class and *petit peuple* of France, it was anathema to the nation's elites. Once the sit-down strikes ended and the right recovered from its fears of insurrection, it began to pour invective on a regime it regarded as little better than bolshevism. Léon Blum became one of the most bitterly hated men in France, the target of insults generously laced with anti-Semitic invective. Like Franklin D. Roosevelt in the United States, so hated by American conservatives that they refused to mention his name, referring to him instead as "that man in the White House," Blum became the personal symbol of everything the French right hated about the modern era. The Popular Front brought not only working-class empowerment but also an unprecedented level of class conflict and antagonism. The hostility between right and left in France was so great that the nation sometimes seemed to be on the verge on civil war.

The regime's greatest weakness, however, was the failure of its economic program. The Popular Front hoped that a shorter work week would help reduce unemployment, and more jobs would pump more money into the economy. Fears of nationalization and the left triggered major capital flights from the country, not only weakening the franc but also cutting government revenue at a time of increasing government expenditures. Although wages went up, thanks in part to the forty-hour week, productivity did not, translating into rising prices that reduced real wages. This triggered further strike actions, which tended to alienate small shopkeepers and their radical representatives. Moreover, the franc remained overvalued. When the government finally went back on its promises and devalued the franc in October 1936, it was a classic case of too little too late. In addition, it alienated many of the regime's middle-class supporters. Unlike Nazi Germany or the Soviet Union, France under the Popular Front lacked the authoritarian structure to turn the economy around, nor did it pursue public investment to the same degree as the Scandinavian countries.

While the Popular Front's weak economic performance hurt the government's popularity, the Spanish Civil War threatened to tear the coalition apart. The popular front was a global crusade for social justice and against fascism, and global solidarity was a key tenet of the movement. One of the poorest and most divided countries in Europe, with a powerful monarchist right and a large anarchist labor movement, Spain had become a republic in 1931 and in February 1936 elected its own Popular Front government. This proved too much for the military, which in July under Gen. Francisco Franco attempted to seize power. The resulting conflict pitted the Spanish right and left against each other and became an international battleground for fascism and antifascism. The Spanish Civil War became the great antifascist cause of the age, as young men from throughout Europe and America flocked to join the International Brigades, military units organized by the Comintern, to fight fascism in Spain. On the other side, in spite of international nonintervention treaties, both Germany and Italy channeled military aid and "volunteers" to aid Franco's forces.

No country was more affected by the conflict than France. The cause of republican Spain was extremely popular among the French left: nine thousand Frenchmen fought in the International Brigades, more than from any other country, and communities along the Spanish border helped smuggle arms and soldiers over the Pyrenees to the republic. In spite of his personal sympathies with the fellow Popular Front government, Léon Blum ultimately chose not to intervene or furnish aid to loyalist Spain, for reasons of both foreign and domestic policy. Many in France feared intervention might lead to war with Italy, Germany, or both, and were not willing to take the risk. The British made it clear that they would not support such a policy, that France would be on its own. Moreover, the increasingly revolutionary nature of the Spanish republic alienated many French radicals, and even some moderate and pacifist socialists, and there was no consensus within the coalition for intervention. For those on the left, however, the Blum government's decision not to intervene in Spain seemed a crass betrayal of the ideals of antifascism and the Popular Front.

By the spring of 1937 the coalition had lost much of its support, and the idealistic days of the previous spring were only a memory. In March Paris police clashed with communist demonstrators, killing five and wounding hundreds, an incident that highlighted divisions in the Popular Front. In June

Blum's government fell after the Senate denied its request
powers to manage the economy. A new Popular Front governm
ical leader Camille Chautemps took power, but sponsored no
and proved incapable of recapturing the excitement of 1936. In March 1938
Blum returned to power, but three months later was again forced to resign,
and the Popular Front coalition disbanded. The new centrist regime of radical Edouard Daladier came to power determined to improve the economy by
reining in striking workers and reassuring business leaders. Finance minister Paul Reynaud pushed through a series of measures providing incentives
for investors and weakening the forty-hour work week. This outraged labor,
prompting the CGT to declare a one-day general strike on November 30.
The strike was a complete failure, largely because few workers supported
it, and in its aftermath French unions lost many of the members they had
gained in 1935 and 1936. The power of labor was broken, and the Popular
Front was dead.

Many commentators at the time, and many historians ever since, have
branded the Popular Front a failure. It did not lift France out of the Depression, and its foreign policies proved largely ineffective. Some, notably Marc
Bloch in his classic *Strange Defeat*, have suggested the bitter atmosphere of
class recrimination during the Front contributed to the nation's collapse in
1940. At its best, however, the Popular Front created a new vision of France,
one whose riches belonged to all. Many of the cultural institutions it created
would survive the war and go on to shape French life in the late twentieth
century. Above all, it made working people part of the nation to an unprecedented degree, providing a new perspective on French universalism.

FOREIGN AFFAIRS AND THE END OF THE PEACE

Had France been able to negotiate its economic and social problems in calm
isolation, the 1930s might have turned out differently. But every French regime had to cope with the increasingly ominous international climate, above
all the rising threat presented by Nazi Germany after 1933. With Britain and
America taking little interest in Continental affairs during the interwar years,
France had been left largely on its own to support the Versailles treaty and
the diplomatic status quo. During the prosperous years of the 1920s it had
been able to partner with Weimar Germany to keep the peace. Depression
and the rise of international fascism left France more isolated, however, especially as Hitler skillfully exploited the contradictions of Versailles and the

divisions between the victors of World War I. In the end the vision of a universal peace created in 1919 had shrunk to one maintained by France alone, a task the nation of the 1930s could no longer sustain.

The international tensions of the interwar years, especially the 1930s, brought a growing number of refugees to France. The nation had a long tradition of hosting foreign exiles, frequently seen as symbolizing its commitment to universal freedom and justice. The years after the armistice brought them in unprecedented numbers, however. Many White Russians, refugees from the Bolshevik Revolution, had settled in France during the 1920s, opening nightclubs in Montmartre and working as taxicab drivers. After 1922 they had been joined by antifascist exiles from Italy, often finding work in the construction industries of Paris and other major cities. The Nazi seizure of power unleashed a new flood of refugees into France, including tens of thousands of German Jews and left-wing intellectuals. A colony of leading German writers, including Thomas Mann, Bertolt Brecht, and Lion Feuchtwanger, settled in the small Provençal port of Sanary-sur-Mer. Especially in Paris, refugees seemed to be everywhere, haunting the cheap cafés, looking for whatever work they could find, hoping for a better day. In his novel *Arch of Triumph* Erich Maria Remarque described living illegally in a Paris hotel full of refugees whose owner thoughtfully provided a rotating display of paintings depending on the political orientations of her guests. The growing numbers of refugees in France, at a time when work was scarce and life difficult, prompted some sympathy but more often resentment from the country's citizens. The crisis of Jewish refugees helped spur the renaissance of anti-Semitism among the far right and the fascist leagues in France. The universal nation had become a universal refuge, with all the conflicts and tragedies of the 1930s reflected in the streets of Paris.

When Hitler came to power, proclaiming his intention to rearm Germany and challenge Versailles, French men and women across the political spectrum opposed the new regime and supported diplomatic measures against it. France initially turned to its allies in the east, hoping to strengthen them and confront Germany with the potential of a two-front war. This policy, led by foreign minister Louis Barthou, collapsed in October 1934 when Barthou and King Alexander I of Yugoslavia were assassinated in Marseilles during the latter's state visit to France. The French government also joined Britain in signing a pact with Italy, but public outrage over Mussolini's invasion of Abyssinia in 1935 forced its abandonment, eventually pushing the Italians into the arms of Nazi Germany. France had greater success in courting another potential ally, the Soviet Union. Even more than in the late nineteenth century, allying with Russia posed major ideological challenges, but the need for support against Germany combined with Stalin's new openness to the west led to the signing of a formal pact between the two countries in February 1936. This brought the French a major new ally, but at the price of undercutting their agreements with eastern nations like Poland and Czechoslovakia.

A month later Hitler defied Versailles by marching German troops into the Rhineland. This was probably Nazi Germany's greatest gamble; although it had begun to rearm in earnest, it still had a smaller army than France and could not have resisted concerted action by the western powers. But the French government chose, fatefully, not to force the issue. The nation was in the midst of a tumultuous electoral campaign and more concerned with economic problems; mobilizing the French army would have cost millions of francs a day. Moreover, the British showed no intention of challenging Hitler's action, since as many pointed out it simply involved Germany invading its own territory. Few people in either Britain or France wanted to risk a major war over what seemed essentially an internal German question.

So the French did not act, with significant consequences to come. Germany's remilitarization of the Rhineland made a French invasion more difficult and limited France's ability to aid its eastern allies in time of war. More generally, it showed Hitler that he could challenge the Versailles system and win, emboldening him to take other steps to advance German interests at French expense. In addition, the incident showed that France would not take diplomatic or military action without the support of Britain. The failure of the Ruhr invasion in 1923 had shown the dangers of unilateral action. Henceforth the French would follow London's lead in dealing with German expansionism.

In 1937 Neville Chamberlain became prime minister of Britain and adopted a policy of trying to meet German demands in order to avoid war. Historians have debated the pros and cons of appeasement, some arguing it was a naive and hopeless attempt to prevent war, others pointing out that in the context of the times it was a rational if ultimately failed strategy. For France, the history of European diplomacy since Versailles showed the nation could not stand on its own against Germany. More significantly, the large majority of people in France, as in Britain, were terrified at the prospect of a new world war, believing that resisting Hitler was not worth the devastation it would bring. In a series of essays in the late 1930s the philosopher Simone Weil argued strenuously for pacifism, contending that the use of military force would only increase oppression both abroad and at home. Whether or not a firmer stance against Hitler could have prevented the war remains one of history's great unanswered, and unanswerable, questions. For a nation so recently traumatized by war, it made sense for its leaders to consider all possible alternatives to a return to the battlefield.

This did not mean that the French chose to do nothing. In 1930 France had begun building the Maginot Line, a massive series of fortifications designed to prevent a future invasion from Germany. A classic example of military planners' tendency to fight the last war, the Maginot Line was in effect an elaborate fortified trench stretching along the German border from Switzerland to Luxembourg. It underscored France's defensive approach to possible war with Germany. Shortly after assuming power in 1936, the Popular Front government began a program of rearmament to prepare for a potential new war. It focused on military aviation, nationalizing the aircraft industry as a priority for national defense. The forty-hour workweek and labor strife slowed production significantly, but by 1938 France was beginning to develop a modern air force.

Nonetheless, French rearmament failed to equal that of Germany, which by the late 1930s was devoting over half of all state expenditures to building a modern military machine. By the end of 1938 German forces were at least as strong as those of France and in some cases, notably modern aircraft, vastly superior. This new balance of power, plus the clear unwillingness of London and Paris to risk war, emboldened Hitler to take further aggressive measures in 1938. In March German forces marched into Austria, annexing that country in violation of the Versailles treaty, which had explicitly banned the Anschluss. Both France and Britain protested, but since most Austrians seemed to welcome the Germans as liberators rather than conquerors, acquiesced to the annexation.

Next Hitler moved against Czechoslovakia, the most stable and prosperous democratic state in eastern Europe and a key French ally. The Sudetenland was a Czech region bordering Germany with a large concentration of German speakers (as well as major fortifications and munitions factories). As Berlin launched a campaign vilifying the Czech government and demanding "justice" for the Sudeten Germans, Neville Chamberlain suggested Britain was willing to compromise while at the same time making it clear that in case of war his nation would not intervene to help the French. Given this, France decided to follow London's lead and acquiesce to Hitler. In September the British, French, and Germans met in Munich to resolve the issue; neither the Soviets nor the Czechs were invited to the conference. The meeting agreed to

Hitler's demands, and Munich has since gone down in history as the classic example of appeasement, of the betrayal of a people in the face of fascist aggression. Yet for most people in France, the conference was a success because it avoided, or at least delayed, the outbreak of a new European war.

Such hopes would be dashed in 1939. In early March what remained of Czechoslovakia collapsed as Slovakia declared independence and Germany occupied Bohemia, in blatant violation of the Munich agreements. Two weeks later Franco's forces triumphed in Spain, crushing the Spanish republic and sending 500,000 loyalists across the Pyrenees to refugee camps in France. The continued expansion of fascism had by early 1939 convinced the majority of French people that appeasement was no longer a viable option, that Hitler would only respect force. The nation thus further increased its commitment to rearmament, trying to make up for lost time. In the summer of 1939 France lavishly celebrated the sesquicentennial of the French Revolution. A million and a half spectators crowded onto the Grands Boulevards of Paris to watch an ostentatious military display proclaiming the might of French arms and French ideals. At the same time France once again allied with Britain, in this case a Britain that had sacked Neville Chamberlain and rejected appeasement, to offer guarantees to Hitler's probable next victim, Poland. At the end of March the western allies pledged to go to war if necessary to safeguard Polish independence.

The final act in the drama leading up to the outbreak of war occurred in late August. Although France and the USSR had been formal allies since 1936, they had never coordinated military strategies. The failure of the western powers to stop Hitler at Munich, while excluding Russia from the negotiations, had revived Stalin's fears about Britain and France using Nazi Germany to attack the Soviet Union. He therefore began his own secret negotiations with Berlin. On August 23, 1939, Hitler announced the signing of the Molotov-Ribbentrop Pact, a nonaggression agreement between Germany and the USSR. The news broke like a thunderclap in France, not least among the French communists who received no advance warning and still adhered to the popular front strategy of broad-based antifascism. For the French people in general, the Nazi-Soviet pact meant nothing could stop Hitler in the east, and that consequently war was imminent.

On September 1, 1939, Nazi Germany invaded Poland. The next day the National Assembly voted unanimously to award war credits to the government of Prime Minister Edouard Daladier. It also issued an ultimatum to Germany to withdraw immediately from Poland. When Germany failed to do so, on September 3 both Britain and France declared war. World War II had begun.

France between the wars was both troubled and dynamic, and much of its dynamism came from its interactions with the broader world. Few periods of the nation's modern history have been more transnational, from the tremendous increase of the immigrant population during the 1920s to the sparkling verve of Paris as the center of the world's avant-garde. The empire was larger and played a more central role in French life than ever before. At the same time, the fate of France seemed tied more than ever to decisions made elsewhere, from the diplomatic suites of London and Berlin to the bankers' palaces of New York. In 1919 Clemenceau and other French leaders had understood that France could not ensure a vision of world peace on its own, but the tragedy of Versailles was that they could not conceive of a universalism that would both protect the nation's interests and prove attractive to other people. Instead, the French would have to contend with alternate universal visions whose view of France ranged from indifferent to deeply hostile.

During the Munich crisis of September 1938 two soldiers, one French and one German, faced off against each other on opposite sides of the Rhine River. The German soldier erected a sign bearing the words *Ein Reich, Ein Volk, Ein Führer*. Observing this, the French soldier responded by putting up his own sign, featuring the words *Liberté, Égalité, Fraternité*.[3] The universal nation had met its ultimate opponent, and the struggle between the two would soon begin.

Suggestions for Further Reading

Berstein, Serge. *La France des années trentes*. Paris: Armand Colin, 1988.

Camiscioli, Elisa. *Reproducing the French Race: Immigration, Intimacy, and Embodiment in the Early Twentieth Century*. Durham, NC: Duke University Press, 2009.

Chafer, Tony, and Amanda Sackur, eds. *French Colonial Empire and the Popular Front: Hope and Disillusionment*. Houndmills, UK: Palgrave, 1999.

Cross, Gary. *Immigrant Workers in Industrial France: The Making of a New Working Class*. Philadelphia: Temple University Press, 1983.

Duiker, William J. *Ho Chi Minh: A Life*. New York: Hyperion, 2001.

Flanner, Janet. *Paris Was Yesterday*. New York: Vintage, 1972.

Frader, Laura Levine. *Breadwinners and Citizens: Gender in the Making of the French Social Model.* Durham, NC: Duke University Press, 2008.

Hyman, Paul. *From Dreyfus to Vichy: The Remaking of French Jewry, 1906–1939.* New York: Columbia University Press, 1979.

Jennings, Eric. *Imperial Heights: Dalat and the Making and Undoing of French Indochina.* Berkeley: University of California Press, 2011.

Johnson, Douglas, and Madeleine Johnson. *The Age of Illusion: Art and Politics in France, 1918–1940.* New York: Rizzoli, 1987.

Lebovics, Herman. *True France: The Wars over Cultural Identity, 1900–1945.* Ithaca, NY: Cornell University Press, 1992.

Lewis, Mary. *The Boundaries of the Republic: Migrant Rights and the Limits of Universalism in France, 1918–1940.* Stanford, CA: Stanford University Press, 2007.

Martin, Benjamin F. *France and the Après Guerre, 1918–1924: Illusions and Disillusionment.* Baton Rouge: Louisiana State University Press, 1999.

Maza, Sarah. *Violette Nozière: A Story of Murder in 1930s Paris.* Berkeley: University of California Press, 2011.

Neulander, Joelle. *Programming National Identity: The Culture of Radio in 1930s France.* Baton Rouge: Louisiana State University Press, 2009.

Nguyen Tut Tranh Gaspard. *Ho Chi Minh à Paris, 1917–1923.* Paris: Harmattan, 1992.

Rearick, Charles. *The French in Love and War.* New Haven, CT: Yale University Press, 1997.

Reynolds, Sian. *France Between the Wars: Gender and Politics.* New York: Routledge, 1996.

Roberts, Mary Louise. *Civilization Without Sexes: Reconstructing Gender in Postwar France, 1917–1927.* Chicago: University of Chicago Press, 1994.

Rosenberg, Clifford. *Policing Paris: The Origins of Modern Immigration Control Between the Wars.* Ithaca, NY: Cornell University Press, 2006.

Stovall, Tyler. *Paris and the Spirit of 1919: Consumer Struggles, Transnationalism, and Revolution.* Cambridge: Cambridge University Press, 2012.

Thomas, Martin. *The French Empire Between the Wars: Imperialism, Politics, and Society.* Manchester, UK: Manchester University Press, 2005.

Vigna, Xavier. *Histoire des ouvriers en France au XXème siècle.* Paris: Perrin, 2012.

Wilder, Gary. *The French Imperial Nation-State: Negritude and Colonial Humanism Between the Two World Wars.* Chicago: University of Chicago Press, 2005.

Notes

1. Eugene Weber, *Movements, Currents, Trends: Aspects of European Thought in the Nineteenth and Twentieth Centuries* (Lexington, MA: Heath, 1992).

2. Janet Flanner, *Paris Was Yesterday, 1925–1939* (New York: Viking, 1972), xx–xxi.

3. Denis Brogan, *The Development of Modern France, 1870–1939* (Gloucester, MA: Peter Smith, 1970), 2:729.

nine

France in World War II: Defeat and Rebirth of the Universal Nation

With the possible exception of the Revolution itself, no other event in the history of modern France has caused as much controversy as the German occupation and the Vichy collaborationist regime of the 1940s. Ever since the 1970s, and especially the 1980s, French historians and social commentators have written obsessively about France's experience in World War II, all the while paradoxically decrying the national "silence" about the period. Its defeat by Germany in 1940, followed by an occupation unprecedented in the modern history of France, constituted not just a military disaster but a national catharsis. For the French, the question became not so much could they claim to be a universal nation, but rather did their nation exist at all.

Much of the debate about occupied France, and particularly about the Vichy regime, has focused on the nature of collaboration. A tradition stretching back to the liberation argued that Vichy was essentially imposed by the Germans. But since the 1970s a group of historians led by Robert Paxton have contended the regime was homegrown, the product of French far-right ideology stretching back to the Dreyfus affair, if not the Revolution. Far from a nation of resisters, France was increasingly viewed as a nation of collaborators.

9.1. German soldiers marching up the Champs-Elysées.
Source: Bundesarchiv, Bild 146–1978–052–03.

More recently, social historians have challenged this viewpoint, noting that while most people in France did not join resistance organizations, they did not support Vichy and strongly opposed the occupation.

Ironically, historians have generally considered occupied France from the perspective of national history and identity, even though it occurred as part of one of the modern world's great global experiences, World War II. Taking a transnational approach on this subject permits us to view it with new insight. The central question of collaboration versus resistance looks different if we explore how to tease out the interrelationship between national and international history—between foreign occupation and national politics. What if the answer to the question of whether Vichy was foreign or indigenous is neither one nor the other, but both? In a similar vein, does the fact that so many members of the French resistance were foreigners suggest that the resistance served as an incubator of a new, transnational vision of France? France during the occupation had important ties to other eras in French history, as well as other places and struggles in a world at war.

France during the 1940s may have been the site of what historian Henry Rousso has termed a "Franco-French civil war," but if so the bounds of this war extended far beyond the nation's borders. The history of Vichy and the German occupation illustrates the collapse of the universal nation as well as its reconfiguration and rebirth. During these years, more perhaps than at any other time in the history of modern France, the struggle for the universal values of the French Revolution and the battle for sheer national survival became inseparable.

PHONY WAR AND COLLAPSE

In September 1939 France experienced none of the celebration and excitement that gripped Paris and other cities in August 1914. Both the dreadful legacy of the Great War and the fearsome threat posed by a powerful and vengeful national enemy left little room for optimism. Instead, the French entered World War II in a spirit of resigned determination. The oft-repeated phrase *il faut en finir*, we must make an end of it, summed up the national mood as the French people geared up for the new test of arms.

Preparing for war involved domestic as well as military mobilization. The government of Edouard Daladier reacted to the Nazi-Soviet pact by concluding that communism was the enemy of the nation. In fact, however, the PCF had no advance knowledge of the pact and did not endorse it before October. By the end of September, the government dissolved the PCF and began suspending communist municipalities and arresting party activists throughout France. These included many foreign antifascists, refugees from Germany, Italy, and elsewhere throughout Europe, who were rounded up and interned in camps alongside republican exiles from Spain. The Soviet Union's invasion of Poland in late September, followed by its attack on Finland at the end of November, unleashed a new wave of anticommunism in France during the winter of 1940. In sharp contrast to the *union sacrée* of 1914, the nation entered the new war divided, unable to resolve the conflicts that had haunted it during the Popular Front.

The other major contrast with 1914 was the initial absence of war on French territory. Instead of invading France, Hitler launched the devastating attack on Poland Germans called *Blitzkrieg*, lightning war. The heart of the blitzkrieg strategy was the use of tanks and aircraft to destroy enemy resistance rapidly, relegating the masses of infantry to a support role. British and French plans to aid Poland, to the extent that there were plans, envisaged mobilizing to attack Germany in the west as a way of relieving pressure on the Poles. Yet the speed and force of the German assault on Poland caught

Paris and London unawares. Polish resistance crumbled within a few weeks, so that by the time France and Britain could have mobilized to take significant action there was no longer a Poland to defend. Therefore, rather than engage in a pointless exercise, France chose to take a defensive posture, waiting to see what Hitler's next moves would be. Blitzkrieg in the east was matched by *Sitzkrieg*, a war without action or movement, in the west.

For the French people, the nine months of the phony war were filled with nervous anticipation, stress, and boredom. Soldiers complained about the lack of action and about workers recalled from the front lines to serve in the war factories. Having lost the opportunity to aid Poland, the government fell back on its primary strategy of waiting for the Germans to attack. This defensive posture emphasized the solidity of the Maginot line, stretching between the Swiss and Belgian borders. However, as critics noted at the time, the strategy had a few key weaknesses. France had not fortified the border with Belgium, not desiring to antagonize an ally. To compensate for this, the army stationed its strongest forces along this border, believing the Germans would attack there. It only lightly guarded the area just north of the Maginot line, including Luxembourg and southern Belgium, believing tanks could not easily negotiate the hills and woodlands of the Ardennes forest. The French military's greatest weakness, however, was its reliance on an outmoded strategy that emphasized infantry and relegated tanks and airplanes to support roles. Only a few voices spoke up for a more integrated military strategy, notably Charles de Gaulle, a tank commander who in 1940 would become France's youngest general. For the most part, however, the French army continued to rely on its traditional defensive posture, ignoring the lessons of blitzkrieg and rendering only token assistance when Germany overran Denmark and Norway in April.

The long-awaited invasion finally happened in May, and it was devastating. On May 10 Hitler's armies advanced into the Low Countries, quickly overwhelming their defenses. The Netherlands collapsed in four days, after a massive Luftwaffe bombing raid tore out the heart of Rotterdam. Belgium lasted a few days longer, but its resistance effectively ceased when German paratroopers seized the great forts that constituted the heart of its defensive strategy. While French forces moved into the Low Countries to counter the invasion, unexpectedly the main German attack occurred farther south, through the lightly defended Ardennes forest. The combination of large numbers of Panzer tanks and close support from Luftwaffe dive bombers proved more than France could handle. Within a few days Germany had shattered

French resistance in the area and its armies began racing to the Englisn C...nel, trapping the bulk of the French and British armies in a giant pocket.

The speed of the attack completely disoriented France, not only militarily but politically as well. The government of Paul Reynaud collapsed on May 9, a day before the invasion, but could not be replaced during the national emergency. It proved incapable of coordinating military strategies with the British government, now headed by the redoubtable Winston Churchill. And as the Germans advanced, military units in the field were forced to fall back without clear instructions from Paris. On May 18 Reynaud fired General Gamelin, replacing him with General Weygand who had been stationed in Syria, but the new commander in chief also failed to stem the German tide. A plan to attack the enemy armies in late May came to nothing due to lack of coordination between British and French forces. The increasing hopelessness of the military situation led the British to evacuate over 300,000 soldiers from Dunkirk to England by early June. Although this included over 100,000 French troops, many in France saw this as evidence that the British were deserting them in their nation's hour of trial.

By the beginning of June the situation was clearly hopeless. On June 10 the government fled the capital for Bordeaux, as it had in 1914. The approach of the Germans and the failure of French leadership triggered a mass flight to the south, or exodus as the French called it. This had also happened in 1914, but the scale of the panic in 1940 reached a new level: as many as 10 million French people, 25 percent of the nation's population, took to the roads with all the belongings they could carry. The population of Lille dropped by 90 percent, and 2 million Parisians fled their homes. Soon the nation's roads were clogged with families and individuals walking, riding horses, pulling carts, and even pushing baby strollers, headed toward the south and some illusion of safety. Primarily women, children, and the elderly, those on the roads of France faced not only shortages of food and water but also constant bombing and strafing raids from German aircraft. Strangely, the great exodus of 1940 replicated in tragic fashion the departures for vacation during the summer of 1936, especially because many of the internal refugees sought out places they had first visited four years earlier. As a result, the population of towns and cities in the south swelled dramatically; the resort town of Pau, in the Pyrenees, grew from 38,000 to 150,000 in a matter of weeks. Many never made it, some 100,000 French people dying during the exodus.

Most at risk were foreign refugees, many of them Jews and antifascist activists, who had flooded into France during the 1930s. For them the collapse of a nation that many had looked to as the last bulwark of democracy in an increasingly fascist Europe was not only a tremendous shock but in many cases placed them in immediate danger. Thousands of anti-Nazi Germans, including leading artists and intellectuals like Heinrich Mann and Max Ernst, feared arrest by the Gestapo. Those detained in camps for enemy aliens in 1939 desperately sought to escape before the Germans arrived. Some French camp commanders let them run away, but others turned them over to the Nazi authorities. The fate of Walter Benjamin, a German Jewish philosopher and leading member of the Frankfurt School, symbolized the tragedy and despair of 1940. Escaping Paris a day before the Germans marched in, with specific orders to arrest him, Benjamin managed to cross the border into Spain. In September, after the Spanish authorities threatened to send him back to occupied France, he committed suicide.

The trauma of the great exodus, of a France in extremis and literally falling apart at the seams, was key to the settlement of 1940. On June 10 Italy declared war against France, leading American president Franklin D. Roosevelt to declare "the hand that held the dagger has struck it into the back of its neighbor." On June 14 German troops entered Paris, parading down the Champs-Elysées in a display that would haunt the French imagination for years to come. This and similar images would circulate globally, making the fall of France one of the world's great news stories in 1940. In Boston, a riot broke out at Filene's department store as women fought for dresses from the last *haute couture* shipment to leave Paris before the occupation. Meanwhile, the French government struggled to respond to the catastrophe. In reshuffling the cabinet, Reynaud brought in Marshal Henri Pétain, the hero of Verdun, who had been serving as ambassador to the new Franco regime in Spain. Members of the administration held different opinions as to how to cope with the disaster: some counseled continued resistance, either from Brittany or more feasibly from a base in the colonies. But Pétain and many others, observing the terrible chaos of the nation, concluded that the war was indeed lost and France must adjust as best as it could to a Europe dominated by Nazi Germany. Increasingly many inside and outside the government looked to Pétain, the war hero and nonpolitician, as the savior France needed in its most desperate hour.

On June 16 the French cabinet voted to request armistice terms from the Germans. Paul Reynaud resigned as prime minister the same day, recommending that Pétain be appointed as his successor. The next day Pétain broadcast his first speech to the French people, saying, "It is with a heavy heart that

I tell you today that we must cease hostilities."[1] On June 22 France signed the armistice, in effect its capitulation, with Nazi Germany. The Germans insisted on doing so in a particularly vindictive manner that presaged the character of the occupation. In November 1918 German representatives had signed the armistice ending World War I in a railway car in the middle of Compiègne forest in northern France. In 1940 the Germans insisted on bringing the same railway car to the same spot and forcing the French to sign the armistice there. Hitler sat in the seat Marshal Foch had occupied in 1918 when he dictated terms to the defeated Germans. The message was clear: France had lost not just World War II but World War I as well.

Not everyone in France accepted this. On June 18 Charles de Gaulle, who had fled to London, broadcast a radio address to the French people calling for continued resistance. Yet for most French people the news of the armistice came as a great relief. It meant the end of France's suffering and the repatriation of 1.5 million prisoners of war captured during the battle of France, not to mention the return of millions of refugees scattered throughout the country. It meant above all that France might be able to put the disaster of 1940 behind it and start building a new future. The outlines of that future would soon become evident.

VICHY AND THE NATIONAL REVOLUTION

The terms of the armistice were simple and harsh. France would be divided into two main parts: the majority of the country—Paris, everything north of the Loire River, and the Atlantic coastline—would be occupied by the Germans, while southern and eastern France would not be occupied but nonetheless subject to German oversight. In addition Germany annexed Alsace-Lorraine and placed regions along the French and German border under special restrictions. Italy occupied Corsica and small parts of the southeast along the Italian border. The French army would be reduced to 100,000 men, the exact same number as that imposed on the Germans by Versailles, and the navy restricted to port but otherwise left alone. France would be required to pay all the costs of the occupation. In some ways things could have been worse. For example, and perhaps most important, the Germans left the French empire intact, in contrast to the Allies' expropriation of Germany's colonies in 1919. Nonetheless, it struck many in France as deeply humiliating and excessively severe. For the first time in many centuries, Paris was no longer a capital city but merely a large urban area. In 1815 Talleyrand had managed to convince

Map 9.1. France, occupied zones, 1940–1944.

Metternich and the victors at Vienna to restore France as a great power. In contrast, 1940 saw the universal nation reduced to an occupied territory, subject to the will of its masters in Berlin.

Nonetheless, the armistice left the French with a semi-independent state and some autonomy to determine their own destiny and place in Hitler's Europe. For many, the catastrophe of 1940 reflected broader failings in French politics and society. The right blamed the defeat on the nation's departure from traditional morality, reasserting its interwar critique of modernity. France had become too urban, too multicultural, too decadent, too feminine. The collapse was often portrayed in gendered terms, with the aggressive masculinity of Germany overwhelming, even raping, a passive, feminized France. Conservative commentators criticized Frenchwomen for preferring consumerism and amusement to motherhood; France lost the war because it had too few babies. The new France would have to address these problems if it wanted to be a great nation again.

For the French right and for Marshal Pétain in particular, the defeat of 1940 provided an opportunity to overthrow republican universalism and implement its own vision of France. In announcing the terms of the armistice to the French people on June 25, Pétain emphasized the importance of national renewal. Technically still a prime minister under the Third Republic, he moved swiftly to establish a new regime and consolidate his own power. Because Bordeaux lay in the occupied zone, the French government had to go elsewhere, and after some consideration it chose the small resort town of Vichy, moving there on July 1. A spa town in the hills of the Auvergne known for its curative waters, Vichy was not the most obvious place for a national capital, but it did have lots of empty hotel rooms suitable for ministerial offices as well as lacking ties to prominent national political leaders or a left-wing working-class population. The idea of a small-town national capital was a radical departure from French tradition, much more reminiscent of American state capitals like Albany, New York, or Sacramento, California, and symbolized a rejection of the evils of Paris and urban civilization.

As prime minister, Pétain had to form a new government, and his most important choice was the leading politician and former prime minister Pierre Laval. Like many Third Republic politicians, Laval had begun his career as a socialist, including serving as mayor of the working-class Parisian suburb of Aubervilliers, then moved steadily to the right. Along the way he acquired a reputation for opportunism; as Parisian wits joked, "from the left or from the right, his name is spelled the same." Prime minister for the Radical party in 1935, when he tried to broker an alliance with fascist Italy (the Hoare Laval pact), Laval was forced out of power by the Popular Front. This reinforced his hatred of the left and his conviction that his political opponents were destroying France. In June 1940 Pétain made him a senior member of his cabinet, and Laval took the initiative in lobbying for the creation of a new regime. On July 10, largely at his instigation, French legislators voted 569 to 80 to grant Marshal Pétain full powers to revise the constitution. The one-sided nature of the vote reflected the anxiety of the times, as well as the fact that the PCF had been outlawed. As with Germany's 1933 Enabling Act, which followed the ban against German communism, in France anticommunism was the first step in the destruction of French republican democracy. The next day Pétain issued several constitutional acts, naming himself head of the French state and effectively destroying the Third Republic. The longest regime in the history of modern France died as it was born, in the throes of a defeat by Germany.

The basic outlines and ideology of the new Vichy state soon became clear. As Pierre Laval stated, "Parliamentary democracy has lost the war. It must disappear and give place to a hierarchical authoritarian regime, national and social."[2] Pétain's initial decrees not only gave him overwhelming power to pass laws, appoint and dismiss ministers, and appoint his successor, they also dissolved the National Assembly until further notice. At the time these acts were generally popular: instead of the squabbling and ineffective politicians of the 1930s, France now had an august father figure (Pétain was 84 in 1940) who would save the nation. Pétain promptly appointed Pierre Laval to serve as his prime minister, a position Laval would hold during most of the occupation.

The new Vichy state of Pétain and Laval had two primary goals: to obtain the best treatment possible from Nazi Germany and to revolutionize French society. The two goals were not the same. Hitler did not require the French to create a collaborationist regime: Vichy was not imposed on France by Berlin. Germany's primary interest in occupying France was to extract resources from the French people and to prevent the nation from aiding the Allied war effort, not to impose ideological conformity. Elsewhere in western Europe the Germans adopted a practice of direct rule over occupied nations. The governments of Norway, the Netherlands, and Belgium fled the occupation for exile in London during the war. Only the Danish government stayed in office, and only until 1943. In opting for collaboration, France chose a path not followed elsewhere on the Continent.

In choosing to work with the Nazi authorities, the Vichy regime hoped to avoid the kind of savage exploitation and repression Germany visited on Poland. It even had fantasies of achieving the status of a junior partner in fascist Europe. The limits of collaboration soon became evident, however. In October 1940 Pétain hosted Adolf Hitler for a meeting in the village of Montoire on the Loire River, the boundary between the occupied and unoccupied zones. Both Pétain and Laval proposed collaboration to Hitler, especially in terms of mobilizing the resources of the French empire in the war against Britain. Hitler made it clear, however, that France was a conquered country, not an ally. Moreover, the Germans did nothing to improve living conditions in occupied France as a result of the meeting, and soon began expelling thousands of people from Alsace and Lorraine into the occupied zone. Most prisoners of war remained in detention in Germany for the duration of the

conflict. Nonetheless, the very fact of the meeting, including phot
and Hitler smiling together and shaking hands, indelibly stamped
collaborationist regime.

What did collaboration mean? The answer varied widely according to
who answered the question. It did not necessarily mean an active embrace of
Nazi ideology. France did have active fascists, notably the former communist
Jacques Doriot and the former socialist Marcel Déat, but they were largely
sidelined at Vichy. Traditional conservatives and reactionaries, especially dis-
ciples of Charles Maurras and the Action Française, dominated the cabinet
Pétain appointed in July 1940. Most of the fascist true believers left Vichy for
occupied Paris, where they could enjoy German subsidies and complain about
the backwardness of the French regime.

Collaboration often meant going along with the German authorities,
accepting and helping implement their policies without protesting. This
occurred across the ideological spectrum. For example, the long-term communist mayor of the Parisian suburb of Bobigny, Jean-Marie Clamamus, broke
with the party because of the Nazi-Soviet pact in 1939 but continued to serve
as mayor throughout the occupation, working closely with the Germans. Especially at the local and regional level, collaboration in France could mean a
lot of different things, ranging from ardent support of German policies to pretending nothing had changed. It often meant negotiating with the Germans
over a myriad of small issues and concerns, ranging from allowing French
citizens to cross the border between the occupied and unoccupied zones to
handling complaints from civilians about the behavior of German soldiers.
After the liberation many Vichy officials argued they were trying to protect
the French people, working for France, just like the resistance. Such claims
were often suspect and self-serving, not to mention morally outrageous, but
the complexity of collaboration meant they could not simply be dismissed out
of hand.

Vichy's other primary goal, what became known as the national revolution,
was also less than straightforward, especially because the leaders and social
forces who supported the regime were by no means unified. In addition to the
traditional reactionaries and the die-hard fascists there were some who saw
the collapse of 1940 as an opportunity to modernize French society, to, in the
words of one French historian, privilege administration over politics.[3] These
technocrats from business and public administration, led by the brilliant *poly-
technicien* Jean Bichelonne, saw in Vichy the opportunity to escape the inefficiency of parliamentary democracy and build an authoritarian regime based

on modern technology. What became the national revolution was the result of endless negotiations and compromises between these three very different groups.

At the heart of the national revolution lay the belief that prewar France was decadent and needed social and moral renewal, as well as a rejection of republican universalism and the political culture of the French Revolution. Nothing better symbolized this than the decision to replace the classic revolutionary slogan "Liberty, Equality, Fraternity" with the words "Labor, Fatherland, Family" (Travail, Patrie, Famille). Vichy rejected the liberal individualism and emphasis on human rights of the Revolution in favor of a focus on organic community; in 1941 it drafted the statement "Principles of Community" as a counterpoint to and rejection of the 1789 Declaration of the Rights of Man. The very idea of a national revolution rejected the global dimensions of 1789, although Vichy had its own transnational inspirations, specifically the "new state" of Portuguese dictator Antonio Salazar.

A new emphasis on family played a central role in the ideology and practices of the Vichy state. From the outset the regime conceived of France as one big family, ruled over by a benevolent grandfatherly figure, Marshal Pétain. France during the twentieth century has known other savior politicians, notably Georges Clemenceau before and Charles de Gaulle after, but the cult of Pétain that developed during Vichy was without precedent. The man's image, featuring his erect military bearing and smiling blue eyes, was everywhere, including on Baccarat crystal and Sevres porcelain, and schoolchildren ritually pledged themselves to serve the savior of France. The song "Maréchal nous voilà" (Marshal, we are here) became the unofficial national anthem of Vichy.

The family model went beyond venerating Pétain to promoting the interests of real French families. Above all, this meant a strong focus on motherhood and a rejection of feminism as corrosive of both the family and the society. Vichy considered France's low birthrate not only a symbol of national decadence but also a key cause of the defeat of 1940, and was determined to make France a fertile nation again. The regime made Mother's Day a major holiday, complete with radio broadcasts from Pétain to the mothers of France, and restricted the ability of women to work in public service. A 1941 law banned divorce in the first three years of marriage. Vichy also continued and reinforced the Third Republic's policies subsidizing large families. It intensified the battle against abortion, prosecuting abortion providers. In July 1942 the state executed Marie-Louise Girard as an abortionist. She was the last woman to be guillotined in French history.

If Vichy's emphasis on raising the national birthrate continu
cies of the Third Republic, it also anticipated the Fourth Repub\
France's birthrate began to rise in 1942, after declining for nearly ___ury.
This trend, which would culminate in the massive baby boom of the postwar
years, is difficult to explain. Having children usually reflects confidence in the
future, something hard to find in wartime France. The surge in the birthrate
perhaps reflects the impact of both Third Republic and Vichy family-friendly
policies. This was one of the central developments in France during the twentieth century, and it underscored the fact that Vichy was not a regime apart
but an integral part of French history.

A focus on the family also meant making the education—intellectual,
physical, and moral—of young people a top priority. Vichy actively promoted
youth sports, ironically continuing the orientation of the Popular Front, arguing that education should develop strong bodies as well as minds. It struggled
to counter the image of French youth as effete, the products of an educational system that focused solely on intellectual concerns while neglecting the
broader physical and moral development of young people. The regime also
purged the public schools of leftist teachers, often considered the standard
bearers of socialism in French politics, and reinserted religious instruction
into the curriculum. At the end of July 1940 Vichy created the Youth Workshops (*Chantiers de la jeunesse*), in part to replace military conscription, which
had been suppressed under the terms of the armistice. The program required
all twenty-year-old Frenchmen to serve for eight months, living in rural camps
and engaging in physical labor and training. The workshops were supposed to
promote the moral formation of French youth by teaching them the value of
hard work and the simple life of the countryside. This fit in well with Vichy's
return to the soil policy, regarding the revitalization of rural life and a rejection
of urban decadence as key to the regeneration of the nation.

The family motif also carried over into economic planning. Like many
other authoritarian and fascist regimes in Europe, Vichy saw the class struggle as profoundly destructive of national unity. It rejected both Marxism and
liberalism, emphasizing cooperation over competition. The regime embraced
corporatism, based on the medieval idea of an economy divided into guilds of
labor and capital that would work together to promote both economic development and social harmony. In October 1941 Vichy abolished trade unions, seen
as seedbeds of radicalism and social division, and banned strikes. It replaced
them and business organizations with organization committees (COs) for specific industries. Each CO would include representatives of capital, labor, and

the state. In theory this provided parity between different economic groups; in practice, the absence of independent unions and the loss of the right to strike placed workers at the mercy of capital. Vichy might run the economy as a family, but it was an authoritarian family, treating working people like children.

Although the national revolution's ideological character was overwhelmingly traditional and backward-looking, the technocrats who clustered around the regime also had an impact on Vichy's policies. Jean Bichelonne and others began to experiment with the idea of centralized economic planning, something that would emerge full-blown in France under the Fourth Republic. Bichelonne became head of the newly created Ministry of Industrial Production in 1942 and began laying out plans to close outmoded factories and channel state resources into more innovative economic sectors. Vichy planners also discussed modernizing French architecture, for a time attracting the participation of the nation's greatest modern architect, Henri Le Corbusier. In 1943 the regime began laying out plans for an outer belt around Paris, both to facilitate traffic flows and to isolate the capital from communist suburbia. The *péripherique*, a classic symbol of life in France during the late twentieth century, originated with the urban planners of Vichy.

To an important extent, both the traditional and modernist visions of the national revolution were fantasy rather than reality and changed little in France. The nation's birthrate rose substantially, but whether Vichy deserved the credit is questionable. Judging from protests by their parents, young people hated the spartan conditions and military-style discipline of the Youth Workshops, and many clung to the ideals of the Popular Front. The rural population did not grow appreciably during these years, and much of French industry remained small-scale and technologically backward. If Vichy had more time to rule, things might have been different, but ultimately the regime had little to show for its goal of national and spiritual renewal.

The national revolution's greatest significance was its demonstration that Vichy arose out of French politics rather than simply being imposed by the German occupation. Technocrats, traditionalists, and fascists all had deep roots in French society, and they saw the regime as a chance to apply these ideas and overthrow the political culture of republican universalism. At the same time, it is clear that without the defeat of 1940 and the occupation, Vichy would never have happened. Moreover, the exigencies of collaboration, of trying to strike the best possible deal with Germany, helped justify many of the regime's policies. Even if Vichy adopted policies the Germans did not necessarily request, the uncertainty and fear of what the occupiers might demand must be taken into account. Ultimately, Vichy's national revolution was a blend of French and foreign influences and exigencies. It demonstrated that the rejection of republican universalism also had its own universal dimension.

VICHY, GERMANY, AND THE JEWS

Nothing more clearly demonstrates the intersection of national and transnational during the Vichy years than its policies toward France's Jewish population, and no aspect of French life during the war years is more complicated, controversial, or tragic. It is crucial that debates over the place of Jews in French life occurred in the context of occupation by a murderous foreign power that implemented the Holocaust, an unprecedented genocide of Europe's Jewish population. Just as Vichy probably would not have happened without the occupation, an independent French regime would probably not have collaborated in the deportation of masses of Jews to the death camps of the east.

In 1940 about 330,000 Jews lived in France, primarily in the Paris area. It was a diverse population. Many came from families that had lived in France for generations and had become highly integrated into French society. Bordeaux, for example, had a small Sephardic Jewish community that dated back to the sixth century, and during the nineteenth century after emancipation large numbers of Jews had embraced French culture. The majority of Jews in France, however, had immigrated during the interwar years, seeking economic opportunity during the 1920s and refuge from Nazism during the 1930s. Most came from central and eastern Europe, although some originated in French North Africa. For the most part they lacked French citizenship, which would become a crucial distinction during the 1940s.

The attitude of the French toward their Jewish population was complicated and at times paradoxical. The French Revolution had emancipated Jews across Europe, and the emphasis on individual equality before the law without regard to race, ethnicity, or religion was a key aspect of republican universalism. France was also the land of the Dreyfus affair, however, and one of the birthplaces of modern anti-Semitism. Whereas World War I had brought increased acceptance of the Jewish population in France, during the 1930s the combination of rising immigration and economic hardship prompted a new wave of anti-Jewish sentiment, led by the nation's fascist leagues. Yet ultimately the pro-Dreyfus forces had triumphed, reinforcing the image of France as a tolerant and accepting nation. In 1920 Joseph Rosencher brought his family from Poland to France. As his son Henri later noted, "My father was looking for justice and equity. He chose France, which had had the courage and the glory of rendering justice to Dreyfus."[4]

In many ways, Vichy represented the victory of the anti-Dreyfusard forces in France, and its attitudes to French Jews made this clear. Right from the outset the regime demonstrated its anti-Semitic character, enacting discriminatory measures against the Jews often independent of the occupation authorities. In October 1940 Vichy promulgated its first Jewish statute, excluding Jews from the army, civil service, and positions in industry and the press, without regard to citizenship. The same month it passed another law permitting the immediate internment of foreign Jews. A second Jewish statute followed in June 1941, banning Jews from more professions and imposing quotas on Jews in universities and professions like medicine and architecture. The next month it set up a census of the nation's Jewish population, breaking with the republican tradition that banned French governments from collecting data about race or religion in the census or other official documents. Such steps, while not imposed by Germany, were often taken with an eye toward currying favor with the occupiers, and in general Vichy did not embrace the fervent anti-Semitic rhetoric so prominent among the fascist collaborators in the occupied zone, notably Paris. The anti-Jewish policies and attitudes of Vichy arose from a complicated mixture of indigenous politics and foreign occupation. Here, as in so many areas of Vichy France, national and transnational came together.

Starting in late 1940 the Nazi authorities did begin to pressure Vichy to impose anti-Semitic measures. In September they forced Jews in the occupied zone to register with the authorities, something that would make future roundups much easier. In October began the "Aryanization" (or expropriation) of Jewish property in the occupied zone, reducing many Parisian Jews to poverty. In March 1941, under German pressure, France created the General Commissariat for Jewish Affairs, headed by veteran anti-Semite Xavier Vallat. In November, the regime created the General Union of French Jews (UGIF). These two bodies would coordinate Jewish policy and ultimately make it easier for the occupation authorities to implement anti-Semitic measures. In 1941 German authorities began rounding up Jews in the occupied zone, interning them in camps in northern France. The first raid took place in May, followed by subsequent roundups in August and December. They primarily targeted Jewish immigrants, although in some cases French Jews were arrested, ostensibly in reprisal for attacks against German soldiers. Over eight thousand

Jews were sent to camps run by French authorities, notably t
Drancy in the Paris suburbs, where they languished in terrible condiu.

In January 1942 Nazi Germany began outlining its plans for "the final
solution to the Jewish problem," elaborating them at the Wannsee Conference
in Berlin. Jews throughout Europe were to be deported to death camps in
the east and exterminated, either through overwork, starvation, or execution.
What had begun as a series of anti-Semitic policies would soon escalate into
the organized genocide of the Holocaust. The first convoy of Jewish deportees from France left for Auschwitz in March 1941. In the summer of 1942
German and Vichy authorities began a series of key negotiations over the fate
of Jews in France. In June occupation authorities required Jews to wear the
yellow Star of David. On July 2 the Germans demanded the right to round up
Jews in the occupied zone and insisted that the French help them do it. Vichy
officials responded by distinguishing between French and foreign Jews and
striking a key agreement with Germany: if the occupation authorities would
leave French Jews alone, in return French police would organize the roundup
and deportation of foreign Jews. This was the devil's bargain that would shape
Jewish life in occupied France.

Within weeks the impact of this decision became dramatically, terribly evident. Starting in the early morning of July 16 and continuing for the next two
days, Paris police began rounding up Jews throughout the capital and interning them in the Vélodrome d'Hiver, a sports stadium on the southern edge
of the city. Nearly 13,000 "foreign" Jews were arrested, including 4,000 children whose capture Laval had insisted on over German objections, saying he
didn't want to break up families. Vichy authorities organized the roundup, and
French police carried it out. The prisoners were held in terrible conditions for
five days in Paris before being transferred to Drancy in the suburbs. After that
they were deported, ostensibly to work camps in the east, in reality to the final
solution. These included Joseph Rosencher, whose tragically misplaced faith
in French justice would earn him a one-way ticket to Auschwitz and death.

The Vel d'Hiv mass arrests constituted the greatest single example of Vichy's persecution of the Jews in occupied France. French police organized further roundups in the unoccupied zone in subsequent months, so by the end
of 1942 over 40,000 Jews had been deported to the east. As the true meaning of deportation and the reality of the Holocaust became clear, the regime's
resistance stiffened somewhat, so by 1944 the Germans took over the main
responsibility for arresting Jews. Ultimately France would send over 75,000
Jews, including 24,000 with French citizenship, to the death camps of Nazi

9.2. In 1942, Jews were required to wear a yellow star. *Source:* United States Holocaust Memorial Museum, gift of the Ruth Renée Heyum Trust.

Europe. To give one example among many, in November 1943 Madeleine Levy, the granddaughter of Alfred Dreyfus, was deported from Drancy after being arrested by the Gestapo in Paris for her resistance work. She died in Auschwitz a few months later. Very few of those deported would ever return.

The fate of France's Jews during the occupation illustrates the transnational character of Vichy. The anti-Semitic character of the regime is beyond question, with a pedigree going back to the reactionary ideology of anti-Dreyfus forces like the Action Française. More complicated is the question of Vichy's complicity with the Holocaust. It is one thing to hate and persecute Jews, another to murder them. French authorities had to function in the context of occupation by a vicious and radically anti-Semitic state, so while it might be possible to resist Nazi demands, the possibilities and consequences of such resistance were never clear. The Vichy regime's distinction between French and foreign Jews also underscored both its differences from German policy and its rejection of universal republicanism. Instead of France's tradition as a haven for the oppressed it focused on the rights of citizenship, emphasizing xenophobia over racism in ways that showed the slippery boundaries between the two. The focus on deportation, replicating earlier expulsions of immigrants such as the repatriation of colonial labor after World War I, also underscored Vichy's rejection of universalism as a part of French national identity.

Finally, three-quarters of the Jews in France, including 88 percent of those with French nationality, survived the war. Comparisons with other parts of Nazi Europe are instructive. Very few countries occupied by Nazi Germany had such a survival rate: Denmark, with a tiny Jewish population, and Italy, only occupied by Germany late in the war. Credit for this belongs mostly to the Jews themselves and to those who aided them, not to the Vichy authorities. Bulgaria, like Vichy an ally of Nazi Germany during the war, simply refused to deport its Jewish population, all of whom survived. Yet France was both an ally and a conquered country at the same time, primarily the latter. Had the French not actively registered and rounded up Jews more might have survived; had they not tried to protect those with French nationality, more might have died. The answers were not clear at the time, and to this day this tragic part of French history remains complex.

EMPIRE BY ASSOCIATION: VICHY AND THE COLONIES

The defeat of France in 1940 and the occupation of the metropole gave France's colonies a greater prominence in national life than ever before. For Vichy the empire was a key aspect of its attempt to retain some autonomy vis-à-vis Nazi Germany; for the resistance, the colonies remained the "real" France, controlled by independent French leaders. Since German troops did not set foot in the empire, with the exception of North Africa, Vichy rule there was much more purely French than in metropolitan France. The regime had a freedom of operation in the colonies unhindered by German pressure, so that to an important extent Vichy's colonial policies illustrate the true nature of the regime. At the same time the resistance scored its first tangible successes in overseas France. The struggle for the future of the nation thus ran directly through the empire.

The armistice of 1940 had left France's colonial holdings untouched, leaving it to the French to decide the fate of their empire. In September the Japanese occupied Indochina but left the administration of the colony to the French. Initially all the colonies rallied to Vichy, seeing it as the legitimate successor of the Third Republic. The major exception was Chad, led by France's sole black colonial governor, Félix Eboué, which pledged its support for de Gaulle and the Free French by the end of the summer. Elsewhere, however, Vichy had full power to shape life in France's colonies.

As in the metropole, but in some ways to an even greater extent, Vichy in the empire represented the rejection of republican universalism and the ascendancy of the far right in French politics. French colonial administrators and settlers seized it as an opportunity to reinforce authoritarian racial hierarchies and suppress attempts to elevate the natives to the status of French men and women. The later years of the Third Republic had already seen a drift away from the republican ideal of assimilation, underscoring the idea that colonial subjects were permanently and unalterably different from the French. Association, in contrast, argued that there were different paths for different peoples, that the natives could never become French but must find their own way to modernity. Whereas in some respects association preached the respect of difference, in the colonial context it all too often underscored racial hierarchy and white supremacy.

Vichy embraced associationist ideology, blending it with its own views on the spiritual renewal of the nation. In the metropole the regime had strongly rejected urban life as decadent, instead promoting a return to the soil. This view had particular relevance in the colonies, which had seen intensive urbanization during the interwar years as a result of widespread land expropriation, and also the rise of native urban elites whose very presence undermined colonial racial hierarchies. In the empire Vichy translated anti-urbanism into a veneration of traditional peasant cultures (ironically, the same cultures colonial rule had undermined or even destroyed), warning colonial subjects away from modernity and republican universalism. Vichy also sought to reinforce traditional hierarchies in its colonies, giving new powers to native elites and rulers. In Madagascar, for example, Vichy not only embraced the island's monarchy but sought to portray Pétain as a type of Malagasy king. As in the metropole, Vichy in the colonies promoted the cult of Pétain, portraying him as a traditional local ruler. The regime also stressed the importance of sports and physical fitness for colonial youth, continuing the tendency of colonial administrators to deemphasize colonial education and intellectual pursuits that would produce discontented and potentially anticolonialist natives.

Vichy's colonial ideology also had a strongly repressive character. Colonial settlers and administrators bitterly resented the rather tepid attempts of the Popular Front to humanize conditions in the empire, and when Vichy came to power they rushed to reverse such policies. Forced labor regained its prominence in colonial life, especially as Vichy used the colonies to supply materials to Nazi Germany. As in the metropole, the regime also stamped out any vestiges of representative democracy and citizenship in the empire.

In the old colonies of the Caribbean and Indian Ocean, Vichy suspended elections and dismissed mayors and other local officials, essentially overturning the citizenship of their inhabitants and recasting them as colonial subjects. This suspension of republican citizenship, in some ways paralleling Napoleon's restoration of slavery after the French Revolution, caused bitter resentment in the nation's Caribbean colonies. Many in Martinique and Guadeloupe concluded that the real agenda of Vichy, in alliance with the *békés*, was to restore slavery outright. Similarly, the regime overturned the Cremieux decree, which had granted French citizenship to Algerian Jews. Vichy applied its anti-Semitic policies throughout the empire, excluding Jews from the civil service, and colonial administrators blocked plans to help desperate refugees fleeing Nazi Europe settle overseas, notably in Madagascar. In the empire, as in its anti-Semitic policies, Vichy's inherent racism found its most extensive expression.

The autonomy of the empire under Vichy also illustrated the regime's foreign policy and relationship to the war in general. This was most important in North Africa, where the regime first allied itself with the Nazis and then shifted to join the British and Americans during the desert war of 1942–1943. But elsewhere as well Vichy had to fight the war on its own. In both Madagascar and the Caribbean colonies of Martinique and Guadeloupe Allied naval blockades combined with local resistance to prompt the overthrow of the Vichy regime. The struggle against Vichy gave France's colonies a new level of global prominence. In 1942 Hollywood awarded its Best Picture award to *Casablanca*, a portrayal of the battle between Vichy and the resistance in colonial Morocco. Under Vichy the colonial and transnational aspects of French life came together in new ways.

Vichy's colonial policies have a significance that goes beyond the story of the collaborationist regime. Writers and scholars ranging from Hannah Arendt to Aimé Césaire and Frantz Fanon have argued that in many ways colonialism and fascism are similar if not identical, or to put it another way that fascism was simply colonialism applied to Europeans. This is in many ways a controversial perspective, one still debated today. Its applicability to wartime France is not clear, especially because to an important extent the Vichy state was more traditional and reactionary than fascist. The history of Vichy and the French empire nonetheless lends some support to it, in two respects. First, there is a strong continuity between the colonial policies of the Third Republic and the Vichy state. Both were essentially authoritarian and based solidly upon racial hierarchies. The colonial policies of Vichy were certainly more extreme, but not fundamentally different in kind. Second, occupied France, and the rest of Nazi Europe, was in many respects itself a colony. Like colonies traditionally, it was controlled by a foreign power that considered itself racially superior, and subject to resource extraction and forced labor. In wartime Paris taxi drivers coped with the lack of gasoline by making pedicabs: the backseat of a cab attached to a bicycle. This European version of the rickshaw underscored the colonial nature of life under German rule. In both senses, therefore, empire became more central to French life than ever before.

LIFE IN WARTIME FRANCE

It is one thing to study the structure and policies of the German occupation and Vichy regime, another to consider how the French people reacted to them. Historians have debated how to understand public opinion under Vichy. Did the people of France support or oppose the regime and the occupation? Should they be considered resisters, collaborators, or something else? The vast majority of French people were neither militant collaborators nor members of the resistance. Instead, they tried to make do the best they could in unprecedented and very difficult conditions. Nonetheless, it seems clear that most opposed the occupation, and while Vichy enjoyed important popular support at the outset, this declined sharply as its essentially collaborationist nature became more evident.

The news of the armistice and the establishment of the new regime in June 1940 came as a tremendous relief to most French people. Vichy had a solid claim to legitimacy, having been chosen by the elected representatives of the nation, and the war hero Marshal Pétain was extremely popular. This did not necessarily mean that the French as a whole embraced Pétain's vision of the national revolution. Rather, people were relieved that the bloodletting and destruction of war would stop, and that hopefully the new regime would secure better conditions for the French people in what seemed certain to be a Nazi-dominated Europe for the foreseeable future.

The armistice did at least temporarily stop the war in the metropole, but the Vichy regime soon proved unable to improve living conditions in France. A million prisoners of war remained in Germany. The division of the country into occupied and unoccupied zones divided families and communities. It became extremely difficult to cross the border between zones or even send mail from one to another. Clocks in the occupied zone were set to German time, an hour ahead, so even timekeeping was divided. The people of Alsace-Lorraine, formally annexed to the Third Reich, were subjected to forced Germanization, including the adoption of German first names. Those who resisted or were judged not capable of adapting to the new order were expelled from their homes into the rest of France. Over 100,000 men were conscripted into the Wehrmacht.

These problems often paled before the central concern for most people in wartime: food. France had traditionally been one of the most productive and well-fed agricultural nations in Europe, but that changed dramatically during the war. As in other occupied nations, Germany requisitioned large amounts of agricultural produce from France. Moreover, many French farmers remained imprisoned in Germany, further hurting food production. The result was a level of food shortages, and hunger, not known in France since the Franco-Prussian War and the siege of Paris. The government imposed food rationing, but stores often ran out of food, so that a central experience of life in wartime was standing in line hoping to buy something to eat. By the winter of 1942–1943 official caloric intake had dropped to 1,200 per day, far short of the norm of 2,000. Essential commodities like butter and meat became scarce by 1941. Certain foods from overseas, notably coffee and tropical fruit, disappeared entirely.

People in cities had less food than those in the countryside, which helped promote the Vichy ideal of return to the soil; worst off were those in cities surrounded by agricultural areas that produced specialized commodities for the market. The situation contributed to a flourishing black market in food, which ensured that those with the money to pay prices several hundred times the official rate could find something to eat. The black market also privileged those with connections to German and Vichy authorities. It served as a major cause of division and resentment in French society during the war.

Food shortages underscored the inability of Vichy to protect its people during the war: the French actually had some of the lowest caloric intake rates in occupied Europe. By the beginning of 1942 it was also clear that the regime had not brought peace to France. Britain unexpectedly survived the Nazi assault, and by the end of 1941 Germany faced two powerful new enemies: the Soviet Union and the United States. In early 1942 the Allies began bombing German installations in France. A March attack on the Renault factory in the Paris suburbs, which was making tanks for Germany, killed over three hundred workers. While France for the most part did not experience the aerial destruction visited on Britain, much of eastern Europe, and ultimately Germany itself, it was clear that the regime could not guarantee the safety of its people.

Vichy also failed to restrain the harshness of German rule in France. Starting in the fall of 1941 the Germans instituted a systematic policy of reprisals, taking civilian hostages (overwhelmingly communists and Jews) and executing them in response to attacks on German soldiers. The Vélodrome d'Hiver roundup of July 1942 horrified the Parisians who witnessed the traumatic scenes of thousands of Jewish men, women, and children being arrested and imprisoned by the Vichy police. Many in France increasingly came to view Vichy as at best unable to protect its people, at worst actively persecuting them. Pétain's meeting with Hitler at Montoire in October 1940 was extremely unpopular with the French. To the extent that the regime was seen as collaborating with the occupation, it lost support among its citizens.

For most people in France, life during wartime consisted of material privations and anxiety about both their own future and that of the nation as a whole. Many families had to make do without husbands and fathers, imprisoned in Germany or after 1943 subject to forced labor there. Women had to stand in line for hours to buy food for their families, and learn to make do with ersatz coffee and other commodities. Community solidarity often broke down, as individuals thought first of themselves and their families. Anonymous letters of denunciation, accusing people of being Jewish, of trading on the black market, or of "immoral behavior" with the Germans poured into the prefects' offices. Those in the occupied zone had to cope with the daily presence of German soldiers, of street signs in German, and other humiliating reminders of the nation's subjection.

Without a doubt, some collaborated with Vichy and the occupation. Some used the new circumstances to take revenge on their neighbors or seize Jewish property expropriated by the regime. Whereas most French people living in the occupied zone gave German soldiers and officials the cold shoulder (Germans called Paris *die Stadt ohne Blick*: the city where no one looks at you), not all did, especially when it became clear that the right contacts could bring solid advantages, like access to food or family members under arrest. Frenchwomen had to negotiate relations with the regime and the occupiers delicately, and accusations of personal collaboration were gendered to a significant degree. In particular, sleeping with Germans, what became infamously known as "horizontal collaboration," brought widespread condemnation, especially if it was seen as bringing special privileges. After the war the leading actress Arletty would defiantly proclaim "my ass is international, my heart is French," but such attitudes found few supporters.[5] This kind of collaboration reflected a desire to survive and take advantage of the wartime situation rather than a commitment to Vichy or Nazi ideology.

For Jews, the occupation years brought isolation from French society and increasing terror at the prospect of deportation. Most chose to obey the new anti-Semitic laws, hoping their good behavior would be rewarded, and many French citizens insisted on believing, despite all evidence to the contrary, that their country would not betray them. As conditions worsened, the fight to survive often meant fleeing their homes into hiding, generally moving from the occupied to the unoccupied zone and taking up new identities or hiding out with sympathetic non-Jewish neighbors. They lived in constant fear of denunciation, of a knock on the door in the middle of the night.

And yet life went on, somehow. French intellectual and cultural life continued during the war years. Paris even experienced a kind of renaissance, fueled both by native intellectuals and German occupiers. Over four hundred plays were produced in Paris during the occupation, often by writers like Jean-Paul Sartre and Albert Camus who would become more famous after the war. Movies became more popular than ever as audiences searched for entertainment and distraction; few addressed politics or wartime conditions. One of the greatest films in French history, Marcel Carné's *Children of Paradise*, was made during the occupation, premièring after the liberation. Artists had to tread carefully during the war, embracing themes that would appeal to audiences but not offend the censors. In Martinique, Aimé Césaire and other *négritude* writers along with surrealist André Breton started the journal *Tropiques*, which emphasized discussions of black culture rather than politics. Jazz survived and even prospered in France, despite Nazi and Vichy scorn for "decadent" music, but often by translating lyrics into French and stripping the music of foreign or American associations. The jazz classic "St. Louis Blues" thus became "La Tristesse de Saint Louis." American culture had dominated both cinema and jazz during the interwar years; the isolation of Vichy helped promote a specifically French vision of these art forms.

One fascinating aspect of life during Vichy France was the rise of a distinctive youth culture. Young people, especially Parisians, interested in jazz began forming their own counterculture, exemplifying café life, distinctive clothing, and its own slang. They took the name Zazou from a swing hit by Johnny Hess in 1939, itself borrowed from a 1933 song by black American musician Cab Calloway. The Zazous adopted the zoot suit, a dramatic clothing style invented by African American youth emphasizing broad padded shoulders, baggy pleated pants, and broad-brimmed hats, as well as growing their hair long. Their life-style, focused on listening to jazz and dancing in cafés, directly challenged the moral Puritanism of Vichy. The Zazous also rejected Vichy's emphasis on national renewal by embracing an explicitly transnational cultural form based on youth. Their true peers were the Swing Kids of Nazi Germany, and the black and Mexican American zoot suiters whose defiance of cultural norms prompted widespread rioting in Los Angeles during 1943. They embodied a globalized cultural alternative to conservative nationalism during the 1940s and anticipated the rise of youth culture in the postwar era.

The Zazous represented both cultural innovation and a spirit of resistance in wartime France. Resistance to Vichy and the occupation took many forms and entailed extreme risk to those who engaged in it. While its actual impact in liberating France from Nazi rule is open to question, it played a key role in redefining France and setting the agenda for the postwar era. During the wartime resistance, a new vision of the universal nation took shape.

THE RESISTANCE AND THE DECLINE OF VICHY

Like collaboration, resistance in wartime France took many forms and is notoriously difficult to define. Just as few French men and women actively supported Vichy and the occupation, few actively opposed them. Historians reassessing Vichy have emphasized its French roots and have tended to discount the Gaullist myth that France was a nation of resisters united in opposition to the occupation. Yet as the example of the Zazous shows, resistance was not just a matter of joining the partisans and taking up arms against the enemy. French men and women manifested their opposition to Vichy and the Germans in a variety of ways ranging from symbolic gestures to armed struggle. While ultimately it would take the might of the Allied armies to defeat Germany and end the occupation, resistance above all made the point that, no matter how beaten down and humiliated, the French would continue to fight for their nation.

If there was an official beginning to the French resistance, it was Charles de Gaulle's radio broadcast from London on June 18, 1940, arguing that France had lost a battle, not a war, and calling on the nation to struggle against the invader. A brave act at the time, it also illustrates some of the complexities of the resistance as it developed during the war years. First, few people actually heard the broadcast; many had fled their homes, and most French placed their hope in Marshal Pétain, who had addressed the nation the day before.

The idea of resistance was thus not immediately popular. Second, de Gaulle appealed for continued *military* resistance to the Germans—for the regular armed forces to continue the fight. He did not at that point anticipate the occupation of France or the prospect of guerrilla warfare against the enemy. A career military officer from first to last, de Gaulle was never comfortable with the idea of civilians taking up arms against the occupier, and this tension between different ways of fighting Vichy and the Germans would last throughout the occupation.

In fact, the resistance to Nazi Germany would take both forms: a military in exile and resistance by armed partisans inside France. From the start, de Gaulle's radio broadcast from London established him as the undisputed head of the former, which would soon take the name Free France. The fact that de Gaulle would take charge of the resistance, and indeed become one of the greatest leaders of France during the twentieth century, was not obvious at the outset. From a conservative Catholic family that had nonetheless embraced the cause of the Third Republic, de Gaulle had distinguished himself as a military officer, becoming in 1940 the youngest general in France. He was one of the nation's few military leaders who embraced the doctrine of mechanized warfare used to such great effect by Nazi Germany, and during the Battle of France his tank unit had scored some of the few French victories during that campaign. It was one thing to be a prominent military officer, quite another to be a national leader, however. De Gaulle had no political experience and no claim to appoint himself head of a government in exile. The Vichy state had come into being through legal channels, via a vote of the nation's elected representatives. In taking up arms against it, de Gaulle was therefore rebelling against the legitimate government of France. This at least was the opinion of the United States, which promptly recognized Vichy and ignored de Gaulle and the Free French until 1942.

De Gaulle did enjoy key advantages, most notably the fact that no one else of his prominence was calling for resistance at the time. Thousands of French citizens fled to England in the summer of 1940, including diplomats, military men, soldiers evacuated at Dunkirk, and fishermen who sailed their boats from the ports of Normandy and Brittany. They rallied around de Gaulle as spokesman for the France they had lost. De Gaulle also benefited enormously from recognition by Winston Churchill. Ten days after his radio address the British government formally recognized de Gaulle's authority over the French resistance, in large part because by making a separate peace with Germany Vichy had violated the terms of its alliance with London. The

British gave de Gaulle a small budget and access to the BBC, and more important credibility as leader of free France. De Gaulle thus took his place among the other Continental governments in exile flooding into the British capital in 1940.

Perhaps most important was the recognition that came from the French empire. Although, as noted above, most colonial governments rallied to Vichy, Félix Eboué had declared Chad's support for de Gaulle in August. During the fall of 1940 he led colonial troops in a successful struggle to win over the rest of French Equatorial Africa to the resistance. In November de Gaulle named him governor general of French Equatorial Africa, and the city of Brazzaville in the Congo became in effect the first capital of Free France. By the end of the year Tahiti and New Caledonia had also declared for de Gaulle. These colonial successes were crucial: they meant that parts of France itself recognized de Gaulle as the national leader and gave him a base to recruit French troops. By the end of the war the majority of Free French soldiers would be colonial recruits. They also underscored the centrality of the empire to the nation, making de Gaulle a legitimate national leader because he controlled part of the national territory. More than ever before in its modern history, the future of France would be decided in its colonies.

During the next two years de Gaulle would work to make Free France a reality, organizing military units and beginning to establish an alternative political structure. He adopted the Cross of Lorraine, a heraldic emblem from the annexed province of Lorraine that had long symbolized French nationalism, as the symbol of Free France. He also struggled to keep positive relations with the British, not an easy task given the enormous power differential between himself and Churchill, and resentments on both sides. In September 1941 he created the eight-member National Committee, which began to take on the appearance of a French provisional government in exile.

Meanwhile, resistance began to develop in occupied France. In one sense, the resistance began at the same time as the occupation, with scattered and spontaneous acts of defiance by French citizens against the Germans. Organized resistance began with small-scale groups of friends and colleagues, people horrified by the national catastrophe and searching for ways to promote the liberation of France. In the summer of 1940, for example, a group of scholars at the Musée de l'homme, the main museum of anthropology in Paris, came together to print anti-German leaflets and organize escape routes to Britain for pilots shot down over France. By the end of the year they had started their own newspaper, *Résistance*. Groups also formed in the unoccupied zone. In the fall of 1940 Raymond and Lucie Aubrac helped create the group Liberation-Sud, which began publishing its own newspaper in 1941.

Internal resistance during these early years was a risky, highly dangerous enterprise. The Germans broke up the Musée de l'homme group in early 1941, executing several of its members a year later. In order to survive, members of the resistance had to assume new identities and isolate themselves from family and friends. Many who took up active resistance activities in these early years were young adults without children or those on the margins of society, and virtually none had any concrete idea of what to do. They had few contacts with the Free French or the outside world in general, and had to figure things out as they went along. To make a mistake could easily mean arrest and death. Only gradually did an organized resistance emerge.

No group played a greater role in the resistance than the French Communist Party. The years from 1939 to 1941 constituted one of the strangest periods in the history of the PCF. Banned in August 1939 as a result of the Nazi-Soviet pact, with the fall of France and the establishment of Vichy it had to negotiate an extremely complicated situation. It was heavily repressed by the new French regime but tolerated by the Germans, thanks to Hitler's alliance with Stalin. Many rank-and-file communists, especially those who had joined during the antifascist Popular Front, resented this political ambivalence and chafed under party discipline. Germany's invasion of the Soviet Union on June 22, 1941, conclusively resolved this situation, however. Almost overnight the PCF shifted from its tortuous antiwar stance to a militant antifascist party of resistance. The policy shift came from Moscow but resonated powerfully with most French communists. Moreover, the PCF also had the skill to undertake resistance work, having developed clandestine networks as well as a quasi-military sense of discipline under the Third Republic. The communists thus brought both a new level of rigor and a large militant popular base to the French resistance, and increasingly played a leading role in the movement.

It was the PCF, for example, that began the practice of systematically assassinating German and Vichy targets. On August 21, 1941, communist militants shot and killed a German naval officer at the Barbès-Rochechouart metro station in Paris. They followed this with several more actions over the next few months, including the assassination of the German military commander of Nantes. This policy became controversial when the Germans reacted by taking civilian hostages and shooting them, leading Gaullists and most other members of the resistance to condemn it. The communists persisted, however, arguing it was important to show the Germans and Vichy collaborators they weren't safe anywhere in France, and that reprisals increased popular support for the resistance. In 1941 the PCF founded the Francs Tireurs et Partisans, a guerrilla army open to all but controlled by the party. It would emerge as a leading military force in the resistance. It also created the National Front as the political arm of the communist resistance, complete with specialty groups for different segments of French society.

There was more to resistance than joining secret organizations, however. Most people in France did not become partisans but manifested their opposition to the occupation and Vichy in symbolic ways. Millions of French people secretly listened to BBC radio broadcasts, especially as it became clear that Germany was not going to win the war right away. De Gaulle's call on the BBC for all people in France to stay at home for an hour on the afternoon of New Year's Day 1941 resulted in empty streets throughout France. The BBC also helped launch the idea of V for victory, which soon began to appear on walls throughout the country. Waiters would arrange silverware in restaurants in the shape of a V. Others would ostentatiously carry two fishing poles (in French, *deux gaules*) to manifest their support for the general. On Armistice Day 1940 thousands of Parisian students gathered at the Arc de Triomphe to sing the "Marseillaise" and shout "Long live de Gaulle!"

Vichy's anti-Semitic measures often prompted widespread condemnation and resistance. Shopkeepers would rush to serve clients wearing the Jewish star, and some Zazous adopted their own yellow star, labeled "Swing." As the persecution of the Jews worsened, many non-Jews crossed the line from symbolic to actual resistance, helping them escape, sheltering them in their homes, or warning them of imminent arrest. Many churches as well as the Paris Mosque hid Jews, especially children, during the war years. The small Protestant town of Le Chambon, high in the French Alps, organized to provide shelter and save some two thousand Jews from deportation.

By the end of 1942 the resistance was growing in strength and size. Various groups began to establish links with the Free French abroad, some leaders traveling in secret to London to meet with de Gaulle personally. By the middle of the year de Gaulle had begun regular contacts, including funding, with various resistance groups, arranged by his personal emissary, Jean Moulin. Large demonstrations on Bastille Day 1942, especially in Lyon and Marseilles in the unoccupied zone, indicated the growing popularity of resistance. Members of the organized resistance constituted only a tiny fraction of the French population and posed no significant military threat to either the Germans or Vichy.

Nonetheless, it was becoming increasingly clear that the occupation would not go unchallenged.

As it grew, the resistance became more diverse both sociologically and ideologically. Originally a heavily urban phenomenon, it began to show some presence in small towns and rural areas. By the end of 1942 people from across the political spectrum, especially communists, socialists, and Christian Democrats, had become involved. Yet if there was no specific party line, many members of the resistance shared a common progressive orientation, very similar to that of the Popular Front. Many saw themselves as fighting not just to defeat the Germans but to construct a more just society after the war, not to restore the Third Republic but to build a new country based on vaguely socialist principles. Poverty and social injustice were the enemy as much as fascism; indeed, for many in the resistance they were indistinguishable. This was true throughout occupied Europe, but the presence in France of a reactionary collaborationist government gave this perspective special significance.

This link between the fight against fascism and the struggle for social justice was most pronounced in the colonies, above all in Indochina. The parts of the empire that remained under Vichy's control began to see resistance movements of their own. In Martinique and Guadeloupe, the combination of local resistance and American pressure led to the collapse of Vichy by 1943. In Indochina, nominally controlled by Vichy though occupied militarily by Japan, antifascism and anticolonialism joined hands. In 1941 Ho Chi Minh and other exiles in China founded the Viet Minh, or Vietnamese Revolutionary Organization, to fight for independence from France. In 1943 the Viet Minh began waging war against the Japanese occupiers, with the aid of both China and the United States. It made it clear, however, that it was fighting a double war against Japanese fascism and French colonialism. For the Viet Minh and their Vietnamese supporters, the struggle for national independence and social justice could only succeed through the destruction of both.

The growth of the resistance by early 1943 was due in large part to the failures of Vichy and its increasing inability to keep the loyalty of the French people. In April 1942 Laval not only proclaimed his hopes for a German victory but announced a voluntary program for French workers to take jobs in Germany. Virtually no one was willing to volunteer, so by September Vichy created the Service du Travail Obligatoire (Compulsory Labor Service, or STO), requiring men between eighteen and thirty-five to register for labor service in Germany. Widespread resistance continued, and in February 1943 the Germans imposed compulsory labor service on all men born between 1920 and 1922.

Several hundred thousand French workers ended up laboring in Germany during the war. Others fled into hiding, however, often swelling the ranks of the resistance. Many joined the Maquis, guerrilla armies operating in the rural and mountainous regions of the country. For the French population, the STO represented the inability or unwillingness of the regime to protect its people.

Even more important was the crisis that erupted in North Africa at the end of 1942. On November 8 Allied forces launched a major invasion of French North Africa, Operation Torch, planning from there to invade Italy and Mediterranean Europe. American and British forces stormed the beaches of Casablanca, Oran, and Algiers, while members of the Free French attacked Vichy forces from the rear. For months the Americans had been negotiating with Vichy leaders in North Africa, hoping to persuade them to switch sides. On November 8 they succeeded in capturing Admiral François Darlan, the commander in chief of Vichy's military, and two days later he agreed to surrender, in effect switching sides to the Allies. News of this "betrayal" infuriated Hitler, who responded by ordering German troops to move into the unoccupied zone the next day, Armistice Day. This new occupation not only erased the distinction between the two main parts of France, it demolished the fiction that Vichy was an independent state. Moreover, the surrender of Darlan meant that the regime had lost control of most of the empire.

By the beginning of 1943 Vichy had little popular support left in France, and was relying increasingly on German power and on repression. In January Laval created the Milice (Militia), a paramilitary police force that took the lead in battling the resistance and rounding up Jews for deportation. Often more ruthless than the Gestapo, the Milice symbolized Vichy's commitment to waging civil war in France against its opponents. The regime looked aside as Germany began to round up more Jews, including French citizens, even as public knowledge of the extent of the Holocaust spread throughout Europe and the world.

It soon became clear that Vichy had backed the losing side in the war. In February 1943 German forces surrendered to the Red Army at Stalingrad, and by May Axis resistance in North Africa had ceased, paving the way for the Allied invasion of Sicily and then the Italian mainland in July. The overthrow of Mussolini later that month showed that for Vichy and all the other allies of Nazi Germany the end was just a matter of time. Laval and the Vichy leaders desperately tried to placate their German masters while at the same time hoping against hope for a compromise peace that would not completely destroy the regime.

As Vichy waned, the resistance grew in power and influence. The situation in North Africa in the aftermath of the Allied invasion was extremely complex, and it was not at first clear that de Gaulle and the resistance would be able to assume control there. The Americans had no love for the Free French and were at first quite content to see Vichy forces remain in power. They initially recognized Admiral Darlan in spite of his unpopularity among the French, but when he was assassinated on Christmas Eve 1942, Roosevelt turned to Henri Giraud, a reactionary general and de Gaulle's military superior. De Gaulle remained in London, infuriated, but gradually outmaneuvered the lackluster Giraud. At the end of May de Gaulle left London for Algiers, where he and Giraud jointly headed up the new National Committee of French Liberation (CFLN). By the end of the year de Gaulle had established sole leadership of the CFLN, which was increasingly taking the form of a provisional government.

In 1943 de Gaulle took systematic control of the resistance inside France. In March his representative, Jean Moulin, again traveled to occupied France, meeting with the leaders of different organizations to persuade them to accept Gaullist leadership and join a unified resistance council. After much negotiation, Moulin's efforts bore fruit on May 27 when the main resistance organizations, including the communists, agreed to join a National Resistance Council (CNR) recognizing de Gaulle as the head of the nation's provisional government. This was Moulin's greatest triumph and also his last; the next month the Gestapo arrested him and other members of the resistance in Lyon and then tortured him to death.

The creation of the CNR came at a time when the resistance was emerging as a national mass movement. The growth of the Maquis gave the movement a presence in the countryside, at a time when French peasants were turning against the regime. Relations with the civilian population were not always easy, since the Maquisards sometimes stole food to survive, and their presence always created the possibility of reprisals. Nonetheless, most peasants supported the rural guerrillas in their attacks on Vichy officials and collaborators, and the Maquis helped make what had started off as a heavily urban movement into one that spoke to all corners of France.

In other ways as well, by the end of 1943 the resistance became more representative of the nation as a whole. From the beginning women took part in both resistance activities and organizations. Several women played leading roles, including Germaine Tillion in the Musée de l'homme group and Lucie Aubrac of Liberation Sud. Most women were not leaders but rather foot soldiers in the movement, and many served in positions such as couriers of supplies, where they were less likely to attract attention than men. In the resistance, as in society as a whole, women had to deal with male ideas about gender, so that few were allowed into combat units like the Maquis. The resistance as a whole may not have challenged patriarchy, but it did provide a space for some women to act outside normal gender roles.

Large numbers of immigrants and foreigners also took part in the resistance, probably in greater percentages than French citizens. Many were already isolated from mainstream society, so opting for a clandestine existence constituted less of a rupture. Some, like the over 100,000 refugees from republican Spain, were seasoned antifascist militants targeted for arrest by Vichy and the Germans. Some two thousand antifascist Germans and Austrians, veterans of the International Brigades in Spain, fought in the Maquis. For many, fighting in the resistance represented their way of claiming French identity. At the same time, many resistance organizations were leery of foreign participation, both because they wanted to emphasis the national character of their movement and also because they didn't want to confirm Vichy propaganda, which argued the resistance was essentially composed of foreign agitators, not loyal French men and women. Jews played a major role in resistance organizations. Many took part in mainstream groups, like Jean-Pierre Lévy, the head of Franc-Tireur. But others joined specifically Jewish resistance groups, especially those directed by the Communist party, which attracted mostly foreign Jews. Still others were active in rescue organizations like the Amelot Committee in Paris. All told, the diversity of the resistance represented a progressive vision of France that was both national and transnational at the same time.

By the end of 1943, the defeat of Nazi Germany was just a matter of time. But no one knew how much time, or what the end of the occupation would look like. The year 1944 would indeed be a year of liberation, but it would also bring great suffering and tragedy to the French people. The rebirth of the universal nation would be a violent act that involved not only major battles but also competing visions of France in the postwar world.

LIBERATION

No matter how much the resistance grew, it never became a military match for the forces of the German occupation. Only a full-scale invasion of the Continent by the Allied armies would liberate France. De Gaulle and the

French resistance had been pressing for the invasion for years, as had the Soviet Union, desperate for relief from the German onslaught. The German invasion of Italy after the fall of Mussolini in 1943 had stiffened what had been considered the "soft underbelly" of Nazi Europe, making the need for an attack in the west greater than ever. Expecting this, Hitler's generals had built the Atlantic wall, a formidable string of fortifications along the English Channel.

The Allies and the Free French agreed on the need for the invasion but not on how it should proceed. Starting in 1943 American general Dwight D. Eisenhower, the Allied supreme military commander, led the planning process for Operation Overlord, the assault on occupied France. Over the next several months the Allies assembled the largest naval invasion force in history, with over 3 million soldiers. The greatest priority was the defeat of Nazi Germany, rather than the immediate liberation of French territory, a point of potential conflict between de Gaulle and the British and Americans. It was also not clear that the Americans would simply hand over liberated territory to the Gaullists. Moreover, whereas de Gaulle advocated the liberation of French territory by the military, in particular the armies of Free France, many in the resistance called for a revolutionary insurrection against the occupier instead. De Gaulle feared that liberation could result in a seizure of power by the powerful communist resistance. By the summer of 1944 it was no longer just a question of winning the war, but equally of planning the postwar era.

On June 5 the BBC broadcast a coded message to France including lines by the poet Verlaine: *Blessent mon coeur d'une langueur monotone* (Wound my heart with a monotonous languor). This was the signal to the resistance that the long-awaited invasion was imminent. The next day, D day, American, British, and Canadian troops stormed onto the beaches of Normandy against fierce German artillery fire. That night de Gaulle, who had not learned of the invasion until the troops were actually on the ground, broadcast a message to the French people proclaiming the battle for France; the same day Pétain also issued a broadcast, asking the French not to fight one another or the Germans. The war for the liberation of France was under way.

The next two months were some of the most difficult of the war for the French people. German resistance was stiff, and the Allied armies were not able to break out of Normandy until the end of July. As a result Norman villages and towns were devastated, suffering the heaviest destruction of the war. Allied bombings killed five thousand people in Le Havre alone, and the majority of Caen was destroyed. The news of the D day landings prompted a flood of new recruits into the resistance, but victory was by no means assured, and many partisan groups were overwhelmed in pitched battles with German forces. In July partisans seized control of Vercors, southwest of Grenoble, only to be defeated and massacred by German troops at the end of the month. Retreating German troops committed the worst massacres of the war, notably at Oradour-sur-Glane in the Haute-Vienne, where on June 10 an SS division killed 642 people, burning women and children alive in the village church and razing the town to the ground. Roundups of Jews also continued until the end; the last convoy of deportees, some 1,300, left Drancy for Auschwitz on July 31.

By that date, however, the Allied forces finally broke German resistance in Normandy and began moving deeper into France. In spite of previous disagreements with the Americans, de Gaulle was able to ensure that liberated territory was placed under the rule of his provisional government. At this point the question of Paris became paramount for de Gaulle and the French resistance. Mindful of the dangers of getting bogged down in urban warfare, Eisenhower wanted to bypass the French capital, instead striking directly for the Rhine. This was not at all acceptable to the Gaullists, who insisted on liberating Paris as soon as possible. Not only would freeing Paris symbolize the liberation of the nation as a whole, but they also feared the prospect of a communist insurrection, indeed a new version of the Paris Commune, if they delayed.

This was no idle fear although, as events would later show, the PCF was not interested in seizing power in 1944. Nonetheless, by the end of July Paris was falling apart. Urban systems like the Metro were breaking down, and food was scarcer than ever. On August 10 strikes broke out throughout the city and its suburbs, culminating in a strike by the Paris police on August 15. Firefights began to erupt between the resistance and the German forces, and by August 19 the resistance occupied the prefecture of police in the center of the city and launched a full-scale revolt. Fighting broke out throughout Paris, especially in the Latin Quarter. Attempts by Swedish diplomats to broker a truce failed after a few days, and on August 22 fighting resumed more fiercely than ever. Hundreds of barricades went up around the city, and the Germans fought back, burning the Grand Palais to the ground. The specter of Warsaw, at the time fighting a battle for its life against the Germans that would end with the destruction of most of the city, hung heavily over the French capital.

At this point the French entreated the Allied military commanders to change their plans and allow Free French troops to march on Paris. On August 23 they agreed to do so, allowing General Leclerc's 2nd Armored Division the honor of invading the capital, along with American troops. The Americans also demanded, interestingly, that black colonial soldiers be excluded from the liberation of Paris. As a result, the "French" division that marched into the city was composed largely of Spanish republicans. Street fighting continued in the city until Leclerc's forces arrived in Paris on the morning of August 25. That afternoon the German commander of Paris, Gen. Dietrich von Choltitz, who had defied Hitler's orders to burn the city to the ground, formally surrendered. De Gaulle arrived in the city that same afternoon, going to city hall and proclaiming, "Paris! Paris humiliated! Paris broken! Paris martyred! But now Paris liberated!"[6] The next day, in one of the great moments of modern French history, de Gaulle led a march of a million French men and women down the Champs-Elysées as the bells of Notre Dame pealed in celebration. The war was not yet won; sniper fire broke out during the march, and much of France remained under German control. Yet there was no longer any doubt about the nation's future.

By the end of September most of France had been liberated, sometimes by resistance forces on their own. As the Germans retreated, they took with them Marshal Pétain and Pierre Laval, who found refuge in the castle of Sigmaringen overlooking the Danube. In April 1945 the last pockets of German resistance in France were wiped out, and on May 8 Nazi Germany surrendered unconditionally. The war in Europe was over; what the peace would look like was not yet clear.

During World War II France experienced defeat, terror, genocide, and rebirth. To a greater extent than any other time in the modern era the very existence of the nation, and the very meaning of French identity, was a stake. Defeat destroyed the Third Republic, the longest regime in the history of modern France, and challenged the universalist political culture that originated in the Revolution. In a sense the war years and the struggle between Vichy and the resistance represented the last and greatest battles between French men and women over the character of the nation. Like the Dreyfus Affair, the war years revealed both the powerful conservative, even reactionary, currents in French society, and the power and ultimately the triumph of universal republicanism.

To a much greater extent than ever before, the French struggles of the war years took place in a global context. Both Vichy and the resistance owed their existence in large part to forces beyond the nation's borders. Moreover, the resistance triumphed by mobilizing the margins of French life, both foreigners and colonials, to an unprecedented degree. In more than one sense, the salvation of France in 1944 came from over the sea. After liberation the French would wrestle with defining French identity in the aftermath of Vichy and the resistance: how to emphasize national unity and integrity in an increasingly globalized world. This challenge would lead to new perspectives on the universal nation in the postwar era.

Suggestions for Further Reading

Aubrac, Lucie. *Outwitting the Gestapo*. Lincoln: University of Nebraska Press, 1994.

Azema, Jean-Pierre. *From Munich to the Liberation*. New York: Cambridge University Press, 1984.

Bloch, Marc. *Strange Defeat: A Statement of Evidence Written in 1940*. New York: Norton, 1968.

Burrin, Philippe. *France Under the Germans: Collaboration and Compromise*. New York: New Press, 1996.

De Gaulle, Charles. *Complete War Memoirs*. New York: Simon & Schuster, 1968.

Diamond, Hanna. *Fleeing Hitler: France 1940*. Oxford: Oxford University Press, 2008.

Ginio, Ruth. 2006. *French Colonialism Unmasked: The Vichy Years in French West Africa*. Lincoln, NB: University of Nebraska Press.

Jackson, Julian. *France: The Dark Years, 1940–1944*. Oxford: Oxford University Press, 2001.

Jennings, Eric. *Vichy in the Tropics: Pétain's National Revolution in Madagascar, Guadeloupe, and Indochina, 1940–1944*. Stanford, CA: Stanford University Press, 2001.

Marrus, Michael, and Robert Paxton. *Vichy France and the Jews*. New York: Basic, 1981.

Paxton, Robert. *Vichy France: Old Guard and New Order*. New York: Norton, 1972.

Rousso, Henry. *The Vichy Syndrome: History and Memory in France Since 1944*. Cambridge: Harvard University Press, 1994.

Sweets, John. *Choices in Vichy France: the French under Nazi Occupation*. Oxford: Oxford University Press, 1994.

Thomas, Martin. *The French Empire at War, 1940–1945*. Manchester, UK: Manchester University Press, 2007.

Zuccotti, Susan. *The Holocaust, the French, and the Jews*. Lincoln: University of Nebraska Press, 1999.

Notes

1. Julian Jackson, *France: The Dark Years, 1940–1944* (Oxford: Oxford University Press, 2001), 126.

2. Gordon Wright, *France in Modern Times* (Chicago: Rand McNally, 1974), 397.

3. Jackson, *France,* 147.

4. Susan Zuccotti, *The Holocaust, the French, and the Jews* (Lincoln: University of Nebraska Press, 1999), 1.

5. Jackson, *France,* 335.

6. Gregor Dallas, *1945: The War That Never Ended* (New Haven, CT: Yale University Press, 2005), 21.

[ten]

THE FOURTH REPUBLIC:
NEW CHALLENGES FOR
THE TRANSNATIONAL NATION

IN HER IMPORTANT STUDY OF 1950S FRANCE, *FAST CARS, CLEAN BODIES*, literary scholar Kristin Ross points out that questions of empire were central to the history of France in the decades after World War II, but from two different perspectives. Under the Fourth Republic the nation had to contend both with the loss of much of its empire while at the same time taking its place in a world dominated by the United States, the new imperium of Pax Americana. Algeria and America would shape much of French life as the nation rebuilt itself from the traumas of occupation and collaboration and sought a new place in the world.

Few eras of modern French history were more clearly shaped by transnational pressures and concerns than the years of the Fourth Republic, from 1946 to 1958. World War II ended in 1945, after an unprecedented destruction and loss of life in Europe and Asia, only to give rise to a new conflict between the United States and the Soviet Union. Even more than the struggle against Germany and Japan, this new cold war was fought on a global scale, so that all the nations and peoples of the world were pressured to choose sides. At the same time European colonialism faced a wave of challenges

Map 10.1. France today.

from independence movements throughout Asia, Africa, and the Middle East. Within a generation after the end of World War II, little remained of the formal empires that symbolized the global dominance of Europe at the start of the twentieth century. The contest between capitalism and socialism and the struggle against empire would interact in a variety of ways, together reinforcing the integration of global affairs in the late twentieth century.

For the French at the end of World War II, the overwhelming priority was rebuilding their nation: achieving greatness in world affairs and pursuing prosperity and justice at home. In key ways the story of the Fourth Republic is one of success at home and failure abroad. While it laid the foundations for impressive economic growth and social transformation, at the same time it fought and lost two disastrous colonial wars and found itself increasingly integrated into the American sphere of influence. Like the Third Republic, it would collapse under the weight of military defeat. During the middle of the twentieth century the vision of France as a universal nation would be challenged by the global processes of decolonization and the cold war. The universalist ideal in France was not dead, however. The translation of resistance ideology into welfare state benefits for all testified to its continued hold on the French imagination. Nonetheless, what role the universal nation could and would play in a period of global turmoil remained unclear.

FROM LIBERATION TO THE FOURTH REPUBLIC

A central irony characterizes France's transition from war to peace after liberation. The two French forces that had led the nation out of the darkness of the occupation were the Free French of Charles de Gaulle and the internal resistance. Both had strong claims to shaping the future of the nation. Yet when the dust of the immediate postwar period had settled, neither was in power. Instead, for all the fervent calls for change and renewal, the new Fourth Republic bore an uncanny resemblance to the Third. This was even stranger, given that public opinion polls of the French at the end of the war revealed an overwhelming desire to use this moment of national renewal to create a fundamentally new and different France. Yet once the euphoria of liberation had faded, achieving consensus on what this new path should be proved more difficult than anticipated.

When the German troops left, taking their Vichy allies with them, they were replaced by liberation committees representing the provisional government established by de Gaulle. One concern was whether or not local resistance groups, often led by communists, would try to seize power on their own. This did not happen, in large part because the PCF cooperated with the Gaullists in restoring order throughout France. In November 1944 Maurice Thorez, leader of the French communists, returned to Paris from his wartime exile in Moscow and made it clear to his followers and the French in general that the party's task was to rebuild France, not start a revolution. The PCF's attitude ensured that the transfer of power after liberation went smoothly. Some members of the resistance, however, determined to punish collaborators, particularly members of the Milice, took matters into their own hands. During the fall of 1944 a wave of summary arrests and executions swept across France, claiming as many as 10,000 lives. Conservatives claimed the number was far higher and charged that a new red terror was abroad. These unofficial purges often targeted women accused of "horizontal collaboration": sleeping with Germans. Particularly in small towns, many were manhandled by jeering crowds, had their heads shaved bare, and were driven from their homes.

One of the first tasks of the provisional government was to deal with the possibility of civil war by setting up orderly mechanisms for dispensing justice to the collaborators. Formal trials of accused Vichy officials began in early 1945, and several hundred thousand were brought before the courts in the next few years. Both Pétain and Laval were captured and returned to France for trial. Pétain was convicted but spared the death penalty due to his advanced age (89), while Laval was executed after unsuccessfully attempting suicide. All told, less than a thousand collaborators were executed, a small number compared with the nearly 300,000 French men and women killed by the Nazis and Vichy. The official purge focused on those who played major leadership roles or spoke out publicly for Vichy, targeting ideologues while largely sparing technocrats.

In the final analysis, however, punishing people for past crimes was less important than tackling the problems of the present. In many respects France was comparatively fortunate at the end of the war. With the exception of Normandy the nation had suffered less physical damage than the rest of Europe, and de Gaulle had enabled it to make an orderly return to self-rule. Nonetheless, conditions were far from normal. Over 2 million prisoners of war and conscript laborers remained in Germany for several months. France suffered from a near economic collapse in 1944–1945: industrial production was 40 percent below that of 1938, and in some crucial sectors like coal even less. The war had devastated the nation's transportation network, especially its railroads, which resistance fighters had at times blown up to hinder German troop movements, and millions of homes had been destroyed or rendered uninhabitable. Agriculture also suffered, thanks to a lack of manpower and to fighting in the summer of 1944 that disrupted the harvest and damaged many farms. The result was major shortages of food and fuel, made all the worse by the exceptionally harsh winter of 1944–1945. Material conditions in France during the first year after liberation seemed harsher than they had been under Vichy. Not until the end of the decade did economic and material conditions return to prewar levels.

The government responded to the shortages by rationing essential commodities, which helped ameliorate the worst impacts of the crisis. At the same time, however, rationing contributed to the return of the black market, at times more robust than it had been during Vichy. This of course privileged those who could pay high black market prices. Growing inequality, especially benefiting those considered "economic collaborators" during the war, undercut the promise of liberation. The resistance had emphasized improving conditions for ordinary people, yet in the immediate postwar era patriotic French families suffered continuing deprivation while those who had prospered during the war continued to grow fat. The economic crisis was thus a political problem; as *New Yorker* Paris correspondent Janet Flanner noted, "Butter has taken on political qualities."[1]

By 1945 the joy of liberation was a distant memory, as France turned to the arduous task of building the future. One of the most somber examples of the new sobriety was provoked by the return of Nazi concentration camp survivors. The revelations of the Nazi death camps and the Holocaust at the end of the war shocked people in France and throughout the world. The terrible physical and emotional condition of many survivors, not to mention the fact that so many (over 95 percent of deported Jews) never returned at all, underscored the horrors of the war and the hard work required to recover from it. The final conclusion of World War II with the nuclear obliteration of Hiroshima and Nagasaki, as well as rapidly cooling relations between the United States and the Soviet Union, suggested that the postwar world would be a dangerous place.

This was the context in which de Gaulle and the French political leadership sought to create a new political structure for the nation. The war years had drastically changed the face of French politics. The Communist party, until the Popular Front only a minor political sect, emerged from the war as one of the most powerful political forces in France. Both its own dynamic role in the resistance and the tremendous prestige of the Soviet Union as the primary victor over Nazi Germany brought it an unprecedented mass following. Municipalities throughout the country named streets after the battle of Stalingrad in homage to the Russian ally. The socialists had also come out of the war with their national power and influence reinforced by their commitment to the resistance and to social equality. Perhaps most dramatic was the emergence of a new progressive Catholic party, the Mouvement Républicain Populaire (People's Republican Movement, or MRP), reflecting both the growth of the Christian left during the interwar years and the engagement of many

Catholics in the resistance. Most significant, of course, was the disappearance of political conservatism, discredited by its proximity to Vichy. Even the Radical party, the quintessential center of the Third Republic, lost much of its support after the war. Liberation and resistance thus provoked a massive shift to the left in French politics.

And then of course there was Charles de Gaulle, the man who symbolized the rebirth of the nation. While the French admired and even revered the great general, some feared he might want to become a postwar strongman. Had he fought Pétain only to replace him? Many others feared the new prominence of the French Communist party, especially as communist parties in eastern Europe began establishing "people's democracies" under the sponsorship of the Soviet Union. Some suspected the PCF had similar designs for France. Both de Gaulle and the communists represented clear alternatives to the Third Republic, but both alternatives had their risks.

In October 1945 France held its first elections since the war, voting to elect a Constituent Assembly and whether or not to restore the Third Republic. For the first time in history Frenchwomen exercised the right to vote. De Gaulle's provisional government had decreed female suffrage in 1944, and the new regime would make it a permanent part of national politics. Voters overwhelmingly rejected the idea of returning to the Third Republic, instead endorsing a popular referendum to approve a new constitution and thus a new regime. Each of the three main parties won roughly a quarter of the vote; the PCF came in slightly ahead, establishing the clear leftist dominance of postwar politics.

At this point a basic disagreement over the structure of the new regime surfaced. De Gaulle and those closest to him wanted to establish a republic with a strong executive, which would avoid the weakness and instability of the Third Republic. It required no great stretch of the imagination to guess who this strong executive would be. But the political left, above all the PCF, wished for a strong legislature, preferably centered in a united house elected by direct suffrage. Both models were deeply rooted in French history, one looking back to Bonaparte, the other to the Jacobin republic. De Gaulle denounced the legislative model, and in January 1946 abruptly resigned as leader of the provisional government. To his surprise, the assembly did not beg him to return, and a year and a half after his triumphal return to Paris the great general exited the stage of French politics.

The Constituent Assembly debated the issue for several months before coming up with a system that favored the option of a strong unicameral legislature, submitting it to popular referendum in May 1946. Supported by the PCF and SFIO, it was vigorously opposed by the MRP who feared it might pave the way to a communist seizure of power. Thanks largely to the MRP, French voters defeated the constitution, forcing the election of a new Constituent Assembly and the development of a new constitutional proposal. Many political conservatives, seeing no other viable alternative, chose to vote for the MRP, so that it emerged from the new elections as the largest party in France. More months of debate and negotiation followed until the legislators wrote a new constitution, one with a bicameral legislature and a weak presidency. All three main parties ultimately accepted this proposal, only to be opposed by de Gaulle himself, increasingly supported by the French right. On October 13 the new constitution narrowly won approval, with a third of the electorate abstaining. The new Fourth Republic was at long last a reality.

COLD WAR AND COCA-COLONIZATION: FRANCE BETWEEN THE SUPERPOWERS

The grand alliance that won World War II was always a marriage of convenience rather than conviction. The Soviet Union and the United States in particular had little in common beyond a mutual desire to destroy Nazi Germany, and much that had historically divided them. As the war neared its end and victory became more certain, these differences increasingly emerged into the open, culminating in the global conflict known as the cold war.

Americans and Soviets had experienced the war in fundamentally different ways. For the Soviets the German invasion was a catastrophe that cost the lives of at least 20 million people and destroyed much of the industrial infrastructure so painstakingly built up since the 1917 revolution. One-third of the population of Leningrad had died, mostly from starvation and disease, during the German siege. For Soviet dictator Joseph Stalin, the top priority was ensuring that Russia never again faced such a devastating invasion from Europe. This meant the demilitarization of Germany but also the establishment of reliable, friendly regimes throughout eastern Europe. Stalin was less concerned about spreading revolution as the Red Army swept west toward Berlin but was determined to control the region between Russia and Germany.

For the United States, in contrast, World War II confirmed the global supremacy hinted at by World War I. Not only had America not suffered invasion or wartime damage (its population in 1945 was bigger than in 1941), but its economy had expanded so much that it was far and away the wealthiest country in the world. Whereas other nations in 1945 confronted the problem of rebuilding their economies, the United States faced the challenge of maintaining wartime levels of production. In the opinion of many American political and business leaders, this could only be done by ensuring the access of national goods to global markets. The United States also regarded the war as a victory for democracy, and looked with increasing suspicion on Soviet moves to create satellite regimes along its borders.

As tension increased between the US and USSR, the Soviets began applying more pressure to eastern Europe. Between 1945 and 1948 the states of the region gradually fell under communist domination. At the same time the United States became involved in a civil war in Greece, pitting the communist resistance movement against the established monarchy. This commitment led US President Harry Truman to proclaim the Truman Doctrine in March 1947, signaling America's intention to resist communist expansionism in the postwar era. In 1948 the United States enacted the Marshall Plan to provide aid to rebuild western Europe and thus prevent communist subversion there. In 1949 the US led western Europe into the North Atlantic Treaty Organization (NATO), an anti-Soviet military alliance, to which the USSR responded in 1955 by creating the Warsaw Pact. Also in 1949 the two superpowers effectively divided occupied Germany into two client states: West Germany and East Germany. That same year saw the triumph of the communist revolution in China. By 1950 Europe and the world were divided into competing blocs, and the cold war would dominate international relations during the late twentieth century.

The location of France in western Europe, liberated by American rather than Soviet troops during the war, placed it firmly in the capitalist bloc. Stalin recognized this. The Soviet dictator was less interested in world revolution than in Russian dominance of eastern Europe, and he was quite willing to see the United States control the western part of the Continent. He made this clear to the United States and Britain at the end of the war, looking for a quid pro quo arrangement. Moreover, Stalin hoped that if he accepted American dominance of western Europe, the US might be willing to continue wartime aid that the USSR badly needed to rebuild its shattered economy. For this reason, he instructed the PCF in 1944 to accept the leadership of de Gaulle rather than trying to move from resistance to revolution. Stalin viewed an independent France as a valuable postwar asset that could resist American pressure and also hold the line against any future German resurgence. Both global and local factors thus prevented French communists from attempt to seize power during the liberation.

A key part of the history of the cold war is how nations other than the two superpowers reacted to the growing conflict between America and Russia. Having fought strenuously during the war for French independence, de Gaulle was not interested in seeing France become a satellite of any other nation, and his fellow citizens agreed. The resistance, like the Popular Front before it, had emphasized a broad-based progressive coalition opposing fascism and supporting social justice, and rejected dividing the world into rival capitalist and communist blocs. Starting in January 1946 the three progressive parties in France ruled together in a grand coalition known as tripartism. This represented nothing less than the rebirth of the Popular Front, and the hope that in spite of the looming cold war the spirit that had animated the resistance could lead France into the postwar era. A tripartite government also ruled Italy briefly after the war, and in both countries the movement suggested that at least part of Europe could carve out a third way between the great powers.

Tripartism in France was carefully structured to enable each of the three parties to play a major role in, but not dominate, the government. In eastern Europe communist parties had used control of key ministries, notably defense and the interior, to gradually establish one-party rule, and great care was taken to ensure that the PCF could not repeat this pattern in France. The coalition invariably chose socialists to serve as prime minister, both because the SFIO was the smallest of the three parties and because it stood ideologically between the PCF and the MRP. The three parties achieved some success in working together, most notably in creating the structure of the Fourth Republic. The growing antagonism between the superpowers, however, and its ramifications for France, would ultimately doom this attempt to continue wartime unity.

The challenges to tripartism came from both the metropole and the empire, and in both cases centered around the role of the Communist party. In November 1946, after a year-long struggle to reassert French control over Indochina, France bombarded Haiphong harbor in Vietnam, subsequently unleashing a full-scale war against the Viet Minh (see next section). The Indochina war dramatically highlighted the differences between the PCF and the other tripartite parties. The Soviet Union fully backed the Viet Minh, leaving the French communists in an impossible position. The PCF generally supported movements of colonial liberation, especially the Viet Minh, with its shared history of communist resistance to fascism. Yet it was also part of the French government engaged in war against them. Increasingly observers in both France and abroad came to view the first Indochina war as less a colonial conflict and more a part of the cold war, leaving the PCF awkwardly straddling both camps.

Ultimately, however, domestic considerations doomed tripartism. With the announcement of the Truman Doctrine the US government began pressuring both France and Italy to rid their governments of communist participation. Continued US economic aid might be imperiled by a failure to do so. For France, still impoverished, hungry, and struggling to rebuild, this pressure had an impact, directly linking political conformity to material well-being. It reinforced the hesitation some members of the SFIO and MRP had about the wisdom of their alliance with the PCF.

More important, however, was the increased restiveness of many French workers as bad times continued in the postwar years. Not only were food and fuel in short supply, but rapid inflation was reducing their ability to buy those commodities available. Starting with the liberation, the PCF exhorted French workers to place the national interest above their own by working to restart the national economy before demanding wage increases; the successful battle for France must give way to the new "battle of production." Yet as time continued and inflation ate away at real wages, working people became less willing to accept this, especially as the wealthy continued to consume extravagantly. In March 1947, for example, fashion models and photographers staged a fashion shoot in Montmartre's Rue Lepic market to publicize Christian Dior's New Look, which had been launched a month prior. A crowd of housewives, outraged at the display of such luxury when they could barely get food for their families, attacked the session, trying literally to strip the clothes off the models' backs. These were the PCF's constituents, and ultimately it could not continue to ignore or try to placate their anger for the sake of the national interest, or its own place in the coalition government.

Matters came to a head in the spring of 1947. Socialist prime minister Paul Ramadier had enacted a series of deflationary measures, notably wage freezes, to combat inflation. In May the communist-controlled CGT staged major strikes on the railways and at the Renault auto plant, both state industries since the war, against the plan and for wage increases. The PCF had to choose between its coalition partners and its constituents, and after much hesitation it chose the latter, the four communist ministers voting no confidence in the Ramadier government. Ramadier responded by firing them and accusing the PCF of trying to overthrow the government. This action ended the tripartite experiment. Freed from its double bind, the PCF now moved into opposition and strikes broke out across the country. This massive strike wave against austerity crested in November, when 3 million French workers staged work actions that turned violent in Marseilles and some other areas. The government responded by mobilizing troops to battle striking coal miners, proclaiming that the strikes were a communist attempt to seize power. In less than a year Paul Ramadier had gone from being Léon Blum to Georges Clemenceau.

The defeat of the strike wave and the isolation of the PCF from the mainstream of French politics, which would last until the early 1980s, ended tripartism, as well as the attempt to create a broad progressive coalition in French politics that had begun with the Popular Front. It also marked the revival of the right in French politics. In April 1947 de Gaulle would found the Rassemblement du Peuple Français (Rally of the French People, or RPF). For the rest of the Fourth Republic power would be held by a series of center-left coalitions dominated by the SFIO and MRP. Both the communists and Gaullists would be consigned to the sidelines.

These developments reflected national tensions and international developments. In June 1947 the US government announced that France would receive a major infusion of funds under the Marshall Program, something that would have been much less likely had communists remained in the government. In December the CGT split, the dissidents creating their own anticommunist union organization: the CGT-Force Ouvrière; aid from American unions and the CIA played an important role in engineering this break. American pressure thus facilitated the collapse of tripartism, but so did internal tensions in French society. For both local and global reasons, therefore, by 1948 France had definitively chosen the American side in the cold war.

What did the alliance with the United States mean to postwar France? Americans had lived in France since the era of Thomas Jefferson and Benjamin Franklin, and both world wars had brought masses of American soldiers to French soil. French intellectuals had long debated the significance of American culture both for France and the world, often viewing it critically as a symbol of capitalist modernity. During the postwar years the French encountered a nation more than ever determined to play a dominant role in world affairs. This meant using America's economic might, and Europe's need for reconstruction aid, to integrate the west into a US international sphere. In 1946 Washington pursued negotiations with Britain and France toward this end. At the beginning of the year a high-level French delegation headed by

Léon Blum traveled to the United States to request financial assistance. The French requested a loan of $3 billion and were disappointed to receive $650 million, although the agreement annulled over $2 billion in debt. The Americans took aim at the French film industry, which had heavily restricted foreign imports before the war and prospered during the occupation. Under the terms of the Blum-Byrnes accord France had to open up its theaters to foreign films, a move that helped ensure Hollywood dominance of the nation's screens for years to come.

The Blum-Byrnes agreement promoted America's economic and cultural influence on France. In 1948 a controversy over "Coca-Colonization" erupted. Few products have signified the American way of life to a greater extent than Coca-Cola. The syrupy soft drink from Atlanta had been largely unknown in Europe until World War II, when it became part of the commodity baggage associated with the liberating American armies. In 1948 Coca-Cola applied for permission to open a bottling plant in Marseilles, something it was doing all over Europe. The French government initially refused, and a furor soon erupted seeing Coke as another symbol of American imperialism. The communists led the charge, inventing the term "Coca-Colonization" to make the point that Coca-Cola was not simply a beverage but an assault on French culture. They were joined by France's powerful wine industry, which viewed the soft drink as an unwelcome competitor. Heavily imbued with cold war political tensions on both sides of the Atlantic, this "tempest in a Coke cup" would come to symbolize French fears of American cultural imperialism in the postwar period. Coca-Cola would not receive permission to open a bottling factory in France until the early 1950s.

American influence in postwar France went far beyond soft drinks. The Marshall Plan poured billions of dollars of aid money into the country, which it then used to buy American products. US aid included a technical assistance program; American experts trained French managers and administrators in fields like statistics. Aid programs from the United States also helped shape French intellectual life, with an eye toward weakening the influence of Marxism. Both the Rockefeller and Ford foundations created French programs, helping to fund the social sciences in particular. In addition, American culture remained popular, not only Hollywood movies but also jazz and popular fiction like crime novels.

Yet interactions between France and the United States were not a one-way street, especially where culture was concerned. French intellectual life after the war demonstrates this clearly. The immediate postwar period became one of the great eras of the Parisian intelligentsia during the modern era. Existentialism, a philosophy founded in the nineteenth century by the Danish thinker Søren Kierkegaard and refined during the interwar years by the German scholar Martin Heidegger, became the dominant intellectual mood of the era. Led by Jean-Paul Sartre, whose 1943 treatise *Being and Nothingness* became the bible of the movement, existentialism took a bleak view of human existence, arguing that man must struggle to be free but that the struggle usually ended in failure. Its pessimism aptly summed up postliberation disenchantment, and the anxiety about the cold war and the nuclear age, felt by many in France and elsewhere.

For the most part existentialism espoused determinedly leftist perspectives, and many in the movement harshly criticized US politics and culture. Yet at the same time existentialists embraced certain parts of American life, notably jazz, blue jeans, and other aspects of popular culture. Their support of African American writers like Richard Wright served both to praise American culture and criticize American racism. Existentialism fascinated many young Americans as a cultural mood rather than a strict philosophy. The center of the existentialism phenomenon, the Left Bank neighborhood of Saint-Germain-des-Prés in Paris, became known for its café life. There young people would sit around discussing politics and philosophy, dancing the jitterbug to jazz bands, and cultivating an air of worldly *anomie*. This image of the Gauloise-smoking beret-clad youth became a worldwide sensation. It was the successor to the wartime Zazous, and played a central role in inspiring the Beat generation of America in the 1950s. Precisely because it represented an alternative to, even a rejection of, postwar American culture, existentialism found a receptive audience among domestic critics.

The example of existentialism underscores the fact that when France finally chose sides in the cold war, it did so for domestic reasons as well as international pressure. Even after the end of tripartism the PCF remained influential in France, usually winning at least 20 percent of the vote in national elections, and it harshly opposed American influence. Many French intellectuals sympathized much more with the Soviet Union than the United States. The debates over Americanization would intensify during the 1960s, when increasing prosperity enabled many in France to practice the kind of consumerism pioneered across the Atlantic. But the very intensity of these debates, starting with that over Coca-Cola, showed the importance of national culture in a globalizing world. Americanization, both politically and culturally, challenged universalist ideas of French national identity. French responses defended these ideas in ways that attracted support in France and throughout the world.

BUILDING A NEW FRANCE

Seen from the perspective of the late 1940s, the Fourth Republic did not have a lot to recommend itself. The economy remained depressed, the leader of the Free French had been exiled into the political wilderness, the nation seemed increasingly subject to the will of the United States, and the regime was embroiled in the first of the major colonial wars that would ultimately bring about its ruin. For all the hope for change and renewal, the new republic replicated the structural weakness and instability of its predecessor. For all the struggles that had brought about the salvation of France during the war, the fruits of victory seemed few and far between.

The Fourth Republic did renew and even revolutionize the nation in important ways, however, above all when it came to economic performance. It laid the structural basis for what would become one of the greatest periods of economic expansion in the history of modern France. Known as the *trente glorieuses*, or the thirty glorious years stretching from the late 1940s to the mid-1970s, this era not only ushered in unprecedented national prosperity but fundamentally transformed the nation. These changes would become most evident during the 1960s and 1970s under the Fifth Republic, but the Fourth laid the groundwork. Capitalist expansion did not bring about the resistance vision of social justice, for in many ways France remained a highly stratified society after the war. But postwar prosperity did make real improvements in living standards throughout the country, as well as restoring the sense of national self-confidence so badly damaged by the war years.

The economic boom of the mid-twentieth century went far beyond France. During the 1950s the United States, western Europe, and Japan achieved impressive rates of economic growth. The defeated Axis powers, West Germany and Japan, grew fastest of all, taking advantage of American aid and the destruction of their old industries to build anew from the ground up. As a result, West Germany's gross national product (GNP) grew 300 percent between 1950 and 1964. Nations in Mediterranean Europe, especially Italy and Spain, also racked up significant growth and economic development. In contrast, victorious Britain began a sustained period of relative economic decline; from the world's workshop in the nineteenth century, it became increasingly regarded as the economic sick man of Europe.

The French rate of economic growth was less impressive than that of West Germany and some other European nations. It nonetheless compared favorably with that of Britain, and represented the most sustained period of economic expansion in the nation's history since the late nineteenth century. Several factors helped produce this dynamism, but one stands out. As noted in the previous chapter, during the war years the French birthrate began growing for the first time in a century. After the war ended natality rates accelerated, producing an unprecedented number of infants. This was part of what became known as the worldwide postwar baby boom, as the US and Europe experienced sharp rises in natality. The French case was special because the nation's birthrate had been declining so long, and French society had become accustomed to fewer and fewer children. The number of births in France grew from roughly 600,000 per year in the 1930s to over 800,000 by 1950. So notable was the nation's new fertility that comedians joked the new national slogan should be "Liberty, Equality, Maternity."

A number of factors help explain the French baby boom, including state policies favoring large families under both Vichy and the Fourth Republic (after the liberation the state continued subsidizing families with more than two children) and the large number of prisoners of war and workers who returned from the war. Many babies born in 1946 were known as "children of the return." As the baby boom accelerated, the new generation began moving like an enormous lump through the snake of French society, stimulating industries and services along the way. France's hospital and medical care sector was the first to feel the pinch, followed by the dairy industry, day care centers, and schools. As families grew, they began searching for more spacious housing, providing a major stimulus to that industry. By the 1960s the new generation would play a key role in the development of modern consumer society.

Population growth and the demand it stimulated was a major factor in postwar economic expansion, but production also had to be organized, providing for more resources and more efficient business practices. During the interwar years most of French business had used traditional production and marketing methods, while in some sectors innovation had become more common. Under the Fourth Republic, however, an increasingly interventionist state pushed for more modern approaches to industry. In particular, after the liberation France turned to centralized economic planning, a strategy generally associated with authoritarian regimes like Nazi Germany and the Soviet Union. Many in the resistance had advocated the traditional socialist demand for widespread state control over industry, and after the liberation the provisional government did nationalize some firms, including the Bank of France and the major utilities. An even more important inspiration, however, was Vichy, which had created France's first state economic planning agency in 1941. Thus the policies that became known in postwar France as *planisme* had a diverse ideological pedigree.

The founder of postwar state economic planning was Jean Monnet, a prominent businessman who joined the Free French in London during the war. Monnet had started his professional life as a brandy merchant from Cognac before carving out a distinguished reputation as an international financier between the wars, working for several years in China with the government of Chiang Kai-Shek. During the war he collaborated closely with both Winston Churchill and Franklin D. Roosevelt. In August 1945 Monnet proposed to de Gaulle to create a centralized planning office to oversee French reconstruction. De Gaulle agreed, and in January 1946 the Commissariat général du plan (the General Planning Commission) was born.

For Monnet, *planisme* had nothing to do with socialism or promoting equality. Most of French business and industry remained in private hands. Rather, it was matter of making the national economy, and capitalism in general, function more efficiently and productively by targeting financial and material resources to sectors where they would have the maximum impact. The commissariat was a body of forty individuals representing private industry, labor, and the public sector, appointed by the prime minister and directly answerable to him. Thus, as under Vichy, centralized economic planning under the Fourth Republic was largely exempt from parliamentary oversight. The commissariat would identify targets and key sectors, and companies that cooperated with the plan would get priority in the allocation of resources. Unlike under authoritarian regimes, targets would be negotiated between industry and labor, and meeting them was voluntary. For business centralized planning represented a positive alternative to nationalization, whereas for labor it had traits of public control of the economy.

The commissariat got to work immediately at the beginning of 1946, and within a year had restored the nation's productive output to prewar levels. Later in 1947 it unveiled France's first five-year plan, emphasizing key industries like coal and electricity. Monnet used funds from the Marshall Plan to provide crucial investment capital. The commissariat not only recognized that financing and raw materials were important, but also increased resources in management, administration, and information. The five year plan thus created the National Institute of Statistical Studies (INSEE) to develop advanced economic data sets. It also founded the National Administration School (ENA) to train the industrial managers and high-level civil servants of the future. Created in the tradition of the *grandes écoles* like the Ecole Normale Superieure and the Ecole Polytechnique, ENA would become one of the most prestigious educational institutions in postwar France; under the Fifth Republic many would refer to the nation as an ENArchy.

A key aspect of the first five-year plan was an emphasis on boosting basic production over improving the standard of living. Material conditions in France were still very difficult, and many basic commodities like bread were rationed until 1949. Housing was in desperately short supply, creating not only widespread homelessness but squatters' movements in several cities. As we have seen, this material deprivation was a major reason for the collapse of tripartism. Yet, as elsewhere in Europe, France's governments after liberation gambled that only increased productivity could raise living standards, and therefore basic production had to be the first priority. By 1952, when the plan came to an end, Monnet could point to some solid successes even if the commissariat had not achieved all of its goals. The gross national product was 39 percent higher than in 1946, output of coal and electricity was up significantly, and France had repaired and modernized its transportation sector. Above all, the plan demonstrated that centralized economic planning could work in a democracy.

Immediately after completing the first five-year plan, Monnet launched a second one. The new plan, from 1952 to 1957, concentrated on consumer goods and agriculture, seeking to improve the national standard of living. It built on the first plan, investing much of the nation's growing wealth in improving the lives of its citizens. The plan invested in modernizing agriculture, promoting the use of fertilizers and farming machinery like tractors, and favoring larger farms. It also tackled the knotty housing issue, a major problem since the nineteenth century. The French had traditionally spent less of their budgets on lodging than other Europeans, so that as a result the nation had some of the most antiquated housing stock on the Continent. Under the second five-year plan France built over 1 million new housing units, mostly in the form of *habitations à loyer modéré* (low-cost rental housing, or HLM). These modern, often high-rise housing blocs sprang up in the suburbs of Paris and other French cities, dramatically altering the nation's urban skylines and streetscapes. Although they did help ease the housing shortage at the time, most were cheaply built and began to fall apart within a generation.

10.1. Postwar public housing in Toulouse. Postcard circa 1960.
Postcard Lapie. Courtesy of Kenny Cupers.

Centralized economic planning thus melded the legacies of Vichy and the resistance to create the foundations for the nation's postwar renewal. It took place in an international context, specifically two aspects of postwar economic policies. The Marshall Plan played a critical role in providing the capital for reconstruction. Moreover, its emphasis on the systematic allocation of resources and the development of technical and managerial skills closely coordinated with Monnet's ideas about planning. While the economic recovery was not made solely in America by any means, the Marshall Plan did play a critical role at a critical time.

More important, certainly for the long term, were the beginnings of European integration. Many individuals contributed to this new beginning for Europe, but none was more important than the French statesman Robert Schuman. Born in Luxembourg of an Alsatian family, Schuman had personally experienced border conflicts between France and Germany. He became a French citizen when Alsace rejoined France in 1919, only to be deported to Germany after the defeat of 1940. He escaped the Dachau concentration camp to join the French resistance. As a result of his wartime experiences Schuman became convinced that the historical antagonism between France and Germany must be ended, and believed that economic cooperation would make this possible. In a speech he gave in the Alsatian capital of Strasbourg in 1949, Schuman argued for a transnational solution to national conflict:

> Our century, that has witnessed the catastrophes resulting in the unending clash of nationalities and nationalisms, must attempt and succeed in *reconciling nations in a supranational association*. This would safeguard the diversities and aspirations of each nation while coordinating them in the same manner as the regions are coordinated within the unity of the nation.[2]

In 1950, as foreign minister, Schuman called on France and West Germany, together with all the nations of Europe, to manage their coal and steel industries jointly as a first step toward creating a supranational democracy in Europe. The next year the Treaty of Paris created the European Coal and Steel Community, including not only the two classic rivals but also Italy, Belgium, the Netherlands, and Luxembourg. This was the precursor to the 1957 Treaty of Rome, in which these six nations joined together to create the European Economic Community (EEC), or Common Market.

Helping create the EEC was another way in which the Fourth Republic laid the foundations for the consumer prosperity of the 1960s and beyond. The EEC became a large united economic zone, free of tariffs between its member states, and it began to resemble an economic superpower like the United States more than individual nations. The increased size of the EEC markets facilitated the growth of French exports, stimulating those industries modern enough to compete beyond the national borders. At the same time, it provided a level of national security unknown after World War I. The creation of a Franco-German economic alliance ended the fearsome rivalry that had torn Europe apart for over half a century; in European international relations after 1945, peace and prosperity reinforced each other. France took the lead in creating a united Europe, and this initiative represented an important aspect of French universalism in the contemporary era.

Another contribution made by the Fourth Republic to the development of postwar prosperity was the creation of the welfare state. The idea of government providing for the material welfare of its citizens had a long history, and between the wars France had experimented with a variety of policies, including subsidies for large families. After liberation the French government sharply increased these programs, creating what became known as *l'état providence*: the providential state. Much of this was the work of the provisional government, which in 1945 created the nation's first comprehensive system of national health insurance. It also enacted pensions for the elderly, disability assistance, family allowances, and workers compensation. The Fourth Republic reaffirmed these benefits and extended them to the entire population. The creation of this social safety net infused money into the economy by creating the thousands of jobs needed to administer the programs. It also encouraged consumers to spend more freely, since they no longer needed to worry about supporting themselves in illness, disability, or old age. Providing basic security for the nation's citizens had been a key goal of the resistance and a socialist tradition since the 1800s. In the mid-twentieth century under the Fourth Republic France moved to make it a reality.

A final important dimension of postwar prosperity was the use of immigrant labor. Reconstruction required labor; by 1947 policy makers estimated France faced a shortage of over 300,000 workers. Immediately after the war some 1.7 million foreigners lived in France, mostly Europeans from Italy, Spain, Poland, and Belgium. Within thirty years that number would double to 3.4 million. In 1945 the provisional government drew up a nationality code that paved the way for future immigration, while distinguishing between permanent and temporary migrants. The code represented a compromise between two visions of immigration: the immigrant as future Frenchman, helping to renew the national population, versus the immigrant as a dispensable source of manpower. Most immigrants went into the industrial sectors prioritized by the plan, such as coal, steel, and transportation. Their labor was crucial to the renewal of French productivity in the early years of the Fourth Republic, helping to lay the basis for postwar prosperity. However, as we will see in the next chapter, they drew relatively little benefit from it.

The growing presence of immigrant workers provides another example of the transnational character of economic reconstruction under the Fourth Republic. Making a new France would involve both capital from the United States and labor from eastern and southern Europe, as well as increased access to markets in western Europe. At a time when France was struggling to reassert its national identity, the bases of that renewal would owe more than a little to forces beyond its borders. In the late 1940s France was no longer an occupied nation, but it remained part of a complex web of global forces whose dynamics helped shape national policy and destiny.

One of these key dynamics was the push for independence among Europe's colonies in Africa and Asia. Decolonization became the key concern of the Fourth Republic, especially during the 1950s. It would force the French to

discuss how France should define its boundaries, as well as its ve
as a nation, in the postwar era. The upsurge of anticolonial nation.
empire also offered a different perspective on wartime resistance & ... its legacies. In confronting decolonization, France would have to reconsider what it
meant to be a universal nation.

THE REVOLT AGAINST EMPIRE

On May 8, 1945, Algerians gathered to celebrate the end of the war in Europe. In the market town of Sétif, east of Algiers, several thousand Arabs
marched not only to hail the victory but also to demonstrate against colonial
rule. Marchers fought with French police who tried to confiscate nationalist
banners. A full-scale riot soon broke out, and over the next several days Algerians attacked French settlers in the area, murdering roughly one hundred.
The French army soon counterattacked, attacking Algerian individuals and
communities across the country. Official sources claimed roughly 10,000
casualties, but as many as 45,000 Algerians may have perished in the repression. On the same day the war in Europe ended, a new war for colonial
liberation began.

Along with the cold war, decolonization was the defining global event of
the postwar era. The speed of the process was startling; whereas in 1945 European nations still controlled the majority of the planet's land era, twenty
years later their formal holdings had shrunk to small bits of territory scattered
around the globe, the confetti of empire. In 1947 India, the jewel in the British crown, would achieve independence as the separate states of India and
Pakistan, and ten years later Ghana would emerge from the colonial Gold
Coast as the first modern independent nation in sub-Saharan Africa. In part
the end of empire reflected the decline of Europe in the postwar era, split
between two superpowers both of which rejected formal colonialism. It also
underscored the globalization of the idea of national self-determination that
first became prominent in World War I. Then European powers had been able
to deny this ideal to the people of their colonies, but they would not be able to
do so a second time. By the end of the 1960s formal colonialism had become
a symbol of national weakness rather than strength; the largest remaining empire belonged to Portugal, the poorest country in western Europe.

The French experience has often been viewed as a case study in how not
to decolonize. The nation became involved in two major colonial wars, together lasting sixteen years, and lost both of them. Britain's peaceful retreat

from India and much of Africa is often contrasted with France's brutal war in Algeria. This view has major problems: it neglects the violence that often attended British decolonization (notably the bloody partitions of India and Palestine and the brutal repression of the Mau Mau in Kenya), and on the other side fails to acknowledge that much of the French empire made the transition to independence peacefully or in some cases opted for full integration into the metropole. Moreover, the end of formal empire was not as sharp a break as is sometimes assumed; French influence continued in many of the nation's former colonies as the old idea of imperial rule gave way to a new emphasis on *Francophonie*: political, social, and cultural interchange.

As noted in the previous chapter, the French empire played a greater role in national life during World War II than ever before; de Gaulle had in effect liberated mainland France from a colonial base. Few people in the metropole acknowledged the central role played by the colonies during the occupation or in national life generally. The myth of the resistance, propagated by both the Gaullists and the left, argued not only that most French people had been resisters but that France had liberated itself. This image of "France" generally did not include the people of the colonies, whose contributions to the liberation were usually ignored. At the end of November 1944 the French army responded to salary demands from a group of African soldiers stationed at Thiaroye in Senegal by massacring thirty-five of them.

Many French leaders, however, felt holding onto the colonies was more important than ever in the postwar era. France's pretensions to being a great power had been badly shaken by the defeat of 1940, and the nation ardently desired to resume its nineteenth-century status as one of the world's most important and powerful countries. The only feasible way of accomplishing this in the era of the superpowers was to remain a great imperial power; unlike the metropole, the "nation of 100 million Frenchmen" could still aspire to global dominance. Moreover, many felt the material resources of the colonies were vital for national reconstruction after the war. Both the military and the French colonial lobbies fought strenuously to keep the empire, as did French settlers living in the colonies.

This did not mean that the colonized agreed on the importance of remaining French. The interwar years had seen the beginnings of anticolonial nationalist movements in the empire, especially Indochina and North Africa. The war itself, fought in the name of national self-determination and against Nazi racism, could not help but feed colonial desire for independence. In 1941, after the British defeated Vichy forces in Syria and Lebanon, they forced the Free French to recognize the independence of those nations. When American soldiers landed in North Africa in 1942 they brought with them Arabic language copies of the Atlantic Charter, a document drawn up by the Allies calling for popular self-determination. Shortly thereafter local nationalists issued the Manifesto of the Algerian People, whose first demand was the abolition of colonialism. In January 1943 President Roosevelt publically came out in support of Moroccan self-determination. In addition, French defeats at the hands of Germany in Europe and Japan in east Asia weakened the empire's prestige among its subjects.

For all these reasons, the future of the empire occupied a large place in the provisional government's debates about creating the Fourth Republic in 1945. Like the Popular Front before it, the provisional government emphasized reforming colonialism rather than fundamentally challenging it. The constitution of the Fourth republic abolished the empire, at least in theory, replacing it with the French Union. It also made some important changes in imperial practice. The constitution ended forced labor, and a related series of laws between 1944 and 1947 finally did away with the Indigénat, or native code. The Fourth Republic made colonial natives citizens of the French Union, much as it had granted the franchise to Frenchwomen, although this was in reality second-class citizenship. In Algeria, for example, the electoral system was heavily skewed to protect the power of the French settler minority. Only a small minority of colonial citizens could vote in national elections.

Most notably, the new constitution permanently changed the status of the four "old colonies": Martinique, Guadeloupe, Guiana, and Réunion. On March 19, 1946, the French government passed a law granting full departmental status to the old colonies, making them integral and equal parts of France. A key advocate for this change was the great *négritude* poet Aimé Césaire, who represented Martinique in the national government as a delegate for the Communist party. For Césaire and the people he represented, departmentalization represented the achievement of their dream and long political campaign for equality within the French nation, not separation from it. Martinique and Guadeloupe had been part of France since the early seventeenth century, and during the war had mobilized to defeat Vichy rather than demand independence. Many felt their islands were too small to be viable independent nation-states, and they had the example of impoverished, US-dominated Haiti to warn them of the perils of trying to go it alone. The creation of overseas departments represented a new vision of France as a global nation.

The Fourth Republic's ideas about the empire had some merit but fell far short of what many in the colonies wanted and of global trends in general. The French Union would have retained the classic colonialist division between a dominant metropole and dependent overseas territories. French politicians refused to consider African proposals for a Eurafrique, in which all citizens of the union would be equal, because then the union might not remain under French control. The French Union might have constituted a revolutionary proposal during the interwar years, but for many in the 1940s and 1950s history had passed it by.

This soon became clear in Indochina after the liberation. France struggled to reimpose colonial rule over the territory. During the war Vichy maintained administrative control of the colony, although Japanese troops had occupied it in 1940, while the Viet Minh waged war against both. In March 1945 the Japanese overthrew the Vichy administration, imprisoning many of its members. They then declared Bao Dai, the emperor of Annam, ruler of independent Vietnam. Over the next months, as the defeat of Japan seemed inevitable, the Viet Minh achieved increasing influence, especially in northern Vietnam. Japan surrendered on August 15 and in Indochina it turned over much of its positions and weaponry to the Viet Minh. On August 19 the Viet Minh began the August revolution, seizing control of Hanoi and attacking French positions throughout the north. A few days later Bao Dai's government agreed to resign, and on September 2 Ho Chi Minh proclaimed the Democratic Republic of Vietnam and independence from France.

From the beginning what would become the first Indochina war was a complicated global affair. The Viet Minh declaration of independence took place in the absence of an effective French presence in Indochina; the few French troops there were still in the Japanese prisons they had inhabited since March. In September Chinese soldiers moved into northern Vietnam. The same month the first French troops landed in the south, brought in by British detachments, and seized control of Saigon on September 21. Indochina was now divided between the Viet Minh in the north and the French in the south. The Chinese withdrew early in 1946, leading to a tortuous series of negotiations between the two increasingly antagonistic parties.

The failure of the negotiations and the outbreak of war between France and Vietnam is strange in several respects. Indochina was a valuable colony, but it was also several thousand miles distant, and mounting a major military campaign there would require resources France could scarcely afford when it was recovering from the occupation. Even more curious was the fact that the conflict was between two groups rooted in wartime resistance against fascism. The tripartite government that began the first Indochina war not only included the PCF but was organized around the principle of upholding the unity of the resistance. Yet it chose to go to war against a nationalist movement equally committed to national liberation. The power of special interests in French politics, notably the so-called Saigon clique and other colonial interests, helps explain this to a certain extent. The transition from resistance to cold war was also highly significant, so that the increasing strains in the French government between communists and noncommunists both produced and arose out of the question of Indochinese independence. The Americans, who during World War II had aided the Viet Minh and favored Vietnamese independence, began after 1945 to see Vietnam as a case of communist expansion rather than anticolonialism, a shift that would have major implications for French policy.

The main goal for the French was to reestablish colonial rule in the north, against the wishes of the Viet Minh if necessary. At first some in Paris were willing to grant the Viet Minh a measure of autonomy, at least in the north, in the context of continued membership in the French Union. Ho Chi Minh spent several months in France pleading the nationalist case. Eventually, however, hard-liners prevailed, leading to a suspension of negotiations in June 1946. Over the next several months the French began preparations to retake the north by force. In November the French issued an ultimatum to the Viet Minh ordering it to withdraw from the main port city of Haiphong. The Viet Minh defied the order and subsequently the French navy bombarded the city, killing several thousand inhabitants. The army then launched a land invasion, capturing Hanoi in April 1947. The Viet Minh retreated to the countryside, resuming the same kind of guerrilla warfare they had practiced against the Japanese.

For the next few years the war essentially stalemated. The French forces had overwhelming military superiority, including tanks, artillery, and aircraft. They quickly overran the major cities in the north, forcing the Viet Minh to withdraw into isolated jungle and mountain retreats. The Viet Minh, in contrast, were familiar with the local terrain and could move faster, so French efforts to apprehend the leadership and defeat the insurgents in regular battles generally failed. Above all, however, the Viet Minh had overwhelming popular support. Many Vietnamese did not especially like communism, but most hated the French. As one young woman noted in describing her brother's political views:

Hac, the oldest, followed the nationalist movement . . . he felt the Viet Minh was the only group with enough leadership to defeat the French. Since the goal was independence, he felt duty-bound to render his services. Besides, he admired Uncle Ho and his closest aides, so he put aside his political disagreements, trusting that the Viet Minh would mend its ways after the colonialists were gone.[3]

In true Popular Front fashion, the Viet Minh downplayed its Marxist ideology during the war to win broad popular support in the struggle against colonial rule. This not only enabled it to recruit much larger numbers of soldiers than the French, but also frequently gave it the advantage of surprise, since the local peasants would describe French troop movements. This advantage was translated into launching short surprise attacks before blending back into the countryside. The Viet Minh also moved into Vietnamese villages as administrators and civic leaders, creating an infrastructure for postcolonial rule during the war. French forces might win battles, but the Viet Minh had the loyalty of the Vietnamese people. The course of the war thus graphically illustrated the failure of France's colonial mission.

For most French people, the Indochina war existed on the other side of the world, far away from their concerns. The primary example of, and reason for, this, was the nature of "French" forces in Indochina. At the beginning of the conflict the French government decided not to use troops from the metropole, for fear of provoking an antiwar backlash at home. Consequently, most of the French soldiers in the Indochina war were colonial subjects, and a majority were Vietnamese. The French Foreign Legion also played a significant role in the conflict, using non-French soldiers from throughout Europe and the world. Ironically enough, many of the Legionnaires were of German and Austrian origin, former prisoners of war who chose the Legion as a way to get out of POW camps and start a new life. The struggle for the future of Vietnam was thus both a local civil war and a broader transnational conflict.

In the late 1940s France had other problems in its empire. In March 1947 an anti-French insurrection broke out in Madagascar. In 1942 British forces had overthrown the Vichy regime on the island, installing Free French forces. This damaged the prestige of the colonial administration in Malagasy eyes. In elections in 1945 a new independence party, the MDRM (Democratic Movement for Malagasy Renewal) won several seats in local elections. In 1946 it proposed holding a referendum granting Madagascar the status of an independent nation within the French Union. The French government refused to accept this, pushing the MDRM into armed rebellion. The revolt began on the night of March 29, as thousands of Malagasy fighters, many armed only with spears, attacked French centers throughout the island. The French fought back brutally, bringing in army units from elsewhere in the empire and unleashing a wave of terror across Madagascar. French soldiers raped, tortured, and executed suspected rebels, sometimes burning down entire villages. They succeeded in suppressing the revolt by the end of 1948, at a cost of as many as 100,000 Malagasy dead.

Despite its success in Madagascar, France proved incapable of scoring an outright victory in Indochina. The year 1949 represented a turning point of the war, especially in its international context. The victory of the Chinese communists in October created a major new ally for the Viet Minh, although in reality Mao Zedong's regime gave less concrete aid than the French feared. Perhaps the most important result of the communist victory in China was the reaction it provoked from the United States. The Americans had long been moving toward a view of the Indochina war as a conflict between communism and the free world, and Mao's victory in China followed by the outbreak of the Korean War the following June convinced them once and for all of this. The US thus sharply stepped up its aid to the French, so that it was soon paying most of the war's costs. After years of unsuccessfully fighting for the hearts and minds of the Vietnamese, the French decided to create their own puppet regime, led once again by emperor Bao Dai, and argued that they were willing to grant the colony its independence but were fighting communist subversion. In 1949 the cold war took over the fight for empire.

Unfortunately for the French, most Vietnamese continued to consider the war an anticolonial struggle and supported the Viet Minh. The ever increasing number of recruits enabled the Viet Minh gradually to move from guerrilla warfare to mounting a regular army, led by the formidable general Vo Nguyen Giap. By the end of 1953 Vietnamese forces had managed to secure control of most of the Red River delta, the heartland of northern Vietnam. The French army became pessimistic and dispirited, considering the war unwinnable. Public opinion in France also began to turn against continuing a conflict that promised to drag on without resolution. In the spring of 1954 the Viet Minh won a major victory over the French at the battle of Dien Bien Phu. General Giap's forces lured French units into a trap in a hilly area of northern Vietnam, occupying the high ground surrounding the enemy and bombarding them from above with heavy artillery. After a siege of two months the French garrison surrendered, and with that France's war effort in Indochina collapsed.

At that point the French realized unless they were willing to make a much larger military commitment they would have to cut their losses. The disaster at Dien Bien Phu caused the collapse of the French government and the new prime minister, Pierre Mendès-France of the Radical party, came to power determined to end the war. In July 1954 representatives of the French and the Viet Minh met for peace talks at Geneva. France agreed to recognize Vietnamese independence and temporarily divide the country between the Viet Minh in the north and Bao Dai in the south, pending elections that would permanently decide the nation's fate. These elections were never held, thanks largely to pressure from the United States, setting the stage for America's own (and far worse) war in Vietnam. After eight years of war, at a cost of over 90,000 French and up to 300,000 Vietnamese dead, France's empire in Indochina came to an inglorious end.

The collapse of French colonial rule in southeast Asia came as a major blow to France's pretensions to be a world power and a universal nation. Henceforth it had no representation on the Asian continent, and the bitterness of the rupture meant that, aside from some architectural legacies, French influence would play a very small role in postcolonial Vietnam. The great irony was that the Viet Minh was in some respects, of all the anticolonial movements in the empire, the one closest to the model of the French resistance. Whereas that model failed at home with the end of tripartism, it triumphed in overseas France. This paradox underscored the contradictory nature of republican universalism, showing how its own principles could come back to haunt it.

THE ALGERIAN WAR AND THE END OF THE FOURTH REPUBLIC

The loss of Indochina in 1954 was a major colonial defeat, but Vietnam was far away and its independence had little impact on life in France. In contrast, North Africa was much closer, on the opposite shore of the Mediterranean, and intimately linked to the metropole by a myriad of political, economic, and cultural ties. As in Indochina, World War II had challenged French rule in the colonial Maghreb, reinforcing nationalist movements across the area. Much more than in Indochina, France made a major effort to hold onto Algeria in particular. The result was one of the most vicious colonial wars of the twentieth century, a military disaster that would bitterly divide France and ultimately destroy the Fourth Republic.

The loss of Indochina persuaded some in France that *
empire were over, and the nation would have to adjust to tł
sweeping the colonized world. Pierre Mendès-France recognizeɑ ɯɪɪ๑, ɑ...
ter Dien Bien Phu he moved to end French rule in Morocco and Tunisia. Both
countries had powerful independence movements that became increasingly
restive after the war. In Morocco the French deposed Sultan Mohammed V
in 1953 for his nationalist sentiments, provoking a wave of riots throughout
the country. Faced with united and increasingly violent opposition from the
Moroccan people, the French brought back the sultan in 1955. A year later
the French peacefully ended their protectorate over the country. Events in
Tunisia followed a similar pattern: after France arrested the nationalist leader
Habib Bourguiba in 1952 his supporters turned to a terror campaign, launching bombing attacks against French facilities. The French government recognized the hopelessness of the situation, and granted Tunisia independence in
March 1956, a few days after Morocco.

Perhaps the greatest tragedy of the Fourth Republic was that the French
didn't follow a similar path in Algeria. For the French, Algeria was fundamentally different from the rest of their empire, legally not a colony at all but
rather three departments of France. It was also the only major French colony
that had a large French settler population, roughly 1 million people, or 10
percent of the country. When asked in opinion polls, most French strongly
opposed the idea of Algerian independence. Even Mendès-France declared
before the National Assembly, "One does not compromise when it comes to
defending the internal peace of the nation, the unity and integrity of the Republic. The Algerian departments are part of the French Republic. They have
been French for a long time, and they are irrevocably French. . . . Between
them and metropolitan France there can be no conceivable secession."[4]

Increasingly this was not the opinion of most people in Algeria. The Muslim population, the overwhelming majority of the country, had long suffered
discrimination and poverty, and this did not significantly change under the
Fourth Republic. The new constitution enfranchised a greater percentage of
Algerians, but the political system remained overwhelmingly dominated by
the *pieds noirs*, or settlers. Algerian cities remained segregated, with the native population cooped up in the *medinas*, or native quarters, while Europeans
enjoyed spacious modern accommodations in the new French neighborhoods.
By the early 1950s Algeria had a number of nationalist organizations, including Ferhat Abbas's Democratic Union of the Algerian Manifesto (UDMA) and
Messali Hadj's Movement for the Triumph of Democratic Liberties (MTLD).

In 1952 after a series of anti-French demonstrations colonial authorities cracked down on dissent, arresting Messali Hadj and forcing other nationalists to flee the country. One of those, Ahmed Ben Bella, a decorated veteran of the French army, founded the Revolutionary Committee of Unity and Action (CRUA). Based in Cairo and clandestinely in Algeria, the CRUA began organizing a war of independence against the French.

For Algerian nationalists the news of Dien Bien Phu came as a thunderclap. Here was concrete proof that a colonial insurgency could defeat the French and win independence. Many Algerian soldiers had fought with colonial regiments in Indochina, and those taken prisoner by the Viet Minh received a strong dose of anticolonial propaganda from their captors. Nationalists renamed the CRUA the National Liberation Front (FLN), organized along both political and military lines. On October 31, 1954, the FLN proclaimed the independence of Algeria and on the next day, the French holiday of Toussaint, or All Saints' Day, it began the uprising that would turn into the Algerian war. A small group of activists launched a series of attacks against French targets and pro-French Algerians. Most notoriously, two French schoolteachers were pulled off a bus and killed.

France reacted with a fury to the violence, sending in 20,000 troops to Algeria to crush the uprising. The FLN was not the Viet Minh. The young organization had barely a thousand members nationwide, and only a small number of firearms and bombs. By the beginning of 1955 French forces had apprehended much of the leadership, and the organization was in disarray. Faced with an overwhelming military disadvantage, in early 1955 the FLN turned to terror as a way to demoralize and ultimately defeat the French, forcing them to withdraw from Algeria. In June FLN guerrillas attacked French settlers in the town of Philippeville, brutally massacring over one hundred men, women, and children. French soldiers, aided by local settlers, responded by rampaging through villages in the area, killing thousands of civilians. This cycle of terror and counterterror became a key feature of the Algerian war, hardening attitudes on both sides and ultimately driving many Algerians into the arms of the FLN.

While engaged in guerrilla attacks against both the French and Algerian rivals, the FLN also sought to reorganize Algerian civil society, reaching out to the people through a variety of specialty groups. At times FLN militants tried to change the behavior of Algerian Muslims, banning wine and prostitution in adherence with Islamic principles. They began campaigns against drunkenness in the Arab neighborhoods of major cities. At the same time they continued the guerrilla war against the French. FLN units would attack both military and civilian targets, usually making surprise raids at night then disappearing back into the general population. They often attacked French settlers living on isolated rural plantations, so that many *pieds noirs* moved into the cities. Increasingly Algeria was a country where violence seemed spontaneous, random, and everywhere; no one felt safe.

The Algerian uprising was part of the broader global revolt against colonialism, and it shared much with the pan-Arab movement shaking the Middle East. Pan-Arabism, the idea that all Arabs constituted a unified nation and culture, had emerged during the late nineteenth century and shaped Arab struggles for freedom from both the Ottoman Empire and the western powers. In 1956 Gamel Abdel Nasser became president of Egypt after helping overthrow the monarchy four years earlier, and he turned his country into the leader of the pan-Arab movement. Ben Bella and other FLN leaders took refuge in Cairo and received both moral and material support from the Egyptian regime. In response, France joined the 1956 invasion of Egypt by Britain and Israel after Nasser nationalized the Suez Canal, only to be forced to withdraw by the United States and the Soviet Union. The idea that attacking Egypt would somehow solve the Algerian crisis was absurd, but it illustrated how the conflict fit into broader global concerns.

In 1956 the French army sharply increased its engagement in Algeria. By the end of the year France had sent nearly 400,000 troops across the Mediterranean in what some called the biggest national armada since the Crusades. In March the French government declared a state of emergency in Algeria, giving the army free rein to defeat the FLN by any means. Military leaders in Algeria, often with the active support of French settlers, undertook a brutal campaign of suppression. They engaged in massive reprisals for FLN activity and forcibly relocated entire villages. Most notoriously, the army began to use torture on a systematic basis to force information out of FLN suspects and break its networks.

In 1957 the army put these techniques to good effect in the battle of Algiers. The FLN had established control of Arab urban ghettos, and increasingly in 1956 and 1957 the army decided to challenge it. The struggle began late in 1956 when the FLN called a general strike and enforced it in urban areas. At the same time, it began sending women disguised in western dress out into the European neighborhoods to plant bombs in cafés. By the end of the year bombs were going off every day in the city, and the French population demanded the army bring an end to this campaign of terror. The army, led

10.2. French paratroopers on patrol during the battle of Algiers, 1957.
Source: Nacerdine ZEBAR/Gamma-Rapho via Getty Images.

by Gen. Jacques Massu, moved in to the Arab neighborhoods and broke the strike by ordering shopkeepers to reopen at gunpoint. It also arrested suspects and tortured them for information, using electric shock, waterboarding, and in the case of women rape. By late 1957 Massu and his troops had effectively destroyed the FLN's infrastructure in the Algerian capital.

This military victory had a political cost, however. Increasingly the FLN was making its case on the international stage. The United Nations held debates about the Algerian question every year starting in 1955, and the French position gradually lost ground, especially among communist and Arab member states. Many American statesmen began to view the French war in Algeria as an international liability, weakening their ability to win over nonwestern nations to the global struggle against communism. In July 1957 US Senator John F. Kennedy, who would soon become the next president of the United States, condemned the war and called for Algerian independence.

At the same time opposition to the war began to develop in France itself, especially among intellectuals and young people. France fought the Algerian war, unlike the war in Indochina, with a conscript army, so that masses of

French young people experienced military service in the conflict. The army's massacres and increasing use of torture, coming barely a decade after Vichy and the Nazis had practiced similar atrocities in France, sparked a national crisis of conscience. In 1955 the writer Claudet Bourdet published an article trenchantly entitled "Is there a Gestapo in Algeria?" Two years later Jean-Jacques Servan Schreiber, the influential editor of the magazine *L'Express*, published *Lieutenant in Algeria*, a searing memoir illustrating the brutal practices of the French army. The same year Jean-Paul Sartre published a series of articles in *Les Temps Modernes* attacking the conduct of the army in Algeria, and soon became a supporter of Algerian independence. His close colleague Francis Jeanson organized a clandestine network of French intellectuals to funnel money from the Algerian community in France to the FLN. For many young people growing up in France during the 1950s, the Algerian war was a key moment of political consciousness raising. Not all French intellectuals embraced the Algerian cause, however. Albert Camus, Sartre's great intellectual rival during the 1950s, came from a *pied noir* family, and while he hoped for a peaceful settlement to the conflict he refused to support Algerian independence or the FLN. As he commented, "I believe in justice, but I would defend my mother before justice."[5]

No one in France better symbolized support of Algerian independence than the young Martinican psychiatrist Frantz Fanon. A student of Aimé Césaire's while in high school, Fanon left Martinique during the war to join the Free French. After the war he completed his education in France and then served an internship at a psychiatric hospital in Blida, Algeria. Fanon's direct experiences with the suffering of his Algerian patients and his growing awareness that their tales of torture were not fantasies but drawn from real life made him a committed partisan of Algerian independence. He joined the FLN in 1954 and worked for a free Algeria until he died in 1961. Shortly before his death he published *The Wretched of the Earth*, a justification of revolutionary anticolonial violence and one of the world's great texts from the era of decolonization.

At this stage French opposition to the Algerian war was still weak; none of the major political parties, including the communists, supported the movement. Things began to change in 1958, the year the war came home. By this point it became clear to many that the French government had lost control of the situation. Like the Third Republic before it, the Fourth Republic was based on a weak executive and strong legislature, a structure that worked during peaceful times but was often incapable of handling crises. Moreover, the marginalization of the significant percentage of the electorate that voted for the PCF narrowed the ability of governments to function effectively. The result was a series of weak regimes: twenty in eleven years. Pierre Mendès-France had some success reforming this system, but after his government fell in 1955 things reverted to normal.

The government was unable to rein in the army in Algeria, which increasingly pursued its own agenda. The army leadership was determined to crush the FLN and feared that the politicians in Paris would not let it finish the job. The precedent of Indochina war still rankled for many, and it was reinforced by the outcome of the Suez crisis, when the French and their allies had scored a military victory over the Egyptians, only to be forced to retreat by political pressure. In addition, many French settlers were terrified at the prospect that their government might even consider change in Algeria, let alone independence. And since they often worked closely with French soldiers their fears reinforced the apprehensions of the military.

Matters came to a head in 1958. On May 13 MRP member Pierre Pflimlin formed a new cabinet, which might be willing to consider negotiating with the FLN. The same day a huge demonstration of settlers took to the streets of Algiers to demand the rejection of the cabinet. The demonstration soon turned into a riot, prompting a group of generals led by Jacques Massu to seize control of the local government that night and proclaim the creation of a Committee of Public Safety. The generals immediately demanded that French President René Coty appoint a new emergency government, to be headed by Charles de Gaulle, to save French Algeria. This coup d'état in Algeria, with the prospect of a similar result in France, shocked the French people and underscored the inability of the Fourth Republic to deal with the Algerian crisis.

De Gaulle had had nothing to do with the coup, although some of his followers supported it. Ever since abandoning politics in 1946, he had spent most of his time at his estate in Colombey-Les-Deux-Eglises writing his memoirs. To the rebels in Algeria, de Gaulle represented both a military hero and a man who stood above politics: someone they could trust to support them and their mission. De Gaulle was interested in returning to power, but not as a dictator. On May 15 he announced that if asked, he was ready to serve his country once again, but only if he was granted extraordinary powers (allowing for censorship, searches, and other extrajudicial security measures) for six months as well as the ability to draft a new constitution. Many on the left feared that de Gaulle would establish an authoritarian regime, while some in the army questioned his intentions regarding Algeria. Over the next two weeks his supporters negotiated with a variety of French leaders to win acceptance of his return to power. At the same time the army continued preparing to seize power in case de Gaulle didn't accept. On May 24 paratroopers from Algeria landed in Corsica, overthrowing the local government and threatening to do the same in Paris. Parisians walked around with one eye warily cocked toward the sky, dreading the sight of airborne troops descending on the capital.

The end came quickly. On May 29 the various sides reached an agreement, and President Coty formally invited de Gaulle to assume power. He did so in the nick of time; had de Gaulle not accepted, the military had scheduled its seizure of power for the next day. On June 1 the National Assembly voted full powers to de Gaulle and empowered him to draft a new constitution. The vote, at 329 in favor to 224 opposed, was by no means unanimous. Nonetheless it was official and binding, and like Pétain in 1940 de Gaulle could claim to have taken power legally. With that vote, after little more than twelve years of existence, the Fourth Republic formally came to an end. For the second time in his life, Charles de Gaulle had come forth as the savior of France.

Like the Third Republic and the Second Empire before it, the Fourth Republic perished in the throes of military disaster, if not actual defeat. It could claim neither the glamour of the second nor the longevity of the first. Moreover, the regime was supposed to make peace after the deadliest conflict in human history, and yet it found itself continually at war. Indeed France was in a state of war almost continuously for a quarter of a century, from 1939 to 1962, and that became the reality that shaped the life and ultimately the death of the regime. The major accomplishments of the Fourth Republic, ranging from the welfare state to economic renewal and European integration, were essentially foundational. Their results would emerge full-blown under the Fifth Republic. The latter would reap what the former sowed.

France under the Fourth Republic had to confront new realities about the relationship between the nation and the broader world. In two contrasting respects it was forced to reconsider its relationship to empire, both the loss of much of its own, and its place in the cold war imperium of the United States. Its attempt at preserving both empire and independence, tripartism, collapsed under the pressure of domestic and global events. Yet the vision of republican universalism was not lost. Charles de Gaulle would attempt to revive it during the next decade, making France once again a nation that stood for both its own distinctive culture and a way of conceiving of the world as a whole. Under his leadership the Fifth Republic would write a new chapter in the history of the universal nation.

Suggestions for Further Reading

De Beauvoir, Simone. *The Mandarins*. Cleveland, OH: World, 1956.

———. *The Second Sex*. London: David Campbell, 1953.

Clayton, Anthony. *The Wars of French Decolonisation*. London: Longman, 1994.

Dalloz, Jacques. *The War in Indochina, 1945–1954*. Dublin: Gill & Macmillan, 1990.

Fanon, Frantz. *The Wretched of the Earth*. New York: Grove, 1963.

Flanner, Janet. *Paris Journal, 1944–55*. New York: Harcourt Brace, 1965.

Gildea, Robert. *France Since 1945*. Oxford: Oxford University Press, 1996.

Horne, Alistair. *A Savage War of Peace: Algeria 1954–1962*. New York: Penguin, 1987.

Kahler, Miles. *Decolonization in Britain and France*. Princeton, NJ: Princeton University Press, 1984.

Kuisel, Richard. *Seducing the French: the Dilemma of Americanization*. Berkeley: University of California Press, 1993.

LeSueur, James D. *Uncivil War: Intellectuals and Identity Politics During the Decolonization of Algeria*. Philadelphia: University of Pennsylvania Press, 2001.

Lottman, Hertbert. *The Left Bank*. San Francisco: Halo, 1991.

Rioux, Jean-Pierre. *The Fourth Republic, 1944–1958*. Cambridge: Cambridge University Press, 1987.

Ross, Kristin. *Fast Cars, Clean Bodies: Decolonization and the Reordering of French Culture*. Cambridge: MIT Press, 1996.

Servan-Schreiber, Jean-Jacques. *Lieutenant in Algeria*. New York: Knopf, 1957.

Shepard, Todd. *The Invention of Decolonization: The Algerian War and the Remaking of France*. Ithaca, NY: Cornell University Press, 2006.

Stovall, Tyler. *France Since the Second World War*. London: Pearson Education, 2002.

Wall, Irwin. *France, the United States, and the Algerian War*. Berkeley: University of California Press, 2001.

Werth, Alexander. *France 1940–1955*. Boston: Beacon, 1956.

Wylie, Laurence. *Village in the Vaucluse*. Cambridge: Harvard University Press, 1957.

Notes

1. Janet Flanner, *Paris Journal, 1944–55* (New York: Harcourt Brace, 1965), 20.

2. The Schuman Project, www.schuman.info/Strasbourg549.htm.

3. Nguyen Thi Thu-Lam, *Fallen Leaves: Memoirs of a Vietnamese Woman* (New Haven, CT: Yale Southeast Asia Studies Center, 1989), 41–42.
4. Todd Shepard, *The Invention of Decolonization: The Algerian War and the Remaking of France* (Ithaca, NY: Cornell University Press, 2006), 6.
5. Robert Gildea, *France Since 1945* (Oxford: Oxford University Press, 1996), 22.

eleven

THE FIFTH REPUBLIC:
A NEW ERA FOR FRANCE

WITH CHARLES DE GAULLE'S RETURN TO POWER IN 1958, FRANCE began not only a new regime but a fundamental transformation of the nation. The Fifth Republic departed significantly from the basic structure of the regimes that preceded it, in some ways looking all the way back to the Bonapartism of the nineteenth century. In its first decade the new regime completed the process of decolonization that had torn the Fourth Republic apart, developing new ways to connect France with its former colonies and current overseas territories and departments. During the 1960s and early 1970s the structural work of remaking the economy began to bear fruit, creating a dynamic new consumer society and transforming the face of the nation. By the end of the *trentes glorieuses* France had over 50 million people, most of them enjoying a lifestyle their grandparents could not have imagined. In addition, France developed new ways of asserting its national identity and its universal values in relation to the United States, Europe, and the rest of the world.

The Fifth Republic began with a decade of peace and prosperity that brought some of the best times modern France has ever known. These good times would not last, however. Ten years into the new regime, the explosion of May 1968 would demonstrate that even prosperity and youthful dynamism could pose problems for French society. By the mid-1970s the postwar boom

11.1. Anti-imperialist poster, May 1968.
Source: Bibliothèque nationale de France.

had run its course, and France had to contend with unfavorable economic factors including slow growth and high unemployment. The Fifth Republic would embark on a new stage after the death of Charles de Gaulle in 1970 in the context of seemingly permanent hard times.

And yet amid all these challenges France would uphold its identity as a universal nation, remaining attached to the idea that French national culture was both singular and important for all people. Charles de Gaulle's emphasis on *la gloire*, national grandeur, underscored the idea that France should not just work well but also inspire both its own people and humanity in general. This would become a major shaper of not just foreign affairs but state policy as a whole under the Fifth Republic. Similarly, France would not simply walk away from its empire but continue to see the cultural space of *Francophonie* as defining the nation's place in (and contributions to) the world. French artists, academics, and writers would inspire intellectuals far beyond the nation's borders. At the same time the French would draw on and integrate political and cultural trends from throughout the world, stamping them with their own Gallic flavor. Revolutions in transportation and communications during the mid-twentieth century would knit the peoples of the world ever closer together, both challenging and reshaping what it meant to be French, while at the same time underscoring the key place of France in the modern world.

BUILDING THE FIFTH REPUBLIC

In May 1958 Charles de Gaulle returned to power after twelve years in exile, largely on his own terms. He had stomped off the national stage in 1946 because the nation rejected his vision of postwar French government. Now, over a decade and two wars later, de Gaulle had a chance to implement that vision. As a result, the Fifth Republic would essentially be de Gaulle's republic. He would serve as head of state for more than ten years, but even after his departure the French regime would bear his stamp.

Above all, de Gaulle wanted a regime with a strong executive branch. This not only fit his persona, but in his opinion (and that of many other French) the failings of both the Third and Fourth Republics could be directly traced to weak governments and fractious legislatures. The traditional *immobilisme*, or inaction of the French state, was inadequate to deal with crises and could not move France into the future. Under the new constitution, accordingly, the president would cease to be a largely ceremonial position as it had been under the preceding republics. The president would be elected for a seven-year term, something unprecedented in modern democracies. Initially, the constitution stated the president would be elected by an electoral college composed of 70,000 members drawn from across France. In 1962 de Gaulle changed that to provide for the direct election of the president by a national vote. The president also had the right to propose referendums for direct vote by the French people, thus going over the heads of the legislature, and the ability to suspend the legislature and rule by emergency decree for six months. In addition, the president named the prime minister, who had to be approved by the legislature. In short, the president of the Fifth Republic would be an elected monarch in all but name. France had not had such a strong executive since the second empire, and the combination of powerful president and a system of referendums reminded more than a few of the nation's Bonapartist heritage.

For all the strength of the executive, however, France under the Fifth Republic remained a democracy. The legislature was divided between the

National Assembly, elected by direct popular vote, and the Senate. The National Assembly did lose the ability to name the government, although the prime minister would come from the dominant political party. It was not clear, however, what would happen if the president's party was not the largest in the National Assembly. During de Gaulle's years in power this was not an issue, but eventually the question of "cohabitation" would surface as a potential weakness of the regime.

De Gaulle drew up the constitution of the Fifth Republic at a time of national crisis; the legislature had little to do with it. The new constitution went public on September 4, 1958, the eighty-eighth anniversary of the founding of the Third Republic. Not all members approved; the PCF was frankly hostile and other leading politicians, notably Pierre Mendès-France, called on voters to reject it. The French people overwhelmingly backed the new constitution, however, voting 80 percent in favor. The first legislative elections under the new republic took place in December 1958, and they were a triumph for de Gaulle. His followers had created a new political party, the Union pour la Nouvelle République (Union for the New Republic, or UNR) just before the election, and it came in first in the balloting, winning over 40 percent of the seats. Along with allied parties, including the Radicals, the MRP, and the SFIO, the Gaullist coalition headed by the UNR controlled over 75 percent of the National Assembly, whereas the PCF dropped from 150 to 10 seats. The same month the first presidential election gave an overwhelming victory to de Gaulle. The former general was now as powerful as any leader of modern France, and he wasted no time in using that power to reshape the nation.

FROM DECOLONIZATION TO A FRANCOPHONE WORLD

De Gaulle's first priority as head of state was to end the war in Algeria, and he began moving on this issue within days after assuming power. On June 4, 1958, he flew to Algiers and held a public meeting to win the assurances of the army and the settlers. *Je vous ai compris* (I have understood you), he declared, although as commentators noted such a statement could be interpreted in more than one way. Nonetheless, this was enough to reassure the French in Algeria that they had backed the right man: de Gaulle would stand up for continued colonial rule. He agreed to continue military operations against the FLN, which by the end of 1958 was clearly losing the war on the ground. Meanwhile, however, he was coming to realize that France had forfeited the loyalty of Algeria's Muslim majority and could only hold onto the colony by force. Therefore he had to look for a political solution. On assuming power, de Gaulle announced a program of social and political reform in Algeria and called on the FLN to negotiate a compromise. His actions did nothing to mollify Algerian nationalists, who had long since decided nothing less than complete independence from France would suffice.

If the FLN was losing the war on the ground, it was winning the political struggle. Antiwar sentiment was spreading rapidly in France, so that by 1959 a clear majority of the population favored negotiating with the FLN. De Gaulle realized that the army and settlers in Algeria would never agree to independence, so ultimately he decided that France would have to move on without them. In September 1959 he announced for the first time that he would accept the principle of Muslim self-determination in Algeria after the end of the war. This statement hit France and Algeria like a bombshell. The army and the settlers felt personally betrayed by the very general they had hoped would keep Algeria French, no matter what, and they began organizing to defy him. For the settlers in particular, Algeria was the only home they had ever known, and the idea of living under Muslim rule or abandoning it was simply unthinkable.

The storm broke in January 1960. To defuse the conflict de Gaulle had recalled General Massu, but this infuriated the French in Algeria. On January 24 several generals staged a new insurrection in Algiers, building barricades and threatening again to overthrow the government. This was the acid test for Charles de Gaulle and the young Fifth Republic: could he control the army in Algeria where the preceding regime had failed? He met the test brilliantly, giving a speech on national television (one of the first times this new electronic medium played a major role in French politics) demanding obedience and in effect speaking over the heads of the rebellious generals to the troops. The sight of the veteran general and savior of France, dressed in his military uniform, calling on the soldiers to follow his orders was too much for the revolt, which fizzled after a week.

The failure of barricades week showed de Gaulle's determination to end the conflict, but a final resolution took two more bloody years. The French government began negotiations with the FLN to pursue a settlement. Meanwhile, in response to their defeat, rebellious settlers and soldiers founded a new organization, the OAS (Secret Army Organization), to pursue a campaign of terror against anyone, French or Algerian, who espoused the cause of independence. They launched a bombing campaign, including letter bombs and plastic explosives, against their opponents. Violence was now common in France as well as Algeria. The FLN pursued a campaign of assassinating its political opponents among the Algerian community in France, and French police often arrested and tortured Algerians. The escalating brutality in the metropole exploded on the night of October 17, 1961, when the Paris police savagely attacked a demonstration of Algerians in the heart of the city. Scores of men, women, and children were summarily shot or thrown into the Seine to die, which the police referred to as "drowning by bullets." As many as two hundred people died that night, and police authorities banned any mention of the "incident," effectively suppressing any discussion of it for over a generation. In February 1962 the Paris police assaulted a demonstration of French communists at the entrance to the Charonne metro stop, killing eight people and injuring hundreds.

By 1961 the French people had clearly had enough of Algeria. In a national referendum organized by de Gaulle in January, 75 percent voted in favor of Algerian self-determination. On April 22, the OAS seized power in Algiers, but like the revolt a year before it soon collapsed in the face of de Gaulle's determined opposition. Assured of national backing, the French continued negotiations with the FLN, resulting in the Evian Accords (March 1962) granting formal independence to Algeria. In April the French voted massively to approve the agreement in a national referendum. The months between the signing of the agreement in March and the formal granting of independence on July 5 saw a vicious terror campaign by the OAS, which staged more than one hundred bombings every day. The FLN often responded in kind, massacring thousands of French settlers when it marched into Oran in July. This final spasm of violence led to the exodus of the French settler population across the Mediterranean to a France they had never known. It was a terrible end to a terrible war, but it was the end; Algeria was now independent, France was free of the North African quagmire, and Charles de Gaulle had successfully met one of the greatest challenges of his career.

Algeria was by far the knottiest colonial issue the new Fifth Republic had to confront, but there was more to decolonization than resolving the Algerian conflict. The new constitution, like that of the Fourth Republic before it, reformed the relationship between France and its colonies. De Gaulle scrapped the French Union, replacing it with the "French Community," which promised full citizenship to residents of the empire. In changing the administration of the colonies, the new French government also offered residents a series of choices about their continued relationship to France. They could remain

French territories, directly administered from Paris; they could elect to become member states of the community, self-governing and autonomous; or they could choose full departmental status as the old colonies had done in 1946. Colonial citizens were also given a fourth choice, immediate independence, but de Gaulle made it clear that choice would carry with it the termination of all aid from France.

As in the metropole, people in the colonies voted on the new constitution, and their future relations with France, in a referendum. Held on September 28, 1958, the referendum was a victory for Gaullist imperial policy. While several colonies, notably French Polynesia and New Caledonia, opted to remain territories, virtually all of the Africans voted to become member states of the community. The one exception was Guinea, led by the dynamic Sekou Touré, great-grandson of Samory Touré, one of the leading rebels against French colonial expansion in nineteenth-century Africa. Famously saying to Charles de Gaulle, "We prefer poverty in liberty to riches in slavery," Touré led his people to choose immediate independence.[1] Paris reacted harshly to this rebuke; French administrators left Guinea precipitously, taking with them everything they could carry, including telephones and lightbulbs.

Within two years, the remaining African colonies became independent in their turn. After the referendum colonial leaders like Felix Houphouet-Boigny of the Ivory Coast, who was also a deputy in the French National Assembly, began pushing for formal independence while at the same time preserving economic, cultural, and diplomatic ties with France. Africa was changing, and powerful movements for the end of European rule were organizing across the continent. Sensitive to these winds of change, de Gaulle agreed to accept African proposals for independence, realizing that by accepting the inevitable France could continue its influence over this part of the world. As a result, in 1960 France granted independence to no fewer than fourteen African colonies. French diplomats flew from one colonial capital to the next, lowering the French flag and witnessing the raising of the new banners of independent states. Thus 1960 became the great year of African independence and a landmark in the history of decolonization. In granting independence to the African colonies, de Gaulle helped transform France from a symbol of resistance to decolonization to one of its enlightened advocates. Since the choice for independence essentially emptied the French Community of its members, after less than two years the organization ceased to exist. Its end marked the last gasp of the French empire; in 1960, after centuries of overseas expansion, France gave up its imperial vision for good.

Or did it? Many anticolonial activists at the time, and many historians since, have argued that the conclusion of formal European rule during the era of decolonization did not necessarily bring about the end of empire, contending instead that colonialism gave way to neocolonialism. Certainly for France granting independence to its colonies did not necessarily mean that it renounced the nation's presence beyond the borders of the metropole. After 1960 the French flag continued to fly over a wide variety of overseas departments and territories throughout the Caribbean, the Indian Ocean, and the Pacific, so that to a significant degree overseas France ended as it had begun, on the shores of distant islands. The residents of these areas are French citizens, and many of them live in the metropole. During the 1960s the French government encouraged and organized immigration from the Caribbean overseas departments to the metropole, for example, ostensibly to relieve overcrowding in those islands. Paris has also continued to provide a range of economic subsidies for its overseas areas as a way of encouraging them to remain French.

Perhaps more important, after 1960 France retained close ties with its former African colonies. In negotiating independence the French usually retained some access to raw materials, and the new African states remained important trading partners. While the nation's foreign commerce has tended to focus more on Europe and the United States since the start of the Fifth Republic, trade with Francophone Africa has helped the French balance of payments and promoted continuing influence in the region. In many cases the national currencies of the new states were linked to the French franc, thus closely connecting their economies. In addition, the French military has intervened on numerous occasions in African wars since 1960. Finally, French culture has been a major means of continuing French influence in former colonial Africa. Many members of the African elites speak French and are educated in French universities. The rise of the Francophone movement in the 1980s, emphasizing the global community of those who speak and write in French, has underscored France's global influence. At the same time, as we will see in more detail in the next chapter, this influence has not been one way; the end of empire led to former colonial residents and cultures making an impact on France itself.

In the end, French decolonization brought about a new vision of France as a universal nation. In many ways it revealed France at its worst, and French influence in Algeria and especially Vietnam has never recovered from the trauma of the massive colonial wars under the Fourth Republic. But de Gaulle learned from these disasters and steered the nation into a new relationship with its colonies. In doing so, he reaffirmed the idea that France was a world power: that French civilization was a key part of the heritage of humanity as a whole. This emphasis would shape de Gaulle's approach to foreign policy during the 1960s, creating a new vision of France as a great nation.

LA GLOIRE: DE GAULLE, FRANCE, AND THE WORLD

As noted in the previous chapter, the defeat of 1940 and the German occupation were an unprecedented trauma for the French people. The nation went from being one of Europe's, and the world's, great powers to being the colony of stronger country. The postwar fight to preserve the empire was a response to this national humiliation, but it ultimately failed in its turn, reinforcing rather than assuaging France's loss in World War II. By 1960, therefore, France had been engaged in warfare for nearly a quarter of a century, and it had suffered one defeat after another. How could it possibly regain its status as a great power and a universal nation?

To restore France's place in the world, to reemphasize *la gloire*, the grandeur of the French nation (a term he did not hesitate to use over and over again), was Charles de Gaulle's great mission during the 1960s. It had been his goal ever since the spring of 1940, when as an exile without troops or status he worked tirelessly to persuade the British, the Americans, and everyone else not only that he was the leader of Free France but that France remained a great nation in spite of everything. To reduce it to a matter of personal vanity, as some of his critics both within and without France at times implied, was a fundamental error. In a world dominated by two superpowers, de Gaulle, with the support of most of the French people, wanted to ensure the ability of France not just to determine its own fate but also to remain influential on the world stage. This desire arose out of the tradition of republican universalism, which World War II had challenged and then reaffirmed. In order to reclaim its standing as a universal nation, France had to aspire to greatness, not just in global power politics but in all fields of human endeavor.

Above all, this meant addressing Franco-American relations. Open hostility had existed between de Gaulle and Franklin Delano Roosevelt during World War II, and a variety of issues, including the Coca-colonization controversy, had caused friction since then. At a time when to be anti-American equaled being pro-Soviet in the eyes of many, the desire of the French to preserve their own national autonomy came across as strange, even suspicious, to some in the United States. But de Gaulle was certainly no fellow traveler of the Soviet Union, and France considered itself firmly in the western camp. During the Cuban missile crisis of 1962 de Gaulle strongly supported the American position that stationing Soviet missiles in Cuba was an unacceptable threat to the United States and the free world.

At the same time, de Gaulle recognized that, precisely because America dominated western Europe, the French had to insist on their own independence. One flashpoint was NATO, set up in the late 1940s to coordinate military opposition to Soviet aggression against the western powers. By the late 1950s the prospects of a Soviet invasion of western Europe had diminished considerably, so that many came to see NATO as an arm of US domination rather than a mutual defense organization. In March 1959 de Gaulle asked that decisions over deploying nuclear weapons be made by all NATO member states, not just America. When the Americans refused, France banned NATO from stationing nuclear weapons on French territory, and then a few months later withdrew the nation's Mediterranean fleet from NATO command. Seven years after that, in March 1966, de Gaulle withdrew French troops from NATO and expelled all NATO forces from French territory. France remained a member of the alliance, continuing to station troops under its aegis in West Germany, but it would no longer allow foreign troops on its own soil. For the French, this underscored the fact that unlike West Germany they were in no sense an occupied nation, but in charge of their own military destiny.

Closely related to de Gaulle's estrangement from NATO was his emphasis on making France a nuclear power in its own right. During the decades after World War II possession of nuclear weapons was a key factor in defining a nation as a global power, and the fact that both the US and the USSR held them defined the essence of the cold war. Right after the liberation France's provisional government had created an atomic energy commission to develop nuclear power resources. In 1952 Britain became the world's third nation to explode a nuclear bomb, increasing the pressure on France to follow suit. Two years later, in the aftermath of the humiliating defeat at Dien Bien Phu, the French government decided to develop its own nuclear force. De Gaulle strongly supported this idea, and when he returned to power in 1958 he pushed for the development of a nuclear strike force, the *force de frappe*. It would be operated by France independently from NATO. Development proceeded quickly, and in February 1960 the French exploded their first atomic bomb in the Algerian desert. This caused some friction with the United States, especially when the French asserted that their missiles could be pointed in any direction. France continued aggressively developing its nuclear weapons program during the 1960s, exploding its first hydrogen bomb in 1968. Membership in the world's most exclusive club—nations with nuclear arms—underscored its great power status and its independence from the United States.

De Gaulle also asserted French power and independence in relations with Europe, especially West Germany and the United Kingdom. De Gaulle supported and pursued the work of the Fourth Republic in ending the historical enmity between France and Germany, building an alliance based on economic cooperation and mutual benefit. De Gaulle found a kindred spirit in West Germany's Konrad Adenauer, who served as chancellor from 1949 to 1963. The two developed a close relationship, solidifying the postwar Franco-German alliance, and in 1963 signed a formal friendship treaty between the two nations. De Gaulle believed in the importance of reconciling with Germany, but at the same time he also considered West Germany an ideal ally. The Federal Republic was economically powerful yet militarily and diplomatically weak. Consequently, in an alliance between Paris and Bonn the French could play the dominant role.

Relations with the British were more complicated. The two nations had a lot in common, and during the war London had given crucial support to de Gaulle and the Free French. Yet the closeness of the UK's postwar alliance with the US concerned the French, who feared that America could use Britain to increase its dominance over European affairs. In particular this could threaten French plans for the European Economic Community. Based on the Franco-German alliance, France hoped to see the EEC develop not just as an economic trading bloc but ultimately as a geopolitical counterweight to American power. Consequently, in both 1963 and 1967 de Gaulle vetoed the UK's application to join the EEC. Not until 1973, after de Gaulle's death, would Britain be allowed into the Common Market.

Ever since the liberation many Europeans had dreamed of a third way between American capitalism and Soviet communism. Charles de Gaulle hoped to make Fifth Republic France a world leader in developing such a geopolitical alternative to the cold war. This meant courting the third world. The term itself was coined in 1952 by French demographer Alfred Sauvy, drawing on the historical parallel of the Third Estate during the Revolution. The end of the Algerian war and the successful decolonization of Africa had given France a more positive image in newly independent Africa and Asia, not to mention a bloc of Francophone African states that would often, if not always, support the French position at the United Nations and in global affairs generally. Under de Gaulle, therefore, France set out to claim a leadership role in the nonaligned movement. France recognized communist China in 1964, much to the displeasure of the United States, and by the mid-1960s had emerged as a critic of American imperialism. De Gaulle traveled widely in Latin America, criticizing the hegemony of the United States there, and began to attack America's war in Vietnam. The French also began lobbying support in the Arab world, something possible only after the Algerian war. In 1967 France turned its back on its long-standing support of Israel, imposing an arms embargo on that country after its victory in the Six Day War. In 1968 Paris would begin hosting peace talks between the United States and North Vietnam.

In addition, de Gaulle enjoyed strutting the world stage, dispensing the wisdom from Paris. At times this got him into trouble. In November 1967 he referred to the Jews as "sure of themselves and domineering." This provoked a furious storm of protest, including from his long-time supporter Raymond Aron. Referring to de Gaulle's own considerable ego, some joked that he meant it as a compliment. Perhaps his most famous gaffe also took place in 1967, during a state visit to Canada. Speaking before a large crowd in Montréal, de Gaulle shouted *Vive le Québec* libre! (Long live *free* Quebec!) to roars of approval. This prompted a diplomatic incident with the Canadian government, although many in Quebec argued it was a seminal moment forcing greater discussion of the plight of Canada's Francophone minority. For many French, de Gaulle's larger-than-life persona and outrageous statements spoke to the importance of France in global affairs.

For not only de Gaulle but the people of the Fifth Republic as a whole, grandeur meant that France still counted for something in the world. Politics and foreign affairs were not the only way of asserting this. Shortly after he assumed power de Gaulle named novelist and adventurer André Malraux as his minister of culture. During his ten years in the position Malraux worked tirelessly to promote French culture both at home and abroad. Concerned that years of neglect and increasing automobile pollution had left Paris's most famous monuments gray and grimy, he implemented a massive sandblasting project of the Louvre and other buildings to restore them to pristine condition. He also arranged to send the *Mona Lisa* on a well-publicized tour of the United States. For Malraux, and for de Gaulle, culture as well as military and political prominence made France a great nation. As Malraux put it, culture was the "basis of the French nation acting for all of humankind."[2]

The gleaming buildings of the refurbished capital city vividly illustrated the importance of Paris as a world city, and France as a universal nation. They also reflected the new prosperity of the country, which in the 1960s made dramatic changes in French life. Ideas of French glory must rest on a solid foundation, and during the first decade of the Fifth Republic France became more affluent than ever before in its history. The average French person might marvel at the monumental beauty of a refurbished and cleaned up Paris, but increasingly she could also drive her own car home to a big new apartment or house. A solid decade of unparalleled prosperity created its own self-confidence, which in many respects more than made up for the traumas of the recent past. At the time it was easy to imagine that France, and much of the world, had moved past the tragedies of history to embrace a bright new future that showed no signs of coming to an end. In this decade a new France was born.

PROSPERITY AND CONSUMER SOCIETY

The 1960s were a golden era for France. In December 1958 the government unveiled its latest planning effort, the Pinay-Rueff Plan. The new plan emphasized balancing the French budget, severely strained by the costs of the Algerian war, stabilizing the franc, and boosting French exports by gradually abolishing protectionism. It achieved all these goals, with impressive results. During the 1960s the government continued to invest heavily in the economy, restructuring traditional industries like iron and steel and promoting new technologies. In agriculture it promoted the consolidation of small farms into larger units and provided credit to support mechanization, so that between 1946 and 1974 the number of tractors in France rose from 120,000 to 1.3 million.[3]

As in earlier years, the modernization of the French economy was not universal, and the nation still had many old-fashioned factories and farms. Nonetheless, France's ability to compete in international markets improved significantly. Exports grew from 10 percent to 17 percent by 1970, and foreign investment increased sharply in France as well. Thanks largely to the EEC other European countries, notably West Germany, replaced the former colonies as the nation's most important trading partners. From 1958 to 1970 the national economy grew at a rate of roughly 5.8 percent a year, outstripping even West Germany to become the most dynamic economy in Europe.

Economic growth translated into plentiful jobs. The nation's unemployment rate stayed below 3 percent during the 1960s, so that in essence France enjoyed full employment. Low unemployment rates and high productivity also meant higher wages for most French people. Since inflation generally stayed modest, although it began to creep up toward the end of the decade, real wages grew at a robust rate. This did not necessarily translate into greater social parity; as in most periods of capitalist economic expansion, some benefited more than others. A rising tide may lift all boats, but not equally. Nonetheless, the new prosperity was real for most people in France, enabling them to live in ways undreamed of by their parents and grandparents.

The combination of full employment and high salaries made it possible for the French to think about buying new things to an unprecedented degree. In addition, the increased availability and acceptability of consumer credit meant the ability to purchase big-ticket items previously seen as unaffordable. Moreover, the creation of a new level of social stability by the welfare state meant that people didn't have to worry about saving for disability, illness, or old age, so they could devote more resources to consumer goods. The creation of the welfare state and the expansion of the public sector created thousands of well-paid, secure jobs, further encouraging higher levels of consumption.

And then there was the impact of the baby boom. Between 1946 and 1975 France added over 10 million new citizens, growing from 40 million to 52 million inhabitants. Children, and the families who raised them, proved an inexhaustible market for consumer goods. Not surprisingly, the number of toys sold in France skyrocketed during the *trentes glorieuses*. Young families made many costly purchases. Washing machines and refrigerators were probably the most popular appliances, and both were tied to the idea of saving time for young mothers, who would presumably have to spend less time shopping and going to commercial laundromats. Families that received state subsidies for having large numbers of children generally spent them on big appliances. Many French families bought their own cars, which became more practical with the dramatic growth of the suburban population.

Other popular consumer goods included televisions, gradually replacing the hearth and the radio as the center of family life. By the end of the 1960s TVs had become a leading source of news and entertainment, and in a land that prided itself on fine dining it became surprisingly popular for families to eat dinner while watching television. Finally, the French spent increasing amounts of money on vacations. The Popular Front had invented the practice of a national paid vacation for two weeks. This was raised to three weeks in 1956, and four in 1963. In 1967, 21 million people in France took vacations away from home. Mostly they went to other parts of France, and many camped rather than staying in hotels, but 3 million traveled outside the country as well. By 1975 90 percent of all French households had a refrigerator and nearly 75 percent owned a car, washing machine, and television.[4]

To a great extent, the explosion of consumerism reflected not just the growth of families with children but also the new importance of the home in French life. Traditionally the French had spent a smaller portion of their budgets on housing than other Europeans, prioritizing food and clothing instead. The Fourth Republic had invested massively in building new housing during the 1950s, and much of the new consumer spending focused on making these new homes more accessible (private cars) or more comfortable (TVs, refrigerators, washing machines). Housing became a greater part of the family budget, rising from 16 percent in 1959 to 20 percent in 1975. The increased efficiency of French agriculture meant that people could eat just as well for less money, therefore leaving them free to spend more on their homes.

Not everyone in France approved of the new consumerism. In 1965 the writer Georges Perec published *Things*, a novel about contemporary consumer culture. He described the lives of two young people, Jérome and Sylvie, who found work in a new field created by the economic boom: consumer market research:

> For four years and maybe more they explored and interviewed and analysed . . . There was washing, drying, ironing. Gas, electricity and the telephone. Children. Clothes and underclothes. Mustard. Packet soups, tinned soups. Hair: how to wash it, how to dry it, how to make it hold a wave, how to make it shine. Students, fingernails, cough syrup, typewriters, fertilisers, tractors, leisure pursuits, presents, stationery, linen, politics, motorways, alcoholic drinks, mineral water, cheeses, jams, lamps and curtains, insurance and gardening . . . These were their great days of conquest . . . they were discovering the riches of the world.[5]

The world of Sophie and Jérome, and by extension all of France, was a world of endless commodities that increasingly defined the meaning of life.

Few aspects of the new prosperity came in for greater criticism than the rise of postwar suburbia. Much of the nation's population growth in the postwar era took place in the suburbs, so much so that suburban housing estates became the true face of contemporary France. This was especially true in the Paris area. The city of Paris had been losing population ever since the 1920s, whereas its suburbs continued to grow by leaps and bounds. In 1946 more than twice as many Parisians lived in the suburbs as in the center city; by 1975 this gap between suburbanites and urbanites had grown to over three and a half times. By the 1960s the French government was building more than 300,000 new housing units each year, mostly in the form of the *habitations à loyer modéré* (low cost rental housing, or HLMs). The growth of the high-rise HLMs contrasted sharply with the low-rise nineteenth-century buildings of French cities, as did the lack of street life and convenient public transportation. Perhaps most notorious of these was Sarcelles, a massive housing project built north of Paris as part of the government's new towns initiative. As one novelist described the area, "These really were towers! This was a housing estate for the future! For kilometre after kilometre after kilometre, house after house. Alike. Aligned. White. Still more houses. Houses houses houses."[6] Whereas many praised the new suburban housing, especially in contrast to the collapsing tenements it replaced, others argued it was cheaply built, ugly, and uniform. Social commentators invented a term, "Sarcellitis," to describe the malaise of living in such a depressing environment. In his 1965 science fiction film classic *Alphaville*, director Jean-Luc Godard labelled HLMs "hospitals for long-term maladies" and implied that they lobotomized their inhabitants.

The focus on children and the home during the postwar years highlighted women's changing role in French society. Women had fought actively in the resistance, and after the war the provisional government acknowledged that role by granting them the vote. In 1949 Simone de Beauvoir, existentialist pioneer and longtime companion of Jean-Paul Sartre, published *The Second Sex*, a ringing manifesto that had a global impact and would contribute to the rise of second-wave feminism in the 1960s and 1970s. Yet the prevailing political and social trends of the early Fifth Republic did not fundamentally challenge patriarchy or gender inequality. Women had the vote but very few took a leadership role in politics; by 1968 only 2 percent of members of the National Assembly were women. In general, a glass ceiling kept women out of the upper reaches of public administration, private industry, and academia. The French Academy, admission to which constituted the ultimate honor in the nation's intellectual life, only invited the first woman, the novelist Marguerite Yourcenar, to join its ranks in 1980. Moreover, significant legal barriers to gender equality remained. Until 1964, for example, a married woman needed her husband's permission to open a bank account.

For all these signs of discrimination, however, feminism made little headway in France during the 1960s. As in other western societies, the strong focus on family and domesticity tended to reinforce the idea that a woman's place was in the home. For many if not most women, the concrete material improvements in women's lives resulting from the rising standard of living and the availability of new household appliances trumped concerns about equal treatment of the sexes. Magazines catering especially to women, like *Marie-France, Marie-Claire,* and *Elle,* focused on issues like romance, child rearing, and fashion, not education and career. They emphasized that the modern woman was one who knew how to keep a modern, clean home, aided by the latest household technologies. There were some changes, notably the 1967 repeal of the law banning contraception. But for the most part many French women as well as men saw feminism as an Anglo-Saxon ideology, one that preached that women and men should not just be equal but the same. In a climate that valued women above all as housekeepers and mothers, few paid much attention to Simone de Beauvoir.

Not everyone in France shared in the prosperity of the 1960s. The economic dynamism of those years owed much to the labor of immigrant workers, who by the mid-1970s composed over 6 percent of the nation's population. During the 1960s the majority of them came from Mediterranean Europe, especially Italy, Spain, and Portugal. By the early 1970s France had some three-quarters of a million Portuguese, the largest group of immigrant workers in the country. At the same time the percentage of workers from outside Europe, principally France's ex-colonies and overseas *départements,* rose from 12 percent in 1946 to 23 percent in 1968 and 39 percent by 1975. These came above all from the Maghreb, continuing a tradition of North African immigration that dated back to the interwar years. By 1975 nearly a third of immigrant workers in France came from North Africa.

Most immigrants were unskilled and took the jobs no one else wanted. They were concentrated in heavy industry, such as the giant Renault auto plant outside Paris. They also labored in low-paid but highly visible service occupations, such as the Arabs and the black men who swept the streets of Paris. Most immigrants were young single men who had little knowledge of French and were therefore alienated from the mainstream of French society. Many found housing in cheap hotels in neighborhoods like the Goutte d'Or in Paris's eighteenth arrondissement. Others, especially those with families, ended up in the *bidonvilles,* shantytown developments in the suburbs. Made of corrugated tin, cardboard, and other cheap materials, the *bidonvilles* had no running water, utilities, or toilet facilities. North Africans in particular found housing here. After 1964 the French government launched an initiative to close the *bidonvilles* and move their inhabitants into HLMs, but as of the early

11.2. Algerian immigrant woman in Paris suburbs.
Source: AP Images.

1970s thousands of people still lived there. Isolated from French people both on the job and at home, most immigrant workers in France lived on the margins of the new prosperous society, which their labor helped make possible.

Immigrant workers were one of the most segregated population groups in France during the 1960s, but to an important extent this social isolation applied to the French working class as a whole. The number of French workers grew sharply during the *trentes glorieuses*, surpassing 8 million people, or 38 percent of the working population in general, by 1975. The French Communist party, whose base was heavily working class, remained one of the largest political parties in France, regularly winning 20 percent of the vote in national elections and controlling large numbers of municipalities in the Paris red belt and elsewhere. Working-class living standards rose and their housing conditions improved as many moved from prewar tenements into the new HLMs. Moreover, the geography and sociology of working-class France changed during these years. During the 1960s the French government promoted industrial development in the provinces, so that whereas the Paris area lost working-class

jobs, areas like Brittany, lower Normandy, and the Loire valley gained new factories. The internal composition of the working class also shifted with the rise
of a new skilled labor force concerned not just with wages but also the quality
of the work experience. At the same time industrial development increased
the need for unskilled labor, increasingly provided by immigrants.

Improved living standards did not add up to greater social equality, however. Economic growth during the 1960s tended to increase class divisions,
so that in relative terms French workers fell behind the nation's dynamic
new middle class. They worked longer hours for lower pay than most other
industrial workers in western Europe. Unions were legal under the Fifth Republic, but the union movement was divided between several organizations
and unionization rates were low compared to other developed nations. The
PCF was large and well-established but relegated to the margins of politics, not participating in any French governments between 1947 and 1981.
Moreover, the consumer revolution largely passed working people by in the
1960s; not until the early 1970s could workers and their families buy things
like new washing machines and cars. For most French workers living and
working conditions were better than before the war, but increasing social
inequality continued to make them a class apart.

The growth of the working class was one example of broader changes in
the sociology of France under the early Fifth Republic. Most striking was the
sharp decline of two groups that had composed the heart and soul of the nation during the nineteenth century: peasants and small shopkeepers. The rural
exodus that had done so much to shape modern France reached its apogee in
the postwar era, with roughly 100,000 farmers leaving the land every year. By
1974 the agricultural population had dropped to 2 million from 6 million in
1946; less than one French person in ten worked the land for a living. Those
who remained tended to run more productive and mechanized farms, and
played a greater role in politics and rural activism.

Independent shopkeepers and small business owners also saw their numbers decline in the postwar years, squeezed by the increasing concentration of
industry and the growth of chain stores and shopping centers. In 1963, for example, the French company Carrefour opened the nation's first shopping mall
in the Paris suburbs, and chain stores like Monoprix and Prisunic challenged
the small butchers, bakers, and food sellers that still delight foreign tourists.
During the early 1950s a small town shopkeeper named Pierre Poujade had
launched a national tax revolt to protect independent businessmen. He soon
created a political party that won 2.5 million votes in the 1956 elections,

before collapsing in 1960. The failure of Poujadism not only demonstrated its leader's political inexperience but also testified to the decline of its social base.

In contrast, during the 1960s the most dynamic and fastest growing segment of society was the salaried middle class, the so-called *cadres*. These people were well-educated, reflecting the expansion of both secondary and higher education in the early years of the Fifth Republic, and they mostly worked in the services sector, the source of the majority of new jobs in the 1960s. The elite members of senior management generally graduated from the *grandes écoles*, especially ENA, and went on to lucrative positions in both private business and public administration. Much more numerous, and less well paid, were the members of middle management, the *cadres moyens*, who held university degrees and occupied a variety of administrative positions. The growth of the French state and large corporations created an ongoing need for these white-collar workers, whose salaries funded the consumer revolution of the 1960s. They constituted the key social base of the Fifth Republic, much as the small shopkeepers and self-employed middle class had formed that of the Third.

The changing nature of French life also played a role in reshaping the nation's intelligentsia. During the 1950s and 1960s the idea of *engagement*, that intellectuals should involve themselves in political questions, remained powerful in the literary and philosophical circles of the Parisian Left Bank. In the early years this meant a strong affinity for Soviet communism, born in large part during the resistance. The Soviet invasion of Hungary in 1956, widely criticized by Sartre and other Parisian intellectuals, tarnished the communist ideal for many, and in the late 1950s and 1960s anticolonialism and third world politics became popular. French intellectuals played a leading role in the movement against the Algerian war. This political activism did not go unchallenged. In 1951 Albert Camus published *The Rebel*, a critical view of political activism, and began a famous feud with Jean-Paul Sartre that the two literary lions never resolved.

Perhaps more significant was the challenge posed to *engagement* by a new philosophical school, structuralism. Based in linguistic theory, structuralism argued that cognitive and institutional structures shaped all aspects of human life: that the internal structures of language inexorably shaped human understanding and therefore action. In 1958 anthropologist Claude Levi-Strauss published *Structural Anthropology*, emphasizing the basic conceptual and mythic structures common to all cultures. Writers in other fields, such as Roland Barthes in literary criticism and Jacques Lacan in psychoanalysis, published works from a similar perspective. In contrast to the existentialists, who emphasized individual agency and responsibility, the structuralists tended to see man as the prisoner of forces beyond his control. In times of stability, it was the structures that counted rather than the desire to make change. Structuralism made sense in the new France of the 1960s, as the heroic struggles of the past seemed to have given way to the seamless prosperity of the present.

The most dynamic group in French society was not occupational, however, but generational. By the early 1960s the first members of the baby boom generation were reaching adolescence, constituting a massive new fact in French life. In order to provide for the more sophisticated modern economy, in 1959 the French government raised the school leaving age from fourteen to sixteen, in effect making at least some secondary education mandatory for all young people. France also created a new, comprehensive type of middle school, the *collège*, which enabled upwardly mobile working-class youth to aspire to white-collar jobs. This openness had its limits, however, and higher education remained mostly reserved to members of the social elite.

These reforms reinforced the idea of adolescence as a new factor in French society. In earlier generations children moved directly into adult life, but by the 1960s France had large numbers of postpubescent young people who were still in school and not yet recognized as adults. The rise of youth as an independent group would reshape French society, and the western world as a whole, during the 1960s. During the occupation the Zazous had begun creating their own youth culture, followed by the "existentialist" young people of Saint-Germain-des-Prés in the late 1940s and 1950s. In the early 1960s a new, much larger form of adolescent culture arose. Like the Zazous and the Beatniks it was part of a global phenomenon, in this case dominated by rock music imported from Britain and the United States. In 1960 Jean-Phillipe Smet, a seventeen-year-old from Paris, released his first album under the American name Johnny Hallyday. Billing himself as "the French Elvis," Hallyday soon became a national and international sensation, appearing on the *Ed Sullivan Show* two years before it launched the Beatles in America. On June 22, 1963, the popular youth-oriented radio show *Salut les Copains!* (Hello Pals!) sponsored a mass rock concert in Paris's Place de la Nation. At least 150,000 dancing, singing teenagers showed up, overwhelming the police and leading *Le Monde* to declare that the *yé-yé* age had arrived.

The changing face of French society in the 1960s underscored the fundamental transformations in national life wrought by the postwar era and the early years of the Fifth Republic. A nation with a young, dynamic, and growing population, an urbanized society of skyscrapers, housing projects, superhighways, and shopping malls, a country led by a strong president, almost an elected monarch, allied with Germany and without a formal empire, the France of the late 1960s would have been almost unrecognizable to the people of the Third Republic. A regime of peace, prosperity, and stability, the Fifth Republic seemed to have banished the demons that had haunted so much of the history of modern France. Yet as would become clear in 1968, the history of France and the world had not yet come to a happy ending.

REVOLUTION IN FRANCE?

Like 1848 and 1919 before it, 1968 was a revolutionary year in world history, as the established order faced major challenges across the globe. In the United States the continuing Vietnam conflict had produced a powerful antiwar movement that forced President Johnson not to seek reelection and triggered widespread rioting at the Democratic Party convention in Chicago that summer, while in Vietnam the National Liberation Front launched a major new attack, the Tet Offensive, on American positions. The assassination of African American civil rights leader Martin Luther King Jr. in April sparked rioting in more than fifty cities. The fact that the United States, the stronghold of global capitalism and the postwar world order, experienced such turmoil underscored the depths of discontent. In eastern Europe Czech communist leader Alexander Dubçek tried to liberalize party rule in his country, creating what he called "socialism with a human face," only to be overthrown by the Soviet invasion of Czechoslovakia in August.

Everywhere college students seemed to be at the heart of the protests. In Mexico City a clash with the police during the summer Olympics resulted in the massacre of hundreds. Students generally took the lead in the American antiwar movement, and major protests broke out at Harvard, Columbia, and other universities. In West Berlin students took to the streets to protest the attempted assassination of popular Berlin student leader Rudi Dutschke in April (an act inspired by the murder of Martin Luther King Jr. weeks earlier), and in Italy protests over overcrowding and poor conditions forced the closure of universities across the country. In general the protests took a strongly anticapitalist tone, but many opposed Soviet communism as well. The search for a third way out of the cold war was revived by what became known as the New Left, and no group embraced it more eagerly than university students.

Nowhere did the turmoil of 1968 loom greater than in France, which once again seemed poised to claim the mantle of world revolution. The explosion of May and June 1968 shook the Fifth Republic to its foundations, presenting Charles de Gaulle with one of the greatest challenges of his political life. It started with college students but soon spread to mobilize discontent throughout the society. At one point it seemed that the young revolutionaries of May and their allies might actually overthrow the regime. The power and vehemence of the May movement came as a great surprise to people both in France and throughout the world. After all, the country had experienced one of the most affluent decades in its modern history, it was at peace after many years of war, and the government was extremely stable; in other words, the usual triggers for revolution were nowhere to be found. Most members of the New Left and other radical groupings looked to the third world, notably communist China, for revolutionary inspiration. Few expected to find it in an advanced capitalist country like France. Yet in retrospect it's clear that underneath all the prosperity there were currents of dissatisfaction that with the right opportunity would explode onto the surface of national life.

The strains experienced by French universities in the 1960s provided the spark for the May explosion. By the middle of the decade the baby boom had rolled into the nation's high schools and universities; the number of college students tripled between 1958 and 1968. The French government was forced to scramble to handle the ever-growing enrollments, creating new universities and branch campuses throughout the country. The University of Paris expanded beyond the historic center of the Sorbonne in the Latin Quarter, creating several new campuses. Yet expansion was not accompanied by any serious rethinking or modernization of higher education. French university administrations tended to be conservative and highly centralized, and teaching very traditional and often uninspired. In spite of the rapid growth of new universities, most campuses were overcrowded. Students found it hard to negotiate the thick web of university bureaucracy, and the majority of those admitted never graduated.

Such conditions produced a crisis at the University of Paris branch campus in Nanterre. Established in 1964, Nanterre was located in a working-class suburb of Paris best known for having one of the worst *bidonvilles* in the country. Like many of the suburban HLMs it so closely resembled, Nanterre was constructed in the middle of an empty field. It was designed to be an American-style university with its own campus and student housing, but it was isolated from the Latin Quarter, the traditional center of Parisian student life, and offered none of the cultural amenities and diversions of that neighborhood. The university grew rapidly, from 4,000 to 15,000 students in three years, so that it soon suffered from the same overcrowding as its more well-established peers. Nanterre students resented packed classrooms and dorms, as well as restrictions like the ban on students of the opposite sex in their rooms (de Gaulle would later derisively comment that the students were striking for the right to have mistresses).

In 1967 a group of student activists took over the local chapter of the National Union of French Students (UNEF), affiliated with the PCF, and pushed it in a militant direction. Naming themselves the *enragés*, they critiqued the idea of the modern university as a cog in the capitalist machine rather than as an institution devoted to education and scholarship. They also took radical positions on global issues; unlike the SFIO and PCF, which called for peace in Vietnam, the *enragés* supported the victory of the Viet Cong. Their heroes were not the Soviets but rather third world revolutionaries like Mao Zedong, Che Guevara, and Malcolm X. In January 1968 the *enragés* began a series of demonstrations against the Vietnam War on the Nanterre campus. On March 18 students from Nanterre stormed into Paris, attacking the offices of American Express and burning the American flag. When police arrested one of the students, fellow radicals responded by occupying the administration building on March 22. For the next month the *enragés* plunged the university into chaos, interrupting classes and debating political issues. They shouted down a member of the PCF who came to plead for order. Sometimes brawling broke out, especially between the radicals and neofascist militants who came up from Paris to pick fights. By the end of April the administration had enough, and on May 2 it closed the university for the rest of the academic year.

This decision turned out to be a major mistake. Locked out of the university, Nanterre's student militants left for Paris, transferring the movement from a suburban backwater to the heart of the French university system. That afternoon they occupied the central courtyard of the Sorbonne, in the heart of the Latin Quarter. The administration responded by calling in the police the next day to clear the site, a move that outraged many who did not necessarily support the militants but believed in academic freedom and the autonomy of the university. Students and professors came out in large numbers to support the right to demonstrate, and they were joined by students from local high schools as the movement began to spread beyond the Sorbonne. Over the next few days violent clashes erupted between demonstrators and police, proving to many the validity of the *enragés'* claim that the university was a tool of capitalist repression. This series of confrontations culminated on the night of May 10 when students attempted to retake the Sorbonne from the police, building barricades throughout the Latin Quarter. The police responded with force, beating and gassing demonstrators throughout the night. The fighting was so intense that tear gas drifted down through air ducts into the subway system, causing commuters to break spontaneously into tears. Paris had not seen such street battles since the liberation.

These events quickly became national news, broadcast around the country by newspapers, radio, and television. French people could witness scenes of police brutality on their TV screens, and many reacted with sympathy for the students. The publicity also helped spread the movement to provincial universities, and soon college students throughout the country were challenging their own administrations. President de Gaulle, outraged by what he considered youthful hijinks out of control, wanted to send in the army, but his prime minister, Georges Pompidou, persuaded him to reopen the Sorbonne in the hope that once police repression was no longer an issue the movement would run out of steam.

That didn't happen. After police vacated the Sorbonne on May 12, students triumphantly reoccupied the building, turning it into a 24/7 forum for people to discuss capitalism, revolution, or whatever else was on their minds. An assortment of Marxists, Maoists, anarchists, feminists, environmentalists, and others talked endlessly about their personal grievances and their views on how to remake the world. Professors and students met as equals, and activists from throughout the city came to take part. Students also occupied other facilities in the Latin Quarter, notably the School of Fine Arts. Student artists began creating posters that appeared on walls all over the city and sought to express the spirit of the movement. Slogans like "Be a realist! Demand the impossible!" and "It is forbidden to forbid!" emphasized the attack on authority and the desire for both political and personal liberation. Some also attacked the government: one showed a silhouette of de Gaulle clapping his hand over the mouth of a young man, saying, "Be young and shut up!" The posters, which were created and distributed spontaneously, encapsulated the carnivalesque nature of the movement, its rejection of all authority. Their images portrayed May 1968 as a joyous festival: an anarchist celebration of youth and revolution.

Although movement emphasized a lack of hierarchy and collective decision making, leaders did emerge. None became more famous, or notorious, than Daniel Cohn-Bendit, soon known as "Danny the Red." Born near

Toulouse in 1945 of German Jewish refugee parents, Cohn-Bendit had grown up in France but opted for German nationality as an adult. In 1966 he began his studies at Nanterre in sociology, a prestigious discipline at the time that attracted many leftist students. Completely bilingual, he traveled back and forth between West Germany and France, becoming a critical link between the student movements in both countries. He grew close to several German student leaders, notably Rudi Dutschke and Karl-Dietrich Wolff, whom he invited to speak at Nanterre in the spring of 1968. The interconnections between members of the New Left in France, West Germany, Italy, and elsewhere provided an alternate vision of European unity to that advocated by de Gaulle and Adenauer.

At this point the May movement was like many other student upheavals around the world during that tumultuous year, but it quickly took on an entirely new and much more serious dimension. On May 13, the day after the reopening of the Sorbonne, several hundred thousand protesters marched through Paris, shouting slogans like "De Gaulle! Ten years is enough!" and "We are all German Jews!" On that day French unions staged a one-day general strike, and students marched out from the Latin Quarter to the Renault factory outside Paris, calling on the workers to come join them. Many trade unionists and members of the traditional left, especially the communists, mistrusted the student radicals as spoiled bourgeois youth and remained largely deaf to their appeals. Rank-and-file workers, in contrast, often sympathized with the students as victims of police brutality. Perhaps more significantly, many looked at their own lives and resented the lack of autonomy they had at work, the boring, repetitive nature of life on the job, and could identify with the idealistic challenges posed by the *enragés* to the system; they knew how it felt to be cogs in the machine.

As a result, in a movement that was both massive and spontaneous, workers starting going on strike. The strike wave started in the provinces, beginning with a sit-down strike at an aviation factory near Nantes on May 14. It soon spread to large factories throughout the country, and then beyond the industrial economy to all sorts of offices, stores, and other places of work. White-collar workers staged strikes demanding more room for creativity on the job. In the countryside farmers blocked roads with their tractors to show their support of the movement. Even the nation's professional soccer players joined in, occupying the offices of the National Football Federation, demanding *Le football aux footballeurs!* (Soccer to the soccer players!) In most cases, salary was less of an issue than the pace of labor and the lack of workplace democracy. Those who went on strike often occupied their factories, taking symbolic possession of them. By the third week of May France was witnessing the largest strike wave in its history, akin to the sit-down strikes of June 1936 during the Popular Front, but much more massive. Some 10 million French women and men had joined the movement, and some both inside France and abroad began to wonder if this prosperous capitalist country was on the verge of a revolution.

No one was more surprised by the strike wave than the trade unions and political parties of the left. The strike movement happened without their input and was beyond their control. They could no longer dismiss it as an affair of bourgeois youth, but they had no idea what the strikers wanted or where events were headed. The PCF, for all its rhetorical commitment to the idea of revolution, feared the consequences of anarchy on the job and in the streets. The government was also caught completely unaware. De Gaulle, having assumed that the crisis had ended with the reopening of the Sorbonne, left May 14 for a state visit to Romania. Television news showed him watching Romanian folk dancers while his own country was falling apart. More and more, not only the government but all the major national institutions seemed disconnected from the situation and desires of the French people.

Cutting his visit to Romania short, de Gaulle returned four days later to a nation in chaos. Garbage was piling up on the streets because sanitation workers were on strike, food and gasoline were in short supply, and the movement seemed to grow from day to day. On May 24 the president made a major televised address to the nation, calling for calm and promising reforms. At the same time Prime Minister Pompidou began negotiating with the unions about ending the strikes. On May 27 these negotiations produced the Grenelle Accords, modeled on the Matignon Accords of 1936, which made generous concessions to workers: more paid vacation, wage increases, especially in the minimum wage, and increased union representation on the job. For the union leaders, this represented a major victory, and they confidently assumed their workers would accept it.

They were wrong. Renault workers booed the head of the CGT when he presented the agreement, and everywhere the strikes continued to grow. At this point many concluded France had entered a revolutionary situation that would only end with the fall of the regime. In Nantes, where the workers' movement had started, strikers' representatives essentially took over running the city. Various politicians on the left announced their willingness to form a provisional government and assume power, and people throughout the country assumed that the presidency of Charles de Gaulle, if not the Fifth Republic itself, had come to an end.

But de Gaulle was not finished. On May 29, at the height of the turmoil in France, he suddenly disappeared. Many believed he had returned to Colombey-les-Deux-Églises; some even speculated he had fled the country and the revolution had triumphed. In fact, de Gaulle flew to Baden-Baden, where he met with General Jacques Massu, head of French forces in West Germany and the former leader of France's war effort in Algeria. He wanted to make sure that the army would step in to prevent any attempted revolution by students, communists, or anyone else. Massu agreed to support de Gaulle, but in return he demanded that the president amnesty the four generals arrested for leading the attempted coup d'état in Algiers in January 1960. De Gaulle agreed and then flew back to Paris, where he went on television again to speak to the French nation. Instead of announcing his resignation, as many expected, de Gaulle threw down the gauntlet. He reiterated his pledge of reform but at the same time insisted on the need for order, saying the nation had to choose between him and civil war. He also accused the PCF of plotting to overthrow the government and announced he was dissolving the National Assembly and scheduling new elections for June.

It was a powerful speech, but much of it was not new. More important was the fact that things had changed in the last few weeks: many had become weary of the shortages, the stinking garbage piled up in the streets, and the constant turmoil. Letting off steam and demanding more democracy in daily life was one thing; confronting revolution and civil war quite another. Above all, there was no idea where all this was headed. Consequently, support for de Gaulle and for ending the movement was dramatic and immediate. That evening a spontaneous demonstration of half a million Parisians wound its way down the Champs-Elysées loudly cheering the president and denouncing the students ("Cohn-Bendit to Dachau" was one of the more memorable slogans).

Events of that evening sucked the momentum out of the movement. As May turned to June, workers drifted back to their jobs, happy to accept the Grenelle Accords, and students went back to take their final exams. In the legislative elections held at the end of June the Gaullists scored an overwhelming victory. Forming a new party, the Union of Democrats for the Republic (UDR), they won 75 percent of the vote. The established parties of the left, the SFIO and PCF, were soundly repudiated at the polls, having failed either to support the May movement or to provide a convincing alternative to it. By

July many began leaving on vacation, and the movement had melted away like a snowman in the sun.

The rise and fall of the near revolution of May 1968 is one of the stranger episodes in the history of modern France. It was a powerful social movement born of affluence and stability, not poverty, despair, or defeat. It was easy to conclude that it was simply a flash in the pan, a dramatic manifestation of both the nation's revolutionary heritage and the growing pains of a rapidly changing society. The real meaning of May 1968 goes deeper, however. It revealed a strong desire for democracy that went beyond the ballot box to embrace personal empowerment and social equality. It gave voice to many in French society, including women, immigrants, and gays, whose demands would be pressed more assertively in the years to come. Finally, it took place in the context of a worldwide revolt of students against the contradictions of modern capitalist society and the roles it prescribed for the huge postwar generation. The May movement saw itself as concerned not just with French society but equally with fighting oppression abroad, symbolized by its beginnings in the struggle against the American war in Vietnam. For a brief time in the spring of 1968, the movement that started with a few student radicals at Nanterre made France once again the center of the world.

THE END OF POSTWAR PROSPERITY

By July 1968 Charles de Gaulle had triumphed over the young radicals of May, and the Fifth Republic had survived a major challenge. He would resign less than a year later, however, bringing a final end to the greatest political career of twentieth-century France. In April 1969 de Gaulle submitted another referendum to French voters, this one proposing increased powers for regional councils, and made it clear that if it was rejected he would step down as president. The referendum failed and de Gaulle left public life for the last time, returning to his estate at Colombey-les-Deux-Églises, where he would die in November 1970 at the age of seventy-nine. The great leader had helped bring a new France into being, but in the end it no longer needed him.

Although de Gaulle had personally shaped the Fifth Republic, his departure did not cause a major crisis. His prime minister, Georges Pompidou, easily won the presidential election of April 1969, ensuring the continuity of the republic and Gaullist control. Prime minister since 1962, Pompidou was an able administrator but a rather colorless politician, certainly nothing like his great mentor. Unlike de Gaulle, who was sincerely interested in addressing complaints that surfaced in May 1968, Pompidou resisted democratizing university administrations or the work culture of state-owned factories. He was more interested in developing major technological and building projects, especially for the capital. Pompidou sponsored the building of the Montparnasse Tower, the first major skyscraper in the historic center of Paris, which opened in 1973 to the kind of scorn that greeted the Eiffel Tower a century earlier. He also built the ultra-modern Pompidou Center right next to the Marais district on the Right Bank, and sponsored the transfer of the city's central market place, Les Halles, to the suburbs and its replacement by a modernist shopping mall. Major national projects included France's network of high-speed trains (*trains à grande vitesse*, or TGV) and the Ariane space program. In one major respect, European policy, Pompidou departed significantly from de Gaulle's legacy. He dropped France's opposition to British membership in the EEC, and in January 1973 the United Kingdom along with Denmark and Ireland joined the Common Market.

Pompidou's focus on splashy technological projects reflected the optimism of the final years of the *trentes glorieuses*, as unemployment remained low and the French economy overtook Britain's. By the time of his premature death in April 1974, however, the world's economic situation had changed dramatically. To an important extent, the postwar recovery of Europe had been tied to American dominance of European economies. The Bretton Woods agreements of 1944 had tied European currencies to the dollar. This system worked when the US economy was dominant, but as the European nations became more prosperous during the 1960s, and America struggled under the cost of major social programs at home and the Vietnam War abroad, it became untenable. In August 1971, consequently, America abandoned Bretton Woods and devalued the dollar, causing a major shock to the global economy.

International finance and trade had not yet recovered when the oil crisis of 1973 hit the west. In October 1973 the Yom Kippur war broke out between Israel, Egypt, and Syria. In response to US aid to Israel the Arab-dominated Organization of Petroleum Exporting Countries decided to cut back sharply on oil production. As a result, the price of crude oil skyrocketed, more than quadrupling over the next two years. France, which imported 75 percent of its oil, was particularly hard hit, but the world economy as a whole suffered. In 1979 the Islamic Revolution overthrew the shah of Iran, followed by war between Iran and Iraq the next year. Iranian oil production collapsed, triggering new shortages and price increases in international oil markets. This plunged the world economy into a second major recession between 1979 and 1981.

By the early 1980s the price of crude oil on world markets was at least twenty times what it had been a decade earlier, triggering at the same time major inflationary spirals and a sharp decline in production. The era of "stagflation" had arrived, and governments throughout the world scrambled to deal with a vastly changed economic situation.

By 1974 the crises of the world economy had pushed France into recession, ending the *trentes glorieuses*. The last quarter of the twentieth century and the new century to come would be dominated by economic stagnation. Annual GDP growth of nearly 6 percent shrank during the late 1970s and 1980s to 2 percent and sometimes lower. Moreover, the recession exposed some structural problems in the French economy that prosperity had tended to paper over but became significant during the economic downturn. Not all industries and businesses had modernized during the boom years, and in some sectors productivity rates remained low. Inflation had already been a problem during the 1960s, pushed by the rising living standards and the new consumerism. French wages were relatively high, especially after the Grenelle Accords, making French goods less competitive on international markets. As the international economic outlook worsened, these weaknesses became evident.

The end of prosperity came as a shock to the French people. The length of the postwar boom meant that the nation had not experienced hard times in a while, and much of its population had never known them at all. Prices of consumer goods rose rapidly, eating sharply into family budgets. Above all, unemployment became a major national concern for the first time since the Depression. During the years of prosperity French unemployment rates had rarely risen above 3 percent. The nation had to import millions of immigrant workers to supply adequate labor for the growing economy. This changed after 1974. By 1980 unemployment rates rose to 6 percent, and by 1985 to 9 percent of the labor force. Joblessness continued to grow for the rest of the century, reaching a high point of nearly 12 percent, or 3.4 million people, by the mid-1990s.

Not all shared in the burden of unemployment equally. Young people were particularly hard hit: youth unemployment rates reached 15 percent by the early 1980s, rising to well over 20 percent by the mid-1990s. Increasingly a nation that had looked to its youth as the hope of the future now saw it as a burden on society. Working-class French men and women also suffered, especially those in older industries or regions like the steel factories of Lorraine or the coal mines of the Nord. By the early 1980s deindustrialization—the decline or collapse of older industrial areas in the face of recession and increased competition from cheaper industries in the developing world—had become a major concern for large parts of France. In 1978 the government decided to close several old steel mills in Lorraine, throwing thousands out of work and prompting major riots. High jobless rates meant the decline of the working class in general, so that by the 1990s it constituted less than a third of the working population of France. Hard times also hurt French farmers, particularly those who had not adopted modern agricultural techniques. Between 1975 and 1990 France lost over half a million farmers, completing the destruction of the traditional peasantry.

Perhaps most important of all, the postwar sense of dynamism and faith in the future largely disappeared in the recession years of the 1970s and beyond. The era of ever more dynamic growth and full employment would not return, making it harder to believe in the idea of France as a universal nation. In a world of stagnation and decline, many French tended to retreat into a narrower view of their country, one that might insulate it from a harsh new world. In an increasingly globalized era, however, the problems of France resounded far beyond its borders, and at best the French could hope that its solutions did too.

Dealing with the economy became the number one political issue in 1974 after the death of President Pompidou. The presidential election of that year also raised fundamental questions about the nature of the Fifth Republic: after sixteen years of Gaullist leadership, was it even possible to imagine a government led by another political party? In 1974 socialist leader François Mitterrand ran against the Gaullist candidate for president, Jacques Chaban-Delmas, but was defeated by the centrist leader Valéry Giscard-d'Estaing. A highly trained technocrat, graduate of both ENA and the Ecole Polytechnique, Giscard d'Estaing became the first non-Gaullist president of the Fifth Republic, showing the regime could adapt with the times.

In addition to reviving the economy, the new leadership had to address the needs of young people and the grievances that led to the May movement. Although the near revolution of May 1968 collapsed spectacularly in June, it did not disappear without a trace. During the 1970s a number of social movements developed in France, often led by veterans of May 1968. Many former *enragés* poured their energy into grassroots activism around local issues. In 1971 peasants on the Larzac plateau in southwestern France decided to resist the expropriation of their lands by a military base, and were joined in their ultimately successful campaign by tens of thousands of leftist activists.

In another example, when workers at the Lip watchmaking factory near Besançon learned it was about to close, they occupied the plant and began making watches on their own, quickly dubbed "self-winding watches."

The 1970s saw the rebirth of feminism in France, as in other nations in Europe and America. In 1969 a group of French feminists founded the Mouvement de Libération des Femmes (Women's Liberation Movement, or MLF). One of their major concerns was securing abortion rights. In 1971 a group of noted women, including Simone de Beauvoir and actress Catherine Deneuve, signed the "Manifesto of the 343," declaring publicly that they had undergone abortions and demanding the right for all women. The decade also saw new efforts to campaign for gay rights in France. The first gay pride celebration took place in Paris in June 1977. Another generational change was the decline of religion in French life; by the end of the decade the vast majority of young people in France, although baptized Catholic, never went to church.

In many respects the new president appealed to France's new generation. At forty-eight, Giscard d'Estaing was one of the youngest heads of state in French history. Early in his presidency he lowered the voting age to eighteen. Moreover, he adopted a moderate, often progressive position on social issues. He appointed Simone Veil, crusader for women's rights and Holocaust survivor, minister of health, and in 1975 passed laws legalizing divorce and limited rights to abortion. In addition, Giscard d'Estaing implemented significant educational reforms, creating public nursery schools and enabling more young people to complete their secondary education. He also halted the construction of skyscrapers in Paris after the furor over the Montparnasse Tower, ensuring that the complex of massive office buildings named La Défense was built outside city limits west of the Arc de Triomphe. Yet Giscard was no leftist in disguise. He strongly supported investments in nuclear power, both civil and military, partly in reaction to the increased price of oil.

For all its attempts to embrace new ideas and ways of governing France, the presidency of Valery Giscard d'Estaing was ultimately judged on its economic performance, and this was not positive. Giscard d'Estaing appointed Raymond Barre as his prime minister, one of the top economists in the country. Barre implemented a classic deflationary program to strengthen the franc and revive the economy. He imposed wage and price controls and cut government spending. After 1978 he lifted the price controls in order to encourage private investment. As during the Depression of the 1930s, deflation was both unpopular and ineffective. It failed to stop inflation, especially after the second round of oil price increases in 1979. By the end of the decade, many in France were searching for an alternative to the enlightened capitalism of Giscard d'Estaing, and increasingly they looked to the left to provide it.

THE SOCIALISTS TAKE POWER

The May 1968 movement was a disaster for the parties of the French left. The student revolutionaries had widely condemned the PCF as Stalinist and out of touch, and the SFIO as irrelevant. After their crushing defeat in the elections of June 1968 left-wing parties, especially the socialists, had undertaken major reforms. In 1971 the socialists voted to recreate themselves as the French Socialist party (PS) and deemphasize their classic Marxist message. This effort was led by François Mitterrand, who now became the leader of the PS. In 1972 the PC and the PCF signed an electoral alliance, the Common Program, hoping that by joining forces they might win the right to govern for the first time in a generation.

Mitterrand, who would become the most important French socialist leader since Jean Jaurès, represented the new face of the party. From a conservative middle-class Catholic background, Mitterrand had briefly worked for Vichy during World War II before joining the resistance. After the liberation he had joined the Radical party as a protégé of Pierre Mendès-France. He had no real history with any trade union or other working-class organization. An ambitious politician, Mitterrand had first run for president as the candidate of the left against de Gaulle in 1965. As leader of the new Socialist party, he worked skillfully to craft a new progressive message that would appeal far beyond the traditional working class.

Mitterrand also used the alliance with the PCF, controversial in many quarters, to outflank that party on the left. During postwar years the communists had been the dominant left-wing party in France, regularly getting 20 percent of the vote from their working-class constituents. Yet by the 1970s the French communists, and the international movement to which they belonged, were showing their age. Moscow's invasion of Czechoslovakia in 1968 had proved to many that communism had lost its progressive edge and become repressive. During the mid-1970s the eurocommunism movement challenged the traditional subordination of communist parties to the Soviet Union and began to experiment with internal party democracy. The PCF embraced some of these new ideas, although hesitantly and to a lesser extent than its fellow parties in Italy and Spain. Its resistance to change began to erode its popular base and electoral support, and by the end of the decade the socialists had emerged as the leading left-wing party in France.

The reconfiguration of the French left was especially evident among the nation's intellectuals. The French intelligentsia played a major role in the uprisings of May 1968. Theorists like Henri Lefebvre and Guy DeBord challenged structuralism, emphasizing the cultural dimension of Marxism and attacking consumer culture as dehumanizing. Many, like Sartre, took to the streets during that heady era. Yet the failure of the May movement seemed to reaffirm the basic pessimism of structuralism. During the 1970s structuralism evolved into poststructuralism, a new philosophical approach that emphasized the infinite multiplicity of power relations over straightforward political conflicts. Led by philosophers like Michel Foucault and Jacques Derrida, poststructuralism was a philosophy of the disenchanted, generally disavowing the idea of political revolution. In some ways it represented a return to the liberalism of Raymond Aron and Albert Camus, although it also embraced the struggles of marginalized groups. It both contributed to and drew inspiration from the new identity politics of the 1970s, especially around feminism and gay rights.

This turning away from revolution went together with a more critical attitude toward the Soviet Union. In 1974 *The Gulag Archipelago* by Alexander Solzhenitsyn was published in French, prompting a horrified reaction to Russia's penal camps and the Soviet system in general. This was not the first revelation of the evils of Soviet communism in France, but it now fell on fertile ideological soil. A new group of intellectuals, many of them veterans of May 1968, began to challenge the revolutionary tradition generally. In 1977 Bernard Henri-Lévy published *Barbarism with a Human Face*, arguing that ultimately all revolutionary ideology was Stalinist. At roughly the same time a group of historians led by François Furet began attacking the legacy of the French Revolution, portraying Robespierre as a twentieth-century-style totalitarian dictator. By the beginning of the 1980s French intellectuals had fervently embraced anticommunism, enthusiastically supporting the Polish independent union Solidarity, for example.

The new conservatism of the French intelligentsia, and the decline of the PCF, worked to the advantage of the socialists. Mitterrand could convincingly argue that the left stood for reform, not revolution. This was aided by the breakup of the Common Program in 1977, a split initiated by the communists once they realized that the alliance was not benefiting them but the socialists. As a result, the left did poorly in the 1978 municipal elections. But the government of Giscard d'Estaing had problems of its own, notably hostility from the Gaullists led now by Jacques Chirac. Giscard d'Estaing also suffered from his cozy relationship with brutal African emperor Jean-Bedel Bokassa, especially when it came out that he had accepted a personal gift of diamonds from the dictator. Moreover, the end of the Common Program mattered less in the presidential elections of 1981, when on the second round leftist voters of all persuasions voted for Mitterrand. As a result, on May 10, 1981, François Mitterrand won the presidential election by 52 percent to 48 percent for Valery Giscard d'Estaing. The legislative elections awarded the socialists an absolute majority in the National Assembly, while the PCF lost half its seats. The Socialist party, divided and weak at the beginning of the Fifth Republic, now scored the greatest victory in its history.

The elections of 1981 marked a turning point for the Fifth Republic. The left had taken power for the first time, demonstrating that the regime was flexible enough to represent voices from across the political spectrum. It also meant that the republic had freed itself from the shadow of its founding father, Charles de Gaulle. The election results caused an explosion of joy in France. Massive crowds thronged the Place de la Bastille in Paris, traditional symbol of the French Revolution, waving roses and cheering on the victorious socialists. Mitterrand celebrated his victory by walking to the Pantheon alone to pay homage to the nation's illustrious republican dead. Like the Popular Front before it, the new socialist administration represented a major political change and hopes for a different future. Also like the Popular Front, however, it would soon discover that calling for change was easier than making it happen.

A new France was born during the first two decades of the Fifth Republic, a country that differed sharply in many respects from its past. The stability of the regime demonstrated this; by 1981 it had already lasted longer than any other government in modern French history except the Third Republic, and even with crises like May 1968 and the recession after 1974 it showed no signs of running out of steam. Paradoxically, this stability rested on far-reaching changes in French society and culture. Grounded in a period of rising living standards, the social structure changed radically, replacing groups like small shopkeepers and peasants that symbolized traditional France with a new salaried middle class. Paris grew enormously, reaching an aggregate population of 9 million by the mid-1970s, but this reflected the tremendous suburban growth that transformed cityscapes across France during the postwar era. Adolescents and college students became a major factor in French life, and new types of political movements gained traction, especially after 1968.

A key part of this change was a major shift in France's place in the world. The Fifth Republic built on the previous regime's *rapprochement* with West Germany and investment in European integration. It completed the process of decolonization and at the same time laid the groundwork for post-imperial relations between France and former colonies in the Third World. In addition, de Gaulle's insistence on both political and cultural independence from the United States, in a global era of increasing Americanization, provided a model for how to embrace the modern age without completely surrendering national culture. Under the Fifth Republic France seemed to recover the self-confidence and national greatness lost during the occupation and the conflicts over decolonization. But the end of the twentieth century and the beginning of the twenty-first would bring new challenges, once again reshaping what it meant to be a universal nation.

Suggestions for Further Reading

Atkin, Nicolas. *The Fifth French Republic.* London: Palgrave, 2005.

Berstein, Serge. *The Republic of de Gaulle, 1958–1969.* Cambridge: Cambridge University Press, 1993.

Bess, Michael. *The Light-Green Society: Ecology and Technological Modernity in France 1960–2000.* Chicago: University of Chicago Press, 2003.

Boltanski, Luc. *The Making of a Class: Cadres in French History.* Cambridge: Cambridge University Press, 1987.

Cohn-Bendit, Daniel. *Obsolete Communism: The Left-Wing Alternative.* New York: McGraw Hill, 1968.

Crozier, Michel. *The Stalled Society.* New York: Viking, 1973.

Duchen, Claire. *Feminism in France from May '68 to Mitterrand.* London: Routledge, 1986.

Gifford, Prosser, and William Roger Louis. *The Transfer of Power in Africa: Decolonization, 1940–1960.* New Haven, CT: Yale University Press, 1982.

Hecht, Gabriel. *The Radiance of France: Nuclear Power and National Identity After World War II.* Cambridge: MIT Press, 1998.

Henri-Lévy, Bernard. *Barbarism with a Human Face.* New York: Harper & Row, 1979.

Hirsh, Arthur. *The French New Left.* Boston: South End Press, 1981.

Kuisel, Richard. *Capitalism and the State in Modern France.* Cambridge: Cambridge University Press, 1981.

Lacouture, Jean. *De Gaulle.* New York: Norton, 1990.

Ross, Kristin. *May '68 and Its Afterlives*. Chicago: University of Chicago Press, 2002.

Seidman, Michael. *The Imaginary Revolution: Parisian Students and Workers in 1968*. New York: Berghahn, 2004.

Singer, Daniel. *Prelude to Revolution*. New York: Hill & Wang, 1970.

Touraine, Alain. *The May Movement: Revolt and Reform*. New York: Random House, 1971.

Notes

1. Mohamed Camera, "Sekou Touré," *ThinkAfricaPress*, December 19, 2013.
2. Lebovics, *Mona Lisa's Escort: André Malraux and the Reinvention of French Culture* (Ithaca, NY: Cornell University Press, 1999).
3. D. L. L. Parry and Pierre Girard, *France Since 1800: Squaring the Hexagon* (Oxford: Oxford University Press, 2002), 227.
4. Ibid., 232.
5. Georges Perec, *Things: A Story of the Sixties* (Boston: David Godine, 1990), 37–38.
6. Christiane Rochefort, *Les petits enfants du siècle* (Paris: Hachette, 2001).

[twelve]

POSTCOLONIAL FRANCE: A NEW UNIVERSAL NATION?

ON BASTILLE DAY, JULY 14, 1998, A MASSIVE CROWD OF 1.5 MILLION people packed the Champs-Elysées, laughing and crying in rapturous celebration. Similar festivities took place all over France in the biggest public outpouring of joy since the liberation. For the first time in its history, France had won the World Cup, the greatest prize in soccer. Led by an Algerian, Zinédine Zidane, with players from Senegal and Guadeloupe, the team represented a new multicultural vision of France. As such, it had come under criticism from the right-wing press, which cast doubt on the team's ability and discipline. Zidane and his teammates triumphed, however, sweeping such doubts away with a convincing victory over Brazil, a nation often viewed as a multicultural success story. As one young man declared that night in Paris, "France loses when she discriminates. Here, we were forced to win, forced."[1] A France that embraced its global and postcolonial heritage had become champion of the world.

In the years since François Mitterrand and the socialists took power in 1981, France has grappled with a number of challenges, most importantly, the meaning of French universalism and French national identity as the world moved into the twenty-first century. Profound global transformations, including the collapse of the Soviet Union and its satellites in eastern Europe, the

12.1. New Year's Eve, 2000: France celebrates the
new millennium. *Source:* AP Images/Michel Euler.

decline of American political and military power worldwide, the rise of Islamic
fundamentalism, European integration, and the birth of a globalized information economy, would shape not only how France dealt with the outside world,
but also how it conceived of itself. At the same time, the end of formal empire
created a large population in the metropole of colonial origin, especially but
not only from North Africa, transforming the character of the nation's suburbs
and, increasingly, of France as a whole. By the beginning of the twenty-first
century minarets rose above urban landscapes throughout the country, and
black and brown men, women, and children were a common sight in the nation's schools, shops, and streets. The empire might be over, but the colonies
had come home, creating a new vision of France as a postcolonial nation.

Many scholars and cultural commentators, in France and abroad, have
viewed postcolonial multiculturalism and universalism as fundamentally opposed to each other, and consequently have seen the concept of the universal

nation as in decline since World War II. The contradictory nature of republican universalism as exemplified by the French Revolution and the Third Republic, based on the subjection of women and the exclusion of colonial subjects and racial minorities from full citizenship, is no longer tenable in the contemporary era. Moreover, the end of other universalisms, notably that of Soviet communism, calls into question the ability of any political or cultural philosophy to encapsulate the human experience in all its diversity. At the same time, questions about the idea of the nation-state in an era of globalization have further weakened the concept of the universal nation.

In this final chapter we will explore how the French have grappled with challenges to the idea of republican universalism in the contemporary era. In spite of the demands of a new era, the political culture of republican universalism has remained strong, at times surprisingly so. As noted elsewhere in this book, universalism in France has often been championed by groups on the margins of society, a fact to keep in mind while considering contemporary debates around multiculturalism and French society. France at the beginning of the twenty-first century is a nation struggling not just to integrate new population groups but to reconcile the basic contradictions at the heart of republican universalism. Although the future of this struggle remains to be seen, the ideal of the universal nation still forms the core of French identity.

THE NEW GLOBALISM AND THE END OF THE "SHORT" TWENTIETH CENTURY

Just as in many ways the twentieth century really started with World War I, so it essentially ended in the late 1980s. By the beginning of that decade, the global economic downturn had brought to power a new wave of conservative politicians in the west. In 1979 Margaret Thatcher was the first woman ever to be elected prime minister of the United Kingdom; in 1980 Ronald Reagan became president of the United States; and in 1982 Helmut Kohl chancellor of West Germany. All three, but especially Reagan and Thatcher, acted to implement a right-wing agenda by repressing unions, privatizing public industries, and challenging the idea of the postwar welfare state. Such policies did little to resolve the economic crisis but did contribute to greater political and social polarization in the United States and western Europe.

The biggest political shift, however, took place in eastern Europe, and it was one of the great events of the twentieth century. Since the late 1940s the lands behind the "iron curtain" had been isolated from the rest of the world and frozen in time. Periodic revolts had taken place, notably Hungary in 1956 and Czechoslovakia in 1968, but the communist regimes and Soviet power structure seemed unshakeable. In 1980 a revolt broke out in Poland, when steelworkers in the port city of Gdansk demanded and got the right to form an independent labor union. The movement attracted great support in Poland and in the west, often, paradoxically, among those doing their best to suppress unions at home.

Real change, however, would have to come from the Soviet Union, and this happened in 1985 when Mikhail Gorbachev took power in Moscow. Significantly younger than previous Soviet leaders, Gorbachev realized the USSR could not continue the policies of the past, so he began a process of economic and political liberalization unprecedented in the history of the USSR. One major aspect of this was a new willingness to let the nations of eastern Europe determine their own fate. In particular, Gorbachev revoked the policy of military intervention in the satellite countries. Without Soviet support, in 1988 and 1989 the local communist regimes began toppling like dominoes. In Poland, Solidarity won a sweeping victory in free elections, and powerful but peaceful mass movements overthrew communist rule in Hungary and Czechoslovakia. In November 1989 East Germany agreed to allow free emigration to the west, and on November 9 crowds from both sides of divided Berlin stormed the city's famous wall and tore it down. The next year elections throughout Germany formally united the country after over forty years. Two years later the Soviet Union itself collapsed, as the system proved incapable of adapting to Gorbachev's reforms. The great Russian Revolution, which dominated so much of the history of twentieth-century Europe, was dead; the cold war was over, and the west had won.

Or had it? In some ways certainly; economic and military pressure from the west, not to mention the glaring gap in living standards between the two parts of Europe, helped precipitate the collapse of Soviet communism. The 1987 image of Ronald Reagan in West Berlin proclaiming, "Mr. Gorbachev, tear down this wall!" was powerful and influential. But even though the United States was the world's only superpower after 1991, it never regained the global dominance it had exercised in the aftermath of World War II. The communist takeover of Vietnam in 1975 signaled the limits of American power, followed by revolutionary Iran's seizure of fifty-two American hostages for over a year at the end of the decade. The rise of Islamic fundamentalism as a political and military force led to a number of attacks on the United States, culminating with the destruction of New York's World Trade Center, and the deaths of almost three thousand people, on September 11, 2001. The attack sparked American invasions of Afghanistan and later Iraq in the first decade of the twenty-first century, invasions that initially succeeded but ultimately only prompted greater turmoil in the region.

In short, the west's victory in the cold war failed to bring either greater prosperity or greater global security. Communism collapsed in the Soviet bloc but survived elsewhere, notably in China, where in 1989 the regime overwhelmed the pro-democracy forces symbolized by the stand-off at Tien-An-Mien Square in Beijing. Although China rejected political democratization, it enthusiastically embraced a capitalist reorganization of its economy, leading to massive economic growth during the 1990s and the first decade of the new century. The great nation, the largest on earth, thus came to represent a successful political and economic hybrid unimaginable at the height of the cold war.

At the same time, the end of the twentieth century saw a major leap in the interconnectedness of people throughout the world, so that the term "globalization" became one of the leading themes of the era. As many, including this author, have argued, globalization did not just happen in the late twentieth century; flows of people, goods, and ideas across borders, continents, and oceans have occurred for centuries. But the last few decades have witnessed an increased focus on globalization, as the world seems to become ever more closely knitted together. Mass air travel and tourism, the rise of multinational corporations and global transfers of wealth, and international immigration have all reinforced the idea of an interconnected planet.

But nothing better symbolizes the new globalism than the rise of the Internet and the new international information economy. By the early 1980s personal computers were common in Europe, and fax machines were sending documents instantaneously anywhere in the world. A number of US government agencies collaborated to invent the Internet, which became adapted for personal and commercial use by the early 1990s. By the beginning of the twenty-first century the Internet had revolutionized not just global communications but the world economy in general. Companies and individuals developed their own websites, transforming commerce and professional development, and the rise of social networking sites like Facebook created new forms of individual and community interaction. In addition, the Internet and the personal computer industry generated tremendous wealth, transforming the economies of regions like the San Francisco Bay Area and countries like India and Israel. It enabled anyone with a personal computer, smartphone, or tablet to search for products, services, or ideas throughout the world.

Because the new globalism developed during a period of conservative ascendancy, many have criticized globalization as a phenomenon promoting capitalist hegemony by lowering wages, turning large numbers of people into immigrants lacking citizenship rights, and flattening out the unique contributions of local and national cultures. In the absence of a powerful globalized union movement, it has often been viewed as an attack on workers' rights and standard of living. As a result, a widespread antiglobalization movement developed by the end of the twentieth century. Since the late 1980s protests against neoliberal globalization have taken place around the world, notably 1999's "battle of Seattle," where thousands of demonstrators protested a conference of the World Trade Organization.

For France, globalization and the new shape of international politics after the cold war posed multiple challenges. The rise of a postcolonial population at home forced the French to rethink how they defined their national identity. At the same time, the new globalized economy and culture threatened the basic underpinnings of the nation-state itself, leading some to conclude it had become irrelevant to life in the twenty-first century. Finally, French leaders had to confront major shifts in international politics, ranging from German unification to Islamic fundamentalism, and their implications for France's place in the world. All of these considerations challenged the idea of the universal nation and its continued viability.

THE ROSE REVOLUTION:
ACHIEVEMENTS AND DISCONTENTS

When French socialists took power in 1981, they had to deal with not just the nation's economic troubles but also the unfavorable alignment of international politics. In a western world dominated by Ronald Reagan and Margaret Thatcher, which emphasized deflation and weak unions, mounting a progressive solution to the recession was a challenge. Like the Popular Front nearly half a century before, the Rose Revolution made a promising and dramatic start based on the ideals of the French universalist left, only to be forced to come to terms with a challenging global conjuncture.

The new government, dominated by the Socialist party but also including several communist ministers, made a number of changes in its first year. Its first priority was to address the recession, and it did so in classic socialist fashion. The government implemented a wave of nationalization, taking over important industries like armaments, steel, and banking. It also passed legislation increasing wages, strengthening unions, shortening the work week from forty to thirty-nine hours, and granting employees an additional week of paid vacation, raising the total number to five. In addition it increased pensions and family allowances, as well as lowering the retirement age and raising taxes on the wealthy. The government hoped that giving average citizens more purchasing power would pump more money into the economy and lift the nation out of recession.

The new government did more than just address economic problems, however. It established a ministry for women's affairs and passed legislation requiring equal pay for equal work. It also abolished the death penalty, at long last retiring the guillotine from active service: the "national razor" was no more. In addition, the new government implemented a far-reaching decentralization plan, delegating more power to mayors and departments. Some of its most noteworthy actions dealt with culture. Mitterrand appointed the energetic Jack Lang minister of culture, and Lang initiated a series of initiatives designed to bring culture to the French people. These included a national musical festival, still celebrated every year on the summer solstice, when all were asked to make music in their own way, and legislation designed to protect independent booksellers. The government also ended centralization and state control of the air waves, launching the famous *radios libres*, or free radio stations. All sorts of groups, including ethnic, religious, political, neighborhood-based, and language-based, could have their own radio station, which went a long way toward bolstering community organizations in France.

The cultural reforms, which included subsidies to different cultural institutions all over the country, were seen as a success even if the number of French people who patronized concerts or the theater did not grow appreciably. The economic program was another matter, however. Like the Popular Front, the Mitterrand administration faced significant opposition from the right wing in politics and in business. A major flight of capital ensued after the election, as some wealthy people transferred funds to banks in Switzerland or elsewhere outside the country. Much of the money the government pumped into the working and middle classes was spent on imports, hurting the nation's balance of trade deficit. The national wage increases and pro-union legislation also hurt investor confidence, especially compared with the economic policies of the US and the UK. In 1982 the Social Democratic government in West Germany was replaced by that of Helmut Kohl, who proceeded to implement a similar deflationist program. All of these problems put major pressure on the franc, forcing Mitterrand, like Léon Blum before him, to devalue before the end of his first year in office. More generally, the attempt to adopt a Keynesian economic strategy while the rest of the western world was pursuing a deflationist program that was more appealing to international investors proved unworkable. As a result, both inflation and unemployment continued to rise in the first two years of the Mitterrand administration. France could not survive as a socialist island in an increasingly capitalist sea.

Confronted with these realities, the Mitterrand administration executed a striking about-face between 1982 and 1984. Although it couldn't easily reverse the measures it had taken in the heady aftermath of its 1981 victory, by 1984 it had abandoned the reflationist approach to the recession, taking a series of deflationist measures instead. These included enacting wage and price freezes, slashing public expenditures, and lowering taxes on businesses. In order to make older, nationalized industries competitive, the government reorganized them and laid off thousands of workers. The socialist regime thus dealt with deindustrialization, the decline of traditional industries during the 1980s, much like other governments in Europe and America, by getting rid of their increasingly obsolete workforce.

In spite of this sharp turn to the right, the Mitterrand administration tried to maintain its socialist identity by continuing to democratize French public life, especially in the field of culture. But even here it encountered resistance. Education minister Alain Savary proposed increasing state control over private schools, but the government was forced to backtrack on these initiatives after a firestorm of public protest brought a million demonstrators into the streets of Paris. Mitterrand reacted to this setback by replacing Prime Minister Pierre Mauroy with a newcomer, Laurent Fabius. The difference between the two men was instructive. Mauroy was a traditional socialist, a schoolteacher from the working-class city of Lille. Fabius, in contrast, came from an affluent background and held degrees from both ENA and the Ecole Normale Supérieure. He seemed more like a technocrat, a socialist version of Valéry Giscard-d'Estaing, and unlike Mauroy he argued socialism must be based in market economics. By appointing Fabius prime minister, Mitterrand sent a powerful signal to France and the world that French socialism was willing to adapt to global realities.

However, this gambit failed to win the support of the French electorate. The municipal elections of 1983 showed a big swing to the right, reinforcing the Mitterrand administration's policy shift. This new direction did not, however, prevent the right from winning a major victory in the legislative elections of 1986, forcing Mitterrand to name Gaullist leader and mayor of Paris

Jacques Chirac prime minister. This represented the first time in the history of the Fifth Republic that the president and prime minister came from different political parties, a weakness in the basic structure of the regime. The next two years witnessed a tricky "cohabitation" between Mitterrand and Chirac. It forced both Gaullists and socialists to move toward the center, not taking any major new initiatives and continuing the shift in ideological orientation already taken by Mitterrand's government. Ultimately it illustrated the durability of the Fifth Republic: in spite of its difficulties the Mitterrand administration did not simply collapse as Léon Blum's had fifty years earlier.

In 1988 Mitterrand won reelection as president, in part because he convinced voters that the socialists had evolved into a true centrist party. As in 1981, he immediately dissolved the National Assembly and held new legislative elections. The PS won these, although much less handily than seven years earlier, and with the other left parties was able to cobble together a bare majority. This brought an end to cohabitation, but the new government lacked the dynamism of 1981. The socialists succeeded in reinventing themselves as the party of the center, the equivalent of the Radical party during the Third Republic. France in the 1980s was very different from France in the 1880s, however, and changes in French society brought new political challenges to the forefront of national life.

IMMIGRATION AND RACE AT THE END OF THE TWENTIETH CENTURY

As we saw earlier in this book, immigration played a key role in the nation's economic revival after World War II. Mostly from Mediterranean Europe during the years of the Fourth Republic, by the late 1960s more and more immigrants were coming from outside Europe, especially France's former colonies and overseas *départements*. With the end of postwar prosperity in the early 1970s French public opinion began to view immigrants less as an asset to the nation and more as a source of competition for scarce jobs, even though few French men and women were willing to take such positions at the bottom of the economic ladder. The increasing nonwhite character of the immigrant population also contributed to this more negative view. As a result, in 1974 the French government abruptly terminated legal immigration into the country.

Far from resolving the immigrant "problem," however, these restrictions created new challenges for French society. For one thing, illegal immigration into France continued, especially from Africa. Employers still needed to fill the least desirable jobs, and illegals were even cheaper and less aware of their rights as workers than legal immigrants. Moreover, during the 1970s the French government continued to allow resident foreigners to bring their families to France. Family reunification was seen not just as a humanitarian gesture but also as a way of integrating what was primarily a single male population into national life, and rendering it less socially threatening. The racially inspired goal of creating more acceptable immigrant life thus worked at cross purposes with the desire to get rid of immigrant labor. As women and children from outside France settled in the country they created communities that were clearly permanent, impacting not only housing but also schools and other social services. Paradoxically, in spite of concerns about unemployment, the nation's population of foreign origin increased during the recession of the 1970s.

By the early 1980s this new population had transformed large areas of France. Its impact was felt most powerfully in the suburbs of Paris and other cities, areas that had expanded dramatically during the *trentes glorieuses*. By the late 1970s the number of immigrants from the former French colonies, above all North Africa, was increasing sharply, although the nation still had large Portuguese and Italian populations.

As working-class French families became more affluent during the 1960s and early 1970s, they tended to move out of the HLMs, often to be replaced by immigrant families. Many of these settled in the suburbs, which became increasingly identified not just with immigration but social problems in general. The specter of *la banlieue*, the impoverished and increasingly multicultural outskirts of Paris and other cities, haunted French society at the end of the twentieth century.

The suburbs came to represent the intersection of concerns about race and class in contemporary France. This was not new: the heavily working-class population of the suburbs in the late nineteenth and early twentieth centuries had often been portrayed as racially Other, as the barbarians lurking outside the gates of urban civilization. The rise of a large nonwhite population there by the 1980s sharply reinforced this image. It is worth remembering that during the 1950s the suburbs had been seen as symbols of progress and modernity. By the early 1980s, however, many of the housing projects were starting to decay, and schools were overburdened and struggling to teach a new diverse student body. Above all, the plentiful jobs that had formed the basis of postwar prosperity had largely disappeared. Increasingly France's suburbs, like the inner-city ghettos in the United States to which they were often compared by

French commentators, encapsulated problems of poverty, race, and the interactions between them. At the same time the suburbs were a massive physical and demographic fact. By the early 1980s, for example, over 7 million people lived in the Paris suburbs alone, nearly 15 percent of the nation's population.

At the heart of the immigration problem in France during the 1980s was the so-called second-generation immigrant. This term usually designated young people born in France to non-European immigrant parents. Above all, it was applied to those of North African heritage, never those whose parents came from elsewhere in Europe. The phrase itself is nonsensical and illustrative at the same time. After all, people cannot immigrate to the country of their birth, so it is literally impossible to be a second-generation immigrant. Its widespread use, however, testified to the fact that by the 1980s immigration was seen as a problem of race, not nationality. Second generation immigrants were those who could never become truly French, due to the color of their skin, their religion, or other cultural attributes, and would always remain "immigrants." The universalist logic of French colonialism, which refused to accept as equal citizens those who refused to embrace French civilization, found its postcolonial reflection in the suburbs of the late twentieth century.

These were young people who were born and raised in France, knowing no other home or language, yet considered foreigners. Even youth of Caribbean background, originally from islands that had been French since the early seventeenth century, were often mistaken for immigrants and treated accordingly. Concentrated in suburbs hit hard by economic decline and deindustrialization, they suffered high unemployment, the lack of jobs reinforced by the reluctance of employers to hire people who didn't look or sound like them. Young men often got into trouble with authority figures, either teachers at school or police on the streets, and some turned to crime, reinforcing the reputation of the suburbs as a danger zone. Young women also experienced numerous problems, ranging from high unemployment to patriarchal pressure from both their families and French society as a whole.

Young people in the suburbs also created their own cultural forms, notably French hip-hop, to express their experience and often their alienation from mainstream French society. This included Verlan, a reverse language that became popular in the suburbs. Verlan functioned by reversing syllables to form new words. One of the most popular was *beur*, the Verlan form of *arabe*, which became a standard designation for young people of North African heritage.

Social pressure, racism, and unemployment led to an explosion in 1981, the first of many in the French suburbs since the end of postwar prosperity.

France was not the only European country grappling with integrating minority working-class youth in the late twentieth century. In April 1981 rioting broke out in Brixton, a predominantly black neighborhood in London. That summer the first major suburban rioting erupted in France, in the Lyon suburb of Les Minguettes. Nicknamed the "rodeo riots," they involved young people throwing rocks at the police as well as stealing and burning hundreds of cars. A second wave of rioting occurred in the Paris and Lyons suburbs in the early 1990s, so that by the end of the century conflicts with police and burning cars had become endemic in the *banlieue*.

Islam played an important role in the rise of postcolonial society in France. The religion of most North Africans and many Africans in France, by the 1980s Islam had become the second largest religion in the country with millions of believers, and France had become the largest Muslim nation in Europe outside Turkey. Muslim cadis were a common sight in immigrant suburbs and urban neighborhoods, as were mosques with minarets rising above suburban skylines. Although France embraced a proud secular tradition, it still saw itself as part of Christian Europe, and the new prominence of the Islamic faith came as a shock. Hostility to Islam had deep roots in French society, going back as far as the Crusades, and was reinforced by the colonial experience in North Africa. At the same time, the rise of fundamentalist Islam and the increasing conflict between it and the west played into suspicions that French Muslims wanted to turn France into another Iran. Interestingly, Islam was seen as a threat not just by Christians in France but by defenders of secularism, who viewed it as challenging the separation of church and state. Like the battles between church and state in the late nineteenth century, conflicts over Islam in France have often pitted one universalism against another.

This erupted in spectacular fashion in 1989. On October 3 three girls walked into a middle school in Creil, in the Paris suburbs, wearing Muslim headscarves (*foulards*). The principle, Eugène Chenière, expelled them, claiming that wearing an Islamic symbol in a secular public school constituted a violation of secularism (*laicité*) and an attack on republican universalism. This prompted a firestorm of media attention and soon turned into a major political and cultural crisis, splitting France in two. Some, including Danièle Mitterrand, the president's wife, supported the three girls in the name of religious toleration and diversity while many others argued the school had been correct in upholding the principle of secular universalism. Many in the latter camp identified with the political left, with the tradition of republican universalism they saw threatened by Muslim fundamentalism. Feminists also often attacked the girls for adopting what they considered a symbol of patriarchy, and many argued they were forced to do so by either their conservative families or a patriarchal North African culture in the suburbs that considered unveiled girls immodest and subjected them to sexual harassment. The French government resolved the Creil affair by ruling that religious symbols could be worn in public schools as long as they were not "ostentatious." This vague decision led to further controversy until a conservative regime in 2011 banned wearing the face-covering veil, becoming the first nation in Europe to do so.

Controversy over the veil in contemporary France revealed tremendous hostility to Islam: the conviction that no one could be Muslim and French at the same time. Racism played a role but was not the only factor at work. The school principal whose actions started the 1989 affair was a black man from the French Caribbean, and public opinion polls consistently showed that a large percentage of French Muslims also opposed wearing the veil in public school. Alain Finkelkraut, a leading intellectual and the son of Holocaust survivors, strongly supported what he considered a defense of universalism and human rights. Moreover, as Joan Scott has recently noted, the 1989 veils affair took place in the context of a global opposition between Islam and the west, including Iranian Ayatollah Khomeini's fatwa against Salman Rushdie's *Satanic Verses*, a novel condemned by Muslim fundamentalists for satirizing their faith, and the outbreak of the first Palestinian intifada against Israeli occupation. France thus seemed to occupy a central position in what Samuel P. Huntington would soon call the "clash of civilizations."

The veil affair, and the broader issue of race and immigration in contemporary France, also spoke to the nation's relationship with the United States. Many in France, on both right and left, opposed multiculturalism and considered it an American import that was fundamentally opposed to French republican universalism. In France the traditional resistance to *communautarisme*, viewing citizens as members of distinct communities as well as individuals, fueled opposition to ideas of ethnic or racial solidarity. French people should consider themselves citizens of the republic, period. Unlike the United States, France refused to collect official statistics about race or religion, arguing that such information enabled Vichy to round up and deport Jews during World War II. At the same time, French social commentators often argued that France was not racist because it did not recognize the concept, that racism was an American problem. Therefore, a refusal to see racism as a problem in France also constituted a defense of French culture against American influence. At the same time, many French nonwhite youth enthusiastically embraced the cultures of US minorities, especially that of African Americans, which they viewed as the model of a racialized minority in western society. The idolization of Bob Marley and the Black Panthers, and the widespread adoption of hip-hop music and dance, underscored the transnational dimensions of racial difference in France.

Questions of immigration and race soon had a major impact on French politics. Although the far right had emerged from the World War II greatly diminished, it never completely disappeared in France. In 1972 a number of neofascist parties came together to create the National Front (Front National, or FN). Like its namesake in Britain, founded five years earlier, the French National Front seized on the issue of immigration, essentially non-European immigration, as what was wrong with French society and politics. It was led by Jean-Marie Le Pen, a veteran of both Indochina and Algeria, who had been active in the Poujadist movement of the 1950s, and its intellectual pedigree stretched back to the Action Française. Violently racist and anti-Semitic, the National Front made no bones about its hostility to anyone not considered authentically French. Le Pen was fond of making outrageous statements, calling the Holocaust a mere detail of history, and claiming that nationalist activists in New Caledonia wanted replace the French tricolor with their own flag featuring a banana in the middle.

Initially confined to the lunatic fringe of French politics, the National Front broke through to the mainstream in the early 1980s. The climate of economic decline and high unemployment provided fertile soil for its message blaming immigrants and foreigners for France's problems. In 1983 the FN, led by a local activist who had belonged to the Milice during the war, won control of the municipal council of Dreux, a small city near Paris. In 1984 it won 11 percent of French votes for the European Parliament, and in the early 1990s was regularly scoring 15 percent and more of the vote in national elections. By this point it consistently outscored the French Communist party, and won the votes of some white workers in the suburbs who had previously supported the PCF.

Moreover, the rise of the National Front shifted the entire political spectrum to the right on immigration. In 1986 Charles Pasqua, Prime Minister Chirac's interior minister, dramatically rounded up and deported over a hundred immigrants from Mali, giving them one-way tickets home and driving them straight from the police station to the airport. In addition, Pasqua proposed revoking the tradition of *jus soli*, that all those born on French soil automatically become French citizens. Both actions uncomfortably recalled Vichy's

Jewish policies. In 1991 Chirac himself, trolling for white working-class votes, characterized the typical immigrant family as "a father, three or four wives, about 20 kids, earning $10,000 a month without working . . . if you add to this the noise and the smell, it's enough to drive the poor French worker living next door crazy."[2]

By the end of the twentieth century France was becoming a multiracial society, and for many that took some getting used to. A department like the Seine-Saint Denis in the Paris suburbs had a population that was nearly 40 percent Muslim, and Sarcelles was home to people from sixty different countries. It was this diversity that the 1998 World Cup victory celebrated. Yet France was also home to one of Europe's most powerful neofascist parties. Intellectual and political discussions about the meaning of this new diversity for France's national identity raged at the end of the century, giving a new energy to debates about the meaning of republican universalism. It remained to be seen, and still does to this day, whether new postcolonial France would overcome the contradictions of colonial-era republicanism to create at last a truly universal nation.

MEMORIES AND LEGACIES OF WAR

One aspect of the critique of traditional universalism that surfaced during the late twentieth century was a reassessment of the nation's recent history, especially World War II and the occupation. For decades after the liberation, the Gaullist myth that the French people had united in resistance to Vichy and the Germans dominated public discourse about the war. The resistance may have failed to master the postwar politics of the Fourth Republic, but Charles de Gaulle's return to power in 1958 helped reinforce this idea. Starting in the 1970s, however, and culminating over the next twenty years, a variety of voices in French society began to question the resistance myth, taking a more complicated and sometimes painful look at how France experienced one of the most tragic episodes in its history. A reconsideration of the Holocaust, and of the role of French Jews in the life of the nation, played a key role in this process. By the end of the century this process of introspection began to reconsider the history of another national trauma, the war in Algeria, and the legacy of French colonialism more generally. The process of rethinking France's recent history called into question traditional narratives of republican universalism, while at the same time making the nation more inclusive and truly universal.

The reassessment of resistance myth began, appropriately enough, less than a year after the death of Charles de Gaulle. In 1971 the director Marcel Ophuls released the great documentary film *The Sorrow and the Pity*, which showed in more than four hours of interviews and commentary that many in France had supported Vichy and the Nazi occupation, as well as at least tolerating anti-Semitic policies. The fact that the film gave roughly equal time to collaborators and resisters outraged many and challenged the classic resistance myth. In 1973 *Vichy France: Old Guard and New Order*, by American historian Robert Paxton, was published in France. Paxton shocked the French by arguing, backed up by extensive documentation, that Vichy was not simply imposed on France by the Germans but came out of a long tradition of right-wing antirepublican politics in French history. Moreover, he showed that Vichy officials had often pursued collaboration with the Germans and had initiated many anti-Semitic policies, notably organizing the deportation of Jews from France to the east. Both the documentary and the historical study provoked agonized discussions in France, forcing people to take a more realistic look at the wartime experience and confront the complex nature of French identity, not just during Vichy but in the modern period overall. The tradition of universal republicanism might be dominant during the twentieth century, but it alone did not shape the history of modern France.

The reassessment of Vichy and the war prompted new appraisals of the position of the nation's Jewish community in French life. As noted in Chapter 9, roughly 80 percent of the French population survived the occupation. More than in most other European countries, many Jews in France had lived through and remembered the Holocaust. At the same time, many were ambivalent about addressing the Jewish experiences of hiding, deportation, and genocide, often preferring to focus on their contributions to the French resistance and their integration into the resistance myth. By the 1970s, however, this attitude had begun to change. After 1962 hundreds of thousands of Jews from North Africa immigrated to Israel. They were generally less attracted to the idea of assimilation into French universalism, tending to see themselves as Jews who lived in France rather than French people who happened to be Jewish. In 1967 Israel's victory in the Six Day War led to a new sense of assertiveness among Jews throughout the world, including in France. The new openness toward the history of the war enabled many Jews to speak out about their own experiences and note that it was French police, not Germans, who rounded them up and sent them to the camps. Jewish communities also debated how to remember their important role in the resistance. Some pushed for a greater acknowledgment of the fact that they fought Vichy and the Nazis *as Jews* while others emphasized that they fought above all for France and should be recognized as French men and women who made sacrifices for their country.

During the 1980s a series of highly publicized war crimes trials in France underscored the nation's attempts to come to terms with its occupation legacy. In 1987 the French government placed Klaus Barbie, the "butcher of Lyon" on trial for crimes against humanity during the war. Barbie had been head of the SS in the city, where he tortured members of the resistance and deported Jewish children to concentration camps. He also helped set up the assassination of Jean Moulin in 1943. After the war Barbie escaped France with the aid of the US government, which used him to fight communism in Latin America. He settled in Bolivia, where he became involved in right-wing and anticommunist politics, and was rumored to have helped arrange the murder of Che Guevara in 1967. In 1983 the Bolivian government extradited him to France. After an extensive, grueling trial Klaus Barbie was convicted of crimes against humanity and sentenced to life in prison, where he died four years later. Barbie was a German, but his trial underscored not only the horrors of the Holocaust in France but also the fact that French people helped make it possible.

Two years later came the turn of Paul Touvier, a leader of the Milice during the war. Touvier exemplified the gruesome work of wartime collaborators, arresting Jews and murdering members of the resistance. Tried in 1994, he was the first French citizen to be convicted of crimes against humanity. The Touvier trial underscored the fact that France had not been a nation of resisters during the war. In 1997 the French government turned to Maurice Papon, who had worked for Vichy in Bordeaux during the war, helping deport over a thousand Jews. Unlike Barbie or Touvier, Papon had continued to work as a French civil servant after the war and had served with distinction. De Gaulle had personally decorated him in 1956. His case thus revealed how far collaboration had gone in France, and to what extent collaborators had survived the downfall of Vichy.

The Papon trial unexpectedly revealed another hidden side of recent French history. During the Algerian war Papon had served as prefect of the Constantine department, where among other things he tortured FLN prisoners. In 1958 he became police prefect of Paris. In that role he ordered both the police action at the Charonne metro stop in 1962 and the massacre of October 17, 1961. The latter incident had been covered up by the police, and even though it happened in the middle of Paris few had ever heard of it. Thanks to Papon's trial the official government documentation on the massacre was opened to the public for the first time, forcing the French to discuss this particularly ugly incident, and the history of the Algerian war in general.

This was not the only overlap between the histories of Vichy and of French colonialism. During his trial Klaus Barbie had been defended by Jacques Vergès, a half-Vietnamese radical lawyer who used the trial to condemn the brutalities of France's colonial past as a way of "normalizing" Barbie's own crimes. At the same time, as Vergès's strategy reveals, these different historical reckonings could work at cross purposes, opposing groups that had been victimized by France in the past. During the 1980s a number of attacks against Jewish institutions took place in France, starting with the bombing of a synagogue in Paris's Rue Copernic in 1980, as well as the attack on Goldenberg's, a prominent restaurant in the heavily Jewish Marais neighborhood of the capital, in 1982. These acts were the work of Arab terrorists, reflecting both the global ramifications of the conflict between Palestinians and Israelis as well as tensions between France's Jewish and Arab communities, often related to the history of colonial Algeria, where many in both groups had once lived. These tensions have continued to the present day, showcasing the interaction of local and global conflicts in contemporary French society.

In the 1990s French authorities responded to the new discourses on war and colonialism by issuing formal apologies. In July 1995 President Jacques Chirac formally accepted the responsibility of the French state for the deportation and murder of French Jews in World War II. In 1997 the French Catholic Church and the French police also apologized, in an extraordinary wave of national remorse for the past. The new century saw the beginning of similar statements concerning the sins of French colonialism. In 2001 France passed a law, written by Guyanese assemblywoman Christiane Taubira, declaring slavery and the slave trade a crime against humanity, and that same year issued an apology to the *harkis*, Algerians who had fought for France during the Algerian war and then had been massacred by the FLN as traitors while the French government stood by and did nothing. On October 17, 2001, Paris Mayor Bertrand Delanoë place an official plaque on a bridge over the Seine commemorating Algerians who had died in the massacre forty years earlier.

The reassessment of French history that took place at the end of the twentieth century challenged in fundamental ways the universalist narrative, showing how French people had been treated and abused as Others in spite of their membership in the national community. At the same time, the willingness of the French to address the more sordid chapters of their past suggested the possibility of a new universalism, one that would resolve the paradoxes of the past and create a France that could truly claim to be a universal nation.

FRANCE, EUROPE, AND THE WORLD AT THE END OF THE TWENTIETH CENTURY

François Mitterrand began his second term as president of France during a time of momentous change in Europe. Within a year after his second inauguration the communist state system in eastern Europe had cracked dramatically and irreversibly, and two years after that the Soviet Union vanished into history. The end of the twentieth century was also marked by an intensification of European integration, culminating with the weakening of national borders and the creation of the euro as a common currency in 1999. Whereas the changes in eastern Europe were sudden and tumultuous, those in western Europe were deliberate and well-planned. The combination of the two, nonetheless, meant that Europe as a whole had not witnessed transformations on this scale since the end of World War II. In the 1990s, therefore, France confronted a vastly different world.

During this time of momentous change internationally, France celebrated a momentous event of its own: the bicentennial of the French Revolution in 1989. It was a huge, extravagant series of festivals, capped off by a massive march down the Champs-Elysées featuring everything from Scottish pipers playing to African American musicians moonwalking down the famous avenue. Particularly poignant were hundreds of Chinese students wearing headbands with the Chinese characters for "Liberty, Equality, Fraternity" a month after the crackdown at Tien-An-Mien Square. Yet underlying the festivities was a somber tone. Part of it came from new, critical attitudes to the Revolution itself. In a world era of conservative hegemony, the great revolution was often seen either as a precursor to totalitarianism or simply no longer important; in the harsh glare of the late-twentieth-century recession, Utopia increasingly had a bad name. If the seminal event that launched republican universalism no longer counted, how could France still claim to be a universal nation?

At the same time, domestic conditions in France were far from ideal. Government policies had some success in improving economic conditions during the 1980s, but a renewed international downturn sent unemployment rates shooting back up to 11 percent by the early 1990s. Socialist efforts to promote centralization gave real power back to local governments, but one unfortunate side effect was increased political corruption at both regional and national levels. The mayors of Grenoble and Nice were imprisoned for financial improprieties. One particularly shocking and tragic example of government ineptitude was the tainted blood scandal that erupted in 1991, when it came out that state doctors had used blood contaminated with the HIV virus for transfusions, thus infecting 1,300 people. Even France's vaunted intellectual life seemed to have run out of steam. For all the lively chattiness of TV book programs like *Apostrophes*, no new major conceptual and theoretical breakthroughs followed deconstruction, and most French intellectuals strongly resisted new global trends like postcolonial studies. Mitterrand himself, now well into his seventies, showed little of the dynamism that had galvanized the PS and the nation in 1981. Instead, he seemed to retreat into the confines of the Élysée palace, so much so that people began referring to him as the Sphinx.

Both this sense of *anomie* at home and the great events transpiring abroad tended to give new impetus to foreign affairs and foreign policy in France during the 1990s. Most in France applauded the collapse of Soviet communism, and intellectuals greeted it as a new wave of human liberation, especially when a major playwright and philosopher like Václav Havel took power in Czechoslovakia. But the new shape of Europe also raised some concerns, especially the issue of German reunification and its impact on European integration.

After 1945 French governments had strongly supported the alliance with West Germany, seeing it as a way of taming German nationalism and promoting economic growth in western Europe. The alliance had always viewed the Federal Republic as a junior partner, however, wealthy and prosperous but weak militarily and diplomatically. With the end of the cold war, reunified Germany became bigger and stronger, free to develop an independent path in the world. The idea of it remaining subordinate to France became less and less viable, leading Mitterrand and other French leaders to express reservations about German unification. Would a united Europe now become a vehicle for German hegemony in Europe, rather than French hegemony? Germany and France had developed strong ties during the decades since 1945, and the two countries remained allies into the twenty-first century. Nonetheless, the emergence of a new Germany implied the loss of French hopes to use dominance of European affairs as a way of playing an independent global role equal to that of the superpowers.

France's relationship with the United States became less tempestuous during the 1990s. The end of the cold war left the US as the world's only superpower, removing the Soviet Union as a potential counterweight and thus giving France less room to maneuver diplomatically. It is a curiosity of postwar history that right-wing governments often seemed more hostile to the Americans than those of the left. Even though Mitterrand continued to support many third world causes, he did not deliberately provoke Washington the way de Gaulle had. In 1982, for example, he revised de Gaulle's tilt against Israel by becoming the first French president to visit the Jewish state. In 1991 France along with other European nations joined the US in attacking Iraq after it invaded Kuwait. France also joined America in intervening in the conflict in the former Yugoslavia at the end of the decade, French planes participating in the bombing of Belgrade in 1999. Yet while France generally went along with the main lines of US foreign policy during the Mitterrand era, the country still criticized American policies at times, cautioning Washington about the potential of civilian casualties during the Yugoslav war, for example. During his visit to Israel, Mitterrand called publically for a Palestinian state, a position deeply unpopular with Jerusalem and Washington at the time, but later accepted by both.

Mitterrand's most important achievement in foreign policy was leading France into a unified Europe. European leaders and diplomats had been carefully planning this process for decades, and neither German reunification nor the collapse of Soviet communism proved capable of derailing the process. The leaders of western Europe took the first major step in 1985 by ratifying the Schengen agreement, which abolished border controls between the Low Countries, France, and West Germany. More importantly, in 1992 France played a leading role in drafting the Maastricht treaty. The treaty formally abolished the European Economic Community (EEC), replacing it with the new European Union. It also provided for a common European citizenship as well as a unified new currency, the euro.

The socialist leadership strongly supported these moves toward European unification, believing that this was the best way to perpetuate the global prominence of the French nation in post–cold war Europe. Public opinion polls at the time showed strong support for European integration. Maastricht had to be formally approved by each participating nation, so in September 1992 the French voted in a national referendum on the treaty. The communists, Gaullists, and National Front opposed it as an affront to national sovereignty, a neoliberal plot against social welfare and citizenship, and a power play by Germany and the "Eurocrats" of Brussels. The socialists and the centrist parties called for a yes vote, saying Maastricht was the wave of the future and would benefit the French economy. The treaty barely passed in France, by a vote of 51 percent to 49 percent. The wealthier, more urban, and younger segments of the electorate tended to vote yes, while rural and poor areas as well as the elderly generally opposed the treaty. The nation was clearly of two minds about the benefits of European integration. It was not alone in that regard: Ireland and Denmark also held referendums on Maastricht, and whereas Ireland voted massively in favor, the Danes rejected the treaty by a slender margin before reversing themselves and approving it the next year.

Nonetheless, France remained a leader in the push for a united Europe. Jacques Delors, economics and finance minister during the first Mitterrand administration, helped pioneer the creation of a single European currency. This took several years to finalize, involving complex negotiations between the participating nations with a view to making as smooth a transition as possible. Yet all went well, and in 1999 the euro was born. Some nations, notably the United Kingdom, abstained, but most of Europe took part, and over the next few years France and other nations phased out their national currencies. The French franc, created in the fourteenth century, officially ceased to exist in January 2002.

European integration was not total, of course: France retained its own government, its own laws, and its own military. In casting their lot with a united Europe, however, the French opened up the possibility of a fundamental reconceptualization of the universal nation. While France may not have achieved the Gaullist dream of dominating the Continent, it did have a powerful voice within European affairs and could help Europe serve as a counterweight to American power. Moreover, the principles of liberal democracy and human rights that the French had pioneered were firmly enshrined in European political ideology and culture. In a postcolonial era, a united Europe provided an alternative for global influence to the former French empire. It promised that the ideals of republican universalism would continue to resonate far beyond the borders of metropolitan France.

FRANCE ENTERS A NEW MILLENNIUM

On January 8, 1996, François Mitterrand died of cancer at the age of seventy-nine. The previous year he had stepped down after completing two full seven-year terms, making him the longest-serving president of the Fifth Republic. Mitterrand dominated French politics during the last quarter of the twentieth century, and only Charles de Gaulle loomed larger in the history of France since World War II. Both men stood for an imperial presidency, almost an elected monarchy that continued the tradition of savior-politicians in twentieth-century France starting with Georges Clemenceau. Befitting such a strong leader, Mitterrand left his mark on the national capital with a series of major construction projects, including the construction of the Orsay Museum, a new opera house in the Bastille neighborhood of Paris, a massive new building for France's National Library, and I. M. Pei's dramatic glass pyramid at the entrance to the Louvre. The pyramid provoked a firestorm of controversy for situating modern architecture in the middle of a classic monument. More generally, Mitterrand shepherded France into a new era marked by a stagnant economy and an increasingly postcolonial society at home as well as European integration and the collapse of Soviet communism abroad. Throughout all these changes, Mitterrand continued to assert France's prominence as an exceptional nation among nations.

His successor, Jacques Chirac, elected president in 1995, was cut from different cloth. Born in 1932, Chirac was the first president of postwar France not old enough to have served in the resistance. A member of the PCF in his youth, he served in the Algerian war before graduating from ENA and then going into government service. Before being elected president, Chirac served twice as prime minister, once under Giscard d'Estaing and once during the period of cohabitation under Mitterrand, as well as serving as the mayor of Paris from 1977 to 1995. Chirac was thus a man of profound and diverse political experience, and by 1995 he had managed to unite most of the French mainstream right behind him.

Like Mitterrand before him, Chirac started his tenure in office by trying to address the nation's grave economic problems, and like Mitterrand before him his approach soon got him into political trouble. During his campaign he criticized social inequality, or *la fracture sociale*, and the impact of capitalist economics on the poor. As president, however, he made it clear he would adopt standard right-wing policies. After winning the presidency Chirac dissolved the National Assembly, holding new legislative elections that returned a strong conservative majority. Based on a strong right-wing trend in the electorate, Chirac named Alain Juppé, a fellow ENA graduate and experienced administrator, as prime minister. Juppé soon instituted a major program of budget cutbacks, notably in social security and health benefits. The goal of the Juppé plan was to reduce the state's budget deficit in accordance with the requirements of the Maastricht treaty. The plan, widely interpreted as a frontal attack on the French welfare state, provoked a massive firestorm of protest. Students protesting cuts in education and public sector workers outraged by proposed pension cuts and industrial restructuring joined the movement. The protests started in October, and by the beginning of December some 2 million French workers had gone on strike, paralyzing much of national life. It was the biggest protest movement to hit France since 1968, and it forced the new government to backtrack on its commitment to the Juppé plan. Events signaled that powerful forces in French society, more than elsewhere in Europe, would resist neoliberal globalization and the attack on the welfare state.

The protests proved a disaster for Chirac and his government. In the spring of 1997 Chirac unwisely called for new legislative elections. The vote was a calamity for the two rightist parties, the RPR (the Rally for the Republic) and the UDF (the Union for French Democracy), and a huge success for the PS, which pieced together a parliamentary majority with the help of the PCF and the Green party, who scored enough votes to obtain parliamentary representation for the first time in France. At the same time, in contrast to the mainstream right-wing parties, the National Front continued to poll strongly, winning 15 percent of the vote on the first round of the elections. Lionel Jospin, leader of the PS, became the new prime minister as France entered its second round of cohabitation.

The left had come back to power in France, and over the next few years Jospin tried to revive the socialist principles that had powered the Rose Revolution. But this was 1997, not 1981. On one hand, it was hard to recover the joyous optimism of Mitterrand's historic victory. On the other, the French economy experienced substantial growth at the turn of the century. Moreover, the international political conjuncture was more favorable, the age of Reagan and Thatcher in the 1980s giving way to that of Bill Clinton and Tony Blair in the 1990s. The biggest economic problem facing France was unemployment, which in spite of economic recovery remained over 11 percent in the late 1990s. Jospin's government addressed this problem by cutting the work week from thirty-nine to thirty-five hours, without reducing wages. The experiment was not entirely successful, but joblessness did decline slightly by 2002. In addition, Jospin's government increased the minimum wage and cut employee contributions to health insurance, thus putting more money in working people's pockets.

The Jospin government had more success in regard to the social and cultural innovations that had so distinguished the first Mitterrand government. It implemented a wide variety of initiatives, ranging from increasing national child care facilities to beefing up antidiscrimination legislation to conform to EU requirements. Of particular note were the new laws on civil marriage and gender parity. The government revoked the Pasqua Law of 1993, restoring automatic French citizenship to those born in France. In 1998 the government proposed the Civil Solidarity Pact (PACS), a form of civil union that gave rights traditionally linked with marriage to unmarried couples. The proposal generated fierce opposition on the right, which saw it as a stalking horse for gay marriage, but in 1999 the National Assembly voted it into law. Since then the overwhelming majority of *pacsé* couples have in fact been heterosexual.

The government's proposed parity law also generated widespread controversy. Shortly after it came to power in 1981, the Mitterrand administration had passed a law requiring that all candidate lists for municipal elections be at least 25 percent female. This did not last long, however; in 1982 the Constitutional Council, a rough equivalent of the US Supreme Court, struck it down as a violation of the Declaration of the Rights of Man. Opponents argued the law contravened the equality of all citizens by creating a quota system based on gender. In 1999 the Jospin government submitted a revised version of the parity law, emphasizing equal access to political representation for women and men and requiring that most electoral lists in France have equal numbers of both. Some, including prominent intellectual Elisabeth Badinter, opposed the law as a violation of republican universalism and an embrace of American-style affirmative action. These transatlantic references were somewhat ironic given the increasing antiaffirmative backlash in the US during the 1990s, symbolized by California's 1996 passage of Proposition 209, banning the use of racial categorizations for admission to public universities. But public opinion polls consistently showed strong popular support for the idea, which was supported by both Jospin and Chirac. Consequently, in 2000 the law passed with a large majority and gradually began to make a difference in female representation in French politics. In 2007 socialist Ségolène Royal became the first major female candidate for president in the nation's history. More generally, it prompted a debate about France's universalist tradition that addressed one of its classic paradoxes, and began to point the way toward a new, more inclusive idea of universalism.

The progressive social initiatives of the Jospin government reflected the rise of new grassroots movements in French society by the turn of the century. The campaign for parity, for example, arose from feminist activism in the 1990s, and the creation of the PACS owed a lot to a view that it could provide much in the way of gay rights without directly confronting political homophobia and the rejection of gay marriage. The 1990s also saw the emergence of the Green party and political environmentalism as a permanent force in French politics, led by, among others, an older Daniel Cohn-Bendit. Although a minority phenomenon, regionalist movements challenged traditional ideas about French identity. In the 1990s the Corsican separatist movement embraced terror, launching a series of bombings that culminated with the assassination of the departmental prefect in 1998. New Caledonia, Guadeloupe, and Martinique all saw the growth of independence movements in the 1980s and 1990s, also at times tinged with violence.

One of the most fascinating of the new French political activists in the late twentieth century was also one of the most unlikely. José Bové, originally from southern France, had spent much of his childhood in Berkeley, California, before returning to France and embracing anarchist politics as a young man. He became one of the New Left veterans who moved in the 1970s to Larzac, where he started a career as a sheep farmer making Roquefort cheese. Bové soon became an agricultural union activist and then active in the slow food and anti-globalization movements by the 1990s. He took part in the anti-WTO demonstrations in Seattle in 1999, and that same year became internationally notorious by destroying a McDonald's restaurant in the southern city of Millau with his tractor. For Bové and his followers, McDonald's represented a threat to both French culture and decent food in general. Like another person with roots in Berkeley and France, Alice Waters, whose restaurant Chez Panisse helped launch the slow food movement, José Bové stood for a world in which local culture and cuisine would be a universal value.

By the end of the 1990s, France was a country struggling to come to terms with its past and exploring new directions for the future. In a mood of cautious optimism, the nation took part along with the rest of the world in celebrating New Year 2000, marking the beginning of a new century and a new millennium. As with the bicentennial in 1989, the government planned a massive celebration. It did not go off without a hitch: a series of powerful rainstorms left much of the nation without power, and the special clock set up to count down the seconds to the new year broke down just before completing its task. In spite of such glitches France marked the occasion with style, illuminating the Eiffel Tower with a flashing light bright enough to be seen across a large part of the nation. Symbolically at least, France could still claim to be a light to all the nations of the world as it entered the new millennium.

THUNDER ON THE RIGHT

The dynamism of Jospin's government contrasted sharply with Chirac's activities as president under this second round of cohabitation. Chirac achieved some important changes, reducing the length of the presidency from seven to five years and abolishing mandatory military service, bringing to an end a key component of French citizenship that dated back to the Revolution. But a series of scandals in Chirac's party sapped his government's energy. In 2001 the party lost control of the Paris municipality to socialist Bertrand Delanoë, who would become the city's first openly gay mayor. Chirac also provoked controversy by his decision to resume nuclear testing in French Polynesia.

In 2002 the French went to the polls to elect a new president. Most assumed that after the first round of elections it would be a contest between Jacques Chirac and Lionel Jospin. But the voters decreed otherwise. During the electoral campaign a number of commentators focused on the issue of crimes committed by immigrant youth, frequently accusing Jospin of being soft on criminals. At the same time the progressive vote was badly splintered, with several left parties like the Greens and the Trotskyists getting between 4 and 5 percent of the vote. As a result, during the first round of voting on April 21 Jospin's Socialists came in third with 16 percent of the vote, outdistanced by Jean-Marie Le Pen, who won 17 percent for the National Front.

The results caused an uproar in France and sent shock waves around the world, as it seemed the nation might elect a president widely considered to be a neofascist. Massive demonstrations against the National Front took place over the next few weeks, including a May Day march of over half a million people in Paris. Many French across the political spectrum decided to vote for Chirac, in spite of his problems with corruption and conservative policies, rather than risk a Le Pen presidency. The left-wing daily *Libération* ran the headline "Vote for the Crook, Not the Fascist," and some advocated going to the polling booths with clothespins over their noses.[3] As a result, Jacques Chirac won the presidency in a landslide, winning over 80 percent of the vote in the second round of the elections.

Notwithstanding its eventual defeat, the dramatic success of the National Front in the 2002 elections pushed the political spectrum to the right. A lot of people in France saw the nation as threatened by immigrants, integralist Islam, and European integration, and the mainstream Gaullist right felt compelled to address these concerns while emphasizing its disdain for the National

Front. After his reelection Chirac appointed as his interior minister Nicholas Sarkozy, a rising young politician of Hungarian and Greek origin. Sarkozy tried to reach out to minorities in France, creating the French Council for the Muslim Religion with the goal of promoting a French and modern vision of Islam. He also spoke out in favor of affirmative action, known in France as "positive discrimination." At the same time Sarkozy often showed himself insensitive to difference, arguing, for example, that Turkey was too Muslim and too Asian to be a part of the European Union. Given the concerns of many in France, the role the nation would play in an increasing globalized world remained open to question.

In the first decade of the twenty-first century France continued to assert its independence and distinctiveness as a nation in world politics. A prime example of this was the notorious "freedom fries" episode of 2003. In 2002 president George W. Bush of the United States declared he had evidence that Iraq was producing weapons of mass destruction, and that consequently its allies should participate in an invasion to overthrow dictator Saddam Hussein. Jacques Chirac rejected this proposal, arguing that there was no convincing evidence of such weapons, and threatened to veto such a resolution at the United Nations. Although many other nations, notably Russia and Germany, also refused to join the anti-Saddam coalition, public and political anger in the United States centered on France as the enemy, unleashing a wave of anti-French hostility in 2003. As a protest, the cafeteria of the US Congress decided to rename French fries "freedom fries." The French responded by noting that French fries were Belgian in origin. The majority of Americans, many of whom had opposed the war, thought the whole affair patently silly; one restaurant in Santa Cruz, California, even rolled out a new menu item, "impeach George W. Bush fries." Nonetheless, the French could take pride that, with the discrediting of the so-called evidence for weapons of mass destruction and the disastrous results of the war in Iraq, that they had been on the right side of history.

In 2005 the French took another, much more serious position that underscored the nation's independence. In the spring of that year countries throughout the European Union voted on whether or not to approve a formal constitution for the EU. Both France and the Netherlands held referendums on the question, and both countries rejected it by solid majorities. In France much of the left, including a sizable fraction of the PS, opposed the constitution as designed to reinforce neoliberal globalization, whereas the National Front and part of the mainstream right rejected it as subordinating national interests to Europe. The vote was seen not only as a stumbling block for European integration but also as a personal defeat for Jacques Chirac, who had strongly supported the measure.

A more serious event at the end of the year underscored the weakness of the regime. For years the impoverished and multicultural suburbs of Paris and other French cities had languished in poverty, unemployment, and despair, despite periodic government attempts to improve conditions. On the night of October 27 two teenagers, Zyed Benna and Bouna Traoré, were electrocuted at a power station in the Parisian suburb of Clichy-sous-Bois while fleeing the police. News of the incident soon spread throughout the Seine-Saint-Denis prompting young people, of both French and immigrant origin, to torch cars and throw rocks at the police. Sarkozy did not help matters, to say the least, when he characterized suburban youth as "scum" (*racaille*), and threatened to clean out the housing projects with a power hose. In response the *banlieue* exploded, and soon Chirac's government was facing a nationwide wave of suburban riots. Youths throughout the country attacked police stations, schools, power stations, and other institutions. Much of the international coverage of the riots blamed them on Muslim youth and Islamic fundamentalism. Some French commentators even targeted polygamy as the cause, saying African immigrants had too many children and let them run wild in the streets. In reality, high unemployment, persistent racial discrimination, and anger at being ignored by French society fueled the riots. On November 8, Chirac's government declared a state of emergency, using a law first enacted in 1955 to deal with the war in Algeria, a parallel between colonial and postcolonial unrest noted by many. Armed with these special powers, Nicholas Sarkozy brought in extra police to question and arrest suspects as well as imposing curfews in troubled areas. By the end of November the rioting had died down, after the arrest of nearly three thousand individuals, the deaths of two men, the torching of thousands of cars, and hundreds of millions of euros in property damage.

New protests broke out in the spring of 2006, primarily among university students. The government, in an attempt to address the problem of high unemployment among young people, proposed a new law that would have made it easier to fire people under twenty-six during their first two years on the job. The intention was to facilitate hiring the young, but many saw it instead as discrimination and reacted with a firestorm of protests. By March universities across the country had shut down and massive demonstrations took place in major cities, including one of over 700,000 in Paris. Unions joined

12.2. Young residents of Villiers-le-Bel, a northern Paris suburb, face riot police during clashes on November 26, 2005. *Source:* AP Images/Thibault Camus.

the movement, so that over a million workers walked out on strike. Faced with this ferocious public reaction, Chirac withdrew the proposed law.

The 2005 riots underscored two of the central problems of contemporary France: lack of economic opportunity and racialized exclusion, and the interactions between them. Unfortunately, the riots did not lead to a systematic approach to dealing with these problems. Instead, Nicholas Sarkozy won widespread approval for his stand-tough approach to the rioters, propelling him to victory in the 2007 presidential election against socialist candidate Ségolène Royal. As president, Sarkozy demonstrated the same combination of toughness and openness he had shown as interior minister. His cabinet was unusually diverse, including not only women but people of color. Fadela Amara, a feminist of Algerian origin who organized Ni Putes, Ni Soumises (Neither Whores Nor Submissives) to fight for the rights of poor women in the suburbs, became secretary of state for urban policies.

Sarkozy also launched several projects to investigate and reconsider French identity in the twenty-first century, projects that usually provoked controversy. In 2007 he opened the Cité nationale de l'histoire de l'immigration, a museum of the nation's immigrant history situated in the old colonial building of the former Museum of African and Oceanic Arts in Paris. The new museum proved controversial from the outset, and several historians denounced it. In November 2009 Sarkozy launched a national debate on French identity, featuring a government website titled "What Is French?" A year later he was forced to back down after critics on the left charged he was targeting immigrants and people of color as not French. In 2011 Sarkozy suggested building a National History Museum as one of his administration's legacies. Again there was controversy. As one history professor at the Sorbonne noted,

> The very idea of a specifically French history museum is ideological . . . To know about French Algeria you need to know about Algeria before France arrived there . . . If we need any history museum, it would be a world history museum, not a French history museum, to give us a real perspective on who we are, and what is France today.[4]

The impassioned debates over Sarkozy's projects to reconceptualize French identity and history underscored the centrality of such questions in contemporary France, as well as the conflicted perspective on its future as a universal nation.

Although he mainly focused on economic liberalization, after the global downturn of 2008 Sarkozy began calling for greater state intervention, while denying he had suddenly become a socialist. Sarkozy also presented himself as pro-American, seeing the US as a land of upward mobility and progress. In 2008 he, and France in general, fervently embraced US presidential candidate Barack Obama during his visit to Paris. He also continued the French tradition of leadership in foreign affairs, helping broker a truce after the Israeli invasion of Gaza in 2009, and pushing successfully for international military intervention in Libya to overthrow dictator Muamar Khaddafi in 2011. Sarkozy led a rather flamboyant lifestyle, characterized by his marriage to Italian supermodel Carla Bruni, and showed no reticence about making blunt and inflammatory statements. Critics responded by labeling him "President Bling-Bling." The son of immigrants, not a graduate of ENA, Sarkozy personified a new generation of French leaders.

To his misfortune Sarkozy was unable to resolve the economic crisis after 2008. The nation's unemployment rate, which had declined to under 8 percent in 2007, soon climbed back up to 10 percent by the end of the decade. In 2012 Sarkozy lost the presidential election to François Hollande, socialist candidate and the former husband of Ségolène Royal. Sarkozy thus became the first president under the Fifth Republic to be defeated after only one term. As time passed, however, it seemed a fair bet that François Hollande would follow him as the second. Like his socialist predecessors during the Fifth Republic, Hollande came to power with radical ideas for changing France, including dramatic tax increases on the wealthy and legalization of gay marriage, something he made good on in 2013. Unfortunately one of his other ideas, abolishing homework for schoolchildren, appealed strongly to a constituency that could not vote. More importantly, the economy continued to decline after Hollande became president, producing some of the highest unemployment and slowest growth rates in Europe by the beginning of 2014. Moreover the PS often seemed adrift, without any significant ideas or proposals. The scandal surrounding the terrible sexual assault committed by Dominique Strauss-Kahn, Hollande's rival, continued to tarnish the party's reputation. The socialists and their allies lost the municipal elections in March by a sizable margin, and Hollande's approval ratings dipped below 20 percent, making him the most unpopular president in the history of the Fifth Republic. Worse was to follow: the May elections to the European Parliament were won by the National Front, now led by Le Pen's daughter Marine Le Pen, with 25 percent of the vote; the PS finished third with 14 percent. By this time, the days of a strong president like Charles de Gaulle or François Mitterrand seemed very far away.

By 2014 the Fifth Republic was fifty-six years old, having lasted longer than any regime in the history of modern France except the Third Republic. All indications suggested that it would last indefinitely, becoming the dominant political framework of the nation in the contemporary era. More than other modern regimes it had had to deal with troubled economic times and the lack of prosperity as an endemic state of affairs. In addition, since the 1980s the Fifth Republic had to confront a fundamental reshaping of the international landscape, and its implications for both the global and local life of the country. In an era of collapsing universalisms, it remained to be seen whether the old universal nation trope would remain relevant in the postcolonial era.

The initial popularity and quick decline of both Nicholas Sarkozy and François Hollande suggested a nation unsure of its direction and its future. France in the early twenty-first century was in many ways a nation divided, finding that the old certainties no longer provided a surefire guide. The rising power of the National Front in French politics worried many and suggested

France might try to reaffirm its national identity by recreating an imaginary France that never existed. At the same time, however, the sometimes anguished debates over how to make universalism truly universal both underscored the continuing importance of that ideology and pointed the way forward to new definitions of it. While race and adjustment to postcolonial society posed major problems for France, the nation seemed capable of adjusting to them, and at least they were debated openly and actively. By contrast, the riots that erupted in 1992 after the beating of Rodney King by the Los Angeles police took place in the middle of a US presidential campaign but were completely ignored by the major party candidates. In short, the global significance and interconnectedness of such questions in France, and the determination of the French people to address them, suggested that the tradition of the universal nation was by no means finished.

Suggestions for Further Reading

Ardagh, John. *France in the New Century*. London: Penguin, 1999.

Bowen, John. *Why the French Don't Like Headscarves: Islam, the State, and Public Space*. Princeton, NJ: Princeton University Press, 2006.

Brubaker, Rogers. *Citizenship and Nationhood in France and Germany*. Cambridge: Harvard University Press, 1992.

Chabal, Emile. "Writing the French National Narrative in the Twenty-First Century." *Historical Journal* 53, no. 2 (2010): 495–516.

Fenby, Jonathan. *France on the Brink*. New York: Arcade, 1999.

Godin, Emmanuel, and Tony Chafer, eds. 2004. *The French Exception*. London: Bergahn, 2004.

Hargreaves, Alec. *Immigration, "Race," and Ethnicity in Contemporary France*. New York: Routledge, 1995.

Keaton, Trica Danielle. *Muslim Girls and the Other France. Race, Identity Politics, and Social Exclusion*. Bloomington: Indiana University Press, 2006.

Kedward, H. R. *France and the French*. New York: Overlook, 2005.

Murphy, David, and Charles Forsdick, eds. *Postcolonial Thought in the Francophone World*. Liverpool: Liverpool University Press, 2009.

Scott, Joan. *Parité: Sexual Equality and the Crisis of French Universalism*. Chicago: University of Chicago Press, 2005.

———. *The Politics of the Veil*. Princeton, NJ: Princeton University Press, 2007.

Silverman, Maxim. *Deconstructing the Nation: Immigration, Racism, and Citizenship in Modern France*. London: Routledge, 2014.

Silverstein, Paul A. *Algeria in France: Transpolitics, Race, and Nation*. Bloomington: Indiana University Press, 2004.

Notes

1. *Le Monde*, July 14, 1998, xvi.
2. *New York Times*, March 18, 1992.
3. *Libération*, April 23, 2002.
4. Nicholas Offenstadt, cited in the *New York Times*, March 8, 2011.

CONCLUSION

IN THE CONTEMPORARY ERA IT HAS BECOME COMMONPLACE TO criticize French universalism and to speak of its decline. These critics focus primarily on its contradictory character, on its extension of universalist principles to some people but not all, particularly women, the colonized, and the ethnically and racially different. The idea that French universalism is in decline arises from the nation's humiliation in World War II, its postwar loss of empire and a leading position on the world stage during the cold war, and challenges from an increasingly diverse and multicultural population by the end of the twentieth century. The rejection of French republican universalism arises out of a broader turning away from all universalist philosophies in the aftermath of the collapse of Soviet communism, a belief that broad attempts to improve and remake mankind have led more often to oppression and totalitarianism than to human liberation.

One of the ironies of this turn against universalism is that it has had its own universalist character, especially in France. French intellectuals like Michel Foucault pioneered the postmodern turn against universalist narratives, with the result that their work became a global intellectual sensation, perpetuating the idea of Paris as the world's center of new ideas. More recently, many French writers and thinkers who challenged Marxist universalism have embraced a kind of neo-republican ideology that reemphasizes some of the key tenets of republican universalism against what it sees as Anglo-Saxon multiculturalism. In an era of global uncertainties, many French thinkers on both right and left have turned to the republican tradition as a key heritage of their country, a renewed vision of the universal nation.

Despite all its trials and mutations since the Revolution, and despite the many challenges facing it today, the tradition of republican universalism is by no means exhausted in France. It is certainly possible to read the history of modern France as a study in the rise and fall of republican universalism. The Revolution combined the universalism of the Enlightenment with a powerful ideology of national citizenship and human rights to create a vision of the universal nation. Struggles over this vision during the nineteenth century led to the triumph of the Third Republic as the high point of republican universalism. During the twentieth century, in contrast, defeat by Nazi Germany, decolonization, and the cold war, as well as postcolonial multiculturalism and European integration, increasingly called into question the idea of France as a universal nation.

As this book has argued, the idea of the universal nation has both shaped and been shaped by France's interactions with the broader world. The military expansionism of the French Revolution, and its desire to carry revolutionary ideas to all of humanity, lay at the core of French citizenship and national identity. This same crusading zeal helped inspire the colonial civilizing mission in Africa and Asia during the nineteenth and twentieth centuries. At the same time the presence of both individuals and ideas of foreign origin, ranging from Empress Eugénie and Ho Chi Minh to global hip-hop, testified to the importance of international factors in shaping French life. Republican universalism emphasized the global influence of French culture and identity, but that culture was equally a product of global interactions.

To contend, however, that French universalism started with the Revolution and ended with Vichy, to view it as a movement whose day is done, is to oversimplify a rich history and complex current realities. It is deeply ironic that the universalist model should be challenged at a time when France is more diverse and globally interconnected than ever before. Even current debates about universalism underscore international comparisons, notably the contrast with Anglo-Saxon models. Such a conclusion ignores the ways in which, over time, France has succeeded in integrating immigrants from Europe and elsewhere in the world into French life, and at the same time tends to overlook the ways in which France itself has been changed by newcomers. The very meaning of French universalism and the French nation has, like everything else in human history, changed over time, as has the world of which it is a part.

In similar fashion, the tendency to oppose French universalism and Anglo-Saxon multiculturalism obscures more than it illuminates. It is based, first, on a simplistic image of British and especially American politics, one that for example ignores the strong and largely successful backlash against affirmative action in the United States. It also tends to ignore the ways in which many in France have embraced multiculturalism, ranging from the parity movement to the creation of racial interest groups like Natives of the Republic and the Representative Council of Black Associations (CRAN). Finally, such opposition promotes a narrow vision of republican universalism, neglecting the fact that many who espouse a more inclusive vision of French life nonetheless remain attached to many republican and universalist values. The antiracism and ethnic cosmopolitanism of French hip-hop is a case in point. The debates and conflicts over French identity that have been so agonized since the late twentieth century have involved the interaction of both national and global concerns. Their very intensity testifies to the continued vitality, in very different form from the eras of the Revolution or the Third Republic, of the ideal of the universal nation.

Historians are not prophets. Our job is to chronicle and analyze the past, not predict the future. In conclusion, permit me to reemphasize the importance of France in the history of the modern nation and the making of the modern world. French history exemplifies not only the creation of national institutions and culture, but equally the transnational dimension of that past. The ideal of the universal nation may be problematic and contradictory, but it has played a key role in the history of modern France and may continue to do so into the twenty-first century and beyond. As the millions of foreign tourists who flock there every year understand, France is an important part of the human heritage, and this historian can only hope that it will continue to be so for many, many years to come.

INDEX

CPSIA information can be obtained
at www.ICGtesting.com
Printed in the USA
LVOW10s1215301216
519247LV00014B/28/P